Pearson New International Edition

Check-In Check-Out
Managing Hotel Operations
Gary K. Vallen Jerome J. Vallen
Ninth Edition

Pearson Education Limited
Edinburgh Gate
Harlow
Essex CM20 2JE
England and Associated Companies throughout the world

Visit us on the World Wide Web at: www.pearsoned.co.uk

© Pearson Education Limited 2014

ISBN 10: 1-292-02110-1
ISBN 13: 978-1-292-02110-2

British Library Cataloguing-in-Publication Data
A catalogue record for this book is available from the British Library

Printed in the United States of America

Table of Contents

GLOSSARY

Words in *italic* in each definition are themselves defined elsewhere in the Glossary. (Words not listed might be found in the Index.) cf. means "compare."

A card A form once used with the *NCR front-office posting machines* to reconcile and report cash at the close of the first shift and alternate shifts thereafter; see also *B card*.

account balance The difference between the *debit* (charge) and *credit* (payment) values of the *guest bill*.

account card See *guest bill*.

account receivable A company, organization, or individual, *registered* or not, who has an outstanding bill with the hotel.

accounts receivable ledger The aggregate of individual *account receivable* records.

acknowledgment Notice of a *confirmed reservation* by telephone, fax, email, letter, postcard, or preprinted form.

ADA See *Americans with Disabilities Act*.

adds Last-minute *reservations* added to the reservation list on the day of arrival.

ADR See *average daily rate*.

adjoining rooms Rooms that abut along the corridor but do not connect through private doors; cf. *connecting rooms*.

advance deposit A deposit furnished by the guest on a room *reservation* that the hotel is holding.

advances See *cash paid-outs*.

affiliated hotel One of a chain, *franchise*, or *referral* system, the membership of which provides special advantages, particularly a national reservations system.

after departure (AD) A *late charge*.

afternoon tea A light snack comprising delicate sandwiches and small sweets served with tea, or even sherry; cf. *high tea*.

agency ledger A division of the *city ledger* dealing with *travel agent* (agency) accounts.

agent Representative of an individual or business; term that is a popular substitute for clerk, as in guest-service agent rather than room clerk.

AH&LA See *American Hotel & Lodging Association*.

AIOD Telephone equipment that provides *Automatic Identification of Outward Dialing* for billing purposes.

All-inclusive *Plan* that includes all hotel services: room, food, beverages, entertainment for one price.

allowance A reduction to the *folio*, as an adjustment either for unsatisfactory service or for a posting error. Also called a *rebate*.

amenities Literally any extra product or service found in the hotel. A swimming pool, *concierge* desk, health spa, and so on are all technically known as amenities. However, this term is used primarily for in-room guest products: as soap, shampoo, suntan lotion, mouthwash, and the like.

amenity creep The proliferation of all guest products and services when hotels compete by offering more extensive *amenities*.

American Hotel & Lodging Association (AH&LA) A federation of regional and state associations that are composed of individual hotel and motel properties throughout the Americas.

American plan (AP) A method of quoting room *rates* where the charge includes room and three meals.

American Resort Development Association (ARDA) A professional association of *timeshare* developers.

American Society of Association Executives (ASAE) An organization of the professional executives who head the business and *SMERF* associations in the United States.

American Society of Travel Agents (ASTA) A professional association of retail *travel agents* and wholesale tour operators.

Americans with Disabilities Act (ADA) Established in 1990, the ADA prohibits discrimination against any guest or employee because of disability.

application service provider Supports *central reservation systems* and *global reservation systems* with hardware and software.

arrival, departure, and change sheet A pencil-and-paper form to record guest *check-ins*, *check-outs*, and *changes* under a hand audit system; sometimes three separate forms.

arrival time The hour which the guest specifies as the time that he or she will arrive to claim the *reservation*.

ATM Automatic teller machine provides self-service banking services. Often located in heavily trafficked public areas such as hotel lobbies or casino/hotels. User must have a *PIN*.

attrition The failure of a convention *group* to fill its reserved *block* of rooms.

authorization code (1) Response from a credit-card issuer that approves the credit-card transaction and provides a numbered code referral if problems arise; (2) a code for entry to a computer program.

available The room is ready.

available basis only (1) Convention *reservations* that have no claim against the *block* of convention rooms (see *blanket reservation*) because the request arrived after the *cutoff date*; (2) no reservations permitted because the rate being granted is too low to guarantee space, employee *reservations*, for example.

available rooms The number of guest rooms the hotel has for sale—either the total in the hotel or the number unoccupied on a given day.

average daily rate (ADR) The average daily *rate* paid by guests; computed by dividing room revenue by the number of rooms occupied. More recently called *sales per occupied room*.

back to back (1) A sequence of consecutive *group* departures and arrivals usually arranged by tour operators so that rooms are never vacant; (2) a floor plan design that brings the piping of adjacent baths into a common shaft.

bank Coins and small bills given to the cashier for making change.

bank cards Credit cards issued by banks, usually for a smaller fee than that charged by *travel and entertainment cards*.

batch processing A computer procedure that collects and codes data, entering it into memory in batches; cf. *online computer*.

B card A form once used with *NCR front-office posting machines* to reconcile and report cash at the close of the second shift and alternative shifts thereafter; see also *A card*.

bed and board Another term for the *American plan*.

bed and breakfast (B&B) Lodging and breakfast offered in a domestic setting by families in their own homes; less frequently, the *Continental plan*.

bed board A board placed under the mattress to make a firmer sleeping surface.

bed night See *guest day (night)*.

bed occupancy A ratio relating the number of beds sold to the number of beds available for sale; *occupancy* measured in available beds rather than in *available rooms*.

bellcaptain (1) The supervisor of the bellpersons and other uniformed service personnel; (2) a proprietary in-room vending machine.

bellcaptain's log See *callbook*.

bellstand The bellperson's desk located in the lobby close to and visible from the front desk.

Bermuda plan A method of quoting room *rates*, where the charge includes a full breakfast as well as the room.

best available A *reservation* requesting (or a confirmation promising) the best room available or the best room to open prior to arrival; cf. *available basis only*.

B folio The second *folio* (the individual's folio) used with a *master account*.

blanket reservation A *block* of rooms held for a particular *group*, with individual members requesting assignments from that *block*.

block (1) A number of rooms reserved for one *group*; (2) a restriction placed in the *room rack* to limit the clerk's discretion in assigning the room.

book To sell hotel space, either to a person or to a *group* needing a *block* of rooms.

bottom line The final line of a profit-and-loss statement: either net profit or net loss.

box Reservation term that allows no *reservations* from either side of the boxed dates to spill through; cf. *sell through*.

breakage The gain that accrues to the hotel or tour operator when meals or other services included in a *package* are not used by the guest.

brunch A meal served after breakfast but before lunch and taking the place of both.

bucket See *cashier's well*.

budget motel See *limited service*.

building cost rate formula A rule-of-thumb formula stating that the average room rate should equal $1 for every $1,000 of construction cost; see also *rule-of-thumb rate*.

C-corporation Used to distinguish standard corporations from nonstandard corporations, such as non-taxpaying *REITs*.

cabana A room on the beach (or by the pool) separated from the main *house*; may even be furnished as a sleeping room.

café complet Coffee snack at midmorning or midafternoon.

California length An extra-long bed, about 80 to 85 inches instead of the usual 75 inches. Same as *Hollywood length*.

call accounting system (CAS) Computerized program that prices and records telephone calls on the guest's electronic *folio* through a *property management system (PMS) interface*.

callbook The bellperson's record of calls and activities.

call sheet The form used by the telephone operator to record the room and hour of the *morning call*; replaced by automatic systems.

cancellation A guest's request to the hotel to void a *reservation* previously made.

cancellation number Coded number provided by the hotel or *central reservations office* to a guest who cancels a *reservation*.

case goods Furniture that provides storage.

cash advance See *cash paid-outs*.

cash disbursement See *cash paid-outs*.

cashier's drop A depository located in the front-desk area where others can witness cashiers depositing their *turn-ins*.

cashier's report The cash *turn-in* form completed by a departmental cashier at the close of the *watch*.

cashier's well The file that holds paper-and-pencil *folios*, often recessed in the countertop; also known as *tub*, *bucket*, or *pit*.

cash paid-outs Monies disbursed for guests, either advances or loans, and charged to their accounts like other departmental services.

cash sheet The *departmental control sheet* maintained by the front-office cashier.

casualty factor The number of individual or *group reservations* (*cancellations* plus *no-shows*) that fail to appear.

central processing unit (CPU) The *hardware/software* nucleus of the computer.

central reservations office (CRO) A private or chain-operated site that accepts and processes *reservations* on behalf of its membership.

central reservations system (CRS) The sophisticated *hardware* and *software* used by a *central reservations office* to accurately track and manage *reservation* requests for member properties.

change Moving a party from one guest room to another; any change in room, *rate*, or number of occupants.

chargeback Credit-card charges refused by the credit-card company.

check-in All the procedures involved in receiving the guest and completing the *registration* sequence.

check-out All the procedures involved in the departure of the guest and the settlement of the *account*.

check-out hour That time by which guests must vacate rooms or be charged an additional day.

city ledger An *accounts receivable ledger* of nonregistered guests.

city-ledger journal The form used to record transactions that affect the *city ledger*.

class The quality of hotel, with *average daily rate* the usual criterion.

closeout hour Also called *close of the day*.

close of the day An arbitrary hour that management designates to separate the records of one day from those of the next.

closet bed See *Murphy bed*.

collar hotel Identifies location of a hotel on the collar (outside rings) of a city.

colored transparency A colored celluloid strip placed in the *room rack pocket* as a *flag* or indicator of room status, replaced by PMS.

commercial hotel A *transient hotel* catering to a business clientele.

commercial rate A reduced room *rate* given to businesspersons to promote occupancy.

commissionable Indicates the hotel will pay *travel agents* the standard fee for business placed.

comp Short for "complimentary" accommodations—and occasionally food and beverage—furnished without charge.

company-made (reservation) A *reservation* guaranteed by the arriving guest's company.

concession A hotel tenant (concessionaire) whose facilities and services are often indistinguishable from those owned and operated by the hotel.

concierge (1) A European position, increasingly found in U.S. hotels, responsible for handling guests' needs, particularly those relating to out-of-hotel services; (2) designation of the sleeping floor where these services are offered.

condominium A multiunit dwelling wherein each owner maintains separate title to the unit while sharing ownership rights and responsibilities for the public space.

conference center A *property* that caters to business meetings, corporate retreats, and conferences. Generally considered smaller in size and more personable in nature than a convention hotel.

confirmed reservation The hotel's *acknowledgment*, maybe in writing, to the guest's *reservation* request.

connecting rooms *Adjoining rooms* with direct, private access, making use of the corridor unnecessary.

consortium A new organization, formed by existing organizations (banks, developers, hotels) to carry out a particular enterprise.

continental breakfast A small meal including some combination of: bread, rolls, sweet rolls, juice, or coffee. Often set up in bulk by the innkeeper or host; continental breakfasts are usually self-service.

Continental plan A method of quoting room *rates* where the charge includes a *continental breakfast* as well as the room rate.

convention rate See *run-of-the-house rate*.

convertible bed See *sofa bed*.

corner (room) An *outside room* on a corner of the building having two *exposures*.

corporate meeting package (CMP) An *all inclusive plan* quoted by *conference centers* and hotels for corporate meetings.

correction sheet A form once used with *NCR front-office machines* to record posting errors for later reconciliation by the *night auditor*.

cot See *rollaway bed*.

coupon (1) A checklike form issued by *travel agents* to their clients and used by the clients to settle their hotel accounts; (2) a ticket issued by *tour groups* for the purchase of meals and other services to be charged against the *master account*. Also called a *voucher*.

credit An accounting term that indicates a decrease in the *account receivable*; the opposite of *debit*.

cutoff date The date on which unsold rooms from within a convention's *block* of reserved rooms are released for sale.

cutoff hour That time at which the day's unclaimed *reservations* are released for sale to the general public.

daily rooms report See *room count sheet*.

day rate A reduced charge for occupancy of less than overnight; used when the *party* arrives and departs the same day. Also called *part day rate* or *use rate*.

D card A form once used with *NCR front-office posting machine* as the machine equivalent of the *transcript*; the term is still used for the daily revenue report prepared now by the *property management system*.

dead room change A physical change of rooms made by the hotel in the guest's absence so no tip is earned by the *last* bellperson.

debit An accounting term that indicates an increase in the *account receivable*; the opposite of *credit*.

deluxe A non-U.S. designation implying the best accommodations; unreliable unless part of an official rating system.

demi-pension (DP) A non-U.S. method of quoting room *rates* similar to the *modified American plan (MAP)* but allowing the guest to select either luncheon or dinner along with breakfast and room; also called *half pension*.

density board (chart) A noncomputerized *reservation* system where the number of rooms committed is controlled by type: *single*, *twin*, *queen*, and so on; obsolete.

departmental control sheet A form maintained by each *operating department* for recording data from departmental *vouchers* before forwarding them to the front desk for *posting*. Replaced by *point-of-sale* terminals.

departure *Check-out*.

deposit reservation See *advance deposit*.

destination clubs Costly up-front fees and annual dues give members access to upscale private resort homes for longer periods than typical *timeshares*, but without the equity position of *fractionals*.

destination hotel The objective of—and often the sole purpose for—the guest's trip; cf. *transient hotel*.

did not stay (DNS) Means the guest left almost immediately after *registering*.

difference returnable See *exchange*.

dine-around plan A method of quoting *AP* or *MAP* room rates that allows guests to dine at any of several different but cooperating hotels.

display room See *sample room*.

D.I.T. Domestic independent tour or domestic inclusive tour; cf. *F.I.T.*

double (1) A bed approximately 54 by 75 inches; (2) the *rate* charged for two persons occupying one room; (3) a room with a double bed.

double–double See *twin–double*.

double occupancy (1) Room occupancy by two persons; (2) a ratio relating the number of rooms double occupied to the number of rooms sold.

double-occupancy rate A *rate* used for tours where the per-person charge is based on two to a room.

double-up A designation of *double occupancy* by unrelated parties necessitating two *room rack* identifications and/or two *folios*.

downgrade Move a *reservation* or registered guest to a lesser accommodation or *class* of service; cf. *upgrade*.

downtime That time span during which the computer is inoperative because of malfunction or preemptive operations.

ducat See *stock card*.

due back See *exchange*.

due bank See *exchange*.

due bill See *trade advertising contract*.

dump To *check out* early; with reference to *groups*.

duplex A two-story *suite* with a connecting stairwell.

duvet A bed comforter, much like a large pillow, filled with feathers in a washable cover.

early arrival A guest who arrives a day or two earlier than the *reservation* calls for.

EBITDA See *house profit*.

economy class See *tourist class*.

Ecotourism Responsible travel to nature areas that conserves the environment and improves the well-being of local people.

efficiency Accommodations that include kitchen facilities.

Elderhostel Study programs for senior citizens that include travel and classes, often held on college campuses.

electronic data processing (EDP) A data handling system that relies on electronic (computer) equipment.

ell A wing of a building at right angles to the main structure.

emergency key (E-key) One key that opens all guest rooms, including those locked from within, even those with the room key still in the lock; also called the great *grandmaster*.

English breakfast A hearty breakfast of fruit, cereal, meat, eggs, toast, and beverage generally served in the United Kingdom and Ireland, but less often of late.

en pension See *full pension*.

en suite Forming a suite; adapted to mean a room with a bath.

European plan (EP) A method of quoting room *rates* where the charge includes room accommodations only.

exchange The excess of cash *turn-in* over *net receipts*; the difference is returnable (due back) to the front-office cashier; also called *due back, due bank*, or *difference returnable*.

executive floor See *concierge* (floor).

executive room See *studio*.

exempt workers Employees (supervisors) not covered by wage-and-hour laws.

exposure The direction (north, south, east, or west) or view (ocean, mountain) that the guest room faces.

express check-out Mechanical or electronic methods of *check-out* that expedite *departures* and eliminates the need to stop at the desk; also called *zip-out*.

extra meals An *American plan* charge made for dining room service over and above that to which the guest is entitled.

family plan A special room *rate* that allows children to occupy their parent's room at no additional charge.

family room See *twin–double*.

fam trip Familiarization trip taken by (offered to) *travel agents* at little or no cost to acquaint them with *properties* and destinations.

farm out Assignment of guests to other *properties* when a *full house* precludes their accommodation.

fenced rates One of several tools used by the reservations department to maximize room revenues under *yield management* systems, including nonrefundable, prepaid *reservations,* and *reservations* not subject to change.

first class A non-U.S. designation for medium-priced accommodations with corresponding facilities and services.

F.I.T. Foreign independent tour, but has come to mean free independent tour, a traveler who is not *group* affiliated; by extension, frequent independent traveler, or full inclusive tour; cf. *D.I.T.*

flag (1) Designating a hotel's membership in a chain or *franchise*; (2) a device for calling the room clerk's attention to a particular room in the *room rack*.

flat rate (1) See *run-of-the-house rate*; (2) same price for *single* or *double* occupancy.

float The free use of outstanding funds during the period that checks and credit-card charges are in transition for payment.

floor key See *master key*.

floor (release) limit The maximum amount of charges permitted a credit-card user at a given *property* without clearance; the limit is established for the property, not for the user.

folio See *guest bill*; also called an *account card*.

force majeure (forz mazhoer) An unexpected and disruptive event that frees parties from contractual obligations; an act of God.

forecast A future projection of estimated business volume.

forecast scheduling Work schedules established on the basis of sales projections.

forfeited deposit A *deposit reservation* kept by the hotel when a *no-show* fails to cancel the reservation; also called a *lost deposit*.

fractionals Shared ownership of resort real estate that includes periodic access; differs from *timeshares* in which one buys only the right to use.

franchise (1) An independently owned hotel or motel that appears to be part of a chain and pays a fee for that right and for the right to participate in the chain's advertising and reservation systems; (2) the chain's right (its franchise) to sell such permission; or the permission itself, or both.

franchisee One who buys a *franchise*.

franchisor One who sells a *franchise*.

free sale Occurs when a *travel agent*, airline, or other agency commits hotel space without specific prior confirmation from the *property*. See also *sell and report*.

from bill number ... to bill number A cross-reference of *account* numbers when the bill of a guest who remains beyond one week is transferred to a new *folio*.

front The next bellperson eligible for a *rooming* assignment or other errand apt to produce a *gratuity*; cf. *last*.

front office A broad term that includes the physical front desk as well as the duties and functions involved in the sale and service of guest rooms.

front of the house (1) The area of the hotel visible to guests in contrast to the back of the house, which is not in the public view; (2) all of the functions that are part of the *front office*.

full day The measure of a chargeable day for accounting purposes; three meals for an *AP* hotel, overnight for an *EP*.

full house Means 100% *occupancy*, all guest rooms sold; cf. *perfect fill*.

full pension A European term for the *American plan*.

full service Means a complete line of hotel services and departments are provided, in contrast to a *limited-service property*.

futon A Japanese sleeping mat made of many layers of cotton-quilted batting that is rolled up when not in use.

garni A non-U.S. designation for hotels without restaurant service except for *continental breakfast*.

general cashier The chief cashier with whom deposits are made and from whom *banks* are drawn.

general manager (GM) The hotel's chief executive.

ghost card Nonexistent credit card or credit-card charges not supported by a signature.

global distribution system (GDS) The *hardware, software*, and computer lines over which *travel agents*, airlines, online subscription networks, and others access *central reservations systems* and individual *property management systems*.

grande dame French for an aristocratic lady; hence, an elegant, grand hotel.

grandmaster One key that opens all guest rooms except those locked from within; see also *emergency key*.

gratuity A tip given to an employee by a guest, sometimes willingly and sometimes automatically added to the charges; see also *plus, plus*.

graveyard A work shift beginning about midnight.

greens fee A charge for the use of the golf course.

group A number of persons with whom the hotel deals (reservation, billing, etc.) as if they were one party.

guaranteed rate The assurance of a fixed *rate* regardless of the hotel's *occupancy*, often given in consideration of a large number of *room nights* per year pledged by a company.

guaranteed reservation Payment for the room is promised even if the occupant fails to arrive.

guest account See *guest bill*.

guest bill An accounting statement used to record and display the charges and payments made by registered guests (*accounts receivable*) during their hotel stay. Also known as *folio* or *account card*.

guest check The bill presented to patrons of the dining rooms and bars and, when signed, often used as the departmental *voucher*.

guest day (night) The stay of one guest for one day (night); also called *room-night* or *bed night*.

guest elevators Lobby (front) elevators for guest use exclusively; employees are permitted only during guest service, as bellpersons *rooming (a guest)*; cf. *service elevators*.

guest history A record of the guest's visits, including rooms assigned, *rates* paid, special needs, credit rating, and personal information; used to provide better guest service and better marketing approaches.

guest ledger All the *guest bills* owed by registered guests (*accounts receivable*) and maintained in the *front office*, in contrast to the group of *city-ledger* bills (nonregistered guests) maintained in the accounting or back office.

guest night See *guest day*.

guest occupancy See *bed occupancy*.

guest-service area See *front office*.

half-board See *modified American plan*.

half-pension See *demi-pension*.

handicap(ped) room A guest room furnished with special devices and built large enough to accommodate guests with physical handicaps.

hard copy Computer term for material that has been printed rather than merely displayed.

hard goods Guest-room furniture: beds, chairs, and so on; cf. *soft goods*.

hardware The physical equipment (electronic and mechanical) of a computer installation and its peripheral components; cf. *software*.

HFTP Hospitality Financial and Technology Professionals, an association specializing in hotel accounting, finance, and technology; formerly the IAHA, International Association of Hospitality Accountants.

hide-a-bed See *sofa bed*.

high season See *in-season rate*.

high tea A fairly substantial late afternoon or early evening meal; cf. *afternoon tea*.

HITIS An acronym for Hospitality Industry Technology Integration Standards, which are computer *interface* standards developed to facilitate the *interface* of computer systems from various vendors onto the hotel's *property management system*.

HOBIC An acronym for Hotel Outward Bound Information Center, the telephone company's long-distance hotel network.

holdover See *overstay*.

Hollywood bed *Twin* beds joined by a common headboard.

Hollywood length An extra-long bed of 80 to 85 inches instead of the usual 75 inches. Same as *California length*.

Hospitality Sales and Marketing Association International (HSMAI) An international association of hotel sales and marketing managers.

hospitality suite (room) A facility used for entertaining, usually at conventions, trade shows, and similar meetings.

hostel An inexpensive but supervised facility with limited services catering to young travelers on foot or bicycle; cf. *Elderhostel*.

hotelier Innkeeper or hotelkeeper.

hotel manager Hotel executive responsible for the front of the house, including *front office*, housekeeping, and uniformed services; also called rooms manager, house manager, or guest-services manager.

hotel operating hours Twenty-four hours per day; 7 days per week; 365 days per year.

hotel rep See *rep(resentative)*.

hot list A list of lost or stolen credit cards furnished to hotels and other retailers by credit-card companies.

house A synonym for hotel, as in *house bank, house count, house laundry*; see also *property*.

house bank See *bank*.

house call Telephone call made to the outside of the hotel by a member of the staff doing company business; not subject to a *posting* charge, as guest calls are.

house count The number of registered guests; cf. *room count*.

housekeeper's report A report on the status of guest rooms, prepared by the *linen room* and used by the front desk to verify the accuracy of the *room rack*.

house laundry A hotel-operated facility, usually on premises, in contrast to an *outside laundry* that contracts with the hotel to handle *house* and/or guest laundry.

house profit Net profit before income taxes from all *operating departments* except *store rentals* and before provision for rent, interest, taxes, depreciation, and amortization; renamed as "earnings before interest, taxes, depreciation, and amortization (EBITDA)" by the 1977 edition and subsequent editions of the *Uniform System of Accounts* for hotels; see also *bottom line*.

house rooms Guest rooms set aside for hotel use and excluded, therefore, from *available rooms*.

housing bureau A citywide reservation office, usually run by the convention bureau, for assigning *reservation* requests to participating hotels during a citywide convention.

Hubbart room rate formula A basis for determining room *rates* developed by Roy Hubbart and distributed by the *American Hotel & Lodging Association*.

HVAC Acronym for heating, ventilation, and air-conditioning.

ideal average room rate This formula assumes a hotel sells an equal number of rooms from both the least expensive upward and from the most expensive downward. The resulting average rate is a theoretical benchmark against which to compare actual operating results.

imprest petty cash A technique for controlling petty cash disbursements by which a special, small cash fund is used for minor cash payments and periodically reimbursed.

incentive (group, guest, tour, or trip) Persons who have won a hotel stay (usually with transportation included) as a reward for meeting and excelling their company's sales quotas or other established standards.

inclusive terms (1) Phrase that is sometimes used in Europe to designate the *American plan*; (2) indicates that a price *quote* includes tax and *gratuity*.

independent A *property* with no chain or *franchise* affiliation, although one proprietor might own several such properties.

information rack An alphabetic listing of registered guests with a room number cross-reference.

in-house On the premises, such as an in-house laundry; cf. *off premises*.

in-season rate A *resort's* maximum rate, charged when the demand is heaviest, as it is during the middle of the summer or winter; cf. *off-season rate, low season, shoulder*.

inside call A telephone call that remains within the hotel; cf. *outside call*.

inside room A guest room that faces an inner courtyard or light court enclosed by three or four sides of the building; cf. *outside room*.

inspector Supervisory position in the housekeeping department responsible for releasing *on change* rooms to ready status.

interface Computer term designating the ability of one computer to communicate with another; see *HITIS*.

International Association of Travel Agents (IATA) A professional affiliation which both lobbies on behalf of the travel industry and identifies/verifies legitimate *travel agents* to other vendors.

Internet telephony Telephone capability on Internet access; also called VoIP, Voice over Internet Protocol.

interstate call A long-distance call that crosses state lines.

interval ownership See *timeshare*.

intrastate call A long-distance telephone call that originates and terminates within the same state.

in-WATS See *wide area telephone service*.

IT number The code assigned to an inclusive tour for identification.

joiner A guest who joins another guest or *party* already *registered*.

junior suite One large room, sometimes with a half partition, furnished as both a *parlor* and a bedroom.

king An extra-long, extra-wide bed at least 78 by 82 inches.

kiosk An information site (originally a booth) that may be staffed, but more likely provides access to the hotel's property management system for self-registration and self-check-out.

lanai A Hawaiian term for "veranda"; a room with a porch or balcony, usually overlooking gardens or water.

last The designation for the bellperson who most recently completed a *front*; cf. *front*.

last-room availability A sophisticated reservations system that provides real-time access between the chain's *central reservations system* and the hotel's *in-house property management system*.

late arrival A guest with a *reservation* who expects to arrive after the *cutoff hour* and so notifies the hotel.

late charge A departmental charge that arrives at the *front office* for billing after the guest has *checked out*.

late check-out A departing guest who remains beyond the *check-out hour* with permission of the desk and thus without charge.

LEED Leadership in Energy and Environmental Design is a benchmark created by the U.S. Green Building Council for buildings that meet energy and environmental standards.

light baggage Insufficient luggage in quantity or quality on which to extend credit; the guest pays in advance.

limited service A hotel or motel that provides little or no services other than the room; a *budget hotel (motel)*; cf. *full service*.

linen closet A storage closet for linens and other housekeeping supplies usually located conveniently along the corridor for the use of the housekeeping staff.

linen room The housekeeper's office and the center of operations for that department, including the storage of linens and uniforms.

lockout (1) Denying the guest access to the room, usually because of an unpaid bill; (2) a key of that name.

log A record of activities maintained by several *operating departments*.

lost and found An area, usually under the housekeeper's jurisdiction, for the control and storage of lost-and-found items.

low season See *off-season rate*.

maid's report A status-of-rooms report prepared by individual room attendants and consolidated with other reports by the *linen room* into the *housekeeper's report*.

mail and key rack An antiquated piece of *front-office* equipment where both guest mail and room keys were stored by room number.

maitre d' The shortened form of maitre d'hôtel, the headwaiter.

market mix The variety and percentage distribution of hotel guests—conventioneer, tourist, businessperson, and so on.

market niche Identifiable, but often poorly served, subset of a market.

master account One *folio* prepared for a *group* (convention, company, tour) on which all group charges are accumulated.

master key One key controlling several *pass keys* and opening all the guests rooms on one floor; also called a *floor key*.

master franchise A *franchisee's* right to resell pieces of the *franchise* to other *franchisees*.

menu An array of function choices displayed to the computer user, who selects the appropriate function.

message lamp A light on the telephone, used to notify an occupant that the telephone system has a message to relay.

meters See *square meters*.

mezzanine financing A high-interest, unsecured, temporary debt that may become equity in the hotel; often paid off when a regular mortgage is obtained.

minisuite See *junior suite*.

minor departments The less important *operating departments* (excluding room, food, and beverage) such as valet, laundry, and gift shop.

miscellaneous charge order (MCO) Airline *voucher* authorizing the sale of services to the guest named on the form, with payment due from the airline. The manual form has been replaced by an automated MCO on ticket stock.

modified American plan (MAP) A method of quoting room *rates* in which the charge includes breakfast and dinner as well as the room.

mom-and-pop A small, family-owned business with limited capitalization in which the family, rather than paid employees, furnishes the bulk of the labor.

moment of truth A popular term describing the interaction between a guest and a member of the staff, when all of the advertising and representations made by the hotel come down to the quality of the service delivered at that moment.

morning call A *wake-up call* made by the telephone operator or automatically by the *property management system* at the guest's request.

move-in date The date that a group, convention, or trade show arrives to begin preparing for their meeting or exhibit; cf. *move-out date*.

move-out date The date that a group, convention, or trade show vacates the *property* after a meeting or exhibit; cf. *move-in date*.

Ms An abbreviation used to indicate a female guest without consideration of marital status.

Murphy bed A standard bed that folds or swings into a wall or cabinet in a closet-like fashion; trademarked.

NCR front-office posting machine A mechanical device used to *post folios* and automatically accumulate *account receivable* and revenue balances; two models, the NCR (National Cash Register Company) 2000 and the NCR 42(00), neither of which are manufactured today, were replaced by electronic *property management systems*.

NCR paper No carbon required; paper is specially treated to produce copies without carbon.

net rate A room *rate quote* that indicates no additional commissions or fees are to be paid to *travel agents* or other third parties.

net receipts The difference between cash taken in and *cash paid-outs*.

night audit A daily reconciliation, which is completed during the *graveyard* shift, of both *accounts receivable* and incomes from the *operating departments*.

night auditor The person or persons responsible for the *night audit*.

night auditor's report An interim report of *accounts receivable*, room statistics, and incomes earned; prepared by the *night auditor* for the *general manager*.

night bird Euphemism for prostitute.

night clerk's report Another name for the *room count sheet*.

no reservation (NR) See *walk-in*.

no-show A *reservation* that fails to arrive.

occupancy (percentage of occupancy, occupancy percentage) A ratio relating the number of rooms sold (*room count*) to the number of *rooms available* for sale.

occupied (1) A room that is sold or taken and is not available for sale; (2) someone is physically in the room at this time.

ocean front A front room with an *exposure* facing directly on the ocean; cf. *ocean view*.

ocean view Other than a front room, but with some view of the ocean; cf. *ocean front*.

off line See *batch processing*.

off premises Not on the *property*; cf. *in-house*.

off-season rate A reduced room *rate* charged by *resort hotels* when demand is lowest; cf. *in-season rate, shoulder*.

off the shelf Standardized, not customized, computer software.

off the street (OS) See *walk-in*.

on change The status of a room recently vacated but not yet available for new occupants.

one- (two-) pull dialing One (two)-digit telephone dialing (or Touch-Tone) that connects the caller to hotel services such as room service and bellstand.

online (computer) Computer facilities hooked directly to input and output devices for instantaneous communication; cf. *batch processing*.

opaque A reservation website, not operated by the hotel, that identifies the actual hotel being booked only after the guest (who is shopping rates) commits a final payment.

open credit Credit based only on a guest's signature.

operating departments Those divisions of the hotel directly involved with the service of the guest, in contrast to support divisions such as personnel and accounting.

organic search results By anticipating the user's key words and phrases, a website listing appears close to the top of the Internet display naturally, without artificially gaining placement through paid advertising. Also known as "pure results" or "natural search results."

out of inventory (OOI) A significant problem has removed this room from availability. Whereas *out of order (OOO)* rooms are usually available in only a matter of hours, OOI rooms may be unavailable for days or weeks.

out of order (OOO) The room is not available for sale because of some planned or unexpected temporary shutdown of facilities.

outside call A telephone call from outside the hotel; a call that terminates outside the hotel; cf. *inside call*.

outside laundry (valet) A nonhotel laundry or valet service contracted by the hotel in order to offer a full line of services; cf. *house laundry*.

outside room A room on the perimeter of the building facing outward with an *exposure* more desirable than that of an *inside* room.

out-WATS See *wide area telephone service*.

over or short A discrepancy between the cash on hand and the amount that should be on hand.

overbooking Committing more rooms to possible guest occupancy than are actually available.

override (1) Extra commission above standard percentage to encourage or reward quantity bookings; (2) process by which the operator bypasses certain limits built into the computer program.

overstay A guest who remains beyond the expiration of the anticipated stay.

package A number of services (transportation, room, food, entertainment) normally purchased separately but put together and marketed at a reduced price made possible by volume and *breakage*.

paid in advance A room charge that is collected prior to occupancy, which is the usual procedure when a guest has *light baggage*; with some motels, it is standard procedure for every guest.

paid-outs See *cash paid-outs*.

paid search results Advertisers position their websites at the top of the Web page by purchasing key words or phrases from search-engine companies.

parlor The living room portion of a *suite*.

part day rate (guest) See *day rate*.

party *Front-office* term that references either the individual guest ("Who's the party in room 100?") or several members of the group ("When will your party arrive?").

pass key (1) A sub *master key* capable of opening all the locks within a limited, single set of 12 to 18 rooms, but no other; (2) guest key for access to public space (spa, pool).

PBX See *private branch exchange*.

penthouse Accommodations, almost always *suites*, located on the top floor of the hotel, theoretically on the roof.

percentage of occupancy See *occupancy.*

perfect fill *Occupancy* of 100%, with every room actually occupied; cf. *full house* in which 100% *occupancy* might reflect guaranteed reservations that didn't actually show.

permanent guest A resident of long-term duration whose stay may or may not be formalized with a lease.

personal digital assistant (PDA) Handheld computer, often with wireless capability.

petite suite See *junior suite.*

petty cash See *imprest petty cash.*

pickup (1) The procedure once used with *NCR front-office posting machines* to accumulate the *folio* balance by entering the previous balance into the machine before posting the new charges; (2) the figure so entered; obsolete.

PIN Personal identification number. A secret combination of numbers and letters chosen by an individual as identification for accessing electronic equipment such as *ATMs.*

PIP See *product improvement plan.*

pit See *cashier's well.*

plan The basis on which room *rate* charges are made; see *American plan* and *European plan.*

plus, plus Shorthand for the addition of tax and tip to the check or price per cover.

PMS Property Management System.

pocket A portion of a manual *room rack* made to accept the *room rack slips* and provide a permanent record of accommodations and *rates;* obsolete.

point-of-sale (POS) terminal An electronic "cash register" providing *on-line* communications to the *property management system* from remote sales locations, in contrast to an input device at the *front office.*

porte-cochère The covered entryway that provides shelter for those entering and leaving a hotel; French: coach gate (port-ko-shâr).

porterage (1) Arrangements made to handle luggage; (2) the charge for luggage handling.

post(ing) The process of recording items in an accounting record, such as a *folio.*

power of the pen Right to *comp* guest services.

preassign *Reservations* are assigned to specific rooms that are *blocked* before the guests arrive; cf. *prereg(istration).*

prereg(istration) Registration is done by the hotel before the guest arrives, although the actual *(reg)istration card* is not completed. Used with groups and tours to reduce *front-office* congestion, since individual guests need not then approach the desk; cf. *preassign.*

private branch exchange (PBX) A telephone switchboard.

product improvement plan (PIP) Standards established by franchisors. A franchisees must meet PIP or risk losing its franchise.

projection See *forecast scheduling.*

property Another way to reference a hotel; includes physical facilities and personnel.

property management system (PMS) A hotel's, that is a *property's,* basic computer installation designed for a variety of functions in both the back office and *front office.*

published rate The full *rack rate* quoted or published for public information; the rate quoted without discounts.

quad Accommodations for four persons; see also *twin–double.*

quality assurance A managerial and operational approach that enlists employee support in delivering a consistently high level of service.

quality circle A group of persons from different but related departments who meet on a regular basis for dialogue and problem resolutions as part of a *quality assurance* program.

quality management See *total quality management* and *quality assurance.*

quality of the reservation Differentiates *reservations* on how likely they are to be honored by the guest: *paid in advance reservation* vs. *guaranteed reservation* vs. 6 PM *cutoff hour,* and so on.

queen An extra-long, extra-wide bed, about 80 to 85 inches long by 60 inches wide; see *California length;* see *king.*

queuing theory The management of lines (queues of persons waiting their turn) in order to maximize the flow and minimize the inconvenience, but doing so with attention to operating costs. Also called *waiting-line theory.*

quote To state the cost of an item, room *rates* in particular.

rack See *room rack.*

rack rate The full *rate,* without discounts, that one *quotes* as a room charge; so called because the *room rack* is the source of the information.

rate The charge made by a hotel for its rooms.

rate cutting A reduction in *rate* that attracts business away from competitors rather than creating new customers or new markets.

real estate investment trust (REIT) A form of real estate ownership (public corporation) that became popular during the real estate recovery of the mid-1990s because of income tax advantages.

rebate See *allowance.*

recap A summary or recap(itulation) of several *transcript* sheets in order to obtain the day's grand totals.

referral A *central reservation system* operated by *independent* properties in contrast to that operated by chains and *franchisors* for their *affiliated hotels.*

registered, not assigned (RNA) The guest has *registered,* but is awaiting assignment to a specific room until space becomes available; see *on change.*

register(ing), registration (1) Indication (completing and signing the *registration card*) by a new arrival of intent to become a guest; (2) register: the name for a book that served at one time as the registration record; obsolete.

(reg)istration card A form completed during *registration* to provide the hotel with information about the guest, including name and address, and to provide the guest with information about the hotel, including legal issues.

REIT See *real estate investment trust.*

reminder clock A special alarm clock that can be set at 5-minute intervals across a 24-hour day; once used by the *front office* for *wake-up calls.*

rep(resentative) Short for *hotel rep*resentative: An agent under contract, rather than an employee under salary, who represents the hotel in distant cities or for special activities, chiefly marketing activities, but sometimes gaming related.

reservation A mutual agreement between the guest and the hotel, the former to take accommodations on a given date for a given period of time, and the latter to furnish the same.

reservation rack A piece of *front-office* equipment, largely replaced by the *property management system,* providing an alphabetic list of anticipated arrivals with a summary of their needs, filed chronologically by anticipated date of arrival.

residential hotel A hotel catering to long-stay guests who have made the *property* their home and residence; see also *permanent guest*.

resident manager See *hotel manager*.

resort hotel A hotel that caters to vacationing guests by providing recreational and entertainment facilities; usually a *destination hotel*.

RevPar Short for revenue per available room, a ratio of room revenue to the number of *available rooms*.

road warrior Slang for a frequent traveler battling the hardships and indignities of being on the road, that is, of traveling, for long periods of time.

rollaway bed A portable utility bed approximately 30 by 72 inches; also called a *cot*.

rondoval A *suite* in the round, special to honeymoon *resorts*.

room charge sheet See *room count sheet*.

room count The number of occupied rooms; cf. *house count*.

room count sheet A permanent record of the *room rack* prepared nightly and used to verify the accuracy of room statistics; also called a *night clerk's report*.

rooming (a guest) The entire procedure during which the desk greets, *registers*, and assigns new arrivals, and the bell staff accompanies them to their rooms (rooms them).

rooming slip A form issued by the desk to the bellperson during the *rooming* procedure for guest identification, and left by the bellperson with the guest to verify name, *rate*, and room number.

room inspection report A checklist of the condition of the guest room prepared by the *inspector* when the room attendant has finished cleaning.

room-night See *guest day (night)*.

room rack A piece of *front-office* equipment, now replaced by the *property management system*, in which each guest room is represented by a metal *pocket* with colors and symbols to aid the room clerk in identifying the accommodations.

room rack slip (card) A form prepared from the *registration card* identifying the occupant of each room and filed in the *pocket* of the *room rack* assigned to that guest; obsolete; cf. *room rack*.

rooms available See *available rooms*.

room service Food-and-beverage service provided in the privacy of the guest room.

rooms ledger See *guest ledger*.

rule-of-thumb rate A guideline for setting room rates with the hotel charging $1 in rate for each $1,000 per room construction costs; see also *building cost rate formula*.

run-of-the-house rate A special *group* rate generally the midpoint of the *rack rate* with a single, flat price applying to any room, *suites* excepted, assigned on a *best available* basis.

ryokan A traditional Japanese inn.

safe deposit boxes Individual sections of the vault where guests store valuables and cashiers keep house *banks*.

sales per occupied room See *average daily rate*.

sales rack A piece of *front-office* equipment, now replaced by the *property management system*, used for the storage and control of *stock cards* (*ducats* or *sales tickets*); obsolete.

sales ticket See *stock card*.

salon European designation for *parlor*.

sample room A guest room used to merchandise and display goods, usually in combination with sleeping accommodations.

Scottish breakfast See *English breakfast*.

seamless connectivity The next step beyond *last room availability*. *Travel agents*, airlines, online subscription networks, and others can access a *property*'s room availability right down to the last room.

search engine optimization Gaining maximum exposure on the Internet by an artful blending of *paid search results* and *organic search results* using the key words and phrases that most closely match the user's expected input.

season rate See *in-season rate*.

segmentation The proliferation of many hotel types as the lodging industry attempts to target its facilities to smaller and smaller market niches (segments).

sell and report *Wholesalers*, tour operators, *reps*, airlines, and *central reservation systems free sell* rooms, periodically reporting the sale to the hotel; also called status control.

sell through Denoting days for which no *reservation* arrivals are accepted; reservations for previous days will be accepted and allowed to stay through the date; cf. *box date*.

sell up Convince the arriving guest to take a higher-priced room than was planned or reserved.

service charge A percentage (usually from 10 to 20%) added to the bill for distribution to service employees in lieu of direct tipping; see also *plus, plus*.

service elevators Back elevators for use by employees (room service, housekeeping, maintenance, etc.) on hotel business and not readily visible to the guests; cf. *guest elevator*.

share More than one person occupying the guest room.

shoulder Marketing term designating the period between peaks and valleys; the time on either side of the *in-season rate* or the leveling off between two sales peaks.

Siberia Jargon for a very undesirable room, one sold only after the *house* fills and then only after the guest has been alerted to its location or condition.

single (1) A bed approximately 36 by 75 inches; (2) a room with accommodations for one; (3) occupancy by one person; (4) the *rate* charged for one person.

single supplement An extra charge over the tour *package* price assessed for *single* occupancy when the total price was based on a *double-occupancy rate*.

sitting room See *parlor*.

size The capacity of the hotel as measured by the number of guest rooms.

skip See *skipper*.

skipper A guest who departs surreptitiously, leaving an unpaid bill.

sleeper A departed guest whose record remains active, giving the appearance of an *occupied* room.

sleeper occupancy See *bed occupancy*.

sleep-out A room that is taken, *occupied*, and paid for but not slept in.

slide An error caused by a misplaced decimal, as when 36.20 is written 3.62.

smart card A credit card or other card containing a microprocessor capable of interfacing with the *PMS* or other computer configurations.

SMERF Marketing reference to Society, Military, Educational, Religious, and Fraternal organizations.

sofa bed A sofa with fixed back and arms that unfolds into a standard *single* or *double* bed; also called a *hide-a-bed*.

soft goods Linens; cf. *hard goods*.

software The programs and routines that give instructions to the computer; cf. *hardware*.

special attention (SPATT) A label assigned to important guests designated for special treatment; see *very important person*.

split rate Division of the total room *rate* charge among the room's several occupants; see *share*.

split shift A work pattern divided into two work segments with an unusually long period (more than a rest or mealtime) between.

spread rate Assignment of *group* members or conventioneers using the standard *rate* distribution, although prices might be less than *rack rates*; cf. *run-of-the-house rate*.

square meters Measurement used in the metric system: 0.093 square meters equal 1 square foot; 10.76 square feet equals 1 square meter.

star rating An unreliable ranking (except for some well-known exceptions) of hotel facilities both in the United States and abroad.

star reservation Indicates the arrival of a *very important person*, SPATT.

stay See *stay-over*.

stay-over (1) Any guest who remains overnight; (2) an anticipated check-out who fails to depart; also called *holdover* or *overstay*.

stock card Once used with a *sales rack* to represent the content of the *room rack pocket* when the room rack was distant and therefore inaccessible to the room clerk; also called a *ducat*; obsolete.

store rentals Income earned from shop leases; cf. *concession*.

studio (1) A bed approximately 36 inches wide by 75 inches long without headboard or footboard that serves as a sofa during the day; (2) the room containing such a bed; cf. *sofa bed*.

suite A series of *connecting rooms* with one or more bedrooms and a *parlor*; very large suites include additional rooms such as dining rooms; see *hospitality suite*.

summary transcript sheet See *recap*.

supper (1) A late-night meal; (2) the evening meal when midday service is designated as dinner.

swing The work shift between the day *watch* and the *graveyard* shift; usually starts between 3 and 4 PM.

T&T See *trash and towels*.

take down Cancel *reservations* that are without an *advance deposit* after the *cutoff hour*; also called "dump"; cf: *dump*.

tally sheet See *density board*.

TelAutograph A historical piece of communication equipment that transcribes written messages; obsolete.

timeshare (1) A method of acquiring accommodations by which each occupant purchases the right to use the facility (room or apartment) for a specified period; an interval ownership; (2) term for users who share computer facilities.

time stamp A clock mechanism that prints date and time when activated.

to-date Designates a cumulative amount; the sum of all figures in the current period (usually monthly or annually) including the day or date in question.

total quality management (TQM) A way to continuously improve performance at every level of operation, in every functional area of an organization, using all available human and capital resources. See also *quality assurance*.

tour group See *package*.

tourist class A non-U.S. designation for *limited-service* hotels whose accommodations frequently lack private baths; also called *economy class*.

trade advertising contract An agreement by which hotel accommodations are swapped for advertising space or broadcast time; also called a *due bill*.

traffic sheet A *departmental control sheet* once used by the telephone department before *call accounting systems*; obsolete.

transcript A pencil-and-paper form once used by the *night auditor* to accumulate and separate the day's charges by departments and guests.

transcript ruler The headings of a *transcript* sheet attached to a straightedge and used as a column guide at the bottom of the long *transcript* sheet.

transfer (1) An accounting technique used to move a figure from one form to another, usually between *folios*; (2) the movement of guests and/or luggage from one point to another (e.g., from the airline terminal to the hotel); see *porterage*.

transfer from The *debit* portion of a *transfer* between accounts or ledgers.

transfer journal A *front-office* form once used to record *transfer* entries between different accounts or different ledgers.

transfer to The *credit* portion of a *transfer* between accounts or ledgers.

transient guest A short-term guest; see *transient hotel*.

transient hotel A hotel catering to short-stay guests who sometimes stop en route to other destinations; cf. *destination hotel*.

transient ledger See *guest ledger*.

transmittal form The form provided by national credit-card companies for recording and remitting nonelectronic credit-card charges accumulated by the hotel.

transposition A transcription error caused by reordering the sequence of digits, as when 389 is written as 398.

trash and towels References basic service fee paid for each stay by occupants of *timeshares*.

travel agent (TA) An entrepreneur who *books* space and facilities for clients in hotels and public carriers for which hotels usually pay a 10% commission.

travel and entertainment card (T&E) A credit card issued by a proprietary company, or bank, for which the user pays an annual fee; cf. *bank card*.

Travel Industry Association of America (TIAA) A nonprofit association of many travel-related agencies and private businesses working to develop travel and tourism in the United States.

tray service The fee charged *American-plan* and *all-inclusive* guests for *room service*.

tub See *cashier's well*.

turn away (1) To refuse *walk-in* business because rooms are unavailable; (2) the guest so refused is a turn-away.

turn-downs An evening service rendered by the housekeeping department, which replaces soiled bathroom linen and prepares the bed for use.

turn-in The sum deposited with the *general cashier* by the departmental cashier at the close of each shift.

turnkey A facility (computer, *franchise*, entire hotel) so complete that it is almost ready for use at the turn of a key.

twin (1) A bed approximately 39 inches wide by 75 inches long to sleep a single occupant; (2) a room with two such beds, *twins*.

twin-double (1) Two double beds; (2) a room with two such beds capable of accommodating 4 persons; see *quad*.

twins Two *twin* beds.

type The kind of market toward which the hotel is directed, traditionally: *commercial, residential,* and *resort*.

understay A guest who leaves before the expiration of the anticipated stay.

Uniform System of Accounts for the Lodging Industry A manual and dictionary of accounting terms, primarily incomes and expenses, to ensure industrywide uniformity in terminology and use.

United States Travel and Tourism Administration (USTTA) A division of the Department of Commerce responsible for promoting travel to the United States; successor to the U.S. Travel Service (USTS).

unoccupied (1) An unsold room; (2) a room that is *occupied*, but is temporarily vacant, the guest is out.

u-owe-me See *exchange*.

upgrade Move a *reservation* or a currently registered guest to a better accommodation or class of service; cf. *downgrade*.

upsell See *sell up*.

use rate See *day rate*.

user-friendly Computer design, application, or implementation that minimizes the user's fears, encouraging purchase and use of the equipment.

vacancy The hotel is not fully *occupied*, so there are rooms available for sale.

very important person (VIP) A reservation or guest who warrants *special attention (SPATT)* and handling.

VoIP Voice over Internet Protocol. See *Internet telephony*.

voucher (1) The form used by the *operating departments* to notify the front desk of charges incurred by a particular guest; (2) form furnished by a *travel agent* as a receipt for a client's advance *reservation* payment; see *coupon*.

waiting-line theory See *queuing theory*.

wake-up call See *morning call*.

walk (a guest) To turn away guests holding confirmed *reservations* due to a lack of available rooms.

walk-in A guest without a *reservation* who requests and receives accommodations.

walk-through A thorough examination of the *property* by a hotel executive, *franchise* inspector, prospective buyer, and so on.

watch Another term for the work shift.

WATS See *wide area telephone service*.

who An unidentified guest in a room that appears vacant in the *room rack*.

wholesaler An entrepreneur who conceives, finances, and services *group* and *package* tours that he or she promotes (often through *travel agents*) to the general public.

wide area telephone service (WATS) Long-distance telephone lines provided at special rates to large users; separate charges are levied for incoming and outgoing WATS lines.

worldwide travel vouchers (WTVs) Form of payments drawn against a well-known financial institution (usually a major credit-card company).

xenodoghcionology The study of the history, lore, and stories associated with inns, hotels, and motels (zeno-dog-hi-on-ology).

yield The product of *occupancy* times *average daily rate*.

yield management (1) Controlling room *rates* and restricting *occupancy* in order to maximize gross revenue *(yield)* from all sources; (2) a computerized program using artificial intelligence.

youth hostel See *hostel*.

zero out To balance the *guest bill* as the guest *checks out* and makes settlement.

zip-out See *express check-out*.

The Traditional Hotel Industry

From Chapter 1 of *Check-In Check-Out,* Ninth Edition. Gary K. Vallen, Jerome J. Vallen. Copyright © 2013 by Pearson Education, Inc. All rights reserved.

The Traditional Hotel Industry

Over eons of time, wanderers and single travelers found security and accommodations in trees and caves, castles and churches, homes and estates. Greater political and economic freedom eventually increased their numbers. Soon, the courtesy of friendly hosts gave way to commercial enterprise. The hotel industry was born carrying this culture of hospitality. So *hospitality* and *hotels* are related concepts, deriving from the same Latin root. However, the word "hotel," which comes from the French *hôtel*, meaning large house, didn't appear until the 18th century.

UNDERSTANDING THE HOTEL BUSINESS

The Service Culture

The hotel industry has flourished through the centuries by adapting to the changing environment that marks human progress. These stages have been labeled: The 18th century was the agricultural age; the 19th, the industrial age; and the 20th century the age of service, including medicine, education, and hotelkeeping. The 21st century opened with that same service culture, but will likely close as the age of technology. Innkeeping has started to adapt its hospitality heritage to the new age. The shift translates into newer kinds of, but less personal, services.

A Cyclical Industry

Hotelkeeping is a cyclical industry that closely follows economic phases. Wide swings carry the innkeeping industry between peaks of exceptional profits and troughs of outright distress. This rollercoaster has been most evident over the past half century. The entire travel industry was brought to its knees by the oil embargo of 1973. Innkeeping then cycled from bankruptcy to recovery. A decade later, in the early 1980s, the industry witnessed a second such distress when the federal government changed the income tax laws on real estate. (Remember, as hotels are pieces of real estate, any change in real estate will directly affect the hotel industry.) Dominant companies bought distressed properties at that time and recovery followed once again. By the late 1990s, hotel profits had reappeared. Just as the recovery was being consolidated came the tragedy of 9/11, the attacks on the World Trade Center (2001). Travel and tourism bottomed out again. Although recovery was faster this time, it was short-lived. First, a stumbling prosperity and then a dramatic downturn in the U.S. economy in 2008 halted travel once again. Business began an upward crawl anew in late 2010.

Hoteliers stop building during downturns. Three years is the typical span between planning and opening a hotel. It's even longer if there are special financing, zoning, or environmental issues. Over half of the announced projects are never built. For instance, Taj Hotels took 18 months just to renovate The Pierre in New York. When occupancy and profits boom, the competition begins to rev up new properties. So new rooms often come on line—three years later—just as the cycle peaks. That increased supply exaggerates the next downward dip. Supply and demand play their traditional roles in hotel economics as they do for general business. Overbuilding (excess supply) exaggerates the downturns far more often than does insufficient demand (fewer customers).

How Hotels Count and Measure

Within the cycles, new hotels and hotel rooms are built and old rooms are removed. One can never say for certain how many hotels or hotel rooms are available at a given time. Governmental agencies (Bureau of the Census) and trade associations (American Hotel & Lodging Association (AH&LA)) track and report the numbers. Other interested parties include the World Tourism Organization (WTO), the International Hotel and Restaurant Association (IH&RA), and private firms such as Smith Travel Research and PricewaterhouseCoopers. None of the figures ever agree; some not even close.

The Bureau of the Census counts once every decade and takes several years to report. By then, the numbers become inaccurate. The 2010 count, for example, was made during a horrific downturn cycle when many hotels had closed.[1] Still, estimates are possible. The previous count approximated 65,000 hotels in the United States with some 5,500,000 hotel rooms. The typical hotel, about half of which are small, nonchain affiliated, has about 85 rooms. Figures get skewed, however, because convention hotels (large hotels) number less than 2% of all U.S. properties, but contain about 12% of all hotel rooms.

Hotels are valued on a per-room cost, either the cost per room to build or the resale price per room—called the *per-key cost*. Valuing each room at, say, $250,000—unchanged in the past several years because costs rose substantially and then fell even more so—U.S. hotels are worth nearly $1.5 trillion.

Together, Europe and the United States once accounted for two-thirds of the world's total rooms. However, their leadership has been challenged by the robust growth of tourism and business travel in other areas, such as Asia and South America. For example, international companies built 50 five-star hotels in Beijing for the 2008 Olympics. Marriott Hotels opened seven of them, with its Great Wall property alone having 1,300 rooms. Growth like this changes the world's balance.

OCCUPANCY Occupancy, a measure of supply and demand, gauges the industry's economic health. While robust demand encourages construction of new rooms, falling demand seals the fate of old hotels. Worn-out rooms are kept in place only during boom periods, when there is a room shortage. They fall to the wrecker's ball or are converted when they are competitive no longer. Many were renovated into dormitory rooms when American universities were in their boom years. In the 1990s, condo conversion was the hot move as luxury residential units were more valuable than luxury hotel units. One of the most publicized of these conversions was that of the New York City's famous Plaza. The hotel's 800 rooms were converted into 152 residential condo units and 282 guest rooms. However, the downturn that began in 2008 put an end to condo conversions.

At any given time, the number of rooms available for sale reflects the mathematics of the old and the new. During the upward cycle, more guests are buying, but fewer rooms are available. Room rates rise. Just the opposite happens in a downward cycle: There are fewer buyers and more rooms, so rates fall. Customer demand is measured by the *number of rooms occupied*, also called the *number of rooms sold*. Hoteliers count this figure every night.

Hoteliers also count the number of rooms in their hotels. Although the number of rooms is just an estimate worldwide, hotel managers know their own numbers. Whether for the world, the region, or the individual hotel, that number is called *the number of rooms available for sale*.

The relationship (or ratio) between the *number of rooms sold* (demand) and the *number of rooms available* (supply) measures the property's health. It is a closely watched value that asks, "How well did we sell rooms relative to the number of rooms that could have been sold?" That big mouthful has a shortcut called the *percentage of occupancy*, or *occupancy percentage*, or just *occupancy*.

---

[1]Facts about the lodging industry are reported in the *SC Series*, but results of the 2010 Census were not yet available for this publication.

The occupancy calculation is a simple division. The number of rooms available for sale is divided into the number of rooms sold (see Exhibit 1):

$$\frac{\text{number of rooms sold}}{\text{number of rooms available for sale}} = \text{a percentage of occupancy}$$

Occupancy can be computed by one hotel for one night, one month, or one year. Citywide, regional (the Northeast, for example), and national occupancies are tracked by many agencies. Among them are hotel chains, convention bureaus, and state tourism offices.

Values become less accurate as the count moves from the individual property to a worldwide number. Nevertheless, everyone is engrossed in occupancy figures. More so when estimates suggest that a mere 1% rise in chain occupancy represents millions of dollars of improved profits.

SALES PER OCCUPIED ROOM Occupancy measures quantity, that is, the hotel's share of the market. *Sales per occupied room*—also called *average daily rate* (ADR)—measures quality. Its formula (see Exhibit 1) is:

$$\frac{\text{total dollar room sales}}{\text{number of rooms sold}} = \text{ADR (a dollar value per room sold)}$$

Given	Number of rooms in the hotel available for sale	800
	Number of rooms in the hotel	820
	Number of rooms sold to guests	600
	Number of dollars received from guests for rooms	$72,000
	Number of employees on staff	500
	Number of guests	700

Computations

Percentage of occupancy is 75%.

$$\frac{\text{number of rooms sold (to guests)}}{\text{number of rooms (in the hotel) available for sale}} = \frac{600}{800} = \frac{3}{4} = 75\%$$

Sales per occupied room (average daily rate, ADR) is $120.00.

$$\frac{\text{room sales (as measured in dollars)}}{\text{number of rooms sold (to guests)}} = \frac{\$72,000}{600} = \$120.00$$

Sales per available room (RevPar) is $90.00.

$$\frac{\text{room sales (as measured in dollars)}}{\text{number of rooms (in the hotel) available for sale}} = \frac{\$72,000}{800} = \$90.00$$

Mathematical check:

$$\text{ADR} \times \text{occupancy} = \text{RevPar} \qquad \$120 \times 0.75 = \$90.00$$

Number of employees per guest room is 0.625.

$$\frac{\text{number of employees (on staff)}}{\text{number of rooms (in the hotel) available for sale}} = \frac{500}{800} = 0.625$$

Percentage of double occupancy is 16.6%.

$$\frac{\text{number of guests} - \text{number of rooms sold}}{\text{number of rooms sold}} = \frac{700 - 600}{600} = 16.6\%$$

EXHIBIT 1 Hoteliers track the health of the industry through the measures and ratios shown. Outside of the United States, bed occupancy percentage (number of beds sold ÷ number of beds available) is often substituted for the percentage of room occupancy. Bed (or guest or sleeper) occupancy of 50% approximates room occupancy of 70%.

The health of the industry is reflected in both occupancy and price. Price, ADR, ($) increases as occupancy (%) increases. The more rooms sold—that is, the greater the demand—the higher the room rate. That's because lower-priced rooms sell first. Conversely, as occupancy falls, so does the ADR. Supply and demand are at work.

REVPAR (REVENUE PER AVAILABLE ROOM)   RevPar is an old industry standby that once was called *average rate per available room*. RevPar (or REVPAR) measures management's ability to keep rates high even as occupancy declines. Hoteliers are fond of saying, "hotels fill from the bottom up," meaning that guests elect lower rates when an empty house allows it. Superior managers strive to keep rates high even as occupancy dips within the cycle. Management does this using *yield management*. RevPar reflects the revenue (sales) relative to the total rooms available for sale. In contrast, ADR measures the revenue per room relative to the number of rooms actually sold. (Remember, "rooms sales" and "room revenue" are interchangeable terms.) Exhibit 1 illustrates the computation.

$$\frac{\text{total dollar room sales}}{\text{number of rooms available for sale}} = \text{RevPar (measured in dollars)}$$

Both of the values, room sales and number of rooms available, are easily misstated. Total room sales must not include taxes or the value of free breakfasts or parking. Similarly, the number of rooms available must include vacant rooms, but not those permanently assigned to other uses such as offices.

Before 2008, RevPar was rising steadily, increasing at the top of the cycle aided by inflation. That value took a nose dive in 2008–2011 when the average price of a hotel room fell about 16%.

RevPar does not reflect management's ability to control costs or produce sales in other departments. RevPar is an ideal measure for rooms-only hotels (those with no bars, no laundries, and no restaurants).

DOUBLE OCCUPANCY   Exhibit 1 continues with the occupancy calculations. Spoken as "double occupancy," the value is really a "percentage of double occupancy."

$$\frac{\text{number of guests} - \text{number of rooms occupied}}{\text{number of rooms occupied}} = \text{percentage of double occupancy}$$

"Multiple occupancy" is a better term than "double occupancy" because more than two guests may be housed in one room. If the number of guests is greater than two, the formula falters. Assume, for example, two rooms occupied by three persons in one room and one person in the other. The calculation would be 4 (guests) − 2 (rooms) ÷ 2 (rooms) = 1 or 100% double occupancy. In fact, it is only 50%, one room in two.

Double occupancy's impact on room revenue is much clearer. Additional charges (a double rate) is usually levied when families, skiers, and tour groups double up. Casino/hotels want bodies on the casino floor, so they rarely charge double occupancy rates. High double occupancy is associated with resort properties, giving them a higher ADR.

Another statistical fudge occurs when comps (complimentary—free rooms) are counted as occupied. The occupancy percentage increases but ADR decreases because there are no dollars earned. Similarly, averages for the entire industry are slanted when large hotels are counted along with hotels of 50 rooms or less.

BREAK-EVEN POINT   To break even is to have neither profit nor loss. Inflows from revenues match exactly outflows from costs. Hotels have large fixed costs including interest on debt payments, licenses, taxes, and fixed salaries and wages. Reducing fixed costs drops the level of occupancy needed to break even. Similarly, increasing sales from food, beverage, spa, and so on reduces the pressure on room sales. Increasing RevPar also contributes, provided the percentage of occupancy is maintained.

Break-even points are important, because there is no profit until that point is reached. Once the point is reached, profits accumulate quickly. Each sales dollar before the break-even point is used to pay off debt, pay utilities, and pay the staff. Thereafter, each dollar contributes to profits.

Break-even points are expressed in percentage of occupancy. That value has been declining over the past decades. Better hotel design and better financing have held down both variable and fixed costs. Changes in market mix and higher room rates have improved revenues, the other component of break even. So break-even points fell throughout the past quarter-century. Recently, however, rising debt and shrinking revenues boosted the break-even occupancy—at the very time when occupancy nosedived.

Special Characteristics of the Hotel Business

Several special characteristics limit management's flexibility. While some are lodging-only issues, some are found in other industries as well.

PERISHABILITY   Vacant rooms are perishable. The industry's mantra is "an unsold room tonight can never be sold again." Unlike a can of fruit which inventories on the grocer's shelf, hotel rooms are time restricted. No way to take last night's empty room to meet an overflow tonight. Like empty airline, theater, or arena seats, unsold hotel rooms cannot be stored, cannot be saved, and cannot be used anew.

LOCATION   According to Ellsworth Statler, who sold his Statler chain to Hilton, "Location, location, location" are the three most important aspects of [hotel] real estate. Good locations are not easy to acquire. Changing neighborhoods and shifting demographics sometimes doom a hotel whose original location was good. Unlike an airline seat, there is no way to move the hotel room. A fixed location in an uneven neighborhood requires astute management and a heavy dependence on marketing and sales.

FIXED SUPPLY   Just as the hotel's location is fixed, so is its supply of rooms. Airlines adjust to demand by adding or removing flights. Not so with hotels. What you see is what you must manage.

HIGH OPERATING COSTS   Unlike manufacturing, which offsets high labor costs with large capital investments, hotels are both capital- and labor-intensive. The result is, in the jargon of the trade, a *large nut*. Large built-in costs continue regardless of occupancy levels. Innkeeping's break-even hurdle is high.

SEASONALITY   Throwing away the key is a traditional practice when a new hotel opens. The act signifies that the hotel never closes. Yet, hotelkeeping is a very seasonal business. Cyclical dips hit commercial hotels every seven days as they struggle to offset poor weekend occupancy. The federal holiday law that extended weekends into Mondays certainly didn't help.

Occupancy computations must account for this weekend phenomenon. Especially since the business traveler—the very person not registered during the weekend—still accounts for the bulk of the industry's business. Given the usual profile of the commercial, urban hotel (see Exhibit 2), national occupancy in the 70–80% range remains an elusive goal. Annual cycles compound the problem. Commercial occupancy falls off between Thanksgiving and New Years and from May Day to Labor Day.

Monday	100%
Tuesday	100
Wednesday	90
Thursday	90
Friday	40
Saturday	20
Sunday	20
Total	460%
Average per 7 days	66%

EXHIBIT 2   The difficulty of achieving a national occupancy in the mid-70% range is highlighted by the typical cycle of weekly occupancy for commercial hotels. The challenge is convincing groups, whose members work all week, to hold conventions on the weekends. (*Smith Travel Research* now tracks U.S. occupancy daily and weekly as well as annually.)

Resorts have an opposite pattern: They have busy weekends, but slower midweeks. The slack months of the commercial hotel is the very season of the resort hotel. At one time, resorts opened Memorial Day and closed Labor Day. Winter resorts (December 15–March 15) fared no better. Bad weather devastated both the 100-day seasons.

Both summer and winter resorts have extended seasons with groups, conferences, and special events. Most remain open year-round. Hotels that operate on the four-day season may be worse off than the seasonal hotels. At least the latter have a higher double occupancy.

TRADITIONAL CLASSIFICATIONS

Lodging is an industry of rapid transformation. The inns of old evolved from private homes located along the traveler's route. Today's hotel is often a point of destination even as it serves its traditional role of accommodating those in transit. Yesterday's tavern offered meals with the family. Dining today is a created experience in design, décor, and menu. Early inns were indistinguishable from their neighbor's homes. Today's edifice is a sharp contrast in style and packaging (see Exhibit 3).

The industry still delivers the basic accommodations of shelter, food, and hospitality. It is the means of delivery that has changed. These variations have been marked by shifting terminology: *hostel, tavern, public house, inn, guest house, hotel, resort, motel, motor lodge, motor inn, bed and breakfast,* and *condo.*

The industry's trade association has undergone similar shifts in identity. The American Hotel Association became the American Hotel & Motel Association, more recently the American Hotel and Lodging Association. "Motel" has been replaced in the professional vocabulary with new hotel types.

Changes notwithstanding, several traditional classifications have withstood the test of time. They are size, class, type, and plan. These are not definitive, objective measures. Nor are they self-exclusive. Hotels fall into all categories or into just some. Each category impacts differently on how managers manage.

Size

The number of rooms available for sale, the very same figure used in occupancy computations (see Exhibit 1), is the standard measure of size. Measures such as the number of employees or gross dollar sales are simply not used. Counting available rooms is not as certain a gauge

EXHIBIT 3 Unlike the inns of yesteryear, today's hotels are often architectural attractions, creating a buzz that helps assure their success. *Courtesy of the Singapore Sands, Singapore.*

as one would first believe. More rooms may be advertised than are actually available. Older hotels have rooms that are no longer saleable. Newer properties lose guest rooms to unplanned offices and storage. As a rule, the older the hotel, the fewer rooms available relative to total room count.

Hotels are grouped by size for financial reporting, for the U.S. Census and for trade association dues. Traditionally, large hotels are 300 rooms, or more. Medium hotels are 100–300 rooms and small hotels are less than 100 rooms. Recognizing that these definitions are getting dated, the AH&LA boosted its definition of small to 150 rooms. About 25% of its membership falls into the small category.

For hotels seeking government loans, the Small Business Administration's (SBA) definition of "small" for lodging enterprises is $7 million dollars in annual sales. That value changes periodically. An 80-room hotel with 70% occupancy and an ADR of $100 would qualify. It would only generate $2,044,000 annually (80 rooms × 70% occupancy × $100 ADR × 365 days per year).

Visualizing small- and medium-sized hotels as *the* lodging industry is difficult when one thinks of famous hotels such as the Waldorf=Astoria in New York City with 1,852 rooms, or the New Otani in Tokyo, 2,057 rooms (see Exhibit 4). Small hotels are more common in Europe where they have been traditionally family owned and operated.[2] The shift to chains and franchised hotel names has accelerated recently in both Europe and Asia and is changing the structure of the business there. Still, only one-third of Europe's hotels are branded versus three-fourths in the United States.

Hotel	Number of Rooms[a]	Location
Venetian/Palazzo[b]	7,100	Las Vegas
MGM grand/Mansion/Signature[b]	6,850	Las Vegas
Asia-Asia[c]	6,500	Dubai, United Arab Emirates
First World Hotel	6,100	Genting Highlands, Malaysia
Wynn/Encore[b]	4,750	Las Vegas
Luxor	4,400	Las Vegas
Mandalay Bay/The Hotel[b]	4,350	Las Vegas
Ambassador City	4,200	Jomtien Beach, Thailand
Excalibur	4,050	Las Vegas
Aria	4,000	Las Vegas
Bellagio	4,000	Las Vegas
Circus Circus	3,700	Las Vegas
Planet Hollywood (nee: Aladdin)	3,700	Las Vegas
Shinagawa Prince	3,700	Tokyo
Flamingo	3,550	Las Vegas
Hilton Hawaiian Village	3,400	Honolulu
Caesars Palace	3,350	Las Vegas
Las Vegas Hilton	3,200	Las Vegas
Mirage	3,050	Las Vegas
Opryland Hotel	3,000	Nashville
Monte Carlo	3,000	Las Vegas
Venetian	3,000	Macau
Cosmopolitan[d]	3,000	Las Vegas

[a] Room numbers have been rounded to 50.
[b] Built and marketed as separate hotels.
[c] Announced, but not opened.
[d] Opened but not complete.

EXHIBIT 4 Megahotels, once exclusive to Las Vegas, are now worldwide. Still, many of these behemoths rely on gaming for their financial success. The Opryland Hotel, which bills itself as the largest U.S. hotel outside of Nevada, is part of Gaylord Entertainment. The world's tallest hotel opened in 2011: The Hong Kong Ritz-Carlton has 118 floors.

[2]Family-owned hotels account for 94% of Italy's hotel companies.

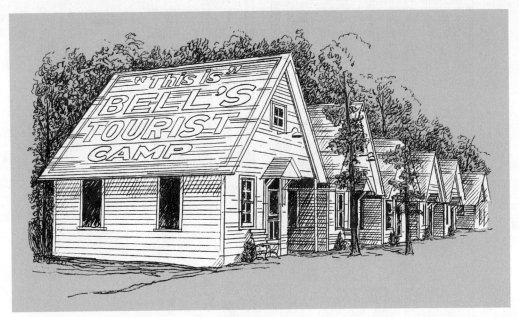

EXHIBIT 5 Tourist courts predated the highway motel, which gained momentum from the federal, interstate road construction boom following World War II. Kemmons Wilson's Holiday Inn chain (1952) set the initial standard for motels. Then came amenity creep.

MOM-AND-POP MOTELS   The term "motel" (motor + hotel) was coined after World War II when Americans took to the highways. The concept was refined by Kemmon's Wilson who created the Holiday Inn chain. Motels replaced the very limited facilities known as tourist courts (see Exhibit 5). Many "motels"—the term has now fallen from favor—were family owned and operated. Whence comes the term "mom-and-pop." There were some 60,000 mom-and-pop motels along the 1960s highways. Rising construction costs and difficult financing headed a list of hurdles that such small entrepreneurs could not overcome. They did not purchase in quantity; they were unable to advertise widely; and they competed against the better management talent that worked for their chain/franchise competitors.

Class

The class of hotel is sensed as often as it is measured, but two yardsticks quantify the appraisal: They are price (ADR) and rating systems.

AVERAGE DAILY RATE   Delivering class, elegance, and service costs money. Larger rooms, upgraded furnishings, and extra employees incur larger financing costs, depreciation, energy, wages, and more. So too do better levels of maintenance, 24-hour room service, saunas, and similar extras. All must be recovered by higher rates. More than just a generalization: The better the class of hotel the higher the rate.

Driven by inflation, ADR has been increasing industry-wide for decades. So a higher room rate over time is not the measure. A higher rate relative to competition is critical. Location, location, location also plays a role. Hotels in small towns are different than their big-city counterparts. A $75 rate in Los Angeles conjures up a totally different class of lodging than does that same rate in a small rural town. However, at a given time and with concern for size, type, and location, ADR is a fair measure of class. So published rates help classify the nation's hotels (see Exhibit 6).

FULL-SERVICE TO LIMITED-SERVICE   Hotels are as diverse as the traveling public that fills them. Responding to varied needs, the industry has created a range of accommodations from the full-service high-rise to the squat roadside inn. One group offers nothing more than a clean room and a good mattress. Guests do not need swimming pools, closets, or lobbies, goes that argument. This hotelier offers limited service at minimum price. It does so with new language: Limited service is now "select service," or, better still, "focused service."

Classification of Hotels by Average Daily Room Rate

Deluxe Hotels (typical room rate: $650 plus/night)
- Fairmont Hotels
- Four Seasons Hotels
- Ritz-Carlton Hotels

Upper Upscale Hotels (typical room rate: $450/night)
- Le Meridien Hotels
- Sofitel Hotels
- W Hotels

Upscale Hotels (typical room rate: $350/night)
- Hyatt Hotels
- Marriott Hotels
- Omni Hotels

Midprice Hotels with Food (typical room rate: $160/night)
- Four Points (Sheraton)
- Garden Inns (Hilton)
- Best Western

Midprice Hotels without Food (typical room rate: $95/night)
- AmeriSuites
- Hampton Inns
- La Quinta

Economy Hotels (typical room rate: $70/night)
- Baymont Inns and Suites
- Red Roof Inns
- Super 8

Budget Inns (typical room rate: $65/night)
- EconoLodge
- Microtel
- Motel 6

EXHIBIT 6 ADR, average daily rate, identifies the class of hotel, offering consumers a range of accommodations from the bare-minimum budget facility to the full-service, super deluxe property.

One hundred eighty degrees away is the full-service, upscale property. This hotel has superior facilities and a full complement of services. Limited services means lobby vending machines or a nearby restaurant servicing several properties in the area. Full service has a menu of dining options and a range of extras: lounges, room service, newspapers to the room, exercise facilities, and electronic support. Expense-account travelers patronize full-service properties although something less costly may do when the family travels.

Between the two lies the bulk of facilities. Services are added as competition demands and costs allow. Services are pared as markets shift and as acceptable self-service equipment appears.

NUMBER OF EMPLOYEES Class as measured by full service or limited service refers as much to the size of the staff as to the physical amenities. Thus, the number of employees per guest room is another measure of class (see Exhibit 1).

$$\frac{\text{number of employees on staff}}{\text{number of rooms available for sale}} = \text{number of employees per guest room}$$

Budget properties, those without restaurants or amenities such as bars or room service, operate with as few as 0.25 (one-fourth) employee per guest room. An 80-room house might have as few as 20 employees. There's a limit to how small the staff can shrink. If the property wants the legal benefits of being a hotel, common law requires it to be open 24 hours daily. Now add in staff days-off, plus a minimum housekeeping crew, night security, someone for repairs and maintenance, and the total grows.

Because a minimum staff is needed, a hotel of 60 rooms might have almost the same number of employees as one of, say, 100 rooms. Each property needs a minimum number at the desk, a manager, a head housekeeper, an accountant, and someone in maintenance. Each must provide for vacations and sickness. Housekeeping is staffed differently. If a housekeeper cleans 15 rooms per shift, every additional 15 rooms requires an extra employee and eventually a supervisor. Hotels minimize that number by using and paying for call-in housekeepers only when volume dictates.

The in-between class of hotels uses an in-between number of employees. That ratio ranges from 0.5 (one-half) an employee per room to a ratio as high as 1:1. Depending on the services offered, a 300-room hotel could have as few as 125 employees to as many as 250. Some may be part-time.

Full-service hotels require more employees to staff a variety of departments. All of them have bells, restaurants, turn-down service, marketing, and pools. Still more staff is needed for properties with theaters, acres of grounds, casinos, and 24-hour room service. The employee–rooms ratio may jump then to 1.5. Thus, a 1,000-room hotel/casino operating 24 hours could have 1,250–1,500 employees. No wonder so many localities with low labor usage—Detroit, for example—have voted for local casinos.

Asian hotels have the largest employee–rooms ratio because labor is less costly. The Bangkok Shangri-La, for example, has 1,073 staff members for 697 rooms, a ratio of 1.5:1. Hong Kong's Peninsula Hotel operates with 655 employees for its 300 rooms. That's better than 2:1. The Singapore Sands (see Exhibit 3) has a nearly 4:1 ratio: 10,000 employees for 2,560 rooms. (No wonder, Singapore's few hotel/casinos generate more earnings than all of Las Vegas' hotels combined.)

Worldwide, the workforce is huge. The United States alone has some 2 million hotel workers. The privately funded World Tourism and Travel Council (WTTC) estimates 225 million employees in the world's tourism industry. That includes about 13% of Europe's total labor force.

RATING SYSTEMS Room rates provide good guidance to the class of hotel even when formal rating systems exist. Some rating systems have been publicized; some have not. Some are government-run; some are not. Most are standardized within the single country, but not so across borders. Members of the World Tourism Organization have done much to standardize their systems by adopting the WTO's five recommended classes. Deluxe or luxury class is at the top. First-class, which is not top-of-the-line despite its name, comes next. Tourist class, sometimes called economy or second class is actually third in line. Third and fourth class (really the fourth and fifth ranks) usually have no private baths, no centralized heat, not even carpeting.

International travelers avoid third- and fourth-class facilities. They also know to discount the deluxe category of many Caribbean properties. Similarly, experienced travelers limit stays in Africa and the Middle East to deluxe properties.

Worldwide There are some 100 rating systems worldwide. Most of them rank by using stars; others use coffee pots, alphabets, and even feathers. Britain uses ticks for its holiday parks, which are upscale RV (recreational vehicle) parks.

Europe's system is the most developed. Its four- and five-star hotels have restaurants and bars. *Hotel garni* means no restaurant but a continental breakfast is usually served. That's the usage in England as well as on the Continent and both correspond to the U.S. phrase, "breakfast included."

The Swiss and Mexican Hotel Associations are unique because they are self-rating, private organizations. The Swiss use the World Trade Organization's (WTO) five classifications plus a luxury class termed "Gran Tourism" or "Gran Especial." The Irish Tourist Board takes a different approach, listing the facilities available (e.g., elevator, air conditioning, laundry) rather than grading them. Directories of the European Community do the same and also classify by location: seaside/countryside, small town/large city. European auto clubs go further by distinguishing privately owned from government-run accommodations.

Spain has standardized the rating system of its *paradors* (stopping places) despite a wide range of facilities and furnishings. About one-third of this government-operated chain is at a four-star level.

In 2008, Italy finally adopted a one-to-five-star rating system but left enforcement to individual regions. One of the rating criteria is room size: The minimum size of a four-and five-star hotel room must be 15 square meters (155 square feet). Hotels will rate four- or five stars only if the staff has foreign language capability.

Japanese traditional inns, *ryokans,* are rated according to their rooms and baths and—of all things to Western values—gardens. These hotels offer two meals, which are often taken in the uncluttered guest room that opens onto those gardens. The Japanese Travel Bureau lists about 1,000 ryokans for international guests. Ryokans are not favored by Japanese nationals.

Korea has its own version of traditional, budget-priced lodging called *yogwans.* Most have standard hotel accommodations. Upscale *yogwans* have names that end in *jang* or *chang.*

The United Kingdom has the largest number of rating systems including the National Tourist Board (NTB), the Automobile Association (AA), the Royal Automobile Club (RAC), and commercial enterprises such as Michelin. Some rate by stars; others use pavilions or crowns. Each classification is further divided by grades or percentages. For example, the AA might rate a property as Four Star, 65%.

The U.S. System Unlike the United Kingdom's mix of private and governmental rating systems, the U.S. ratings rely solely on private enterprise. The American Automobile Association (AAA) has been one of two major participants. The other participant Mobil (now named Forbes) was started in the motor-lodge era of the late 1950s as a subsidiary of Mobil Oil. Now, both face a wide range of competitors.

Michelin, which is popular in Europe, now has U.S. guidebooks. Zagat started with restaurant guides and only recently added hotel ratings. J. D. Powers, which is famous for rating consumer goods, has also entered the market. Many websites (Expedia, for one) carry evaluations as do a wide range of publications. Social networks probably do the best job because previous guests "tell it like it is!" on websites for all to read.

There are bed-and-breakfast guides, magazine guides, regional guides, even one by the National Association for the Advancement of Colored People (NAACP). None are government affiliated. All are crowding out the traditional star system of Forbes and the diamond ratings of AAA (see Exhibit 7).

Historically, a good Mobil (Forbes) listing boosted occupancy by 20% or so. Similarly, as much as 40% of room sales in small hotels has been attributed to an AAA listing. Both agencies rely on anonymous, on-site inspections to cover about 25,000 properties. AAA personnel identify themselves after their annual visit. Forbes inspectors come every 18 months but remain anonymous. Online reservation (res) systems such as Priceline also send inspectors, but they solicit business at the same time. AAA includes information for handicapped travelers; the Scottish Tourist Bureau does too using three levels of accessibility. All travel guides encourage input from their users.

By building different facilities for different markets, hotel chains have created internal rating systems, but few consumers recognize them.

Membership in Preferred Hotels, a loosely knit affiliation of independent properties, requires ratings of superior or above from one of the recognized services. By just belonging, the hotel flashes its rating.

Not all guides are consumer oriented. Several list conference and meeting facilities. Others are aimed at travel agents and meeting planners. Among the publications that focus on the trade are the *Hotel and Travel Index,* the *Official Hotel Guide*, and the *Official Meeting Facilities Guide.* Their contents list both objective (number of meeting rooms) and subjective assessments (food, convention services).

We may soon see a new environmental rating. The U.S. Travel Data Service reports that guests are willing to pay more for environmentally friendly lodgings (EFL).

Type

Size and class, two of lodging's four traditional classifications, have just been discussed. Now we examine the third classification, types of hotels. Type has three traditional subdivisions of its own: commercial hotels, resort hotels, and residential hotels. As with so many other definitions in a dynamic industry, there are sharp distinctions no longer.

★★★★★

Every rating has cleanliness, maintenance, service (staff), furnishings, and physical appointments as its base. Ratings must also consider regional differences. A historic inn of New England cannot be compared to a dude ranch in the Southwest or an urban-center highrise. Each star-level must incorporate the best standards of the previous level.

★

One-star establishments should be clean and comfortable even as they offer minimal services at minimal price. Rates should be comparable to local competitors with similar accommodations. Service must be courteous but may not be available around the clock. There is no restaurant. Furniture and linens must be in good condition, but will not be luxurious. Housekeeping and maintenance should set a good standard.

★★

Two-star accommodations must meet the standards of one-star facilities and include some, but not necessarily all, of the following: Better-quality furniture, larger bedrooms, color TV in all rooms, direct-dial phones, and perhaps, a swimming pool. Luxury will usually be lacking, but cleanliness, maintenance, and comfort remain essential. The desk is open around the clock.

★★★

Three-star properties include all of the facilities and services mentioned in the preceding paragraph. Additional service personnel will be apparent. Food service, especially at breakfast, is required. So is a swimming pool. Upgrades in the bath should be apparent. Internet access available. Electronic locking and security systems are in place. Three-star establishment should offer a pleasant travel experience.

★★★★

Four-star and five-star properties make up less than 2% of the ratings! They must be outstanding in every respect. Bedrooms should be extra large; furniture of high quality; all of the essential and extra services (dining, lounges, spas, laundry) should be offered at a stepped-up level. Personnel must be well trained, courteous, groomed, and anxious to please. Rates will reflect these superior standards. A stay in a four-star property should be memorable. No place will be awarded four or five stars if there is a pattern of complaints from customers, regardless of the luxury offered.

★★★★★

There are a very few five-star-award facilities. Those that reach this pinnacle go beyond comfort and service to deserve the description "one of the best in the country." Superior restaurants are required, although they may not be rated as highly as the accommodations. Twice-daily maid service is standard; linens should be no less than 250 count. Rooms will be large and accommodations and toiletries in the bath extra special. Lobbies will be places of beauty, often furnished in antiques. Grounds surrounding the building will be meticulously groomed and landscaped. Guest will feel pampered.

EXHIBIT 7 The authors have created criteria for rating U.S. hotels, which are expressed traditionally with stars and diamonds. Other symbols are used worldwide where rating systems are usually government controlled. Private organizations, such as *Forbes' Travel Guide*, do the job in the United States.

COMMERCIAL HOTELS   Commercial hotels, or transient hotels, make up the largest category of American hotels (see Exhibit 8). They service short-term, transient (not permanent) visitors. Businesspersons are the chief market of commercial houses. Conventioneers, engineers, salespersons, consultants, and small businesspersons form the core of the customer base. Indeed, commercial guests are the backbone of the entire lodging industry. They are equally important to the urban property and the roadside motor hotel. Still, there are plenty of rooms to accommodate leisure guests, and commercial hotels do so with pleasure.

Commercial hotels locate close to their market—the business community, usually an urban area. As business centers have left downtown cities, so has the commercial hotel. Arterial highways, research parks, airports, and even suburban shopping centers have become the new locations for commercial properties.

Many businesspersons relax on weekends, which explains the poor weekend occupancy of the commercial hotel (see Exhibit 2). Attempts to offset this decline with tourists, groups, and special local promotions have been only moderately successful.

Large, commercial hotels are almost always full-service properties. Businesspersons are usually expense-account travelers who can afford four-star and even five-star accommodations. Travel offices of many businesses began to monitor employee travel costs after the downturn following the World Trade Center disaster. Furthermore, Congress has enacted restrictions on the amount of tax-deductible business travel expenses.

EXHIBIT 8 Location, location, location is the mantra of commercial hotels, which serve several markets but chiefly business clientele. Thus, their usual locations are business parks, research centers, ring roads, or urban downtowns. *Courtesy of New York Marriott Marquis, 45th and Broadway, New York, New York.*

RESIDENTIAL HOTELS   Unlike the transient nature of the commercial hotel guest, residential guests take permanent occupancy. This creates a landlord–tenant relationship that differs in legal rights and responsibilities from the traditional guest–innkeeper relationship. In some locales, the room occupancy tax is not payable for residential (sometimes called *permanent*) guests in a transient hotel.

The last census reported that two-thirds of all commercial hotels had permanent guests. New York City's Waldorf=Astoria is a good example. Its Towers (a section of the hotel) houses residential, often famous, guests. Less common is the true residential hotel that solicits overnight travelers.

Extended-Stay Hotels   Extended-stay hotels are different from either commercial or residential properties. Rooms are designed differently because guests are there for long-term stays. But that timing is loosely defined. Guests are not in permanent residency—there is no lease—as they are in residential hotels. Neither are they the transient, two-to-four day commercial guests.

Extended travel and suitcase living quickly lose their glamour. Keeping workers productive and comfortable over long periods takes more than a hotel room. Extended-stay hotels provide kitchens, grocery outlets, office space, fireplaces, office equipment, exercise rooms, and laundry facilities—even secretarial support—but all with maid service. But it may not be daily service.

The all-suite hotel emerged from the extended-stay concept as management/owners sought to broaden an otherwise narrow market. The same building caters to both long-term business travelers and all-suite users (families, interviews, small in-room meetings, etc.).

RESORT HOTELS   Transient hotels cater to commercial guests, residential hotels to permanent guests, and resort hotels (see Exhibit 9) to social guests—at least traditionally they did.

Economics has forced resorts to lengthen their summer or winter season to year-round operations. Groups and conventions are booked at the expense of traditional social guest. Commercial hotels retaliated by shifting markets and designs to lure vacationing guests. As a result of these shifts, mixed-use properties emerged, sometimes in residential areas as part of master-planned communities.

Many believe that the modified resort is the hotel of the future. It is in keeping with social trends and compatible with the traits of modern vacationers. Unlike the formality of the vacationer of an earlier era, today's leisure guest is a participant who seeks a host of activities.

EXHIBIT 9   Resorts have broadened their appeal beyond the "social guests" that persisted through the middle of the 20th century. Amenities, including executive conference centers, spas, tennis clubs, water sports, and more appeal to groups as well as leisure guests. *Courtesy of the Sagamore, Bolton Landing, New York.*

The Megaresort   Megaresorts are large, self-contained resorts. Entertainment and recreational facilities are so numerous and so varied that guests need not leave the property during their entire stay. That's the idea behind large casino/hotels trying to capture players. There are other self-contained resorts of which the Sandals chain in the Caribbean is a good example. Size distinguishes the megaresort from these other all-inclusive accommodations. Although size is a distinguishing part of the Las Vegas hotels, large hotels are found worldwide (see Exhibits 3 and 4).

Plan

Plan identifies which meals, if any, are included in the quoted room rate. Rates are higher, obviously, if meals are provided. Classification by plan is more objective than classification by any of the other three categories: size, class, or type. Either meals are included or they are not.

EUROPEAN PLAN   With few exceptions, hotels worldwide operate on the European plan. No meals are included in the rate quote. Evidence of the widespread use of the European plan is its lack of notice. Rate is not quoted as the European plan; it's just understood.

Continental Plan (Continental Breakfast)   Travelers eat breakfast, more than any other meal, in the hotel. European hotels sometimes include a breakfast with the rate. This *continental breakfast* (Europe being the continent) usually consists of coffee or chocolate, a roll, and a bit of cheese. Cold meat or fish are added in the Scandinavian countries. The continental breakfast is on the wane on the continent even as it gains favor in North America. Many all-suite hotels now offer breakfast, with hot foods. It is a revival of the American view of the continental plan, which took form in the no-restaurant format of the 1950s motel. In-room coffeemakers or coffee and sweet rolls in the proprietor's kitchen were touted as continental breakfasts.

A coffee urn and sweet rolls in the lobby after the dining room has closed is sometimes called a continental breakfast. A similar setup at a group registration desk or at the rear of a meeting room during a speaker's talk might appear on the program as a continental breakfast. Juice is included in the United States or abroad if there are American delegates, but rarely is it served elsewhere.

In some parts of the world, an abbreviated breakfast is called *bed-breakfast*. The *Bermuda plan* includes a full breakfast. A hearty breakfast called an *English breakfast* is served in Ireland and the United Kingdom. It includes cereal, eggs and meat, toast with butter and jam, but no juice. English breakfasts can be negotiated for tour groups, but are not normally included in the room rate.

Café complet, a midmorning or afternoon coffee snack with bread and butter, is mistakenly called a continental breakfast. Café complet is not included in any rate quote regardless of the menu or time of service.

Late afternoon tea has gained some favor over "the happy hour." Many top hotels and most cruise lines have latched onto the British ritual "cream tea." Delicate sandwiches and small sweets are served with tea or sherry. This should not to be confused with "high tea," which is a substantial supper usually containing meat. High tea is a rarity today, even in British hotels.

AMERICAN PLAN Rates quoted under the American plan (AP) include room and all three meals. The American plan, which is occasionally called bed and board, had its origin in colonial America, when all guests ate at a common table with the innkeeper and his family. The plan was still in effect when resorts for the affluent began operating in the Northeast about the late 1800s. They held onto the plan until after World War II. The New England resorts retained the AP for the same reason the colonial innkeepers offered it in the first place. Both were isolated so there was no other option. Better roads and better cars spelled the end of the captive guest.

Europe's full *pension* (pen'-si-own) is like the American plan except it includes a continental breakfast rather than a full English breakfast. The more descriptive *inclusive terms* is used when marketing to U.S. travelers. The pension of Europe is the same as the guest house of Britain or the boarding house of the United States. *Pensiones* are usually longer-stay facilities, closer to our residential hotels, with limited services. Guests join an extended family.

Modified American Plan Many guests view the American plan negatively. It requires them to adhere to the hotel's meal schedule and to pay for meals whether they eat them or not. The modified American plan (MAP) offers a compromise. The hotel retains some of the meal capture of the AP, and the guest feels less restricted. Guests get breakfast and dinner as part of the room rate quote, but not luncheon. Thus, the guest need not return to the hotel for an inconveniently scheduled luncheon nor suffer the cost of a missed meal. To make the difference clear, AP is sometimes quoted as FAP, full American plan. Half-pension or *demi-pension* is the Continent's equivalent of the MAP.

Cruise ships provide American-plan dining, but they don't use that terminology. Neither do the *all-inclusive resorts* of the Caribbean, which quote drinks, tips, and activities for the one price.

A *dine-around* plan is another variation. AP hotels allow guests to dine at other hotels in the vicinity. The cooperating hotels might be members of the same chain or a local consortium of competitors who understands the marketing value of the option. Conference centers, which cater to groups, call their variation CMP, *complete meeting package*. The quoted room rate includes room, meals, coffee breaks, meeting setups, and gratuities. Of the rate quoted, 50% might be attributed to rooms, 33% to food and beverage, 10% to gratuities, and the remaining 7% to meeting space and audiovisual/electronic support. This accounting is for internal use and would not be communicated to the guest.

Variations on the Themes

The hotel business is a dynamic one because it is run by clever hoteliers. They innovate by modifying the standard into something different even as the basic industry remains the same (see Exhibit 10). Bed-and-breakfasts and boutique hotels are two great examples.

BED AND BREAKFAST (B&B) American B&Bs are modern versions of the 1930s rooming houses, once called tourist homes. It is a worldwide theme: *zimmer frei* (room available) in Germany is *minshuku* in Japan. Running a B&B is an adventure for some owners; for others a [h]obby; and for many a livelihood. Guests take beds with private families, who furnish camaraderie [alo]ng with the mandatory second "B," breakfast. The lack of privacy—conversation at breakfast [and] sometimes even a shared bath—forces the host and guests into a level of intimacy that brings [f]riendships along with new business.

Specialty Hotels that Fit No General Category	
Backpackers	And camping
Club Med	Vacation villages
Couples only	Honeymoon resorts and gay groups
Dude ranches	For the horsey set
Eco lodges	Safari lodges; wilderness accommodations
Exclusive-use	Resorts that limited use to one group of guests at one time
Floating	House boats; as hotel rooms in India
Grand dames	Ladies with aristocratic bearings; hence grand, elegant hotels
Historical	Buildings (not only hotels) listed with the National Trust
Ice hotels	Made of ice, popular in Iceland and Canada
Kosher	For Jewish and Muslim diets
Landmarks	Former jails and prisons; famous homes; lighthouses
Luxury camping	With creature comforts
Mi Casa Es Su Casa	Joining families in private homes
Military hotels	The army alone has some 22,000 commercial hotel rooms
National parks	Operations, including rates, set by the government
Native American	American Indian operations
Nudists	Camps, colonies, beaches
Resident clubs	Private facilities, often with golf clubs
Retreats	Centers for rehabilitation from drug and alcohol addiction
Singles	May be religious affiliated
Sleep clinics	For giving polysomnograms, sleep tests
Tree houses	Popular in Turkey
Water Parks	Indoors with attached hotels
Yurts	Round, cloth-covered tents called gers by the nomad Mongols.

EXHIBIT 10 Innovative operators and marketeers have created many new hotel niches that do not fall within lodging's traditional classifications of size, class, type, and plan.

Like the rest of the lodging industry, change is part of the B&B's vocabulary. There are many subcategories because the business is individualized and localized. It changes as it moves from west to east. The B&B Inn, which is larger and usually the owner's primary occupation, is the California version. The east coast has the Country B&B. It tilts toward a boarding-house concept because many Country B&Bs serve all three meals. Between the coasts are a variety of facilities serving their local markets (see Exhibit 11). Like other small businesses (typically eight-rooms or less), B&Bs often lack staying power. The problem gets severe where zoning laws prohibit them from putting up "rooms-for-let" signs. The Yellow Pages now list B&Bs. Heretofore, they were carried under "hotels, motels and tourist homes."

Like hotels, B&Bs fight for business and seek referrals. Governmental agencies rate and refer B&Bs in Europe and Japan. The French call them *café-couette* (coffee and quilt) and rate using coffee pots, not stars. Since there is no U.S. government rating system, private rating systems have emerged. However, they come and go quickly, for they too, like the B&Bs, lack staying power.

EXHIBIT 11 Bed and breakfasts operate under a variety of names. *B&B inns* are popular on the west coast; *country B&Bs* in New England. In between are many wonderful stopping places with award-winning breakfasts and distinctive guest accommodations. *Courtesy of the Inn at 410, Flagstaff, Arizona.*

BOUTIQUE HOTELS   Boutique hotels are the rage among the hip, the chic, and the cool. So sometimes the pool-party buzz that they create hides their true identity. They're just hotels; hotels with niche appeal. Attracting a defined customer/guest and using word-of-mouth and social networking, rather than traditional advertising, contributes to the aura. It is difficult to differentiate their basic services from any other hotel and the distinction grows less evident as the major chains move rapidly into the boutique world.

Boutique hotels have small inns as their prototypes, but they provide the amenities of fine hotels. Although many now number in hundreds of rooms, boutiques still remain fashionable because of their good urban locations. They are proof-positive of "location, location, location." Two reasons account for their popularity in London, San Francisco, and New York. First, being relatively small, they can find affordable land in crowded urban areas. Indeed, once they were called *urban inns. European-style hotels* or, in Britain particularly, *baby grand hotels* were terms once widely used. Second, the boutique's guest is an urban-centric customer, one who willingly pays a 10–15% room premium for the design and excitement of the urban inn and its location.

The term "boutique" has been attributed to Steve Rubell, one of the founders of New York City's *Studio 54.* Asked to describe his hotel, The Morgans, Rubell said that other hotels are large department stores, but Morgans is a small boutique.[3] Boutique suggests something different, very eclectic, always with flair, funky, and artsy (see Exhibit 12). The modern boutique aims to mirror its guests: wannabes who often see themselves experiencing the lifestyle of celebrities. Differences notwithstanding, boutique executives still talk about service, guest experiences, and the quality of the operating team—issues for any hotelier.

Ian Schrager, Rubell's partner, helped develop the boutique concept but left after the idea was widely adopted by the hotel chains. Starwood Hotels introduced the W Hotel ("W"—warm, welcoming, and witty). Meridian Hotels use the term *Art and Tech.* Marriott, long an adherent to standardized operations, added a new brand, *Autograph Collection.* This upscale boutique is the very antithesis of standardization. That's probably why Marriott's name has not yet been attached.

EXHIBIT 12   Boutique hotels have become a distinct segment of the lodging industry. Like the B&B, there is no one standard. Indeed, breaking the stereotype of the hotel is the very appeal of the genre.   *Courtesy of the Georgian Hotel, Santa Monica, California.*

[3]Derived from the Greek for storehouse. "Perhaps that's where the notion that boutique hotels need to be small began." Jeff Higley, editor-in chief, *Hotel Design,* October/November, 2005, pg. 4.

Boutiques have higher RevPar and occupancy figures (lower break-even points) than traditional establishments. That appeals to the chain, but does the chain appeal to the consumer? Can branded chains deliver the unexpected and the quirky, which are the hallmarks of a boutique? Can a hotel with banquet and meeting business maintain that special guest–staff connection? W's New York City property is trying with 722 rooms. More like a department store than a boutique.

TROPHY HOTELS   To their owners trophy hotels are another prize for the mantelpiece. Hoteliers acquire lodging's *grande dames* because they add to professional reputations. They carry a long historical lineage. Some are profitable, ongoing properties for generations, such as Denver's Brown Palace. Others are not, but they offer some tax relief with a listing in the National Register of Historical Places. Some are really trophies: How else to account for a true upscale property, the Conrad Hotel, in Indianapolis except that it is owned by a wealthy investor.

Summary

Hotelkeeping remains a major contributor to commerce and culture even as it undergoes rapid changes. Despite its ongoing transformations, innkeeping still measures success with occupancy (%); average daily rate (ADR); and revenue per available room (REVPAR).[4]

To maximize the values of these measures, management must overcome obstacles inherent in the hotel business. Among them are a very perishable product, an unchanging inventory in a permanent location, a high break-even point because of fixed and variable expenses, and seasonal variations—all operating within a challenging cycle of ups and downs that might last for years.

Understanding the industry's traditional identifications (size, class, type, and plan) helps to identify the new permutations (all-suite, B&B, and boutique) that keep the industry economically sound and exciting as a career. Competition sharpens management skills; rating systems measure the results. With change comes new classifications and new challenges.

Resources and Challenges

RESOURCES

Website Assignment

Use references from websites to update the chapter's statistics. Provide national or local values as assigned by the instructor. Identify the sources of your data, which is to include: the percentage of occupancy, ADR, and RevPar. Categorize your sample by citing its geographic coverage, type of hotel, year of the statistics, and so on.

Interesting Tidbits

- In 2010, President Obama publicly chastised groups for meeting in Las Vegas and other resorts while the economy was in dire financial straits. Many properties immediately dropped the term "resort" from their identity.
- The Marina Bay Sands (Singapore) opened 2,500 rooms in 2010 with 20,000 employees, an unprecedented ratio of eight employees per guest room! *Las Vegas Review Journal*, May 27, 2006, pg. D1. The staff has been whittled down since, the usual arrangement with new hotel openings.
- *Pied-à-terre* [paid-a-tera] is a French term for a second residence such as business travelers might have for frequent visits to a particular city. (The original use meant a romantic hide-away.) If neither the traveler nor the business keeps such facilities, Marriott and other chains (Furnished Quarters) maintain business apartments.

Challenges

True/False

Questions that are partially false should be marked false (F).

_____ 1. The hotel industry has been an economic survivor because, in part, it is contra cyclical: Up when the economy is down; down when the economy is up.

_____ 2. As a generalization: The larger the hotel, the fewer employees per guest room.

_____ 3. "Cost per-key" is another means of expressing ADR.

_____ 4. Boutique hotels have introduced the American plan to urban audiences.

_____ 5. "Hotels fill from the bottom up," so RevPar falls as occupancy climbs.

---

[4]GOPPAR (gross operating profits per available room) is a new suggested measure; it includes profits from all operating departments. It has not been widely adopted.

Problems

1. A natural disaster such as an earthquake or human-made disaster like the attack on the World Trade Center has an immediate effect on hotel occupancy. Explain step by step how you would estimate the loss in room income to New York City's hotels when approached by the news media. (Hint: New York City has an estimated 63,000 rooms. Use figures and values from the chapter and/or make assumptions; assumptions should be identified.)
2. Create a checklist with two dozen objective listings that could be used by an evaluator inspecting guest rooms for a national rating system.
3. Explain where the hotel industry is in its economic cycle. Be specific. Is it at the bottom of the trough? The highest point of its rise? Somewhere in between? If so, moving in what direction? Submit evidence to support your position.
4. Give three to five examples of each type of expense that is used to determine the cost portion of a hotel's break-even point: fixed expenses, semifixed expenses, and variable expenses.
5. How many rooms does the MGM Grand Hotel need to sell annually if it budgets operations on an annual occupancy of 82%? (Hint: See Exhibit 4.)
6. Using information contained in this chapter, justify or challenge the statement of Andrew Young, the former mayor of Atlanta, who said that a 1% rise in room occupancy creates 400 new jobs for that city. (Hint: You will need to know the approximate number of rooms in the city and an estimate of the staff-to-room ratio.)

AN INCIDENT IN HOTEL MANAGEMENT
Hit with a Stinging Towel

The resort was living up to everything the family had heard about it. The view was magnificent, the rooms were large, and the food was great. There were three swimming pools in addition to the beach by the ocean. Getting a towel was the big problem. An in-room sign read,

Please do not take bath towels to the pool or beach; towels are available there.

Except there were no towels for two days straight. The attendant said that the laundry couldn't keep up with the demand because the house was full. It was true the beach and the pools were packed with crowds! So the children took towels from their bath on their final day. Kids! Both left their towels on the beach.

The family's upbeat vacation and positive image of the resort took a wide U-turn when they found a $22 charge on the bill for two towels missing from Room 319. And the dad said so aloud.

Questions:
1. Was there a management failure here; if so, what?
2. What is the hotel's immediate response (or action) to the incident?
3. What further, long-run action should management take, if any?

Answers to True/False Quiz

1. False. The hotel industry is cyclical just as the rest of the economy is. Up when business is good; down when the economy falters. In fact, there are indications that a slowing hotel business first signals an approaching downturn for the whole economy.
2. False. Large hotels require extra staff to operate departments that smaller hotels lack: bells, laundry; pool/spa, food and beverage, and so on.
3. False. Cost per key is a measure of the building's value (cost of the building ÷ number of rooms). ADR (average daily rate) is the hotel's average charge for rooms (room income ÷ number of rooms occupied).
4. False. Boutique's guests are urban-centric customers who pay a premium for the novelty of the urban inn and its location; they don't want their grandparents' lifestyle.
5. False. Hotels do fill from the bottom up meaning lower-priced rooms are taken first. As occupancy increases, higher-priced rooms are sold pushing RevPar higher.

The Modern Hotel Industry

Hotels didn't always serve the role they play today. They originated as resting places for tired travelers moving from place to place. Such was their role even as late as Colonial-America's posthouses when horses were the major means of transport. After the Civil War, Fred Harvey Hotels teamed up with the emerging railroads to bring riders to see the West—with Harvey Hotels their very destination. By recreating itself over and over again, the lodging industry stays viable and forward-looking. Doing so, requires it to adopt new patterns. This chapter examines four: product; market; ownership and management.

NEW PRODUCT PATTERNS

The four patterns are actually interlaced. Changes in one pattern invariably impact the other. New methods of financing may create new management patterns, for example. Or, new products emerge when driven by new markets. Recognizing that no one size fits all, lodging executives began *brand stretching*, later called *brand segmentation*,[1] as one means of offsetting dips in the demand curve.

Segmentation, Brand, and Image

SEGMENTATION To counter falling occupancy during the 1990s, upscale hotels moved vertically downward—that is, stretched their brands—into midscale operations. Marriott introduced Fairfield Inns, for example. Midscale chains moved both upward and downward. Choice Hotels, for example, stepped up with its Clarion brand and down with its Sleep Inns (see Exhibit 1). It also enhanced its Quality brand by upgrading properties and introducing inclusive breakfasts. Adding to the richness—some think confusion—Choice added Cambria Suites, designating it as a "lifestyle chain."

Other chains adopted different strategies. Holiday Inn Hotels launched a new brand, Crown Plaza. That altered its identity. It was no longer just a roadside, motor-inn company, but competed with the urban likes of Starwood's Sheraton and Hilton's Double Tree brands. Hyatt, an urban chain strong on conventions and group business, acquired AmeriSuites, a leisure-oriented chain. (Hyatt, which was privately owned by the Pritzker family heretofore, became a public company with 400 hotels in 2009.) Some resort companies shifted focus into commercial businesses and vice versa.

By segmenting, individual companies follow an industrywide pattern that helps define their business (see Exhibit 2).

BRAND Segmentation creates issues as well as solutions. Identification of new products can be muddled by too many new designs, new logos, and new promotions. Hoteliers realize that putting together a group of like hotels—or even worse, unlike hotels—under one name does not automatically create a brand.

A brand is defined by the customer's recognition of the name and the logo. To that end, hotel chains have poured advertising dollars into the creation of new brands. But how many guests know that Renaissance Hotels are owned by Marriott (see Exhibit 1) or that Le Meridien and Westin are both subsidiaries of Starwood? Like

---

[1]Hoteliers use "segmentation" to mean different hotel products. To economists, the term means a subset of products developed for one market; almost the same.

Brand Names				
Company Name	**Low End**	**Midscale**	**Upscale**	**Suites**
Choice Hotels International	Comfort Inn Econo Lodge Rodeway Inn Sleep Inn	Quality	Clarion Ascend Collection[a]	Cambria Suites Comfort Suites MainStay Suites Suburban[b]
Marriott International[c] Independent Hotels Autograph Collection Luxury Boutique	Fairfield Inn	Courtyard Residence Inn	JW Marriott Marriott Hotels Renaissance Ritz-Carlton	ExecuStay Marriott Apts Renaissance Suites SpringHill Suites TownePlace Suites
InterContinental[d]	Holiday Inn Express	Holiday Inn Hotel Indigo	Crowne Plaza InterContinental	Candlewood Suites Staybridge Suites

[a] Historic, Boutique, and Unique.

[b] Suburban's full name is Suburban Extended-Stay Hotels.

[c] Marriott's list is not complete; among the missing is its timeshare division, spun out in 2011.

[d] InterContinental has had several name changes: From Holiday Inn to InterContinental to Bass Hotels to Six Continents and back to InterContinental Hotels and Resorts.

Note: Read horizontally, not vertically. Brand comparisons are valid only within the same chain. They are not valid between companies. Choice's midscale brand, for example, is not equated to Marriott's midscale brand.

EXHIBIT 1 Hotel corporations stretch up and down to create new brands. More products using more names makes it difficult to identify the host company. That may defeat the very purpose. Adding to the muddle, they use unrelated names for their frequent-guest programs. Exhibit 14 piles on still others.

EXHIBIT 2 The lodging industry can be classified into many segments and still retain size, class, type, and plan as its basic definition. Both individual hotels and whole chains can be so identified, For example: A commercial, three-star property near the airport can be a REIT-owned, chain-managed, and franchise flagged.

A Segmented Industry

Segmented by Activity
- Casino hotel
- Convention hotel
- Dude ranch

Segmented by Financing
- Public corporation
- Private individual
- REIT

Segmented by Location
- Airport
- Highway
- Seaside

Segmented by Management
- Chain
- Management company
- Self-managed

Segmented by Markets
- Business
- Groups
- Leisure

Segmented Miscellaneously
- Collar
- Hostel
- Mixed-use

Segmented by Ownership
- Chain
- Condominium
- Mom-and-pop

Segmented by Plan
- American plan
- Continental plan
- European plan

Segmented by Price (ADR)[a]
- Deluxe
- Midrange
- Budget

Segmented by Ratings
- Five-star
- Four-star
- Three-star

Segmented by Service
- Full service
- Moderate service
- Self-service

Segmented by Structure
- High rise
- Low rise
- Outside corridor

Segmented by Type
- Commercial
- Residential
- Resort

Segmented by Use
- Bed and breakfast
- Extended stay
- Health spa

[a] See also Exhibit 6.

Marriott and Starwood, most large chains have several brands. Some of them have been created, others purchased. There are advantages to multiple brands if the parent company can sell the differences and values of each. Sheraton's Four Points and W's boutique brand are extremes under the umbrella of the still broader brand, Starwood.

Establishing a brand is more difficult when the chain is foreign based. Not only is it unfamiliar to the local traveler, it may use a foreign-sounding name. Try Crowne Plaza in Beijing. Spain's Sol Melia and India's Taj Hotels (see Exhibit 13) are recent entries into North America.

BRAND EQUITY   Brand equity is the inherent value that the shopper's recognition gives to the brand. There is equity (value) in the brand if that recognition carries a positive image. There is no brand equity if guests know the brand but will not stay. Travelodge is a good example of strong brand recognition with weak brand equity. In the United States, it is a Wyndham company, but non-Wyndham Travelodge has both recognition and equity overseas, particularly in Australia.

Four criteria change brand recognition into brand equity. They are instant identification (the Hilton name), broad distribution (Holiday Inn Hotels), consistent quality (Hampton Inns), an assured level of service (Four Seasons).

Branding is more about consistency than about identification with the parent. Branding is more about quality than about advertising. Branding is more about the chain's personality than it is about location. Branding is more about individualizing the experience than it is about cluttering the landscape with numerous properties.

Price—in the lodging industry that's room rate—is the offset to brand equity. With so many choices, buying decisions often depend on nothing more than the quoted rate. When hotel rooms are viewed as a product rather than as a service, they are characterized as a commodity, much like wheat or oil. In the extreme, guests see every hotel room like every other, and brand managers fight an uphill battle for identity. Websites such as *Priceline.com* focus the buyers' attention on price, not brand. When viewed as commodities, hotel rooms lack brand equity and the entire industry suffers.

New Product Segments

New faces on tired properties create neither brand recognition nor brand equity. Hence, hoteliers make more dramatic efforts to identify a new need and match it with an innovation. Among the successful launches have been economy hotels, all-suite hotels, casino/hotels, spas, and conference centers. Let's check into each and see how closely they adhere to the traditional definitions.

ECONOMY (BUDGET, OR LIMITED-SERVICE) HOTELS   Inexpensive hotels date back to the roadside motor courts of the 1930s. Then came Holiday Inn Hotels, a chain of clean, no-frills accommodations. Existing motor-court operators saw the chain very differently. They saw it as *amenity creep*!

Amenities and Amenity Creep   Amenity creep is the history of the industry's ever-improving levels of service. An amenity is a special extra that distinguishes the property from its competitors. It helps establish the brand and gives it equity. After a time, guests expect the amenity. They no longer view it as an "extra." It is soon offered industrywide as competitors meet the challenge. Rather than a marketing advantage, the amenity is now a fixed cost.

Amenity creep explains ever-larger hotel rooms. It explains why free wireless connectivity replaced income-earning in-room telephones and free, flat-screen television replaced yesteryear's coin-operated sets. The list goes on: Air conditioners replaced electric fans and inclusive breakfasts replaced in-room coffeemakers. Two wash basins with soaps, combs, and lotions replaced the disposable shower cap and the free shoeshine cloth. Now, the cost of toiletry amenities may exceed $10.00 per room per night! Exhibit 3 contrasts the amenities of yesteryear to those now in place.[2]

---

[2]Guests demand for amenities grew after liquids and gels were banned at airports. Hotels offered replacements at the desks, in vending machines and lobby shops, but not in all guest rooms.

Signs of Amenity Creep	
One-Time Amenities	**Today's Amenities**
Bathrobe	Sleep CD
Bottle Opener	Flat, Plasma Screen TV
Chocolate Mint on the Pillow	Luxury Bedding[a]
Direct-Dial Telephone	Wireless Internet
Double Sink in the Bathroom	Yoga Mat
In-room Coffeemaker	All-Inclusive Breakfast
Iron and Ironing Board	Ergonomic Furniture
Plastic Shower Cap	Check-in Kiosk
Radio Alarm Clock	Satellite Radio
Shoeshine Cloth	Perfumed Guest Room Spray
Soap and Shampoo	Loan Overnight Pets (Cats, Fish)
Swimming Pool	Spa

EXHIBIT 3 Amenities can be one-upmanship as each hotelier searches for a unique offering. Guests at San-Francisco-based Kimpton Hotels—neither a mass-marked chain nor a boutique—are offered chocolate drinks, Yoo-Hoos, and Twinkies. Its Topaz Hotel (Washington, D.C.) gives horoscopes.

How Budgets Compete   As amenities, franchising fees included, push room rates upward, new, less expensive chains enter the fray at the lower end. Some date this rotation to 1964 when Motel 6 appeared. Motel 6—now owned by Accor—had interior corridors and upgraded heating and air-conditioning. Earlier budget hotels such as Holiday Inn and Ramada suddenly found themselves in midrange.

New hotels start out with smaller rooms. Microtel's hotel rooms are 178 square feet versus the typical 300–325 square feet. Their properties, on less desirable locations and smaller building sites, save on land costs. Nonessential facilities such as pools, lobbies, meeting rooms, and restaurants are omitted. They provide free continental breakfasts as they are less costly than operating the usual money-losing hotel restaurant. Better still, new budgets locate near existing restaurant chains.

More recent budgets focus on design and construction. Economy comes from standardized architectural plans and from using just a few builders. New structures have low ceilings and improved insulation. Better construction has reduced subsequent operating costs. The offset has been amenity creep. Interior corridors, required for better guest security, add substantially to construction costs.

Budgets may employ as few as 20 employees per 100 rooms. Eliminating the dining room is just the first step in labor savings. By using hanging furniture and eliminating the tub (shower only) housekeeping productivity Increases. Fewer guest-room attendants saves labor costs.

A chain requires about 250 properties to become a major brand. To quickly achieve market identity, some chains acquired and then franchised old mom-and-pop operations at fire-sale prices. Days Inns was chief among them (see Exhibit 4).

Hard Budgets   There are degrees within the budget chains. The euphemisms used for very inexpensive accommodations are economy, budget, limited-service, and low-end class. Adding to the confusion of the terminology are "upscale budgets"—an oxymoronic term—(La Quinta, for example), intermediate budgets (Red Roof Inns), and low-end budgets (Super 8).

Hard budgets are found worldwide. They are located at airports and at the hundreds of truck stops that dot the interstate roads. The airports at Los Angeles and Honolulu have budget rooms, measuring 75 square feet, which is less than one-third of a normal-sized hotel room, for rest and showers between flights. Tokyo's airport offers "capsule rooms," the size of railcar sleeping berths, 5′ × 5′. Rooms at a London chain, "Yotel," are 9′ × 12′. New York City has the Jane Hotel (50-square-foot rooms) and the Pod (100-square-foot rooms). Berlin's counterpart is Motel One with free Internet access. Taj Hotels' budget subsidiary, Roots, offers rooms of a whopping 175 square feet.

Among the Budget Chains Are ...		
Name	**Parent Company**	**Approximate Number of Rooms**
Comfort Inn	Choice	165,000
Days Inns	Wyndham	150,000
Econo Lodge	Choice	55,000
Howard Johnson	Wyndham	15,000
Knights Inn	Wyndham	15,000
Motel 6	Accor	100,000
Red Roof Inns	Westmont Hospitality	35,000
Sleep Inns	Choice	25,000
Super 8	Wyndham	125,000
Travelodge	Wyndham	40,000

EXHIBIT 4 Budget hotels, like their larger cousins, are controlled by a few large chains. These ten account for nearly 700,000 rooms. The typical budget hotel is less than 100 rooms in size, located on the highway, and flying the franchise flag of one of these companies.

China uses bath houses as hard budgets. International budget chains gained footholds there during the 2008 Olympics.[3] Hard budgets have caught on in Europe as well. France has the largest number driven by very high payroll taxes. Minimizing labor costs—something that hard budgets do well—drives France's development.

Hard budgets *hostels* are favored by the young, the single, and the not-too-discriminating traveler. However, they fail to attract many guests as the dorms lack privacy. But amenity creep is noticeable. Small rooms are now available for families and friends. Security of personal items, better beds, and even *en suite* baths are attracting new clientele. Hostelling International, representing some 4,000 hostels, has been working to upgrade facilities and assure stricter standards, even sending out inspectors.

ALL-SUITE HOTELS Each segment of the industry offers something unique. Boutique hotels emphasize soft attributes (fashion and spas) over hard values (room size and meeting space). Budgets offer rooms at reduced prices. All-suite hotels offer two rooms for the price of one. To investors in all-suites, the appeal is higher weekend occupancy and profits.

Hometel, the original extended-stay hotel, was conceived in 1969. It became the largest all-suite chain after Holiday Inn acquired it and renamed it Embassy Suites. Hilton bought Embassy Suites when The Holiday Corporation was broken up (1990). Currently, Hilton has Embassy Suites, Homewood Suites, and Hampton Suites (see Exhibit 12). Holiday's other chain, Residence Inns, was sold to Marriott in 1987. Now Marriott also has several all-suites (see Exhibit 1).

Separate living–sleeping accommodations are attractive to executives, who wish to conduct business outside the intimacy of a bedroom. So, a sofa bed and often a second bath were included in the living space. With this the market expanded from being only extended stay to catering to a third market, that is, traveling families seeking economical accommodations

Extended Stay Long-term business travelers, relocating families, and reassigned military personnel are markets for extended-stay properties. So too are company training sessions and employees on long-term but temporary assignments. Among them are movie crews, federal agents, FEMA employees, and utility workers. Leisure travelers fill in the vacancies and broaden the market.

The kitchenette is to the all-suite as the swimming pool is to the motor hotel. Everyone looks for that amenity, but few use it. That makes nearby restaurants a plus. With almost no transient guests, some of these properties close overnight, an action that might prove troublesome because hotels must always be open to gain the legal benefits of innkeeping.

---

[3]China has its own budget brands: Green Tree and Motel 168, whose upgraded sibling is Motel 268.

Corporate Housing Companies often send employees from different departments to one city. Rather than booking hotel rooms, businesses take long-term leases on apartment accommodations that provide hotel services. Such buildings may be exempt from local room taxes and are often permitted in areas not zoned for hotels. Marriott's Executive Apartments, a division of its all-suite Execustay chain, operates in this market.

Mixed-Use Projects and Other Hotel Segments

The dynamic nature of hotelkeeping brings innovation and excitement to the industry. One curious example is Elderhostel programs that have blended hotels with universities. Children's camps within hotels are at the other end of the age spectrum. (They even give frequent-stay points to the kids.) Resorts find teenagers a tougher market; activities for them must be cool and tilted toward adult-like recreation. It's worth it: Vacationing families spend four-plus nights versus the business-guest's stay of one-plus nights.

"Mixed use," a buzz word in real estate, takes innovation to the next step. In one development are apartments, hotels, resorts, condominiums, shopping marts, and business towers. Mixed-use resorts add tennis, golf, skiing, and swimming. Combining residential, business, retailing, recreation, and entertainment is the modern version of a small town. Dual brands are another type of mixed use. They combine transient and extended-stay hotels on one site to draw on two distinct markets.

Demographic shifts make mixed-use communities feasible. Retirees find them to be ideal. Urban centers accommodate working-from-home employees. Marrying vacation environments and residential facilities seems the best of all worlds. It certainly fits for space-challenged cities. "Hotels," in the broadest definition of the word, are at the core of the mixed-used development.

CASINO/HOTELS Not every mixed-use project has a casino/hotel, but the possibility of having it has increased many fold. Casinos have spread across the nation and the world. Tax-starved states have licensed them and Native American tribes have built them. They have fed the wealth of Macau and Singapore. The jobs they create and the taxes they generate have all but silenced their critics.

Casinos are almost never free-standing. They are casino/hotels, more accurately casino/resorts, typified perhaps by the Atlantis Casino & Resort in the Bahamas. Casino/resorts show signs of becoming the dominant segment in the lodging industry. They are certainly the largest hotels around, and their cash flow is immense. It needs to be when the break-even point can exceed $1 million per day!

The focus of casino/hotels is different from that of traditional hotels. Gaming revenue (called win) usually generates more income than rooms do. So having rooms occupied (having potential gamblers in the house) is more important than ADR or even RevPar. Similarly, two guests in the same room double the casino "action." So single and double rates are kept the same and rooms are often "comped" (free). Mixed use may change one casino truism: Higher revenues sometimes come from other than the win.[4]

CONFERENCE CENTERS Conference centers (CCs) first appeared in the 1960s. What began in renovated mansions morphed into highly specialized facilities designed for meetings and conferences. CCs offer dedicated space, audiovisual equipment, theaters, closed-circuit television, and simultaneous translation capabilities (see Exhibit 5).

Unlike convention hotels, conference centers do not solicit transient guests. Food service is not open to the public. The centers number in the hundreds as they serve a special niche in the meeting market, unlike hotels that number in the thousands. Conference centers need not be separate and distinct from hotels, but they must have separate and permanent space. The conference center must occupy at least 60% of a facility for it to gain membership in the International Association of Conference Centers. Hotel space is not usually dedicated. Unlike conference centers, hotels hold various functions including meetings, banquets, trade shows, and weddings (see Exhibit 6).

---

[4]As Las Vegas' gaming revenues fell, income from other departments grew in importance. Not so in Macau where gaming generated $23 billion in 2010. (In Vegas' best year, 2007, $12.8 billion was the take.)

EXHIBIT 5 Conference centers blend business and high-tech facilities in dedicated meeting space with pleasant, resort-like surroundings. Hotels that compete for this market segment do so with multiple-use space (see Exhibit 6). *Courtesy of Barton Creek Resort, Austin, Texas.*

Double occupancy is high in CCs. Two persons in a room encourages familiarity, which is one of the goals of conference planners. Even senior managers are doubled up. Upper and lower managers get to know one another.

Rates at conference centers are bundled. Every expense, including that of guest rooms, meeting rooms, food, drinks, and equipment, is included in the rate quote, called a *corporate meeting package (CMP)*. The CMP is a modern version of the American, all-inclusive plan. But then the conference center itself is a modern marriage of the convention hotel and the traditional resort. Attendees reside and work for five days in a business/convention gathering, followed by a two-day weekend in a resort setting (see Exhibit 5). Much like convention hotels, weekend occupancy is low. The business model is static; it is nothing like the growth in spas!

EXHIBIT 6 The versatile space of convention hotels accommodates meetings and banquets, trade shows and weddings, proms, seminars, and more. Contrast this to the dedicated space of Exhibit 5. *Courtesy of Radisson Hotel Orlando, Orlando, Florida.*

SPAS The term originated in the city of Spa, Belgium, where ancient Romans "took the waters." The resorts of 19th-century New England developed around mineral springs, so the resorts themselves became known as spas. Today's spas are far different from their famous namesakes at Saratoga Springs in New York or White Sulphur Springs in West Virginia. Originally sought for their restorative properties, those resorts became the playgrounds of the rich. Horse racing and casinos replaced the waters as the main attraction. Early spa-goers sought better health in the healing qualities of the waters. That pretty well determined the spa's location. Modern spas are everywhere as their attraction today is not water but Health! Health remains the essence of the spa experience. Attendance evokes an almost religious fervor of health, exercise, massage, and diet.

Spa installations continue to grow because they are profitable. Unlike unused swimming pools, guests take to the spas and pay handsomely to do so. Even modest properties offer them. There are "stay spas," destination spas with a resort component. There are "day spas," which may or may not have lodging facilities. In between are resorts with various amenities, and spas being one of them. According to the International Spa Association, there are seven types of spas: club, cruise-ship, medical, day, destination, mineral springs, and hotel/resort.

The mantra of the spa-goer, stress reduction—no competition—fits perfectly with a new catchphrase of lodging, "lifestyle hotels." aloft Hotels, a division of Starwood's W Hotels, favors that term. Spa designer Bliss (another division of Starwood) is responsible for aloft's baths and showers. So the spa has changed its historical course to become a lifestyle and beauty industry, catering to both men and women (see Exhibit 7).

EXHIBIT 7 Spa services are highly specialized so hotels often lease the space rather than operate it. Services are very personal, individualized, and costly. Many products are similar despite their different names. One leisurely afternoon at the spa might produce $200–$500 on the folio.

Spa Services	
Acupressure	Aromatherapy
Ayurveda[a]	Bikini wax
Body treatment	Body wax
Brow wax	Exfoliation
Facial	Fango[b]
Gommage[c]	Herbal treatment
Hydrotherapy	Lip wax
Loofa scrub	Massage
Mud bath	Nail care
Oxygen treatment	Pedicare
Shiatsu[d]	Wraps

[a] Folk medicine from India.
[b] Rehydration massage.
[c] Japanese acupuncture.
[d] Upgraded mud bath.

FITNESS CENTERS   Spa managers reject the noisy energy of fitness centers although fitness centers are euphemistically called health clubs. These work-out facilities preceded the introduction of the spa. They are less costly to launch and to manage. Indeed, when a few pieces of equipment are in an old storeroom, nothing is managed. A cadre of accredited trainers and expensive equipment is the other extreme. Users are often businesspersons, so staff scheduling must be accommodative; staff must be there early and late. Guests are also annoyed when nonguests overrun the gym (local memberships increase the center's revenues). Portable equipment brought to the guestroom is an expensive amenity offered by some upscale properties.

Minimum equipment includes stationary bikes, treadmills, and stair-climbing machines. Users like to see familiar brands that operate without a learning curve. Management must be diligent about maintenance. It must undertake periodic inspections and repairs to the equipment as it does, say, for ice machines and elevators. Broken and dirty equipment undermine the image of the center. They might even undermine insurance coverage, which is an absolute necessity for spas and fitness centers.

NEW MARKET PATTERNS

Consumers have a rich selection of choice from bottled water, to autos, to lodging accommodations. The challenge lies in enticing fickle consumers in to your property.

Marketing to the Individual Guest

By law, hotels must accept all who come in good condition provided they are willing and able to pay. In practice, hotels cater to particular market segments (niches). What appeals to one type of guest may be of indifference to another. So the guest's very presence tells us as much about the hotel as about the guest.

GUEST PROFILES   Guests have several profiles; they wear different hats under different circumstances. Personas change depending on the stay. Sometimes guests are businesspersons; sometimes they are family members. They may be transient travelers, convention goers, tour group members, or excited tourists. Some guests are urbane, others unsophisticated. They're citizens or foreign visitors, locals or from other states. Each group has its own profile.

Profiles are gathered by many agencies, not just hotels. The typical study focuses on demographics. Information such as the guests' age, income, job, gender, residence, and education and the number of persons in the party can be determined with accuracy. And knowing one's guests is the staring point for servicing them and ensuring their return.

Some patterns are less measurable than demographics. Developers differentiate between upstairs and downstairs buyers. *Upstairs buyers* want larger sleeping rooms and comfortable work spaces. For this, they sacrifice theme restaurants, intimate bars, and other lifestyle accoutrements. Not so with *downstairs buyers*, who use the concierge, want public space above all else, and are more extroverted. Usually, women are upstairs buyers, while men are downstairs buyers. Whatever the type, every guest wants good lighting and a clean room.

Profiles of extended-stay guests show something else entirely. They try to re-create a little bit of their homes by bringing personal items such as photos and stuffed animals. Very long-term guests actually rearrange furniture. Both groups use the kitchenette sparingly.

BUSINESS/LEISURE TRAVELERS   Price is less important—not unimportant, but less important—to businesspersons than to leisure travelers. Businessmen and women do not cancel trips because of high rates, nor make them because of low rates. Theirs is an *inelastic market*: Very little change in demand comes from a change in price. Leisure guests are an *elastic market*. High rates discourage them and low rates attract them.

All guests have some degree of elasticity. Leisure guests are sometimes inelastic as they *must* come for a wedding or funeral. Businesspersons become elastic if their company uses a travel desk to arrange air, lodging, and car rentals. They become more inelastic if they make the booking personally. For everyone, price—elasticity—becomes more important during down cycles. Lower rates—price—drove the industry's nascent recovery of 2012.

Although less and less so, business travelers are traditionally men and tourists are mostly couples. Almost everyone watches television from bed. The business traveler's profile shows greater use of the shower and the movie channel. Tourists take to the pool. Leisure travelers are 5–10 years older than their business counterparts; they make reservations less often and pay less for their rooms.

Women make up about one-third of business travelers. That's a demographic measure. But, how best to please that market is a psychographic issue. Psychographic profiles detail, traits, personalities, and inner motivations. Every profile is flawed because no guest is 100% of the composite study. In fact, the registered guest may not have personally made the reservation. Demographic profiles indicate that compared to their female counterparts, male business travelers make their own arrangements. As both men and women business travelers use their rooms as offices, they give high priority to comfortable furniture and convenient work space. Women executives (upstairs buyers) rank in-room coffee very important! Men don't.

Young, leisure guests are looking for resorts that offer off-beat experiences (mountain climbing and archeological digs) even at higher rates. This contrasts to the preference of the economy market, such as government employees on a fixed per diem (daily) allowance. With them are retirees whose time is more flexible than their budgets. International guests swing between elastic and inelastic status depending upon the dollar's value in the world market.

INTERNATIONAL GUESTS   Globalization requires special attention to the profile of the international guest. Foreign visitors are big business. The World Tourism Organization (WTO) forecasts over 100 million visitors to the United States by 2020. International guests spend about twice the time and money reaching their destination, so they stay longer and spend more than domestic guests. By spending money in a foreign land, tourists help the host country's balance of trade.

Hotels seeking foreign tourists must cater to their needs. Japanese, for example, prefer traveling in groups and finding bedroom slippers by the bed is a big plus! (Japanese visitors have contributed much to the economy of Hawaii and that was felt dramatically during the 2008–2011 downturn, when the number of Japanese visiting Hawaii declined.) Every ethnic group has a different breakfast need and hotels soliciting international guests should make an effort to offer it.

PREFERRED-GUEST PROGRAMS   Preferred-Guest Programs (PGPs) improve guest profiling through electronic recordkeeping and intra-chain networks. Just as frequent-fliers earn points with airlines, guests earn points with hotel chains. Points are turned into gifts and free stays. To qualify, guests provide information about their travel and personal habits. Hotel companies maintain demographic and psychographic profiles on millions of names. The cost is borne largely by franchisees and hotel owners, not the operating chains. (Chains own few hotels, as the next segment of this chapter explains.)

Rewards range from the simple to the expensive. Among the less costly are room upgrades, check-cashing privileges, daily newspapers, late check-outs, and guaranteed rates. Up a step and the reward becomes a fruit basket, a bottle of special water, or free in-room films. Many are awards that even nonmembers can access at times.

Elite-club memberships, achieved by earning many, many points, carry elite awards. Among them are rate discounts, spa memberships, accommodations in the chain's exotic destinations, and even cash. Giving cash or its equivalent raises ethical issues. Hard-core PGP members travel almost always on expense accounts paid with someone else's cash.

PGPs cycle in tandem with economic conditions. Tough times bring additional perks, double or triple points. During the downturns that followed 9/11 and 2009, upgrades were offered throughout the industry. Like other amenities, preferred-guest programs follow the competitors. One chain adds lower brands to the coverage; competitors follow. Some others distribute expensive gift vouchers through catalogs; competitors follow. Tie-ins using hotel points for airline travel are introduced; competitors follow.

During downturns, blackout dates are dropped, elite-travel status is eased, more brands are placed under the one umbrella, and stockholders are automatically included. Responding to the 2009 cyclical dip, Ritz-Carlton Hotels offered points for the very first time.[5] Amenity creep crept in.

---

[5]Including Ritz, Marriott's loyalty program involves about 50% of chainwide stays.

No one really knows how much business loyalty programs represent. It is known that they add name confusion to branding. Wyndham adds *Trip Rewards* to its 19 chain names! Hilton has *HHonors Club* and 12 other brand names. There are two golds: *Gold Crown Club* (Best Western), and *Gold Passport* (Hyatt). Marriott with 19 brands has finally changed its FGP name from *Honored Guest Awards* to *Marriott Awards*.[6]

Despite the cost, the real lack of competitive difference and the uncertainty of their effectiveness, no company dares close its program. Airlines have the same dilemma. Hotels will do what airlines have done: that is, tighten access, increase points, and reduce awards. They'll do that until the next downturn in business.

NONGUEST BUYERS   Nonguest buyers are intermediaries, not guests. They have no intention of becoming guests. These third parties may be actual persons, but just as often they are legal persons (companies and organizations). It's obviously not to the industry's advantage. With intermediaries, hotels are not selling rooms to guests; they're buying guests through new marketing channels.

Nonguest buyers negotiate from strength. The American Automobile Association (AAA) and the American Association of Retired Persons (AARP), for examples, haggle over room rates. They obtain special rates for their members although neither the associations nor the hotels know who those guests will be! So widespread is this practice that almost every hotel grants the guest's request for a special AAA rate. Rarely is the guest even asked to verify AAA membership. Other travel clubs negotiate a different commitment: second nights free.

A second type of nonguest buyer actually buys the rooms, rather than just negotiating rates. Businesses book through "travel desks," discussed earlier. Either the business operates its own desk or employs an outside agency. Whichever, the buyer is not the arriving guest.

Franchisees rely on the franchise's reservation system, another type of nonguest buyer. The room commitment is made by the franchise system, a third party. Quite possibly, that system is not even owned by the franchisor, rather by still another entity.

Group tours, incentive firms, and wholesalers make huge room commitments, but someone else occupies the room. The same is true with travel agents who buy rooms which their clients occupy. Airlines, websites, and auto-rental companies round out a growing list of nonguest buyers.

Marketing to the Group

Group business is a post-World War II innovation that changed the very concept of hotelkeeping. Modern hotels became destination sites as well as providers of transient accommodations. Now, instead of selling one guest one room, hoteliers sell dozens or many hundreds of room-nights at one time. One constant remains: Buyers are either tourist/leisure visitors or business/commercial groups.

TOURIST/LEISURE VISITORS   Rising disposable income and broader travel horizons have made travel appealing to every level of society. Packaging travel and accommodations has brought costs low enough to attract huge numbers of the world's citizens. The travel and hotel industries embarked on the same kind of mass production techniques that increased efficiency in manufacturing. The move was delayed until the transport carriers and the destination hotels were large enough to move and house these large numbers.

The Tour Package   Groups of tourists, especially first-timers, traveling together look to a new entrepreneur, the wholesaler. This nonguest buyer handles the mass movement of leisure guests. Wholesalers buy at wholesale (reduced) prices because they buy in quantity. They buy blocks of rooms (commitments to buy a given number for so many nights), and blocks of airline and bus seats. Then the wholesaler sells the "package" at retail. The offer includes ground handling and baggage along with other goodies that the wholesaler either buys inexpensively or gets without cost from the hotel (see Exhibit 8).

---

[6]These and other brand names used throughout the chapter are registered trademarks.

Vacations—Round the Nation

With the Vallen Chain
☰V
A Vallen Corporation Property

$797.20 *In Las Vegas*	$867.50 *In Orlando*	$993.33 *In Maui*
Round Trip Air	Round Trip Air	Round Trip Air from LA
4 Days/3 Nights	4 Days/3 Nights	5 Nights/4 Days
HOTEL PARADISE	HOTEL CARTOON	THE VALLEN MAUI
Taxes Included	Room Upgrade If Available	6th Night Free
Airport Transfers	$40 Daily Car Rental	Includes Full Breakfast
Free Gaming Lesson	Nonstop Flights from Major Cities	Guaranteed Ocean View or Suite

$815.00 *In New York City*	$717.76 *In Boston*
4 Days/3 Nights	4 Days/3 Nights
2 Broadway Shows	Bottle Champagne Nightly
THE BIGGEST APPLE	FREEDOM TRAIL HOTEL
Apple Before Bed	Guided Walking Tour of Historic Boston
One Breakfast-in-Bed	$25/Day Food or Beverage Credit
City Bus Tour	Surprise Amenity

CALL: 1-888-555-5555 OR YOUR TRAVEL PROFESSIONAL

Rates are quoted per person, double occupancy and are available until September 30. Unless otherwise stated, taxes and service charges are not included. Las Vegas offering is good Mondays to Thursdays only. All vacations earn Club Vallen points. Air trips, where included, require specific flights on carriers of the company's choosing. Other restrictions may apply. The company strives for accuracy but will not be held responsible for errors or omissions in this advertisement.

EXHIBIT 8 Sample of print advertising used by this hypothetical tour operator, *Vacations—Round the Nation,* to sell packaged vacations. Buying in quantity puts this wholesaler at risk of not reselling all of the spaces. But quantity purchasing reduces costs from hotels and airlines making possible huge savings. (See also travel pages of local newspapers.)

Wholesalers promise hotels year-round, back-to-back charters (each departing group is matched by a new, arriving group). Hotel sales executives and accountants sharpen their pencils to accommodate the price. One sale books hundreds of rooms. One correspondence confirms all the reservations. One billing closes the account. Bad debts are minimized and credit-card costs are eliminated. It is a bargain buy for the traveler, a profitable venture for the wholesaler, and great business for the hotel. More importantly, the hotel now has a basic occupancy on which to build its room rates (see the discussion on yield management).

Group tours offer many packages, some reminiscent of the old American plan. Transportation, rooms, food and beverage, entertainment, and tips are offered for one fixed price. (Unlike the all-inclusive plan, not all items are included, see Exhibit 8, so hotels gain from sales outside the package.) Strong bargaining—sharp discounts from hotels, airlines, and ground handlers—sometimes allows the wholesaler to sell the package for less than the airline seat alone.

The wholesaler also benefits from *breakage*. Every guest does not use every part of the package. Some may not play golf; others may not use the drink coupon and still others may skip the buffet. Guests pay the hotel with coupons issued by the wholesaler. If the hotel gets no coupon, it presents none at the time of settlement. The wholesaler doesn't pay the hotel even though the guest has paid the wholesaler as part of the package. That's breakage. Still, everyone has gained. The hotel has a basic occupancy; the wholesaler has a profit (perhaps a loss); guests have had savings. The downside is a loss of guest identity. Even the hotel's staff senses a reduced responsibility when guests are customers of a third party.

Substitute a bus seat for an airline seat and small hotels anywhere can host a tour group. Bus tours are a broad market with the hotel providing two services: It is the bus' destination (while the group tours local attractions); it is the transient accommodation because the stay is a brief night or two before the tour moves on.

The Inclusive Tour (IT) Package   The IT package is marketed to individual guests. Logically, it should have been discussed earlier under the heading "Marketing for the Individual Guest." It is here under the heading "Marketing to the Group" because IT packages so closely resemble the just-discussed wholesaler's tour packages. The tour package requires numerous buyers to make it profitable, whereas the target groups of the IT package are couples or small groups of friends.

Group tours involve financial risks (air and land transportation) outside the hotel's control. The hotel's IT package is the same as the wholesaler's tour package without the risks. Guests get to the hotel on their own. Once there, the package is the same; often it is better. The basics remain: room, food, and beverage. Hotels add "freebies," such as free tennis or golf. Free admissions: tickets to theaters, art shows, formal gardens tours, or spas sweeten the deal. More so if these extras normally require a fee. Casino ITs include one free play at a table. Breakage now accrues to the hotel; the wholesaler is no longer in the picture.

Both the wholesaler and the hotel market directly to the public. Exhibit 8 would be a newspaper advertisement. Exhibit 9 could be used similarly or distributed individually across

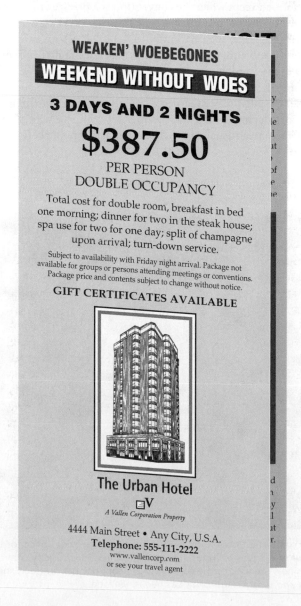

EXHIBIT 9 Inclusive tour (IT) packages enable hotels to compete with tour wholesalers (see Exhibit 8) except transportation is not included. The package is complete within the hotel. IT packages also compete with the hotel's own room rates, so they are offered and withdrawn as occupancy dictates under a yield management system.

the desk, through the mail, or to convention attendees. Travel agents are traditional advertising outlets. They normally receive a 10% commission on rooms booked for their clients. Because ITs do not break out room costs from other services, the hotel pays TAs 10% on the entire package price.

One hotel may offer several IT packages. Each (a golf package, a spa package, a valentine package) is aimed toward a different market. Commercial hotels use them extensively to off-set weekend doldrums—the Run Away with Your Wife package. The contents and price of each varies. Care must be exercised because the hotel competes with itself. Inclusive tour packages are discounted rooms with extra services that sell for less than the normal room rate. So ITs are discontinued during high occupancy periods.

BUSINESS/COMMERCIAL GROUPS Our fondness for forming groups brings people together under many umbrellas. For short, the industry uses either SMURF (societies, military, university, religious, fraternal) or SMERF (social, military, educational, religious, fraternal). Non-U.S. hoteliers use MICE (meetings, incentives, conventions, and exhibits). Each group has numerous divisions that meet, hold shows, and stage conventions. They need a range of facilities because they meet at local, state, regional, national, and international sites.

Conventions Conventioneers assemble for many reasons. Meetings, speeches, delivery of papers, job placements, and socials go on for several days. Some are professional, while others are merely entertaining. Delegates interact individually for professional advancement and work jointly for the organization except when the convention is a private enterprise.

With the growth of mixed-use facilities, both urban and resort hotels vie for convention business. To be competitive, the convention hotel must offer a range of facilities. Meeting spaces, banquet facilities, and audiovisual equipment are minimal requirements (see Exhibit 6). Conventioneers are a captive audience. The more complete the property, the more appealing the site to the meeting planner, who is the eventual buyer.

Sports activities, beautiful scenery, and isolation from the hubbub of the cities are touted by a resort's sales department. Urban properties compete with theaters, museums, and historical locations. Urban areas usually have the advantage of publicly financed convention halls (see Exhibit 10).

EXHIBIT 10 Publicly supported convention centers solicit and provide space for trade shows. Delegates may number in the tens of thousands during a three- or four-day convention. What is good for the local hotel business is good for the community's economic health (see Exhibit 10). *Courtesy of Las Vegas Convention and Visitors Authority, Las Vegas, Nevada.*

Hotels sometimes join with nearby competitors when the convention is too large for one property. Although not the rule, conventions of 50,000 to 100,000 delegates have been recorded. Conventions of that size are usually held with trade shows.

Trade Shows   Trade shows are product lines that the exhibitor shows to potential buyers. Trade shows and conventions are often held together. They are not open to the general public. Shows may require a great deal of space if the displays are large pieces of equipment or house large numbers of exhibitors and attendees. City convention bureaus build halls to accommodate the exhibits, leaving housing to the city's hotels.

Exhibits of small goods such as jewelry or perfume can be housed almost anywhere. They do not need convention halls. Even small hotels can pursue small trade shows. Although not commonly done, guest rooms sometimes are used for exhibition and sleeping. Shoppers visit the room to do business during the day and at day's end, the exhibitor occupies the room as a guest.

Competition for conventions and trade shows is coming from corporate training centers. Not hotels and not conference centers, training centers were built by and run for specific companies. They are in-house training sites that, like hotels and conference centers, abhor vacancies. So the likes of the U.S. Postal Service (Norman, OK) and Aetna Insurance (Hartford, CT) will happily book private guests or groups and trade shows into facilities built for their own training purposes.

The Single Entity   The single entity is neither a tour package nor a convention/trade show. Its members are bound by a different adhesive. Guests belong to the group (a company, an orchestra, a college ball team) before they come to the hotel. The unit (the company, the orchestra, the ball team) makes the reservation and pays the bill. The single entity stays together: It meets, it performs, it plays ball.

Although the visiting ball team is the good example of single entity, hotels cater to other groups as well. There are company sales and technical meetings, new product-line shows, traveling choral groups, and high-school graduation trips. Hotel/casinos have their own form of the single entity, the gambling junket. High rollers are brought in to the property for several days of entertainment and play.

Tour groups offer a contrast. Tour group members have no previous affinity. They come together only for the trip. Each member pays the wholesaler. With a single entity, the entity usually pays the hotel bill, not the individual members. Tour groups dissolve after the trip; single entities retain their original relationships.

Members of some single entities (say, a church group) may contribute prorated costs. Business entities (say, company training programs) would pay the entire cost. Single entities are arranged and paid for by the entity. Tour groups are for-profit businesses. There are similarities between the two: Both commit to a block of rooms and both pay a single bill (called a folio) for those rooms.

Attendees at conventions and trade shows are unlike the tour group and the single entity. The room block is most likely made by a nonguest buyer, a professional trade-show executive. Convention delegates then make individual room reservations *with the hotel* against that room block. Delegates, who represent a wide range of companies and geographies, pay their own bills. Each convention-eer comes and goes without concern for the schedule of other delegates. The subject matter of the convention may be their one common interest. Convention goers may not know other attendees, or they may have come with others from the same company. If there are many representatives from the same organization, they may be billed as a single entity within the convention.

Incentive Tours   Incentive tours are special, highly prized single entities. Businesses run incentive programs to motivate employees. Cash bonuses, prizes, and incentive trips—a free vacation for two—are rewarded to those who meet announced goals. Many winners from one company make up an incentive tour, a single entity.

Resorts covet incentive tours. The winners are the company's top people. Only the best accommodations will do. Unfortunately for the resorts, incentive tours have grown so important that most companies hire incentive-company specialists. Hotels know them as nonguest buyers!

Incentive companies run incentive programs for many businesses. This gives the incentive company leverage against the hotel. The two sides bargain tough when bookings for several incentive groups are possible. The incentive company exerts the same pressure on the hotel/seller as does the tour operator. More than one sale is at stake. Price and quality are the difference. Cost is critical for the wholesaler, quality for the incentive buyer.

NEW OWNERSHIP PATTERNS

The State of the Industry

Historically, the inn was owned and managed by a family. Then, in the 1950s ownership began to separate. Now, those who own hotels no longer manage them! Owners focus on income taxes, depreciation, and rents. Each became more important than hiring, food and beverage, and marketing, which are management issues. The historical hotel has undergone tremendous changes.

TURMOIL AND CHURNING   There are various cycles of hotelkeeping. Good and bad times roll in on waves of change. The cycle is dramatic because unforeseen events come quickly from a variety of causes.

For example: Income tax laws were changed in the 1970s. Before that, speculators bought and sold hotels at ever-increasing values. The gains came from turning the real estate, not from operational profits. When Congress repealed certain tax advantages, trading hotel equity lost its appeal. Rentals were insufficient to pay the mortgage debt on unreasonably high real-estate values. Estimates place about two-thirds of the nation's hotels in financial distress. Prices plummeted and the industry went into shock. For some, there was a silver lining. Bankrupt hotels resold at distressed prices so earnings were adequate to meet the lower mortgage obligations. Distressed hotels closed, so room supply fell. Balanced supply and demand meant a healthy industry once again.

A new cycle of overbuilding (increased room supply) began in 2000. With it, another downward spin. Before the trend was clear, New York City experienced the September 11, 2001 attacks. Travel and tourism fell into unforeseen turmoil. Occupancy and RevPar plunged then as it did again between 2008 and 2011.[7] Searching desperately for business, hotels, and airlines too, allowed another nonguest buyer to gain hold. Websites, online travel agencies (OTAs), started selling hotel rooms.

Churning   Churning is any rapid buying and selling. Buying and selling hotels, for example. Oddly, a major hotel churner is not even a hotel company. The Blackstone Group, a private-equity firm, became interested in hotel real estate when the values plummeted after 9/11.

A small chain, Homestead Village, was its first acquisition; Hilton was acquired more recently (see Exhibit 12). In between, Blackstone bought Extended Stay America, Boca Resorts, Prime Hospitality, and Wyndham Hotels. Each had additional brands. It paid $3.5 billion for La Quinta's 7 brands, including Baymont Inns. Rapidly churning, Blackstone then sold AmeriSuites[8] and the management and franchising rights for Wyndham Hotels. In keeping with its own mission, Blackstone did not sell Wyndham real estate. It did sell Baymont. Many of these deals were negotiated with Cendant Hotels, a churner in its own right, now long out of business.

There are many real-estate churners in the lodging industry. Large hotel companies have no desire to own hotel real estate. So companies such as Starwood Capital—not to be confused with Starwood Hotels—buy and sell chains or individual hotels. Colony Capital, another equity firm, bought the Raffles Hotel Chain (Singapore), the Bahamas-based Kerzner casino company, and the Fairmont Hotel Chain, San Francisco. It is an international business!

The angst experienced in 2001 was felt again in 2008–2012 with collapse, financial reorganizations, or outright bankruptcies. Red Roof Inns, the Maui Prince, and the Four Season Maui, Hawaii, especially, were hit hard. In California alone about 250 hotels verged on foreclosure.

A CONSOLIDATING INDUSTRY   Consolidation—bigger hotel companies and fewer of them—has contributed to the churning and turmoil. Whether the cycle is up or down, the big guys get bigger (see Exhibit 11). Growth comes from acquiring hotels, from adding new properties, and from creating new brands (Hyatt's Andaz, for example).[9] Growth is facilitated when the stock

---

[7]Estimates suggest hotel rates of 2010 fell some 16–20% worldwide, bringing them below the ADR of 2004!

[8]Extended Stay's bankruptcy was lodging's largest ever. Six years later (2010) Blackstone partnered with others to buy Extended Stay again—this time out of bankruptcy; having sold it in 2007. Talk about churning: Buy in 2004; sell in 2007; rebuy in 2010.

[9]In 38 months between 2005 and 2008, 38 new hotel brands were created. *Travel Management*, April 30, 2008, quoting Bjorn Hanson of PricewaterhouseCoopers.

The Big Guys of the U.S. Hospitality Industry

Company Name[a]	Estimated[b] Number of Hotels	Estimated[b] Number of Rooms
Best Western	4,200	310,000
Choice	6,000	490,000
Hilton	3,200	375,000
Marriott	3,150	500,000
Starwood	1,000	290,000
Wyndham	7,100	590,000

[a] Generally used name, not official, registered trademarks.
[b] Figures are estimated and rounded.

EXHIBIT 11 Growth, consolidation, and churning within the lodging industry have created large companies. They're big, tough competitors. These six chains control an estimated 2.5 million rooms. Not listed are the many international chains headquartered outside the United States.

market booms. Shares of hotel companies increase in value. These shares, rather than cash, are used as currency to buy competitors or smaller companies.

The industry is dynamic with "change" being the catchword. Two themes are evident with Hilton Hotels carrying the fundamental story. Hotels are no longer family affairs and the hotel is no longer managed by its owners (see Exhibit 12).

The Hilton Story

A Chronology of Changing Ownership in Hotelkeeping

Hilton—Family-Owned
Family operated rooming house
Conrad Hilton's first hotel, 1919, Mobley House, Cisco, Texas
Family name first used: The Hilton Hotel, 1925, Dallas, Texas
Move Westward, 1938, Sir Francis Drake, San Francisco
Move Eastward, 1943, Roosevelt Hotel, New York City
Purchased the Stevens and Palmer House hotels in Chicago, 1945

Hilton Hotels Corporation
Incorporated 1946 as Hilton Hotels Corporation, headquartered in Beverly Hills
First hotel company to be listed on the New York Stock Exchange, 1947
Acquisition of the Statler Chain, 1954 (Largest real estate deal ever to date.)
Hilton's second large acquisitions: Promus/DoubleTree Hotels (7 brands), 1999

Hilton—International (Visa)
First international hotel, 1953, in Spain
Separated Hilton International in 1964 and sold it to UAL, 1968
UAL sold Hilton International to Ladbroke, 1987
Ladbroke names the chain "Hilton Group, Plc"
Hilton then calls its international hotel chain, "Visa"
Hilton repurchases its international brand, 2005

Hilton Hotels Corporation—Continuing Change
Acquires its first casino hotels in Las Vegas, 1971
Separates gaming from hotels; creates Caesars Entertainment, 1988
Merges with Bally's Entertainment, 1996
Sale of Red Lion to WestCoast Hospitality, 2001
Sale of Scandic Hotels, 2007

Hilton—Still in the Hotel Business
Sells itself (the operating company) to the Blackstone Group for $26 billion, 2007
Blackstone financed in part by Goldman Sachs and Bank of America
Debt of $20 billion threatens solvency during economic downturn
Blackstone and lenders sell off divisions of Hilton, 2011
Ownership is further divorced from operations
Hilton family no longer part of Hilton Hotels, 2007
Headquarters moves from California to Washington, D.C., 2009
Operates almost 3,500 properties in 79 countries, 2011

EXHIBIT 12 Hilton's history exemplifies the hotel industry's path as both shifted from a Mine Host family affair to a separation of ownership and professional management. Blackstone, the world's largest buy-out firm, is also involved with Highland Hospitality Group, Extended Stay Hotels, the La Quinta chain, and Columbia Sussex. The shift from Mine Host to real estate has never been clearer than the path taken by Hilton.

THE GLOBAL VILLAGE   The global village, shorthand for shrinking political differences and interlocking economies worldwide, has enabled businesses to cross borders and jump oceans. Hotel companies have been among the leaders. Consolidation has been possible, in part, because of the global village. Hilton's reacquisition of a British company proves the point (see Exhibit 12). So does Starwood's takeover of Le Meridien, originally French and later British-owned. It now operates in 21 countries. It is the same story with Colony Capital's purchase of Raffles (see Churning). Raffles owns Swissotels, which operates in three-dozen locales.

Who pursues whom depends on the value of international currencies. If foreign investors want a U.S. hotel, they need U.S. dollars. When the dollar is weak, fewer units of the foreign currency are needed to buy the necessary dollars. The international buyer with the strong currency gets a bargain. China is in that position now. Japan was similarly situated 30 years ago. All currencies, including dollars, go up and down in value. The United States started the overseas movement post World War II, when the dollar was very strong.

Many international chains have expanded globally (see Exhibit 13) or have made subtle name changes. Best Western became Best Western International; Quality Inns became Choice Hotels International.

Global acquisitions involve more than currency values. Companies may be after assets (management talent or reservation systems) or new markets. Guests in foreign lands search for familiar names. U.S. citizens do so abroad; foreign visitors do so in the United States. Political stability is another factor. Foreign investors face financial loss from political upheaval. The stability of the United States is particularly attractive to foreign investors. This is especially so because they have longer business horizons than do their domestic counterparts.

Ownership and Financing Alternatives

Large hotels require large amounts of money, sums beyond the means of most families. This was one of the reasons for ownership to separate from management. The corporate form of ownership made the shift that much easier, both coinciding with the construction know-how to build very larger hotels.

INDIVIDUAL OWNERSHIP   There are still large numbers of individually owned hotels. Many are held by members of the Asian American Hotel Owners Association (AAHOA). They are usually small, fall within the economy class of roadside motels, and carry a franchise flag. Best Western International is another affiliation of individual owners, but it is not a franchise group.

Owning a single hotel or even several hotels is not the same as maintaining a family homestead. The issue is not where the family dwells, but where the financing comes from. There are still instances where the cash to buy or build come from an extended family. Uncles and aunts and

Company Name and Identity	Estimated Number of Rooms[a]	Countries of Operation[b]
Accor (France)	500,000	China, France, India, Sweden
InterContinental (U.K.)	620,000	Andorra, Gabon, Kazakhstan, Rwanda
JAL Hotels (Japan)	18,000	China, Germany, Myanmar, Taiwan
Rezidor[c] (Denmark)	84,000	Croatia, Ireland, Senegal, United Kingdom
Sol Melia (Spain)	75,000	Costa Rica, Mexico, Spain, Venezuela, Vietnam
Taj Group (India)	10,000	Malaysia, Maldives, India, Seychelles

Half-Dozen International Hotel Chains That also Operate in the United States

[a] Values are rounded.
[b] Representative; country lists are not complete.
[c] Strategic partnership with Radisson SAS (Carlson).

EXHIBIT 13   Maturing markets abroad and the relative strengths of world currencies encourage both American and foreign chains to operate domestically and internationally.

in-laws are tapped for the equity (the ownership portion). Sometimes local businesspersons in small towns invest out of public pride.

Borrowed funds supplement equity monies. Lenders are local banks and investment groups or even the franchise company bidding for the flag. Small business loans by local and regional banks can be guaranteed by the Small Business Administration (SBA) or the Business and Industry Loan Guarantee Program (Department of Agriculture). Small entrepreneurs borrow more easily and less expensively when the lenders are guaranteed 80% of their loans by these agencies.

More equity money is needed as the project grows. Then the effort shifts from Main Street to Wall Street and the sale of shares (stock). En route, borrowed money comes from regional and national banks, from insurance companies, and from pension funds. At one time, labor unions were a source. Investment bankers, mortgage brokers, and private equity firms join the flow that supports hotel development. During the downturn of the 1980s, when prices collapsed, a new financing vehicle called the REIT reenergized the market.

REAL ESTATE INVESTMENT TRUSTS (REITs) REITs can own hotel properties just as individual owners or corporations do. REITs are public companies that raise capital through the sale of stock. (There are private, nontraded REITs.) Small investors buy and sell REIT shares through the stock market. REITs use the funds to buy hotel properties. Other REITs specialize in buying apartment buildings, office buildings, and shopping-malls. REITs pay no federal income tax, provided at least 90% of taxable income is paid out to shareholders. REITs that move into operations, called C-Corporations, do pay income tax.

In 1993, Marriott split into two parts: Marriott International, the operating company, and Host Marriott—later Host Hotels & Resorts—the REIT. Host has bought and sold hundreds of hotels properties. Host is one of the industry's best churners because it is the world's largest hotel REIT with Felcor Lodging Trust as a close competitor.

CONDOMINIUMS AND TIMESHARES Condominiums (condos) and timeshares (interval or vacation ownerships) are two relatively recent developments. Both have their origins in destination resorts. Condos, an American innovation, first appeared at ski resorts Aspen and Stowe. Timeshare, a later development, is a European idea that took hold in Florida. Foreign ownership there was fueled by a weak dollar and the certainty of American real-estate laws. Although condominiums are worldwide, their largest presence is in the United States.

Condominium Ownership Condos are often confused with timeshares because the physical buildings of both may look alike. They can be differentiated based on ownership of the units, not the blueprint of the building. Condos are real-estate purchases; timeshares are not. The craze for condo ownership was originally nurtured by a favorable income-tax treatment. Taxes changed which slowed growth. Then bankruptcies skyrocketed during the economic malaise that left buildings half empty or half built, especially in Florida.

A condominium is the owner's home, but it may be a second home or a speculative buy. Owners finance and furnish the unit as they would any home purchase. As members of the condo association, they are also owners of the common areas.

The concept of mixed-use facilities grew from these new ownership patterns. Because condo owners are not always in residence, there is an opportunity to rent the unit. Then on-site management is needed to service the transient guest with linens, maintenance, and more. A hotel company is the perfect answer, and adding an adjacent hotel a logical extension. Then, both owners and guests can access all types of services and amenities. Next came retail outlets, health clubs, entertainment venues, and businesses. Thus, the mixed-use development was born.

There are endless permutations to the basic plan. In its simplest form, owners reserve so many days per year for personal use. That could be 100%. The unoccupied times go into the rental pool, or not as owners prefer. Profits, if any, from the participating units are paid to homeowners under some rotating, prorata plan. A round-robin structure has appeared. Homeowners, who have helped the developer finance the construction, now occupy the units as guest/owners and hire a management company to rent the unused space.

A variation on condo ownership is taking place by the swimming pool. Cabanas, poolside huts, at upscale resorts (some with baths and even kitchens) are being sold as timeshares and condominiums. Costs can be tens of thousands of dollars.

Condo Hotels   Condos are visualized within resort projects. Locating them within commercial hotels is a new twist. But urban hotels have joined the movement; residential guests buy condominiums within commercial hotels. It is part of a broader social movement that has residents moving back to city centers. The Ritz-Carlton in downtown Boston is a good example. As with resort condos, those within a transient hotel also help developers in financing. Condo units are prepaid; developers have upfront money. That concept fell apart in 2008 when neither the hotel builder nor the condo buyer had sufficient money to finance the building of condos.

Unlike resort condominiums, the commercial hotel condo is not usually rented to transient guests. These questions remain: What if permanent occupants decide to make their condos available? Is such space computed in occupancy if available but not owned by the hotel? If so, or even if not, how is the occupancy percentage calculated? If left vacant are these room computed in RevPar?

The urban condo movement alarmed city fathers because conversions reduce the number of transient rooms. Fewer transient rooms threaten local tourism and convention solicitation. Moreover, municipal income is lost with fewer transient rooms subjected to room taxes. New York City lost some 10,000 rooms with The Plaza Hotel its most publicized conversion, the famous Plaza Hotel. Pressure from New York officials forced the Plaza to convert fewer transient rooms than first announced.[10]

Timeshares   Unlike condominium deals, timeshares are not real-estate purchases. Buyers do not buy a unit; they buy only the *right to use* a unit for so many days each year over a fixed period. At the end of 20–30 years, the developer—not the guest who had paid upfront money and fees for decades—owns the unit. In contrast, condominium owners have immediate title to the property.

Timeshares started out with sleazy reputations. No real-estate titles meant no oversight by real-estate regulators. Numerous complaints about unethical sales techniques forced state commissioners to act. One critical regulation was a cooling-off periods of 10–30 days. It allowed buyers to rescind purchases made under the high pressure of timeshare sellers. Once credibility was established, large hotel companies entered the business. Disney and Marriott, among others, helped reassure buyers. Timeshare sales entered a new phase, and with it a host of new options such as Deeded Timeshares (with title) and Floating Weeks. All variations on the theme.

Savvy marketing executives contributed to the turnaround by simply changing the name. Timeshares became *interval ownerships, vacation clubs, or vacation ownerships.* More expensive timeshares in golf-course homes with commitments longer than the standard one-or two-week stay are called *private residence clubs* or *fractionals.* They sell for ±$250,000! Timeshare segmentation has stretched into private clubs, *The Phillips Club of New York.*

The popular timeshare remains a very poor investment even at a price of $15,000 plus annual fees. Getting out from those annual costs is almost impossible, resale practically unknown. Buyers who give them back may still be responsible for fees. eBay often lists units for sale at 10% of their original cost. The other major negative, coming to the same place at the same time for 25 years, has been alleviated by exchange arrangements, but at a cost.

Exchanges   Changing places caught on as timeshare owners awoke to the limits of their contracts. Exchange companies—such as Resort Condominiums International (RCI), a well known name—have matured to provide a legitimate service to the once-booming industry. Timeshares can be traded by paying a fee and depositing one's own unit into the exchange pool. Units at both ends of the trade must be affiliated members. RCI advertises 3,700 resorts worldwide.

The importance of swapping was not lost to hoteliers. Hotel companies with timeshares enlarged on the idea by using their preferred-guest programs (PGPs). Timeshare guests can trade vacation units for other PGP values, including airline tickets and, with Disney, even cruises.

Hoteliers have taken to integrating resorts with timeshare facilities. It is so natural that the two building are very often side-by-side. During selling, prospects are offered free or discounted mini vacations at the resort, provided they listen to a timeshare sales pitch. These are long, pressurized sessions. Promised gifts are rescinded if the guests leave early. Many do anyway!

---

[10]"Buy-to-Let" rooms are the London equivalent of condominiums. With city occupancy in the high 80%, demand has driven the unit price to $500,000 and up. GuestInvest is one of the early British chains.

The synergy of hotels and timeshares is the same as that of condos and timeshares. Hotels offer the infrastructure (spas, golf courses, restaurants) that timeshare lacks. The large size of the parties in the timeshares and their 50-week occupancy provide a base to the hotel's business.

Role of the Timeshare   Timeshares and condos are above all financing alternatives for the developer. Converting existing resorts, or parts of them, was the first step in timeshare development. The funds were used to pay debts, upgrade and refurbish facilities, or line the pockets of the owner. This conversion phase failed because buyers wanted more than renovated hotel rooms or even extended-stay facilities with kitchenettes.

Developing new upscale accommodations takes capital. So the developer sets out to sell each unit 50 times, once each week. The more desirable the time purchased, in-season versus off-season, the more the unit costs. An 80-unit property may have as many as 4,000 participants (50 weeks × 80 units). The figure swells when the actual number of persons in each unit (2–6) is added in. A lucky developer might gross $100,000,000 upfront to finance the project: say, $25,000/unit × 80 units × 50 weeks. This substantial sum is offset by vacancies and expensive marketing costs including sales commissions. Fractionals have a different profile: These luxurious, private residences often cost in the millions, but limit occupants to 10 to 14 buyers, not 50.

The upfront calculations must be tempered by several realities. Only a percentage of the units are actually presold and two weeks of the year are held back for maintenance. California law actually requires that. Unlike condominiums, where upkeep is the owner's responsibility, timeshare repairs, services, and furnishings are the developer's costs. Some expenses are offset by weekly maintenance and housekeeping fees levied on the occupants for T&T—trash and towels—and sometimes insurance.

Deeded timeshares is one innovation that improved the industry's outlook. With a deed, owners have the right to exchange, gift, sell (difficult), will, or rent the unit. It might even appreciate in value. That likelihood is so small that the industry's trade group, American Resort Development Association, forbids suggesting it.

Limiting the number of unit users has also been tried. Rather than 50 buyers for 50 weeks, the unit is sold in larger blocks to, say, six buyers for eight weeks each. Rotating weeks is another innovation. Taking advantage of the two-week break in occupancy, time allotments are rolled over. Occupants rotate throughout the years. No one gets the best times always and no one the worst. Of course, it may take a decade to get a one-time chance at Christmas or the July 4th weekend.

JOINT VENTURES AND STRATEGIC ALLIANCES   Joint ventures and alliances are similar to partnerships, except that the participants are not persons. They are legal entities, hotel corporations, for example. Sovereign-wealth funds have become active joint-venture members. These are investments made by the governments of several nations. Especially active in the hotel arena are Singapore[11] and Dubai. Dubai's sovereign fund, Dubai World, was hit hard during the 2008–2010 downturn.

Although not government owned, Kingdom Hotels Investment Company of Dubai (owned by Saudi Prince Alwaleed bin Talal) sometimes appears to be owned by the government, as does another private investor, Sovereign Hospitality Holdings (part of the Kharafi Group of Azerbaijan).

Singapore's fund, GIC (Government Investment Corporation), joint ventured with Host Hotels (a U.S. REIT) in 2010 to bid for London's famous Grosvenor House. Marriott, the management company, did not join the venture. GIC was also busy across the globe bidding for Japan's ANA hotel chain, which Morgan Stanley (USA) had financed.

In 1999, Canadian Pacific Hotels in a joint venture with Kingdom Hotels (Prince Alwaleed bin Talal) purchased Fairmont Hotels and Resorts. As a result of its financial support, Colony Capital, a private investment firm, retains a large stake in Fairmont Hotels.[12]

Joint ventures are usually financial marriages warranted by rising costs and ever-larger megadeals. Strategic alliances spread the risks and tap the capabilities of different organizations.

---

[11]Singapore's investment company bought 7% of Hyatt Hotels when it went public in 2009.

[12]Colony Capital is also the largest shareholder of Accor, the world's fourth-largest hotel group. Colony has moved into the expanding business of boutique hotels with a recent investment in SLS Hotels.

Financial, managerial, operational, and government expertise may not be found in a single company. Gaming management is one such skill. New gaming ventures in Singapore and Macau have recently turned to Nevada expertise to make certain of their success.

NEW MANAGEMENT PATTERNS

The era of the small innkeeper/entrepreneur is waning. Costly and risky enterprises facing intense competition require the management talent and capital access that only large, public companies—hotel chains—can provide.

Hotel Chains

Travel evokes the unknown and the unfamiliar. Within that environment, travelers seek a rather personal service—a bed for the night. Since it is not possible to test the facilities beforehand, the decision rests on the reputation of the individual hotel or, more likely, on its chain membership.

Chain-controlled hotels dominate the U.S. hotel industry (see Exhibit 14). About 75% of all U.S. hotels are under some flag. Overseas, the momentum has just started. Chains comprise about 33% of European hotels, where individuals and families still hold sway.

The reasons are simple. Chains bring strengths in site selection, access to capital, and economies of scale in purchasing, advertising, and reservations. Chains attract the best management talent and provide the consumer with brand recognition. Despite their importance, hotel chains do not build hotel. Those who build may not own, and those who own may not manage. So builders, lenders, and owners turn to the chain.

PARTIES TO THE DEAL   Five different parties are involved in the development and operation of a hotel. That need not be five separate entities. One participant could have several roles. The *developer* (Party number 1) sees an opportunity, acquires the site, and puts the plan together. The

Twenty Hotel Chains: Some Old and Well Known; Some New and Unproven	
Name	**Parent Company**
aloft Hotels[a]	Starwood
Caesars Entertainment	Formerly Harrah's[b]
Disney	Its Own Brand[c]
Element	Starwood
Fairmont	Fairmont Raffles Hotels
Four Seasons	Its Own Brand
Historic Hotels of America	Referral Group
Host Hotels	Its Own Brand
Hyatt[d]	Global Hyatt
Indigo	InterContinental
Loews	Its Own Brand
MGM Resorts	Its Own Brand
Morgans	Its Own Brand
NYLO (New York Loft)	Its Own Brand
Omni	Its Own Brand
Onyx	Kimpton Hotel Group
Renaissance	Marriott
Ritz-Carlton	Marriott
Sheraton	Starwood
Westin	Starwood

[a] Spelled with either a capital- or lower-case letter.
[b] Harrah's, which is a public company no longer, changed its name in 2010.
[c] Companies with their own brands usually name each hotel differently.
[d] Hyatt became a public company in 2009.

EXHIBIT 14   An alphabetical register of hotel chains, some old and some new, untested ones. Several new brands feature "lifestyle alternatives" for Generation X'ers. They're either a really new option or just a new brand name.

hotel might be a project of the community. It might be one element in a business park or a resort in a timeshare complex. The developer could also be the *owner* (Party number 3), which would fold the five parties into four identities.

Many sources provide mortgage loans. Private-equity firms and REITs have been especially active in the past decade, but traditionally loans have come from commercial banks. That *lender* is Party number 2. Some financing might even come from other parties to the deal. Mezzanine financing, a secondary source of borrowed money with higher interest rates, is often used during construction. It falls between equity funds and senior mortgage debt. There may be numerous mezzanine loans and some may convert into equity money.[13] If Marriott, for example, were to be the *management company* (Party number 4), it might lend short-term funds, mezzanine financing, to the project.

Party number 3, the equity or owner, could be any of the others, or an individual, a joint venture, a REIT, a public corporation, or a separate entity making a passive investment.

If none of the others are capable of running the hotel, a management company is needed. If that management company has no recognizable logo—is not known to the public—a franchise license is obtained from Party number 5, the *franchisor*, who provides the brand recognition (see Exhibit 15).

Above all, hotel chains (see Exhibits 11, 13, and 14) supply management talent. They can provide support to the other four parties as well. Chain management helps with development, sometimes holds a piece of the ownership equity, provides brand recognition, identifies possible sites, and operates the reservation system.

CONSORTIA AND MEMBERSHIP ORGANIZATIONS Independent operators are at a disadvantage, fighting the logos and reservation systems of their chain-linked competitors. Battling back, they, too, have affiliated. Their associations are looser, focusing chiefly on common logos, standards, and reservations systems. There is some training and advice, but restrictions are few and autonomy understood.

Reservation referrals are cooperating properties that organize to promote the group. They have a national reservation system, joint advertising, and a recognizable logo. This helps the single property compete but still maintain its independence. There is no interlocking management, no group purchasing, no general financing—nothing but a common sales effort. Unlike the

Representative Franchise Fees[a]

Fee	Representative Terms	Alternative Terms
Application[b]	The greater of $50,000 *or* $400 times the number of rooms	A lesser fixed amount plus a per-room fee over, say, the first 75 rooms
Royalty	4%–6% of gross room revenues	3% of gross revenue, *or a minimum per night, say, $8*
Advertising/ Marketing	1.5%–3.5% of room revenue	2% of gross revenue, *or a minimum per night, say, 1.50 per room*
Training	0.5% of gross revenue plus cost of attending school	None; franchisee bears all schooling costs for employees sent away
Reservation	3% of room revenue plus $5 per reservation	$10 per reservation, *or a minimum per night, say, $10 per room*
Frequent Traveler	1.5%–2.0% of room revenue	

[a] Other possibilities include email costs, global reservation costs, termination costs, accounting charges, and participation in frequent guest promotions.
[b] All or some (90%–95%) of the application fee is returned if the application is not approved.

EXHIBIT 15 Hotel franchisors (those who sell franchise rights) charge franchisees (buyers) a variety of fees that may total 8 to 10% of gross sales. (Reminder: As room rates rise, so does the innkeeper's franchise fees, as a fixed percentage of the higher rate.) Franchisees gain access to national reservation systems, which may account for a large percentage of the franchisee's occupancy.

---

[13]"Hunters" who stalk sick hotels often buy outstanding mezzanine debt at greatly reduced costs and leverage that debt to gain control of the assets.

standardization set by franchises, members have no prescribed limits on buildings or sites as long as each property meets the standards in its own unique design. Still, Best Western International, the largest referral group, has begun suggesting prototype guest rooms.

Best Western (see Exhibit 11) has 4,000-plus independently owned affiliates in 80 countries. Members vote for the board of directors that operates the association, sets standards, and collects fees, even as it allows the uniqueness of each property.

Preferred Hotel and Resorts Worldwide is a different type of membership group. Its room rates are at the other end of Best Western's. Both are international in scope, but Preferred has a much smaller membership, some 700 properties. Subgroups within its banner include Summit and Sterling Hotels and Preferred Residences, upscale fractionals. The Sagamore Resort is a member of the Preferred Hotels group. It is also listed as one of the Historic Hotels of America (HHA) because HHA is a brand of Preferred hotels. HHA, with about 200 properties, is a program of the National Trust for Historic Preservation. Membership in HHA requires that the property be at least 50 years old or eligible to be listed in the National Registry of Historical Places.

Management Contracts and Management Companies

MANAGEMENT CONTRACTS A management contract is an agreement between a hotel owner (Party number 3) and a management company (Party number 4). The contract is a complex legal instrument by which the management company operates the hotel within the conditions set down by the contract. For this, the owner pays the management company a fee of between 2% and 4% of revenues (not profits) plus incentives based on other values: 75% occupancy, for example. Management companies may provide preplanning advice if joined early in the process.

Fees are paid whether there are profits or not. Profits, if any, belong to the owners, as do losses. Since management fees are paid in good times and bad, these companies have profited and grown rapidly. They have very little invested capital and almost no risk. (Risk lies with Parties numbered 1, 2, and 3.) The relationship between the two parties is not always smooth: Lawsuits arise over many issues that the contracts cannot foresee. One example dealt with the revenue earned by the management company's sale of guests' names and address. To whom did that income belong? Another dealt with the rebates from purveyors. To whom did that income belong? Lawsuits are fewer during up cycles, when both parties profit, but they are greater during downturns, when owners suffer the most. Contracts favorable to one of the parties reflect the time in the cycle that the agreement was made. During bad times, owners accept restrictive terms. An improved economy shifts the advantage. Competition among management firms and good cash flows force concessions from the management companies bidding for the contract. Then, owners negotiate shorter contracts, smaller fees, and increased capital to be invested by the management company in upgrading the physical property.

MANAGEMENT COMPANIES Management companies, as distinct from owner/managers, are a relatively recent innovation. Four separate but similar events explain their presence. In each case, lenders took control of hotels when owners defaulted on loans. Lenders/bankers dislike holding physical assets (buildings); that is not their expertise. So they sell them as quickly as possible. Resale values are greater if hotels are up and running, so lenders hire management companies to operate defunct hotels.

Management companies made their first appearance during the Great Depression (1930s) when most of the nation's hotels went bankrupt. Bankers sought help and as a result management companies were conceived. Event #2 was the oil embargo of 1973. Without oil, travel shut down and many American hotels fell to the auctioneer's hammer. Management companies were reborn. The 1980s downturn was Event #3. It, like the downturn of Event #4 (2008–2011), impacted both banking and hospitality. The downturn was caused by overbuilding, overfinancing, and a failing economy. Despite a 30-year gap, federal intervention again saved banks, and thus hotels, and with that management companies matured. Consolidation and brand identification have enabled the better known chains to dominate the management field. The number of independent properties that look to smaller management companies is declining. At the same time, there is greater competition from and among the big guys (see Exhibit 11).

LEASING (RENTING) Management contracts and lease contracts are opposite views of the industry's health. One or the other is popular depending on the position of the economic cycle.

Management companies lease (pay rent) to owning companies for the right to run the hotel and keep the profits. With management contracts, owners pay (hire) management companies to manage; profit or loss remains with the owners. Leases are popular when times are good. The management company wants in; it pays rent but keeps profits. Leases are win/win if the rent is high enough for the owner to pay the mortgage, with some left over.

Historically, hotel chains (Pick, Flagler, Statler) owned their buildings. A new era began in the 1950s as hoteliers entered a sale-and-leaseback phase. The hotel company sold the building and then rented it back. It obtained a cash infusion and kept the operating earnings less the rental fee. The next step is where we are now. Hotel companies sidestepped ownership from the start, focusing on either the lease or the management contract. Hoteliers allowed the other players (developers, owners, and lenders) to carry the burden of the physical building. This enabled management companies to grow rapidly and profitably. Today they are the hotel business.

The dynamics of hotelkeeping allow various combinations. Some companies own and operate while others enter joint ventures. Some just manage; others contribute equity to the deal. Franchising is another option.

FRANCHISING   Franchising is not a new idea, nor is it unique to lodging. Many industries franchise; hamburgers are probably the best known. A franchise buyer (called the *franchisee*) pays for and acquires rights from a seller (the *franchisor*). The franchisee may now use the franchisor's name, products, techniques, and advertising within a fixed geographic area. Buying a franchise allows the franchisee to operate as an independent entity but have the benefits of the chain. Those benefits come with costs.

Franchisees pay a variety of fees beginning with a signing fee. The biggest burden is a royalty on room revenue: So much paid per room per night. As Exhibit 15 points out, other fees are levied for the sign; for bookings made through the res(ervation) system; for amenities with the franchisor's logo (soap); for training and for membership in the frequent-guest program. Management companies that lack a recognizable logo often pay some of the owner's franchise fees in order to win the management contract.

Franchise fees are a major operating expense, upward of 10% of room sales. There is a counterbalance, however. Brand identification adds upward of 10 percentage points to occupancy and $20-plus to ADR.

Franchise fees buy services as well as identification. The number of services offered depends on the franchise purchased. High-end franchises might include feasibility studies, and help with site selection, financing, advertising, and systems design. Some properties gain as much as 50% of all room sales through that res system.

Franchising is growing in Europe and Asia. China joined in as it prepared for the 2008 Olympics. Contrariwise, some American owners are dropping franchises in favor of membership groups. *Membership affiliations*, also called *brand affiliations* or *referral groups*, have shorter contracts and fewer restrictions. Franchise fees typically cost four to five times more than memberships fees. Moreover, franchisors are among the first with costly amenity creep. Owners must pay for these required upgrades.

Best Western International is the oldest, largest, and the best known of the brand-affiliated groups. Two emerging affiliates are Best Value Inns and Payless Lodging. They now coexist with more senior alliances such as Historic Hotels of America, Budget Host, and Utell.

THE FRANCHISE FLAG   Franchising hotels probably began in the late 19th century. Cesar Ritz—ritzy now means the best—gave his name to the small number of hotels that he managed. Kemmons Wilson took the naming idea a step further, Holiday Inn.

Franchising is all about name recognition. The franchisor sells its "flag" to the franchisee. Franchisee and parent are so alike that guests make no distinction. The physical hotels are indistinguishable. The differences lie in the ownership and management. The franchisor (the chain) neither owns nor manages the franchise property. The franchisee, the owner, can manage it, hire the franchisor to manage it, or contract with a management company to do so. Franchisees often buy different franchises (multiple flags) if they own more than one property. Or they may own several properties under one flag.

Each flag denotes a certain type of property, service, and price to the guest. So a franchisee intent on developing long-stay facilities would not shop for a flag that carries the upscale image of, say, Marriott's Ritz Carlton.

Canceling a franchise contract is difficult and expensive. Franchisees are usually small businesspersons. (Large hotels carry the flags of their management companies.) The franchisor is a multifaceted company whose attorneys write the franchise contract. Although competition and court decisions have helped balance the scales, tension often exists between ees and ors. When issues become widespread, franchisees form organizations to counter the strength of their franchise parent. That was the source of the Owners Association of Intercontinental Hotels (IAHI), a franchise owners' group within one brand initially, Holiday Inn. The Asian American Hotel Owners Association (AAHOA) is an owners' group across many brands.

Some of the issues that small business owners fight are as follows:

1. Protection against competitors opening with the same flag within geographic areas supposedly restricted to the initial franchisee.
2. Costs from unexpected upgrades required by the franchisor, particularly when the franchisee attempts to sell the property.
3. High liquidation damages when the franchisee wants out.

Despite some negatives, a franchise is essential for attracting the transient traveler who doesn't know the property and who may never come that way again.

Summary

Hotelkeeping opened the 21st century at the peak of its cycle. New products, new markets, and new ownership/management patterns are still falling into place. These strategic changes allow for rapid responses and decisive moves to meet worldwide competition head-on, at home and abroad. The hotel industry has a willingness to try things new: new products, new marketing techniques, and new ownership patterns that call for new management structures. New flags (brands) are flying even as consolidation shrinks the number of, and grows the size of, surviving hotel companies.

Shifts in lodging take place within the global village, where innovation and competition move swiftly between continents. Their speed and direction reflect the relative strength of currencies and of name recognition. High fees notwithstanding, franchising is one such concept.

Underpinning the global market is the inelastic business traveler. Many predict that the rapidly growing elastic market of international tourism will soon move to the first spot.

New products, new markets, new financing options, and new operational changes are reshaping this ancient industry as they have done for centuries.

Resources and Challenges

RESOURCES

Website Assignment

HVS International has a free website for "The Hotel Franchise Fee Calculator." Try: HVS international franchise calculator.

Select a franchise for your 110-room hotel which has an ADR of $90 and an occupancy of 65%. Make your selection by contrasting two choices from the franchise calculation using two years of comparison and assuming: (1) Every value increases by 2% annually; (2) Frequent travelers account for 10% of the occupancy; (3) Third-party reservations account for 1/8 of total reservations; and (4) The Internet accounts for 5% of reservations.

Explain the reasons for your choice over the second brand by showing your calculations for both and listing any assumptions that you make.

Interesting Tidbits

- *Business Travel News* (May 19, 2008) reported that 42–50% of those surveyed in 2007 and 2008 viewed hotel rooms as a commodity that was to be procured like pencils and paper clips, at the lowest price.
- Marriott's move away from rigid standardization is accelerating using several sub-brands in addition to its Autograph collection: Boutique Arts, Iconic Historic; Boutique Chic, Urban Edge, and Spa & Lodge.
- Private Equity Funds, which have entered the hotel business, are large pools of money from private sources (not public stock markets) that acquire equity (ownership) or sometimes debt (bonds or mortgages) in order to take control of a company.

Challenges

True/False

Questions that are partially false should be marked false (F).

_____ 1. Management contracts and management leases are essentially the same thing; only the participating parties differ.

_____ 2. Room rates (or price) is best viewed as and set as if they were commodities like oil or wheat.

_____ 3. Amenity creep has been the result of a bedbug infestation that has resulted in part from increased international travel.

_____ 4. An elastic buyer is one who has bounced back into travel after an economic slowdown.

_____ 5. By expanding (easing visa requirement) international travel to the United States, the nation could help balance its international trade deficit.

Problems

1. Using the trade press, your own management skills, or Web sites, prepare a list of six amenities, other than those cited in the text, that hoteliers use to attract business. *Hint:* Start the list with "free parking."

2. Identify the advantages and disadvantages to the personal career of a student who takes a job after graduation with a Hilton Inns franchise and passes up an offer from Hilton Hotels, the parent company.

3. Why is Best Western International not listed among the large management companies of Exhibit 15 After all, Best Western has some 300,000 rooms in its brand! Explain in detail.

4. Someone once said, "If you try to be all things to every guest, you'll likely end up as every guest's second choice." Is that an accurate statement? Why or why not? Answer woth special attention to the segmentation of the industry's product line.

5. A traveller driving along Interstate 36 stops at two different hotels on successive evenings. Explain, and differentiate between, the signs posted by the front desk in terms of the text discussion about ownership, management, franchising, and joint ventures.

   Hotel A: This Hampton Inn is owned by Jerome J. Vallen and Sons, Inc., under license from Promus. Richfield Hotel Management.

   Hotel B: This Hampton Inn is owned by Promus. Jerome J. Vallen, General Manager.

6. Obtain a copy of a management contract from a local hotel, or review a book in the library on hotel management contracts. Discuss three terms (for example, life of the contract, payment, maintenance of the property, or investment by the management company) that intrigue you.

AN INCIDENT IN HOTEL MANAGEMENT
Taken for a Ride

The hotel advertised the availability of free shuttle service. A business guest relied on that information when she booked for a meeting at company headquarters about one mile away. She tried to arrange the trip only to be told that first priority went to airline employees. (The hotel has a room contract with the airline.) As a result, she was late for appointments the first day.

The guest complained and was told that the shuttle would be available if she called with a 30–45 minutes lead time. On the second day, she did that from the office, but the pickup was never made; she took a cab back. Arrangements worked both ways the other days. On the last morning, she was stunned to learn that the shuttle was leaving in 5 minutes, not between 30 and 45 minutes after her call. She had not finished dressing and had had no breakfast.

Questions

1. Was there a management failure here; if so, what?
2. What is the hotel's immediate response (or action) to the incident?
3. What further, long-run action should the management take; if any?

Answers to True/False Quiz

1. False. No, the parties do not differ. Both arrangements involve the hotel owner and an outside company. With a lease, the outside company pays rent to the owner and keeps profits, if any, for itself. With a management contract, the owner keeps profits, if any, and pays the outside company to manage the operation.

2. False. Hopefully, no one views the hotel room and its price as a commodity. There are difference in wheat and oil that allow small price ranges, but the variations in hotel accommodations are so great (size, location, services, furnishings, etc.) as to warrant a wide range of (not commodity) pricing.

3. False. Amenity creep is the continued upgrade of hotel facilities and services (and thus price, room rate) brought about by competition and guest expectations.

4. False. An elastic buyer is one who responds readily to price changes. Lower room rates encourage the elastic buyer; higher rates discourage the elastic buyer. Tourists are a good example of elastic buyers. Businesspersons are generally inelastic guests.

5. True. Tourists and businesspersons, including conventioneers, have a difficult time getting visas—part of homeland-security measures. Were visa issues eased, increased international travel would help offset the nation's negative balance of trade.

The Structures of the Hotel Industry

From Chapter 3 of *Check-In Check-Out,* Ninth Edition. Gary K. Vallen, Jerome J. Vallen. Copyright © 2013 by Pearson Education, Inc. All rights reserved.

The Structures of the Hotel Industry

Two structures define the lodging industry. One, the physical structure—the building—is more visible than the other, the organizational structure. Because management focuses on profits, both structures have grown in importance.

THE ORGANIZATIONAL STRUCTURE

A wide range of skills is needed to operate large hotels. The list ranges from plumbers to accountants, and from bartenders to telecommunication specialists. Hotels with thousands of rooms have populations greater than many small towns. Each property structures its human resource, its organization, to achieve the most efficient and profitable design. That said, a pattern emerges based on the industry's best practices. This chapter outlines that design.

The workforce is separated into specialized departments—each entrusted with its share of duties. Good management minimizes the friction that invariably arises among different departments. Poor performance in one unit undermines the efforts of all. Coordinating the whole, unifying the specialties, and directing the joint efforts is the job of the GM, the general manager. GMs get their authority from ownership.

Ownership

From atop, ownership oversees the unfolding pyramid (see Exhibit 1). Ownership may rest with an individual, a partnership, a joint venture, or a public corporation. The term "ownership" refers to the operating company, not the ownership of the building. Of course, they could be the same. Management companies vary in size: They may range from a few individuals to the 800 million shares authorized for the Marriott Corporation.[1] Companies that own or manage a hotel can also own other companies, by acquiring the shares of those subsidiaries. Thus, Marriott owns Ritz Carlton and Renaissance, its subsidiaries.

Corporations are legal persons and do business as if they were real. Corporations limit the liability of the individual share(stock)holders. If a hotel company fails (and many did during the 2008–2010 down cycle), shareholders may lose their investments, but they are not responsible for the company's debts. The corporate "person" is the responsible party. The corporate person is the one who buys and sells, borrows, pays taxes, and hires the general manager who makes the organization work.

---

[1]The Marriott family owns about 25% of the 350,000,000 shares issued and outstanding. J. W. (Bill) Marriott, who is 79 years old (2012), is the company's chief executive officer (CEO). His father, J. Willlard Marriott, was the company's founder. No family member is waiting in the wings, so the next chief executive is likely to be a nonfamily member.

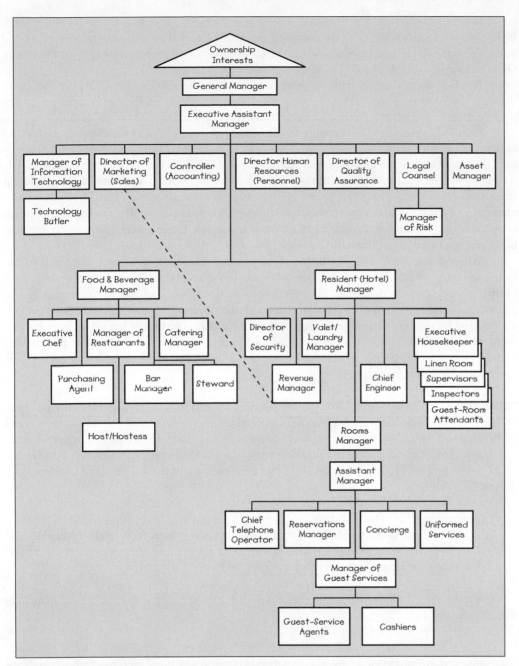

EXHIBIT 1 Hotel organizations are changing to keep pace with social and economic shifts. Flatter organizations (fewer supervisory levels) notwithstanding, new positions are being added even as older ones are being retrenched. The chart is incomplete except for the resident manager's line, which is the thrust of the chapter. Even here, flatter organizations are the trend, so many hotels lack all of the intermediate managers discussed in the chapter.

The General Manager

Management titles vary, often based on size. Large chains use corporate titles similar to those found in other businesses: CEO (chief executive officer), CFO (chief financial officer), COO (chief operating officer).

General manager (GM or *The* GM) is the title at the unit level, which is the operating hotel. If the GM is also an executive of the company that owns either the management contract or the hotel, the title used might be *president* (of the corporation) *and general manager* (of the hotel). *Owner-manager* is used for a GM who actually owns the hotel.

The GM deals directly with ownership or through the CEO or the COO, or indirectly through layers of corporate titles. Among them are vice-president for operations; area vice-president; food and beverage manager, eastern division; regional director of marketing.

Standing alone, the GM is simply the employee most responsible to whatever ownership structure is in place. The GM is responsible for all that happens in every department. To help the GM, there may be an *executive assistant manager*. Like the boss, the executive assistant has responsibility over the entire organization. The job of an executive assistant manager is different from that of the *assistant manager,* who is not the assistant manager, despite the title. The assistant manager is a rooms division post that works directly with the guest public (see Exhibit 1). Small hotels lack both executive assistants and assistant managers. Large hotels have several assistant managers to cover the desk around the clock.

"Around the clock" because hotels never close: 7/24/365 places great demands on the time and energy of hotel executives. Their work week is open ended. In contrast, the work week of operative employees is defined by federal and/or state labor laws and union contracts. An *executive-on-duty* program offers relief for salaried executives and their assistants. Slow periods are covered by rotating executives in various positions including that of the GM. Every department head listed in Exhibit 1 takes a turn as GM with overall responsibility. The reservoir of management talent is deepened; the experience of the individual is broadened; and quality time spent with the family is increased.

FROM HOST TO EXECUTIVE   With time, the GM's position has undergone many changes. During the period of one-person ownership, general managers personified their hotels. He (and in those far-off days, the GM was a he) was known as "Mine Host." His name was in the advertising. His personality was part of the aura. His presence was the hotel's very identity. Hotels were small so the property reflected the qualities, the personality, and the very essence of this special person (see Exhibit 2).

> How different from today, when …
> "… the amount of time spent with customers versus budgets is totally reversed.
> In fact, one room clerk working at a hotel for more than six months … [said] she had never seen the general manager [at] the front desk."[2]

A statement like this reflects the reduced importance of being a "greeter" in the manager's overall responsibility.

> "… the term "Hotel Greeter" appears to have been rather loosely defined. In the 1930s and 40s … the Association of Hotel Greeters was open to any hotel employee whose work involved meeting the public—most were in management …[3]

The issues are also different today. Labor and law, community relations, energy, and more—all cited in Exhibit 2—preempt executive time and account, in part, for the demise of privately owned establishments. Chain resources, not family finances, are needed to fund the expensive expertise that supports the individual GMs.

Mobility also accounts for the decline of Mine Host. Long tenures enabled GMs of yesteryear to mark their properties. Not so today. Managers are transferred to other hotels based on the company's needs and the manager's expertise. F&B may be the strength of one manager; marketing another; finance a third.

Guests have changed too. Mass marketing and one-time arrivals make Mine Host less relevant.

---

[2]Jeff Weinstein. "Old-Fashioned Hotelkeeping." *Hotels,* February, 2001, p. 5.

[3]Joy Kingsolver. *Web Site for Archives and Archivists,* March 3, 2000.

What Has Become of Our Genial Hosts?

What was it in bygone days
That served the famous hoteliers?
Smiles and friendships, *bon mots* and more.
To know them, guests flocked through the door.

Schooled in the fine art of conversation
Made hotelkeeping an endless vacation,
Chatting and supping and drinking one's fill
While the cream of society fattened the till.

What has become of our Genial Hosts?
Alas, conditions have altered their posts.
They rarely see their fashionable clients.
Their careers have become mathematical science.

Occupancies, percentages, rooms income,
Wages, break-even, taxes, and then some!
Their carefree pasts have become archaic.
The Innkeepers' life is today algebraic.

Each acts like an Einstein, a judge, and a foreman,
A housekeeper, a chef, an art critic, a doorman.
And there on the desk, a great volume about:
Hotel management; titled, *Check-In Check-Out.*

Consultants and salespersons vie for a visit
Then the new decorator with the latest what-is-it.
They're umpires and referees; they pacify all
From the board of directors to the charity ball.

And leaving the office, they find in the corridors
Anxious sales staffers and tired night auditors.
And if that's not enough, alack and egad
There's always the competitor's TV ad!

What's to be done about REITS and franchisees,
And what about the competition overseas?
Consolidation? Segmentation?
Rising prices of electrification?

Hearing the reverberations about minimum wage
Helped bring the change from host to sage.
Entertainment centers, computerization, what more?
Environmental concerns and a concierge floor.

What has become of our Genial Hosts?
What else: they're figments, relics, ghosts.
And when will they rest from their toil so hard?
When they hang o'er their tombs a "Do Not Disturb" card.

EXHIBIT 2 The shift from hotel host/greeter to hotel manager/executive is described lightly in this well-known ditty, which the authors have changed to modernize the phrasing. Time has not changed the numerous disciplines required of the general manager even as qualifications shift from specialist to generalist and back again.

STRENGTH AND SALARIES Outsiders still believe that the GM's job is all about meeting celebrities and enjoying free dinners and drinks. But another night of cocktail parties is not a hotelier's idea of a great evening. Sixty-plus hour work weeks wreak havoc with marriage and family, reduce productivity, and make an evening out just more work.

Studies point out the importance of a manager's people skills. That means, in part, developing the social and communication arts required of an important community person. These skills are equally critical to managing the hotel's human resources. Many staff members work at minimum wage and depend on uncertain tips. Low wages, which account, in part, for the high rate of employee turnover, may be offset somewhat by an empathetic executive communicating company values.

Providing incentive bonuses and rewards is one technique for supplementing employee wages and retaining good employees. The same is true for general managers. Executive incentives and bonuses range between 20% and 40% of annual income. GM salaries are dependent on several criteria: the size of the hotel, the ADR that the manager delivers, and the revenue (both gross and net) generated by the property. Salaries for general managers of non-casino hotels range between $75,000 and $150,000 plus bonuses and/or incentives.

Salary packages are negotiated. Housing (no rent, no telephone or utility bills) may supplement cash salaries. Free laundry and dry cleaning are common benefits. Membership fees for local clubs/associations are appropriate if the manager is to be a visible community leader. Stock options (shares sold to the manager at reduced prices) is another salary add-on, a fringe benefit of corporate ownership. In the end, the salary reflects the manager's strengths.

SUPPORT DEPARTMENTS   GMs contend with a growing list of issues that require special knowledge and expertise. Although Exhibit 2 treats these lightly, managers are supported with experts in law, employment, environment, taxes and technology. Some of these specialists are available only at organizational levels higher than the operating hotel. Others are part of the property's organizational chart (see Exhibit 1). If the general manager carries a corporate title, so may the support staff. A GM with a title of president and general manager may have vice-presidents of: marketing, human resources, and so on rather than directors of marketing or managers of human resources. Whatever the titles, the organization is almost certainly a corporation.

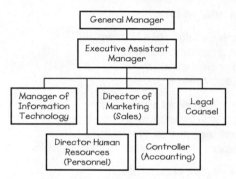

Staff managers work for the operating departments as well as the general manager. The resident manager, discussed below, looks to human resources for filling job openings. The marketing department fills the resident manager's guest rooms; accounting department oversees billing and collection. Staff also has guest contact; they are not isolated. Legal counsel gets involved with accidents, accounting with unpaid bills, and technology with guest support.

THE FOOD AND BEVERAGE (F&B) DEPARTMENT   Unlike the advisory nature of the support staff, the *food and beverage manager* has direct operating (line) responsibilities. Where present, F&B is one of the hotel's two operating departments (see Exhibit 1). The rooms department, the thrust of this text, is the other.

Of late, the importance of F&B is waning. Many hotels have no F&B departments, although food and beverage once accounted for nearly half of hotel revenues industrywide. Its importance has shrunk (see Exhibit 3) because many hotels either offer no meals or include breakfast within the room rate. Food revenues have fallen even in full-service hotels.[4] F&B's declining

---

[4]Responding to guest surveys, Holiday Inn has made its bar "the social hub," where a limited menu served by bartenders (reducing wait-staff costs) is being tested. The goals: A gathering place for downstairs guests, increased food service and income, and labor savings. The move is part of a general re-do of the brand that has shed franchisees who were unable to fund the estimated $250,000 needed to upgrade outdated properties.

Holiday Inn follows Starwood (small meeting spaces within the lobby), Courtyard (media booths within the lobby), and Days Inn (communal seating) in creating lobbies for "hanging out."

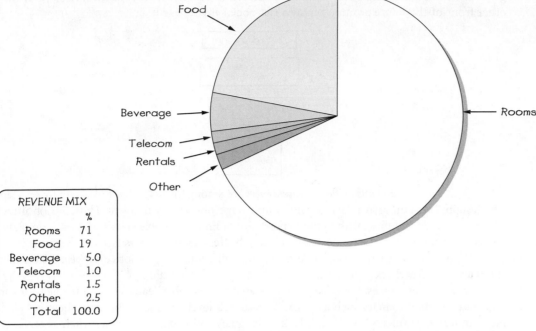

REVENUE MIX	
	%
Rooms	71
Food	19
Beverage	5.0
Telecom	1.0
Rentals	1.5
Other	2.5
Total	100.0

EXHIBIT 3 Rooms is the lodging industry's largest revenue earner and the most profitable department, approximately $0.70 of each dollar sale. The percentage of nonroom revenue is higher in full-service properties and resorts because they offer many additional services. Food and beverage sales have fallen as a percentage of industry revenues because many hotels have done away with restaurants. Similar declines have occurred in telephone revenues because guests have increased their use of wireless communication devices.

importance means fewer middle managers there. So many day-to-day decisions are pushed onto operating employees.

The Hotel (or Resident) Manager

The hotel manager, also called the *house manager* or *resident manager,* is the front-of-the-house counterpart to the food and beverage manager, if one exists. All operating departments, other than F&B, report to this person. Exhibit 1 illustrates the scope of the resident manager's responsibilities. Every department that services guests falls within the purview of this manager, who, in turn, reports to the GM.

Like other industries, lodging has been moving toward flatter organizations. Fewer management levels between the top and the bottom of the chart speed communications and decision making and hold down costs. So very few hotels have all the positions shown in the exhibits. Small hotels do not need them and large hotels cannot afford them all. In the absence of a resident manager, department heads (housekeeper, security, etc.) report directly to the GM. A still smaller house would do away with some department heads. Supervision would be left to a senior employee, or operative employees would turn directly to the general manager.

All positions are retained here to facilitate the discussion. Besides, large hotels do have resident managers and all the support positions. Included are housekeeping; security; rooms; engineering (repairs and maintenance); laundry and valet; revenue control; shops, rentals, and business centers; concierges; pools; and spas.

HOUSEKEEPING Responsibility for the delivery of the hotel's basic product, a clean room, rests unconditionally with housekeeping. Yet it has never enjoyed the status afforded other units within the resident manager's orbit. This is because the job entails physical labor such as servicing guest rooms and cleaning public space. Besides, housekeepers usually work in isolation, while other front-of-the-house positions enjoy a rich social environment.

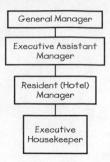

Guest-room attendants or *floor housekeepers* are among the hotels least paid employees. Tips, which supplement the salaries of other minimum-wage jobs, are less frequent. Thus, the job attracts the less educated and those with limited knowledge of English. Simple clerical duties—completing forms for minor in-room maintenance—add to job stress. Housekeepers face another problem: A great deal of work is part-time/call-in. As occupancy falls, housekeeping jobs disappear. Uncertainty about a weekly pay check is piled atop physical labor and low job status.

Despite these issues, housekeeping does an amazing job. Cleanliness is a prime factor for high ratings from agencies such as AAA. This superb level is achieved because the crew works hard under watchful supervision. A lack of language skills does not lessen their motivation; minimum salary does not mean minimum commitment. But those factors, when combined with high turnover, do make management's job more difficult.

Organization of the Department   The manager of the housekeeping department is called the *housekeeper. Working housekeeper* is the title used if this supervisor also cleans rooms. Large hotels favor the title *executive housekeeper.* (Similar titles are found in the kitchen: *working chef* and *executive chef.*)

Housekeeping's responsibilities are in flux when compared to that of other departments. Assignments are added or deleted depending on the inclination of the GM and the capabilities of the current housekeeper. Traditionally, housekeepers have been women who have risen in rank from guest-room attendants. This still holds true in small hotels, which rely chiefly on the housekeeper's menial skills. Large hotels require more management skills. After all, housekeeping is the largest department in the hotel.[5] This recognition has opened the competition to professional managers, men as well as women, who have never worked the floor.

The size of the hotel, the ability of the housekeeper, and the biases of the general manager dictate the housekeeper's span of responsibility. The position may or may not be responsible for:

… laundry and valet;
… swimming pools, outdoor ponds or water attractions;
… guest-room design and décor;
… purchasing;
… functions that might otherwise be engineering's, furniture repair.

To emphasize the importance of the job being done, some GMs have the housekeepers report directly to them. Others hold to the more traditional resident manager reporting line of Exhibit 1.

Duties of the Department   Housekeeping is charged with the general cleanliness of guest rooms, corridors, and public spaces such as lobbies and restrooms. Attendants may also service employee locker rooms, bathhouses, and spas. Housekeeping in food and beverage is the responsibility of that department's stew*ard* (not ste*wart*).

Guest-room attendants service 12–18 rooms per day, taking about 30 minutes per room (see Exhibit 19). Rooms being readied for new occupants take more time than do stay-overs. Union contracts may limit the number of rooms that guest-room attendants service to 12 and require extra pay for servicing additional rooms. Otherwise, 14–15 rooms (7+ hours) and one or two

---

[5]Housekeeping at the Excalibur, 4,000 rooms, has 750 on-staff. Housekeeping at Caesars Palace uses a computer program to track the costumes of its uniformed employees. Both hotels are in Las Vegas.

breaks make up the busy workday. Some hotels use two-person teams. This cuts down the prep time and offsets job isolation, which may improve worker morale and boost productivity. Equally important, teams make the job safer. Isolated, hotel maids have been attacked by both men and animals. Some hotels have started issuing wireless signal devices, which housekeepers can buzz to call security. Maids especially dislike turn-down assignments, which means preparing beds at night. Sending housemen along has been one response, especially if the property management system indicates a pornographic film is on the room's TV.

Housemen help with heavier work, including wall washing, vacuuming, and shampooing. Some jobs, window washing in particular, may be outsourced to specialty firms. Housemen move clean and soiled linens between the laundry and the floors, storing them in the floor closets, or maids' closets (see Exhibit 15, adjacent to room 11).

Besides linens, floor closets hold a variety of supplies, all charged against the housekeeper's budget. Some are guest supplies (soaps and toilet tissues) and some cleaning supplies (sprays and cleansers). Also stored are vacuum cleaners, electric brooms, pails, and so on. Replacements, based on occupancy, are either purchased by the housekeeper directly or by the purchasing department on orders from the housekeeper.

Daily guest-room cleanliness is not the department's sole responsibility. Dry cleaning drapes and bed covers, disinfecting after illness or animal occupancy, pest control and clean-ups that follow deaths and fires are just the start of a long list of duties. The department monitors sick guests, a job often done by the housekeeper personally. Working closely with security, it maintains lost-and-found.[6] Working closely with the laundry, it monitors linen use. Counting and weighing linens (about 9 pounds in a midrange room) are crucial tasks if the hotel has no in-house laundry. Outside laundries base charges on weight and/or linen count. Hotels often rent their linens from these very laundry companies. Renting linen, rather than buying it up front, reduces the capital (dollars) needed to open.

Linen repair is handled by a seamstress working in the *linen room*. There is no special "linen room," that is the name of the department's office. All uniformed staff come to the room to get their uniforms fitted and to trade soiled ones for fresh issues.

Working with the Desk   Housekeeping's coordination with the front desk is essential to the sale of rooms. Hundreds of arrivals and departures take place daily. Rooms must be serviced quickly to placate waiting guests and maximize room revenue. A *floor supervisor* or *floor housekeeper* inspects (hence also *inspector*) and approves rooms recently vacated and cleaned by the guest-room attendants. Rooms are held *on-change* by the desk until approved by the inspection. Once approved, then, the room status is changed to *ready* and new guests are assigned. Waiting guests may be assigned to on-change rooms, but not actually housed in them. In rare cases, baggage of new arrivals may be taken to on-change rooms. This check-out/check-in sequence is critical to control and security. Most property losses, both the hotel's and the guest's, originate in guest rooms. Security awareness must be part of the department's training and supervision.

SECURITY   Automation and structural changes have altered the industry's organizational charts. At one time, security was the eyes and ears of bellpersons, elevator and telephone operators, and floor room clerks. As these jobs disappeared, as street crimes entered the hotel, as liability claims and insurance costs rose, security departments grew in size and importance.

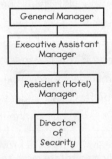

---

[6]Legionnaire's Disease, which led to the closing of Philadelphia's most luxurious hotel Bellevue Stratford Hotel in 1976, has haunted the industry. The most recent outbreak came in 2009 at the Epic Hotel in Miami, also rated a top-class property.

The lost-and-found department of Chicago's Hyatt Regency (2,000 rooms) cataloged 113 pieces of underclothes, 31 pairs of eyeglasses, 30 cell phones, and 2 sets of dentures each month! *H&MM*, November 6, 2000, p. 142. Mobile-device chargers (called black spaghetti by housekeepers) are the left-behinds of 2012; a typical commercial hotel gets nearly one per day. They are given away to guests who left theirs behind elsewhere.

Floor Housekeepers Must:

…Block open doors with linen carts;
…Deny room access to keyless guests;
…Inform management of illegal paraphernalia in guest rooms;
…Keep floor closets locked;
…Leave guests' personal items untouched;
…Prevent guests from entering rooms that have been opened;
…Report suspicious persons and/or activities;
…Secure master keys by attaching them to their persons.

EXHIBIT 4 Housekeepers have always been at the front line of security. More so today because there are fewer bell positions, traditionally the most mobile positions in the organization.

Guest-room attendants and floor supervisors are now among the hotel's first lines of defense. Holding master keys, they are also hit with the first level of suspicion. It is a matter of self-interest for these floor crews to follow basic security measures (see Exhibit 4). It is a matter of self-interest for their employers to adequately screen new hires in all departments because housekeeping is just one segment of a diverse structure.

Hotels expanded security staffs and improved electronic surveillance after several catastrophic events. Among them were the World Trade Center (2001), which took out the Marriott Hotel, and the bombings in Mumbai, India (2008), which took out the Oberoi and Taj Mahal hotels. Actually, measured changes were underway long before. Earlier incidents such as the in-hotel rape of a well-known actress and disastrous hotel fires in San Juan and Las Vegas had moved security higher on management's radar. The single house detective[7] or night watchman walking a fire patrol had been replaced by an upgraded security staff. The move gained traction from the increase in hotel/casinos, which always had larger security departments.

Physical upgrades accompanied personnel changes. Early efforts included observation ports (peepholes in guest-room doors), electronic locks in place of mechanical ones, and public-address systems into rooms. Perimeter lighting was improved. Smoke alarms and sprinkler systems were mandated. Properties that fail to comply were downgraded by rating agencies, lost their franchise affiliation or were closed by local authorities. Throughout, better security measures were implemented everywhere (see Exhibit 5).

SECURITY CHECKLIST	
Item	**Advantage, Concern, or Solution**
Above-street elevators	Use room key to limit access to guest sleeping floors
Above-street lobbies	Allows for prelobby screening at entry level
Alarms	Loud enough to be heard over ambient noise
Atrium design	Glass elevators improve visibility of guest-room doors
Babysitters	Licensed child care
Badges	No one on convention floor without identity
Cameras	Must be monitored 24/7, including elevator-mounted cameras
Communications	Alert community members to scams, employees to issues
Counterfeit litigation	Train to identify "professional" litigants
Conventions	Identify and monitor everyone on the floor

EXHIBIT 5 Common law holds innkeepers to a high standard of security, requiring them to provide safe premises. This duty cannot be delegated away. Heightened security concerns among the traveling public necessitate more than just a minimum response to this security checklist.

[7]The house detective plays an important role in Arthur Hailey's fictional book and later film *Hotel*. A must read.

SECURITY CHECKLIST

Item	Advantage, Concern, or Solution
Cribs	Require high maintenance and properly sized bedding
Crowd control	For visiting VIPs, protestors; emergencies
Data security	Frequent guest; registration; credit cards
Defibrillators	Quick response to heart attacks
Employees	All vetted; training to include security awareness and detection
Equipment	Secure sliding glass doors; inspect sprinkler and alarm systems
Exit signs	Fire exit signs at floor level for those crawling below the smoke
Fire	Directions and exits posted on inside of guest-room door
Force majeure	Convention contracting and planning for acts of God
Gambling	Organized by guest in their rooms or by employees
Garage	Electric gates; install emergency telephones
Grief counseling	For employees and guests following incidents
Guest awareness	Guest receives a security message when turning on the television
Guest-room attendants	Allow no one into the room without proper identification
Guest-room safety	Peepholes; fire and smoke alarms; inside locks that retain keys
Handicapped	Provide for needs of handicapped during emergencies
High-tech	Coded passes, parking passes, panic buttons; secure with password
Homicides	Rank third against desk clerks, after cabbies and cops
Identity theft	Rampant, so it's not a lodging industry issue alone
In-house losses	Some may be attributed to employees
Inspection	Investigate any occupied guest room not cleaned for 24 hours
Keys	Unnumbered plastic types have replaced numbered metal types
Lighting	Adequate-plus everywhere, especially exterior
Locks	Electronic
Master keys	Secured and accounted for, including guest-room attendants
Messages	Wait until writer leaves before placing message in cubbyhole
Mutual aid	Cooperation among competitors and law enforcement agencies
Notices to guests	By means of rooming slips, in-room tents, guest-service manuals
Patrols	Random schedules; escort guests to parked cars
Pickpockets and prostitutes	Keep photo lineups available with desk and security personnel
Planning	For the unexpected emergency: cyclones, flood, hurricane, tsunami
Safety	Inspections: wet, slippery floors, bathroom fixtures, etc.
Spot checks	Identifications, baggage, packages, purveyors
Staffing	Security needed regardless of hotel size
Swindlers	Make false claims; pass bad checks and currencies; rob and steal
Teens	Balancing legal right to occupy with destructive behavior
Thefts by guests	Taking home more than memories; pranks; falsified value of loss
Training	All employees get security-awareness training
Unexpected	Foreign visitors, foreign languages; health alerts
Valuables	In-room safes
Video	Cameras strategically placed; incidents accurately recorded
Visibility	Uniformed personnel as well as security in mufti

EXHIBIT 5 Continued

A second phase of upgrades included installation of CCTV (closed-circuit television). Improved video cameras allow one security person to monitor corridors, parking areas, and public spaces. In-room alarms, telephones, and radios for the hearing and visually handicapped are now in use. Remote card readers control access to garages, swimming pools, rec rooms, and even stairwells. Biometric room-key systems are in the pipeline. Still, balance must be maintained. Hotels hesitate to install heart defibrillators, fearing an increase in lawsuits because the devices often fail. The FDA has had nearly 30,000 such reports and has issued dozens of recalls. Nevertheless, 20% of the states require them in health clubs.

Security has morphed from a hidden issue to a visible response. Plain-clothed personnel have been replaced in part by uniformed staff. Security now wears distinctive blazers in lobbies, by the elevators—where a room key is required for access—and on patrol. Not that everyone switched. Some still dress in mufti, in keeping with their prior backgrounds as federal agents, officers, and police investigators. Obviously, many of the actions taken remain invisible to the public. That includes the increased number of security staff holding degrees in criminology.

Security's Charge   Security is charged with the protection of persons, both guests and staff, and of property, both guests' and hotel's. Good security has a strong market appeal; everyone wants to feel safe. The hotel's reputation suffers from security lapses, but even more so from the bungling of poorly trained personnel. Lawsuits often originate in the failure of security or the desk to respond compassionately and professionally to guest injuries or their properties losses. It takes both training and foresight on part of the personnel. Kona Village in Hawaii has a red emergency switch above the bed so guests can signal the desk to dispatch security.

Protecting persons has a higher priority than protecting property. Still, property losses far outweigh personal injuries. Employees are one source of larceny, but many guests take home more than memories. Pilferage is so costly that some hotels tag property with minute circuits for tracking. Both employees and guest are petty thieves of towels and even of furnishings that are not secured. So lamps and pictures are bolted down. Several chains have reduced losses by simply removing their name from the towels. Although the term usually refers to larger, more valuable assets, "asset management" is a buzz word among hotel executives. An industry that loses an estimated $100 million a year from petty theft must certainly focus on asset management.

Theft against guests is not always carried out by the hotel employees. A class of professional thieves specializes in hotels. They know how to obtain room keys from the desk or steal from guests' belongings by the pool. Guests are not all innocent. Some lose valuables and accuse the hotel while others feign insurance losses.

An Ever-Widening Role   Petty thieves and pickpockets still demand attention, but new flash points add to the job of security. Security now umbrellas and trains for such risks as elevator failures, presence of hazardous materials, food poisoning, bomb threats, fire, and crowd control. Security works with police in solving robbery, murder, and suicide cases. It interfaces with insurance companies about accidents and claims and maintains the records and logs so vital to court cases. Internally, it focuses on risk management, workman's compensation, and compliance with ADA (Americans with Disabilities Act). It prepares for and manages natural disasters and simple power failures.

Old assignments and new mesh in an ever-broadening role of security. Helping the credit manager with lockouts and luggage liens has been part of the old. So, too, has been policing *night birds* (prostitutes) and helping drunken guests. A greater openness about security has enlisted guests in the campaign. In-room notices alert them to evacuation routes. Signs warn against elevator use during fires. In-room safes minimize property losses. Fire-exit signs are being relocated near the floor, making them more visible to those crawling under the smoke.

Competitors have also been enlisted because thieves generally work one area before moving on. Neighbors/competitors are alerted by the hotel that has been attacked first. Even, convention and visitor bureaus are part of the network. Convention crowds of hundreds or thousands of delegates have always created medical emergencies and petty theft. Now, public safety has become a deciding criteria in site selection. With it has come increased sensitivity to booth security. Convention hotels and convention halls employ bomb-sniffing dogs, metal detectors, and package searches. New paragraphs have been added to standard convention contracts to reflect these—and ADA's—growing requirements. New contract provisions for unexpected and disruptive events, force majeure (forz ma-zhoer), are redefining what has previously been understood to be "acts of God."

Everywhere, hotel chains are enlisting outside experts and consultants to develop and/or review security plans. Disasters such as flood, fire, hurricane, earthquake, bomb threats, and hostage-taking must be anticipated and security procedures set in place. Then, they must be tested. Staff must have a clear knowledge of who gives the orders, where emergency supplies are stocked, who comprises the disaster team, and how communication will be relayed. Emergency evacuation arrangements must be simulated, drilled, and critiqued. Preplanning considers many facets, as diverse as police cooperation, fire-resistant furnishings, and building design. Atrium lobbies (see Exhibit 10), for example, present both advantages and problems for security.

Hotel security has grown in importance even as other departments have been downsized. However broad its charge, it must function still as a deterrent first; then as a restraint, and only rarely as a police force. Hotel security remains an iron hand in a velvet glove.

OTHER DEPARTMENTS   The organizational chart of Exhibit 1 reflects the hotel manager's oversight of all operating departments except F&B. Not shown is the manager's role of landlord. Hotels are real-estate investments above all else; hotels rent space. There are numerous tenants in large hotels and in casino/hotels. Some tenants such as florists, beauticians, and clothing shops need retail space. Commercial firms lease office space. Airlines, auto, and tour desks require lobby space. If the business center is not a hotel unit, it, too, may be a tenant. Renters turn to the hotel manager with their issues because hotel managers are the designated landlords. Supported by hotel staff in accounting and law, they negotiate leases and rental contracts.

Thousands of people pass through hotels each week. So, medical emergencies must be anticipated. It is another job for the hotel manager, although the job may be delegated as are other responsibilities. If so, it is probably assigned to the concierge, who may enlist the services of *Hotel Docs*. Private physicians come to the hotel at no charge; ill travelers pay for their own care as they would at home.

A facilities manager, if one exists, is another member of the hotel manager's staff. Reporting lines might be through engineering or housekeeping because the job oversees all physical plant from the boiler room to the garden. Very few hotels staff this position.

The Rooms Manager

The *rooms manager*—where one exists—oversees four departments: reservations, uniformed services, concierge, and telephones.

Few hotels actually have all the levels discussed here. Many duties are folded into one job. One person may play the roles of resident manager, rooms manager, and front-office manager. Consolidation is especially true when the industry is in a down cycle. If several management levels exist, the *manager of guest services*, once called the *front-office manager*, takes direct control of the desk. Exhibit 6 combines the several jobs since each calls for managers with superior people skills.

A Vallen Corporation Property

DEPARTMENT OF HUMAN RESOURCES

COMBINED JOB DESCRIPTION: Hotel Manager, Rooms Manager, and Manager of Guest Services

RESPONSIBILITY: All these positions have broad responsibility for the operation of the Rooms Division and of the Front Office.

QUALIFICATIONS

REQUIRED:
- No less than 5 years of industry experience, or 2 years with a college degree
- Previous supervisory or middle-management experience

DESIRABLE:
- Able to stand and work for long hours
- Approach problems with innovative solutions
- Demonstrate open-mindedness; willing to test ideas regardless of source
- Earned reputation for honesty; good credit rating
- Evidence good communication skills, especially verbal
- Exhibit self-confidence, poise, and an ability to retain composure under stress
- Have knowledge of computer equipment and can make minor repairs
- Is an effective listener
- Meet deadlines of all types
- Possess some level of foreign language capability
- Read professional journals and the business press
- Think quantitatively, good math skills; some understanding of accounting
- Warm guests, employees, and visitors with outgoing personality

DUTIES:
- Acknowledge and resolve complaints quickly and professionally
- Add and remove special hotel packages as demand warrants
- Approve and monitor budgets of departmental managers
- Arrange outside medical support as needed
- Assume full management responsibility during manager-on-duty assignments
- Attend and contribute to interdepartmental meetings
- Call the hotel from outside to uncover areas that warrant training
- Coordinate the duties of all staffers within the span of control
- Conduct employee appraisals, evaluations, and counseling sessions
- Develop and work within standards of industry's best practices
- Ensure that all operations fall within the guidelines of the company manual
- Hire, train, supervise, and discharge, where necessary
- Hold security drills with the cooperation of the city's safety department
- Implement and manage recycling and conservation programs
- Increase ADR and RevPar by astute use of yield management
- Inspect employee dress and uniform standards
- Interface positively with other department heads
- Maintain a constructive interaction with the union and its membership
- Monitor the bell department's call sheets
- Oversee preparation of reports and recordkeeping
- Negotiate rentals and other leases, including charges that clear the desk
- Participate in and train for emergencies
- Post job openings and develop staff from within
- Prepare both oral and written reports
- Receive and attend to VIP guests

EXHIBIT 6 The guest-service manager by whatever title (front-desk manager, rooms manager, etc.) has a broad range of responsibilities. These are described here at length because flatter organizations incorporate additional duties from positions that may no longer exist.

- Review and submit payroll records
- Safeguard arriving packages and mail
- Stem scams by cooperating with credit-card companies and police agencies
- Support the company's preferred guest program
- Train staff in their duties and the operation of their equipment
- Uncover fraud and dishonesty among employees and guests
- Unify the work of reservations with rooms and sales and marketing
- Uphold all company standards of dress, courtesy, and operations
- Visit restrooms to check cleanliness, supplies, and appeal
- Walk property and note needs of repairs and maintenance

EXHIBIT 6 Continued

ROOM RESERVATIONS Prospective guests request accommodations through the reservations department. Inquiries are received, processed, and confirmed by the department under the supervision of a *reservations manager* or other executive if that post has been eliminated.

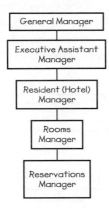

Hotel reservations are made via letter, fax, email, twitter, and occasionally in person. Most come by telephone either directly to the hotel or, more frequently, through its central reservation office (CRO) via a toll-free number. CROs started with chains and franchises, but are used universally now. With so many external sources, on-site reservation departments are shrinking, combined with other front-office jobs.

The importance of the guest's initial contact cannot be overlooked. Reservationists need strong telephone personalities. They must be good salespersons and have full knowledge of the hotel and the community. The quality of the reservationists' disembodied voices must close the sale, convincing the caller to commit to the room. Weak English-speaking skills won't do it!

Res departments track anticipated arrivals by dates and length of stay. That information and the type of accommodations needed is sent to the front desk on the guest's arrival date. Estimating the number of rooms sold and the number still available for sale is a major responsibility of the department. Groups and individuals must be balanced to achieve maximum occupancy and rate. Sales, reservations, and the front desk work together to bring about a full house (100% occupancy) without overbooking (committing more rooms than are available).

Detailed reservations are maintained on a day-to-day basis for a year and in less detail for as much as three to five years. Computerization has made the job easier and decisions more accurate.

THE UNIFORMED SERVICES The ranks of the service department (or uniformed services or *bell department*) have been waning. At one time, there were baggage porters, pages, transportation clerks, and operators for both guest and service elevators. What remains is organized around a few bellpersons and an occasional door attendant.

Changes in the structure of the travel industry have eliminated the once-important role of the service department: arranging travel. Furthermore, wheeled suitcases and lighter luggage mean most guests handle their own baggage. Self-service is part of the culture. No help is needed to move luggage a few floors by elevator. Fewer calls for baggage assistance means fewer tips, less job appeal, and a smaller workforce.

Bringing ice to a room, a time-honored assignment for generating tips, is no longer a "front" (tip-earning) call. In-room refrigerators and floor ice machines reinforce the idea of self-service. Group arrivals and departures remain the department's best moneymakers. Sales departments add a contractual charge (a tip) to group bookings for each bag in and each bag out. Funds are collected and distributed to the bells whether tour guests use the service or not.

Management cost-cutting has also contributed to smaller departments. Today, every employee is paid a minimum wage, whereas tips alone constituted the salary of an earlier era. Reducing staff cuts labor and fringe benefits, which add about one-third more to payroll costs. So the doorman at the entry is rarely found around the clock and the motor inn without any uniformed services is the new norm.

In urban properties with separate parking, someone needs to be at the door to handle garaging. Few urban hotels own their own parking spaces. Either they lease space or contract with a parking concessionaire who provides the attendants—reducing department size once again.

If available, uniformed personnel will be the guest's first contact with the hotel. Whether it is a door attendant, a bellperson, or a van driver (another department member), first impressions stick. The condition of the uniform, the speech and personality of the employee, and the quality of the greeting portray the standard of the hotel to the new arrival. In this respect, human resources departments make better hires for the doorpersons and bellpersons than they do for van drivers.

The manager of the service department has that very title: *manager of services* or *superintendent of services*. However, neither of the titles is as romantic as the traditional title, *bell captain* or its shorter version, *captain*.

Some services that were previously handled by the bell captain have migrated to the desk of the concierge. With them have gone the flow of money because tour operators and auto rental agencies pay commissions to the desk that books the business.

CONCIERGE   Not many U.S. hotels have a concierge. The position is limited to larger, upscale properties. It is more popular in small hotels overseas, especially in France.[8] Great Britain calls the front desk the front hall, so the concierge becomes the head hall porter. Listing what a "concierge" does (see Exhibit 7) is easier than trying to pronounce the word, *kon syerzh*.

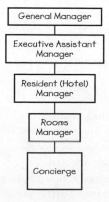

---

[8]The International Union of Concierges was founded in Paris in 1952; the U.S. chapter in 1978. Members wear the Golden Keys (Les Clefs d'Or), their professional symbol.

A...	as in	Art supplies and restoration
B...	as in	Babysitting services for vacationing parents
C...	as in	Churches for all denominations
D...	as in	Dinner reservations at sold-out restaurants
E...	as in	Errand and courier services for speedy delivery
F...	as in	Flowers for that special occasion
G...	as in	Galleries for antiques and arts
H...	as in	Helicopter services
I...	as in	Interpreters for an international symposium
J...	as in	Jewelers from whom one can buy with confidence
K...	as in	Kennels for a cherished pet
L...	as in	Libraries for source materials
M...	as in	Maps to navigate the city or the subway
N...	as in	Newspapers from distant cities and foreign countries
O...	as in	Orchestra tickets at the last minute
P...	as in	Photographers for that special occasion
Q...	as in	Queries that no one else can answer
R...	as in	Restaurants of every specialty
S...	as in	Scuba diving sites and services
T...	as in	Transportation: air; auto; bus; limo; taxi; train
U...	as in	Umbrellas on a rainy day
V...	as in	Virtual reality equipment
W...	as in	Wedding chapels
X...	as in	Xeroxing a last-minute report
Y...	as in	Yoga demonstrations and instructions
Z...	as in	Zoo directions for an outing with the children

EXHIBIT 7   Concierge service runs the gamut from A to Z.

Concierge comes from the Latin *con servus*, meaning "with service." Another translation is "building guard." The Count of Cierge was in charge of prisons under the French monarchy making him the "keeper of keys."[9] Thus, the European concierge began as a door attendant (building guard) and then became keeper of keys, porter, and, eventually, provider of services.

The U.S. version of concierge, called the lobby concierge (see Exhibit 8), provides a variety of information and personal services, nothing to do with keys. Travel assistance, conveying messages, tickets and reservations to events outside the property, babysitting, and language translation and more fall within the concierge's duties. The concierge also arranges for pet care, hair stylist, flower delivery, or attending physician (see Exhibit 8).

As hotels retrench and automate services, the post of concierge grows more important for upscale hotels. Guests have no one else to question. Elevator operators, floor clerks, bells and transportation desks have disappeared. Many of the gratuities that had gone to those uniformed services have been redirected to the concierge. The concierge is tipped by the guest and commissioned by the service companies (theaters, rentals, tours, etc.).

Several hotels have created the job of *compcierge*, with the *comp* part standing for computer. A compcierge comes in two forms. One is an information technology (IT) expert, who

---

[9]Marie Antoinette was in the Concierge Prison (the Palais de Justice) during the French Revolution.

EXHIBIT 8   Pleasant working conditions and an aura of capable service highlight this lobby photo of a concierge at work. Some hotels limit concierge service to a specially designated concierge floor, which offers extra services at higher rates.   *Courtesy of the Wynfrey Hotel, Birmingham, Alabama.*

provides personal computer support to conventioneers and guests. A "computerized console," which provides local information, is the other use of the term. A computer/concierge either stands alone in the lobby or supports a concierge's desk, freeing the real person for complex services.

The Concierge Floor   The concierge floor is a special accommodation available at a premium room rate or made available without charge to frequent-guest members. Included among the extras are free continental breakfasts and evening cocktails. Terrycloth bathrobes, shoe shines, larger guest rooms, and expedited arrival and departure procedures are other add-ons.

Access to the floor is restricted and requires a special elevator key. The concierge is usually seated by the elevators adding security as *floor clerks* (see Exhibit 15) did before World War II. In this respect, the concierge floor is a throwback to the original intent of the concierge: keeper of the keys. The entry of Asian hotel companies into the U.S. market has added another variation, the floor butler or floor steward. Providing round-the-clock coverage, the floor butler helps with more personal services, such as unpacking. Guests summon the butler with room bells or switches on the bed-side console.

All upscale chains offer concierge floors. Hilton calls them "The Towers," after the famed Waldorf=Astoria Towers, one of Hilton's trademarks. Hyatt uses "Regency" and Radisson uses "Plaza Club." Add these to the names of the frequent guest programs and mix in the brand name of chains. Confusion is the result; no one even tries to remember which name is which.

THE TELEPHONE DEPARTMENT   Hotels have telephones, lots of telephones. Guest rooms may have two with another in the bath. Even as the number of instruments has grown, the size of the telephone department has shrunk. Computerization and social change (everyone carries a cell phone; pay phones have disappeared from lobbies) have downsized this department. Direct-dial, automatic equipment handles the few calls that still originate in-room. The same is true for calls between guest rooms or to hotel departments, such as room service. Billing is also done electronically. Gone is the old position of *charge operator.*

In no other hotel department has the installation of costly/complex equipment been so rapid, so complete, and worked so well. Supervising the few employees still left is the *chief operator* or *telephone supervisor*.

Live operators may still take incoming calls, but even these have been automated. Unanswered rings are switched to the electronic "mailbox" of the guest's room. Operators intercede as necessary but no longer hand-transcribe messages. Previously, a *message operator*, another position long gone, placed messages in the cubbyholes at the front desk. Electronic messaging on the guest-room telephone compensates for the missing operator's garbled language, poor handwriting, and strong foreign accent.

Alarm clocks in each room have almost eliminated morning wake-up calls. Some guests still prefer the assurance of human intervention, which the operator provides with an automated wake-up call.

Manager of Guest Services

One final level of management is needed for our full-service-hotel illustration. Reporting to the rooms manager is the *manager of guest services,* once called the *front-office manager.* Large hotels support this position with *assistant managers,* who cover the desk around the clock (see Exhibit 1). Smaller hotels and/or job consolidation assigns the assistant's job to a senior *guest-service agent* (once called a senior *room clerk*). It is the guest-service agents who face the public and operate the desk (see Exhibit 14).

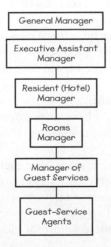

STRUCTURE OF THE FRONT OFFICE   Physically, the front office is an easily identifiable area of the lobby. Functionally, it is much less so despite constant reference to it as the "hub and heart" of the hotel. The front desk is, in truth, the very face of the hotel—the nerve center of guest activity. Through it flows communications with every other department, from it emanates instructions for guest services, and to it comes billing and settlements.

The front office is important because room sales earn over two-thirds of total revenue (see Exhibit 3). This is more than that of all other departments combined! In budget hotels, almost 100%

of the revenue comes from rooms. Even hotels with large F&B sales from meetings and conventions depend on room sales: Site selections begin with blocks of rooms. Rooms are not only the largest sales producer but also the most profitable department. Each sale dollar nets over 70¢. Food and beverage nets about 20¢ per dollar sale.

Guests relate to the front office and this adds to its importance. Guests—who rarely see housekeepers, who never see cooks, who know nothing of bottle recyclers—know the hotel by its front desk. They are received there and they depart from there. It is to the desk that guests complain, and from the desk they expect remedies.

Better to define the front office as a bundle of duties and guest services rather than a fixed position in the lobby. Some of its divisions—reservations, for example—can be located elsewhere without losing its "desk" identity. Computerization's instant communication reduces the need for all segments to be within hailing distance.

Someone once said that the front office was so named because it was close to the front door. Simple enough, except new terminology, *guest-service area,* has been adopted to emphasize the real role of the desk. This extension accounts for renaming the front-office manager as the *manager of guest services* (see Exhibit 6) and room clerks as *guest-service agents.*

WORKING HOURS   A hotel never closes. Its legal definition requires that it does not. Work schedules at the desk accommodate that requirement, but only a few other departments cover the whole day. Desk schedules must also provide for the peaks and valleys that bring daily, sometimes hourly, fluctuations to the desk.

The Shift (or Watch)   Most desk employees work an eight-hour shift, which creates a mathematical balance of three shifts per 24-hour day. The workweek is five days with two successive days off. Sick leave, vacations, and days off are covered by others, some of whom work part time. Although there are variations, especially in resort areas that have special wage-and-hour laws, the model follows that of other industries:

Day Shift	7:30 AM – 3:30 PM
Swing Shift	3:30 PM – 11:30 PM
Graveyard Shift	11:30 PM – 7:30 AM

Most employees prefer the day shift because it fits society's rhythm. Bellpersons opt for the swing shift when arrivals and tips are the heaviest. Even senior guest-service agents choose the swing shift if tips are customary, as they might be at resorts.

The graveyard shift has the slowest guest activity, but the desk is busy with the night audit. The night audit is more specialized than the usual desk duties. So night auditors cannot use the general policy that allows senior employees to select their shifts. Few workers actually prefer graveyard hours. Applicants increase when a meal from the kitchen is included.

Rotating personnel and shifts, wherever possible and where union contracts allow, builds camaraderie and morale among employees. It also reduces the chance of collusion, which increases when the same staff always works together. Sometimes day and swing shifts are switched en masse. If so, the switch is made once each month as employees' days off allow. Shifts are not changed on two successive work days because rest time is inadequate. A guest-service agent who closed the swing shift at 11:30 at night would need to be back for the day shift at 7:30 the following morning. Large city commutes makes this impractical; state labor laws make it illegal. Shift rotations should follow the clock: day, swing, graveyard; day, swing, and so on.

Cashiers, clerks, and supervisors usually change shifts in concert. Overlapping arrivals and departures by, say, 15 minutes increases continuity. A seamless transition is lost if everyone leaves and arrives simultaneously. If there are several persons in each job, individual shifts should be staggered by 15 minutes. If there is only one staff member, complementary jobs could be overlapped. The cashier might change at 3:15 PM and guest-service agent at 3:30 PM, for example.

The Split Shift   Employees working a split shift report for work, get off, and return for a second shift the same day (see below, Employee A). Wage-and-hour laws, unionization, distance of travel between home and hotel, and the inability of finding staff have eliminated the split shift. Isolated, seasonal resorts may still use this schedule if labor laws exempt seasonal worker and commuting distance is not an issue because seasonal staff lives at the resort. Split shifts are not just for the desk. Where used, kitchen, dining room and housekeeping also schedule that way.

Employee A	7:00 AM–12:30 PM
Employee B	12:30 PM–6:30 PM
Employee A	6:30 PM–11:00 PM
Night auditor	11:00 PM–7:00 AM

The split shift is advantageous for small properties using one person to cover the desk. That employee need not be relieved for meals. He or she eats either before or after the shift. Where the split schedule is in place, staff members rotate daily between the A and B positions (see schedule above).

FORECAST SCHEDULING   Building work schedules for a large staff is part science and part art. Both improve with experience, but the starting point is a forecast of room occupancy. The schedule builder gets this information from the reservations department. Personnel needs can be envisioned once the daily number of rooms occupied has been forecasted. New computer programs help match room demand to staff numbers, even accommodating individual employee preferences for days off.

Days off are scheduled during the slowest periods. Several employees may be off on a particular day, but none on busy days. Scheduling must reflect organization and operations. Is the bell department supported by a concierge's desk? Does housekeeping change linens daily even for stay-overs? Is occupancy determined chiefly by reservation-holders or walk-ins? With answers, management sets numerical standards for each department. The ratios vary with the size of the house and its level of luxury (ADR). If one bellperson is needed per 65 anticipated hourly arrivals and one guest-room attendant is need per 13 occupied rooms and one guest-service agent is needed per 60 occupied rooms, the number of staff to be scheduled is quickly calculated. The experience of each hotel then dictates what hours, what overlapping schedules, what day's off, what overtime to schedule with what mix of full- and part-time staff.

Staff needs vary throughout the day and even within the same shift. Cashiers are busiest during the morning check-out and less busy in the afternoons when guest-service agents are involved with check-ins. Cashiers at commercial hotels are slower on Mondays when agents are busier and busier on Thursdays when agents are slower. Staff members who have been cross–trained can fill both positions either on different days or on a given day when traffic patterns reverse. Two job descriptions are then reduced to one.

DESIGN OF THE LOBBY   Lobby use and design have gone through phases as guests' use of them and management's vision of them have changed. Computerization accounted for much of the switch. It reduced drastically the mountain of paper and clutter that typified the old. In so doing, it shrunk the amount of floor space needed and with it the old-fashioned, bank-teller look. Today's desk is compact and efficient (see Exhibit 9).

New designs have brought renewed activity including food and beverage sales to the once-sterile lobbies that had no chairs. Action and eye appeal have recreated the lobby (see Exhibits 10 and 11) into the important gathering place that it was over a century ago.[10]

Well-designed lobbies act as town centers. Small furniture groupings assure privacy for cell-phone use and intimate cocktail meetings. Big tables, chairs, and sofas have been replaced

---

[10]President Ulysses Grant (1869–1877) frequently walked from the White House to the Hotel Willard, now an InterContinental Hotel, to have a cigar and a drink. Petitioners, waiting to argue for their constituents, hovered in the lobby to catch the president—hence the term "lobbyist."

EXHIBIT 9 The typical front desk of a medium-sized hotel is open to encourage a sense of welcome and enhanced security. The work level is lower than the desk level to reduce worker fatigue and encourage guest–staff eye contact.

with smaller eye-appealing settings. Women travelers, usually upstairs guests, are more comfortable in lobby bars than lounge bars. So hotels have expanded lobby bar service to include food, afternoon teas, and continental breakfasts. Adding an unusual landmark turns the site into a popular meeting place for appointments. All this structured around the lobby's basics: baggage, restrooms, comfortable seating, and the front desk.

EXHIBIT 10 Atria have vitalized stodgy lobbies into dining spots and social centers while still retaining the lobby's basic services: registration, baggage, telephones, restrooms, and seating. Design elements, including lighting, differentiate the zones. Hyatt Hotels pioneered atrium architecture, first designed by John Portman for this very hotel. *Courtesy of Hyatt Regency Atlanta, Atlanta, Georgia.*

EXHIBIT 11 The familiar front desk of Exhibit 9 gives way to the open lobby where registration pods increase staff accessibility, making the lobby more hospitable. *Courtesy of Delta Hotels, Toronto, Ontario, Canada.*

DESIGN OF THE DESK   The desk is the focal point of the lobby. Its counter top is 40–42 inches across and some 45 inches high. The work side of the desk is lower by 6 inches (see Exhibit 9), which enables the guest-service agent to carry out clerical duties more comfortably. It also drops equipment below eye level, improving the face-to-face interaction between the guest and the agent. The desk's running length is determined by the size of the hotel, even up to 100 feet long!.

Informal registration pods (see Exhibit 11) have been tested as replacements for the standard desks of Exhibit 9. Conversion costs are high so pods have appeared primarily with new construction. Pod designs enable agents to walk into the lobby, greet guests, handle luggage, and sit together. Well-trained receptionists become strong salespersons, regaining some of the Mine Host characteristics of Exhibit 2. Pods improve access for the handicapped and reduce the social barrier of the usual configuration. It also makes supervision more difficult, demanding a high-quality employment process. Pods are not widely used.

As self-computerized-registration gains acceptance, the use, design, and purpose of the desk will change along with the lobbies that contain it. Still, the desk's design and location must account for the security of both guests and staff. Guest security is enhanced when the desk staff has unobstructed views of the lobby and the elevator doors (see Exhibit 19). Atrium hotels have an edge because all entry doors are in full view (see Exhibit 10).

Notwithstanding the many new means of communication, face-to-face interaction remains a critical part of handling the desk's business. That's why most designs center the guest-service agent in the hub position (see Exhibits 12 and 13). From here, agents coordinate the flow from reservations to departures.

Tours are an exception. Group registrations may be handled on the arriving bus. Hotels with very large tour business sometimes build satellite lobbies where busloads arrive and depart.

The front desk must provide a comfortable and practical workspace within an aesthetic design. Architects use lights, form, and materials to convey the image of the hotel as being comfortable, open, organized, and professional—the very traits of the guest-service agents who staff them.

GUEST-SERVICE AGENTS   Next in the line organization is the *guest-service agent*. That title has replaced America's long-time favorites, *room clerk* and *front-office clerk*. Hyatt has tried *gallery-host*, which fits well with its atrium design (see Exhibit 10). *Receptionist* is the favored term outside the United States because elsewhere the function of this position is called reception, not registration.

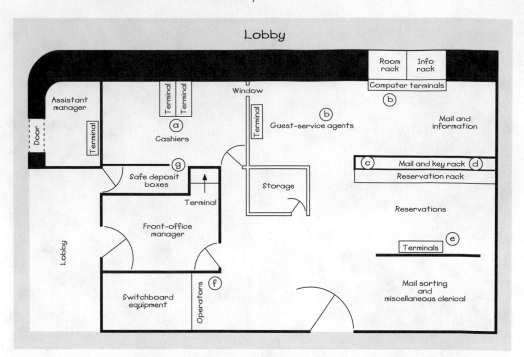

EXHIBIT 12 This schematic illustrates the design and, with Exhibit 13, highlights the functions of a typical front desk. Match the job description throughout the chapter with their locations at this desk. Letter references key together the two illustrations, Exhibits 12 and 13. Not to scale.

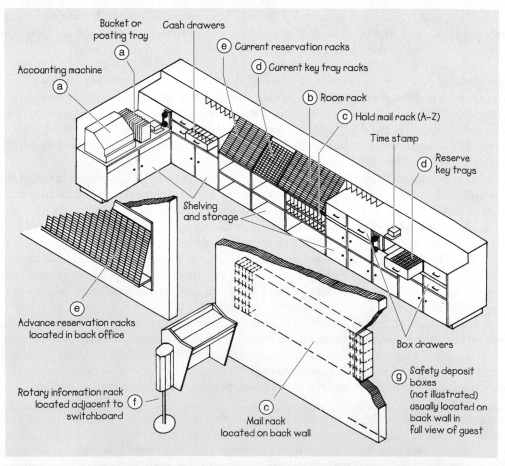

EXHIBIT 13 Similar to Exhibit 12, this illustration points up the tasks of the desk and identifies the relative locations of the staff. Computers have replaced the physical items identified as a, b, c, d, e, and f, but not their functions. Not to scale.

Duties are concentrated in four functions as detailed in Exhibit 14: room sales, guest relations, records, and coordination. Agents bring together the commitments made by reservations, the spaces delivered by housekeeping, the minor repairs handled by engineering, and the billing/collection required by accounting. They adjust minor problems and buffer management from the first blasts of major complaints. Agents are part salespersons, part psychologists, part accountants, and part managers.

Guest-service agents face a wide range of difficult person-to-person encounters, many originating in other departments. Guests raise complaints such as, "The laundry burned my shirt"; "The bellman lost my important papers"; "Housekeeping never made the room last night." Unhappy guests confront the guest-service agent. Where else would they go but to a "guest-service" agent! The situation is frustrating and stressful to both the guest and the agent, who is not in a position to resolve the problem. Rigid policies often curb the clerk's discretion. (But sometimes not, because of employee empowerment.) In most instances, agents must communicate with housekeeping, plead with engineering, track down someone in food and beverage, or implement arrangements that sales and marketing had promised. Decisions do not come promptly, and so waiting guests grow impatient and angry.

JOB TITLE: HOTEL, MOTEL, AND RESORT DESK CLERKS

NATURE OF THE WORK

Hotel, motel, and resort desk clerks perform a variety of services for guests of hotels, motels, and other lodging establishments. Regardless of the type of accommodation, most desk clerks have similar responsibilities. They register arriving guests, assign rooms, and check out guests at the end of their stay. They also keep records of room assignments and other registration-related information on computers. When guests check out, desk clerks prepare and explain the charges, as well as process payments.

Front-desk clerks always are in the public eye and typically are the first line of customer service for a lodging property. Their attitude and behavior greatly influence the public's impressions of the establishment. And as such, they always must be courteous and helpful. Desk clerks answer questions about services, checkout times, the local community, or other matters of public interest. Clerks also report problems with guest rooms or public facilities to members of the housekeeping or maintenance staff for them to correct the problems. In larger hotels or in larger cities, desk clerks may refer queries about area attractions to a concierge and may direct more complicated questions to the appropriate manager.

In some smaller hotels and motels, where smaller staffs are employed, clerks may take on a variety of additional responsibilities, such as bringing fresh linens to rooms, which usually are performed by employees in other departments of larger lodging establishments. In the smaller places, desk clerks often are responsible for all front-office operations, information, and services. For example, they may perform the work of a bookkeeper, advance reservation agent, cashier, laundry attendant, and telephone switchboard operator.

WORKING CONDITIONS

Hotels are open around the clock creating the need for night and weekend work. Extended hours of operation also afford the many part-time job seekers an opportunity to find work in these establishments, especially on evenings and late-night shifts or on weekends and holidays. About half of all desk clerks work a 35-to-40 hour week—most of the rest work fewer hours—so the jobs are attractive to persons seeking part-time work or jobs with flexible schedules. Most clerks work in areas that are clean, well lit, and relatively quiet, although lobbies can become crowded and noisy when busy. Many hotels have stringent dress guidelines for desk clerks.

Desk clerks may experience particularly hectic times during check-in and check-out times or incur the pressures encountered when dealing with convention guests or large groups of tourists at one time. Moreover, dealing with irate guests can be stressful. Computer failures can further complicate an already busy time and add to stress levels. Hotel desk clerks may be on their feet most of the time and may occasionally be asked to lift heavy guest luggage.

TRAINING, OTHER QUALIFICATIONS, AND ADVANCEMENT

Hotel, motel, and resort desk clerks deal directly with the public, so a professional appearance and a pleasant personality are important. A clear speaking voice and fluency in English also are essential, because these employees talk directly with hotel guests and the public and frequently use the telephone or public-address systems. Good spelling and computer literacy are needed, because most of the work involves use of a computer. In addition, speaking a foreign language fluently is increasingly helpful, because of the growing international clientele of many properties.

EXHIBIT 14 The U.S. Department of Labor holds to the older *desk clerk* nomenclature rather than the more modern *guest-service agent* terminology in this excerpt from the Bureau of Labor Statistics, *Occupational Outlook Handbook, 2006–2007 Edition.* (Other job descriptions can be found in the *Dictionary of Occupational Titles.*)

Most hotel, motel, and resort desk clerks receive orientation and training on the job. Orientation may include an explanation of the job duties and information about the establishment, such as the arrangement of sleeping rooms, availability of additional services, such as a business or fitness center, and location of guest facilities, such as ice and vending machines, restaurants, and other nearby retail stores. New employees learn job tasks through on-the-job training under the guidance of a supervisor or an experienced desk clerk. They often receive additional training on interpersonal or customer-service skills and on how to use the computerized reservation, room assignment, and billing systems and equipment. Desk clerks typically continue to receive instruction on new procedures and on company policies after their initial training ends.

Formal academic training generally is not required so many students take jobs as desk clerks on evening or weekend shifts or during school vacation periods. Most employers look for people who are friendly and customer-service oriented, well groomed, and display the maturity and self confidence to demonstrate good judgment. Desk clerks, especially in high-volume and higher-end properties should be quick-thinking, show initiative, and be able to work as a member of a team. Hotel managers typically look for these personal characteristics when hiring first-time desk clerks, because it is easier to teach company policy and computer skills than personality traits.

Large hotel and motel chains may offer better opportunities for advancement than small, independently owned establishments. The large chains have more extensive career ladder programs and may offer desk clerks an opportunity to participate in a management training program. Also, the Educational Institute of the American Hotel and Motel Association [American Hotel & Lodging Association] offers home-study or group-study courses in lodging management, which may help some obtain promotions more rapidly.

EXHIBIT 14   Continued

Flatter organizations, which have removed many of the management levels discussed in this chapter, never eliminate the guest-service agent. The post is too important. Yet, hotels which spend large sums on design and upgrades often overlook their most visible asset, the guest-service agent/cashier.

CASHIERS   Front-office cashiers work at the desk, but report to accounting, that is, either to the *controller* or to the *general cashier*. Contrary to the basic rule of organization that everyone should have but one boss, cashiers have a second reporting line. Their location at the desk also puts them under the control of the guest-service manager. With computerization, the two jobs, that of an agent and a cashier, are rolled into one.

Posting charges (recording them on guest bills), presenting final statements, resolving minor protests by departing guests, and handling cash and credit-card transactions have been the major assignments. Today, most posting is done electronically. At one time, cashiers cashed checks and took checks in payment. They even made small cash loans. None of that is done today. Even accessing safe-boxes (see Exhibit 12) is a duty no longer; in-room safes are in widespread use.

As guest-service agents have been the guest's first contact, cashiers have been the last. Computerization is changing both ends. Guests check in electronically—no need to see the agent—and check out electronically (express check out)—no need to see a cashier. More than ever, both positions are being combined as they have always been in small hotels.

THE BUILDING STRUCTURE

Hotels operate with two configurations: an organizational structure and a building structure. Every hotel has both guest rooms and an organization to deliver those rooms. But the similarity ends there. The differences in the physical buildings and in the delivery systems distinguish one property from another. It is such differences that segment the industry into its many parts.

The Old Versus the New

There is a huge variation between hotels built before World War II and those built since, especially hotels of very recent vintage. Today's hotels require more land—they have a larger *footprint* (the real-estate term)—because they are more open and because guest rooms are much larger. Exhibits 15 and 16 illustrate the differences. Some very famous hotels in the old design still exist. New York's Waldorf=Astoria (1931) and Chicago's Drake (1920) are good examples.

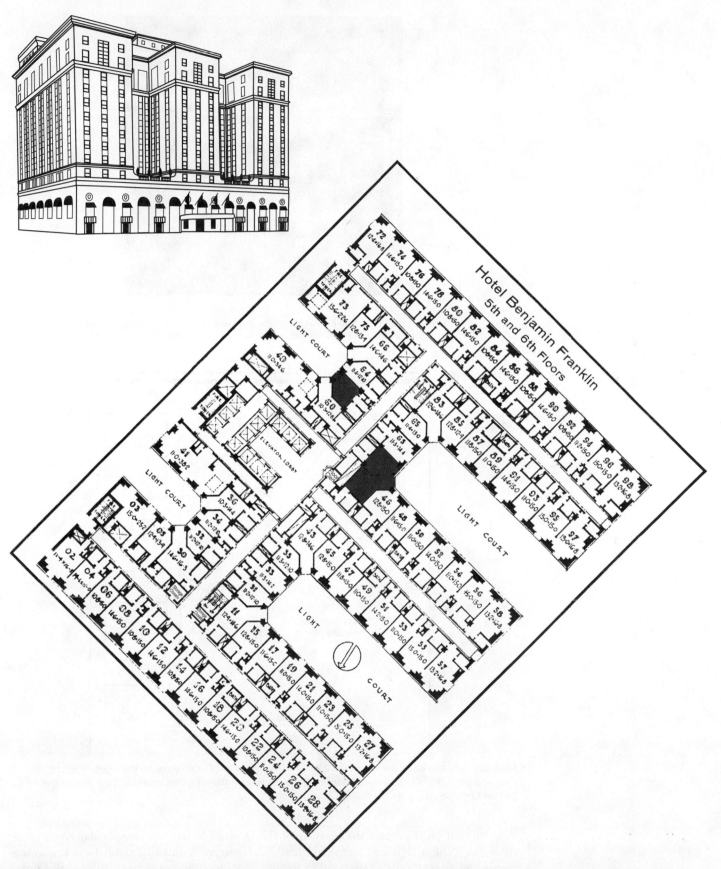

EXHIBIT 15 Typical of hotel construction between 1925 and 1945, this once upscale, commercial hotel had guest rooms smaller than today's budget inns. Light courts designed to maximize land use created oddly shaped rooms such as 44, 61, and 62. Note the floor closets (for linens and engineering supplies) on the corridor corners adjacent to rooms 11, 30, 66, and others and the floor clerk's position opposite the elevators. The job is no longer prevalent.

The Sofitel is a commercial hotel providing its business center and banquet/meeting facilities on the third floor. Special stairwells and extra elevators service the banquet floor, but (for security) not the sleeping floors.

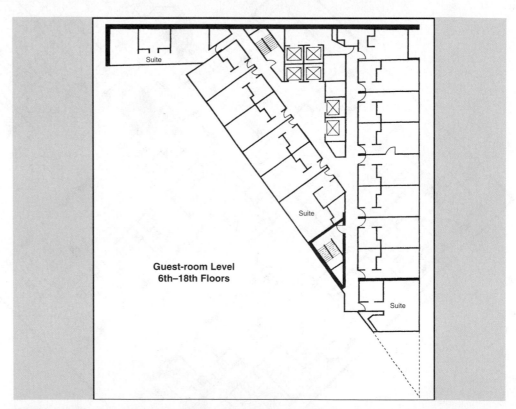

Guest-room Level
6th–18th Floors

EXHIBIT 16 The open design of the 21st-century urban hotel has replaced the light courts of its predecessors (Exhibit 15) and standardized the shape and size of guest rooms.   *Courtesy of the Sofitel Chicago Water Tower Hotel, Chicago, Illinois.*

Exhibit 16 illustrates the exterior of the modern hotel. The rectangular room shape viewed in Exhibit 16 is a modern-day standard. Compare rooms in Exhibit 16 to the strange shapes and sizes of rooms portrayed in Exhibit 15, especially rooms 30 to 36. It took a dozen different room rates to distinguish the accommodations of the old hotel. Three or four rates do the same job today, easing the desk's task of quoting rates and assigning rooms.

Just as room shapes have been standardized, room sizes have increased over the decades. Size is measured by square footage and square footage translates into cost of construction. Higher construction costs obviously lead to higher room rates. Although modern rooms are larger overall than those of 50 years ago, hotels of different classes still offer different sized rooms.

THE OLD: INSIDE ROOMS Rooms 58 to 97 in Exhibit 15 form a U-shape of inside rooms around a *light court*. As illustrated, inside rooms are enclosed by wings of the building. The view is downward toward the roof on the lower floor, which is often dirty and unsightly. Inside rooms are affected by the changing position of the sun, which casts shadows into these rooms even early in the day. Inside rooms are no longer used. Similarly, the semiprivate (shared) baths (bathrooms) of the 1930s have been replaced by today's private, often luxurious, baths.

THE NEW: SUITES AND ALL-SUITES The traditional suite has a parlor (living room or sitting room) and one or more sleeping rooms. A small, modern suite is illustrated in Exhibit 17 and by room numbers 72 to 74 in an older hotel (Exhibit 15). The suite's traditional definition of more than one room has been challenged by modern designs. Some assign suite terminology to just one room if a 600–700-square-foot facility is divided into "two rooms" either by a low wall or by strategically placed furniture. Holiday Inn's Staybridge Suites accomplishes this with a right-angle building that separates the living and sleeping segments.

Larger suites add second and third bedrooms and additional living space. Very luxurious accommodations include kitchens, formal dining rooms, saunas, libraries, and even swimming pools. Most basic suites contain wet bars and several bathrooms. Balconies and patios (lanai suites) are common amenities. Fireplaces may be in suites of hotels that are situated in cold regions. Two-floor suites, some with interior elevators, offer a truly opulent experience. The two-floor suite of the Netherland Plaza (1931) has a panoramic view of Cincinnati. A moderate-sized suite may measure 1,500 square feet (approximately 140 square meters), the size of someone's home. Contrast this with the typical hotel room of ±300 square feet.

Suites are often named, not numbered. "Bridal suite" and "presidential suite" are popular names. Historical figures and local references emphasize the hotel's theme: The Kit Carson suite, for example.

All-suite hotels are another product altogether. They are designed for a different market and a different use (see Exhibits 18). All-suites compete against standard rooms, not against hotel suites. To compensate for their larger rooms, all-suites have less public space. They allocate about 20% of the building to public space (lobbies, corridors, restrooms, vending areas, etc.)

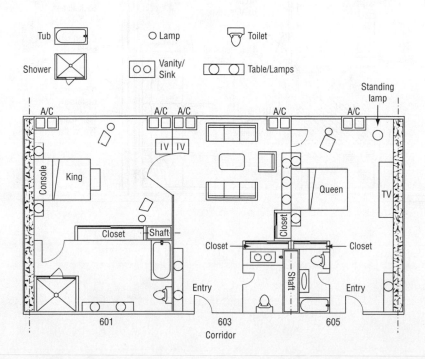

EXHIBIT 17 Illustrates a typical two-bedroom suite. Room 605, the second bedroom, is self-contained. Locked off, the two units can be sold separately. Together, the suite can sleep more than four if sofa beds are the parlor (room 603) furniture (see also Exhibit 18). Note the back-to-back utility shaft; the separate stall shower; the window air-conditioning rather than a central air-handling system and the smaller bath in the parlor. Approximate scale only.

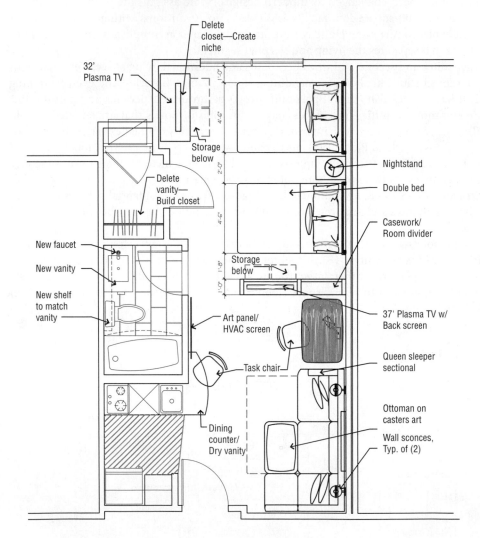

Delete closet—Create niche

32' Plasma TV

Storage below

Delete vanity—Build closet

New faucet

New vanity

New shelf to match vanity

Art panel/ HVAC screen

Task chair

Dining counter/ Dry vanity

Storage below

Nightstand

Double bed

Casework/ Room divider

37' Plasma TV w/ Back screen

Queen sleeper sectional

Ottoman on casters art

Wall sconces, Typ. of (2)

EXHIBIT 18 All-suite facilities appeal to both transient and long-stay guests to whom the concept was originally marketed. Sofa beds provide extra sleeping accommodations. This executive double is being remodeled as part of Gencom's upgrade program after acquiring the chain in 2006. *Courtesy of The Gencom Group, Miami, Florida.*

whereas 40% is the typical figure for full-service properties (including meeting rooms, banquet space, shops, etc.)

All hotels fall back on a building technique invented by Ellsworth Statler in 1923. Back-to-back utility shafts reduce the space required for piping, electrical, electronic, and heating/air-conditioning lines in baths, kitchenettes, and wet bars. Exhibits 15, 16, and 17 illustrate this feature.

CORNER ROOMS   Corner rooms are the most desirable rooms on the floor. They provide double exposure. Facing in two directions, they command a premium rate. To enhance that rate differential, architects either make the room larger or make it part of a suite (see Exhibit 16). Corner rooms are more common in older hotels because the sharp angles of the floor plans create them (see Exhibit 15). Modern building have fewer corners and fewer corner rooms.

MOTOR INNS   The highway hotel is a child of the motel, which makes it the grandchild of the earlier tourist court (see Exhibit 5). Its lineage has given it a unique design. Although not applauded by architects, the simple floor plan (see Exhibit 19) provides easy access to outside parking, which is the market being served.

Room rates are lower because both land and construction costs are lower. Land costs are held in check by careful site selections. Low-rise buildings and simple designs keep construction costs down. Building a U or L-shape (see Exhibit 19) helps with exterior appeal. First impressions are critical because much of the traffic is impulse buying, not reservations. Attractive exteriors rely on landscaping, facing materials and color. First impressions are made by the driveway, the port-cochere, and the entry. Cleanliness and maintenance of grounds, windows, and outdoor signs (all the bulbs lit?) set expectations.

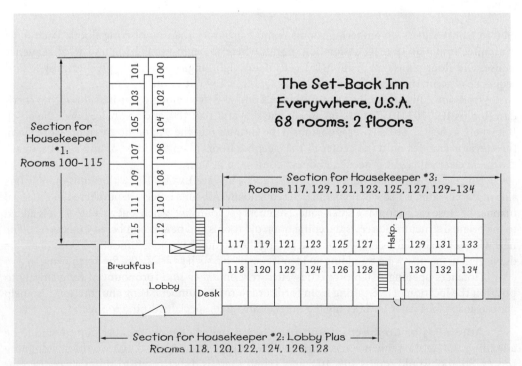

EXHIBIT 19   The typical design of a small, often two-story motor inn of 50–75 rooms is represented by this sketch. Ownership might be a small company or even a mom-and-pop. Most properties such as this are franchise flagged. The design anticipates three housekeepers per floor at full occupancy. The desk and the housekeeper's office are strategically located to monitor the doors. Not to scale.

Numbering for Identification

Everyone, guests and staff alike, uses the guest-room number for identification. Guests depend on the room number to locate themselves. Desk personnel address guests by their names, but use their room numbers within the confines of the desk. The floor number comes first followed by the room number, 1012.

Floors are numbered sequentially in ascending order, but usually reflect the culture of their location. Most Western hotels omit the unlucky number 13 from both floors and guest rooms. The unlucky number in the Orient is 4. So 13 and 4, and in the East any number that adds to 4, may be omitted as room numbers. Better to assign guests to rooms with lucky numbers: 7 in the United States; 6 in the Far East.

FLOOR NUMBERING   Americans number the first sleeping floor as floor one regardless of the number of intervening levels between it and the ground. Mezzanine, upper-ground floor and shopping levels are used without any standards. That sequence adds alphabetic buttons to the elevator, such as *M*, for mezzanine. Others might be LM, SB, and S2 (lower mezzanine; subbasement; and subbasement 2).

The ground floor is floor 1 to the rest of the world. Even without counting the intermediary floors, the 10th floor in the United States is the 11th floor everywhere else. Numerous floor numbers are skipped in Asia because of that bad-luck number four. So the top floor in a 46-story building in Hong Kong was actually numbered the 88th floor.

Numbering gets quite involved for hotels that have several low-rise buildings. Identically numbering each low-rise unit of, say, three or four stories, is one technique. Then each building is given a different name and keys are color coded. Others prefer to number the floors in sequence, moving from one building to the next. Confusion reigns because only one building has a first floor. Ground floors of the other units may start numbering in the teens or twenties.

Hotels with two or three towers have the same option. The towers can be differentiated by name (the river tower) or direction (the east tower), and numbered identically. Or the ground floor of the second tower can be numbered in sequence after the top floor of the first tower. Careful signage is essential whichever technique is used. That need is there for both guests and emergency workers.

ROOM NUMBERING   Numbering rooms is more arbitrary than numbering floors. Each hotel is architecturally unique. Its design determines where to begin numbering and what sequence to use. Old floor plans (see Exhibit 15) with many right-angled corridors preclude any logical sequence of room numbers. Even a design as simple as Exhibit 19 offers choice.

Tradition calls for rooms to be numbered odd and even along opposite sides of the corridor. Rooms 101, 103, 105, and so on are on one side and 102, 104, and so on are down the other. But where to begin? The answer is obvious if the elevator is at the end of the corridor. More often, the elevator empties onto the center of the sleeping floor. Then the logic of any system breaks down. So clear signage it is needed to direct guests and visitors.

No rules govern room numbering. An atrium hotel (see Exhibit 10), with rooms on only one side of the corridor, is likely to be numbered sequentially. All-suite hotels are numbered in the usual manner because each room is a small suite. Numbers get confusing when a new wing or ell is added to the original structure. Rarely is the entire floor, old rooms and new, renumbered in sequence. The new wing is usually numbered without interfacing the old numbers. Sometimes the old numbers are duplicated in the new wing by adding an identifying prefix, such as an N 408, for north wing.

Hoteliers opening Asian properties often rely on a *feng shui* (pronounced fung shway) to position the location of everything from furniture to room numbers. Feng shui masters also help choose auspicious dates for opening the hotel or any of its specialty dining rooms.

Adjoining or Connecting Rooms   Rooms that abut along the corridor are said to be adjoining. Using the sequence mentioned above, rooms 101, 103, and 105 would be adjoining rooms. So, too, would rooms 102, 104, and 106. If there is direct room-to-room access (a door between rooms) without using the corridor (see Exhibit 15, rooms 53, 55, and 57 in the center tower), the rooms connect. Obviously, every connecting room adjoins, but not every adjoining room connects.

ELEVATORS The first hotel elevator, almost the first elevator anywhere, was installed in New York City's Fifth Avenue Hotel (1859). Elevators facilitated the growth of skyscrapers, so hotels were enthusiastic buyers. Elevators became automated in the 1950s, and with it the post of the elevator operator disappeared. In 1985, elevators with transparent walls and views of the buildings innards had a role in developing the atrium lobby (see Exhibit 10). By 2000, television and cartoons had replaced the ubiquitous Muzak music during the few claustrophobic moments of an elevator ride. Speeds can be adjusted for smooth stops and starts or for rapid jumps from start to full speed in just four seconds. Everything is open to testing so long as the ride remains an awkward huddle with a dozen strangers.

Architects pay special heed to the distance from the registration desk to the elevators and from the elevator landings to the guest rooms. The 2,600-room Planet Hollywood (Las Vegas) has a dual elevator core that puts all guest rooms within seven door of any elevator. Room design and door insulation must shield against noises and loud voices caused by guests exiting close-by elevators.

Buttonless elevators, known as *destination elevators*, are designed to speed rides and reduce waiting time. They are already in place in New York's Marriott Marquis. Guests choose their floor number before entering the car. The computer reads the entry and directs the guest to a waiting elevator. No changing of floor numbers once the doors close. Guests need not wait for others to enter or depart. However, a slew of elevators is needed to whisk a solitary party up, say, 15 floors.[11]

Room Shape and Size

Hotels sell guest rooms. So the shape and size of the room is a factor in guest satisfaction and, thus, in business volume. Size, especially, separates the industry's offerings into different products. Hard budgets have small rooms; deluxe accommodations have large rooms. Size even differentiates rate classes within a hotel.

ROOM SHAPE Little has changed in the shape of guest rooms. Interior rooms take shape from the exterior design (concave, square, round) of the hotel.[12] Research may eventually show greater guest satisfactory or reduced wear from certain shapes. Until then, the parallelogram remains the classic favorite with the room depth approximately twice its width. Increases in room size are first made by adding to the depth. Width is increased next, bumping the standard 12- or 13-foot width to 16 feet—a luxurious room.

Round building may have an exterior appeal, but present internal problems. The outer walls are rounded and the inner walls are angled. That's the only mean of accommodating the bath and the central core within the cross-section of too small a diameter.

Rooms get a more spacious look when there is a balcony, either real or false, with French or sliding doors. The balcony also adds interest to the façade.

ROOM SIZE Room shape is architecturally driven but room size is a financial/marketing decision. Economy class hotels have capitalized on smaller accommodations and smaller rates, resisting the general movement to ever-larger rooms. The room's size, furnishings, and amenities structure the rate. Markets vary hotel to hotel. The twin double beds of the family-oriented hotel would not appeal to upscale business travelers.

Comparing room sizes among hotels highlights the difficulty of classifying the world's hotels as one industry. Capsule rooms are of 5 feet in width, 5 feet in height, and less than 7 feet in length. That's less than 35 square feet–75 cubic feet! Rooms in London's easyHotel chain are 60 square feet. Most other hard budgets are larger. Accor's Ibis chain (chiefly Europe) has rooms of approximately 130 square feet (12 square meters). Compare that to rooms in Econo Lodges and Super 8s, which are almost 200 square feet (nearly 19 square meters).

---

[11]The hotel has 22 elevators; 12 are scenic. Speeds attain 1,000 feet (300 meters) per minute. Waiting time is under five minutes.

[12]The W Hotel in Sydney, Australia, was converted from a 100-year-old wool warehouse. It required 33 different shapes for its 104 rooms.

Surprisingly, today's budget rooms are as large as those of a first-class commercial hotel of 100 years ago. The Benjamin Franklin Hotel (Exhibit 15) had rooms of 150–175 square feet. Rooms in today's Sleep Inns, Choice Hotels' budget chain, are bigger at 210 square feet.

The Far East has rooms at the other end of the scale. A standard room at Hong Kong's Shangri-La is 500 square feet, which includes the bath. This size is immediately recognized as super luxury. To generate a luxurious feeling, room size must exceed 400 square feet.

New York City's Four Seasons hotel compares favorably with its worldwide cohorts. Room and bath total 600 square feet (55.75 square meters). This contrasts with the typical room and bath of 250–350 square feet (23.3–32.5 square meters).

Total Square Footage A hotel's total square footage cannot be determined by simply multiplying the size of the average guest room by the number of rooms. Service areas, lobbies, corridors, storage, offices, and public space must also be computed. Total space of a hotel is almost double that needed for guest rooms alone. Even then, allowances must be made for the size, type, and class of hotel. Full-service, convention properties compute total space needed at 900–1,200 square feet per room, which is three to four times a room's actual measurement. Economy properties with no public space are the other end of the spectrum. Total footage is calculated at about 600 square feet per room: two to three times the typical guest-room size.

All-suite hotels are a contrast to standard hotels and even to each other. All suites are segmented into economy, mid-market, and upscale groupings. Size is the distinction because the rental unit's content (bedroom, parlor, bath, kitchenette) is the same for the three segments. Guest Quarters pioneered the type with a 650-square-foot unit. The budget room of AmeriSuites is about 380 square feet. Fireplaces carry Homewood Suites to 550 square feet. Extended-stay suites that measure 400–650 square feet are the size of a standard apartment in many large cities of the United States!

How the Room Is Used Hotel chains build models before proceeding with construction or renovation. They test guest acceptance, preview costs, and seek out flaws before the major project gets underway. One side result has been a focus on how the room is used.

Different kinds of guests use rooms in different ways. Within the same dimensions, a destination hotel furnishes more storage space than a transient property. A transient hotel allocates more space to sleeping and less to the living area than a destination inn. Such would be the case in New York City where the typical daily use of the room is eight hours (for sleep). Extreme climate conditions increase usage of the room.

The use of the room dictates the type of furnishings. A destination resort wouldn't need a desk, but business travelers use their rooms as offices. Hotel rooms actually serve as company offices in developing countries. In most surveys, business guests give high priority to a comfortable work environment.

Designers are good at making small rooms look larger. Eliminating nightstands is one example. Bedside lamps are then mounted on the wall. Mirrors create a perception of space. Wall-to-wall drapes and limited patterns add to the feeling of roominess. Mirrors and balconies also expand the sense of space. Still, it requires about 20 extra square feet (1.86 square meters) before an occupant notices the larger size and before a rate boost can be justified.

Clearly, there is no one standard room. The industry is moving in several directions. Miniprices use modular units measuring 12 feet center to center. Luxurious operations opt for 15-foot centers and lengths of 30–35 feet. (Standard carpet sizes of 12 and 15 feet dictate dimensions unless the plan calls for custom work.) Costs of energy, labor, and borrowed funds become part of the decision. So does the marketplace.

Bed and Bath

Increases in bed sizes—Americans are getting bigger—account in part for the increase in room sizes. Bathrooms, which have become major weapons in the competitive wars, have also contributed to total-square-footage creep.

THE BED Bed types, coverings, and sizes vary across the world and over time. Quilted beddings appeared in Japan about 1500. The nomads of the Middle East likely used some form of stuffed animal skins (early futons) even before the 16th century. American hotel rooms have gone through periods that first favored double beds, then twin beds. Queen and king beds are today's favorites and queen doubles, not twins, are used if two beds are needed. Larger beds mean larger rooms. Larger rooms mean higher construction costs. Higher construction costs mean higher room rates.

Beds are being lowered as well as lengthened. Mattresses and box springs are usually 22–24 inches from the floor. Chairs stand about 17 inches. Lowering the beds to 17 inches keeps all pieces on the same horizontal plane making the room look much larger. The offset is shorter mattress life because guests then sit on the bed. Several good chairs will help, but mattress management has its role. Mattresses must be rotated head to foot and top to bottom. Good housekeeping does that as part of its deep cleaning once in every quarter. The position of the mattress (head versus toe and top versus bottom) is tracked by arrows attached to the side of the mattress.

BED SIZES AND SYMBOLS   Older hotels typically had a variety of beds and furnishings. That had to be communicated to the guest-service agent who assigned rooms to new arrivals. The symbols that were created for the manual room racks have been carried into the computer age. They are used less frequently in modern hotels because most rooms are similarly designed and furnished. Nevertheless, language and symbols that are easy for the desk still cause confusion among some guests. "Single" is one such term.

A single room is one occupied by a single person. It makes no difference whether the bed is a single, a queen, or a king. The ambiguity arises because the terms "single" and "double" refer equally to (1) the room rate, (2) the number of guests occupying the room, (3) the number of guests who could occupy the room, and (4) the size and type of beds in the room. A single occupant in a queen bed would be charged a single rate even if the room had queen doubles and could sleep four persons. The single-room configuration—one single bed for one person—is unknown today. Thus, to the innkeeper, "single" means either single occupancy or single rate.

Single Bed   The once single bed, symbol S, slept one and measured 36 by 75 inches. Older hotels might still have rooms that contain one twin bed or one double bed, but a single bed is unlikely. To meet AAA standards, the single bed (not the twin and not the double) would need to measure at least 39 by 72 inches.

Twin Bed   A twin room, symbol T, has two beds each accommodating one person, but it could be sold to a single occupant. Just as two persons could be assigned double queens. Twin beds measure 39 by 75 inches each and use linens 72 by 108 inches. The old-fashioned 72- or 75-inch-long mattress has been replaced in almost all beds by the California (or Western) length, which stretches to 84 inches long.[13] This increases linen sizes, which increases laundry costs that are based on weight. Higher room rates is the outcome.

Twins are flexible and once accounted for nearly 70% of all rooms. To have two beds, twins were gradually replaced with double-doubles and then queen-doubles. Single business travelers prefer the doubles. They sleep in one and spread papers on the other. A survey done some time ago by Sheraton showed that the second bed was used only about 15% of the time.

Double Bed   Double beds, D is the symbol, have a width between 54 and 57 inches. An important 3 inches for those sharing! As with most beds, the length has increased from 75 inches to the California 84 inches. Double beds take linen 90–93 inches wide and 113 inches long. Half a double bed is 27–28 inches, narrower even than a single bed. That alone explains its disappearance; guests are getting larger and heavier. Because doubles (double-doubles or double-queens) can accommodate four persons, they are also called *quads* or *family rooms*.

Queen and King Bed   Queens and kings (symbols Q and K) are extra wide, 60 and 72 inches respectively, and extra long. They made popular the California length, also called the

---

[13]The standard king or Eastern king is 16 inches wider than a queen, but not longer. The California or Western king is 4 inches longer than the queen.

European King. Although designed for two persons, three or four might squeeze in when part of a family room.

Both beds require large rooms since the critical distance of at least 3 feet between the foot of the bed and the furniture (called *case goods*) is required. Larger sheets, 108 by 122.5 inches, are needed. Rates go up to pay for "larger" rooms, beds, mattresses, linens, and laundry costs.

Hollywood Bed   Two beds joined by a common headboard were called *Hollywood beds*. They used the same twin symbol, T, because that's what they were, twins. They were difficult to make because the room attendant could not get between them. To overcome this, the beds were placed on rollers, which causes rapid carpet wear. Because the total dimension is 78×75 inches (two twins), Hollywood beds were quickly converted into kings by laying one king mattress across both bedsprings. The era of the Hollywood bed passed quickly, but not the design: King mattress are often laid across dual springs.

Studio Bed (Room)   A studio bed is a sofa by day and a bed by night. During the day, the bed is slipcovered and the pillows stored in the backrest. Both the headboard and the footboard disappear when the bed is rolled away from the sofa's frame. These rooms were once popular with business travelers who used the room during the day. So they were also called *executive rooms.* Neither the bed nor the sofa was ever comfortable so the concept gave way to the all-suite configuration.

Sleigh Bed   Any bed can be a sleigh bed, so named because of the sleigh-like design of the headboard and the footboard. There is no change to the integral part of the bed. The use of sleigh-shaped beds is a designer's choice.

Daybed   Add sleigh ends to a twin bed and one almost has a daybed. Daybeds, also called fainting couches or chaise lounges, were once common to the family living room. They may be found today in homes and in very large hotel rooms as an addition to the furnishings. It is possible to sleep in a daybed, seated in a semi-upright position. Visualize a slender, more fashionable recliner and a daybed comes to mind.

Sofa Bed   A sofa bed is similar to a studio bed. It is a sofa first of all. At 17 inches from the floor, the seating quality is far more comfortable than the studio bed, which is 22 inches off floor. Unlike the studio bed, which rolls away from its frame, the sofa bed opens in an accordion fashion from the seat. Since it unfolds, and requires more space than the studio bed, it is less convenient but more comfortable both for seating and sleeping.

Parlors and all-suites are often furnished with sofa beds (see Exhibit 18), but a studio bed is a room unto itself. Sofa beds come in all sizes, single, double, even queen size. The single is almost a three-quarter bed, measuring 48×75 inches.

Sofa beds are sometimes called *hide-a-beds*, so the symbol is H. Large rooms that contain standard sleeping accommodations and a sofa bed are *junior suites.*

Rollaway Bed (Cot)   A cot or rollaway is a portable bed that is added to the usual furnishings on a temporary basis. A rollaway sleeps one, and a comfortable one measures 34 by 75 inches. It uses twin sheets. Cots are usually smaller, 30 by 72 inches, with linen 63 by 99 inches.

Setting-up is labor intensive, chiefly because the storage area is not convenient; not a top priority of architects. Depending on the type and class of hotel, about one cot is needed for every 20 guest rooms.

Crib   As with rollaways, cribs are added as needed. Deaths from unsafe cribs have made them a sensitive issue. The Consumer Product Safety Commission reported (2000) that many hotel cribs were unsafe. Crib recalls have reached nearly 3 million nationwide.[14]

Using regular-size sheets in cribs is as dangerous as crib sides that slide unexpectedly catching small heads between too-small mattresses and the frames. Management must monitor general maintenance (loose parts, protruding screws, and broken slats) on both cribs and rollaways. Lawsuits are too costly after the fact.

---

[14]The drop-side crib, which has had many recalls, was outlawed in 2011. Hotels were given two years to make replacements. Children younger than two years represent an estimated 7 million room nights per year!

Water Bed   In two decades, water beds jumped from a novelty to a hot item and fell back again. Even then, it was a western phenomenon, rediscovered by a Californian who used starch and gelatin as fillers. Water beds substitute for traditional mattresses, except hotels have never used them. Their weight and potential problems make them unusable for hotel rooms.

Futon   The Japanese futon, a cotton-quilted bed, is another addition to America's sleeping design. Like the water bed, futons are found in private residents, not in U.S. hotels. Japanese ryokans still offer this bed, a thick layer of batting laid on the floor, that is easily rolled and stored.

Wall Bed   Like many other copyrighted brands that identify generic products, *Murphy beds* have come to mean any fold-up wall bed. Their popularity waxes and wanes. They are great for dormitories, but like futons and water beds are not found in hotels. When the bed is folded into the wall, the unit becomes a meeting room, office, or display unit. Wall beds are full size, giving them an edge over the studio bed.

Warm air cushions that support the sleeper without frames, mattresses, labor, linen, or laundry might be tomorrow's bed. What a revolutionary thing; what a cost savings! What innovative hotelier will pick up the idea?

THE BATH   "Bath" is the industry's jargon for the bathroom. "Bath" does not refer to the bathtub nor to the activity that takes place in the tub. It is, rather, the industry's reference to the room containing a toilet (sometimes called a water closet), a sink (lavatory), a tub (bathtub), and a shower. The hotel bath has undergone many changes across time, but its position as a sound barrier between the room and the corridor remains. Abutting the corridor saves construction costs and leaves the outside wall for windows and balconies. Modular construction of the bath has gained in popularity. The unit is prefabricated away from the building site and installed as one unit.

Stall showers, which adapt to small spaces, gained favor as old hotels converted from rooms without baths. They fit easily into old closets or corners of renovated rooms. Tub and showers meet the cultural needs of all guests. The Japanese, for example, favor tubs, just as they choose separate beds over all other choices. Bidets (feminine cleanliness), which are in the baths of many countries, have not found favor in the homes or hotels of North America.

Baths account for about 20% of the room size. That works out to some 35 square feet in hard budgets, 70 square feet in mid-range properties, and 120 square feet in luxurious accommodations. What a contrast this is to the hotels of the last century when public baths served whole floors. Very early hotels had baths in the basements because the mechanics of pumping water to higher floors was not yet in place.

Even as some hotels have cut back on low-cost amenities (soap and shampoo) others have built ever-larger bathrooms with expensive appointments including in-floor scales, electric shoe-shine equipment, no-fog mirrors, and plush bathrobes. Chicago's Palmer House added his-and-her baths during its renovation several years ago. New York City's Four Season Hotel features tubs that fill in one minute!

The same "revolution" that brought untold changes to the room's beds and bedding has impacted the bath, with the shower taking center stage. Shower rods were the beginning. Curving the rod outward keeps the sticky curtain from body contact. This minor change launched the dramatic battle of the showers, with almost no concern for the increases in housekeeping costs. Glass-enclosed showers replaced curtains. Multishower heads (see Exhibit 20), "rain showers," which direct the water onto different parts of the body, changed the very meaning of a shower.[15] Similarly, sculptured tubs with multiple outlets were turned into quasi-spas.

The most dramatic changes have taken place in boutique hotels. The walls between bedroom and bath have been eliminated or been replaced by glass panels. For those who dislike living on the edge, the glass panel may be filled with liquid crystals that turn it opaque. For other

---

[15]Federal regulations (1992) limit shower heads to 2.5 gallons per minute. However, there is no restriction on the number of shower heads per shower. Forcing air to mix with the water in the shower head deceives the bather into thinking the pressure is pre-1992.

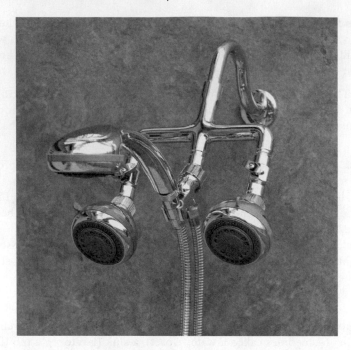

EXHIBIT 20 America's hotels are undergoing a revolution in bath design and comfort. Upgraded showers are part of the amenity wars, and multiple shower heads are at the forefront of comfort. *Courtesy of Zoe Industries, Scottsdale, Arizona.*

avant-garde properties, the bath's frosted window panes have become clear glass overlooking gardens and fountains (and some of the neighbor's windows). By enclosing the toilets, some semblance of privacy has been retained. Questions remain whether these changes with their sexual implications can be sustained, especially for an aging population. After all, not all guests are honeymooners.

The bathroom craze has been carried into the nightclub/lounge scene where unisex bathrooms, one-way glass on the wall of the stall, a 2,000 square-foot room, a glass floor that allows the user to see his or her date at the bar below have been introduced.

As the bath has grown larger, so has the ancillary space. Dressing areas and second lavatories outside the bath proper have added to the room's overall dimensions. Replacing closets with open hanger space has helped compensate. Consolidating furniture has also saved space. One vertical piece can incorporate several horizontal space-users. Into armoires have gone television sets, bars and refrigerators, desks, and drawers for clothing. Flat-screen TVs have reversed this emphasis. Armoires are no longer needed for TV storage. Without them, the room looks larger and more chic.

Whatever the final design, it must reflect guest needs. Some may be in for a two-night stay with a hanging garment-bag. Resort guests need more space and more drawers. Business travelers base their decisions on work space and electronic connectivity and computer support.

Summary

Two designs structure the modern hotel. One, the building, is obvious at once. Its architecture may even be its very attraction. The other structure is organization. Unlike the building, it is not visible at first. Its significance becomes evident only after the guest has stayed awhile. The first structure provides physical comfort; the second reassurance. Both structures undergo constant change because lodging is a dynamic industry. More space and new baths are coming from one of the industry's two structures; fewer personnel and balanced service from the other. W Hotels's appointment of a fashion director to its organizational structure is one simple example. Robots to vacuum and mop is a dramatic projection.

Good building designs evolve from the diverse needs of the consumer. So not all hotels offer the same accommodations. Each structure is designed to attract portions of the traveling public, striving to cast as wide a market net as possible. Thus, hotels range from hard budget hotels with rooms of 150 square feet to upscale accommodations of 600 square feet. (Square meters replace square feet outside of the United States: 0.093 square meters [m^2] equal 1 square foot [ft^2].)

Good organizational designs are equally dynamic, changing as customer demand, technological advancement, and services require. Today's guests are less inclined to wait for personal service. Less service has slashed the workforce. Bells and telephone departments have been reduced because automation and electronics have altered the work of the front desk.

Security is one department that has grown both in size and responsibility. Worldwide events have focused management's attention on security. Although hotels are not insurers of guest safety, they must exercise reasonable care to protect guests and their property. The hotel industry has responded with better trained staff and larger departments. Prevention and deterrence reduce the number of security incidents and, equally important, document those that are unavoidable.

Resources and Challenges

RESOURCES
Web Site Assignment

Using websites, or any other references, prepare a list of no less than five items detailing (1) security measures that hotels have put into place in response to generalized heightened security concerns and/or (2) security measures that hotels might put into place to prepare floor housekeepers for disasters such as earthquakes, floods, fires, or health emergencies.

Interesting Tidbits

- Hotels have been the backdrop for several historic shootings: President Gerald Ford in front of the St. Francis Hotel (San Francisco), presidential candidate Robert Kennedy in the kitchen of the Ambassador Hotel (Los Angeles), civil-rights leader Martin Luther King on the balcony of the Lorraine Hotel (Memphis), and President Ronald Regan outside the Hilton Hotel (Washington).

- Britain's "Loo of the Year" award points up the decline in the number of public toilets, an issue for both locals and tourists. After all, it was a Brit, John Harington, who invented the flush toilet in 1596. Many mistakenly attribute this invention to Thomas Crapper, a plumber who popularized the flush toilet almost a century later.

Challenges

True/False

Questions that are partially false should be marked false (F).

_____ 1. The hotel manager (also called house manager or resident manager) is the front-of-the-house counterpart to the food and beverage manager; each heads the respective areas.

_____ 2. Large hotel rooms measure as much as 350 square feet or about 32.5 square meters because 10.76 divided into square meters equals 1 square foot.

_____ 3. *Guest-service agent*, *room clerk*, *receptionist*, and *front-office clerk* are different terms used to identify the same position.

_____ 4. In most hotels, housekeeping has the largest number of employees.

_____ 5. Registration pods have swept the lodging industry, replacing the traditional desk in almost every large hotel in Canada and the United States.

Problems

1. With special attention to front-office activities, prepare a list of duties carried out by one (or more) of the fictional staff in the book *Hotel* by Arthur Hailey (Garden City, NY: Doubleday & Company, Inc., 1965; also available through Bantam Books).

2. Using information provided in this chapter or acquired elsewhere, sketch to approximate scale a typical room with furnishings that Choice Hotels might be building in Europe. (This requires dimensions to be in meters and square meters.) Above the drawing, list the several assumptions as $1, 2, 3, \ldots n$ that your drawing relies upon. Cite references external to the text if used.

3. Using information provided in this chapter or acquired elsewhere, *estimate* the total square feet of New York City's Four Seasons Hotel. Show the several mathematical steps and label all of your figures.

4. Either as part of your travels this term or as part of a field trip, contrast the size, shape, bedding, price, and characteristics of two or more hotel rooms. Discuss the differences.

5. Interview a hotel manager or a front-office employee. From the information obtained, construct the organizational chart of the front office, and prepare a description of any one front-office job, using Exhibits 6 and 14 as a guide.

6. This question is intentionally excluded in this edition.

AN INCIDENT IN HOTEL MANAGEMENT
Lost-and-Lost

The mother has called three times to inquire about a Fossil watch that her son had left in the shower of room 223. He was part of a school group (three boys to a room) that checked out on the 28th. This information was taken on her first call. A promise was made then to call back, but never fulfilled. Now the mother is on the telephone with the general manager.

The housekeeper told the GM that lost-and-found had only socks, Jockey shorts, and a cap from room 223. The assistant manager, who fielded the second call, explained that he hung up when the "lady" grew belligerent and used very strong language such as the hotel staff was a bunch of thieves, the assistant was an ass, and worse.

Caller: "I realize people misplace things, but that happens with old people in retirement homes, not with a 17-year-old in a hotel."

Questions:

1. Was there a management failure here; if so, what?
2. What is the hotel's immediate response (or action) to the incident?
3. What further, long-run action should management take, if any?

Answers to True/False Quiz

1. True. The hotel manager heads up the rooms division of the organization; the food and beverage manger does the same for that department. In a good-sized property they would be equal level executives.

2. False. To convert square feet into square meters, divide 10.76 into the square foot measure: $10.76 \div 350 = 32.5$. However, although a 350-square-foot room is good size; it doesn't measure up to "a large room."

3. True. *Guest-service agent*, *room clerk*, *receptionist*, and *front-office clerk* are different terms used to identify the same position. The term *receptionist* is preferred almost everywhere outside of the United States.

4. True. In most hotels, housekeeping has the largest number of employees, but many of them are call-in workers who report to work only when occupancy warrants additional personnel on the guest-room floors.

5. False. Registration pods have not been widely adopted. The illustration in the text emphasizes how the lobby area is undergoing change, but the traditional role of the desk—an actual desk—holds sway.

Forecasting Availability
and Overbooking

Forecasting Availability and Overbooking

E very reservation begins with an available room. No rooms available, no reservation can be taken—or can it? Fully committed hotels continue taking reservations because overbooking is actually more conservative than just selling to 100% occupancy. Cancellations and simple no-shows often leave unexpected vacancies. Whether to overbook or not is not the issue. The real question is, "How many rooms should be overbooked?" Management answers by forecasting the number of rooms available for sale.

FORECASTING AVAILABLE ROOMS

The concept behind rooms inventory begins with a one-to-one match between rooms in the hotel and rooms committed either to incoming reservations or *stay-over* rooms. Each day's available rooms inventory is equal to the number of rooms in the hotel less the total number of stay-overs plus incoming reservations.

The system, which is rather simple, becomes complicated when guests change their plans for any untold number of reasons. Some guests stay an extra day or two in spite of their original intention to check out. Others depart earlier than anticipated. A few guests cancel their reservations just hours before arrival (or, worse yet, fail to cancel their reservation and simply never show up). Still others arrive a day or two earlier than expected. Added to these circumstances is the chance for human error—"Oh, I thought you said November 17th, not November 15th," further complicating the situation.

The Simple, Unadjusted Room Count

There are two common methods for forecasting room availability: the simple, unadjusted room count and the adjusted room count. It makes sense to start with the simple approach, where none of the more sophisticated adjustments (such as overstays, understays, cancellations, etc.) have yet been introduced. They will be introduced later in the chapter.

The simple, unadjusted room count compares rooms available in the hotel against anticipated stay-overs and expected arrivals. If any rooms remain uncommitted (i.e., there are more rooms available than are committed to stay-overs and reservations), they are considered available for sale that day.

AUTOMATED INVENTORY TRACKING SYSTEMS   At a moment's notice, the reservations department must be able to determine the number (and types) of rooms available for sale on a given date. Automated property management systems offer various status reports under the reservations module. Status reports generally include the following:

- A 7-, 10-, or 14-day room availability report which shows each room type and the number of rooms available for sale by date.

Business: MAY 25				1-Day Room Inventory Mon MAY 25—				MAY 25 17:15:49	
Room Type	Room Cnts	Rooms Offmkt	Rooms Sold	Rooms Avail	Rates 1per	Rates 2per	Close Level	Host Status	CTA MLOS
DDSU	15	1	5	9	85.00	85.00	4	Open	
DDSN	47	13	34	0	85.00	85.00	1	Closed	
KSU	10	0	5	5	75.00	75.00	3	Open	
KSUN	33	10	19	4	75.00	75.00	3	Open	
KHCN	3	0	1	2	75.00	75.00	2	Open	
DDHN	1	0	0	1	85.00	85.00	1	Open	
KEX	1	0	0	1	85.00	85.00	1	Open	
KEXN	5	2	1	2	85.00	85.00	2	Open	
D1HN	2	0	1	1	75.00	75.00	1	Open	
Totals:	117	26	66	25		Current occupancy 72.5%			

Key stroke action: 1 = Forward 1 Day   2 = Back 1 Day

EXHIBIT 1 An example of a one-day rooms inventory screen. This is an actual Multi-Systems, Incorporated Property Manager screen (PM Version 8.11) from a 117-room all-suite hotel. Notice that 26 rooms are off market (out of inventory due to an in-house renovation project), 66 rooms are sold (either to incoming reservations or stay-overs), and 25 rooms are available for sale. The various room types are listed in the first column from DDSU through D1HN. DD is two double beds, K is one king bed, S or SU indicates suite, EX stands for executive room type, N means nonsmoking (in the absence of N, the room is smoking), and H or HC means handicapped accessible.   *Courtesy of AmeriSuites Incorporated, Patterson, New Jersey and Multi-Systems, Inc., Phoenix, Arizona.*

- A current or one-day inventory report which details all rooms in the hotel and their particular status (see Exhibit 1).
- A reservations forecast report which projects revenue and occupancy for each of several days into the future. This report usually displays the room and house count (number of guests in house) as well as projects the number of stay-overs for each day. As the report reads further into the future (three to five days from today), the forecast becomes less accurate because it is based on each day's assumed check-outs and stay-overs (see Exhibits 6 and 7).
- A general manager's daily report which identifies for the current day group rooms picked up, guaranteed and nonguaranteed reservations, anticipated stay-overs, out-of-order and out-of-inventory rooms, walk-ins, early check-outs, and more.
- An arrival list which details each reservation scheduled for that day's arrival. Reservations are listed alphabetically and can also be reviewed by affiliation: group reservations, travel-agent bookings, late arrivals, and so on.

COMPONENTS OF THE SIMPLE ROOM COUNT Through the property management system (see Exhibits 6 and 7), the room count is scrutinized several days prior to the actual date of arrival. Taking a more precise look over the preceding days prepares the reservations department for problems that may lie ahead. On the date of arrival, the reservations department reviews the room count throughout the day. Common times for review are before the day's arrivals begin (around 6 AM), just after the check-out hour (around 11 AM for many properties), and immediately before and after 6 PM for hotels that allow nonguaranteed (6 PM) reservations. If the hotel has rooms *available for sale* (*a plus count*), it is important to know the number and types available so the reservations department and front desk can better sell the remaining rooms. Maximum rates are charged as the hotel sells its last few remaining rooms (a yield management approach).

Forecasting Availability and Overbooking

When no rooms remain available (*an even* or *zero count*), it is important to be forewarned, lest the hotel find itself in an overbooked situation (*a minus* or *negative count*). Overbooking occurs when there are more reservations and stay-overs than there are rooms available. With advance knowledge, the hotel arranges supplementary accommodations at other hotels, alerts its front-office staff to the sensitive situation, and encourages the reservations department to monitor the room count and note cancellations as they occur.

Committed Rooms The room count process tracks the number of rooms that are committed. The hotel is *committed* to guests staying over from last night (*stay-overs*) and to today's reservations. If the total of these (stay-overs plus reservations) is less than the total number of rooms in the hotel, there is a plus count. If the hotel has more commitments than rooms available for sale, there is a minus count (overbooked).

Overbooking is a strategic decision made by the reservations manager in concert with the front-office manager, the sales manager, and the general manager. Hotels overbook hotel rooms for much the same reason that airlines overbook flights. Both know that some percentage of customers will not arrive (no-show) and others will cancel. The goal, therefore, is to project how many reservations will cancel, no-show, and so on, and to overbook the hotel just enough to result in full occupancy on the day of arrival. Too conservative a projection, the hotel is left with unsold rooms; too aggressive a projection, the hotel is forced to walk overbooked guests.

Refer to Exhibits 2 and 3. Exhibit 2 demonstrates a simple, unadjusted room count. The simple count looks at nothing more than rooms available, rooms committed to stay-overs, and rooms committed to incoming reservations. These same figures are then reused in Exhibit 3. Exhibit 3, however, demonstrates an adjusted count, including adjustments for overstays, understays, cancellations, no-shows, and early arrivals. Although Exhibits 2 and 3 start with the same numbers, the end result is quite different.

Adjusted Room Count

The reservations department collects data over time, which become the basis for statistical adjustments. These adjustments change from day to day, depending on the day of the week and the week of the year. Percentages change with the weather, with the type of group registered, and

---

Given

A 1,000-room hotel had a total of 950 rooms occupied last night. Of those 950 rooms, 300 are due to check out today. In addition, there are 325 reservations for today. There are 5 rooms out of order (OOO).

Required

Develop a simple, unadjusted room count utilizing the given information above.

Solution

Rooms available in hotel		1,000
Occupied last night	950	
Due to check out today	300	
Equals number of stay-overs		650
+ Today's reservations		325
Total rooms committed for today		975
Equals rooms available for sale		25 (with 5 OOO)
Occupancy/ forecast is 975 ÷ 1,000, or 97.5%.		

EXHIBIT 2 A simple, unadjusted room count. This is the first of two sample problems utilizing the same basic information (also see Exhibit 3).

By subtracting committed rooms (650 stay-overs and 325 incoming reservations) from rooms available (1,000 rooms are available despite that 5 rooms are out of order), the reservation manager knows there are 25 rooms available for sale today (1,000 minus 650 minus 325 equals 25).

Compare these results (25 rooms) with the findings from Exhibit 3. Although the same basic information was used for Exhibit 3, the end result is a substantially different room count.

Given

A 1,000-room hotel had a total of 950 rooms occupied last night. Of those 950 rooms, 300 are due to check out today. In addition, there are 325 reservations for today. There are 5 rooms out of order (OOO). Note: This is the same information given in Exhibit 2.

Historical Adjustments

The hotel has developed the following historical adjustment statistics: understays, 6%; overstays, 2%; cancellations, 2%; no-shows, 5%; and early arrivals, 1%.

Required

Develop an adjusted room count utilizing the given information and historical adjustments above.

Solution

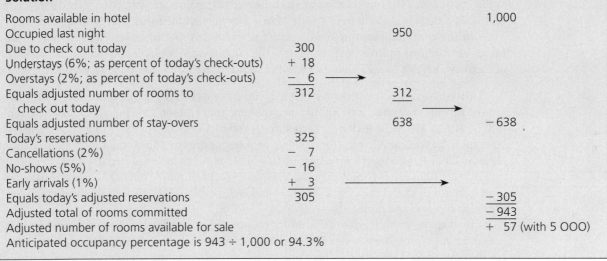

Rooms available in hotel			1,000
Occupied last night		950	
Due to check out today	300		
Understays (6%; as percent of today's check-outs)	+ 18		
Overstays (2%; as percent of today's check-outs)	− 6		
Equals adjusted number of rooms to check out today	312	312	
Equals adjusted number of stay-overs		638	− 638
Today's reservations	325		
Cancellations (2%)	− 7		
No-shows (5%)	− 16		
Early arrivals (1%)	+ 3		
Equals today's adjusted reservations	305		− 305
Adjusted total of rooms committed			− 943
Adjusted number of rooms available for sale			+ 57 (with 5 OOO)
Anticipated occupancy percentage is 943 ÷ 1,000 or 94.3%			

EXHIBIT 3 An adjusted room count. This is the second of two sample problems utilizing the same basic information (see Exhibit 2).

Using the same figures provided in Exhibit 2, this room-count calculation incorporates a series of adjustments. Stay-over rooms, for example, are adjusted by understays (6% of rooms due to check out today) and overstays (2% of rooms due to check out today). Incoming reservations are adjusted by cancellations (2% of today's reservations), no-shows (5% of today's reservations), and early arrivals (1% of today's reservations).

The net result (57 rooms available for sale) is far different from the 25 rooms found in Exhibit 2.

even with the news (think September 11, bed bug infestations, and the state of the economy). Gathering the data is the first step; interpreting it is the second.

Each element in the projection is refined over and over by using additional data and with varying interpretations. Recomputing the count with these adjustments makes a substantial change in room availability (compare Exhibits 2 and 3).

DEFINING ROOMS AVAILABLE   The actual number of hotel rooms available for sale (1,000 rooms for the continuing example shown in Exhibits 2 and 3) varies from day to day. Rooms available for occupancy one day may be closed to occupancy another day. When the reason is unexpected, the removal of such rooms from inventory can have a detrimental effect on the hotel's ability to accommodate reservations.

Rooms removed from availability are categorized either as *out of order* or as *out of inventory*. In either case, when a room is removed from availability, management needs to understand why it is unavailable and how long before it is returned to availability. Short-term repairs (returned to availability the same business day) are defined as out-of-order rooms. Longer repair horizons, or problems which affect guest safety and security, are considered out-of-inventory rooms. Minimizing out-of-inventory rooms is a critical function of rooms management, because they impact the day's occupancy statistic. Too many out-of-inventory rooms may affect management bonuses and even stock prices of publicly traded hotel companies.

Out-of-Order Rooms Out-of-order (OOO) rooms are generally repairable within a short time. A minor problem such as poor TV reception, a clogged toilet, a malfunctioning minibar refrigerator, or a noisy air conditioner will usually classify a room as out of order. Out-of-order rooms pose a special problem to management because in sold-out situations they must be repaired and returned to the market quickly. In periods of low occupancy, management may wait several days before returning such rooms to inventory.

Out-of-order rooms are, by nature, minimally inoperative—the problem that placed the room out of order is slight. When a hotel is close to sold-out, out-of-order rooms are actually sold to the public on an "as is" basis. Management will sell the room with a slight discount to compensate the guest for the inconvenience. (A broken TV set, for example, may warrant a $25 discount, but it is all negotiable. No out-of-order room would ever be sold if it posed a hazard to the guest.

Because OOO rooms can be readily returned to market, they are included in total rooms available for sale. When calculating room count and occupancy statistics, out-of-order rooms are treated as if there is nothing wrong with them—they are included with marketable rooms.

In the continuing example, note that five rooms are out of order. Because out-of-order rooms are counted in inventory, there are still 1,000 rooms available for sale in the hotel. The occupancy of 97.5% (see Exhibit 2) has not changed in the 1,000-room denominator.

Out-of-Inventory Rooms Out-of-inventory (OOI) rooms cannot be sold "as is." Out-of-inventory rooms have significant problems that cannot be repaired quickly. Examples of OOI situations might include a carpet destroyed by flood and drywall in a room, a fire that blackened the walls and left a strong odor, a broken guestroom door lock, an inoperative sliding glass door, or even a criminal investigation in which the police have ordered the room to be sealed until further notice. It is common practice to place blocks of rooms out of inventory during hotel remodeling projects where carpet, window and wall coverings, bathroom tile, and countertops are being repaired and replaced.

By their very nature, out-of-inventory rooms are not marketable. The problem that placed the room out of inventory is significant enough to remove the room from marketability until it has been repaired. These rooms, therefore, are not included in the total figure for rooms available for sale. In calculating room count and occupancy statistics, out-of-inventory rooms are removed from the total of rooms available for sale.

Remember there are five rooms out of order in Exhibits 2 and 3. Out-of-order rooms are not removed from rooms available for sale when calculating room count and occupancy. Out-of-inventory rooms are removed from rooms available, resulting in a change in both the room count and occupancy statistic. To illustrate this point, refer to Exhibit 4. The same ongoing example has one key difference—five OOO rooms have been changed to five OOI rooms.

The distinction between out-of-order and out-of-inventory rooms is an important concept. To further illustrate the point, Exhibit 5 provides three sample problems. Each problem is shown in two parts (a and b). The first part of each problem shows the calculation assuming the rooms were simply out of order. The second part shows a different calculation assuming the rooms were out of inventory. Two of the problems are shown with detailed calculations and final answers. Work through the third problem on your own.

COMPUTING THE NUMBER OF STAY-OVERS To compute the number of stay-overs, the night auditor or guest-service agent begins with the number of rooms occupied last night. Rooms occupied last night is a precise number verified through the hotel's night audit function. Rooms accounted for in front-office records (whether revenue rooms or comp rooms) are counted as occupied last night. Rarely, a situation may exist where the front-office records and the physical house count are off by a room or two. Examples may include a person who acquired a room key through some illegitimate means (usually a hotel employee) or a legitimate guest whose front-office records were not entered into the property management system. Occupied rooms for which the front office has no record are often called *whos*.

Simple, Unadjusted Room Count

Rooms available in hotel		1,000
Less out-of-inventory rooms		5
Equals marketable rooms		995
Occupied last night	950	
Due to check out today	300	
Equals number of stay-overs		650
Plus today's reservations		325
Total rooms committed for today		975
Equals rooms available for sale		20 (with 5 OOI)

Occupancy percentage is 975 ÷ 995, or 98.0%.

Adjusted Room Count

Rooms available in hotel			1,000
Less out-of-inventory rooms			5
Equals marketable rooms			995
Occupied last night		950	
Due to check out today	300		
Understays (6%; as percent of today's check-outs)	+ 18		
Overstays (2%; as percent of today's check-outs)	− 6		
Equals adjusted number of rooms to check out today	312	312	
Equals adjusted number of stay-overs		638	638
Today's reservations	325		
Cancellations (2%)	− 7		
No-shows (5%)	− 16		
Early arrivals (1%)	+ 3		
Equals today's adjusted reservations	305		305
Adjusted total rooms committed for today			943
Adjusted number of rooms available for sale			+ 52 (with 5 OOI)

Anticipated occupancy percentage is 943 ÷ 995, or 94.8%.

EXHIBIT 4 The example continues with one key difference. In this exhibit out-of-order rooms have been changed to out-of-inventory rooms.

Occupancy is calculated by placing rooms available for sale in the denominator of the statistic (rooms sold ÷ rooms available for sale). Because out-of-inventory rooms reduce the number of rooms available for sale, the result is always a higher occupancy statistic. Compare the results above with Exhibits 2 and 3. The same holds true with the sample problems shown in Exhibit 5.

The number of rooms scheduled to check out today is far less precise than the number occupied last night. Rooms due to check out are based primarily on the guests' initial plans at the time they made their reservations. A well-trained guest-service agent reconfirms the departure date during the check-in process. But changes still occur. Corporate guests who complete their business might depart a day or two early. Leisure guests may decide to stay in town a bit longer (or shorter) than originally planned. Emergencies also occur, where guests need to catch the next flight home, regardless of their original intentions.

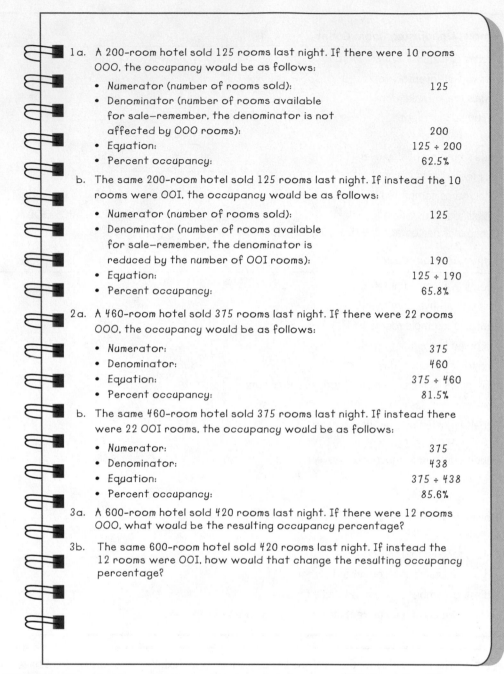

1a. A 200-room hotel sold 125 rooms last night. If there were 10 rooms OOO, the occupancy would be as follows:

- Numerator (number of rooms sold): 125
- Denominator (number of rooms available for sale—remember, the denominator is not affected by OOO rooms): 200
- Equation: 125 ÷ 200
- Percent occupancy: 62.5%

b. The same 200-room hotel sold 125 rooms last night. If instead the 10 rooms were OOI, the occupancy would be as follows:

- Numerator (number of rooms sold): 125
- Denominator (number of rooms available for sale—remember, the denominator is reduced by the number of OOI rooms): 190
- Equation: 125 ÷ 190
- Percent occupancy: 65.8%

2a. A 460-room hotel sold 375 rooms last night. If there were 22 rooms OOO, the occupancy would be as follows:

- Numerator: 375
- Denominator: 460
- Equation: 375 ÷ 460
- Percent occupancy: 81.5%

b. The same 460-room hotel sold 375 rooms last night. If instead there were 22 OOI rooms, the occupancy would be as follows:

- Numerator: 375
- Denominator: 438
- Equation: 375 ÷ 438
- Percent occupancy: 85.6%

3a. A 600-room hotel sold 420 rooms last night. If there were 12 rooms OOO, what would be the resulting occupancy percentage?

3b. The same 600-room hotel sold 420 rooms last night. If instead the 12 rooms were OOI, how would that change the resulting occupancy percentage?

EXHIBIT 5 Out-of-order rooms do not affect inventory (rooms available for sale), while out-of-inventory rooms do. These three examples illustrate the difference this distinction can have on the resulting occupancy percentage. Each example is calculated two ways: First, the occupancy is calculated assuming the rooms were OOO; then the occupancy is recalculated assuming that the rooms were OOI. Try the third example on your own.

Changes, though difficult to project on a guest-by-guest basis, generally form an historical trend over time. Although it is impossible to project if Mr. Jones in room 2144 will stay an extra night, it is somewhat more certain to say that historically 2% of our scheduled check-outs do not depart (they overstay).

Each property collects historical data in order to project understays and overstays. Rather than a constant number of rooms per day, this data is often expressed as a percentage of those rooms scheduled for departure. For example, in Exhibit 3, the understay percentage is 6% (0.06 times 300 rooms due to check out equals 18 understays). The overstay percentage is 2%

(0.02 times 300 rooms due to check out equals six overstays). Although these are both fictitious percentages, a real hotel would develop similar statistical projections over time.

Understays Some guests leave earlier than the hotel expected; they are known as understays (sometimes called *earlys)*. When calculating the number of rooms due to check out, understays are added to the projected check-outs.

Overstays Some guests stay past their scheduled departure date; they are referred to as overstays (sometimes known as *holdovers*). When calculating the number of rooms due to check out, overstays are subtracted from the projected check-outs.

Occupied last night		950
Due to check out today	300	
Plus understays (6%)	+ 18	
Less overstays (2%)	− 6	
Equals adjusted number due to check out today	312	−312
Equals adjusted number of stay-overs		638

By including understays and overstays in the continuing example, the number of rooms due to check out changes substantially. In the simple, unadjusted room count shown in Exhibit 2, the number due to check out today was 300. Once understays and overstays are included in the computation, that number changes to 312. Similarly, the number of stay-overs changes from 650 (in the simple, unadjusted room count; Exhibit 2) to 638 (in the adjusted room count; Exhibit 3).

COMPUTING TODAY'S RESERVATIONS Just as some departing guests change plans and overstay or understay, some of today's arrivals do not adhere to their original reservations. Guests often cancel reservations, arrive a day or two earlier than expected, or never arrive at all. Each of these variables must be assessed and adjusted according to historical data.

No-Shows A guest with a reservation who never arrives is referred to as a no-show. No-shows may result from a change in business or personal plans, inclement weather or closed roads, canceled or stranded flights, illness, or death. It is also possible that they simply forgot they had made a reservation.

No-shows present the hotel with a unique problem—it is difficult to know when to classify the reservation as a no-show. For nonguaranteed reservations, the industry standard is 6 PM. Nonguaranteed reservations that fail to arrive by 6 PM are considered no-shows, and those rooms are sold to walk-in guests.

Guaranteed and advance-deposit reservations are another story, because these types of reservations are held by the hotel all night long. Therefore, it is impossible for a guest-service agent to determine when a guaranteed reservation changes from an expected arrival to a no-show. A reservation that has not arrived by 11 PM, midnight, or 1 AM is probably a no-show. But, there is always a chance the guest has been detained and will still arrive in search of the room.

Asking for an estimated time of arrival at the time of reservation is one partial solution. By documenting the guest's expected arrival time, the hotel is better equipped to make difficult decisions about possible no-show guests. The earlier such decisions are made, the better the hotel's chances of selling the room to a walk-in.

Cancellations Cancellations are infinitely better than no-shows. Guests who cancel on the day of arrival are providing the hotel an opportunity to resell the room. The earlier the cancellation is received, the better the chance of reselling the room.

Cancellation policies may require notice at least 24 hours in advance of the reservation's arrival date. Depending on policy, cancellations made on the day of arrival may be charged one room night. As a courtesy, most corporate hotels allow business guests to cancel, without penalty, until 6 PM the day of arrival.

Early Arrivals   Cancellations and no-shows reduce the number of expected arrivals. Early arrivals increase the number of expected arrivals. Early arrivals are guests who arrive at the hotel one or more days prior to their scheduled reservation date.

There are a number of reasons for this. Maybe the reservations department had a different date for the reservation than the guest understood. Possibly the guest's plans changed and he or she decided to arrive one or more days early. Whatever the reason, the front office should attempt to accommodate the early arrival guest.

Even in periods of 100% occupancy, front-office personnel strive to find accommodations for the early arrival. Not only is that good guest service, but early arrivals often represent a number of room nights to the hotel—many early arrivals stay through the end of their originally scheduled departure. An early arrival who arrives two days early for a three-night reservation may stay all five nights.

Adjusting Today's Reservations   The continuing example in Exhibit 2 shows an unadjusted reservation count of 325 rooms. Assuming a cancellation rate of 2%, a no-show rate of 5%, and an early arrival rate of 1%, the numbers change significantly (see the following table and Exhibit 3):

Today's reservations	325
Less cancellations (2%)	−7
Less no-shows (5%)	−16
Plus early arrivals (1%)	+3
Equals adjusted number of reservations	305

A certain amount of mathematical rounding is necessary to convert these equations into whole numbers (whole rooms). A 2% cancellation rate for 325 reservations results in 6.5 cancellations (rounded to 7). No-shows rounded from 16.25 to 16 and early arrivals rounded from 3.25 to 3.

The Adjusted Result   With all the adjustment components in place, the adjusted room count (57 rooms available for sale; see Exhibit 3) shows a substantial change from the unadjusted room count (25 rooms available for sale; see Exhibit 2). Exhibit 3 could just as easily have projected a change in the opposite direction. Second-guessing the actions of the guest is the reservations department's responsibility. Projections are made from historical data gathered by the property and forecasted on the basis of experience. Data must be accumulated in a chronological fashion, day of the week matching day of the week. It is important for the second Tuesday in April, for instance, to match the second Tuesday in April of last year, irrespective of the calendar dates of those Tuesdays.

Dates do have importance, of course. The Fourth of July holiday is a more important date than the day on which it falls. Similarly, the days before and after such a holiday must be identified with other before and after days of previous years.

At best, the projection is a composite of many previous days and may prove disastrous on any given day. A cautious projection with too few walk-ins accepted results in low occupancy and empty rooms despite guests who were turned away earlier in the day. An optimistic projection accepts so many walk-ins that the reserved guest who arrives late in the day finds no room.

This is the dilemma of overbooking: the need, on the one hand, to maximize occupancy and profits, and the pressure, on the other hand, to keep empty rooms for reservations who may never arrive. Selective overbooking, 5–15% depending on historical experience, is the hotel's major protection against no-shows, double reservations, and "guaranteed reservations" that are never paid.

PUTTING THE ROOM COUNT TO USE   Room forecasting starts with an annual projection and ends with an hourly report. In between are monthly, biweekly, weekly (see Exhibit 6), three-day, and daily forecasts. Ten-day reports (see Exhibit 7) are sometimes used in place of the biweekly projections, but most reservation managers prefer to see two weekends included in a report.

Every department of a hotel uses the room count projections as a tool for labor planning and sales forecasting. Most departments depend on room occupancy for their own volume. This is certainly the situation with valet and laundry, room service, lounges, in-room minibars, and uniformed services.

Hotel at the Greens Weekly Forecast for February 3 to February 9							
	3	4	5	6	7	8	9
Rooms available for sale	1,206	1,206	1,206	1,206	1,206	1,206	1,206
Rooms occupied last night →	1,121	1,190	1,193	890	480	140	611
Less anticipated departures	444	396	530	440	350	55	20
Stay-overs	677	794	663	450	130	85	591
Reservations	498	386	212	25	10	501	552
Estimated out of order	3	3					
Rooms committed	1,178	1,183	875	475	140	586	1,143
Estimated walk-ins	12	10	15	5		25	63
Rooms occupied tonight →	1,190	1,193	890	480	140	611	1,206
Group Arrivals							
National Water Heater Co.	80	140					
Play Tours of America			68				
Chevrolet Western Division					5	183	
PA Library Association						251	396
Chiffo-Garn wedding party							23

EXHIBIT 6 This room-availability forecast demonstrates why statistics that depend on the cumulative results of previous days' forecasts grow less reliable the further the projected horizon. Each day's values build on estimates from previous day's (see arrows). If the actual number of rooms occupied in any preceding day is different than the mathematical base—and it always is—later forecasts become less and less accurate, since they begin with invalid figures.

For example, if the rooms occupied on February 3 are actually less than the 1,190 projected (less because of fewer walk-ins, more understay departures, etc.), then the rooms occupied on February 4 will also be lower than projected. The count for February 4 is based upon the number of rooms occupied the night before (1,190). If the count for February 4 is lower than projected, then the count for February 5, 6, 7, and so on may also be lower than projected.

Housekeeping's schedule is clearly a function of room sales. So, too, are the number of breakfasts served correlated with the previous night's room count. Early scheduling of shifts and days off helps build good employee relations, and the two-week forecast is generally used for that purpose. A two-week lead time may be required in hotels covered by union contracts.

The reservations department has its closest partnership with marketing and sales. Without that alliance, the property has little opportunity to maximize yield management. For example, how many discounted rooms has the sales department committed to wholesalers during a high-occupancy (thus, high-rate) period? The marketing department should be able to help reservations forecast no-shows, walk-ins, early arrivals, and so on, as they pertain to a particular group. Group adjustments differ from adjustments for individual guests and vary from group to group.

Periodic Recounts The longer the period between the preparation of the forecast and its use, the less reliable it is. Without periodic updating, all the departments, but especially the desk, act on information that is no longer accurate. The three-day forecast permits a final push for sales and a tightening of labor schedules throughout the property to maximize occupancy and minimize costs.

By the time hourly projections are being made, responsibility has moved entirely to the front office. Overbooking problems, additional reservations, walk-ins, and stay-overs are being resolved by front-office personnel.

Periodic or hourly forecasts improve the system in two ways. Obviously, the information is more current (see Exhibits 6 and 7). Less obvious is the increased accuracy in percentage adjustments as the day wears on. If 80% of all the check-outs are usually gone by noon, a better

Occupancy Forecast Report

Santa Rae Ranch
Ann Parker

Occupancy Forecast Report
For the Period from 03-JAN- to 12-JAN-
Percentages Include Out-of-Order and Off-Market Rooms
Percentages Exclude Tentative Group Rooms

	FRI JAN-03	SAT JAN-04	SUN JAN-05	MON JAN-06	TUE JAN-07	WED JAN-08	THUR JAN-09	FRI JAN-10	SAT JAN-11	SUN JAN-12
Total Rooms	236	236	236	236	236	236	236	236	236	236
– OOO	3	2	3	3	2	2	3	1	1	0
– OFF	0	0	0	0	0	0	0	0	0	0
Rooms Available	233	234	233	233	234	234	233	235	235	236
Rooms Occupied	94	90	83	44	33	27	21	30	42	27
– Non-Group Departures	11	18	34	14	4	5	17	2	13	4
– Group Departures	12	3	14	1	2	2	0	1	5	4
+ Non-Group Arrivals	18	13	9	4	0	1	15	14	3	0
+ Group Arrivals	1	1	0	0	0	0	12	0	0	0
Net In-House	90	83	44	33	27	21	31	41	27	19
+ Estimated Pickup	0	0	0	0	0	0	0	2	2	2
+ Excess Committed	82	60	1	0	0	0	19	9	14	0
+ Tentative Grp Rooms	5	0	0	0	0	0	2	0	0	0
Net Rooms Reserved	172	143	45	33	27	21	50	52	43	21
Net Rooms Available	61	91	188	200	207	213	183	183	192	215
Non-Group										
Projected Revenue	7113.00	6527.50	3438.50	2757.50	2446.00	1810.00	1341.88	4265.37	3415.99	2913.49
Avg. Rate	103.09	101.99	88.17	95.09	97.84	86.19	70.63	137.59	162.67	171.38
Group (Reserved)										
Projected Revenue	1064.00	965.00	221.00	175.00	47.50	0.00	1148.00	1100.50	590.00	190.00
Avg. Rate	50.67	50.79	44.20	43.75	23.75	0.00	95.67	100.05	98.33	95.00
Group (Excess Committed)										
Estimated Revenue	5340.00	3925.00	20.00	0.00	0.00	0.00	1945.00	845.00	1280.00	0.00
Avg. Rate	61.38	65.42	20.00	0.00	0.00	0.00	92.62	93.89	91.43	0.00
Group (Tentative)										
Estimated Revenue	375.00	0.00	0.00	0.00	0.00	0.00	150.00	0.00	0.00	0.00
Avg. Rate	75.00	0.00	0.00	0.00	0.00	0.00	75.00	0.00	0.00	0.00

Occupancy Forecast Report

	TEN/DEF	FRI JAN-03	SAT JAN-04	SUN JAN-05	MON JAN-06	TUE JAN-07	WED JAN-08	THUR JAN-09	FRI JAN-10	SAT JAN-11
Group (Totals)										
Projected Revenue	6779.00	4890.00	241.00	175.00	47.50	0.00	3243.00	1945.50	1870.00	190.00
Avg. Rate	59.99	61.90	40.17	43.75	23.75	0.00	92.66	97.28	93.50	95.00
Totals										
Projected Revenue	13892.00	11417.50	3679.50	2932.50	2493.50	1810.00	4584.88	6210.87	5285.99	3103.49
Avg. Rate	76.33	79.84	81.77	88.86	92.35	86.19	84.91	121.78	128.93	163.34
% Occupancy Reserved	38.63	35.47	18.88	14.16	11.54	8.97	13.30	17.45	11.49	8.05
% Including Commits	73.82	61.11	19.31	14.16	11.54	8.97	21.46	21.28	17.45	8.05
American Building Consult	DEF	30/0	20/0							
Bavarian Bakeoff	*DEF	0/1								
Bob's Bablo Island Tour	*DEF	5/4	0/3							
Brady Tours	DEF							5/0		
Cardinal Group	DEF	1/0	1/0	1/0						
Cups & China	DEF	10/0								
Honda	DEF							25/11	20/11	20/6
MIPS	DEF	6/5	5/5							
Micro Data	TEN							2/0		
Presentations Now	DEF	5/0	5/0							
Sky Line Displays	TEN	5/0								
Clowns Inc	DEF	25/2	25/2							
US Water Polo Team	DEF	12/1	12/1							

* This group's commitments must be cleaned up or all availability reports will be out of balance.

EXHIBIT 7 This computerized reservation forecast report displays a 10-day view of rooms activity. It details arrival and departure projections for individual as well as group rooms. Usually, such forecast reports also provide an estimate of each day's anticipated rooms revenues. (Note that unlike the treatment suggested by the authors, this example shows out-of-order rooms reducing rooms available.) *Courtesy of Geac Computers, Inc., Tustin, California.*

guess of understays and overstays can be made at noon each day than at 7 AM. Similar refinements are possible with cancellation percentages, no-show factors, and so on. It is possible to improve the accuracy of no-show forecasts by separating the total reservations into three categories—advance deposit, guaranteed, and nonguaranteed—before applying a different no-show percentage to each.

Adjusting by Reservation Quality   The adjusted room count can be improved even further by segregating reservations by quality. The quality of a reservation correlates with its likelihood of no-show. Higher-quality advance deposits and guaranteed reservations have lower no-show statistics than nonguaranteed reservations.

It is more accurate to maintain historical projections for each type of reservation rather than taking a 5% no-show factor across all 325 reservations. Assume that 20% of nonguaranteed reservations are no-shows, 4% of guaranteed reservations are no-shows, and 1% of advance deposits are no-shows. The total number of no-shows would now change from 16 in Exhibit 3 to 28. This is calculated by taking 20% of 100 nonguaranteed reservations (20), plus 4% of 175 guaranteed reservations (7), plus 1% of 50 advance-deposit reservations (0.5 rounds up to 1). See the table below.

Today's nonguaranteed reservations	100	
Today's guaranteed reservations	175	
Today's advance-deposit reservations	50	
Equals today's reservations	325	325
Less cancellations nonguaranteed reservations (0%)	−0	
Less cancellations guaranteed reservations (4%)	−7	
Less cancellations advance-deposit reservations (3%)	−2	
Equals total cancellations	−9	−9
Less no-shows nonguaranteed reservations (20%)	−20	
Less no-shows guaranteed reservations (4%)	−7	
Less no-shows advance-deposit reservations (1%)	−1	
Equals total no-shows	−28	−28
Plus early arrivals (1%)		+3
Equals today's adjusted reservations		291

Accuracy can also be improved by attention to the character of the market. The type of group clues the reservations department to the no-show projection. For example, teachers are very dependable. Tour groups are nearly always full because volume is as important to the tour operator as to the hotel. That generalization must then be balanced by knowledge about specific tour companies. Allocations versus utilization should be computed individually on wholesalers, incentive houses, associations, and other group movers.

Market research may prove that bookings from certain localities are more or less reliable. Variations would depend on transportation, weather, distance, and the kind of guest the hotel is attracting, water park visitors, for example (see Exhibit 8). Commercial guests have a different degree of dependability than tourists, who differ again from conventioneers. A large permanent or extended-stay guest population needs to be recognized in any computations involving stay-overs and anticipated departures.

Cancellations are also correlated with the quality of the reservation. Cancellations are more common with guaranteed and advance-deposit reservations, because such guests have an incentive to call and cancel (it will save them a no-show charge). Cancellations are less common with nonguaranteed reservations. The guest has nothing to lose with the nonguaranteed reservation, because the reservation is basically a courtesy hold until 6 PM. Few guests take the time to notify the hotel that they are not arriving when they have a 6 PM hold (nonguaranteed) reservation. In our continuing example (Exhibit 3), assume 0% of all nonguaranteed reservations call to cancel, 4% of guaranteed reservations cancel, and 3% of advance-deposit reservations cancel. The total number of cancellations changes from 7 to 9. This is calculated by taking 0% of 100 nonguaranteed reservations (0), plus 4% of 175 guaranteed reservations (7), plus 3% of 50 advance-deposit reservations (1.5 rounds up to 2).

EXHIBIT 8 Indoor water parks are one of the latest trends hoteliers are using to boost reservations and occupancy levels. Indoor water parks attached to hotels were once confined to the upper Midwest, where they offered a warm local retreat from the cold Wisconsin and Minnesota winters (shown here is the Grand Lodge in Minneapolis). Today they are popping up everywhere, with projects underway in such sunny states as Texas, Arizona, and California—and being constructed by such hotel chains as Hilton, Holiday Inn, and even Super 8!

In 2000, there were fewer than 25 indoor water parks attached to hotels, measured at 2,500 square feet or larger. By the end of 2011, that number had climbed to well over 225. They are expensive to build and operate, with construction costs running more than double the cost per square foot of conventional hotel swimming pools. But they work well in attracting local families to spend a night or even a weekend. Many properties claim the indoor water parks increased their hotel occupancies by 10% per year, an increase that dwarfs the overall industry growth rate.   *Courtesy: Wirth Companies, Brooklyn Center, Minnesota.*

OVERBOOKING

Even when hotel records show 100% occupancy, there are usually a few unoccupied rooms in the hotel. The hotel shows 100% occupancy because it has sold every available room, not necessarily because every available room is physically occupied. Rooms held for guaranteed reservations provide revenue in the form of no-show charges even when the guest fails to arrive. The *perfect fill* or the *perfect sell-out* occurs when every available room is physically occupied.

The Perfect Fill

Reaching the perfect fill is a challenge because guests are notoriously undependable. To compensate for this lack of dependability, hotel managers sell more reservations than the number of rooms physically available. Look back at the five adjustments covered in the first half of this chapter: overstays, understays, cancellations, no-shows, and early arrivals. These adjustments are designed to compensate for guest behavior by second-guessing the guest and selling more reservations than the number of rooms physically available. The difference between Exhibit 3 (57 rooms available for sale) and Exhibit 2 (25 rooms available for sale) is 32 rooms—32 more reservations than the number of rooms physically available.

Look at the strategy differently. Selling the exact number of rooms physically available in the hotel would be a mistake, adjustments resulting in more available rooms (no-shows, cancellations, and understays far outweigh adjustments requiring additional rooms (overstays and early arrivals). So managers oversell, that is, *overbook*, their properties.

Overbooking is standard practice in the lodging industry as it is in the airline industry. Overbooking means that a hotel knowingly sells more reservations than it has rooms available. When a hotel overbooks a sold-out date, it is taking a calculated risk that more guests will

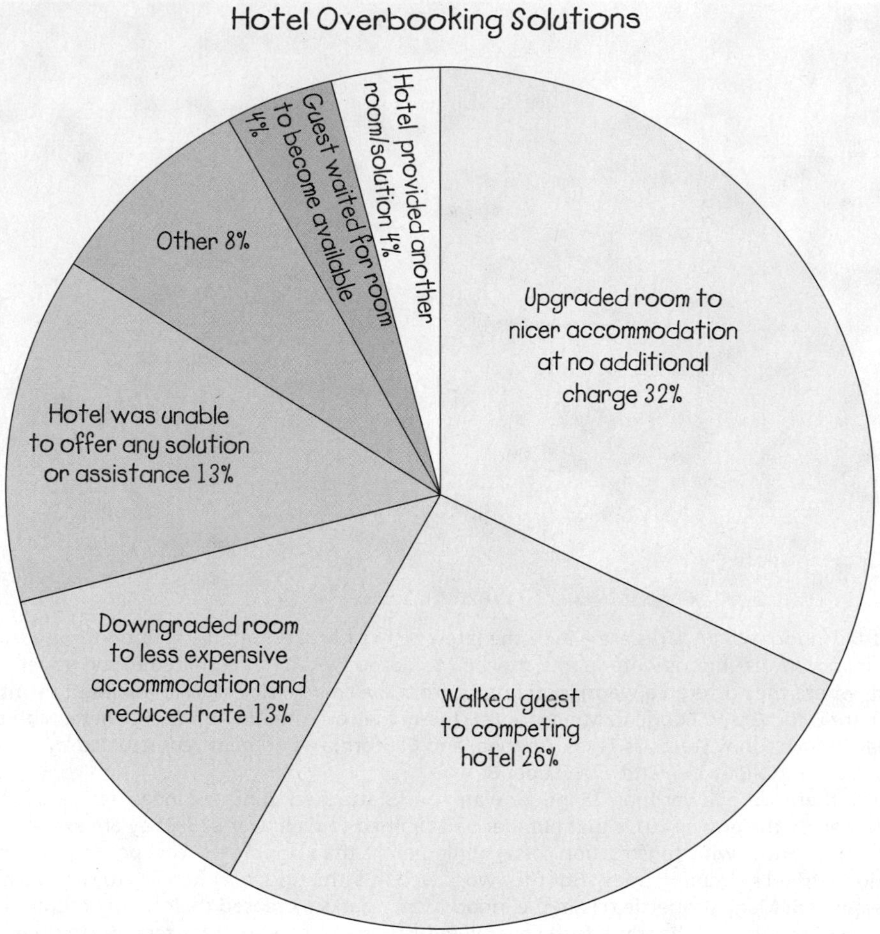

Hotel Overbooking Solutions

Pie chart segments:
- Hotel provided another room/solution 4%
- Guest waited for room to become available 4%
- Other 8%
- Hotel was unable to offer any solution or assistance 13%
- Downgraded room to less expensive accommodation and reduced rate 13%
- Walked guest to competing hotel 26%
- Upgraded room to nicer accommodation at no additional charge 32%

EXHIBIT 9 In a survey designed by American Express Travel Trends Monitor, an amazing 22.0% of all travelers stated they have arrived at a hotel with confirmed reservations only to find the hotel did not have a room available for them (or did not have the exact room type originally reserved). As a follow-up to that question, travelers were asked how their particular situation was handled; that information is shown in the pie-chart above.

Note that many of these overbooking problems were handled internally because other room types were available to accommodate the guest (solved by either upgrading the guest to a nicer room at no additional charge or downgrading the room type and adjusting the guest's rate accordingly). But a dismal 13% of these situations were poorly handled because the overbooked hotels were "unable to offer assistance." *Source: American Express Travel Trends Monitor.*

understay, cancel, or no-show than the number of rooms by which the hotel has overbooked. A conservative overbooking policy rarely places the hotel in a compromising situation. More aggressive overbooking, however, can force both the hotel and the unlucky guest(s) into an unpleasant scenario. (See Exhibit 9).

Reservations Are Legal Contracts

Courts consider room reservations to be legal contracts. The request constitutes the offer, and the promise of accommodations represents the acceptance. Either the promise to pay or the actual transfer of a deposit is the third important element of a contract: consideration. Such promises may be verbal (as with a telephone confirmation) or written (as with an e-mail or letter of confirmation.[1] All the elements of a binding contract are in place.

---

[1]Hotel reservations are legal contracts whether they are oral (see *Dold* v. *Outrigger Hotel and Hawaii Hotels Operating Company*, 1972) or in writing (see *Rainbow Travel Service, Inc.* v. *Hilton Hotels Corp.*, 1990). Although most cases show damaged customers or tour operators suing hotels for overbooking, hotels have also been known to sue guests for their failure to arrive (*King of Prussia Enterprises, Inc.* v. *Greyhound Lines, Inc.*, 1978).

If one party breaches the contract, the innocent party should be compensated for the injury. However, for many years, recovery by either party has generally been limited to the natural or expected costs that the parties anticipated at the time of the agreement.

There have been few legal cases involving breach of reservation contract. There is little to be gained by bringing suit. If the guest breaches the contract by failing to show up for the room, the hotel may have an opportunity to resell the accommodation. Even if the room cannot be resold, the monetary loss to the hotel is minimal. Similarly, if the hotel breaches the reservation contract by failing to provide a room, the guest is free to seek accommodations elsewhere. Even if a room cannot be found, the actual cost to the guest is still quite small (possibly limited to taxi fares and time spent making telephone calls in search of alternative accommodations). And courts have not been willing to compensate the guest for inconvenience and depression.

In very few cases (usually involving group reservations or tour operators) have negligence or fraud in room reservations been alleged and then proven. The threat remains, however, especially for those hotels that overbook as a matter of operational policy. If the complaining guest can show that the hotel consistently overbooked, there might be adequate grounds to recover in a tort action.

This is also true in cases where the plaintiff can demonstrate foreseeable damage. For example, if the hotel overbooked and walked the guest during a sold-out period in the city (say, during the Olympics or the World Series, if either were being held in the city), the hotel could reasonably foresee the difficulty the guest would have in finding an alternative room. After exhausting all possibilities, if the guest decided to sleep in his or her car and was subsequently attacked and harmed, the hotel might be found liable for significant damages.

THREAT OF LEGISLATION   In the early 1980s, the Federal Trade Commission (FTC) threatened to legislate hotel overbooking, as it did airline overbooking. Having witnessed the restrictive regulations the government placed on airlines, the hotel industry took quick action. The hotel industry lobbied the FTC to allow lodging chains and individual properties the freedom to develop their own internal overbooking policies. Policies in place today look remarkably similar across the industry (see Exhibit 10).

State Legislation   In response to consumer outcry, many state attorneys general have mandated certain hotel industry overbooking practices. Florida, for example, has enacted such legislation. In addition to monetary penalties, Florida law requires the hotel to reimburse guests for prepaid reservations whether paid directly to the hotel or to a travel agency. New York and Georgia have legislated refunds for unaccommodated guests. Pennsylvania, Michigan, and Florida permit punitive damages. Hawaii, Puerto Rico, and others have enacted eviction laws permitting the physical ejection of guests who overstay their reservation. This puts the ball in the hotel's court. No longer can the excuse for overbooking be laid on stay-over guests.

Whose Fault?   The fault for overbooking is not the hotel industry's alone. Tour operators, convention housing committees, and individual guests are all to blame. Each, the hotel included, attempts to maximize its own position at the risk of overbooking.

Tour operators negotiate room commitments with hotels months in advance. Yet no one knows exactly how many rooms the tour operator will fill on any given night. Convention executives tend to overstate the number of rooms their event will require as a strategy for obtaining better room rates. To forecast the group's room pick-up rate more accurately, hotels share previous years' histories with each other. The group is also encouraged to adjust its room count periodically over the weeks and days before the event, because the group will often be charged an attrition fee for each unsold room.

Guests are probably the most to blame. Guests are known to make reservations in more than one hotel and, if they do show, change their length of stay without notifying the desk. Second-guessing guests' moves means occasional overbooking will occur, no matter how carefully statistics and previous experiences are projected.

OVERBOOKING POLICIES   The burden of *walking* an arriving guest—sending that person to another hotel—falls to the room/guest-service agent (see Exhibit 11). Too often management leaves it at that, making no provision to train the agent. Where this is a frequent affair, the staff grows immune to the protests and even finds a bit of humor in walking one guest after the other.

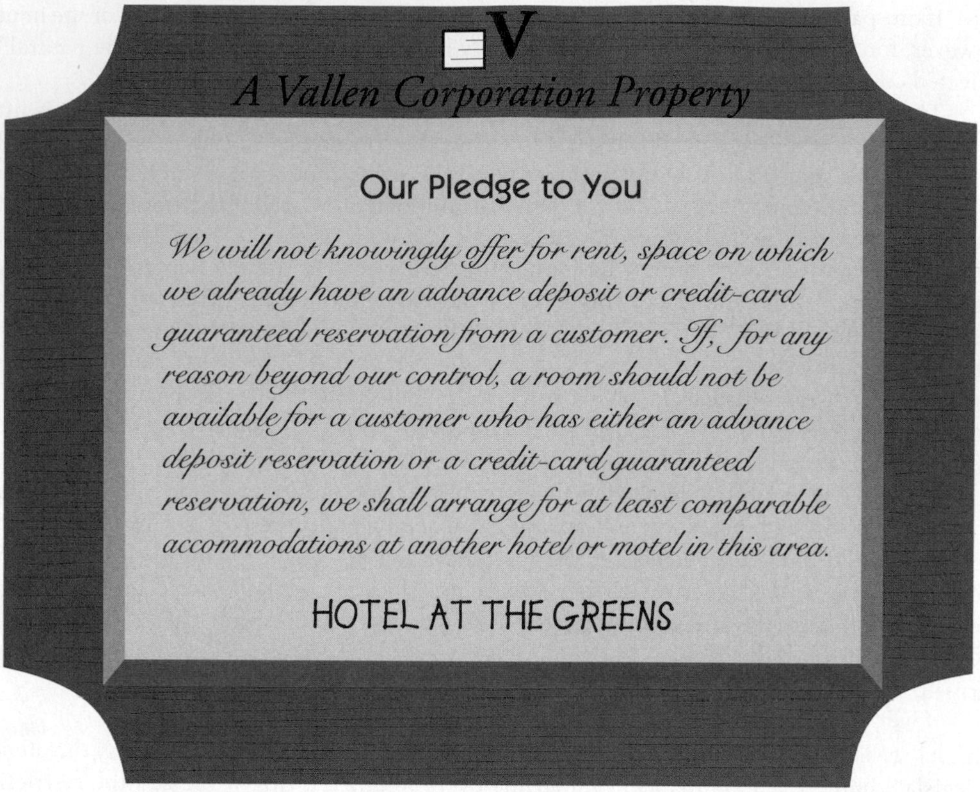

A Vallen Corporation Property

Our Pledge to You

We will not knowingly offer for rent, space on which we already have an advance deposit or credit-card guaranteed reservation from a customer. If, for any reason beyond our control, a room should not be available for a customer who has either an advance deposit reservation or a credit-card guaranteed reservation, we shall arrange for at least comparable accommodations at another hotel or motel in this area.

HOTEL AT THE GREENS

EXHIBIT 10 Nonoverbooking pledge. The American Hotel & Lodging Association encourages all hotels to adopt similar policies. Reading between the lines, this pledge allows the hotel to overbook nonguaranteed (6 PM) reservations. That makes sense, in light of the extremely high no-show rate associated with nonguaranteed or "courtesy hold" reservations. According to this pledge, however, guaranteed and advance deposit reservations are not to be oversold. *Courtesy of the American Hotel & Lodging Association, Washington, D.C.*

EXHIBIT 11 An overbooked hotel is no laughing matter!

In doing so, the staff reflects the apparent attitude of an unconcerned management. The situation should never be treated lightly, even if a number of guests were walked that day.

No matter how well managed a hotel is, or no matter how well it made the forecasts, overbooking will occur. Preplanning for overbooking reduces guest irritation and even offers some chance of retaining business. Arranging substitute accommodations elsewhere is what the clerk should do. Providing the training to anticipate the incident is what management should do. Preparation includes preliminary calls to neighboring properties as the situation becomes obvious. Many smaller properties depend on this type of overflow business. Affiliated properties usually refer each other before overflowing rooms to competitors—even to the extent that a full-service chain property may walk guests to one of the same chain's budget operations and vice versa.

Managers need to be alert to unethical practices involving walked rooms. Some properties give a commission or kickback to clerks of oversold properties when they walk guests their way. Even though the oversold hotel may specify to which properties guests can be walked, $10 or $20 from a competing operation is incentive enough to disregard the rule. Some unethical clerks have been known to refer walk-in customers to the other hotel even when rooms remain available at their own property.

Overbooking and the Antiservice Syndrome   While the majority of hotels prepare their employees to handle oversold days, poorly managed properties place the "blame" on the guest. The classic antiservice approach for an overbooked situation is to act as if the reservation never existed. The guest-service agent's pretense is what guests find so frustrating. To play out the charade, the clerk consults with coworkers, types on the computer, and pretends to check racks and other resources. Finally comes a proclamation—there is no reservation! And therefore the hotel has no further responsibility.

It is this cavalier attitude that concerns the industry. A few highly publicized incidents could renew the FTC's interest in industrywide legislation. Although the great majority of hotels have established fair and consistent overbooking policies, these are voluntary guidelines. Websites have done the same (see Exhibit 12).

Sample Cancellation Policies for Discount Travel Websites

Discount Travel Site	Change/Cancellation Policy
Expedia.com	• Changes or cancellations are charged a $25 fee. • Cancellations or changes within 72 hours of time of arrival are charged a one-night fee.
Hotels.com	• Changes or cancellations are charged a $10 fee (recently reduced from a previous $50 fee).
Hotwire.com	• Changes or cancellations are not an option—all hotel reservations are final.
Lowestravel.com	• Changes or cancellations are always charged a fee, but the exact fee depends partly on what the hotel's individual policy requires.
Orbitz.com	• Changes or cancellations are charged no fee (other than what the hotel's individual policy requires).
Quikbook.com	• Changes or cancellations are charged no fee (other than what the hotel's individual policy requires).
Travelocity.com	• Changes or cancellations are charged a $10 fee. • Cancellations or changes within 72 hours of time of arrival are charged a one-night fee.
Trip.com	• Changes or cancellations are charged no fee (other than what the hotel's individual policy requires).

EXHIBIT 12   A sampling of hotel reservation cancellation policies for some of the biggest names in travel Websites. One of the most punitive aspects of making such reservations is the 72-hour cancellation policy shared by several discount travel sites. Customers should be very certain they know their travel plans before making such reservations.

Forecasting Availability and Overbooking

No-Show Policies   Hotels overbook, in part, to compensate for no-shows—guests with reservations who neither arrive nor cancel. Industrywide, no-shows run about 8%; they can reach as high as 25% in some cities on occasion.

There is a direct correlation between no-shows and the types of reservations a hotel accepts. Lower-quality, nonguaranteed reservations have the highest rate of no-show. As such, hotels have become less willing to accept nonguaranteed reservations (see Exhibit 13). When nonguaranteed reservations don't show, the hotel is left with no revenue except for reselling the room to a walk-in guest after the 6 PM hold. No-shows with guaranteed or advance-deposit reservations, on the other hand, do provide the hotel with revenue.

Guests with guaranteed or advance-deposit reservations are penalized for failing to cancel (or use) their reservation. Hotels usually charge the cost of one room night (one room night plus tax is the amount normally requested for an advance deposit). For advance deposits, it is a simple

Managing Your No-Shows

 Accept only guaranteed or advance-deposit reservations. Accept few nonguaranteed reservations.

 All reservations guaranteed against credit cards should be carefully documented—name, card number, expiration, security code (CCID Number), and billing address. Consider charging the card during the reservation to ensure its accuracy.

 The hotel faxes, scans, e-mails, or downloads the form to the guest for signature, and once the form has been returned, the guaranteed reservation becomes activated.

 To minimize clerical errors, train reservationists always restate reservation details: room type, dates of arrival and departure, rate, applicable discounts, and all other pertinent information before finalizing the reservation.

 Be certain reservationists explain the hotel's cancellation and no-show charge policy with each and every reservation. Some hotels go so far as to have reservationists initial a computer screen field after these policies have been explained to the guest.

 Provide guests a confirmation number and recommend that they keep this number in their records.

 Fax, email, scan, or mail confirmation to ensure all information has been provided to the guest.

 In the event a no-show or cancellation fee is charged, the hotel should immediately send a copy of the charge to the guest via fax, email, or mail.

 Guests who cancel in an appropriate timeframe should be provided a distinct cancellation number and be advised to keep the number on file.

EXHIBIT 13   Well-operated hotels take active steps toward reducing their incidence of overbooking. One of the primary catalysts for overbooking is the negative impact hotels experience from no-show rooms. Here are some steps designed to minimize no-shows while maximizing the hotel's chances of recovering rooms revenue from no-show guests.

matter for the hotel to claim the deposit. With guaranteed reservations, the process is less certain. Collecting against guaranteed reservations can be difficult when guests are unwilling to pay the charge against their credit card or corporate account. This disagreement often results in a fight between the guest and the hotel over the amount of one night's lodging. Even when the hotel wins, it loses, because the guest may forever be lost as a customer. Exhibit 13 illustrates the steps a well-operated hotel should take to ensure no-show revenues are properly collected.

Cancellation Policies   Cancellation policies are another source of guest irritation. After taking the time to contact the hotel and cancel the reservation, guests may be told they will still be charged one room night. Cancellation policies differ by chain, hotel, market, and destination. The cancellation policy adopted by a hotel often reflects the quantity of walk-ins it has experienced. Liberal cancellation policies allow the guest to cancel until 6 PM on the day of arrival. Such policies are generally found at corporate and chain-affiliated properties. In contrast, many resorts and isolated destination properties mandate more stringent cancellation policies. Some request notification 24–48 hours in advance. Others require as much as 7–14 days notice. Still other resorts completely restrict cancellations, notifying the guest of the policy and then charging the full stay at the time of reservation, with no refunds available.

The major credit-card companies mandate cancellation times for properties that guarantee reservations against their cards. Discover, MasterCard, and VISA all require properties to accept cancellations until 6 PM on the day of arrival (resort operations are given the option of requiring cancellations up to three hours earlier). American Express and Diners Club understand that different markets may require different cancellation policies. These two companies allow hotels to establish their own cancellation times, provided that the hotels clearly explain the policies and procedures to guests at the time of reservation. And oral descriptions are not necessarily sufficient. VISA, for one, requires written notice of cancellation policies for reservations made at least 72 hours in advance. Exhibit 14 charts the policies of the several credit-card companies.

Minimizing the Overbooking Problem

There are no perfect solutions to the problem of overbooking. As long as hotels overbook to compensate for no-shows and last-minute changes in occupancy, there will be walked guests. The answer is found not in eliminating overbooking as a management tool but in minimizing the need to overbook on most occasions.

Unfortunately, guests want the best of both worlds. They want the flexibility to understay or overstay as plans change, but they also want liberal cancellation and no-show policies for the times when they don't arrive. This leaves the hotel in a difficult position. If it charges a no-show guest for the unoccupied room night, the guest might never return to the hotel. If the hotel refuses a request for an overstay or tries to charge a fee to an early-departing understay, it may also create ill will. The answer is proving to be found in more restrictive reservations policies and third-party involvement.

INCREASINGLY RESTRICTIVE POLICIES   Certainly, the airlines are strict about their flight policies. Most tickets are nonrefundable and must be paid at the time of reservation. Courtesy (nonguaranteed) hold on reservations usually expire within 24 hours of the time they were made. No-show guests (and cancellations) face $100 "change" fees when they attempt to reuse their tickets. Unused tickets are only valid a year.

The lodging industry is slowly beginning to adopt similar policies. Merely adopting such reform, however, is not enough. The airlines went through a long period of passenger education. The lodging industry will have a somewhat easier time educating their guests (because the airlines already broke much of the ground). Competition between chains will surely affect the success of industrywide reservations policies reform.

Slowly, such changes are taking place. One chain puts its toe in the water, and soon another follows suit. Yield management "fences" (nonrefundable reservations, 21-day advanced purchase, and stay over Saturday night) are some of the first toes. Early departure charges are also being tested.

Early Departure Fees   Several major lodging chains, including Starwood, Hyatt, and Hilton, have recently experimented with early departure charges. Such fees are designed to make

Credit-Card Company

	American Express	Diners Club	Discover Card (Novus)	MasterCard	VISA
Name of guaranteed reservations program	Assured Reservations	Confirmed Reservation Plan	Guaranteed Reservation Service	Guaranteed Reservations	VISA Reservation Service
No-show charge policy	Will support no-show charge if "assured reservation no-show" is written on signature line	Will support no-show charge if "confirmed reservation—no-show" is written on signature line	Will support no-show charge if "no-show" is written on signature line	Will support no-show charge if "guaranteed reservation/no-show" is written on signature line	Will support no-show charge if "no-show" is written on signature line
Cancellation policy	Property may determine its own cancellation times	Cancellations by 6 PM (4 PM for resorts) on day of arrival	Cancellations by 6 PM (property may select up to three hours earlier) on day of arrival	Property may determine its own cancellation times	Cancellations by 6 PM if reservation made in past 72 hours; otherwise, property may set its own policy
Overbooking policy	Property must: • Provide and pay for room in comparable hotel for one night • Provide one 3-minute call • Forward guest contacts to new hotel	Property must: • Provide and pay for room in comparable or better hotel for one night • Provide one 3-minute call • Provide transportation to new hotel	Property must: • Provide and pay for room in comparable hotel for one night • Provide one 3-minute call (if requested) • Forward guest contacts to new hotel • Provide transportation to new hotel	Property must: • Provide and pay for room in another hotel for one night • Provide one 3-minute call • Provide transportation to new hotel • Neither hotel can charge guest. Hotel 1 pays Hotel 2.	Property must: • Provide and pay for room in comparable or better hotel for one night • Provide one 3-minute call • Forward guest contacts to new hotel • Provide transportation to new hotel

EXHIBIT 14 Third-party reservation guarantees are supported by the major domestic credit-card companies. If the room is guaranteed and the guest does not cancel within the established parameters, the hotel has the right to receive compensation for one night's stay. Of course, this means that the hotel must hold the room available for the guest until check-out time the following day. As long as hotels abide by the policies established by each credit-card company, they will be upheld by the credit-card companies in all but the most unusual customer chargeback disputes.

guests think twice before departing early. Early departure fees are also expected to improve the accuracy of the reservation on the front end; once aware of an early departure penalty, guests will probably be more conservative in estimating the number of nights they plan to stay.

As with cancellation and no-show policies, early departure or understay fees must be clearly detailed at the time of reservation booking. Credit-card companies expect properties to explain the policy in detail, include a comment about the policy with mailed confirmations, and have guests sign a statement reiterating the standard during the check-in process. When these procedures are followed, credit-card companies generally support the hotel with regard to guest disputes and chargebacks (see Exhibits 13 and 14).

THIRD-PARTY GUARANTEES   There is some logic in removing the hotel from direct involvement with the guest when fees or penalties are involved. It is easier for the hotel to charge a credit-card company or travel agent the no-show than to assess it directly against the guest or the guest's corporate account. Although the guest still pays the charge in the end, the hotel is one step removed from the negative connotations associated with collecting such fees.

Trip Insurance   The increasing popularity of trip or travel insurance is predicated on this same logic. By placing a third party into the picture, some of the negative feelings associated with paying a penalty fee are assigned elsewhere and the hotel looks a little less the bad guy.

Although less common in the United States, travel insurance is quite popular in Europe. Some explanation about the benefits associated with travel insurance is provided at the time of reservation, or is mailed with the confirmation. The benefits are simple enough: For a small fee, a third party becomes responsible for cancellation, no-show, understay, or reservation change fees assessed for a given trip. The reasons for guests changing their plans are usually described with the insurance and may include illness, death, a change in business plans, or even inclement weather. Some of the more popular companies offering travel insurance include HTH Worldwide, TravelGuard, Travel Safe, and Access America.

Credit-Card Disputes   When the hotel charges a guaranteed no-show against the guest's credit card, it may be the start of a potentially long process of guest disputes. Such disputes place the credit-card company in a third-party position between the hotel and the guest. The dispute starts when the guest contacts the credit card's customer service department claiming, "I never made the reservation" or "I canceled that reservation days in advance."

Once the claim has been made, the third-party credit-card company issues a temporary credit to the guest and an offsetting debit to the hotel. Temporarily, the guest does not have to pay the charge and the hotel does not receive the income.

At this point, the guest's statement is copied to the hotel and the property has an opportunity to respond. Many hotels stop at this point, believing that the case will never be settled in their favor or that the revenue is not worth the hassle. If the hotel chooses not to respond, the guest automatically wins the decision. Even when the hotel does respond, the case is still found in favor of the guest much of the time. Some critics believe that credit-card companies uphold the guests because they want to retain their customers. That is really not the case; if the hotel follows the credit-card company's standard procedure, it should never lose a chargeback dispute (see Exhibit 14).

Best Western, for example, always provides separate confirmation and cancellation numbers (unlike some chains, which simply add an "X" to the confirmation number to signify cancellation). In this way, Best Western can insist that the credit-card company ask the guest to provide the cancellation number. No cancellation number (I lost it, I threw it away, they never gave me a number), no excuse. Similarly, Best Western does not accept the excuse, "I never made the reservation." As a company, they find that excuse questionable—after all, how did the chain get the guest's name, address, phone number, and credit-card number?

Travel Agent Guarantees   A different type of third-party guarantee utilizes the travel agent. When a guest makes the reservation through a travel agent, the hotel removes itself from dealing directly with the customer. In the event of a no-show, the hotel receives payment directly from the travel agent. Whether or not the travel agent then charges the no-show customer is the travel agent's problem.

The only drawback of this system is that the hotel must have a credit relationship with the travel agent. In today's fast-paced travel environment, there is rarely enough lead time for the travel agent to send a check and for the hotel to clear the funds.

ADVANCE-DEPOSIT RESERVATIONS Probably the best of all methods for reducing the industrywide problem of overbooking is to encourage advance deposits. Advance-deposit reservations (also known as paid-in-advance reservations) have historically maintained the lowest percentage of no-shows. Guests who pay a substantial amount in advance (usually the first-night's room charge, although some resorts charge the entire payment up front) have a strong motive to arrive as scheduled.

Advance-deposit reservations require an extra clerical step not found with other reservation trackings. If the guest responds by sending a deposit, the reservation must be changed from tentative to confirmed. If the guest doesn't respond, the reservation office must either send a reminder or cancel the reservation. Sending a reminder starts the tracking process all over again.

Handling the money, usually a check, involves bank deposits, sometimes bounced checks, and accounting records. Refunds must be made in a timely manner when cancellations are requested. Processing and writing any check represents a measurable cost of operation.

For many hotels, these operational burdens are inconsequential compared to the benefits that accrue from advance-deposit reservations. However, even those hotels using advance-deposit systems would probably switch if and when new guarantee systems become available. And that is apt to happen as new electronic systems and new innovations in money substitutes appear.

Summary

Accepting a reservation is only half the battle. Tracking the reservation and forecasting house availability are also important components in reservations' life cycle. Forecasting room availability is as much an art as it is a science. It is a simple matter to count committed rooms (those sold to stay-overs and incoming reservations) as a means of forecasting the number of rooms available for walk-ins and short lead-time reservations. However, such a simple approach leaves untended a number of costly variables. When the reservation manager begins to consider the potential for such variables as no-shows, cancellations, early arrivals, understays, and overstays, the art of forecasting becomes a bit more scientific.

An error in predicting the number of cancellations and no-shows may prove disastrous to a nearly full hotel. Rooms may be overbooked, necessitating that guests be walked to a nearby property. When this is a rare occasion, the employees treat the situation with compassion and the walked guest is a satisfied one. However, when walking guests become a routine daily occurrence, employees become jaded, guests are shown little concern, and dissatisfaction inevitably results.

The lodging industry has done a superior job reducing overbooking complaints in recent years. Partially from fear of government regulation (as with airline overbooking policies), and partially from a desire to create lasting relationships and repeat business in a highly competitive industry, few overbooking complaints have become public scandals.

Resources and Challenges

RESOURCES

Web Assignment

Type "hotel overbooking" into Google and you'll find better than 100,000 results. Find an example of an overbooking incident in the search results. Be prepared to both describe the incident as well as explain, in your opinion, which party was right and why.

Interesting Tidbits

- Hotels that overbook in Florida are obligated under state law to make "every effort" to find suitable accommodations for the injured party, refund the party's deposit, and potentially pay a $500 state-levied fine. The Bahamas Hotel Association (BHA) formalized its own areawide policy. Recognizing that being stranded on an island with no room was not going to encourage tourism, the new policy states that BHA hotels must pay walked guests for air taxi transportation to another island if local accommodations are fully booked. A $25 cab ride is cheap compared to an air taxi in the middle of the night!

- In a landmark case, *Rainbow Travel Service v. Hilton Hotel Corporation* (1990), Hilton Hotels argued that their Fontainebleau Hotel was not responsible for the overbooking incident in question because it was due to factors beyond its control. Many experts believe it was the Fontainebleau Hotel's own policy manual that turned the tide of the trial against Hilton (Hilton eventually lost the trial and paid restitution to Rainbow Travel). And no doubt, that is true. The policy manual read:

  Overboard

  We never tell a guest we overbooked.

  If an overboard situation arises, it is due to the fact that something occurred that the hotel could not prevent.

  Examples:
  1. Scheduled departures did not vacate their rooms.

  2. Engineering problems with a room (pipe bursted, thus water leaks, air-conditioning, heating out of commission, broken glass, etc.).

  Always remain calm and as pleasant as possible.

- Finding any room available, no matter what the cost, can be the paramount issue in certain lodging markets. Cities like Las Vegas, Bangalore, and New York run sustained occupancies at or near 100% for long periods of the year. Corporate travelers are forced to negotiate room commitments with hotels as much as one year in advance in order to secure guaranteed accommodations. Some hotels won't even agree to this "bird-in-the-hand" arrangement for fear it will obligate them to a lower rate than the actual rate during these substantially overbooked periods.

- An AH&LA study on customer satisfaction ranked overbooking just 19th in the frequency of guest complaints against hotels.

Challenges

True/False

Questions that are partially false should be marked false (F).

_____ 1. The term *walking* an overbooked guest means virtually the same as the term *walk-in* guest.

_____ 2. A simple, unadjusted room count does not consider understays, overstays, cancellations, no-shows, or early arrivals in the calculations.

_____ 3. A *perfect fill* (a sold-out night where every hotel room is physically occupied by one or more guests) is not the same thing as 100% occupancy. Therefore, it is theoretically possible for hotel management to show 100% occupancy without actually attaining a perfect fill.

_____ 4. Understays and overstays both affect the room count in the same direction. They both allow the hotel to sell a few more rooms to compensate for the projected understays and/or overstays.

_____ 5. Reservations are only legal contracts if the guest mails in a deposit (or has the credit card charged at the time of reservation) and the hotel returns a receipt and/or written confirmation.

Problems

1. What is the difference between out-of-order and out-of-inventory rooms? Explain why one of these designations affects the occupancy count while the other has no bearing.

2. Prepare a simple unadjusted plus count from the following scenario: A 700-room hotel had 90% of its rooms occupied last night. Of those occupied rooms, 260 are due to check out today. In addition, there are 316 reservations scheduled for arrival today, and 10 rooms are currently out of order.

3. The rooms forecast committee is scheduled to meet later this afternoon. You have been asked to prepare remarks on group no-shows. Contrast the likelihood of no-shows for (a) business groups, (b) tour groups, and (c) convention groups. How would your remarks differ if the group reservation had been made by (a) the vice-president of engineering, (b) an incentive travel company, or (c) a professional convention management company?

4. The rooms forecast is a tool for managers throughout the hotel; it is not for the front office alone. List and discuss how several other nonroom departments (housekeeping, food and beverage, etc.) would use the rooms forecast.

5. A chain's corporate office launches a national campaign advertising its policy of honoring every reservation. Each property is notified that overbooking will not be tolerated. What policies can be implemented at the hotel level to meet corporate goals and still generate the maximum occupancies on which professional careers are built?

6. Two hours before the noon check-out hour, a walk-in party requests five rooms. The following scrambled data have just been completed as part of the desk's hourly update. Should the front-office supervisor accept the walk-ins?

General no-show factor	10%
Rooms in the hotel	693
Group reservations due (rooms)	250
Rooms occupied last night	588
Total reservations expected today from all sources (including group rooms)	360
No-show factor for groups	2%
Understays minus overstays as a percentage of occupied rooms	8%
Early arrivals expected	2
Rooms that are out of inventory	7
Total forecasted departures for the day	211

AN INCIDENT IN HOTEL MANAGEMENT
Tell Me Why I Should

The accounting office received a call from a couple who said they had been at the hotel about five weeks earlier. They were calling to complain about a charge on their latest credit-card statement. The hotel has billed them as a no-show. The guests stated that they had, indeed, been there! Now they wanted a credit against the charge.

Apparently, they had two reservations. One was made directly to the hotel and one through the reservation center. The caller said that both were 4:00 PM holds and that they came on one, but did not bother to cancel the other hold since they knew it would be taken down at that time.

The person answering the telephone knows the hotel has 6:00 PM holds, not 4:00 PM holds. Furthermore, how did the Central Reservation Office get their credit-card number if they had a hold reservation, not a guaranteed one?

"No, we don't have the cancellation number, since we didn't cancel a hold."

"No, we don't have a copy of our bill during that stay; we don't keep everything!"

"No, sorry! We don't recall the room number we were in."

"Well, we were there sometime during the week of the 11th."

Questions:

1. Was there a management failure here; if so, what?
2. What is the hotel's immediate response (or action) to the incident?
3. What further, long-run action should management take, if any?

Answers to True/False Quiz

1. False. Walking a guest is what the hotel must do when no rooms are available and the guest needs to be accommodated at a different hotel elsewhere in town. A walk-in guest is a person who arrives without a reservation and yet is still accommodated because rooms are available.

2. True. Simple, unadjusted room count does not consider those adjustments listed. Understays, overstays, cancellations, no-shows, and early arrivals are only considered in the adjusted room count equation.

3. True. The question defines the perfect fill correctly. Hotels can claim 100% occupancy by showing revenues from no-show and late cancellation charges even when rooms remain physically unoccupied.

4. False. Understays do increase the number of rooms available for sale on any given day. Overstays do just the opposite and decrease the number of rooms available for sale.

5. False. Although it is good advice for consumers to use a credit card when making reservations and for hotels to send (mail, fax, even email) written confirmations with hotel cancellation policies clearly detailed, they are not required for the reservation to become a legal contract. When the offer is made and accepted (even orally, by telephone) for future remuneration, a contract has been established.

Global Reservations Technologies

Rapid advancements in technology have changed the manner in which hotel rooms are booked. Just a few years ago a hotel's posted available rooms were manually adjusted and sold on a daily (even hourly) basis, whereas today rooms are sold electronically through myriad channels with little or no human interaction (see Exhibit 3). This represents a substantial change in methodology over a few short years. What does the future hold for hotel reservations? Imagine the following rather futuristic scenario:

> Heading to the airport for a hastily scheduled business meeting, a technologically savvy corporate businessman accesses the Internet on his smartphone. Through the mobile phone, he checks availability at his favorite New York City hotel, discovers that rooms availability is tight, but manages to reserve a Parlor Queen room for $345 that night. His credit-card guarantee is transmitted automatically, and the return confirmation number is conveniently stored in the smartphone for later retrieval. As he waits for the airplane, our corporate executive downloads a podcast from the New York City hotel, complete with a virtual tour, greeting from the general manager, and highlights of dinner and drink specials he'll enjoy that evening.
>
> Several hours later, this futuristic scenario continues as our business traveler arrives at the Holiday Inn Wall Street. The moment he steps foot into the hotel's lobby, his mobile phone alerts him that a message is waiting. The text message on his telephone asks if he would like to proceed with electronic check-in. No wonder he loves this hotel. Of course he readily agrees, and simply types "yes" into his cell phone and enters a preprogrammed personal identification number (PIN). Then, in one last attempt to up-sell to the guest, the hotel's property management system prompts him with several additional room-rate options. He decides to treat himself to an Executive King Suite for $425 and indicates as much on the phone's screen.
>
> As he walks across the lobby (secretly boasting because he's avoiding the growing check-in queue), his text message provides him the room number and even directions to the room (not that he needs directions—after all, this is his favorite hotel). As he exits the elevator, the hotel's short-range radio-wave technology senses him and prompts his telephone by again requesting his PIN. As he approaches the guestroom (within, say, 15 or 20 feet), the door automatically unlocks itself.
>
> Relaxing in his room a few minutes later, his smartphone again alerts him to a text message. It is the hotel's food and beverage department prompting him through the guest history database to see if he would like the same breakfast he ordered last visit—two eggs scrambled, dry wheat toast, juice, and coffee—delivered at the same time, 6:30 AM?

What a truly seamless series of transactions our corporate guest experienced. Each transaction was fully electronic—both paperless and faceless (no printed receipts or mailed confirmations, and no one-to-one or guest-to-employee interactions). Quite futuristic, you must agree! But wait...this technology is already in place at many hotels across America today. The technological innovations mentioned in the above scenario are available and accessed regularly by today's corporate guests. The future is here!

GLOBAL DISTRIBUTION

Understanding the channels through which hotels receive reservations is challenging. There are numerous *channels of distribution* available for hotels today, with new types being introduced every year. Today, travelers can make reservations by telephoning the property directly or the chain's central reservations office, through email, via the hotel's website, with a travel agent, on the chain's website, or through any number of other online travel sites (see Exhibit 1).

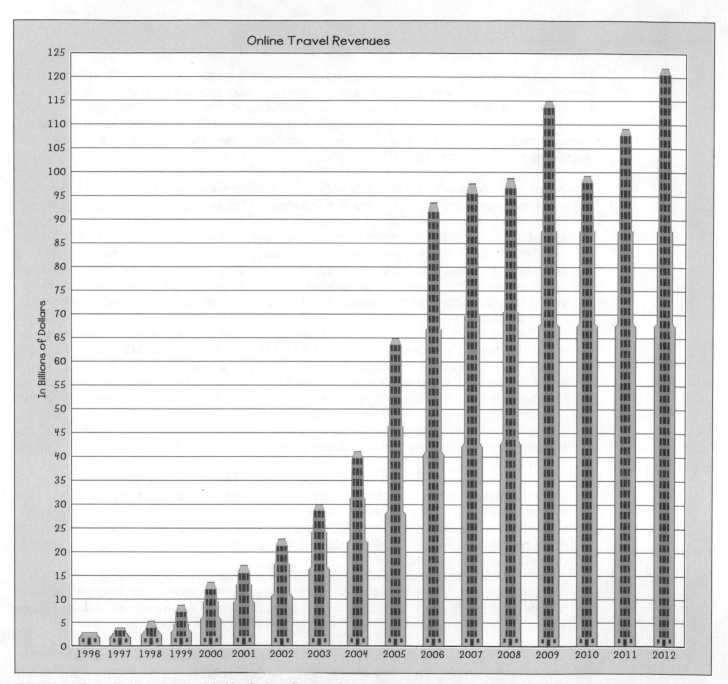

EXHIBIT 1 The United States is the global leader in online travel reservations. Online travel expenditures grew at roughly 43% per year between 1996 and 1999. The growth slowed in 2006 for several years, due in large part, to the lackluster economy. Growth in 2011 and 2012 is estimated at 10% per year. The above figures are for U.S. online travel revenues. Worldwide, the number is closer to $300 billion annually, which equates to more than 1 billion transactions per year (or better than 2,000 transactions per minute)! The three major GDS companies; Amadeus, Sabre, and Travelport employ more than 23,000 persons.

A Brief History

Hotel reservation technologies owe their beginning to the airline reservation systems of the early 1960s. The lodging industry has historically followed the airline industry into adopting new technologies (reservations, inventory control, revenue management, etc.), waiting for the more capital-intensive airlines to perform expensive research and development before wading in. By choosing to wait on the sidelines in the early stages of development, hotel chains saved time and money. This holds especially true for the development of the airlines' global distribution system (GDS).

Travel agents were the first step in the development of today's GDS. Airlines, in an attempt to improve efficiency over telephoned reservations, began installing reservation terminals in travel agencies. This allowed the travel agency access to the airlines' seats inventory and a means by which to electronically ticket clients. Larger agencies, with access to more potential bookings, received more dedicated computer terminals than did smaller agencies. More terminals meant access to more airlines, because each airline had a dedicated proprietary system.

Travel agents enjoyed the increased efficiencies associated with computer access. It was a vast improvement over telephoned reservation, the method smaller travel agencies were still required to use. It was not long before airlines were also offering select hotel rooms and rental cars through their fledgling global distribution systems. American Airlines' Sabre and United Airlines' Apollo were the original two global distribution systems (see Exhibits 2 and 3).

Not all hotel chains joined the early GDSs, because many thought it was cost prohibitive. Hoteliers were accustomed to paying a per-reservation fee for rooms booked through the

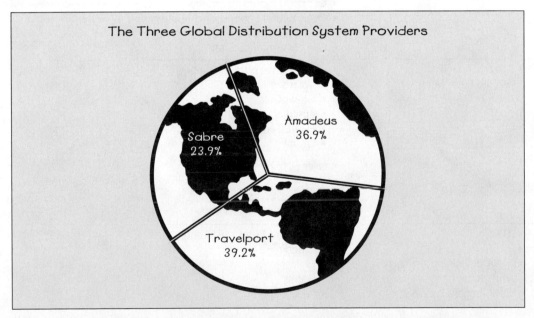

EXHIBIT 2 American Airlines developed the first automated booking system in 1946. Since then, the three major Global distribution system providers have evolved dramatically. Here are some examples from recent years:

- There were four major GDS Systems until 2006. Here's what has happened in the last 10 years;
  - In 2005, Cinven and BC Partners, two private equity firms, took control of Amadeus for roughly $6 billion.
  - In 2006, Cendant Corporation sold Galileo to the Blackstone Group, a private equity firm, for $4.3 billion. Galileo became better known by the name: Travelport. By the way, Cendant only owned Galileo since 2001 when it purchased the GDS for $2.9 billion.
  - Travelport also merged with Worldspan in 2006, essentially creating 3 major GDS Systems.
  - American Airlines sold its Sabre GDS to Silver Lake Partners and Texas Pacific Group for $5 billion in 2007. By the way, Sabre generates about $3 billion in annual gross revenues.

At this time, all 3 major GDS Systems are controlled by private equity firms.

Name	Originally Created by	Also used by

Amadeus	• Air France
	• Iberia
	• Lufthansa
	• SAS
		• Online travel sites, including:
		  • Anyfares
		  • CheapOair
		  • ebookers
		  • Cheap Tickets
		  • Expedia
		  • Flights
		  • Opodo
		  • Jetabroad
		  • Tripsetc
		  • Air-Savings
		
		• Over 500 individual airlines
		• Over 99,000 travel agencies in more than 195 countries
		• Over 86,000 hotels
		• Over 24 Rental Car brands

Sabre	• American Airlines	• Online travel sites, including:
		  • Volaris
		  • Travelocity
		  • zuji
		  • Lastminute.com
		  • Travel Guru
		  • Priceline
		
		• Over 800 individual airlines
		• Over 55,000 travel agencies in more than 100 countries
		• Over 88,000 hotels
		• Over 24 rental car brands

Travelport's Galileo	• United Airlines' Apollo Reservations System	• Online travel sites, including:
		  • Volaris
		  • CheapOair
		  • ebookers
		  • Flight Centre
		  • Orbitz
		
		• Over 500 individual airlines
		• Over 44,000 travel agencies in more than 100 countries
		• Over 60,000 hotels
		• Over 24 rental car brands

Travelport's Worldspan	• Delta
	• Northwest
	• TWA (Following its merger with American Airlines, TWA began using Sabre).
		• Online travel sites, including;
		  • Expedia
		  • Hotwire
		  • Hotels
		  • Priceline
		  • Orbitz
		
		• Over 500 individual airlines
		• Over 44,000 travel agencies in more than 100 countries
		• Over 60,000 hotels
		• Over 24 rental car brands

EXHIBIT 3 Along with the 3 major GDS Systems (listed here as 4 systems to demonstrate the history of Galileo and Worldspan, now operating together under the name Travelport), there are a handful of smaller GDS systems operating around the world. Included among these smaller systems are:

- Abacus (primarily Nippon Airways, Cathay Pacific Airways, China Airlines, Malaysia Airlines, Philippine Airlines, Singapore Airlines, and others).
- KIU (primarily Latin American airlines, including; Sol Líneas Aéreas, Aeropostal, Maya Air, and others).
- Patheo (primarily Finnair, KLM, Lufthansa (now with Amadeus), and others).
- TravelSky (primarily Air China, China Southern Airlines, China Eastern Air, Hainan Airlines, and others).

Imagine how much longer the list would be if we added rail carriers (Amadeus lists over 50), tour operators (Amadeus lists over 180), cruise lines (Amadeus lists 130), and so much more.

chain's central reservations office. And hotels were accustomed to paying a commission to travel agents (usually 10% of the room rate for each night of the guest's stay). But this new fee, paid for each sale over the airline's GDS, seemed an expensive way to attract reservations.

Seamless Connectivity

Another early issue for hotels was the outdated rooms inventory information listed on the airline reservations system. Because rooms inventory had to be updated manually on the airline global distribution system (GDS), this information was always outdated. Not only was this manual updating prone to error, it created time lags between the creation of new data and its appearance on the GDS. Even when the hotel's inventory and pricing was regularly updated, it was the source of many problems. Hotels needed to close availability on the GDS when only a few rooms remained, or else they could find themselves oversold. Hotels were not able to alter rates at a moment's notice. And hotels were only allowed to sell a few categories of room types.

An important step occurred in 1989 when the airline GDSs and the central reservations system (CRS) of the major hotel chains began exchanging real-time information. Now travel agents working through the GDS could view the same information a reservations agent working in the hotel chain's central reservations office (CRO) was able to see (see Exhibit 3).

This was a slight improvement, but unfortunately, hotel central reservations system in the late 1980s were also out of date with regard to the rooms inventory information they carried. The hotel chain's CRS required constant manual updating from each property's in-house reservations department. The hotel's in-house reservations department was responsible for tracking the rooms sold by the CRO and manually adding them to its first-generation property management system. Once added, a new rooms availability count was calculated. The CRO never knew how many rooms a given hotel had available; it just knew that rooms were still open for sale. This placed an important responsibility on the property's in-house reservation manager to manually notify the CRO when room availability began to tighten.

LAST-ROOM AVAILABILITY Because it was manual, communication between each hotel in the chain and the central reservations office was anything but efficient. In-house reservation managers were continually monitoring rooms availability for all dates. When a date began to show signs of filling, the hotel's in-house reservation manager closed availability with the CRO. Sometimes the decision to close availability came too soon and the hotel found itself with rooms left to sell. Sometimes the decision to close availability came too late and the hotel found itself oversold. In either case, this lack of efficiency was expensive to the chain.

Interfacing the central reservations system with each of the chain's individual properties was also expensive. This was especially true in the 1980s, because the individual hotels within the chain were often using dozens of different property management system (PMS) software vendors. Writing programs that electronically linked each hotel's PMSs with the CRS was the next step.

It was a costly step, however. Because each chain had to invest in their own proprietary systems, there were no industry economies. Software was developed at the corporate level so each hotel's PMS interfaced in real-time with the CRS. But at the property level, investments also ran high. Chains mandated only certain PMS software and related hardware would be supported by the chain. Individual properties were faced with large investments, though many chains assisted their properties with a portion of the costs or with inexpensive loans.

The idea behind this substantial investment (running in the hundreds of millions of dollars for the larger lodging chains) was if the CRS could view each property's rooms inventory in real-time, it could sell each property's very last room (hence the name "Last-Room Availability" technology). Those last few rooms sold by the CRO represented almost pure profit to the hotel and therefore the chain. In spite of the substantial cost, the investment had a relatively short-term payback.

Lodging chains also came to realize that real-time information from each property had other advantages as well. Electronic access directly into each hotel's PMS allowed chains to perform research and corporate wide developments, including revenue management, inventory control, and guest history.

ELECTRONIC SWITCH TECHNOLOGY As the computer eclipsed the telephone as the preferred method for making airline and hotel reservations, travel agencies soon found themselves crowded with various computer terminals. With a dedicated computer for each hotel chain and airline the travel agency represented, large travel offices were supporting literally dozens of separate computers. Each of these systems was developed uniquely, and that meant a different set of rules, computer codes, and procedures for each. Not only did this growing number of terminals take up space and require training to learn each system, but travel agents also found themselves spending time moving back and forth between terminals comparing prices and availability.

It took a new innovation, *switch technology*, to get all the companies speaking the same language. The original electronic switch system, THISCO (The Hotel Industry Switching Company, known today as Pegasus Solutions), was introduced in the early 1990s (see Exhibit 3). It was developed by 11 major lodging chains namely Best Western, Choice, Days Inns, Hilton, Holiday, Hyatt, La Quinta, Marriott, Ramada, Sheraton, and Forte in conjunction with Rupert Murdoch's electronic publishing division. Switch technology functions like a clearinghouse. All reservation transactions are processed through the switch. The overwhelmed travel agent now needed access to just one terminal to communicate real-time reservation requests and confirmations to any of hundreds of airlines, hotels, car rentals, and other related services (see Exhibits 3 and 4). Switch technology functions as a translator as well as a real-time communicator. It translates codes from all the various hotel CRS into one common switch language. Thanks to switch technology; when a travel agent books a room with, say, two queens, the agent does not need to remember the exact input code for the particular chain in question. One chain might identify two queens with a QQ code, another chain might use 2Q or DQ for double queen. The electronic

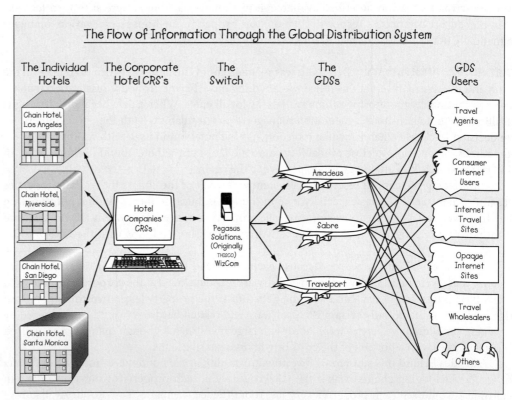

EXHIBIT 4 The global distribution system is enormous. Each of the three airline GDS systems processes over 100 billion transactions per year (that's about 300 million requests for information per day).

The flow of information works like this: The supply side of the flow begins with the hotel where information (rate and availability) flows through the chain's CRS to the switches. The switches provide that information to the three GDSs. Travel agents, consumer Internet users, Internet travel sites, opaque Internet sites, travel wholesalers, and myriad other end users (still to be invented) access the information through the GDSs. The demand side of the flow works in the opposite direction, with the resulting room reservation finally coming to rest in the hotel's reservations system.

switch allows the user to learn one system of codes and translates that information across each chain's particular CRS language.

The introduction of the switch has allowed seamless connectivity across the spectrum of reservations. Now travel agents, airline reservationists, hotel central reservations agent, and in-house hotel reservation clerks access the same information at the same speed. So too do all Internet applications (including travel websites) and channels of distribution. All reservations are made in real time and the rooms inventory updated the moment the reservation is confirmed (see Exhibit 4).

Application Service Providers

The evolution of hotel CRSs from stand-alone call centers in the mid-1960s to today's seamlessly connected systems has only been possible at a substantial price. Because of the heavy investment required, not all hotel chains are in the same place today in terms of their respective levels of sophistication.

Last-room availability software requires an ability to integrate all of the chain's hundreds (if not thousands) of individual hotel property management systems. Some chains are still dealing with the mistakes they made decades ago, allowing each hotel—franchised or corporate-owned—to select its own PMS (hardware and software). Different hardware and software applications across each property in the chain requires a myriad of programming and hardware changes to get all systems speaking the same language. It is this challenge that has lent itself to the successful introduction of application service providers (ASPs). Application service providers are software companies (Pegasus' RezView and Swan's Unirez are two such examples) that offer a suite of software applications via Internet-based access. No longer is it necessary for a hotel chain to purchase and maintain specific PMS hardware and software for each hotel. Rather, through a website, each hotel runs off the same suite of software by simply using any Internet-ready computer—even a laptop!

Generally, ASPs offer four primary functions in their arsenal of applications: a CRS, GDS connectivity, connections to "alternate" distribution systems, and Internet reservations. Hotels simply subscribe to the system, and all property-specific data are stored off property in ASP-maintained warehouses (see Exhibit 5).

Numerous benefits are associated with ASP applications. Hotel chains do not have to make large capital investments in hardware and software. Nor do they have to employ a fleet of specialized software engineers to maintain the system and program new applications. Because every hotel uses the same software, new software enhancements are implemented immediately at the ASP site and made available to all users instantaneously.

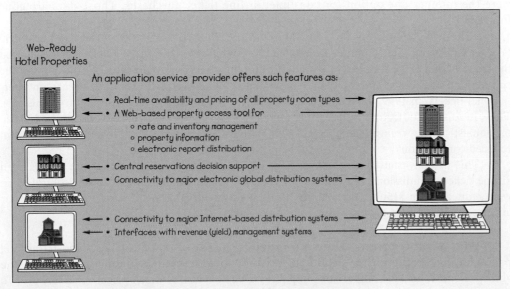

EXHIBIT 5   Features provided through an application service provider.

SINGLE-IMAGE INVENTORY   The biggest benefit associated with ASP applications is single-image inventory. Similar in concept to last-room availability, single-image inventory allows all users to feed from the same database. One inventory—price and availability—is viewed by the GDS, central reservation call centers, and Internet-based distribution systems. The result is a lower error rate in reservation bookings and a resulting improvement in overall customer service.

Although last-room availability and single-image inventory (also known as *true integration*) appear quite similar, they are fundamentally different. The difference is that last-room availability uses PMS inventory for its information. With single-image inventory, all reservation applications as well as PMS applications look at the same database and draw from the same well of information.

As such, the rooms inventory can become available for others to access. One result of having an accessible inventory is an overall savings on reservation commissions. Imagine negotiating a special corporate rate with Pepsi, for example. Rather than having Pepsi book its special rates through a travel agent (and paying commissions to the travel agent and fees to the GDS and other distribution system providers), the hotel could provide Pepsi a unique access code. All reservations booked against the inventory using this special code would be virtually commission-free to the hotel!

Similarly, access to inventory can be made available to corporate or tour and travel group room blocks, giving groups the ability to develop their own rooming lists. Groups can then manipulate their room blocks, change names as often as needed, and simply send the hotel a completed rooming list at the touch of a button.

Traditional Reservation Channels

The explosion of the Internet, advancements in airline global distribution systems, and the increasing sophistication of switch technology have all played a role in changing the hotel industry's reservation landscape. As websites and online bookings grow in reservations volume (see Exhibits 1 and 6), other traditional channels have decreased in revenues and altered the traditional manner by which rooms are sold.

THE CHANGING ROLE OF THE TRAVEL AGENT   On August 30, 2001, just days before 9/11, almost every travel agent office in America closed for part of the day as a symbol of protest. The travel agents' National Day of Awareness was designed to alert consumers to the substantial airline commission changes impacting the travel agent industry. Until just a few months before their day of protest, travel agents were generously paid by the airline industry. They enjoyed a mutually beneficial relationship that created a market in which travel agents were the number one option for consumer airline ticket purchases. Those days are gone forever.

Historical commissions for a $1,500 round-trip, first-class domestic ticket had been $150 (10% commission). That commission eroded in a few short years. In 1995, Delta Airlines started the trend with a $50 cap on its 10% domestic commissions. Two years later, the airlines cut the commission rate to 8%, and then in 1998, instituted a first-ever $100 commission cap on international tickets. In 1999, most airlines cut domestic and international commissions to just 5%. Then, in August 2001, American Airlines (and its subsidiary, TWA Airlines) reduced the $50 cap on domestic ticket commissions to just $20. Within days other fleets followed with their own reduced commissions.

This was devastating for the travel agent industry. Its bread and butter has always been airline ticket commissions, but now (using the $150 commission example above) commissions were reduced from $150 to just $20. In 2002, they lost even that paltry sum when most major airlines simply stopped paying commissions altogether.

Why Airline Commissions Changed?   Increased operating costs and rising fuel prices have squeezed airline profitability. Competitive pressures among carriers and the ability of consumers to comparison shop fares have kept airline ticket prices relatively low. To

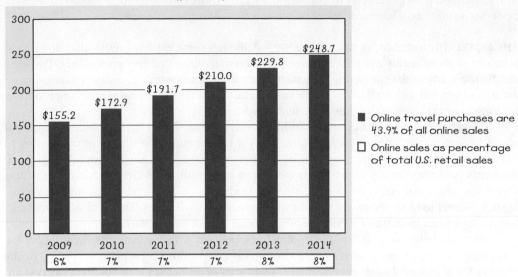

EXHIBIT 6 In the late 1990s online travel purchases outpaced online personal computer purchases, for the first time. Travel has been the leading Internet sales category for better than a decade, and continues to grow at the fastest rate, representing 43.9% of all online sales. That's because online travel bookings make sense. According to Internet experts, the travel industry is a natural for online bookings. Through the Internet, clients can readily compare prices, amenities, and other features before making their purchase.

But hotel bookings lag behind airline bookings in terms of online purchases. This is due, in part, to the fact that hotel bookings are more complicated. Air is the simplest online purchase, followed by rental cars, with hotels coming up third for "ease of use." As such, just one out of every three or so Internet air bookings is accompanied by a related hotel booking.

"All Other Online Sales" includes, in order by revenue, computer hardware, apparel, office supplies, consumer goods, electronics, books, software and games, event tickets, and furniture/appliances.

stay profitable when prices are low and operating costs are high requires saving money wherever possible. Doing away with the 10% travel agent commission was a logical cost-saving measure.

Whatever the reasoning, certainly the airline industry has been successful in moving consumers away from travel agent bookings toward self-directed Internet bookings. Attractive and easy-to-use airline websites have helped simplify the do-it-yourself process. Discounts, double frequent flier miles, and Internet-only specials have also played a critical role in motivating consumers to visit airline websites.

Changes Still to Come Once there were 500,000 travel agencies across the world. In the past decade, and with increasing frequency, the travel agent industry has experienced numerous bankruptcies and going-out-of-business signs. The biggest change for consumers has been an increased fee structure—consumers now pay travel agents $10–$25 per airline ticket booking fee.

In a move similar to the elimination of travel agent commissions, most airlines also reduced or eliminated commissions to Internet travel sites (Travelocity, Orbitz, etc.). Where airlines had generally been paying travel sites a 5% commission (maximum $10 cap per ticket), most now pay none at all. Internet travel sites now add a surcharge similar to the booking fees charged by travel agents.

It is hard to predict what such changes will mean to travel agents, consumers, travel websites, the airline industry, and the hotel industry, but we can make a few conjectures. Travel agents will attract consumers from higher economic strata. These consumers will appreciate (and pay for) higher levels of service. The travel agents' expertise, the ease and convenience of one-stop shopping, and familiarity with the customer's unique needs and wants are the products that travel agents sell. As the travel agent industry evolves, larger agencies will absorb smaller ones. The resulting few mega agencies will undoubtedly carry more clout then we see today in terms of price/fee negotiations, wholesale travel prices, Internet websites, and more.

THE HOTEL–TRAVEL AGENT RELATIONSHIP   Although some experts predict that hotel commissions to travel agents will go the way of airline commissions, that appears unlikely. There are simply too many hotels competing with each other. Even hotels within the same chain or brand are in competition with each other. Hotels cannot afford to limit their chances of selling rooms by limiting their exposure to the global distribution system.

Travel agents are a major source of hotel reservations. Travel agent bookings represent about 15% of all hotel rooms booked. Hotels pay a 10% commission—more in off-seasons to generate volume—for all rooms booked by an agency. Fees are not governmentally regulated. Amounts paid vary from property to property and even within the same property over time. *Overrides,* additional points of 10–15%, are paid to encourage high levels of business from one agency. Guests used to pay no fee to the travel agency for its services. This is almost unknown today. Most agencies charge a service fee for all bookings, not just airline tickets.

Many hoteliers believe they are in direct competition with travel agents, fighting for the same business and paying a commission to boot. This kind of thinking is being supported by the appearance of powerful mega agencies and consortiums of agencies. Large-volume dealers stand toe to toe with national hotel chains. By securing the travel contracts of small and large corporations, these mega agencies squeeze discounted rates from the national hotel chains anxious to get or retain a piece of the business. This has become especially true with high-demand periods in selected cities. Certain major markets, New York City for example, have such high demand during key periods of the year that corporate buyers are using travel agency room blocks as one approach to guaranteeing room availability.

Travel Agent Commissions

The classic argument between hoteliers and travel agents revolves around commissions. Travel agents argue that hoteliers are slow in paying commissions and when the check does arrive, it is often inaccurate. Studies show that from 15% to 50% of all hotel commissions are inaccurate. Hoteliers argue that certain travel agents provide so little business that the commission check costs the hotel more in processing fees than the value of the check.

The advent of travel management software tools (a popular one is Kalypso, by ECommissions Solutions) have deflated most of these arguments. Hotels are better able to track business from travel agencies, choosing to accept business from those with which the hotel has a better relationship and possibly denying business from low producers. Travel agents are paid quicker and with more accuracy. Furthermore, both the hotels and the travel agents are able to evaluate annual business levels and choose with which operators they prefer to do business.

CENTRAL RESERVATION CENTER   Although there is a distinction between the terms central reservations system and central reservations office, today's jargon has made them virtually interchangeable. Technically, the CRS is the electronic system, including the last-room availability interface with individual chain properties. Included are the switch technology connections with the GDS and the chain's Internet websites. The CRO is the actual office site(s) at which chain reservationists reside (see Exhibit 7). Most hoteliers simply refer to all these activities as the CRS.

Outsourcing Call Centers

Central reservations office reached their peak demand in the mid-1990s. Today, even though many chains have grown in size and volume, their CRSs see less business than a decade ago. The result has been a reduction in CRS staffing and the closing of select central reservations office around the globe (see Exhibit 7).

Reduced CRS staffing has created a new trend in call centers—*outsourcing.* Outsourcing the CRS means room reservations are sold through call centers or reservationists not directly staffed by the chain. Two techniques are proving quite popular. The first is outsourcing to a complementary, noncompetitive industry. An excellent example of this relationship is Choice Hotels' outsourcing arrangement with 1-800-Flowers.com. Choice overflows CRS call volume to 1-800-Flowers.com and vice versa. The two organizations find their business cycles to be very complementary.

EXHIBIT 7 The Beardsley Operations Center is one of three remaining international reservations centers operated by BWI. As call volume has dropped, so have the number of call centers worldwide. At its peak, Best Western operated five call centers, including Beardsley (shown above), and call centers in Glendale, Arizona (on the campus of Glendale Community College); Dublin, Ireland; Milan, Italy; and Sydney, Australia. Today, Best Western operates just three call centers: Beardsley, Milan, and Manila, Philippines. *Courtesy: Best Western International, Phoenix, Arizona.*

Choice is busiest in the summer season, posting its largest call demand between the months of May through September. This is the slowest season for the flower industry. Flower demand is highest between October and May, with surges in call volume from Thanksgiving to Mother's Day. By training operators at each company to handle double duty, each chain benefits from the relationship. The operators/reservationists benefit as well, because their job has more variety, there are fewer slow periods, and the two products are widely disparate.

Another outsourcing technique takes advantage of the work-at-home revolution. Driven by expanded broadband access to the Web, cheaper computer technology, improved call-routing systems, and increased dependence on ASP providers, CRSs are beginning to find their answer to overflow call demand in at-home workers. Flexibility is the primary attraction for at-home workers. Access to skilled labor, often without the need to pay costly employee benefits, is the draw for the hotel chains.

Some 70–80% of at-home reservationists have a college degree, compared with 30–40% of reservationists working CRS call centers. The employee turnover rate is lower with at-home workers as well. There is still the boredom of taking call after call, but at-home reservationists temper the monotony with the benefits of staying home every day. The result is a growing dependence on stay-at-home reservationists, approaching one-fourth of all reservationists on the job today.

Processing the Call   Reservations agent receive incoming calls and process them in two to three minutes. They are assisted with sophisticated telephone switching equipment. To save labor, automated telephone systems answer the call and segregate the caller according to a variety of options. The caller listens to the options and selects a specific number on the telephone keypad. Large chains use the telephone system to segregate callers according to the hotel brand in which they are most interested. Another common way to separate callers is according to whether their reservation is for a domestic hotel property, a European hotel, an Asian property, a Latin American operation, and so on.

Once callers have been routed, they may be placed on hold for the next available reservationist. During the holding period, a recording provides information about the chain, special discount periods, new hotel construction, and the like. In recent years, more and more recordings recommend callers visit the website to save time and view special Internet-only discounts. Automatic call distributor equipment eventually routes the telephone call to the next available reservationist.

Time is money, with labor and telephone lines the primary costs of CROs. Reservation management constantly battles to reduce the time allotted to each call. A sign in the office might read: "Talk time yesterday 1.8 (meaning minutes). During the last hour, 2.2. This hour, 2.1." Even more sophisticated devices are available which monitor each agent, providing data on the number of calls taken, the time per call, and the amount of postcall time needed to complete the reservation.

Employee evaluations are not judged on time alone. Systems often evaluate the percentage of the agent's calls that result in firm bookings and the relationship of the agent's average room rate to the average being sold by the entire center. Remember, CROs charge a fee for each reservation. Since the CRO is usually a separate subsidiary of the corporate parent, even company-owned properties pay the fee of several dollars per room-night booked. Franchisees pay more than just the booking fee, including a monthly fee on each room, a percent of gross rooms sales, and other national and regional marketing costs. Though franchisees may complain about the fee schedule, the CRS and its interface to the global distribution system and other channels of distribution is the major attraction of franchising.

IN-HOUSE RESERVATIONS   Whether chain affiliated or independent, all hotels accept direct or *in-house reservations*. In many properties, the number of in-house reservations is minimal. Others—especially nonaffiliated, independent hotels and resorts—may sell the bulk of their rooms through in-house reservationists (see Exhibit 8). In-house reservations are also handled in quantity by hotels with large sales departments. Such business is generated by the hotel's own sales department, and those bookings often bypass the CRS. Bypassing the CRS improves the profitability of each room sold by eliminating fees associated with the reservation.

EXHIBIT 8 Because hotels pay commissions on reservations booked through the CRS, a website can drive traffic directly to inhouse reservations. Shown here is a popular independent resort in Arizona. In spite of the attractiveness of the Web page, you'll notice the guest cannot actually check availability or book a room online—this still requires a call to the property. *Courtesy: Rio Rico Resort and Country Club.*

Where group rooms are deeply discounted, this small savings on each reservation amount to a boost in annual earnings.

Experienced shoppers often call the hotel directly. The in-house reservationist is more informed about the property. He or she has one hotel, whereas the CRS agent has hundreds or even thousands. If the hotel is full, reservations might be refused by the CRS but still be accepted on site.

Although it doesn't make sense, reservation calls directed to the property are being discouraged by, of all entities, the property itself! The hotel, which should encourage callers to bypass the CRS, is often too poorly staffed at the front desk to accept in-house reservations. The caller, waiting on hold to speak with an in-house reservationist, is unknowingly re-routed to the CRS. This can be especially frustrating when the caller has made the effort to look up the individual hotel's telephone number, called the operator, and asked for reservations, only to have the line redirected to the corporate CRO. This approach makes sense during busy or understaffed periods. But systems which send all reservations to the CRS are doing both the property and the guests a disservice.

- Over two-thirds of all Internet hotel bookings are for rooms selling below $100 per night.
- While the ADR for hotel rooms has been growing at roughly 7% per year, online Internet hotel room rates have been growing more slowly—only 5% per year.
- Hotel rooms booked over the Internet sell for an average 21% lower rate than hotel rooms booked through other GDS channels.
- For rooms selling for $301 and higher, the Internet actually sells a higher ADR than for hotel rooms booked through other GDS channels.
- The average length of stay for Internet hotel room bookings is 2.1 nights. Hotel rooms booked through other GDS channels have an average length of stay of 2.2 nights.

EXHIBIT 9 Some interesting facts related to Internet hotel bookings.

INTERNET- AND WEB-BASED RESERVATIONS Internet users have a staggering array of options for booking hotel rooms. Travel-related bookings make up the largest category of Internet transactions (see Exhibits 1 and 6). And each year, the Internet attracts a larger share of reservations away from more traditional sources—growing at a rate four times faster than the rest of the industry (see Exhibit 9).

Over its relatively short business cycle, Internet travel bookings have experienced significant changes and increasing sophistication. One factor in the success of a hotel's online marketing performance is search engine optimization. The use of search engines by guests seeking accommodations is growing at a rate of roughly 50% per year.

Search Engine Optimization Some 80% of all Web visits start in a search engine. Search engines such as Google, Bing, and Dogpile scour or *mine* the Web for a list of sites which match the search criteria requested by the user. The search criteria is a key word or words, or a phrase, such as "Hotels at LAX." The user hopes that search phrase will identify hotels located at or near Los Angeles International Airport. In fact, a quick search on Google with the phrase "Hotels at LAX" actually turned up 3,900,000 results!

The goal of search engine optimization is to juggle all the components of a search strategy so the hotel's website migrates toward the top of the search. Even the top 1% of a search with 4 million results isn't good enough. For the hotel to be found by potential buyers, it needs to make its way into the top 5–20 listings. Statistically, that means, for this example, making it into the top-listed 0.0005% of all results! Users will view most of the first page, rarely the second page, and then revise their search if they haven't found what appeals to them.

The hotel's search engine strategy will usually have both a paid and an organic component. Organic searches are the purest and most trusted kind. When the user looks up "Hotels at LAX," one or more paid listings will appear at the very top. These are usually distinguishable to the experienced user because they are a different color, have added graphics, or are listed on the sides of the top page. Experienced users often ignore these paid commercials and opt for organic results.

Organic results are different from results based on who paid the most to be listed at the top of the page. Organic, sometimes called "pure" or "natural," search results are based on which websites appeared most relevant based on the nature of the content search. Organic results boast a higher reservation conversion rate than paid results because users trust organic results more. Organic results are often very accurate and detailed—for example, adding words like swimming pool, free breakfast, and free airport shuttle to the original search of "Hotels at LAX" dropped the 4 million results to under 90,000. A few more criteria—free parking or club room—and the search will be further refined.

Paid searches can be costly. Hotels pay both for key word placement and for each customer click on the search engine to the hotel's website (called click-throughs). Software packages are available to help hoteliers compare costs for Internet placement versus increased returns in room sales. If the reservation is the final goal, and the manager knows what each reservation is worth, the software will estimate the profitability of the search strategy. It calculates two variable components: the click-through rate of each search engine and hotel's website's reservation conversion rate.

Search engine optimization strategies employ a blended mix of paid and organic results. But search is only half the battle. The hotel's website needs to be attractive and user-friendly enough to get the potential guest to open it, linger a bit, and ultimately book the reservation (see Exhibit 8). The website should be up to date with regard to photographs and video images that showcase the property's ambiance. Information should be updated frequently and detailed enough to explain amenities and provide seasonal information. Information should be written in a variety of languages which parallel languages used by the hotel's guests. And the website should enable guests to make other on-site reservations (golf and dining, for example). No wonder the hotel's website is being called the front desk of the new millennium.

Hotel Websites   Hotel managers realize the importance of spending marketing dollars on the Web just as they spend on billboards, print media, brochures, and so on. A realistic goal for a property is to spend approximately 40% of its annual marketing budget in online products. A worthy goal, though today's industry is not yet there. In a recent study (see Exhibit 10), most hotels stated they were spending only $1,000–$35,000 annually in online marketing. That approaches only 10% of the average property's annual marketing budget.

Spending online in such areas as search optimization, regularly updated content, rich imagery, and interactive maps can return substantial profits. When a guest books directly into a hotel's proprietary website, profits rise because the reservation has lower, if any, associated costs or fees. A $100 room booked through the property's website is worth $100 (less nominal pay-per-click fees charged by the search engines). A $100 room booked through an Internet travel site (Expedia, for example) may be worth just $60 or less!

Chain Websites   In the early years of the Internet, lodging chains lost ground quickly to third-party travel sites and lodging aggregators like Expedia, Orbitz, Hotels.com, and Travelocity (see Exhibit 11). Early on, these third-party travel sites attracted greater demand from Internet users than chain websites. By establishing certain inventory and room-rate pricing rules that all hotels were required to follow, heavily promoting low-price guarantees, and investing substantially in attractive and easy-to-use websites, the travel sites were running before the chains could react.

Times have changed, however, as third-party travel companies have begun losing Internet demand back to the chain websites. The catalyst for this change was a gutsy move by Intercontinental Hotels Group in November 2004. Intercontinental announced it would provide the best room prices on its own website. Shortly thereafter, most of the other major lodging chains followed suit, undercutting the biggest attraction for third-party travel sites, lowest rate guarantees (see Exhibit 12).

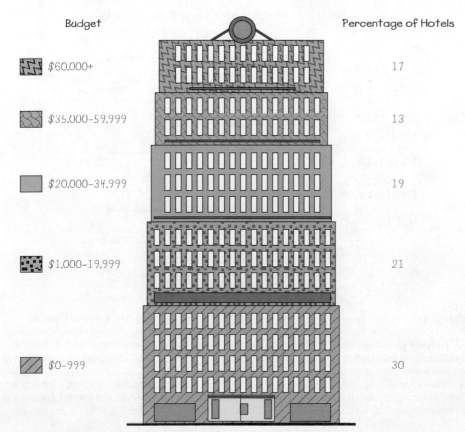

Budget	Percentage of Hotels
$60,000+	17
$35,000–59,999	13
$20,000–34,999	19
$1,000–19,999	21
$0–999	30

EXHIBIT 10   The weighted average annual expenditure by hotels for online marketing is just $26,400. This correlates to only about 10% of the average hotel's overall annual marketing and advertising budget. Online expenses are projected to grow as a percentage of a hotel's overall marketing budget for years to come.

141

Global Reservations Technologies

EXHIBIT 11 The top 10 Internet travel sites by gross annual revenues. New competitors with unique ways of scouring the Internet for lowest rates are constantly threatening these proven brands. A recent study found that newly designed AAA.com offered the lowest rates more often than Expedia, Travelocity, or Orbitz!

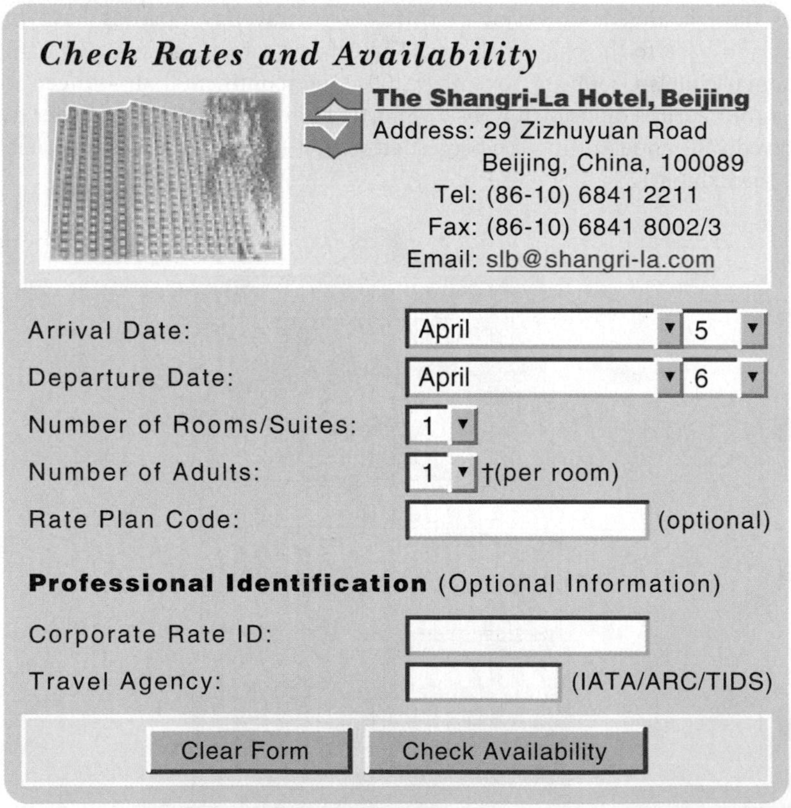

Check Rates and Availability

The Shangri-La Hotel, Beijing
Address: 29 Zizhuyuan Road
Beijing, China, 100089
Tel: (86-10) 6841 2211
Fax: (86-10) 6841 8002/3
Email: slb@shangri-la.com

Arrival Date: April ▼ 5 ▼

Departure Date: April ▼ 6 ▼

Number of Rooms/Suites: 1 ▼

Number of Adults: 1 ▼ †(per room)

Rate Plan Code: (optional)

Professional Identification (Optional Information)

Corporate Rate ID:

Travel Agency: (IATA/ARC/TIDS)

Clear Form   Check Availability

EXHIBIT 12A Making reservations online is as easy as it is widespread (see Exhibits 1 and 6). This Shangri-La Hotels & Resorts online reservation form walks the guest through the process step by step. First we pulled up www.shangri-la.com. Then we selected Beijing, China, and clicked on "reservations." At that point, an availability screen popped up (Exhibit 12A). Once availability was assured, we were given a choice of any different room types and rates. Each room type was detailed: including rate; room description; bed type; and amenities; such as computer, Internet connections, hairdryer, minibar, voicemail, even shoe shine availability. Once we selected our room type, a "required fields" screen pulled up for us to complete and send the reservation (Exhibit 12B). *Courtesy of Shangri-La Hotels & Resorts, Hong Kong.*

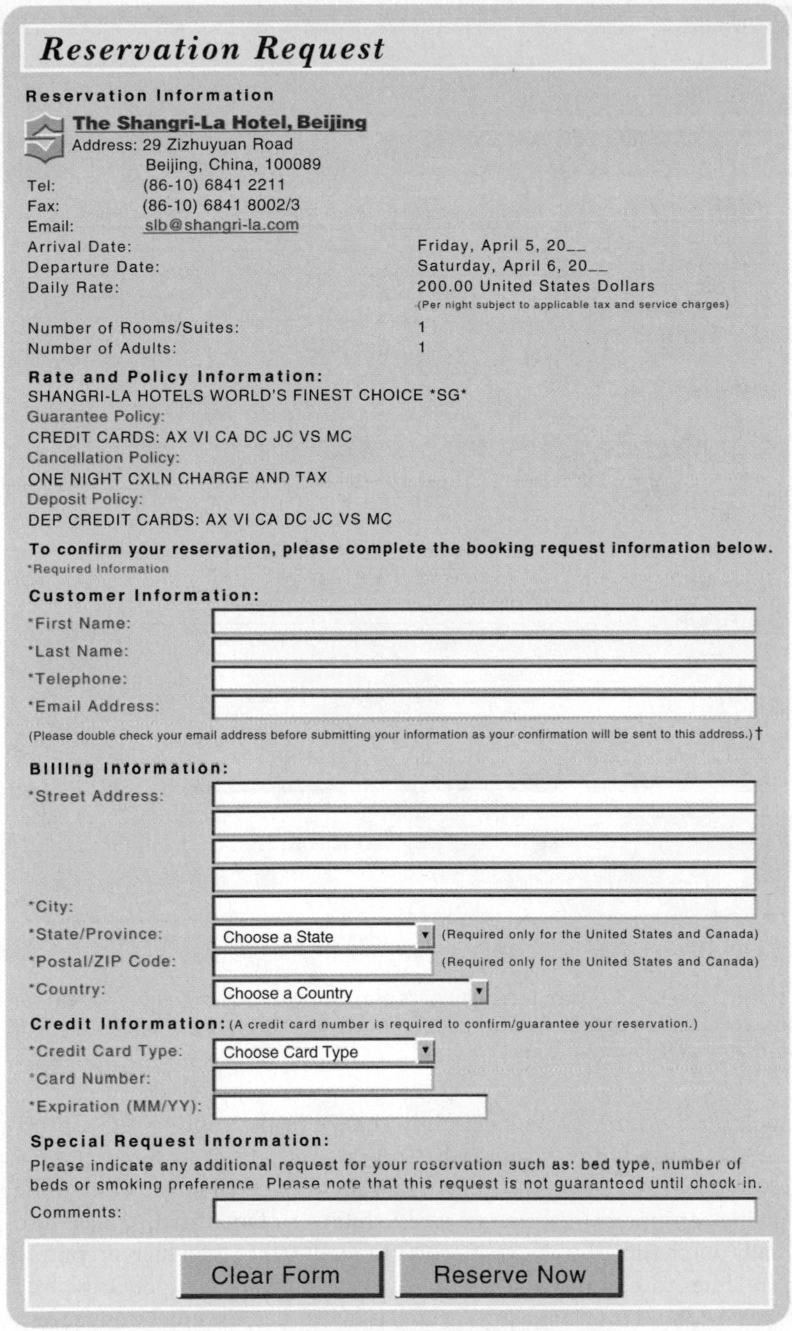

Reservation Request

Reservation Information

The Shangri-La Hotel, Beijing
Address: 29 Zizhuyuan Road
Beijing, China, 100089
Tel: (86-10) 6841 2211
Fax: (86-10) 6841 8002/3
Email: slb@shangri-la.com

Arrival Date: Friday, April 5, 20__
Departure Date: Saturday, April 6, 20__
Daily Rate: 200.00 United States Dollars
                                           (Per night subject to applicable tax and service charges)

Number of Rooms/Suites: 1
Number of Adults: 1

Rate and Policy Information:
SHANGRI-LA HOTELS WORLD'S FINEST CHOICE *SG*
Guarantee Policy:
CREDIT CARDS: AX VI CA DC JC VS MC
Cancellation Policy:
ONE NIGHT CXLN CHARGE AND TAX
Deposit Policy:
DEP CREDIT CARDS: AX VI CA DC JC VS MC

To confirm your reservation, please complete the booking request information below.
*Required Information

Customer Information:
*First Name:
*Last Name:
*Telephone:
*Email Address:

(Please double check your email address before submitting your information as your confirmation will be sent to this address.) †

Billing Information:
*Street Address:

*City:
*State/Province: Choose a State ▼   (Required only for the United States and Canada)
*Postal/ZIP Code: (Required only for the United States and Canada)
*Country: Choose a Country ▼

Credit Information: (A credit card number is required to confirm/guarantee your reservation.)
*Credit Card Type: Choose Card Type ▼
*Card Number:
*Expiration (MM/YY):

Special Request Information:
Please indicate any additional request for your reservation such as: bed type, number of
beds or smoking preference. Please note that this request is not guaranteed until check-in.
Comments:

[Clear Form]   [Reserve Now]

EXHIBIT 12B

Chain websites have other improvements ahead of them if they hope to challenge successfully the third-party travel sites. Hilton Hotels Corporation, for example, recently enhanced each of its various brand websites to enable users to search for all hotels on one page and then compare them side by side. Marriott International, Inc., has enabled its websites to track Marriott's Rewards points in real time. And Westin's website allows users to search by interest or amenities with such terms as "spa" or "family" (see Exhibit 13).

Third-Party Travel Websites   Even as online travel bookings increase, reservations through third-party travel sites have slowed. One reason bookings via third-party travel sites are down is that direct bookings to hotel proprietary websites are up. Good news for hotels (direct bookings cost less in commissions), but a major concern for third-party travel vendors. Third-party travel sites have met this news with a renewed commitment to make their sites the best for consumers in terms of usability, price, selection, and attractiveness.

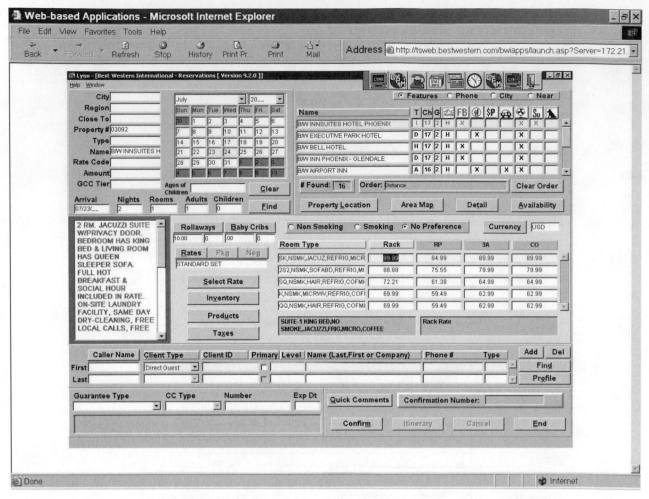

EXHIBIT 13 A sample reservations screen from Best Western International's proprietary Lynx reservations system (version 9.2.0). Exhibit 7 shows individual reservations work stations at Best Western International's Beardsley Operations Center in Phoenix, Arizona. *Courtesy: Best Western International Phoenix, Arizona.*

Although business models will certainly change in the coming years, third-party travel sites will continue to use a proven approach. Contract with the hotel for a set number of rooms (*inventory aggregation*) at a deeply discounted rate and then resell those rooms online at websites known for giving consumers the best rate (see Exhibit 11). One variation has third-party travel vendors actually purchasing the blocks of rooms to resell rather than merely contracting for their availability. In either case, this was a winning concept—selling a product the travel sites don't own (and have no control over) for a price which is lower than the hotel would ever sell rooms on the open market. So why did hotels flock to partner with these third-party travel sites? Because hoteliers hoped this concept was their answer for selling distressed inventory. They believed it was a sure-fire method of enhancing occupancy during slow periods. It gained credence during the post–9/11 period when occupancies plummeted.

Hotels with rooms available most nights were prime candidates to sign with one or more travel sites. Even successful properties with high occupancies contracted with third-party vendors, because they still had nights with unoccupied rooms. The travel sites had some basic rules and rooms commitments, but at first glance these policies seemed reasonable to the hotel operators. Each third-party travel site had its own proprietary rules, but two standards were fairly common across all vendors. The hotel was required to commit at least 5% of its entire rooms inventory for the year, and the hotel could not—through any of its numerous channels of distribution—advertise its rooms at a rate lower than the rate on the travel website. In exchange, the travel websites provided a steady source of occupied rooms the hotel could readily depend upon.

What the hotels did not consider, until it was too late, was how this concept impacted the consumers' view of their product. There is an old adage in the lodging industry: "Once a customer has experienced a discounted rate, it is hard to get him to return to regular price." This was the case with Internet-savvy users who found it easier and less expensive to shop with third-party sites than to visit hotel or chain websites. It has taken the lodging industry the better part of a decade to change that trend and to regain the confidence of customers that chain websites do, indeed, offer the lowest available rates (see Exhibit 9).

The 5% room commitments were also hard on properties. Those hotels that contracted with multiple third-party vendors (Expedia, and Hotwire, for example) were sometimes committing 20% of their inventory to deeply discounted rates. Although the travel websites allowed hotels to black out certain dates for which the property anticipated sold-out occupancy, the number was limited to somewhere between 5 and 15 dates per year. For low-season periods, this might make sense. But on an annualized basis, hotels were experiencing increased occupancy at the expense of profitability. With such deep discounts, even when a hotel was only reaching 80% occupancy, these significant room commitments were eating into profitability, ADR, and RevPar statistics.

Today's industry managers have come full circle. Third-party websites, initially viewed as saviors, then later scorned, are now seen for what they are: another channel of distribution. If used wisely they do provide an avenue for unloading distressed inventory. So long as the hotel operator considers this as just one arrow in a quiver of online reservation channels, it makes sense.

OPAQUE SITES   For hotels that are reluctant to compromise their rate integrity by selling distressed inventory at deeply discounted rates, opaque websites are especially appealing. These sites disassociate the name of the hotel from the deeply discounted rate until the transaction has been complete; hence the name "opaque." Pioneered by Priceline.com, opaque travel sites attract price-sensitive shoppers who are more interested in steep discounts than in specific hotel brands.

Consumers enter general purchase parameters in the opaque website, along with a proposed purchase price. The opaque website then attempts to match hotels which meet the parameters with the price bid by the patron. If there is a match, the patron's credit card is charged and the transaction becomes nonrefundable. If no match is made, the consumer is asked to increase the bid price to a higher rate.

Purchase parameters are designed to place the guest into an appropriate hotel. Parameters start broadly (northwest region, downtown, near major attractions, etc.) and become more specific (2 ½ star, 3-star, or 3 ½ star; swimming pool; two queen beds; etc.). In rare cases, these parameters allow the guest to decipher which property is being offered—there is only one 3-star hotel with a swimming pool in downtown Seattle! But for guests who are wholly price-sensitive and have no brand loyalty, opaque travel represents one of the best approaches for overall low rates.

META-SEARCH TECHNOLOGY   The newest category in the arena of third-party travel sites are the meta-search sites, led by SideStep, Kayak, Mobissimo, and TravelZoo. These sites employ a unique technology which uses advanced search techniques to find all the links on the Internet where hotel prices lurk. This includes third-party travel sites, the GDS, the hotel's own proprietary website, and the chain's website. The lowest prices are then presented to the potential guest, along with a rate and features comparison against other hotels in the area.

The growth in meta-search sites is potentially hazardous to unwitting hotels. Meta-search sites exploit rate differences in those hotels which have not ensured rate integrity across all channels of distribution. And meta-search sites have substantially increased the number of hits on hotel websites. This increase in hits not only degrades the speed of the website response but also substantially increases marketing costs through search engines which charge on a "look-to-book" basis. At one time, hotel look-to-book ratios were as strong as four to one. For every four users viewing rates on the hotel's website, the hotel averaged one booking. Today, due in part to meta-search sites, the look-to-book ratio is thousands to one. To shield the hotel's website from increased hits, hotels and lodging chains are beginning to create separate, but parallel, systems which maintain and continuously update property data. The parallel system carries room type, rate, and availability data for every hotel in the chain. As long as third-party travel sites are confident that these parallel systems are up to date, they can program their proprietary software to search these parallel systems, thereby leaving the website without costly hits.

INDEPENDENT RESERVATION SERVICES   Membership in a CRS is one of the major advantages that chain-affiliated properties have over independent operations. The CRS provides each affiliated property access to the GDS, chain websites, professional assistance with the hotel's own website, a convenient toll-free telephone number for potential customers, automated rate and inventory data, and a wealth of other automated benefits. Yet CRSs are extremely expensive. Costs reach tens or hundreds of millions of dollars, which is prohibitive for most small chains and independent operations.

Smaller chains can provide better guest service at a lower cost by leasing the reservation service. For hotel rep companies—Utell International is the world's largest—this is a natural extension of their primary role and provides economies of scale for hotel clients. UtellVision is a computerized reservation system for Utell member hotels. The system displays two screens simultaneously. The top screen is a series of high-resolution pictures of the member hotel and maps of the surrounding areas; on the bottom is an online reservation availability screen.

Independent hotels and small chains that join a private reservation service (e.g., WorldHotels and TravelClick) generally experience a number of money-saving benefits. They save in hardware and software. They save operating and training costs. Reservation processing is more efficient due to the massive computer capacity of the independent reservation service. And salesmanship is enhanced by joining a group of professionally trained agents. If the independent reservation service is also an ASP, even more benefits are available to the small chain: The property management system database is Web accessible. Single-imaging allows all users access to the same information. Yield management decisions can be made on a chainwide basis—refer to the discussion on ASPs earlier in this chapter (see Exhibit 5).

Hotel Representative Services   Hotel representative services take the independent reservation service one step further. Providing valuable tools to member hotels, hotel rep organizations also provide access to membership for independent, noncompeting hotels. By banding together to market the membership under one flag, the independent hotel garners many of the same benefits which accrue to franchise- or referral-affiliated operations. Preferred Hotel and Resorts and Leading Hotels of the World are two good examples of such memberships.

Utell International is the world's largest hotel representative service, handling thousands of reservations each day for more than 4,000 member hotels. Utell provides member properties with instant global connectivity (through parent company Pegasus) to a telephone reservation network, the global distribution system, and the Internet. Member hotels appear on more than 450,000 reservation terminals, where users gain immediate access to hotel information, rates, and availability.

Other Trends in Electronic Reservations

They say that in just one day, the average American adult is exposed to more information than a person living 100 years ago might have been exposed to in a lifetime. This statistical analogy speaks volumes in terms of the speed and quantity of information available today. And the trend is increasing. For example, the average processing power of a personal computer is expected to grow 1,000-fold over the next five years. In addition, information storage and retrieval capabilities of PCs are anticipated to grow at a compounded rate of 60% per year for the next five years. With these rapid advancements, CROs are facing increasing opportunities for unique and more effective ways of performing their businesses. From smartphone apps to "mapping" software, the future is anyone's guess.

MOBILE APPS   In an attempt to make their chain websites even more attractive, major lodging chains have recently been experimenting with mobile smartphone applications (apps). In light of how many corporate travelers carry smartphones, this is a logical next step.

Smartphones and mobile phones have been used for several years across a number of travel functions—as a boarding pass, flight alert system, weather tracker, room key, and itinerary management tool. But developing hotel reservation software for smartphones has proven very difficult, given the limitations of a 6-square-inch screen. To meet the pent-up demand, booking tool providers have been working furiously to develop appropriate software.

Choice Hotels, for example, recently rolled out its "Choice Hotels Locator" app. With the convenience of handheld technology, guests can now search 4,500 plus hotels of Choice Hotels worldwide, find the right room, and book it—all through the smartphone. The application proved so successful that within weeks, Choice saw a quarter-million adoptions being used in 75 countries. Marriott experienced similar immediate popularity with its Marriott Mobile app.

Certainly smartphone reservations and room booking apps will prove the fastest growing channel of distribution over the next several years. In fact, in its first year of introduction (2010), smartphone room reservations topped $250 million.

The future will likely see hotels attracting traveling consumers via GPS-enabled marketing—although current smartphone users seem wary of this invasion of privacy. Location-based services allow consumers to receive messages and promotions based upon their GPS location. Travelers who are at least 100 miles away from their home base are ideal candidates for hotel promotions, special rates, and so on. (see Exhibit 14).

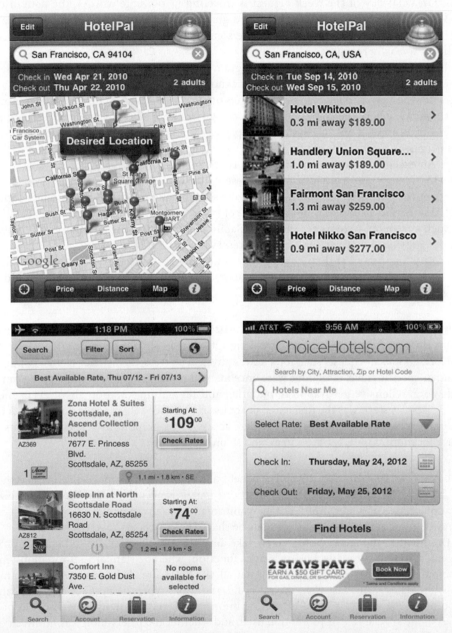

EXHIBIT 14 Two examples of free downloadable hotel reservation Mobile Apps. The top one is HotelPal run by Travelocity. The bottom one is the Choice Hotels Locator App.

Smartphone apps provide the user such information as how close you currently are to the hotel, room rates, pictures of the hotel, amenities, room availability, and a map of the city identifying hotel locations.

VOICE RECOGNITION   Amazing progress has been achieved in the area of automated voice recognition. Currently there are systems in place that can recognize tens of thousands of words spoken by a host of various users. Dragon Systems' NaturallySpeaking and IBM's Via Voice are the two leading personal computer applications. Each can recognize more than 50,000 words with 99% accuracy.

We are closing in on the time when straightforward room reservations will be routinely handled electronically by voice-recognition and voice-synthesis (talking) systems. Thousands of voice-recognition systems are now at work across myriad other industries. The biggest argument in favor of such a laborsaving system is the overall repetitiveness of the reservationist's job. As unique as each reservation might seem, there are more commonalities than differences. Each reservation communicates the city, date, room rate and type, and other basic data. These are functions that a voice-recognition system can logically handle. In fact, the simplest of all voice-recognition software applications utilizes a "command" system. This system recognizes several hundred words from a preprogrammed list of possible commands. On what day of the week a guest is traveling (7 possible words), the date of departure (31 possible words), type of credit-card guarantee (roughly 6–10 possible words), and credit-card number (10 possible words) are some of the common reservation commands a computer can easily recognize.

The voice-recognition reservation program generates a series of questions for the guest to answer. With each response, the program acknowledges the answer, allows the guest to make changes as necessary, and generates a new series of questions based on the previous response. In those situations where the computer cannot recognize the guest's voice due to a strong accent or other impairment, a fail-safe system is in place. The guest might press the zero button twice on the telephone keypad, for example, to alert an operator indicating that personal assistance is needed. An excellent voice-recognition CRO is operated by American Airlines—give it a try at 1-800-433-7300. When American Airlines reservationists are busy, the system probes the key elements of the guest's flight information. It does a fantastic job of understanding originating airport, destination airport, day of travel, time of travel, and so on.

Such computer systems can check availability, quote rates, suggest alternative dates, and thank the guest in a manner similar to the reservationist. Of course, such a system would be significantly less personal than dealing with an actual reservationist. On the other hand, it would surely be less expensive in terms of labor costs, and the computer system would never call in sick!

MAPPING CAPABILITIES   As CRSs gain sophistication, options that were previously unavailable (or manually performed) are increasingly being automated.

Commonplace requests such for a hotel's physical address, its distance from a popular destination, or specific travel directions were once manual tasks. Today, modern mapping functions provide comprehensive geographical, pictorial, and textual information about every member property. Best Western was the first company of its size to offer a mapping feature with its CRS—providing reservations agents with immediate access to geographically related questions about property locations, mileage, travel times, and so on.

GUEST HISTORY DATABASES   Another benefit of an increasingly sophisticated CRS is the ability for hotels to share guest history information. This is especially true if the chain utilizes an application service provider (ASP). Database information is currently utilized only within chains. With ASPs, guest history data could actually be shared across chains.

Even within the chain, hotels rarely take advantage of their wealth of data. All property management systems provide a guest history function, whereby standard information required for reservation becomes marketing data. After all, the hotel already knows the guest's name and address, the dates of the last visit, the rate paid, the room type, the number of guests, and the method of payment. Add a bit of marketing information such as the type of discount package purchased, the special rate or promotion used, and whether the reservation was midweek or was a weekend getaway package, and the manager has an enormous amount of marketing data.

AUTOMATED REVENUE MANAGEMENT SYSTEMS

Technology has also changed the way hoteliers sell available rooms. Rather than the old adage of "placing heads in beds," today's hoteliers need to selectively place the right heads into the right beds at the right price. Despite the fact that rooms are available for sale, not every reservation request is accepted. The decision depends on space and rate ranges available for the specific dates. An occupancy forecast determines the space availability for the day or days in question. Even if only one day of the sequence is closed, the reservation may be refused and an alternative arrangement offered. This is unfortunate if the declined reservation represented a request for a number of days. It is especially unfortunate if the period in question has only one sold-out date. Then the hotel is essentially trading a profitable, long-term reservation against a potential overbooking situation for one sold-out date. In many cases, the reservationist may override the system to book this type of reservation. Obviously, such a decision would be considered on a case-by-case basis.

In other scenarios, salesmanship by the reservationist comes into play. The telephone provides a two-way conversation during which the reservationist can gauge the behavior of the guest. Some guests can be convinced to reserve their chosen date at a slightly higher nightly rate. Other guests can be changed toward a slower occupancy period with the offer of reduced rates. Guests who cannot be accommodated represent lost revenues. The reservationist attempts to salvage lost reservations in a number of ways such as offering other lower occupancy periods, offering another sister property of the same chain in the same town or a nearby community, or when all else fails, offering regrets and best wishes for a chance to serve the guest at another time.

Requests for accommodations are sometimes denied even if the house is not full. Most of the hotel's advertised packages are refused if the forecast shows that the house is likely to fill at standard rack rates. Reservationists must be taught to sell discounted packages or other reduced rates (weekend, commercial, governmental) only on request or when encountering rate resistance from a price-sensitive guest. With a full house, the hotel may *regret* (deny) requests from travel agents, to whom the hotel pays a commission. Busy hotels give preference to higher-paying multiple-occupancy requests over single occupancy.

Casino hotels give preferential treatment to those who are likely to gamble, even to the extent of granting them free accommodations in preference to paying guests who don't play. Noncasino hotels do the same, allotting their scarce space to reservations from certain areas or markets that the hotel is trying to develop.

The Yield Management Revolution

Revenue management, which is the act of controlling rates and restricting occupancies in an effort to maximize gross rooms revenue, is also commonly referred to as *yield management*. In its simplest form, yield management has been around for decades. Any seasoned manager who increased room rates as occupancy rose, or who quoted higher rates for holidays and special event periods, or who saved the last few room nights for extended-stay reservations was using yield management. It is not the practice of yield management that is new, it is the incorporation of revenue managers into dedicated senior staff positions and the automation of yield management into property management systems that is new.

Despite the low business cycle experienced by the lodging industry in the early 1990s, this was the first time hotels began adding revenue managers (or yield managers) to their organizations. Then and now, the position is easily justified by the revenue offset. Some 15–25% of recent ADR growth has been attributed to yield management. To illustrate, a 400-room property with an overall 10% increase in ADR from, say, $118–$129.80 could attribute about $2 of the nearly $12 increase directly to the new yield team. Assuming 70% occupancy, that produces some $200,000 annually (400 rooms × 70% 365 days × $2)—a substantial return on the yield manager's salary and technological investment.

A BRIEF HISTORY OF YIELD MANAGEMENT As with other businesses, price (hotel room rate) is a major factor in the decision to purchase one product over another. That is especially true in an industry as segmented as the lodging industry. Yield management works best when there are distinct market segments to attract. It is the price sensitivity of these market segments that made yield management practices successful in the first place.

The Airlines' Role   Just as it did with GDS and CRS technologies, the lodging industry adopted yield management from the airline industry. Airline rate discounting was widespread in the early 1980s, and that contributed to the array of prices airlines found difficult to track. They began experimenting with adjusted rates based on demand forecasts. Discounted tickets purchased far in advance were used to establish a minimum level of seat occupancy and to forecast overall demand. Low and seasonal periods were also discounted. As the plane filled and the departure date neared, higher and higher fares were charged. Full price—a price that would have been virtually impossible to charge when the plane was empty—will be eventually charged for the remaining seats.

Airlines and hotels are much alike. Both have a relatively fixed supply of product (seats and rooms), and both have products that perish with the passage of time. In the 1980s, airlines had one extra edge—large computer capacity. It takes the computing power of these large systems to simultaneously track occupancy (seat or room) and the variety of price options that both industries market.

Price-sensitive concepts have been employed by hoteliers for a long, long time. Refining the practices and developing them into a computer program with *rules and triggers*, with a historical database and a strategy, awaited the superior computer capability of the airlines. Today, most major lodging chains have developed automated yield management systems that rival the best of the airline systems.

Market Demand   Airlines and hotels did differ in one respect: their view of the guest. Hotels had previously operated on the belief that their customer was not a discretionary traveler. The guest who stayed, hoteliers felt, was someone who had to stay. Guests did not visit merely because the price was reduced enough to lure them in. Urban hotels, which cater to the least flexible guest, the commercial traveler, first evidenced the change. In desperate need of weekend business, these properties began to successfully market weekend specials to discretionary buyers. The yield management revolution had begun.

Yield management has an economic rationale. It assumes that all customers are price conscious—that they are aware of the existence of and the significance of price variations. It also assumes that customers are price sensitive—that their buying habits respond to increases and decreases in price.

All things equal, the guest is motivated by lower prices. Theoretically, when a similar room type is available for a significantly lower rate at an otherwise equal hotel, the guest will select the lower-priced accommodation. In addition, guests who might not have left home at the rack rate are inclined to visit hotels when rates are low. This explains why low-occupancy periods are generally accompanied by lower average room rates.

Each customer class has different degrees of price consciousness and price sensitivity. Earlier discussions on segmentation indicated the wide range of guests to whom the industry appeals. In simple categories, these are the business (corporate) class, the leisure (transient) guest, and the group (corporate and tour) buyers.

Corporate Guests   The business or corporate customer is less sensitive to price— it is not because he or she is not aware of price, just that the customer is less sensitive to it. Businesspersons must travel when the need arises; they do not travel merely because the price is reduced.

Business arrangements may be made only a few days or hours before arrival (see Exhibit 15). Location is critically important, both to save travel time and to present the proper image. Business travelers need to be near the business district, which means high-priced real estate and high room rates. These travelers are away from home a good deal. They seek and probably merit a higher level of comfort than the occasional leisure traveler. In summary, business guests pay higher rates because they are less price sensitive. They have to stay in a specific location at a given time, and that arrangement is often made suddenly, with little advance planning, and therefore little opportunity to obtain discounted rates.

Leisure Guests   The leisure guest, as the name implies, is 180 degrees removed from the corporate traveler. With leisure guests, lead time is long. Reservation bookings are well planned,

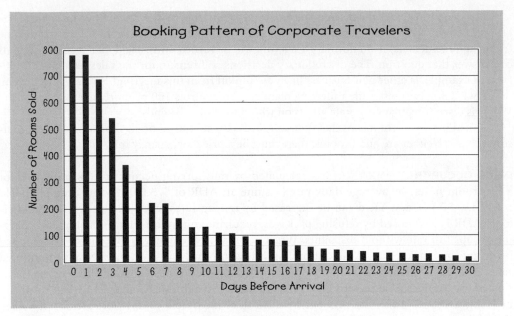

Booking Pattern of Corporate Travelers

EXHIBIT 15 A 30-day booking pattern for corporate travelers. Although some corporate guests book 30 (or more) days in advance, the majority reserve rooms within a few days of arrival. This 275-room hotel receives approximately 60% of its business from corporate guests. In a sample month, some 800 corporate guests make reservations the same day as arrival (0 days). Another 800 book one day in advance.

with adequate time to shop for the best room rates. This class of guest is flexible as to the time of the trip, the destination of the trip, and stopping points along the way. These guests may not even use a hotel. High prices might drive them into camping or park facilities. Poor price value might send them to the homes of friends or family. When prices of accommodations, fuel, toll roads, and gasoline are too high, this guest may just stay home.

Leisure travelers have been the major beneficiaries of the yield management approach offered by both the airline and the hotel industries. The leisure traveler's flexibility with regard to travel dates and itineraries allows him or her to take advantage of deep discounting during off-season and slow demand periods. It is not uncommon to find hotel rooms discounted between 50% and 80% during slow periods. A $250 hotel room in Australia's Kakadu National Park in the tropics, for example, may cost only $100 or so during the rainy season; a $400 golf package in Palm Springs may be discounted to $175 in during summer.

Group Guests *Group business,* the last of the three general classifications, exhibits characteristics from both of the other two categories. This is because the group market forms from components of the business and leisure classifications. From the leisure category come social, fraternal, and hobby associations. From the business segment come professional, union, and governmental groups.

Both types of groups—leisure and business—have their own idiosyncrasies. Generally, business-oriented groups are sensitive to date and place while being less sensitive to rate. This is because business groups usually meet the same week every year. Leisure-oriented groups are more rate sensitive and therefore tend to be somewhat flexible with regard to date and place. Profits can be increased if the sales department, based on good forecasting, can steer the business to the right (right for the hotel) time, place, and rate.

Yield management has changed the interface between the sales department and the group buyer. Based on information from the yield management program, the sales department and/or the revenue manager must decide to take the business, reject the business, or try to negotiate a different time at a different rate. Saturday arrival for a group might actually prove more profitable at $90 per night, for example, than a Monday arrival (which replaces high-rate corporate guests) at $115 per night. A well-programmed yield management system should provide the answer.

At issue is whether the discounted room rates requested by the group plus the value of the group's meeting room and banquet business are valued at more or less than the forecasted income (room and incidentals) from normal guests who will be turned away. Yield management systems can answer that question. The discretionary decisions still remain for the salespersons to evaluate. For example, is other new business likely to spin off from this meeting? Is this a single event, or are we doing business with a meeting planner who controls 100 or more meetings per year? Will this disrupt regular corporate guests on whom the hotel depends?

Yield management means that function rooms are no longer booked on a first-come, first-served basis. Neither are guest rooms; there must be a price–occupancy mix.

PRICE–OCCUPANCY MIX Yield is calculated by multiplying occupancy (assume 65% for a 250-room hotel) by average daily rate (assume an ADR of $75.00). In this example, yield is $12,187.50 per day. Yield can be increased by raising rates when occupancy (demand) is high. ADR is also raised by refusing packages, requiring minimum lengths of stay, and charging groups full rate without discounts. When occupancy (demand) is low, prices are dropped by promoting packages, seeking out price-sensitive groups, and creating special promotional rates. That is the dichotomy of the lodging industry. When times are good (high occupancy), they are very good because with high occupancy comes high rate. Conversely, when times are bad (low demand), times are very bad because all of the hotel's competitors are also lowering their prices.

Since yield is the product of these two elements, equilibrium is obtainable by increasing one factor when the other decreases. Exhibit 16 illustrates the mathematics. Yield in all three cases is identical. To earn the same room revenue, management must choose between high ADR or high occupancy.

All managers will not view the values in Exhibit 16 as being equal. Some would prefer the higher occupancy over the higher rate. Higher occupancy means more persons on property. More guests translate into more food and beverage revenue, more in-room entertainment, more calls for laundry and dry cleaning. More guests mean more greens fees, more amusement park admissions, or more money spent in the casino. For these reasons, many hotels charge the same rate for single or double occupancy.

A different group of operators might prefer to strengthen their ADR. These managers feel that ADR is the barometer of a property's service and quality levels. With the lower occupancy that accompanies higher ADR, hotels save on variable costs like utilities, wear and tear on furniture and equipment, and reduced levels of staffing.

Clearly, price–occupancy mix is not a simple, single decision. Dropping rates to increase occupancy might not be the choice of every manager. Indeed, the same manager might take that strategy at one hotel but not at another. Variations in the facilities of the hotel, in its client base, and in the perspective of its management will determine the policies to be applied.

Revenue per Available Room Yield is usually expressed in terms of gross revenue per day, per month, or per year (see Exhibit 16). However, there is a special advantage to quoting

Hotel	Average Daily Rate	Percent Occupancy	Monthly Gross Revenue[a]	Potential Revenue	Yield Percentage
A	$ 75	65.00	$377,812.50	$620,000	60.9
B	$100	48.75	377,812.50	620,000	60.9
C	$ 50	97.50	377,812.50	620,000	60.9

[a] Revenue or Yield.

EXHIBIT 16 Price–occupancy mix: Yield is the product of occupancy times rate. Management decides whether a higher rate (ADR) or a higher occupancy is preferable. This exhibit assumes 250 rooms and a 31-day month. Potential revenue assumes 100% occupancy at an $80 rate: 250 rooms × 100% occupancy × $80 × 31 days equals $620,000 potential monthly revenue.

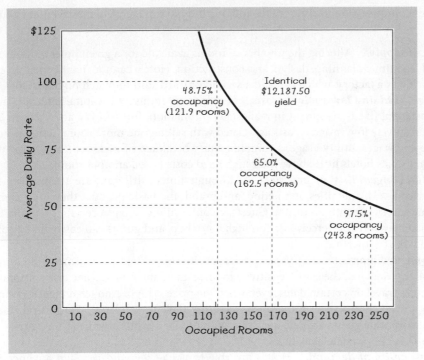

EXHIBIT 17 Referring to the 250-room hotel of Exhibit 16, this graph demonstrates the infinite number of points that make up the daily yield curve.

yield in terms of revenue per available room (RevPAR). RevPAR combines occupancy and average daily rate into a single number. Continuing the illustration discussed earlier, a 250-room hotel at 65% occupancy and $75 ADR produces revenue per available room (RevPAR) of $48.75 (65% × 75).

Before the popularization of RevPAR in the mid-1990s, hotel managers tended toward one of the two camps described above. They migrated either toward higher occupancies or toward higher ADRs. Managers who work toward maximizing RevPAR strive toward a balance or equilibrium between occupancy and rate (see Exhibit 17).

The only difference between calculating yield and RevPAR is that yield defines gross revenues from all rooms sold, whereas RevPAR looks at revenue per available room. In fact, if you take RevPAR for any given day and multiply it by the number of rooms available in the hotel, the product is that day's yield. To demonstrate, take the $48.75 RevPAR found above in our ongoing example and multiply it by the 250 rooms available. The product is the same $12,187.50 yield calculated several paragraphs above in the price–occupancy mix discussion and shown in Exhibit 17.

Contribution Margin The RevPAR calculation is also beneficial to management as a quick glimpse into the hotel's success on any given day. If the hotel knows its fixed costs on a per-room per-day basis (fixed costs include administrative salaries, mortgage debt, fixed franchise fees, and insurance, to name a few), it can quickly gauge how much, if any, of the RevPAR can be contributed toward variable costs and profits. In our ongoing example, if RevPAR is $48.75 and fixed costs are $23.25, then $25.50 per available room can be contributed toward variable costs and profit (commonly referred to as the *contribution margin*). Management can readily see how well the hotel performed on that given day.

IDEAL CONDITIONS FOR YIELD MANAGEMENT Not all industries are successful with managing yield. Unique conditions exist in the lodging and airline industries which set them apart. Perishability of inventory is foremost among these differences. Unlike manufactured goods, which can be inventoried for long periods before being sold, hotel rooms, airline seats, cruise ship berths, ferryboat stalls, and theater and movie seats are all examples of products which perish with time. Hotel rooms, berths, and seats which are not sold tonight are lost forever.

Some unique characteristics of the lodging industry make yield management a successful strategy:

- *Fixed supply.*   Altering the number of rooms available for a given hotel requires substantial lead time, planning, design, and construction. Hotels cannot change their inventory as quickly as a factory, which can add a second or third shift to match high demand.
- *High fixed and low variable costs.*   The lodging industry is capital intensive, requiring substantial fixed investment in real estate, automation, furnishings, and salaries. Yet there are relatively low variable costs associated with selling one more room. Aside from housekeeping wages, utility usage, a complimentary breakfast (if included), and some wear and tear, it costs hotels little above their high fixed costs to sell another room.
- *Interchangeability of products.*   Although hotels differentiate themselves through service levels, amenities, marketing, and brand, the basic product they offer is much the same across the entire industry. Guests are only willing to pay a certain premium for these differences (real or perceived). Too high a markup, and guests can easily find a competing product at a lower rate.
- *Segmented markets with differing price sensitivity.*   Yield management would not work if all travelers had the same sensitivity to price and date. It works because corporate guests need to travel on certain dates, even when the price is high. And leisure guests want to buy low-priced rooms, even if that means altering their travel dates. The general rule here is that corporate guests are date-sensitive, but not rate-sensitive; while leisure guests are rate-senstive, but not date-sensitive.
- *Seasonality of demand.*   Hotels are able to gauge demand through advance reservation sales and historically based projections. And there are clear demand patterns across seasons.

TOOLS FOR MEASURING RESULTS   The revenue manager's daily task is a formidable one. Both average daily rate and occupancy percentage must be maximized internally and ranked against competitive performances. There are two parts to this *competitive market set*. Some hotels are geographic competitors (close by) while others compete on the basic measures: size, class (rate), and type (see Exhibit 18).

Gone are the days when the competitor's performance was measured by counting cars in the parking lot during the day or lighted guest rooms at night. Gone are the days when the staff made telephone calls to competing properties to gauge availability and rates. Today's hoteliers have a large assortment of reports and subscription services that provide a wealth of information. Almost all of the data originate in the global distribution systems. Statistics are the by-product of inventorying and selling rooms through the GDS. It follows that the biggest providers of subscription and information services are the very ones selling millions of rooms—the GDS.

Let's look at some of the most popular reports.

PHASER Complete Access Reports   Provided by TravelCLICK, the *PHASER Report* is one of the several formats available through this company. TravelCLICK is the preeminent provider of digital media and data solutions to the travel industry. By offering hotels and other travel suppliers detailed competitive reports, TravelCLICK helps hotels position themselves more aggressively within their marketplace.

TravelCLICK pulls its competitive information directly from global distribution systems (from Sabre and other GDSs). The report breaks hotel rates into two categories, GDS and CRS, and reports the lowest available rate in each area. *PHASER Complete Access Reports* provide hotel managers with a custom-designed look at their own hotel as it compares with the competitive market set. Hotel managers can select the competing hotels they wish to be included in their market set and set the length of time they wish to be covered in each particular report.

Other features of this report include highlighted rates that have risen or dropped by a user-defined amount (e.g., ± $10). Hotel availability status by day in both the GDS and CRS are included. So, too, are details for every rate offered in the CRS by room type across each competitive hotel during the selected time period.

Smith Travel Research's STAR Reports   Founded in 1985 as an independent research firm, Smith Travel Research (STR) is one of the industry's leaders in providing accurate

EXHIBIT 18 The inviting main pool of the Doubletree La Posada Resort. This three-star and three-diamond property operated in Scottsdale, Arizona. And included in its competitive set are such Scottsdale properties as Hilton Scottsdale Resort and Villas, Sunburst Resort, Doubletree Paradise Valley Resort, and Millennium at McCormick. Its competitive set ranged over many square miles and, interestingly, included two other properties (Hilton Scottsdale Resort and Villas and Doubletree Paradise Valley Resort) licensed by the same Hilton Hotels Corporation that licensed the Doubletree La Posada Resort. The Hilton Hotels Corporation sold the property in 2008 when it was purchased, substantially renovated, and renamed the Montelucia Resort & Spa. *Courtesy of Doubletree La Posada Resort, Scottsdale, Arizona.*

information and analyses to the lodging industry. With the most comprehensive database of hotel performance information ever compiled, STR has developed a variety of products and services to meet the needs of hotel revenue managers.

Although many reports used by revenue managers display future data (rates for a set of dates in the near future), *STAR Reports* (also sometimes referred to as *STaR Reports* and *STR Reports*) are based entirely on historical data. This report answers the following questions: How well did I do in terms of ADR, occupancy, and RevPAR against my competitors for a set period of time? Another key distinction is that *STAR Reports* do not share specific performance data for each competing property. Rather, all data are couched in aggregate, summary findings. In other words, a hotel can see how well it performed against the competitive market set of hotels, but cannot see how well each competing hotel performed individually (only as an aggregate set of hotels).

There are actually a series of *STAR Reports* providing a variety of ways of looking at historical data. The *STAR Trend Report,* for example, compares occupancy, ADR, and RevPAR for a manager's property against the competitive market set for a series of months in the past. This report also provides an index (a measure of market penetration) that shows how well a manager's property performed against the competition. On a scale where 1.0 is performing exactly "on market," a manager would hope to see numbers like 1.2 or 1.3, suggesting his or her property performed 20% or 30% better than the market average.

The *STAR Competitive Set Positioning Report* shares the data listed above, but places the manager's property in rank order against competing hotels. The *DaySTAR Weekday/Weekend Report* compares competitive hotels by their success in filling rooms during midweek and weekends. A number of other *STAR Reports* are available as well. Revenue managers are excited about a new report recently released which compares how well their hotel performs against the competition in terms of transient versus group room bookings.

Travel Information Management Services (TIMS)   The *TIMS Report* also pulls its data directly from Sabre. Rates are gathered through the CRS, and the report displays discounts and lowest available rates for all hotels in the competitive market set.

Hotelligence Report   This is another popular report available through Travel CLICK (see *PHASER Complete Access Reports* above). This report (see Exhibit 19) provides a wealth of information unavailable in other reports. It compares a given hotel's available rooms with those available in the competitive market set. This establishes market share, and much of the report then compares actual history with theoretical market share. Data for the *Hotelligence Report* come directly from Amadeus, Sabre, and Worldspan—and the information from these three sources can be viewed both individually and in aggregate.

THE HOTELLIGENCE REPORT

Data Solutions for the Digital World

Subscriber	Vendor Code	GDS	Total Rooms	Data Exists													Fair Share
				Jan	Feb	Mar	Apr	May	Jun	Jul	Aug	Sep	Oct	Nov	Dec	Jan	
The Premiere Hotel	TC	Amadeus		Y	Y	Y	Y	Y	Y	Y	Y	Y	Y	Y	Y	Y	
First Avenue	TC	SABRE	168	Y	Y	Y	Y	Y	Y	Y	Y	Y	Y	Y	Y	Y	11.4%
Chicago, IL 60601	TC	Travelport		Y	Y	Y	Y	Y	Y	Y	Y	Y	Y	Y	Y	Y	
Competitive Set																	
Luxury Suites	AM	Amadeus		Y	Y	Y	Y	Y	Y	Y	Y	Y	Y	Y	Y	Y	
392 Hampshire Blvd.	AM	SABRE	121	Y	Y	Y	Y	Y	Y	Y	Y	Y	Y	Y	Y	Y	8.2%
Chicago, IL 60601	AM	Travelport		Y	Y	Y	Y	Y	Y	Y	Y	Y	Y	Y	Y	Y	
Presidential Towers	PS	Amadeus		Y	Y	Y	Y	Y	Y	Y	Y	Y	Y	Y	Y	Y	
6457 Washington Square	PS	SABRE	154	Y	Y	Y	Y	Y	Y	Y	Y	Y	Y	Y	Y	Y	10.4%
Chicago, IL 60601	PS	Travelport		Y	Y	Y	Y	Y	Y	Y	Y	Y	Y	Y	Y	Y	
Executive Suites	EX	Amadeus		Y	Y	Y	Y	Y	Y	Y	Y	Y	Y	Y	Y	Y	
893 Circle Bend	EX	SABRE	370	Y	Y	Y	Y	Y	Y	Y	Y	Y	Y	Y	Y	Y	25.0%
Chicago, IL 60601	XE	Travelport		Y	Y	Y	Y	Y	Y	Y	Y	Y	Y	Y	Y	Y	
Capitol Towers	RR	Amadeus		Y	Y	Y	Y	Y	Y	Y	Y	Y	Y	Y	Y	Y	
3000 Wilson Avenue	RR	SABRE	140	Y	Y	Y	Y	Y	Y	Y	Y	Y	Y	Y	Y	Y	9.5%
Chicago, IL 60601	RR	Travelport		Y	Y	Y	Y	Y	Y	Y	Y	Y	Y	Y	Y	Y	
The Tower	TT	Amadeus		Y	Y	Y	Y	Y	Y	Y	Y	Y	Y	Y	Y	Y	
4101 Hurst Avenue	TT	SABRE	237	Y	Y	Y	Y	Y	Y	Y	Y	Y	Y	Y	Y	Y	16.0%
Chicago, IL 60601	TT	Travelport		Y	Y	Y	Y	Y	Y	Y	Y	Y	Y	Y	Y	Y	
Regal Plaza	RQ	Amadeus		Y	Y	Y	Y	Y	Y	Y	Y	Y	Y	Y	Y	Y	
632 Forbes Avenue	RQ	SABRE	288	Y	Y	Y	Y	Y	Y	Y	Y	Y	Y	Y	Y	Y	19.5%
Chicago, IL 60563	RQ	Travelport		Y	Y	Y	Y	Y	Y	Y	Y	Y	Y	Y	Y		

EXHIBIT 19A   TravelCLICK's Hotelligence Report helps hotel executives make both strategic and operational decisions to improve revenue management. These reports are useful for developing effective sales and marketing programs based on competitive information, for evaluating the impact of promotional offers, and for conducting performance benchmarking to fine-tune products and services.

The Hotelligence Report is 13 pages long—shown here are the first two pages. The first page (A) displays both the subscriber hotel (the fictitious Premiere Hotel) and the competing hotels (Luxury Suites, etc.). Information is shown for each property across the dates indicated by Y, as in Yes.

The second page displays the Premiere Hotel's fair market share (11.4%) as compared with its competitive set. However, you'll notice it sold far more rooms (market penetration) than suggested by its fair share—it sold 1.549 rooms for every one room it "should" have been able to sell against its competition. However, you will also note that the Premiere Hotel did less well when it comes to average room rate (bottom left corner of 5-19(B).   *Courtesy of TravelCLICK.*

Note: Total rooms come from the TravelCLICK hotel database. All reservations displayed on the following pages are net of cancels in each GDS. Each reservation represents a stay which occurred during the month shown on the report (date of arrival). "Y" signifies that the hotel received at least one booking from the respective GDS during the month. Fair Share is calculated using the Total Rooms from the TravelCLICK hotel database.

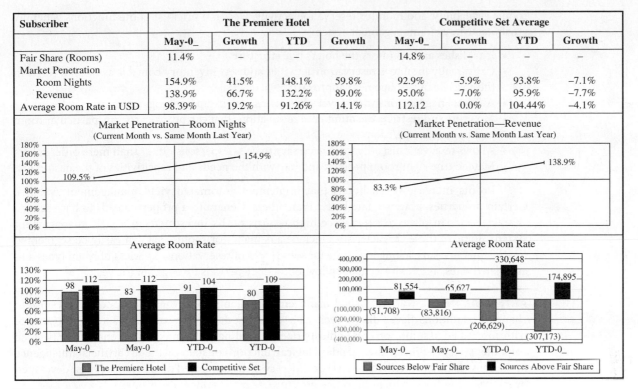

Subscriber	The Premiere Hotel				Competitive Set Average			
	May-0_	Growth	YTD	Growth	May-0_	Growth	YTD	Growth
Fair Share (Rooms)	11.4%	–	–	–	14.8%	–	–	–
Market Penetration								
Room Nights	154.9%	41.5%	148.1%	59.8%	92.9%	–5.9%	93.8%	–7.1%
Revenue	138.9%	66.7%	132.2%	89.0%	95.0%	–7.0%	95.9%	–7.7%
Average Room Rate in USD	98.39%	19.2%	91.26%	14.1%	112.12	0.0%	104.44%	–4.1%

EXHIBIT 19B

Specifically, the report compares room nights sold for the manager's hotel against room nights sold across the competitive set. Again, if the manager's hotel exceeds the theoretical market share, the report will show a market penetration of greater than 1.0. Similar statistics are available comparing overall revenue (yield) in the competitive set of hotels as well as average daily rate. Another thing this report does quite well is to show growth trends for current periods against similar periods the previous year.

Expedia Competitive Price Grid Report   For hotels that sell rooms through Expedia, this has become a valuable report. Rates advertised in Expedia and its competitors help the hotel manage its own website. The revenue manager must be certain that best available rates listed on Expedia are not substantially lower than best available rates listed on the hotel's website. If Expedia is significantly lower, the hotel is encouraging guests to visit other websites as opposed to visiting the hotel's website directly. Remember, the hotel saves numerous commission fees when guests book rooms directly through its website.

Other Reports   Listed here are several other popular reports used by today's revenue managers:

Sabre.Net Reports

Hotel Information Service (HIS) Reports

CheckRate

TrendFx

Automated Yield Management Systems

As far back as 1998, a study of hotel sales and marketing departments found that 80% of hotels were using yield management technology to assist their decision process when booking group business. This figure approaches 100% adoption in recent years. By today's standards, yield management is an expense worth incurring.

Automated yield or revenue management systems are tools that aid management decision making. In the absence of management, these systems can automatically change rates, restrict rooms availability, and monitor reservation activity. Here is a brief list of the functions generally attributable to yield management systems:

- Establishes and monitors the hotel's rate structure
- Continually monitors reservation activities and sets inventory controls as needed (even in the absence of management approval)
- Aids rate negotiations with travel wholesalers and group bookings
- Monitors and restricts the number of reservations that can be taken for any particular room night or room rate/room type
- Allows reservationists the tools necessary to be salespersons rather than mere order-takers
- Matches the right room product and rate with the needs and sensitivities of the customers

Profits increase in all hotels that implement automated yield management systems. Certain properties, however, fare better than others. Generally, a property needs to have several characteristics in place to experience high returns on its investment in a yield management system. Some of these characteristics include a demand for rooms that can easily be segmented into distinct markets, a long lead time for some types of reservations, a variety of room types and associated rates, and high-occupancy/low-occupancy periods throughout the year.

ARTIFICIAL INTELLIGENCE Yield management systems allow for instantaneous response to changing conditions. Seven days a week, 24 hours a day, the system compares actual performance with forecasted assumptions and adjusts rates accordingly. To make these changes, advanced computer systems utilize either standard logical functions or state-of-the-art artificial intelligence operations. Artificial intelligence (AI) or expert systems use stored data that have been developed over a period of time to form rules that govern yield management decisions.

Today's expert systems are truly artificial intelligence. They literally think through demand, formulate decisions, and provide the user with an opportunity to talk with the computer. Below is a list of the special features generally found in an expert yield management system:

1. Is able to deal with quantitative facts and qualitative data
2. Includes an analysis of incomplete data when formulating a decision
3. Explains to the user how a given conclusion was reached
4. Allows a two-way communication interface with the user
5. Applies programmable rules and triggers to its set of facts
6. Can override basic rules and triggers when additional criteria warrant
7. Maintains a database of historical facts, including:

   - Demand for similar periods over a number of past years
   - Room nights lost (regrets) through both in-house reservations and chain (toll-free) sources over a number of past years
   - Changes to demand (by various market segments) as forecasted reservation dates close in
   - Demand for and ratio of transient (leisure) room nights versus corporate room nights over a number of past years
   - Demand for group room blocks (and the ratio of group room block "pickups") over a number of past years

RULES AND TRIGGERS The computer compares actual reservation activity with budgeted forecasts. When a particular date or period falls outside the rules for that time frame, the computer flags it. Once flagged, most systems print a management report identifying periods that are exceptions to the forecast. In addition, expert systems will automatically change rates and other sales tools. The immediacy of the expert system is a major advantage. Hundreds and even thousands of dollars may be lost in the time it takes management to approve a given rate change. The expert system acts first and takes questions later.

To establish rules or triggers for the system to use, management must first segment demand into market types. A typical 250-room property might block 25 rooms for discounting to government guests or IT packages; 50 rooms for transient (leisure) guests; 100 rooms for business (corporate) customers; and the remaining 75 rooms for sale to tours, conventions, or rack rate.

Different guidelines are then placed on each of these market segments. To illustrate, assume that management expects 25% of the transient room block to fill by, say, 181 days out (days before arrival). It also expects that 91 days before arrival, transient rooms will be 60% sold, and by 61 days out, the entire block will be 90% reserved. These are the parameters that management has forecasted for transient rooms. Its expectations for business rooms would be quite different. Once these triggers are identified, they are programmed into the yield management system. The computer then evaluates the effects of changing demand and acts accordingly. If, for example, 181 days out the transient room block is already 35% reserved, the computer would flag the date as a potentially busy period and increase rates for all remaining rooms. How much the rates increase is also subject to advanced programming.

CENTRALIZED YIELD MANAGEMENT   As the trend toward seamless connectivity, single-imaging, last-room availability, and centralized property management systems (ASP's) becomes more prevalent, so too is the trend toward centrally driven corporate yield management systems. Initially, centralized yield management systems look much the same. As rooms are sold through in-house reservations (at the property) or the CRO, changes in inventory are automatically reflected in the centralized yield management system. As room types or dates begin to fill, the centralized system changes rates and inventory restrictions for the individual property. Similarly, nothing prevents the property-level management to tap into its own yield statistics and manually alter rates or restrictions.

What appears quite similar on the surface actually affords the chain and individual property unique advantages. Through centralized yield management, the entire GDS becomes a yield management tool. In essence, the in-house property management system, the CRS, and the GDS are all reading from the same page. The chain can run a whole series of reports, which improves its understanding of certain market segments, lodging categories, dates, and trends (see Exhibit 18). Price-sensitive group room blocks can be moved to sister properties across the chain rather than being lost because one hotel in one particular city was not able to meet the group's price on a given date.

STRATEGIC ACCOUNT MANAGEMENT   Marriott International, Inc., is the industry leader in centralized sales. In December 2007, Marriott unveiled "Sales Force One," which is essentially a dedicated strategic account management approach. Since its introduction, Marriott claims it outperforms all competitors in key markets where the strategy is being fully employed.

Prior to Sales Force One, Marriott's sales managers operated much the same way all hotel sales departments operate, at the property level. Sales departments were situated in virtually every one of Marriott's properties. Larger properties (a JW Marriott, for example) might have six or eight personnel ranging in position from director or vice-president of sales to sales manager to various sales department support staff. Smaller hotels (a Fairfield Inn, for example) would likely have one sales manager performing a myriad of functions. This has been the standard industry model for decades.

A strategic management approach is more centralized. Marriott, for example, has removed most meeting and convention sales managers from the individual Marriott hotels themselves, and placed them in regional (centralized) sales offices in close proximity to its customers. Herein lies the difference; rather than representing a single hotel (say a Courtyard property in San Diego), the sales manager now becomes responsible for a book of business (all major corporate accounts operating in and around San Diego). As these accounts (let's use the San Diego Chargers as an example) set out to find accommodations for their various travel needs, the Marriott Sales Force One executive is at their disposal, matching "appropriate" Marriott properties to their needs across the United States and in 68 other countries around the world.

This approach is more customer centered, creating a competitive edge which Marriott believes will return a $1 billion increase in revenue (long-term) based solely on this centralized sales strategy. The dedicated sales manager grows to understand the client and develops a professional relationship. That means when the San Diego Chargers are sending out scouts who will need to spend several weeks in another town, they will call their dedicated Marriott sales manager, who will reserve them rooms at a Residence Inn or SpringHill Suites. When the Chargers need a full-service property, maybe they will choose a Ritz-Carlton or Marriott Hotels & Resorts. And when a limited or select-service property is most appropriate, the sales manager can sell them toward a Fairfield Inn or Courtyard property. In other words, the Sales Force One strategy means one sales manager representing all hotels within the entire chain.

YIELD MANAGEMENT CONTROLS   Aside from simply adjusting room rates, hotels have several other tools with which they work. One common tool is *boxing* the date. Reservations on either side of the boxed day are not allowed to spill into that date. If Wednesday, April 7, is anticipated as a heavy arrival date, reservations might box it. Rooms sold for Monday or Tuesday must check out by Wednesday; rooms sold for Thursday or Friday cannot arrive a day earlier. Dates are blocked in anticipation of a mass of arrivals, usually a convention or group movement, that could not be accommodated through the normal flow of departures. With such heavy arrivals, no one is permitted to check in before that day and stay through the boxed day, even though there is more than enough space on those previous days.

Another tool available to the reservations department is closing a specific date to arrival. Dates that are *closed to arrival* allow the guest to stay through by arriving on a previous date. Closed to arrival (CTA) is utilized as a technique for improving occupancy on preceding nights before a major holiday or event.

A final example of reservation sales tools is the *minimum length of stay* (MLOS). This technique is designed to improve occupancy on nights preceding and following a major event or holiday by requiring guests to book a minimum number of nights. For example, if New Year's eve has a three-day minimum length of stay, the hotel will probably improve occupancies on December 30 and January 1.

Nests and Hurdles   Also known as *bid pricing, hurdle pricing,* or *inventory nesting,* this sophisticated yield management approach takes normal room allocations to a new level. Referring to Exhibit 20, let us assume that the hotel at the Greens is experiencing an unusually high demand for corporate rooms and has sold out of the $120 rate (Monday) while still offering discounted and rack rate rooms. It would make little sense to turn down a corporate reservation request at $120 while still accepting discounted rooms at $60, but that is exactly what might happen if room allocations are not continually monitored. This is where inventory nesting comes in. By incorporating a set of nesting rules, the property can ensure that high-rate rooms are never closed for sale when lower-rate rooms are still open.

The newest trend in nesting does away with the old concept of room allocations by market segment. Instead, a minimum rate, or *hurdle point,* is established for each day. Reservations with a value above the hurdle are accepted; reservations with a value below the hurdle are rejected. If the hurdle point were set at or below $60 in Exhibit 20, all room types would be available. If the hurdle were raised to $100, the discounted rooms would be closed while corporate and rack rates remained available.

Rather than selling rooms according to unreserved market segment allocations, the hurdle concept sells rooms based on total property demand. When demand is low, the hurdle price is low. When demand is high, the hurdle price is high. In essence, the hurdle price represents the theoretical price of the last room expected to sell that day. If the hotel expects to fill, the hurdle

Data for the 250-Room Hotel at the Greens			
	Discounted Rooms	Corporate Guests	Rack Rate
Normal rate structure	$60	$120	$150
Normal room allocations	75	100	75
Current rooms demand			
Monday (hurdle price is $150)	60	100	57
Tuesday (hurdle price is $120)	53	82	48
Wednesday (hurdle price is $60)	34	51	22

EXHIBIT 20   Inventory nesting prevents higher-priced categories of rooms from being closed when lower-priced categories remain open. Hurdle pricing assumes that each business day has a theoretical rate floor against which reservation requests must be evaluated. If all rooms allocated to corporate guests have been sold, there is no reason to turn down a higher-paying corporate guest when discounted rooms (leisure guests) still remain available for sale.

point might be set at full rack rate. A person making a reservation who is only willing to pay a lower rate is worth less to the hotel than the future value of the last room, and therefore such a reservation would be denied.

The real beauty of hurdle pricing is that hurdles can be added for subsequent days. For example, in Exhibit 20, let's say that the hotel is close to full on Monday (hurdle point $150), somewhat less full on Tuesday (hurdle point $120), and wide open for Wednesday (hurdle point just $60). A guest wishing to stay Monday for one night only would need to pay $150 to get a reservation for the night. However, a guest checking in on Monday for three nights would get the benefit of averaging the hurdles for those three nights. By adding $150 for the first night plus $120 for the second and $60 for the third night, the guest would pay a rate of $110 per night for the three-night reservation or possibly a different rate for each of three nights ($150, $120, and $60, respectively). Try explaining that to a guest!

Fenced Rates   A relatively new addition to the list of reservation sales tools has recently migrated to hotels from the airline industry. Fences or *fenced rates* are logical rules or restrictions that provide a series of options to the guest. Guests are not forced to select these options; their rate is determined by which (if any) options they choose.

As with yield management systems themselves, fenced rates originated with the airlines. Examples of airline fenced rates might include the passenger who chose a lower but nonrefundable fare, a customer who purchased the ticket at least 21 days in advance to receive a special rate, or someone who stayed over on a Saturday night to take full advantage of the best price.

Fenced rates are relatively new to the lodging industry. However, the few chains using them seem quite satisfied with their results. It will probably be standard practice in the future to offer discounts for advanced purchases and nonrefundable and nonchangeable reservations. All of which have been tried.

Summary

Sophisticated automation is changing the method by which reservations are requested and accepted. Never before have hotels had reservations coming into their properties from so many sources. The introduction of last-room availability technology has started a revolution in hotel reservation management.

Last-room availability is real-time communication between CROs and property-level reservation systems. With last-room availability, the CRS can identify room types and rates at a member hotel and can sell to the very last available room. Electronic switch technology has afforded the industry increased access to member hotels. Travel agents, airlines, and subscription online services are all able to access electronically a property's reservation system.

With yield or revenue management (yield equals average room rate times the number of rooms sold), room prices change as a function of lead time and demand. Vacationing families, tour groups, and seniors often know as far as one year in advance their exact date and location of travel. These customers generally book early enough to take advantage of special discounts or packages. Yield management works to their advantage. Conversely, corporate travelers frequently book accommodations at the last moment. In their case, yield management works against them and for the hotel by charging maximum rates to last-minute bookings when the hotel is nearing full occupancy.

Resources and Challenges

RESOURCES

Web Assignment

Attempt to reserve a room at a hotel of your choosing. Search rate quotes across four sources: a third-party travel website (e.g., Expedia), a meta-search site (e.g., Mobissimo), the CRS (e.g., Hilton.com), and the hotel's proprietary website (if available). What conclusions can you draw? Was there rate integrity across all four sources, or were different rates available depending on which approach the traveler took in making the reservation? In completing this assignment, be extra vigilant that you don't actually make a real or fictitious reservation, and please don't provide your credit-card number in the process.

Interesting Tidbits

- Automation does not necessarily improve accuracy. A study last year showed that when it comes to loading next year's hotel room rates into the GDS, about 30% of all negotiated corporate and rates were loaded incorrectly!
- Holiday Inn's Holidex was the industry's first central reservations system (1965). Sheraton Hotels introduced its own CRS later that same year, but with one substantial difference: Sheraton was the first major chain to offer a toll-free telephone number to its customers.
- Travel blogs are a big hit. Sites like TripAdvisor.com and Concierge.com carry blog writeups of many hotel experiences.
- Not all writeups reflect positively on the hotel experience. To combat this, many hotel managers are creating fictitious traveler identities and spinning positive stories on the Web about their recent "stays."
- There are 500 million empty hotel room nights per year in the United States. This provides huge opportunities for mass discounters and last-minute website purchases.
- Although they have been a longtime holdout, luxury hotels are finally starting to offer shopper deals on the Internet. With savings of 50% or more below rack rates, try such sites as allluxuryhotels.com, LuxRes.com, or an opaque site called luxurylink.com.

Challenges

True/False

Questions that are partially false should be marked false (F).

_____ 1. The airline industry was smart, waiting until the hotel industry (primarily Holiday Inns in the early years) developed central reservations system and worked out all the problems. Then the airline industry "borrowed" the existing technology and developed their own automated reservation systems.

_____ 2. The concept of last-room availability (saving the last room until at least midnight each night) was initially started in Washington, D.C. There, hotels catering to Congressional leaders were paid a small nightly fee to keep accommodations available for VIPs until at least midnight.

_____ 3. As of 2002, travel agents were no longer paid a commission (of any size) for booking domestic air travel on most of the major airline carriers.

_____ 4. Central reservations office have experienced higher and higher 1-800 telephone call volume in recent years. Most experts suggest this is partly due to the Internet. Guests first check the Internet for prices and then call the CRS to book the rooms.

_____ 5. In terms of yield management, experts generally consider leisure (transient) guests to be more rate sensitive while corporate guests are generally considered to be more date sensitive.

Problems

1. On busy nights, it is not uncommon for a front-office manager to remove several rooms from availability. Usually, the manager creates a fictitious reservation, thereby "selling" the rooms and removing them from availability. By holding on to a few rooms, the manager feels in a better position to accommodate a special guest or request when the hotel is sold out.

   Granted that the reason management holds rooms may be very honorable, do you believe this practice undermines the very basis of last-room availability technology? Explain your answer.

2. Central reservations system are extremely expensive. Research and development, equipment, and staffing can easily run into hundreds of millions of dollars. How has this prohibitive cost structure changed the hotel industry? How will it change business in the future? And what options are available to the smaller and startup chains in the industry?

3. Several studies indicate quite clearly that reservation calls made to a travel agent, or to the res center, or directly to the hotel may result in three different rate quotes for the same accommodations at the same period of time. Explain.

4. Consider the profitability of a fictitious hotel which charges higher rates but attains lower occupancy compared to a similar fictitious hotel which charges lower rates but attains higher occupancy. Discuss the merits of each hotel, assuming you were (a) the manager of a budget economy property, (b) the manager of a commercial convention property, or (c) the manager of an upscale resort property.

5. Yield management programs often discount rates to the benefit of one segment of guests but charge full rack rate to others who book at the last moment. With attention to the rewards and penalties that such policies carry, discuss a proposed policy that (a) deeply discount rates for noncancellable reservations made 30 days in advance and (b) discount rates for standby guests who are willing to wait until 7 PM for vacancies.

6. Develop a list of fenced rate restriction possibilities. This list may include those currently used by airlines, or create your own possible restrictions.

AN INCIDENT IN HOTEL MANAGEMENT
Take Me Out to the Ball Game

The hotel's website and brochure contain this statement, "…we are close to the ballpark, which is also served by shuttle service…" The central reservations office said, "The ballpark wasn't far," so the reservations was made.

In response to their inquiry, the couple, both senior citizens, is told by the desk that the ball field is about 1.5 miles northwest. The guest-service agent plots the direction on a map. "Oh, yes, there is a shuttle. A city-operated trolley car services the entertainment area and the park. The stop is a short, half-block east. Let me show you on the map."

The couple leaves the hotel in plenty of time and takes the shuttle by a roundabout course to the game. They arrive 15 minutes after the first pitch thrown out by the governor. They also miss the singing of the national anthem by a well-known Hollywood star. The departing crowd is so large that they are unable to get onto the trolley. The few cabs are booked quickly so they walk back at night through a very unpleasant neighborhood.

When they complain softly the next day to the assistant manager in the lobby, she says, "I'm so sorry! You know, of course, we have no control of the public trolley. Why didn't you take our hotel's complimentary shuttle?"

Questions

1. Was there a management failure here; if so, what?
2. What is the hotel's immediate response (or action) to the incident?
3. What further, long-run action should management take, if any?

Answers to True/False Quiz

1. False. This statement is exactly the opposite of the right answer. It was, in fact, the airline industry that first developed central reservations system.
2. False. Last-room availability refers to online communication between each property and the CRS. In such systems, the central reservations office can access real-time rooms inventory for each property in the chain.
3. True. The airline industry began reducing their customary 10% commissions in 1995. By 2002, most major U.S. carriers suspended all domestic commissions. Travel agents now look elsewhere for income.
4. False. Central reservations office have seen a substantial drop in call volume. The Internet is certainly responsible. Internet hotel bookings have been growing at a compounded rate, year after year.
5. True. Corporate guests need to travel when they are scheduled, and will therefore pay the prevailing rate. Leisure guests are more flexible and will book with further lead time in the hope of finding a less expensive date.

Individual Reservations and Group Bookings

From Chapter 6 of *Check-In Check-Out*, Ninth Edition. Gary K. Vallen, Jerome J. Vallen. Copyright © 2013 by Pearson Education, Inc. All rights reserved.

Individual Reservations and Group Bookings

While the number of telephone reservations has declined over the past two decades, the industry has made substantial adjustments to the way it operates call centers. Even as central reservation centers are experiencing numerous layoffs and closures, the industry is renewing its focus on the all-important telephone. Studies show that busy people make hotel reservations by telephone rather than their keyboard. Although the Internet is the best way to shop for distressed inventory, a large contingent of guests (especially the older demographic) still appreciate talking with a reservationist—an experience which provides the caller a sense of place, human interaction, and confidence in the reservation.

Training telephone reservationists to be fast, efficient, and sales-oriented; coupled with continued investment in telephone call systems have proven valuable strategies. This is because the role of the telephone is more critical than ever as lodging chains seek ways to differentiate their products and maintain rate integrity in the face of rampant discounting through third-party vendors.

COMPONENTS OF THE RESERVATION

As telephone call volume drops over time, it is easy for a chain to relegate its central reservation office to second-class status. Changes for the worse, such as understaffing on heavy-call-volume days, closing the CRO during evening and early morning hours, and installing a poorly devised automated phone system, can lead to customer frustration and dissatisfaction (see Exhibit 1).

Automated Phone Systems

Many CROs have addressed their decreased call volume by reducing labor costs, at the same time increasing the amount of self-service required of the caller. Focusing only on the bottom line makes it easy for a central reservation office to lose sight of its basic task—customer service. After running the potential guest through a gauntlet of automated telephone queries, telephone keypad number punching, recorded instructions, and on-hold background messages/music, the reservation agent can easily forget there is someone on the other end of the telephone. To avoid this oversight, one chain actually pastes pictures of real customers on its office walls. It is a wonderful reminder that real people are on the other end of the line.

Certainly there is good reason for utilizing automated telephone systems. Asking the guest to select instructions in English (press "1"), Spanish (press "2"), or some other language (press "3") segregates callers to language-specific reservationists. Further instructions may separate callers by domestic reservations (press "1") versus international reservations (press "2"). Sophisticated voice-recognition systems are capable of understanding more than 100,000 words, and able to separate spoken words from coughs and background noise. Electronically, they ask callers for their cities of choice, date(s) of travel, and number of guests in the party.

Well-designed automated phone systems have met with growing appreciation from most segments of the lodging market. Over time, customers have come to trust the efficiencies offered. Guest self-service has steadily gained acceptance in the lodging industry. Some of that acceptance comes from a change in demographics; younger callers accept change more readily. Mostly, however, the change comes from substantial improvement

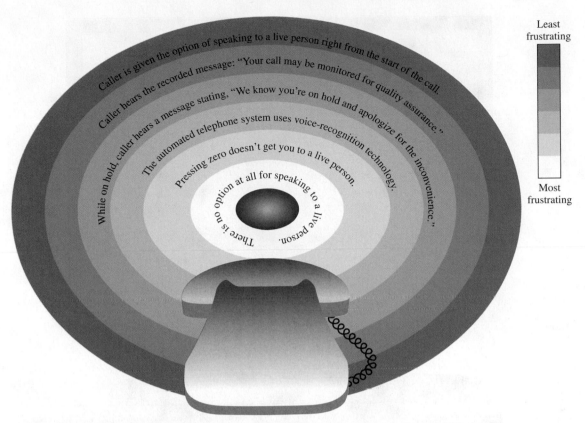

Least frustrating

Most frustrating

Caller is given the option of speaking to a live person right from the start of the call.

Caller hears the recorded message: "Your call may be monitored for quality assurance."

While on hold, caller hears a message stating, "We know you're on hold and apologize for the inconvenience."

The automated telephone system uses voice-recognition technology.

Pressing zero doesn't get you to a live person.

There is no option at all for speaking to a live person.

EXHIBIT 1 Results of a recent study showing the features of automated telephone systems which are the most (and least) frustrating to the caller.

in automated telephone system technologies. The improvement is so dramatic that many callers prefer the automated system over a live reservationist.

Chains love automated phone systems too. Research shows that for every $1 investment in an automated phone system, the lodging company will return better than $2.25 in direct savings. The savings come from reduced labor, shorter call duration, and call self-service.

IMPORTANCE OF TRAINING For all the benefits of telephone technology, one axiom is abundantly clear—the fastest reservation is not always the best reservation. In a study of a major lodging chain's reservation office, agents experimented with changing their initial telephone greeting. The rushed monotone so often associated with call centers was changed to a warmer, friendlier greeting. The results were astounding. Customers responded positively to the inviting greeting they received, and their perceptions of the CRO improved dramatically. The reservation booking rate (ratio of rooms booked to inquiries) improved as well. It took very little extra time for the reservationist to be nice and to "smile" through the telephone. The friendlier greetings added a mere 300 extra seconds (five minutes) to each reservationist's day.

Today's hotel guests, whether corporate, leisure, or group, face more lodging choices than ever before. With so many options available, central reservation offices and in-house reservation centers are realizing that a well-trained reservationist makes a significant difference in guest satisfaction and booking rates.

Seasoned reservation managers know that effective communication skills are more important than basic computer skills. Poorly trained reservation agents miss potential sales by failing to understand the guest's needs. Taking a step away from the rushed script allows the agent to develop a communicative, information-gathering posture. Uncovering personal information (needs) can lead to a successful closing. Reservationists must realize that price is not the only factor that guests consider when determining where to stay. Patiently answering questions, skillfully diffusing objections, and building personal rapport with the customer may prove as important to the decision process as the price of the room.

| HOTEL AT THE GREENS | | | ∗∗NEW RESERVATION∗∗ | | | 10/06/-- 11:29:17 |

(screen fields shown:)

```
HOTEL AT THE GREENS              ∗∗NEW RESERVATION∗∗              10/06/-- 11:29:17

              SOURCE:
            OPERATOR:      ARRIVAL DATE:              # NIGHTS:          C/O DATE:
           ROOM TYPE:         # ROOMS:                     ETA:
          GUEST NAME:                          ADULTS:   KIDS:
         OFFICE PHONE:       (   )  -              CELL PHONE:            (   )

              GTD BY:                               EXP:    /          CORPORATE ID:
           RATE CODE:           PRINT CONFIRMATION:  (N)                  RATE:
        OVERRIDE RATE:             DEPOSIT REQUIRED:  (N)          DEPOSIT AMOUNT:
          GROUP CODE:      MARKET CODE:      VIP ID:                 REQUESTED BY:
        TRAVEL AGT ID:                  AGENT NAME:                   AGENT PHONE:
             REQUEST:
                INFO:

             ADR1 NM:                            ADR2 NM:
            COMPANY:                            COMPANY:
              STREET:                             STREET:
                CITY:        ST:  ZIP:             CITY:                ST:   ZIP:
               EMAIL:                                        OVERRIDE PASSWORD:
```

EXHIBIT 2 Reservation screens are all basically the same. Systems prompt the reservationist with the same basic guest information questions (in roughly the same order). Some fields are "required" and other fields are "nonessential." Review the sample reservations screen in the exhibit above, and try to decide which information is "required" and which is "nonessential." (ADR is an abbreviation for address.)

Training reservation agents to be salespersons is the key to success in the competitive landscape. This is because collecting the guest's reservation data is pretty much the same for all lodging chains. It is easy, too: Basic reservation content where each question to be asked shows right up on the reservation agent's computer screen. The computer literally prompts the agent through each step of the reservation (see Exhibit 2).

Information Contained in the Reservation

The computer prompts the reservationist to ask pertinent questions. As one question is completed, the computer cursor automatically moves to the next question. In this way, essential information cannot be overlooked. This text refers to system-mandated data as "required" fields. If the reservationist attempts to enter an incomplete reservation into the system, the cursor blinks at the beginning of the required information field.

Nonmandated data is called "optional," because the system does not absolutely need this information in order to continue with the reservation. Examples of optional data include high floor versus low floor for a city center hotel, the guest's home telephone or cellphone number, and smoking versus nonsmoking room preference. Smoking preference is generally not mandated by computer systems, yet it is certainly considered of paramount importance to those guests averse to cigarette smoke. Therefore, though data may technically be optional in the computer reservation system, it is not necessarily unimportant to arriving guests.

REQUIRED FIELDS Facts communicated through the reservation form a valuable starting point from which the front office comes to understand the guest's needs. Corporate guests may be placed away from the lobby in a quieter area of the hotel, while guests traveling with children may be roomed near the swimming pool. Late arrivals are noted on the reservation so the front desk is better informed should it need to make difficult overbooking and walked guest decisions. Physical and electronic address information is collected so the hotel can contact the guest for marketing or billing purposes or in the event the guest leaves behind a personal item (see Exhibit 2).

Arrival and Departure Dates   In the chain reservation centers, the questions of arrival and departure dates come third, after "What city?" and "What hotel?" Telephone time is not used to gather the details that follow unless the clerk is certain that space is available at the time and place requested.

Number of Nights   This bit of redundancy prevents later problems if the guest's count of nights is not in agreement with the number of nights calculated between the arrival and departure dates. A common miscommunication occurs when the guest counts the departure day in the number of nights. Many systems ask simply for the date of arrival (say, October 2) followed by a question related to number of nights (say, four nights). Then, the reservationist verifies information with the guest by replying, "So we have you checking out on October 6, is that correct?"

Number of Persons   The number of persons in the party and its relationship help to clarify the type of accommodations required. Two unrelated persons need two beds; a married couple generally prefers one bed. Are there children? Is a crib required? A rollaway bed? Many hotels charge an extra fee for the second, third, and fourth persons in a room. This extra revenue contributes to the bottom line and is easily justified when one considers the added utilities, linens, breakfast, and so on.

Number of Rooms Required   Based on the size of the party and the types of rooms the hotel has available, additional rooms may be required. In many properties, reservationists are authorized to handle requests for up to 10 rooms or so. As the number of required rooms increases above 10, the hotel's group sales department takes over.

Name   The guest's name has become more important in recent years. In the past, the name was used for alphabetical filing of the reservation and was one of several means (confirmation number, date of arrival, etc.) by which the reservation agent or front-desk receptionist could access the guest's reservation record.

Sophisticated reservation systems now use the customer's name as a means of gaining efficiency, saving time, and generating guest loyalty. Many systems integrate guest history into the reservation system. As the guest's name is entered into the reservation, a screen pops up for repeat customers. It shows the guest's address and phone; rate, room type, and number of nights stayed during the last visit(s); and other related information. With most information already in the system, the reservation agent simply verifies that this is the same guest and asks if the information is still accurate. (Refer to the discussion of guest history databases later in this chapter.)

Type of Rooms Required   The question of room type is closely linked to the rate the guest is willing to pay. As the room type increases in luxury, the rate increases as well. Although the specific rate the guest wants to pay is the real question, the reservationist can't simply offer a series of rates. That would be gauche. Instead, the reservationist offers a series of room types.

UPSELLING THE RESERVATION   Reservationists attempt to sell from the top down. This is accomplished by offering the guest the most expensive room first and then waiting for the guest to agree or decline before moving down to the next most expensive room type.

Price   The reservation (the sale) could be lost by the rate quote. The agent may have no negotiating room if the yield management system has eliminated lower-priced options. Quoting the price is not enough. Distinctions between the prices must be accompanied by descriptive matter intended to entice the buyer to the better rate.

At this stage in the reservation, the guest may ask for a specific package or alert the reservationist to a promotional rate. It is also at this stage that the reservationist attempts to upsell the guest to more expensive accommodations (see Exhibit 3).

EXHIBIT 3   Mandarin Oriental is among the finest lodging groups in the world. This exclusive travel package proves it:

- Mandarin Oriental calls it their Fantastic Jet Set Journey Package.
- The package includes nine room nights: three nights each at Mandarin Oriental hotels in Miami, New York, and Washington, D.C.
- At each property and between cities, guests are treated to limousine and helicopter transfers, private jet service for two, and a host of special activities. Activities include:
  - In Miami, guests receive two days' use of a private beach cabana, spa treatments, and a four-hour shopping spree with a personal stylist.
  - In New York, guests are treated with tickets to the Metropolitan Opera, Lincoln Center, and an award-winning Broadway Show. They also enjoy a pretheater dinner at Chef Nori Sugie's Asiate Restaurant.
  - And in Washington, D.C., guests are provided with a private escort through the National Gallery of Art.

Now, imagine trying to sell this package. The cost is a mere $220,000!   *Courtesy: Mandarin Oriental Hotel Group.*

This is where the listening skills of the reservationist are closely tested. By understanding the length of stay, nature of the party, and reason for travel, the reservationist is better able to offer the guest a room type which most closely fits his or her needs. A couple traveling with two children is easily sold the benefits of a junior suite over a standard room with two double beds. The junior suite, complete with a separate living area, allows the parents to enjoy their evening after putting the kids to bed. Corporate guests appreciate rooms with separate desk and workspace areas. Salespersons traveling with product samples appreciate a room with more square footage.

Reservationists are rewarded for their ability to upsell reservations. In this day and age of discounted Internet third-party reservations, it is becoming increasingly challenging to sell guests premium-priced accommodations. Those reservationists whose sales history demonstrates an ability to upsell reservations are provided monetary incentives.

Corporate Affiliation   Commercial hotels are very concerned with identifying all corporate reservations. The typical corporate guest represents far more room nights than does the average leisure guest. In addition, corporate guests usually book their rooms with less lead time (and as such pay a higher average rate) than do leisure guests. Therefore, reservation data related to the guest's corporate affiliation are essential to commercial properties. Asking the guest's corporate affiliation is often the first step in determining the rate to quote. Many corporations negotiate a prearranged nightly room rate.

Quality of the Reservation   Reservations have three quality types—nonguaranteed, guaranteed, or advance deposit. Determination is made either by the guest or the reservationist. The reservationist, for example, may be restricted from accepting nonguaranteed reservations as a function of policy or unusually high business levels. Similarly, the guest may not have a credit card with which to guarantee the reservation or may have a card but not be inclined to use it. In either case, the reservation may fail to materialize because of disagreement over how to guarantee the reservation.

OPTIONAL RESERVATION DATA   Depending on the reservation system in place and/or the amount of reservation activity occurring at the time, certain reservation information may not be required. This less important information is categorized as optional or "nice-to-know" data. Examples of optional information include estimated time of arrival, special guest requests or needs, discounts or affiliations, and smoking or nonsmoking room preference.

Although required fields must be complete for a reservation to be entered into the computer system, optional information is not required. The computer will allow a reservation into the system when nonessential data is missing. In fact, some computer screens display required fields in one color while displaying optional fields in a secondary color. If time permits, the reservationist may request this additional data. Otherwise, it is often overlooked. See Exhibit 4 for a lighter look at guest requests.

Estimated Time of Arrival   By knowing the guests' estimated time of arrival (ETA), the hotel can properly schedule front-desk receptionists to assist with check-in, van drivers to retrieve guests from the airport, and bellpersons to room them. More important, hotels that are filling to capacity can be certain to save rooms for guests who are going to be especially late.

ETA plays its most critical role in overbooking. When the hotel is oversold, front-desk receptionists refer to the incoming guests' ETAs. A room is usually held for those who provided late arrival information. But later in the evening, guests with no ETA (or guests who had listed early ETA but have still not arrived) are declared no-shows, and their rooms are released to cover overbooked reservations.

Special Requests   Guest requests or needs run the gamut from simple requests to essential guest needs. That is why most reservationists provide guests with an opportunity to request any other items of importance before the close of the reservation process. If the request is critical (a handicapped guest requesting a specially equipped room), the guest is usually certain to state the need. In other cases, the request (ocean view, near the Smith's room, below fifth floor) may be forgotten by the reservationist and the guest. Then it becomes the responsibility of the front-desk receptionist. At check-in, each request is handled on a case-by-case basis. Indeed, reservationists generally explain, "I'll note your request on the reservation, but I cannot promise you will get it."

Optional data become required information in those hotels that charge for certain requests. City center hotels or ocean-view properties often charge slightly more for higher-floor view rooms, for example. Recently, some hotels have been experimenting with charging a guarantee fee for certain requests. Rather than responding to the guest, "Your non-smoking request has been noted on the reservation but I cannot promise you will get it," for example, these hotels now offer the option of guaranteeing that the reserved room will be nonsmoking for a small $20 to $30 fee.

Smoking Preference   As mentioned above, smoking has become such a hot-button for guests that many are willing to pay a modest fee to be certain of getting their room of choice. As a result, what was once merely an optional special request has become required reservation data input with many systems. Smokers and nonsmokers alike are committed to their particular

A Room with a View

It's not easy to understand travel professionals these days. And I'm not just talking about the conductors squawking gibberish over the tin-speaker public-address system on the New York City subway. Their messages are crystal clear compared to travel-brochure creators . . . Savvy travelers understand that far-flung lands don't always share the same standards.

Unfortunately, it's hard to plan a journey when you don't really know what you're getting yourself into. Before that next trip, you may want to consult this carefully researched glossary of international travel terms:

At the Hotel:

- Panoramic View: you can see the entire wall of the hotel across the alley.

- Deluxe Accommodation: end of toilet paper roll has been neatly folded to a point.

- All-Night Room Service: that's how long you'll wait for your order.

- Award-Winning Hotel: has been awarded several citations from the health department.

- International Calling Available from Room: available yes, for about $12 per minute.

- Cooled by Ocean Breezes: the window is broken.

- Unrivaled Location: requires a two-hour taxi ride from the airport.

On Tour:

- Must-See: should be called might see, if the other tourists in front of you get out of the way.

- Within Walking Distance: can be reached by foot by elite Kenyan runners in less than a day

- Quaint Village: tourists outnumber locals 9 to 1.

- All-Inclusive: all except drinks, snacks, excursions, activities, and tips.

- Rain Jacket Recommended: Averages three days of sunshine per year.

Shopping and Dining:

- Where Are You From: do you come from a country with a strong currency?

- Special Price: triple what locals pay.

- Bureau De Change: will probably not charge a commission higher than the amount of money you are trying to exchange.

- Establishment Frequented by Locals: locals will try selling you roses for $5 each while you dine with other tourists.

- Tourist Menu: one meal for the price of two.

- Fully Air Conditioned: no matter the temperature outside, the air conditioner will be set on "turbo blast" so you can deep-freeze during your meal.

Getting Around:

- Your Luggage Will Arrive on Carousel 3: some of your luggage will arrive on carousel 3.

- Courtesy Shuttle: if it ever arrives.

- Tourist Facilities Available: gift shops within 20 yards.

- Experienced Driver: hold onto your lunch. He's been to traffic court numerous times.

EXHIBIT 4 Be careful what you ask for... you just might get that room with a view. Here's a spoof on travel industry euphemisms. *Reprinted from* Last Trout in Venice: The Far-Flung Escapades of an Accidental Adventurer *by Doug Lansky, copyright 2001 by Doug Lansky. Reprinted by permission of Travelers' Tales, Inc. and the author.*

preferences. That's why literally all domestic hotels offer smoking and nonsmoking rooms. Some properties offer entire nonsmoking floors, and more than a few chains are completely smoke-free (Westin, Marriott, and some brands within the Choice Hotels Group, to name a few).

Discounts or Affiliations Corporate, AAA (American Automobile Association), AARP (American Association of Retired Persons), or similar discounts are handled during the rate discussion earlier in the reservation process. Many of these organizations require the guest to state his or her discount in advance—the discount is void if the guest forgets to request it at the time of reservation.

Address The guest address and/or phone number(s) are requested by some hotels as a matter of record. Other hotels utilize the information to mail a confirmation letter to those guests who choose not to provide their email address (see Exhibits 5 and 6). In the case of third-party reservations (as when a secretary or travel agent makes the reservation), the address and phone number of the person making the reservation may also be requested.

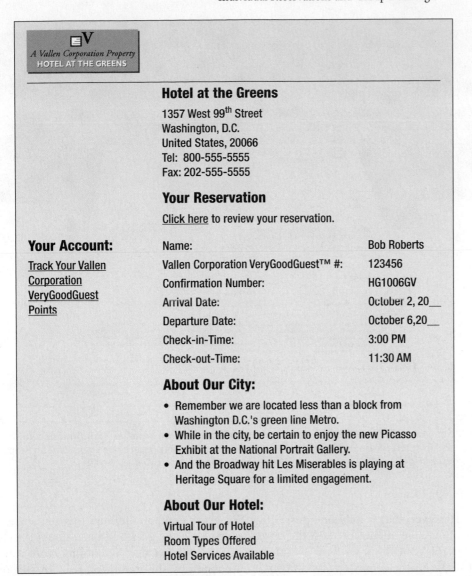

Hotel at the Greens

1357 West 99th Street
Washington, D.C.
United States, 20066
Tel: 800-555-5555
Fax: 202-555-5555

Your Reservation

Click here to review your reservation.

Your Account:

Track Your Vallen
Corporation
VeryGoodGuest
Points

Name:	Bob Roberts
Vallen Corporation VeryGoodGuest™ #:	123456
Confirmation Number:	HG1006GV
Arrival Date:	October 2, 20__
Departure Date:	October 6, 20__
Check-in-Time:	3:00 PM
Check-out-Time:	11:30 AM

About Our City:

- Remember we are located less than a block from Washington D.C.'s green line Metro.
- While in the city, be certain to enjoy the new Picasso Exhibit at the National Portrait Gallery.
- And the Broadway hit Les Miserables is playing at Heritage Square for a limited engagement.

About Our Hotel:

Virtual Tour of Hotel
Room Types Offered
Hotel Services Available

EXHIBIT 5 Emailed confirmations are convenient. They can travel with the guest on his or her smartphone in the unlikely case a disagreement over availability or rate should occur at check-in. Additionally, the email conveniently provides electronic links to valuable guest resources. In this exhibit, for example, the guest can readily manage his VeryGoodGuest points as well as take a virtual tour of the property or learn more about room types and hotel services.

CONFIRMING THE RESERVATION   An emailed confirmation, letter of confirmation, or a confirmation card is sent to the guest by the computerized property management system (or central reservation system) using the information collected during the reservation (see Exhibits 5, 6, and 7). There is a field on the reservation screen that asks "Send Confirmation? Yes or No." The system likely defaults to "Yes" and an email confirmation is sent immediately following the reservation booking. It has become the standard today (see Exhibit 5). However, some guests are still uncomfortable providing their email addresses. Those guests and others for a variety of reasons can be sent mailed confirmation notices, in the form of either a letter or a card, as shown in Exhibits 6 and 7. Of course, mailed confirmations require sufficient lead-time to reach the guest(s) before they depart on travel.

There is actually order to what appears to be random reservation numbers. First on the screen might be the scheduled arrival date, from 1 to 365. February 5, for instance, is 36. Then the individual hotel of the chain might be identified by its own code. The agent's initials sometimes follow, and identification of the reservation concludes with the next confirmation number in sequence. The number, with the pieces set apart, may appear as 36 141 ABC 2366.

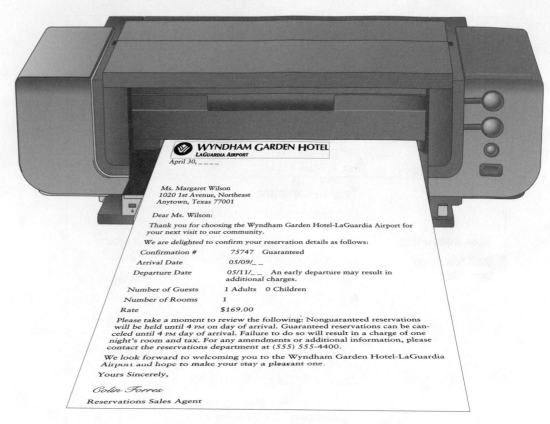

EXHIBIT 6 A letter of confirmation provides the same reservation detail as a confirmation card (Exhibit 7). Such letters are not individually written—this one was prepared as an automatic function of the hotel's Fidelio PMS. *Courtesy of Wyndham Hotels & Resorts, Dallas, Texas.*

However, that is only one possibility. Not every company follows this sequence. The reservation code might start with the first three letters in the guest's last name, and the clerk's identity might be dropped: ROB 36 141 2366. Or the number may be nothing more than the next digits in the sequence (Exhibit 7), accumulated by the month or year. In still other systems, the confirmation number is either completely random or is so complex it is almost impossible to decode.

EXHIBIT 7 As with an emailed confirmation or letter of confirmation (see Exhibits 5 and 6), the "confirmation card" above is prepared from information collected during the reservation. Confirmation cards are sometimes preprinted with hotel information. Blank spaces are then filled in by the computer printer (blank spaces include name and address, room type, etc.). Confirmation cards may be mailed as postcards. This one is designed to be stuffed into a windowed envelope.

			PLEASE CHECK FOR ACCURACY		
□V *A Vallen Corporation Property* HOTEL AT THE GREENS			Your Reservations Have Been Confirmed		
			Accommodations Requested		
Arrival	Time	Departure	No. Guest	Room Type	Rate
6/11/	GTD	6/14/	2	DELUXE KING	120
Special Request: OCEAN VIEW			Group Affiliation: WESTERN ATHLETES CONFERENCE		

We require credit to be established prior to or at registration. For your convenience we accept the following credit cards: VISA, MasterCard, American Express, Carte Blanche, Diners Club, and Discover Card.

PAUL D. LIGAMENT
1234 ACHILLES TENDON WAY
WOUNDED KNEE
SOUTH DAKOTA   12345-6789

A Guaranteed Payment Reservation:
Unless canceled, you will be responsible for payment of room accommodations reserved for one night with the remaining days being canceled.

A 6:00 PM Reservation:
Room accommodations and all remaining days will be canceled at 6:00 PM unless a deposit of $100.00 per room is received in advance.

Reservation #9821-017   **Toll-Free Reservations 800-555-5555**

Check-in time is 4 PM
Check-out is 12 noon

Reservation Information Flow

Once in the system, the reservation appears electronically in myriad formats and printouts until the date of arrival. On the date of arrival, the status of the reservation changes from a future reservation to one of today's arriving reservations. On that date, the overall responsibility for incoming reservations changes from the reservation department to the front-office staff.

An arrival list (Exhibit 8) is printed by the property management system as part of each night's audit. Aside from this hardcopy printout of today's anticipated check-ins, almost all other supporting data are electronic in nature. Only under unusual circumstances will there be a hardcopy support file. Examples of these circumstances include reservation requests by mail or fax rather than telephone or GDS.

With computerized property management systems all the reservation information is stored in computer memory. It can be recalled for viewing on the computer screen if the guest name and the date of arrival are known. In a perfect world, the reservation or confirmation number would be known, and that also will bring the information forward.

Although the majority of reservations remain undisturbed until the date of arrival, a number of reservations are changed. Common alterations include a changed date of arrival or length of stay, a changed guest name (as when an existing corporate reservation is to be claimed by a different employee), a changed room type or discount request, or a cancellation.

No matter what the alteration, the reservationist cannot make a change without first accessing the preexisting reservation. Only under unusual situations is the existing reservation difficult to locate. Difficulty in finding an existing reservation occurs when either the guest or reservationist has made a clerical error. Common clerical errors include incorrect date of arrival or incorrect spelling of the guest's name.

In many cases, these errors are found and rectified. In other instances, the existing reservation cannot be located. If, for some reason, the reservation cannot be found, the reservationist

EXHIBIT 8 Computer display of expected arrivals (reservations) list. Identical hard copies are provided on the day of arrival to the desk, the uniformed services, and even to the dining room if it is an American plan hotel. Note the estimated times of arrival and reservations codes (see Exhibit 6-9). W/ means with.

may actually take a new reservation. This is risky, because chances are there will now be duplicate reservations in the system.

GUEST HISTORY DATABASES   One of the benefits associated with today's electronic systems has been increased data storage capabilities. Customer information, collected during the normal flow of the room reservation, can be stored in guest history databases, manipulated, and used for marketing and guest service/recognition purposes. It makes sense that the hotel's increasing use of guest history data has correlated with increasing computer capacity.

The importance of guest history was first realized at the individual property level. Until recently, centralizing guest history information at the corporate level was too unwieldy to justify. Guest history utilization at the property level was more manageable.

Guest history improves the most basic component of guest service: recognition. Hotels have always known that guests appreciate personal recognition. Imagine the unwavering loyalty that can be gained, then, if the guests' basic needs and requests are recognized in advance. That is the promise of guest history.

In its most common form, guest history is applied during the reservation process. The guest history function is first utilized when the reservation agent pulls up a guest's previous stay information and saves them both the burden of repeating address, credit card, and room type/ rate preferences. However, guest history can accomplish far more than that. In upscale corporate and luxury properties, guest history databases inform front-office personnel of the various likes and dislikes of the guest. Simple preferences such as ground-floor room, feather as opposed to foam pillows, extra pears in the fruit basket, and so on go a long way toward generating loyalty and a sense of belonging.

It makes good business sense, too. Not only does the hotel gain the benefits of enhanced guest loyalty and repeat visitation, but guest history databases are valuable marketing resources as well. Imagine the potential a mailed marketing campaign might have when focused on certain historical parameters. For example, a hotel facing a slow autumn might mail a special promotion to those corporate guests who visited their property at least two times last year during September and October—now *that's* pinpointing the market.

Centralized Guest History

In the past decade, the industry has seen increasing centralization of guest history information. What one property in Washington, D.C. knew about a particular frequent corporate traveler has now become available through the chain's central reservations system to, say, a sister property in Olympia, Washington.

Corporate travelers have been demanding improved guest service (recognition) to compensate for rising room rates. Chains such as Marriott Hotels and Resorts, Ritz-Carlton, Preferred Hotels and Resorts, and Carlton Hospitality Worldwide saw the need to centralize guest history databanks and took an early lead in this area of automation. These chains banked on the premise that when frequent guests at one property are recognized like family in another of the chain's properties, the increased guest satisfaction translates into increased brand loyalty.

Chain-wide guest history databases have been developed from a variety of directions. Marriott's, for example, was designed around their existing Marriott Rewards frequent guest program. Since this program was already in place, Marriott thought it made sense to use it as the starting point. As such, when Marriott rolled out its original guest history program, it already had guest profiles of more than 9 million members. However, Marriott's guest history database system initially stored only basic guest information such as bed type and smoking preference.

Smaller chains had an initial operational advantage over Marriott because of their relative size. Ritz-Carlton, for example, took the complete encyclopedia of guest history information it had developed at individual properties and integrated it into a centralized database. Ritz-Carlton (the Ritz-Carlton Hotel Company is a wholly owned subsidiary of Marriott International) calls this database its Customer Loyalty Anticipation Satisfaction System, or CLASS. Before the implementation of CLASS, regular Ritz-Carlton guests who were visiting a different Ritz-Carlton hotel for the first time would have been treated like first-timers. Now, repeat customers at one property are repeat customers at all the Ritz properties. Any front-desk receptionist at a Ritz-Carlton can call up the guest's latest visit (say, last month at the Laguna Niguel), and say, "I see in Laguna Niguel you requested a 6:30 AM wake-up call with a pot of decaffeinated coffee, skim milk, and a bagel delivered at 7 AM. Shall we provide the same for you tomorrow morning?" Wow!

GUARANTEES AND CANCELLATIONS   The most common method for holding a reservation is to guarantee it against the guest's credit card. The procedure requires the reservation agent to input the guest's credit-card number and expiration date into the appropriate fields in the reservation screen. Nothing is processed or charged at this time. The card will only be charged if the guest is a no-show. Assuming the guest arrives as expected, credit will be established at registration.

Experienced travelers soon realize how much of a game the reservation process has become. Busy properties almost always insist on credit-card guarantees rather than on a 4 PM or 6 PM hold. Credit-card guarantees reduce the number of no-shows.

At the same time, guests know that most properties do not actually charge the card at the time of the reservation. If the guarantee is not processed until the expected night of arrival, unethical travelers can take advantage of the practice. They provide the hotel with an inaccurate credit-card number. In this way, if they fail to show, the hotel cannot actually charge them. On the other hand, if they do arrive and their false credit-card number is challenged, they can blame it on poor communication or a clerical error: They invent the false credit-card number by changing the sequence or transposing two digits on their real credit card, which makes for a fairly believable excuse. For example, if their VISA card number were 4567 890 123 456, they could simply change the number to 4567 809 123 456. Now they have a workable excuse in the event they do show up for their reservation—but a fictitious number in the event of a no-show.

Most hotel chains and individual properties are wise to this game and intercept "errors" at the time of the reservation. They accomplish this by interfacing the reservation system with their credit-card merchant bank. During the several minutes the guest is on the telephone with the reservationist, the credit-card number is input and an approval verification is received. If the approval is denied, the reservationist gives the guest another opportunity to read the correct credit-card number.

Advance Deposits   Advance deposit reservations are most readily used by properties which have either a high ratio of no-shows or a hotel cancellation policy that is more restrictive than the norm (e.g., 48- or 72-hour cancellation as opposed to 6 PM same-day or 24-hour cancellation). The advantages to an advance deposit reservation are clear—the hotel has the guest's money days or weeks in advance, and there is a higher certainty of guest arrival with advance deposit reservations.

Advance deposit reservations have some disadvantages as well. For one thing, they require a longer amount of the reservation agent's time because of the added step of collecting the deposit. This issue is exacerbated in those properties which experience high cancellation rates. Not only does the advance deposit add time on the front end when making the reservation, it requires even more time if a cancellation needs to be processed with a credit to the guest's card or a check cut in the unlikely chance the advance deposit was mailed in by check or money order.

Charging the guest credit card for payment of an advance deposit is preferred to asking for a mailed check. The 2–4% fee is viewed as a reasonable trade-off to requiring guests to mail money orders or checks. Handling cash or checks requires a disproportionate amount of both the hotel and the guest's time and postage relative to the slight economic gain.

Cancellations   Cancellations require a change to the existing reservation. This is not necessarily a problem unless somehow it is improperly handled. Handling anything at the front desk in an improper manner generates problems as well as bad public relations. This is especially true with cancellations: Imagine yourself in the shoes of a guest who previously cancelled the reservation. The hotel improperly recorded the cancellation and your credit-card statement now reflects a $150 no-show charge for the unoccupied room night. That is exasperating!

Encouraging cancellation calls is in the best interest of the hotel. Such calls reduce the no-show rate. Fewer no-shows generate more room revenue from walk-in guests and reduce complaints from the antiservice syndrome of overbooking.

The cancellation number, which is formulated like the confirmation number (discussed earlier), is the only major difference between a cancellation call and any other reservation change. Even then, its importance is limited to guaranteed reservations. The system must protect the guest who has guaranteed the room with a credit card (or advance deposit) from being billed if the reservation is canceled in a timely manner. Nonguaranteed reservations are not generally provided with a cancellation number.

Reservation Coding

The reservation's journey ends at the front desk. Sometimes the journey is long, as when the reservation was made a year in advance. In other cases, the reservation lead time is extremely short, as with reservations made minutes before arrival. In any case, the front desk is the final stopping point in the reservation's journey.

The first step in linking the reservation with the front desk is to change the status of the reservation from future reservation to arriving reservation. In a computerized system, this change occurs automatically as a step in the night audit process.

It is at this moment that guests' special requests and needs become the concern of the front desk. Armed with the knowledge of which rooms are clean and vacant, which rooms are due to check out, and which rooms are staying over, specific room assignments are developed in accordance with guest requests. Even in an automated property, the assigning of special rooms to match special requests is a manual operation. It is the clerk, operating with good judgment, who ultimately determines which requests can be met and which requests will be declined.

SPECIAL CODING   Not all reservations are the same. They may be different in their method of payment, in the guests' specific requests, in the fact that they are *commissionable* to a travel agent, in their time of arrival, or in their affiliation. Whatever the case, the front-desk clerk needs to be alert to unique circumstances.

The difference is generally highlighted somewhere on the reservation where a property-specific coding scheme is used. In this case, advance-deposit reservations will be indicated with one code number (see Exhibit 9, code 40) and travel agent reservations with another code (say, code 55). Following is a brief discussion about some of these special codes.

Advance Deposits   Reservations with an advance deposit need to be specially noted, because establishing guest credit at check-in is handled differently. The front-desk agent needs to be certain the guest's folio reflects the advance deposit credit at the outset of the visit.

Late Arrivals   If front-desk personnel know that a given reservation is due to arrive late, they will be less likely to assume it is a no-show as the evening progresses.

Corporate Guarantee   The right to guarantee rooms with a corporation's good credit must be prearranged with the hotel. In case of a no-show, the room charge is billed to the corporation's city ledger account.

Travel Agents   Special-coding of travel agent (TA) reservations expedites the internal office procedure. After the guest departs, the hotel pays the travel agent's commission. (When the travel agent owes the hotel—an *account receivable*—the hotel bills the balance less the travel agent's commission.) When the reservation is placed, the agent identifies the agency, providing name, address, and *International Association of Travel Agents (IATA)* reference number.

Reservations are confirmed to the agency, not to the guest. In some cases, the hotel lacks the guest's address until registration time. To maintain accountability with the agency, the hotel sends a notice whenever one of the TA's clients fails to appear.

VIPs   Very important persons (VIPs) are generally coded. These may be well-known dignitaries, celebrities, other hoteliers, or important members of an association that the hotel hopes to book later. VIP designations are made by a member of management or by the sales department. *Star reservation* is also used. A *contact reservation* is a VIP that should be met (contacted) and escorted to his or her room by management.

Riding Reservation   Reservations for which the date of arrival is vague may be allowed to "ride." The probable date is booked and then the reservation is carried until the guest shows or an allotted period of time passes, usually less than one week. Seldom used, riding reservations are almost exclusively set aside for VIPs, celebrities, influential guests, or senior managers from the hotel's corporate offices.

Computer Code	Internal System Meaning	Actual Printout on Guest Confirmation
11	VIP	
12	Group buyer	
13	Honeymooners	
14	Comp	
20	Connecting rooms	*Connecting rooms, if possible*
21	Adjoining rooms	*Adjoining rooms, if possible*
22	Rooms on same floor	*Same floor, if possible*
23	Need individual names	*Please advise names of individuals in your party*
24	PS	*Petit suite*
25	RS	*One-bedroom suite*
26	LS	*Two-bedroom suite*
30	Send liquor	
31	Send champagne	
32	Send flowers	
33	Send gift	
34	Send fruit	
40	Require deposit	*Please send one night's deposit to guarantee your reservation*
41	Due bill	
42	No credit, require advance payment	
43	Walk-in	
44	Late arrival	*Anticipated late arrival of guest*
50	Special rate	*Special rate*
51	Airline rate	*Airline rate*
52	Press rate	*Press rate*
53	Convention rate	*Convention rate*
54	Nonconvention rate	*Convention rate applies to convention dates only*
55	Travel agency	*Travel agency*
60	Cot	*Cot will be provided*
61	Crib	*Crib will be provided*
62	Bedboard	*Bedboard will be provided*
63	Wheelchair	*Wheelchair will be provided*
70	Casino guest	
80	See correspondence for very special instructions	
99	Print special message	*(Whatever that message is)*

EXHIBIT 9 Actual listing of reservations codes from a major hotel/casino. Code numbers correspond to an internal system description, policy, or abbreviation. Some codes (e.g., code 54) print onto a special "comments" section of the confirmation sent electronically or by mail to the guest. Other codes (e.g., code 11) are designed for in-house use only.

Convention Delegate *Group affiliation* is a better term than *convention delegate* because the members of a group need not be part of a convention. Hotels cater to tours, company delegations, wedding parties, and other groups that need to be identified. Several codes are needed when different groups are booked at one time. The next section of this chapter discusses groups in detail.

CONVENTION AND TOUR GROUP BUSINESS

The term *group business* represents a variety of options. Group business can range from major conventions and expositions (trade shows), to midsized corporate meetings, conferences, and incentive travel packages to smaller tour groups and corporate retreats (see Exhibit 10). From large to small, group business is a major player in today's lodging industry.

Group Room Revenues

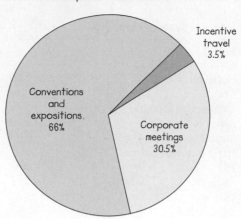

EXHIBIT 10 About two-thirds (66.0%) of all group room revenues come from conventions and expositions. The remaining one-third is composed primarily of corporate meetings (30.5%), with incentive travel (3.5%) making up the difference.

For the rare property, group business may be nonexistent. Such hotels or motels could have limited or no meeting facilities, might be located in remote areas, and face difficult group travel logistics, or be so busy with leisure travel that there is no room for discounted group business. Conversely, major convention properties may derive upward of 90% of all hotel revenues from group activities. Although different types of properties have varying degrees of dependence on group business, the industry as a whole derives a significant portion of its revenues from this growing segment (see Exhibits 11 and 12).

Incentive travel, tour groups, conventions, and trade shows have become mainstays of hotel sales in the United States and abroad. Such gatherings are clearly defined as group business. Business meetings and corporate retreats, though smaller in scale, are included in this broad definition.

EXHIBIT 11 The average expenditure per delegate per convention for all conventions in the United States is $1,196 per event ($337 per day). The average length of stay for delegates is 3.6 nights. This exhibit shows how the average delegate spends his or her travel dollars.

Hotel rooms and incidentals	$569.30 (47.6%)
Community food and beverage	$224.85 (18.8%)
Retail stores	$131.56 (11.0%)
Hotel food and beverage	$118.40 (9.9%)
Transportation (rental car, gas, parking, etc.)	$113.62 (9.5%)
Recreation (sightseeing, sporting events, etc.)	$ 38.27 (3.2%)

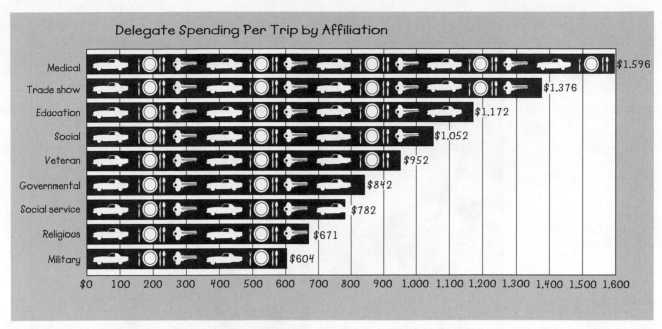

EXHIBIT 12 Convention delegates historically have spent more per trip than corporate or leisure travelers. Depending on the type or purpose of the convention (e.g., medical vs. military), certain delegates spend more than others. *From International Association of Convention and Visitor Bureaus, Washington, D.C.*

Depending on the hotel, smaller gatherings lose the distinction of being classified and tracked as group business. A small wedding party requiring only five or seven rooms, for example, may be considered an individual rather than a group reservation. Several executives meeting in a conference room for a few days are often handled through the hotel's in-house reservation department as individual rooms. Indeed, even a convention meeting planner visiting the property several weeks before the convention is probably handled as an individual (although complimentary) room. Technically, the meeting planner's accommodations should be tracked as part of the overall convention count.

Group reservations are handled differently from individual reservations. One difference is the central reservations office (or any of the GDS channels) may not be entitled to handle the group. Many chains require that group accommodations deal directly with the specific hotel property. Even at the hotel property, midsized and larger operations usually move group reservations from the responsibility of the in-house reservation department.

Most midsized and larger properties have a group sales department designed to handle (among other tasks) group rooms reservations. Depending on business levels, policies, and property characteristics, large groups may be granted special rates and discounts. These special deals are negotiated between the group's representative and the hotel's sales manager, with final approval granted by the general manager of the property.

The Group Rooms Contribution

The contribution of group rooms revenues to total rooms revenues depends on the type of hotel. Some properties—conference centers, for example—are exclusively group oriented (see Exhibit 13). Other operations choose to accommodate groups during slow periods and off-seasons (Exhibit 14). There are very few hotels that refuse to accommodate group business altogether.

Because group business is handled and characterized differently across various hotels and chains, it is difficult to know exactly the impact of group rooms activity on the lodging industry. A fairly large number of group activities are never counted. However, the convention industry (including conventions, expositions, corporate meetings, incentive travel, and trade shows) is conservatively estimated at close to $175 billion annually in the United States alone. According to the U.S. Department of Commerce, that places the convention industry in the top 20 of all industries in the United States. Interestingly, this estimate, $175 billion, remains virtually unchanged since 2008. Thanks to the slow economy and the "AIG Effect"—a growing skepticism with regard to the actual amount of "real" work that gets done during convention gatherings, the convention industry is just returning to 2008 sales levels four years later.

EXHIBIT 13 Convention and meeting facilities come in all shapes and sizes. These two examples range from a cozy roundtable conference room at the Adam's Mark Hotel in St. Louis to the 26,680-square-foot Plaza International Ballroom at the Peabody Orlando. This ballroom can seat 2,420 guests for a banquet. *Courtesy of the Adam's Mark Hotel, St. Louis, Missouri, and the Peabody Orlando, Orlando, Florida. Used with permission.*

THE PERCEPTION PROBLEM The *AIG Effect* is a term coined after the infamous AIG debacle of 2008. AIG, a major insurance firm, sent its corporate officers to a luxury California resort just a week after the U.S. Government paid $85 billion to bail them out of bankruptcy. The result has been long-lasting. All aspects of group travel have suffered a decline due to the nagging perception that the convention industry is an extravagance. Many organizations fear the backlash which might occur should they host their group gatherings at a lavish resort.

In an effort to appear frugal and reasonable, many group meeting planners have lowered their sites in recent years. Mid-scale properties are the beneficiaries; high-end resorts the losers. In an effort to minimize the impact of perception, Loews Resorts officially changed its name to Loews Hotels.

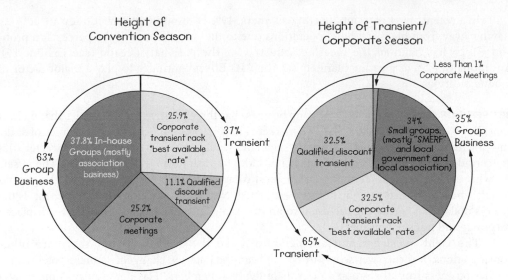

Height of
Convention Season

Height of Transient/
Corporate Season

EXHIBIT 14 Because resorts are generally located in seasonal destinations (e.g., Maui, Hawaii; Aspen, Colorado, or Palm Springs, California) their focus shifts to differing sources of business by season. Resorts can no longer depend solely on transient business to fill their properties 12 months of the year. As such, resorts include meeting space in their overall footprint, and depend on conventions, corporate meetings, and association group business to fill rooms during certain seasons.

The pie chart on the left shows the operation of a resort property in the height of its convention/group season (January through March for Palm Springs, for example). The pie chart on the right shows the opposite demographic, when the hotel will be busiest with transient travel (June through August in Palm Springs).

EXHIBIT 15 An example of advertisements the Las Vegas Convention & Visitors Authority has been supporting in recent months. Las Vegas was one of the hardest hit markets following the AIG debacle. As the largest convention and group travel destination in the world, Las Vegas needs to be serious about its image. That's why, their advertising explains, "so many Fortune 500 companies choose Las Vegas" for their group meetings. *Courtesy: Las Vegas Convention & Visitors Authority.*

In a recent study of group meeting planners, 49% of respondents stated they are actively staying away from high-end hotel operations due to the AIG Effect and the perception problem which has haunted the meeting industry for the past half decade (see Exhibit 15). Additionally, 82% of meeting planners say the AIG Effect continues to play a major factor in today's meetings.

BENEFITS OF GROUP BUSINESS   Group business has three positive characteristics that make it appealing to the hotel industry: (1) The market is large; (2) Groups provide economies of scale; and (3) Group delegates spend more dollars than individual travelers. These macro characteristics are considered by the hotel's sales team as it decides to accept or reject the business. The offsets are what is important. Total income from guest room sales, F&B banquet sales, meeting room rentals, and audiovisual equipment use is estimated. Next is the question of displacement. Is the group's dollar total, including the usual room discounts, greater than or less than the displaced corporate and transient business?

The yield management team helps to make the evaluation, but there are other considerations. If the answer seems to be "no," can the dates be changed? Is there potential for further business from the group and/or its individual members? Has the inquiry come from a meeting planner who holds the potential for other business? The GM, the sales manager, the rooms manager, and the F&B manager huddle to decide.

The first characteristic, group business as a sizable market, was addressed earlier in the chapter (see Exhibits 10 to 12). There is no question that group business, an almost $175-billion industry, is "sizable." And depending on the type of hotel and the market in which it operates, some properties get more than their share of group business (see Exhibit 14).

The second characteristic addresses the incredible economies of scale associated with group business. *Economies of scale* is a term that denotes the economic benefits of mass production. Most items produced in mass quantities benefit from reduced per-item production costs. The same is true for the hotel industry. Selling a bulk of group rooms provides the operator with specific economies of scale. The sales department benefits from the reduced work in booking one large group as opposed to booking numerous smaller visits. The reservation department benefits from having a block of rooms set aside for the group. Even the front office, housekeeping, and uniformed services benefit from group room bookings.

With group arrivals and departures, business levels are clearly understood. With a five-day convention, for example, the front office is especially busy on the first and last days: During the first day, guest registration is busy with heavy check-ins; on the last day, it is busy with check-outs. The middle days, however, are relatively slow for the front-office staff. During these slower middle days, the hotel saves labor costs by reducing its normal staffing levels. The same is true with the housekeeping and uniformed services departments. In most cases, housekeeping spends less time cleaning stay-over rooms than it does cleaning after check-outs. Similarly, the bellstaff is busiest when assisting guests with luggage at check-in and check-out. Uniformed service positions are very slow during the middle days of a convention with the exception of the concierge desk.

The third reason hotels like group business is that group delegates have a higher worth than individual guests. No one understands this quite as well as the casino hotels. Interacting with other conventioneers puts group delegates in a festive mood. The trip is not just business—in many cases there is fun and excitement in the excursion. And what better way to have fun than with an all-expenses-paid trip (see Exhibits 11 and 12)? What a dichotomy; the group camaraderie which puts delegates in a spending mood is the very issue which creates the negative perceptions associated with group meetings.

Many convention, exposition, and conference attendees are visiting the event at no personal cost. Their company or business has funded most or all of the trip. Once at the hotel, delegates have a high likelihood of spending additional money. After all, their basic expenses (meals, lodging, transportation, and convention registration) have been paid. Therefore, they buy a round of golf that they might not ordinarily purchase. They have an extra cocktail and buy more expensive "call" or "premium" liquor brands. They select a souvenir from the gift shop or even a painting from the gallery. And, of course, they might gamble a few extra (or a lot of extra) dollars. Even when delegates attend a convention at their own expense, there are favorable tax deductions that reduce the real cost of the trip.

Casino/Hotels Casino/hotels are an interesting breed. Casino/hotels generally accept only groups that have a high likelihood of gambling. All things being equal, the casino manager may prefer a group of sanitation engineers, police officers, or morticians over a group of doctors, lawyers, or schoolteachers. In fact, the hotel may prefer a few empty hotel rooms over a hotel full of nongamblers. Therefore, even when space is available, certain groups will be refused by casino hotels.

Assuming that the sanitation engineers are considered to be good gamblers, the casino must decide how much they are worth. The question asked always is: Will the group produce more casino revenues than the individual tourists the group is displacing? If the group has a strong reputation for casino play, it will be able to negotiate a better discount than a group with a lesser (or unknown) gaming reputation.

Research shows that different delegates have different spending habits (see Exhibit 12). Industries in which delegates have higher annual salaries (say, physicians) usually see more spending per person during annual conventions than industries with lower annual salaries (say, military officers). This is not always the case with casino gaming. With casino gaming, lower-income delegates often spend more on the casino floor than do wealthier delegates.

The reason can be found in such socioeconomic factors as education, aversion to risk, and moral perceptions among other reasons for which a delegate may or may not gamble. From Exhibit 12, a casino operator may prefer the military group over the physician group if the military has a higher propensity to gamble.

Why Some Hotels Refuse Groups Not too many years ago, select resort operations were less inclined to accept group business than they are today. They refused group bookings because the group alienated nongroup guests staying at the property. That is still often the case. Staying in a hotel that is almost entirely occupied by a large group can be disconcerting to the individual, nongroup guest. Walking the halls, eating a meal, or sitting in the lounge can be self-conscious activities when the nonaffiliated guest is surrounded by loud and boisterous group delegates. Some exclusive resorts will not subject their individual guests to such an uncomfortable situation, especially during high season.

Hotels may be less interested in group business for several other reasons. Group business requires a substantial investment from the hotel. The investment is not limited to construction of the hotel meeting facility. Other investments in group business include kitchen and food service equipment, audiovisual and technology software and hardware, tables and chairs, dance floors, stages and risers, and the like (see Exhibit 13).

Even existing hotel conference facilities are continually investing in new equipment and technologies. To remain state of the art, convention and conference facilities are taking technology to the next level. Not only do guests expect to find Wi-Fi, fax, copier, and printer equipment in every hotel room, but they also expect similar offerings in the conference center. These features might include dedicated amphitheaters in which every seat offers power outlets and Wi-Fi, Bluetooth, or similar technologies which enable attendees to log onto the Web and even download presentations. Sound systems, Internet-ready audiovisual carts with dedicated projectors, computers, and remote-control consoles (to control lighting, projections screens, and even HVAC systems and window coverings) are all investments being made by today's conference centers.

Facilities and equipment investment aside, there is the requirement of additional labor to service the group business. Group hotels require a sales department staffed with corporate, national, and tour group sales managers. They require convention setup persons, banquet coordinators, chefs, food servers, and even conference concierges.

Segments of Group Business

The need to communicate an ever-increasing amount of information has given extra to the convention market. Meeting and speaking with other delegates face to face offers certain benefits that even the most sophisticated social media platforms can only imitate.

The group tour and travel business has been especially strong in light of the ever-increasing numbers of Americans over the age of 55, retired, in good health, and with plenty of discretionary dollars. Lacking the expense account and tax advantages of the conventioneer, the group tourist seeks economy above all else. Group tour and travel rates are often substantially lower than rack rates.

Whereas convention business is sold as a group and guests are handled individually, tour business is sold as a group and guests are handled as a group. One sale, one reservation, one registration, one service, and one billing provide the savings on which the tour concept is built.

TOUR GROUPS   Tour groups are very convenient for the hotel, but that convenience comes at a price. Tour operators demand deep discounts. They get them because the entire burden is on the tour operator, with only minimal risk for the hotel.

The hotel deals with one party—the group tour company or wholesaler. The wholesaler leases the bus or plane, books the rooms, commits land transportation and entertainment, and then goes out to sell the package. Historically, travel agents have been the travel wholesaler's major sales outlets. However, as the travel landscape is changing, so are the distribution channels and sources from which end users (tourists) are finding their information. The travel wholesaler then combines all purchasers (no matter what the source of their business) into one cohesive group. In so doing, the workload at the front office is reduced considerably.

As much as 40% of the tour operator's original room estimate may be lost between the start of negotiations and the date of arrival, perhaps as long as one year later. Consequently, tour operators may be given the right to continue selling rooms up to 7–14 days before arrival. Specific dates are closed when the hotel is full and others may be closed to arrivals. Within the terms of the contract with the wholesaler, the hotel's team can alter the closeout date for the tours, asking for the final rooming list one week, four weeks, or even five weeks before arrival. Nowhere in this process is the hotel's in-house reservation office involved. The wholesaler does all the selling. The deals are negotiated through the hotel sales office, and the CRO is not generally involved.

CONVENTION GROUPS   Arrangements for the convention are made by a representative, meeting planner, or committee of the organization and confirmed to the hotel with a contract of agreement. Large associations have permanent, paid executives in addition to the annually elected officers. These account executives are so numerous that they have their own organization—ASAE, the American Society of Association Executives.

If the organization is large enough to have a paid executive, he or she negotiates the arrangements with the hotel's sales staff. Details focus on many areas, including rooms, food and beverage, and meeting facilities. The organization (club, association, union) contracts with the hotel to buy meeting space (see Exhibits 13), banquet facilities, and rooms to house its own staff. It negotiates with the hotel for a block of guest rooms, but it does not pay for those rooms. Members deal individually with the hotel for accommodations.

The association sells function tickets to its membership for banquets, cocktail parties, and luncheons. The money collected from these events is paid to the hotel at the negotiated price. If the association charges a higher ticket price, it makes a slight profit over the hotel's charge.

In addition, the group benefits from breakage if it sells more tickets than the number of delegates who actually show for the event. On the other hand, if it guarantees a number higher than the number of delegates who show, the hotel will reap the benefit of breakage.

The organization is responsible for its own entertainment (although it may hire people through the hotel or use a destination management company, DMC), its own speakers, films, and so on. For this, it charges the attendees a registration fee. Although some of the fee goes toward the costs of the program, the association usually profits here again.

Further gains may be made through the room rate arrangements. Sometimes organizations require the hotel to charge the attending members more than the negotiated room rate and to refund that excess to the group treasury. This raises many ethical concerns, particularly if the convention guest is unaware of the arrangement.

Room reservations are individually contracted between the hotel and each delegate. Billing is handled the same way, and collections become a personal matter between the conventioneer and the hotel.

The Threat from Discount Travel Sites

The popularity of the Internet has made travel information more readily accessible than ever before. Broad availability of such information has affected the group travel side of the industry far more than anticipated. In the past, the group meeting planner negotiated with the hotel for the best possible convention rate, shared the headquarters hotel information—including rates—with association members and convention delegates months in advance, and assumed reservations against the group block would simply materialize. But the old way is certainly not the current way.

Discount travel sites (e.g., PriceLine.com, Expedia.com, Orbitz.com, and LastMinuteDeals.com) have provided savvy delegates several new options. Let's create a hypothetical situation. Say the fictitious Imperial Arms Hotel at a shore town in New Jersey has the American Billiards Club (ABC) convention visiting from August 3 to August 7. Delegates to the ABC convention likely made their room reservations many months ago at the group-negotiated rate of $139 per night. However, in mid-July, delegates discovered that the same rooms could be purchased over discount Internet sites for just $79 per night. It is a small sacrifice to stay outside of the convention block. Internet-booked rooms sold outside the convention block will not be identified with the convention and therefore will not receive minor convention-associated perks like turn-down service, a daily convention newsletter, or the nightly conference gift. Nevertheless, many delegates canceled their $139 convention room reservations and booked over the Internet at $79.

But the story does not end there. If rooms at the convention headquarters hotel are $79 on the Internet, there are almost certainly other rooms in town at substantial savings as well. It turns out that the fictitious Jersey Shore Hotel (just across the street) has rooms for only $49 on the Internet. Other delegates decide to cancel rooms at the headquarters hotel in favor of an even better rate (although they'll have to walk across the street every day) at the Jersey Shore Hotel.

At this point, the meeting planner faces several serious issues. The availability of substantially lower rates makes not only for an embarrassing situation but a potentially costly one as well. The cost comes through group attrition. If the convention does not generate a certain number of room nights, the difference, the "attrition," is billable to the convention. The ABC group may be liable for thousands of dollars in attrition costs because of the bargain-hunting antics of its delegates.

So what is to be done? Maybe the meeting planner should simply talk to the hotel sales department, explain what has happened in the last few days before the convention begins, and ask for a new contract and better rate. That action has been tried—it does not work. The hotel will stick to its guns and insist on maintaining the negotiated rate and the negotiated attrition clause.

Today's meeting planners therefore must negotiate several clauses into their contracts to combat this growing problem. One clause counts all members of the group against the guarantee. Even if members choose to stay at the hotel as unidentified delegates, if the group (ABC) can prove the members were registered with the convention, the group will receive credit against the room-night guarantee. Another response to the problem of discounted rooms is a clause in the contract stating, "No lower rates shall be offered by the hotel, through any distribution vehicle, during the contracted meeting dates, unless offered to all attendees as well." See a more complete attrition discussion later in this chapter.

EXPOSITIONS AND TRADE SHOWS Expositions and trade shows have many characteristics similar to conventions. In fact, trade shows are often held in conjunction with large conventions. The association (or trade-show entrepreneur) acquires space from the hotel or convention center and leases that space to exhibitors. Those managing the trade show invite guests, exhibitors, and shoppers.

The average guest stay is longer with a show because the displays, which are costly and elaborate, require setup and teardown time. More city ledger charges (direct bill accounts) may occur because the exhibitors are usually large companies that request that type of settlement.

Booking the Convention

Associations book conventions and expositions as many as 5–10 years in advance. Extremely large conventions (with 100,000 delegates or more) such as the National Association of Home Builders (NAHB) or the National Restaurant Association (NRA) may have unconfirmed bookings as far out as 20 years in advance. For small to midsized conventions, two to three years is the norm.

Initially, a blanket reservation is committed by the hotel and a rate is negotiated. For large conventions requiring more than one hotel, a citywide convention and visitor bureau (CVB) negotiates the blanket reservation on behalf of participating hotels (see "Convention and Visitor Bureaus" below). The blanket reservation is little more than a commitment for a set number of rooms at a set rate for a set date. There is little additional detail until a year in advance.

ADJUSTING THE ROOM BLOCK   As the date approaches, some six months to a year in advance, the hotel begins to examine the blanket reservation or room block. After discussions with the association, the hotel may adjust the number of rooms required if the association predicts its convention size to grow or shrink that year. Meetings with neighboring hotels or the CVB may shed light on their management strategies with regard to the room block and the convention's ability to deliver the rooms committed. Finally, communication with other hotels where this group has previously been housed will give some sense of the group's attrition or casualty factor.

Convention hotels usually cooperate by furnishing each other historical information about the group—numbers, no-shows, pick-up rate, and the like. They do this because conventions usually move annually. A hotel in one section of the state or nation is not competing with another if the organization has already decided to meet in another city. Similar information is available through local convention or tourist bureaus, which report to and have access to the files of the International Association of Convention and Visitor Bureaus (IACVB). The IACVB gathers data about the character and performance of each group handled by the member bureaus.

Reservation problems occur despite the best predictive efforts of the marketing and reservations departments. Association memberships change over time, and certain cities prove more or less appealing than previous sites. The casualty factor (cancellations plus no-shows) also varies from group to group, reducing the value of generalized percentage figures.

CONVENTION AND VISITOR BUREAUS   Convention and visitor bureaus (CVBs) are publicly funded, quasi-governmental agencies found in all large and most midsized or small cities. CVBs (sometimes known as convention and visitor authorities) are a centralized entity designed to represent the city's hospitality industries. Usually, CVBs are funded by local lodging or room taxes; they may also receive some government funding and some membership dues. Because the vast amount of funding comes from lodging taxes, hotels are viewed as paying "customers" of the CVB and the CVB is, in essence, working for the betterment of the hospitality industry.

The CVB represents the city through numerous group rooms bids each year (see Exhibit 16). Many of these bids are made directly to the ASAE or a regional counterpart of the same. Hotel sales managers from some of the larger properties (or key properties bidding on a particular piece of business) often accompany CVB representatives on national sales trips.

Expanded CVB Services

In recent years, CVBs have begun vertically integrating more and more group services. Services such as transportation (moving delegates to and from the airport and daily to and from the convention center), on-site registration assistance (temporary staffing of booths), database marketing (identifying who attended and from where they came), telemarketing (swaying potential delegates to attend the convention), promotion assistance (developing videos and print materials), and even special event or off-site banquet planning (managing extracurricular activities outside the convention center) are now being offered by some CVBs.

Meeting planners are generally pleased with the trend toward expanded bureau services. After all, any value-added service included with the price of convention space will ultimately make for a better convention and might save the association money. But at what cost? Though meeting planners are happy about the trend toward vertical integration of CVBs, independent meeting suppliers and destination management companies (DMCs) are less pleased. They argue that CVBs are stepping outside their defined roles as convention and visitor bureaus. The job of the CVB, according to many meeting supply companies, is to bring business into the city. Once the CVB secures the business, independent meeting suppliers should be allowed to handle the details from there.

Certainly the CVBs' expanded role encroaches upon the independent meeting suppliers. When the CVB offers transportation services, that affects the ground-handling companies. When the CVB offers on-site registration assistance, that affects the temporary employment agencies. Others who may be affected by these expanded services include independent research and marketing consultants, video production and media print services, caterers, regional tour operators, and destination management companies (DMCs).

The CVBs understand the problem but often opt for the greater good to the greatest number of persons. You see, if a convention threatens to be lost to a competing city because that city is including additional services, like it or not the CVB will have to match the bid. The alternative is to let the convention, and all its associated community revenues (see Exhibits 10 through 12), slip away. With conventions of 10,000 delegates representing almost

SCHEDULED CONVENTIONS

	Location	Dates	Attendance
Community Associations Institute	Caesar Palace	April 25–May 2	1,000
FORBPO	Aquarius	April 25–30	300
Interop Las Vegas	Mandalay Bay	April 25–29	18,000
Oribe Hair Care Event	Palms	April 25–26	1,000
Prosci Global Conference	M Resort	April 25–28	250
Women's Foodservice Forum	MGM Grand	April 25–28	5,800
Automotive Oil Change Association	Las Vegas Convention Center	April 26–28	2,500
EXAR Corporation Sales Conference	The Mirage	April 26–30	300
Food Distribution Program on Indian Reservations	Rio	April 26–30	250
National Council of Exchangers Conference	Tuscany	April 26–30	200
Post Foods Inc.	JW Marriott	April 26–29	177
U.S. Army Corps Of Engineers	Tropicans	April 26–30	100
Public Employee Retirement Systems	Wynn Las Vegas	April 27–May 7	840
Society of Chest Pain Centers	The Mirage	April 27–30	400
American College of Surgeon	Bally's	April 28–May 2	2,300
Brain Injury Association of America	Signature at MGM Grand	April 28–30	110
Clockwork Home Services Brand Dominance	Caesars Palace	April 28–30	400
Western States Osteopathic	Paris Las Vegas	April 28–May 2	300
American Lung Association in Nevada	Harrah's	April 29–30	250
Bear Tours USA	Flamingo	April 29–May 2	200
Clinical Laboratory Management Association	MGM	April 29–May 6	3,200
Contemporary Forums	Las Vegas Hilton	April 29–May 1	350
Gideons International	Alexis Park	April 29–May 2	400
Public Housing Authorities Directors Association	Paris Las Vegas	April 29–May 6	700
Association of Firearm and Tool Mark Examiners	Green Valley Ranch Resort	May 1–8	350
Emergency Management Issues Special Interest	Renaissance	May 1–9	300
IonWays Super Saturday Training	Suncoast	May 1	100

For a corporate list of conventions, go to www.visitlasvegas.com

EXHIBIT 16 A glimpse at this convention calendar (randomly beginning with April 25th) gives a sense of the wide variety of conventions, associations, and affiliations that meet. Note the numbers of delegates and headquarters hotels listed.

Three large convention centers are located in Las Vegas and host many of the top 200 largest conventions in the world. According to the Las Vegas Convention and Visitors Authority, conventions and trade shows bring in over 5 million delegates a year and generate in excess of $6 billion in nongaming revenue.

$10,000,000 to hotels, restaurants, transportation services, theaters, and shops in a community, CVBs cannot afford to lose business for the sake of a few independent meeting planners (see Exhibit 17).

The Housing Bureau An important division or office within the CVB is the housing bureau (or housing authority). When the CVB is successful in bidding and committing citywide rooms to groups too large to be housed in one hotel, the housing bureau becomes involved. The San Francisco CVB's housing bureau, for example, handles well over one-quarter million room nights per year. It offers its services once a convention reaches 1,000 delegates in three or more hotels.

Each hotel commits rooms toward the blanket reservation and a citywide commitment is made to the association. Rates remain the prerogative of the individual properties (Exhibit 18). Two properties may join forces if the convention is too large for one hotel but does not need a citywide commitment. The property that booked the business becomes the headquarters site

The Meetings and Conventions Industry			
	Number of Annual Meetings	Total Meeting Attendance	Total Meetings Expenditures	Average Expenditures per Delegate
Corporate	1,020,300	79.7 Million Delegates	$ 40.2 Billion	$ 504.98
Association	210,600	37.9 Million Delegates	$ 52.9 Billion	$1,395.84
Conventions	12,700	18.9 Million Delegates	$ 42.5 Billion	$2,249.97
Total	1,243,600	136.5 Million Delegates	$135.7 Billion	$ 993.94

EXHIBIT 17 The meetings and conventions industry is a major contributor to the nation's GNP with aggregate annual U.S. spending topping well in excess of $100 billion.

    While the corporate market holds far more meetings each year than association and convention markets, the average spending per delegate ($504.98) is substantially less than that of associations ($1,395.84) and conventions ($2,249.97).

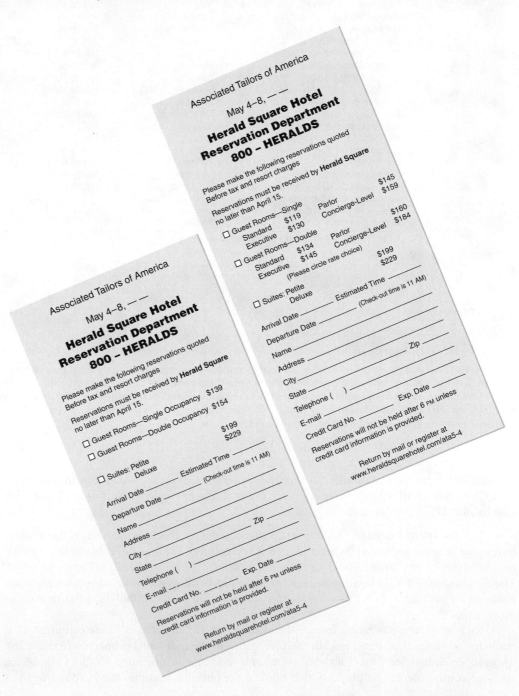

EXHIBIT 18 Here are two sample reservation request cards for individual reservations against the "Associated Tailors of America" (ATA) group room block. Note the card on the left quotes run-of-the-house (flat) rates while the card on the right offers spread rates. One or the other would be emailed or physically mailed to potential delegates depending on contracted arrangements made with ATA. In either case, rooms are quoted as room only; before taxes, resort fees, and additional charges—though resort fees are often waived or substantially reduced as part of the group room negotiations.

and the booking office, with the second hotel (the overflow hotel) honoring the negotiated convention rate. This practice is now considered a violation of the antitrust laws. Joint housing of delegates is permissible, but each property should negotiate its own rates.

OVERFLOW HOTELS   Some hotels request an advance deposit from convention delegates. This is especially true of isolated resorts where there is little chance that walk-ins will fill no-show vacancies. It is also true of overflow hotels.

Small conventions may still be too large to be housed in one hotel. Therefore, the organization finds an additional property to supplement the rooms available at the headquarters hotel. These supplemental properties are commonly referred to as overflow hotels.

Overflow hotels often require an advance deposit sufficient to cover the cost of all nights booked. This is because overflow properties may lose occupancy to the headquarters hotel during the second or third day of the convention. Because of cancellations and no-shows, the headquarters hotel often has vacancies at the outset of the convention (see discussion on attrition below). Rooms available at the headquarters hotel are very appealing to delegates housed at overflow properties. After all, for roughly the same rate, they can conveniently stay in the main hotel with all of the exciting hospitality suites and activities it has to offer.

Advance deposits help overflow properties protect themselves against delegates who check out the second day and move to the headquarters hotel. Overflow properties sometimes protect themselves by charging full advance deposits equal to the entire number of nights the delegate initially planned to stay. They may also change their cancellation policy to reflect 48 or 72 hours' advance notice.

Negotiating Convention Rates

Convention pricing is unique because convention organizers bargain hard to obtain the best rates they can. Yet it is the individual convention delegate who actually reaps the benefit of the discounted rate when he or she pays the room bill. The association executive or meeting planner negotiates with the hotel(s) on behalf of the convention and all its delegates. The sales manager, the director of sales, or even the general manager negotiates on behalf of the hotel.

For most conventioneers, the hotel room is the largest expense item (see Exhibit 11). Therefore, the convention attempts to negotiate a favorable rate so as to attract the most delegates possible. Conversely, the hotel needs to keep its profitability and yield management policies in mind as it sets rate parameters with the group.

If the convention is planned during a slow season for the hotel, the sales department is willing to negotiate. The agreed-upon room rate is also dependent on the number (and profitability) of food and beverage functions planned in association with the convention. Other factors for the hotel to consider are the makeup or demographics of the convention, whether delegates have the potential to return as regular guests, and for casino hotels, whether delegates have a propensity to gamble.

Another variable the hotel considers is the *attrition factor*. Through contacts with other properties that have housed this group in the past, the sales manager gains an understanding of the attrition or *pick-up rate* for this particular group. It makes no sense for the hotel to plan 800 rooms for five nights for the Associated Tailors of America conference (see Exhibit 18) if they'll be lucky to actually sell 650 rooms for an average of four nights. Associations have a tendency to exaggerate the number of rooms needed by delegates. Hotels must ascertain the attrition factor or pick-up rate before committing to a specific room rate.

ATTRITION   The group's attrition factor and the group's pick-up rate are actually mathematical reciprocals of each other. They both provide the sales department with a measurement of the number of rooms actually reserved, in comparison to the number initially set aside in the reservation room block. They just derive this measurement in opposite ways.

The pick-up rate looks at the actual number of rooms sold to convention delegates divided by the number of rooms originally blocked. For example, let's look back to the Associated Tailors' convention. Assume that the blanket reservation blocked 800 rooms for five nights—that's 4,000 room nights. However, at the close of the convention, the hotel discovered it sold only 2,600 room nights. The pick-up rate was just 65.0% (2,600 room nights sold divided by 4,000 room nights blocked).

Conversely, the attrition factor looks at the number of rooms that were not sold or not picked up. The attrition factor measures the remaining unsold delegate rooms by the number of rooms originally blocked. Again, let's look to the Associated Tailors' convention. If 2,600 room nights were actually picked up against a block of 4,000 room nights, 1,400 room nights went unsold to convention delegates. These 1,400 room nights may have ended up being sold to corporate or leisure guests, but only after the agreed-upon closeout date for accepting convention reservations (April 15 in Exhibit 18). The attrition factor for this group was 35.0% (1,400 room nights unsold divided by 4,000 room nights blocked).

Hotels Get Serious about Attrition   Hotel attrition policies are more prevalent (and taken more seriously) than ever before. Groups that fail to fill their contracted room block (usually a 90% pick-up rate is considered acceptable—see Exhibit 19) are charged attrition fees ranging from a few hundred dollars to hundreds of thousands of dollars! After all, when the hotel offers reduced group room rates, it is discounting them against the group's promise to fill them. If the room nights do not materialize, the hotel's bottom line suffers.

Group Room Block Attrition Calculation

	Day #1	Day#2	Day #3	Day #4	Grand Total
Rooms available for sale (this is a 400-room inventory)	395	398	396	394	
Group room block	165	210	225	195	
Net room block (allows for 10% attrition factor per contract agreement)	149	189	203	176	
Sold against group block	152	167	177	144	
Other nongroup rooms	240	194	205	224	
Total rooms sold	392	361	382	368	
Vacant rooms	3	37	14	26	
Group rooms attrition Liability (smaller of net block less group rooms sold **or** vacant rooms)	0	22	14	26	62
Times contracted (negotiated) profit margin per unsold room	$129	$129	$129	$129	
Total attrition liability	0	$2,838	$1,806	$3,354	$7,998

EXHIBIT 19   An example of a room attrition calculation. This example assumes a 400-room hotel is holding a four-night group room block ranging from 165 rooms to 225 rooms per night at a negotiated $169 flat rate. It also assumes each occupied room has a variable production cost of $40, so $129 is the profit margin from each group room night. Please note the contract provides the group a courtesy 10% attrition factor before charges accrue. Also, the contract allows any group rooms sold by the hotel (to transient business) to reduce the attrition liability. Thus, the group is responsible for the lower of unsold group rooms or total hotel rooms unsold each night.

Although attrition policies were rarely enforced a decade ago, today's attrition policies are more serious business. One of the reasons for this increased focus on attrition is the increasing availability of information to meeting planners and association executives. Email marketing and Web-based group registration provide a great deal of information in readily usable form. With online registration, attendees book their own rooms and answer their own housing questions. This releases the meeting planner from these administrative duties—time that can be used to ensure higher pick-up rates.

Room attrition becomes the responsibility of the group. If the group blocked 800 rooms for five nights (4,000 roomnights), and the actual pick-up rate was only 2,600 rooms, the remaining 1,400 rooms are billable to the association or convention group. At $129 per room, for example, the group could be facing a $180,600 charge—less variable costs (see Exhibit 19)! This is where strong negotiations on the part of the meeting planner substantially limit the group's exposure. Negotiating a 10% attrition rate before room charges begin to accrue (90% pick-up rate) is the norm. Asking for 20% or 30% is less common, but known to happen. The dates of the meeting, relationship with the hotel, and competitiveness of the marketplace all carry weight when negotiating attrition rates. Groups which return to the hotel year after year are most likely to receive the most generous attrition rates.

Automated attendee registration (systems like b-there.com, passkey.com, 123sign-up.com, dea.com, regonline.com, cvent.com, dwalliance.com, and emcvenues.com) can alleviate costly attrition fees in several ways:

- Email marketing—You're attending the convention, but are your friends? Please send this email reminder to 10 of your closest associates.
- Targeted marketing—Which attendees who registered last year have failed to reregister this year?
- Cancellation tracking—Who cancelled in the past 10 days, and are any worrisome trends developing?
- Hotel balancing—The Omni is filled to 94% of its block (no attrition fees above 90% pick-up), yet the Radisson sits at just 74%.

COMP ROOMS Complimentary (comp or "free") rooms are one part of the total package. Complimentary rooms for use by the association or convention are usually provided at a rate of one comp unit per 50 sold. The formula applies to tour groups as well.

Many hotels are beginning to take a hard look at how comps are earned and used. Attrition factors, no-shows, and cancellations are no longer counted in the computation. Credit is given only for the number of rooms actually sold; understays do not contribute to the count.

The use of comps is also being restricted. Comps are meant to be used by convention executives and staff during the dates of the convention and possibly several days immediately preceding or following the event. Comps are not designed for use months later as a personal vacation for the convention executive!

RATE QUOTES Rates are quoted as flat or spread (see Exhibit 18). Under the *flat rate*, sometimes called *single rate*, all guests pay the same convention rate, which is usually less than the average rack rate. Except for suites, rooms are assigned on a best-available basis, called *run-of-the-house*. Some pay more for the room than its normal price (with standard accommodations), and others pay less (with deluxe accommodations). Run-of-the-house implies an equal distribution of room assignments. If half the rooms have an ocean view and half do not, the convention group should get a 50–50 split with a run-of-the-house rate. One Hawaiian hotel advertises "run-of-the-ocean" rates. A fair distribution includes an equitable share of standard, medium, and deluxe accommodations.

A *spread rate*, sometimes called a *sliding rate*, uses the standard rack rate distribution already in place. The group negotiates their rate at some amount below the rack rates. Assignments are made over the entire rate spread according to individual preference and a willingness to pay. The range of wealth and interest among the attendees makes spread rates more attractive to larger groups.

MANAGING THE ROOM BLOCK As individual room requests arrive at the hotel, they are booked against the group room block. The hotel and the association reexamine the room commitment several times in the weeks leading up to the convention. Reservations received after the closeout date, 20–30 days before the convention starts, are accepted only if space remains—on an *availability basis only*.

Privacy of information provided with the delegate's reservation—either an electronically submitted reservation or a returned reservation request card (see Exhibit 18)—has received increased attention in recent years. When consumers read stories like the fiasco involving Hotels.com, where a company auditor's stolen laptop compromised the personal information of thousands of customers, the issue becomes increasingly important.

Personal information of meeting attendees is available not only to the hotel(s) involved, but to any vendors servicing the meeting and the association itself. The growing popularity of electronic name badges, scannable name badges, and imbedded name badges has increased the availability of information to many parties. Imbedded name badges, those featuring radio frequency identification (RFID) technology, track the steps of each delegate. Although there is much to be gained by knowing which delegates attended which seminars, when each arrived, how long each stayed, and so on, there is also much controversy surrounding the use of this personal information.

Competitive Clauses Most attendees carry laptop computers and video-capable cell phones. Consequently, no information, personal or corporate, is safe at meetings or conventions, especially where wireless technology is used. This is one reason the industry has seen an increase in the number of competitive clauses in meeting contracts. A competitive clause essentially limits who can book rooms or meetings at the same hotel during a period overlapping with the group in question. A corporation rolling out a new product or technology wants its users to see the product, but wants to keep its competitors from seeing it and potentially stealing it.

UNIDENTIFIED DELEGATES Some delegates slip through the carefully planned system and appear to the hotel as regular guests unaffiliated with the convention. This is often accidental, but some guests deliberately trick the hotel to gain rate or room advantages (see earlier section on The Threat from Discount Travel Sites).

One of two things may happen with these unidentified conventioneers: (1) The reservation might be denied (the convention block is open, but general reservations are closed), and the guest goes elsewhere; or (2) the reservation might be accepted as a nonconvention guest (both the convention room block and the nonconvention categories are open). This second option leaves the hotel with duplicate count.

The situation takes a different twist when the conventioneer accepts space outside the blanket count because all the convention spots have been filled. Once housed, this guest argues to get the special, reduced, convention rate. Too many situations like that, and the carefully balanced yield management system goes awry.

IT PACKAGES The inclusive tour (IT) package is the hotel's move into the lucrative group market. The hotel combines housing, food, and entertainment but no transportation (though sometimes rental cars are included) to offer an appealing multiple-night stay at greatly reduced rates. The IT package affects group bookings, but it is not a type of group business.

IT packages can and do compete with convention reservations. For large conventions, the yield management committee closes the remaining rooms to all but high-priced rates. When relatively few rooms of the hotel are assigned to the convention, all rate classes remain available, including the package, priced at less, and offering more, than the convention rate. Keen convention shoppers book the IT package.

Handling Tour Group Reservations

The workload of the reservation department is affected relatively little by the demands of tour groups. Both the initial sale and its continuing follow-up rest with the hotel's marketing and sales department. That department may have a division called the *tour and travel desk*, which gets involved once the buyer is satisfied with the facilities (see Exhibit 20).

Yield management strategizing is the major role for reservations during the time before the group arrives. Hotels doing a large tour and travel business maintain four-month horizons.

Individual Reservations and Group Bookings

SITE INSPECTION CHECKLIST

ACCOMMODATIONS

Number of Rooms on Property:

	Smoking	Non		Smoking	Non
Doubles	_____	_____	Queens	_____	_____
Kings	_____	_____	Parlors	_____	_____
Suite	_____	_____	Other	_____	_____

Total Number of Rooms Available for Group:

	Smoking	Non		Smoking	Non
Doubles	_____	_____	Queens	_____	_____
Kings	_____	_____	Parlors	_____	_____
Suite	_____	_____	Other	_____	_____

ADA Rooms for the Physically Impaired:

Doubles_____ Queens_____ Kings_____ Parlors_____ Suite_____ Other_____:

Complimentary room policy_____

Sprinklers and smoke alarms in rooms?	≡ **Yes**	≡ **No**
Emergency speakers in rooms?	≡ **Yes**	≡ **No**

Room amenities (list) _____

Emergency lights?	≡ **Yes**	≡ **No**
Hall lighting adequate and exits well marked?	≡ **Yes**	≡ **No**
Walls soundproof?	≡ **Yes**	≡ **No**
Concierge/VIP Club level	≡ **Yes**	≡ **No**

Concierge room amenities (list) _____

Guest phone charge policy/cost_____Long Distance_____

Data port on phone or in room?	≡ **Yes**	≡ **No**

How many telephones in room? _____

Is there a desk with lighting?	≡ **Yes**	≡ **No**
Room Service? (open from _____ to_____)	≡ **Yes**	≡ **No**

Column headings (vertical): Accommodations · Dates of availability · Front desk · Public space · Meeting and banquet space · Food and beverage outlets · Services and parking · Other hotel information · Sports and recreational facilities · Facilities near property · Vendor recommendations · Meeting requirements and history · Site inspection evaluation · Negotiations

MEETING sites RESOURCE — *partners in productive meetings*

EXHIBIT 20 Association executives, professional meeting planners, and tour group operators evaluate numerous hotels before selecting the right property. Each hotel is evaluated for price, availability, size, ability to meet the group's unique needs, and so on. Here is one sample page (Accommodations) from a site-inspection checklist. This particular checklist has 14 pages covering a variety of categories and observations. *Courtesy of Jennifer Brown, CMP; Strategic Site Specialist, Meeting Sites Resource, Newport Beach, California.*

Sell-and-report parameters are adjusted as forecasted demand equals, exceeds, or falls short of historical expectations.

Tour groups are almost always given shares-with rooms, since a premium is charged for single occupancy. The hotel gets a rooming list that shows each pairing. The entire block of rooms is preassigned. If the tour company brings in back-to-back groups, the very same rooms may be used again and again. Keeping the block together in the same floor or wing expedites baggage handling and reduces noise and congestion elsewhere.

Special group arrival sections, even special lobby entrances, reduce the congestion as the group arrives or departs. Transportation is by bus, even if only to the airport. These transfer costs are part of the fee and are arranged by the tour company. Bell fees for luggage-in and luggage-out are also included, levied by the hotel over and above the room charge.

195

Summary

Reservations are contractual agreements, so the hotel or corporate reservationist must be careful to document all pertinent information. Some data, such as the date of arrival, number of persons, type of room, guest's name and rate, are required fields for the reservation. Other information, such as estimated time of arrival, special requests, and discounts, is less important to the reservation and may only be collected in certain cases or by request of the guest.

Once the reservation has been agreed upon between the customer and the hotel or the central res office, its journey begins. In some cases the reservation's journey is short, as with those made a few hours or days before arrival. Other times it is a long journey, as with reservations made months—even years—in advance.

Group business means different things to different hotels, but almost all properties generate some percentage of their revenue through group contracts. Group business is especially beneficial because it is a sizable market (close to $175 billion in annual sales). There are certain efficiencies (economies of scale) associated with group arrivals and departures. Moreover, group delegates generally spend more than individual guests.

Group room blocks may be negotiated years in advance and managed down to the day of arrival. Careful management of group blocks assures a high pick-up rate and little or no attrition charges accruing to the meeting planner or association executive. However, the prevalence of discount websites has made this task substantially more difficult.

Resources and Challenges

RESOURCES

Web Assignment

Choose any three of the following online registration vendors. Determine what tools and information these services provide the meeting planner and explain why they would be substantially more difficult to develop manually, without online registration? Select from event411.com, b-there.com, eventbookings.com, passkey.com, eventregistration.com, dea.com, register123.com, regonline.com, seeuthere.com, cvent.com, dwalliance.com, or emcvenues.com.

Interesting Tidbits

- According to a recent survey, 64% of travelers are verbally informed of the hotel's cancellation policy while booking the reservation. Additionally 44% of hotels go a step further and actually mail a written confirmation. *Source: American Express Travel Trends Monitor.*
- Following the terrorist attacks of September 11, 2011, Videoconferencing and Web conferencing have been growing in popularity as "travel alternatives." Video (and Web) conferences save companies on travel, per diem, ground transportation, and lodging costs by keeping participants at home or nearby in conference-enabled facilities. Additionally, video (and Web) conferencing usually do not utilize the costly services of meeting planners. Such conferences are usually handled internally by the conference users (attendees), creating a substantial cost savings. Specifically, 69% of companies never use a meeting planner to assist with the hosting of video (Web) conferences. Another 20% of companies "rarely" use a meeting planner with video (Web) conferences. Some 5% range from "sometimes" to "often" in their use of meeting planners, and the remaining 5% of companies "always" use a meeting planner with video (Web) conferences.

Source: Business Travel News.

Challenges

True/False Quiz

Questions that are partially false should be marked false (F).

_____ 1. Some reservation information is required, essential to the reservation. The guest's date of expected arrival is one such example. Other information is optional. The guest's date of departure is an example.

_____ 2. As part of the cancellation process for a guaranteed reservation, the reservationist should provide the caller a cancellation number (sometimes a similar number to the confirmation number).

_____ 3. With centralized guest history databases, a chain hotel in New York City can actually retrieve personal information (address, room type and rate, number of nights stayed, etc.) for a guest who last stayed at one of the chain's hotels in Los Angeles.

_____ 4. Meeting planners or association executives who book group business are no longer responsible for room attrition due to the government's Room Attrition Act of 1999.

_____ 5. A hotel that offers delegates this choice—$129 standard is available at the group rate of $99, the $169 deluxe is available at the group rate of $129, and the $199 executive parlor is available at $149—is quoting flat rates (run-of-house).

Problems

1. Many hotels are apprehensive about charging the corporation if a business traveler fails to arrive. Even though a room was held and revenue was lost, the hotel is reluctant to charge the no-show back to the corporation for fear of alienation, and loss of future business.

   Develop a series of strict—but fair—reservation policies that protect the hotel's interests while minimizing conflicts with corporate accounts. In what instances would you charge the corporate no-show? When would you not charge?

2. The use of computerized reservations is far more efficient than the use of manual, handwritten reservations. Compare the manual reservations approach to the automated collection of guest reservation information. List five benefits (efficiencies) created by automated reservation systems.

3. There are economies of scale associated with group room bookings. List 5 such economies and explain how each benefits the hotel's bottom-line profitability.

4. Guests generally prefer the choice associated with spread rates. Hotels find it easier to manage rooms inventory when they use flat rates. Which would you use as a hotel manager? Explain your response.

5. As a prominent hotelier, you have been asked by the CVB to appear before the county commissioners during a CVB budget-review session. The commission is angry that the local CVB spends public funds to maintain a convention housing bureau and that those services are provided without a fee. Do the necessary research to provide hard facts to support your testimony in favor of the CVB.

6. The reservation of an unidentified convention delegate is treated like a corporate or leisure guest reservation. How might this failure to identify the guest as a conventioneer affect the hotel? Could it benefit the guest? Could it hurt the guest? How will it factor into the meeting planner's attrition/pick-up rates?

AN INCIDENT IN HOTEL MANAGEMENT
Don't Box Me In!

A convention exhibitor has shipped display goods to many hotels throughout the years. He knew full well the likelihood that valuable goods *shipped* to the convention through the hotel's receiving dock may not show up on time, or even ever. So he *mailed* two medium-sized boxes to himself marked, "Hold for Arrival" in large print.

Steve, the guest-service agent "sorta remembers" the packages coming about a week back. "They weren't large enough to store with receiving; yeah, I think they went to housekeeping."

Convention Exhibitor: Could you call and find out?

Steve (pointing): The house phones are over there.

The guest returned to report that housekeeping sent them to the desk yesterday so they would be on hand for his arrival. "Well, they're not here; that's for sure!" With hands on hips, Steve waited, slowly chewing his gum.

A second guest-service agent had finished with another guest and realized there was an adjacent *situation*. "The boxes, yes, they're on the mail table in the back room."

Convention exhibitor speaking to the GM's secretary "When I asked for his name, he glared at me, shook his head and pointed to his badge."

Questions:

1. Was there a management failure here; if so, what?
2. What is the hotel's immediate response (or action) to the incident?
3. What further, long-run action should management take, if any?

Answers to True/False Quiz

1. False. Both examples are required. It would be impossible to effectively sell a hotel if we only knew arrival dates and never knew the number of nights intended for the reservation.

2. True. Cancellations for guaranteed reservations should always be provided a distinct cancellation number as proof the cancellation was made.

3. True. In fact, the New York chain hotel could look at the guest's most recent (Los Angeles) stay history and ask the guest if he or she wanted the same wake-up call and the same breakfast.

4. False. Room attrition (usually calculated as less than 90% of the rooms initially blocked for the group actually having sold) has become a more critical issue for meeting planners and association executives. Hotels are serious about charging groups for low occupancy. P.S., there is no such thing as the Room Attrition Act of 1999.

5. False. This hotel is quoting spread rates. If all rooms (standard, deluxe, and executive parlor) were available for a flat rate of, say $129, then the hotel would be quoting flat rates (run-of-house). But a range of rates, as shown in the question, means the hotel quoted spread rates.

Managing Guest Services

Managing Guest Services

T his supervisor–supervised relationship is not going away, but it is changing: It is softening. Everyone realizes that guest service, not amenity creep, is the essence of great hotel management. Guest service relies on and is delivered by line workers.

Guest service doesn't just happen; it must be managed—and it must be managed close to the action. Moving away from a management-imposed culture to an employee-participative one takes commitment. It is slow, hard work. Many workers, even their supervisors, consider guest service to be management's job. But management knows it cannot be the Mine Host of yesteryear from afar. The task has shifted down the organization to rest with the staffers on the floor. Getting those employees to recognize the importance of the task and the mutual interest that it holds is the role of managing guest services. No easy task that!

TOTAL QUALITY MANAGEMENT

The model for actively managing guest relations originated in another broader idea, total quality management (TQM). TQM's focus was manufacturing, producing products with zero defects. Why not adopt that idea—the idea of zero defects—and apply it to customer/employee interactions? Shifting zero defects from manufacturing to service broadened TQM to CRM, customer relations management.

CRM gets special attention when business slumps. Hotelkeeping slumps in cycles. One such period followed the trauma of the World Trade Center. The years between 2008 and 2011 were still worse. Attention to the service-deliverer, the hotel's line employee, gains ground during difficult periods as hoteliers tried to differentiate themselves from competitors. Evidence of the change has been the expansion of the lodging industry's departments of human resources (HR). In twenty-five years, hoteliers have seen the introduction, maturation, and influence of HR departments where there had been none before (see Exhibit 1).

Sensitivity to customer needs is not special to hotelkeeping. Quality service should be a basic commodity of all service industries. In that respect, lodging is similar to banking, medicine, and sales. But it is also dissimilar because lodging's service is in-your-face. That distinguishes it from other service enterprises and separates it completely from manufacturing.

> We are in the people business. Not the hotel business, not the real estate business. Instead of machinery, we have people. Instead of automated convey belts, we have people. Instead of computers that hum and print stuff, we have people. We have not come to grips with this basic concept.[1]

Total Quality Management in Innkeeping

W. Edwards Deming was a pioneering advocate of TQM. He urged a unity of human and technical resources. His famous attention to the size of a worker's shovel has its counterpart in the weight of a housekeeper's vacuum cleaner. Deming advocated a unity of product and process. *Check-in, Check-out* does the same.

---

[1]Steven J. Belmonte, president and CEO, Ramada Franchise Systems, Inc. Talk delivered at several annual conferences of Ramada, including Orlando, Florida, December, 1999.

Why Human Resources Management Has Come of Age
Cultural diversity in the general public and, hence, in the hotel workforce
Expectations of equality in both public and private sectors
Increased empowerment vested in the workforce
Legal, legislative, and government agency requirements
Loss of supervisory (middle-) managers from organizational downsizing
Need to balance high touch with high tech
Recognition of staff's importance to guest satisfaction
Recruitment's high costs
Refocusing on operations after an era of financing and investments
Shortage of good job applicants at lodging's traditional levels
Simply a good business decision
Training added to department's responsibilities
Turnover among hotel staff that may exceed 100% annually

EXHIBIT 1 Industry priorities change over time. The front desk received the most attention before World War II. Food and beverage gained importance after the war, in the 1950s and 1960s. Sales and marketing expanded throughout the 1970s and 1980s, before giving ground to finance and real estate as the 20th century closed. Improved customer relations through human resources management is the current theme. So too is automation.

Executive attention to the employees of the hotel and through them to the guests of the hotels is essential to the successful management of the entire enterprise.

TQM is made of several pieces including *quality assurance* (QA) and *customer relations management* (CRM). The essence of these terms is simple. Every person in the organization has an opportunity to impact positively on the guest. Consider that special terminology. Retailers speak of customers; professionals refer to clients; physicians refer to patients; economists cite consumers; galleries talk of patrons; the corner outlet uses regulars. Only the hotel industry references guests!

Management must make certain that employees have the opportunity to impact the guest just as it has done with other operational innovations. At first, these innovations (elevators, radios, television) were viewed as unique. They are standard products now. TQM is viewed similarly. Quality management and customer relations management were once innovations too. Like TV, they are basic accommodations that no hotel can do without. Thus, the standard of the whole industry moves upward as it does when every hotel has wireless computer connectivity.

EXAMPLES OF QUALITY MANAGEMENT Attending to guest needs has always been part of the industry's buzz although management's concern waxes and wanes. QM grabs greater attention when the economic cycle hits bottom and the search is on for improving profits. And that is what is new: Recognizing the critical role of the staff in reaching profit goals.

Interest in guest service intensified in 1992 when the Ritz-Carlton Company won the first of its two (1999) Malcolm Baldrige National Quality Awards. The award recognizes companies that achieve excellence by emphasizing quality. Ritz-Carlton was the first hotel company and one of the first companies in the country to win the award. It reawakened the entire industry to one of its basic tenets: Service to the guest. Ellsworth Statler, founder of the Statler chain, said, "Life is service. The one who progresses is the one who gives his fellow men a little more, a little better, service."

Other companies followed the Ritz-Carlton example. Sheraton launched its Guest Satisfaction System later renamed Sheraton's Service Promise. The fundamentals of all the programs begin with hiring the right person. Sheraton called hiring Hire Vision; Ritz-Carlton called it Talent Plus. But hiring is just the first step. All programs emphasize: hiring, training, delegating, and rewarding.

Sheraton became part of the Starwood chain, which rolled out a companywide initiative "to integrate the company spiritually and to brand a [Starwood] culture."[2] Not an easy task because Starwood has upscale St. Regis at one end and Sheraton's Four Point Hotels at the other. The same is true with the Ritz-Carlton chain. It is a division of Marriott, which also has a mix of brands. It must now fit into a larger community both as a Marriott subsidiary and as a competitor of brands striving to out-Ritz it,[3] such as the Four Seasons. Marriott's Renaissance Hotel Company coined its own QA program, Savvy Service. Included are 20 principles that associates—Marriott prefers "associates" rather than "employees"—agree to work toward and to recite aloud during training sessions.

Radisson was another early convert to QM, titling it "Yes I Can." It came with a single guest-recognition program, Gold Point Rewards. The move integrated customers of its several businesses: hotels, restaurants, cruise ships, travel management, and resorts. Rewards earned in one venue were valid anywhere within the company. Radisson's program stretched beyond guest relations. It asked employees to extend the same guest-oriented attitudes to fellow workers. Whether greeting or servicing colleagues, staff members were to behave as if their fellow workers were guests.

Basic to all the programs is an improvement in guest service. The best service employees are recruited, trained, and empowered to act. Better service is but one aspect of empowerment. Fewer supervisors are needed if staff members have the authority to make decisions. It is a round robin. Flatter organizations force decisions onto line associates and these decision-making associates reduce the need for supervisors. So the organization gets flatter. Finding and holding workers capable of doing the job requires extensive searches and higher wages. The industry hasn't done that yet. Perhaps when the cycle recovers.

The Real Components of TQM

Guests come to hotels to sleep. Hotel managers must not forget that even as they work on staff–customer relations. Guests will overlook missing amenities if the product that they came to buy is delivered. So TQM begins in the guest room. Dissatisfaction with that basic product cannot be redressed by guest-service agents wearing happy-face buttons.

The search is on—there are plenty of ongoing surveys—for the room that best meets guest expectations. Hilton tested Travel Lifestyle Centers, a takeoff of TLC: Tender, Loving, Care. A second phase, Health-Fit and Stress-Less guest rooms, followed a few years later. But slogans and gimmickry are no substitute for sleep-enhancing designs. So Hilton's rooms also provided blackout curtains, and improved mattresses and dual wake-up systems. To rest well, travelers must be confident about the following morning's alarm clock.[4] Basics met, experimental rooms can add live plants, ergonomic chairs, and aroma therapy. Exhibit 2 broadens the list. What isn't there is the most important of all, renovations.

RENOVATIONS At one time, pink-tiled bathrooms and shag carpets were de rigueur. They are so no longer because remodeling is an ongoing need of the lodging industry. Usually, renovations are not dependent on the ups and downs of occupancy. That said, an unusual surge in remodeling took place between 2004 and 2007 when lodging was near the top of an economic cycle. Of course, new language was ballyhooed along with the upgrades: aloft hotels, Art + Tech, and Creativity Suites. Renaissance Hotels advertised its re-do as the: "Body of a full-service hotel with the soul of a boutique." None of which changed the requirements of a good hotel room.

Certainly, even small amenities such as full-length mirrors and in-room coffee makers add to comfort, but only if basic needs have been met. To achieve minimum expectations, high standards must be set first for bedding, cleanliness, temperature, and noise. Let's examine each.

---

[2]Christina Binkley. "Starwood Sets Effort to Enhance Quality and Improve Cash Flow." *Wall Street Journal*, February 5, 2001, p. PB-4.

[3]A new word, "ritzy," entered the English language when London's elite flocked to the Hotel Savoy, operated by Cesar Ritz, ca. 1889.

[4]Survey after survey rank late or missed wake-up calls near the top of guests' pet-peeves.

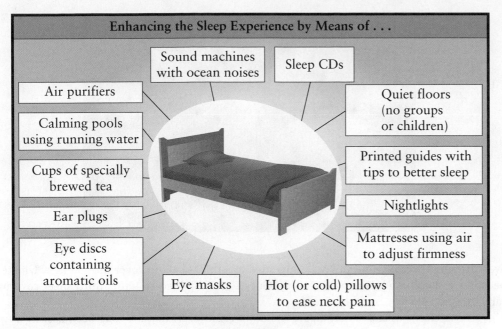

Enhancing the Sleep Experience by Means of . . .

- Sound machines with ocean noises
- Sleep CDs
- Air purifiers
- Calming pools using running water
- Cups of specially brewed tea
- Ear plugs
- Eye discs containing aromatic oils
- Eye masks
- Hot (or cold) pillows to ease neck pain
- Quiet floors (no groups or children)
- Printed guides with tips to better sleep
- Nightlights
- Mattresses using air to adjust firmness

EXHIBIT 2 Sleep is the hotel industry's primary product, so hoteliers have adopted new sleep-enhancing amenities. Quiet is the best amenity of all. It relies primarily on the insulation and pipe-strapping that were installed when the hotel was built.

BEDDING A good night's rest begins with a comfortable bed. The larger beds described there provide the extra inches of mattress (six inches longer than the average height of the sleeper) that experts recommend.[5] The number of beds in each room and their configuration varies with the type and the class of property, but every hotel offers choice.

Beds were replaced at an amazing rate during the last renovation period. Estimates suggest that for several years hotels purchased 1,500,000 beds annually! Marriott alone reported 625,000 beds. A top-quality queen mattress plus bed frame (although many hotels have done away with frames) costs about $2,250. That level of quality assures a mattress life of 12–15 years. The big replacement surge last time around was triggered by design and renovation, not by mattress wear. Buying long-lasting mattresses and matching springs makes sense. Even spread over 10 years, a $2,250 set costs about $0.60 per night.

Mattress quality is measured, in part, by the number of steel coils and the method of tying them down. A 900-coil, pillowtop mattress has been Westin's choice. Wyndham uses 992 coils on its king beds. Marriott has opted for a 7-inch foam mattress with a quilted top. Everyone is using fire-resistant bedding because smokers often fall asleep in bed.

Linens and Pillows There is more to a bed than a mattress. Upgrading requires close attention to the bed coverings (called the soft goods) and especially to the quality of the linen, which is measured by count. The standard count is 180 threads: 80 threads in one direction and 100 in the other. This is a durable product for the hotel and an acceptable quality for the guest, who is probably using that count at home. Jumping to 250 count, or even 300 as some upscale chains have done, makes a noticeable difference.[6] Sheets with that count are smooth and luxurious. Despite the competition, 180–200 count remains the choice of most hotels. But

---

[5]Thomas J. A. Jones. *Professional Management of Housekeeping Operations*, 4th ed. (New York: John Wiley & Sons, 2004). "… today's average American male is about 5 feet 9 inches tall." *The Wall Street Journal*, September 6, 2002, p. A6.

[6]Thread count is but one aspect of evaluating linen. The quality of the yarn, the source of the cotton, the finish, and the blend (of cotton/polyester) all address durability and luxury. Thread count of T-180 is more durable and might be better for high-occupancy properties. Durability is increased further if the linen supply is adequate. Low linen inventory requires the immediate reuse of sheets, but linens wear out less rapidly if they rest a day or two between uses. Recommended "par" inventory is three times the bed count. One set on the bed, one set in the laundry, and one set in the linen closet.

EXHIBIT 3 Improving the sleep experience has prompted a range of bedding upgrades and marketing innovations, including a sleep concierge. *Courtesy of the Benjamin, New York, New York.*

even many mid-scale properties have upgraded to a third sheet to cover the blankets. Unlike a bedspread, sheets are laundered regularly. Guests are delighted to find a third sheet covering rarely washed blankets and bedspreads.

Three sheets of 250 count impact laundry weight (cost) that has long been based on two sheets of 180 count. Introducing fitted bottom sheets reduces weight but adds another laundry issue. Ironing machines are designed for flat sheets. Fitted sheets add labor costs to laundering expenses. Less frequent linen change is the offset. It reduces both laundry loads and housekeeper's time. To accomplish this, guests are encouraged to use "green" tent cards, which tell housekeeping to re-use the linen for a second night.

A bed with linen of 250 count and a top sheet of 180 count is memorable, but not enough to win the bed wars. No longer will just any pillow do. Several pillows, each with distinctive characteristics, including hypoallergenic ones, are on the bed or available on call. Some hotels now offer "pillow menus," with feather and down pillows (see Interesting Tidbits) at the top of the list. Even wedge-shaped pregnancy pillows that lift and support the abdomen are available. The Benjamin Hotel in New York City offers 11 specialty pillows, all delivered and explained by a sleep concierge! (See Exhibit 3.)

Lighter down blankets or comforters, a European favorite, add another dimension to lodging's "new" beds. Cross-ocean borrowing goes two ways. European hotels are introducing king beds—their rooms will be getting larger, too. Housekeepers in Europe put a valance around the bottom of the bed. Their American counterparts call it a dust ruffle; the U.S. valance is above the drapes. Above the drapes in Europe is a pelmet.

Duvets, another European adoption, are enclosed in pillowcase-like covers. Like the third sheet, duvet covers are washable and, if needed, are washed daily. In contrast, traditional bedspreads are dry-cleaned two to four times a year. Reduced dry-cleaning costs help make up for the higher laundry costs of duvets.

The Public Relations of Bedding Bedding is as much a war of advertising/publicity as an issue of design/guest comfort. Westin advertises its Heavenly Bed with pillow-top mattress and its Heavenly Bath with five adjustable jets. Sofitel Hotels (Accor) offer MYBed, "a sea of comfort" in a feather bed with down comforter. Sheraton has a Sleigh Bed. Hyatt's is the Grand Bed. Marriott has, what else, the Marriott Bed.

Hotels advertise their specialty beds everywhere (see Exhibit 4). Westin even has a catalog to sell its beds. The Mondrian Hotel in Los Angeles (Morgans Hotel Group) takes it a step further with an itemized price list in each room![7] This move beats guest theft, which TripAdvisor says occurs with one in five travelers.

CLEANLINESS No architectural design is more attractive than a sparkling bath. A survey of *Tour Book* users (American Automobile Association) ranked cleanliness as their top

---

[7]Morgans carries the recommendation of UrbanDaddy, which reports "a real-time look at the hottest nightlife, restaurants and bars."

RETURN TO B.C. DAYS

(BEFORE CHILDREN)

THE B.C. WEEKEND*

$239
PER NIGHT
INCLUDES:

DELUXE STUDIO SUITE
Retreat to a weekend of divine relaxation in one of
New York's newest luxury hotels – The Benjamin. You'll enjoy
elegant accommodations, a supremely comfortable custom-made
mattress, and our pillow concierge will help you select
from 10 types of pillows for the ultimate night's sleep.

FABULOUS BRUNCH
Indulge in a delectable brunch for two at
Larry Forgione's An American Place.

LUXURY SPA
Enjoy 20% off any spa treatment at the renowned
Woodstock Spa & Wellness Center.

You can also upgrade to a one-bedroom suite for just
$50 more per night.

Call your travel consultant or 1-888-4-BENJAMIN, Ext. 303.
To learn more, take a virtual tour of The Benjamin
at www.thebenjamin.com.

THE BENJAMIN
AN EXECUTIVE SUITE HOTEL

125 East 50th Street ✦ New York, New York 10022
Manhattan East Suite Hotels
Five-globe ECOTEL* certified

*Offer subject to availability and valid weekends, effective 12/22/-- through 3/31/--- Certain restrictions
apply; taxes not included. One brunch for two per weekend stay.
Please book spa treatment at time of reservation.

EXHIBIT 4   The quality of hotel beds has become a major marketing strategy. Here the bed becomes part of the hotel's inclusive tour advertising. *Courtesy of the Benjamin, New York, New York.*

concern.[8] It was ranked ahead of price, location, and amenities. A Wyndham study ranked stale, smelly rooms at the top of their guests' pet peeves. For those with allergies, perfumed housekeeping smells and mists are as bad as animal dander. Hypoallergenic guest rooms may soon replace pillows as the next room amenity. Special cleaning supplies ($H_2Orange_2$) are already in use. Some hotels prepare hypoallergenic rooms an hour before anticipated arrival.[9]

Cleanliness is most noticeable in the bath; guests are sensitized to the quality of the housekeeping there. Tub/showers, toilets, sinks, and bathroom floors demand housekeeping vigilance

[8]Another survey lists bed bugs ahead of dirty hotel as the traveler's pet peeve. Source: *hotel-assist.com.* (A London agency.)

[9]Hypoallergenic amenities include bedding, pillows, linens washed with chlorine, special room filters, wooden floors and blinds, and antimicrobial applications on knobs and hardware as well as attention to the air-handling units. All at a special price.

to remove hair and dirt. Room corners and the areas behind the toilet take extra care. Chrome fixtures, particularly drains in sinks and tubs, must be cleaned daily. Long-term cleanliness may actually begin at construction. Marble countertops, porcelain tile, and latex-enhanced grout are easier to maintain.

Excessive clutter cancels out even the cleanest accommodations. A few simple changes bring order to a bath. Removing nonessentials is a first step. Putting amenities in an attractive container or simply having fewer amenities tidies the scene. A vanity of at least 4 feet with an off-center sink holds everything and leaves an impression of order.

Floor attendants must do more than clean. They will do so if taught to report security issues and guest-room repairs. A leaking toilet or a nonfunctioning tub stopper must receive attention. If quality assurance is in place, a simple reporting system will have been created for non-English-speaking attendants. Otherwise minor, but irritating, repairs will go unreported.

Vacuuming, the final step in cleaning the guest room, may take place only between guests. Stay-over rooms are not vacuumed in some hotels. Elsewhere, vacuuming is daily, check-out or not.

Cleanliness—inside and outside, guest rooms and public space—is taken for granted. Few guests ever compliment sanitation standards on guest-comment cards, but they do complain when it is lacking. That third sheet, which increases laundry costs by 50%, is the first sign of the proprietor's attitude toward cleanliness.

An Old Enemy Has Checked In   A guest that the industry hasn't seen for years has checked in: bedbugs (*cimex lectularius*). The pest nests in mattresses, waiting to feast at night on unsuspecting sleepers. Bedbugs blow in with hurricanes and with international travel, riding on baggage and clothing. They live almost anywhere and go for long periods without food, blood. Bedbugs hide from light—they are nocturnal—so they might rest during the day in dark, protected areas other than the bed. This makes cleanup very difficult. Housekeeping is reluctant to use chemical pesticides, especially in beds. DDT, which was the bugs nemesis, was banned in the 1970s.

A costly solution calls for the destruction of furniture and bedding. Few hotels go to that extreme because solutions are less dramatic although costly. A whole new industry has sprung up selling devices and services, including bedbug-sniffing dogs. Legal claims are sure to follow so procedures must be put in place to verify the guest's complaint, remedy the situation, and compensate—maybe just another room.

Housekeeping's lack of experience accounts for part of the spread. Floor and laundry attendants must look for the telltale signs: tiny, rust-colored blood spots and darker, fecal matter on the linens. Careful examination may turn up skins shed in their hiding places. A sweet, musty odor can be detected in large concentrations.

The pest comes in on persons and luggage, but floor attendants may be the carrier between rooms. Hot water (155 degrees) in the laundry handles the linens, but that's preventative more than curative since the bug's habitat is not limited to the bed. Bedbug control must be part of an integrated pest management program designed to prevent and monitor all types of pests and rodents. So far, the biggest concentrations and worst publicity have come from port-entry cities such as New York.

NOISE, TEMPERATURE, AND DARKNESS   Even "road warriors" (travelers who sleep away from home a great deal) complain about noisy rooms. Poor initial construction, which is not easily remedied, is the major culprit. Budget limitations reduce or eliminate insulation between rooms or around piping in utility shafts. Then back-to-back baths, which reduce construction and maintenance costs, wreak havoc in transmitting noise. Inadequately strapped plumbing means noisy vibrations with every faucet opened.

Poorly insulated rooms bring the neighbor's television program into the sleeper's dreams. Everyday sounds from conversations to children playing come from rooms close by. Hallway noises include the whirr of motors, ice falling into buckets, ringing telephones, and the sound of elevator doors. Late-to-bed revelers add to the din. The worst offenders are there in the room. Fans on the HVAC (heating/ventilation/air-conditioning) systems and mini-bar compressors sing throughout the night.

An inability to control room temperature adds to the sleeplessness. Central HVAC is far superior to individual room units. As with room insulation, construction cost is the determinant. But some room units are not even temperature sensitive; they either run or they are off; no adjustments.

Construction noise and street noise—commuter buses running by an urban hotel—join in-room noise to test the QM challenge. QM's toughest trials come when guests are roomed near ongoing construction because work begins early in the morning. Management must forestall the complaint by alerting the caller at reservations, reminding the guest at registration, and reflecting the circumstances in the rate.

In-room lighting is another comfort gauge. One that takes on special meaning for an aging population. Rarely do guest rooms have architectural lighting, relying instead on lamps and hanging sconces. Specifications for these fixtures must include high wattage. Otherwise, the room is poorly lit, even for young eyes. The same holds true for the bath, where downlights over sinks and vanities are applauded by both men (shaving) and women (applying makeup).

These same eyes like darkness for sleeping. Blackout curtains must block both the morning light and the evening's flashing neon. To counter light leaks between the drapes and noise from within, some properties offer ear plugs and eye masks (see Exhibit 2).

Exhibit 2 also notes that air purifiers are offered in some guest rooms. Companies have responded to the national nonsmoking movement. Guests who violate the terms of no-smoking rooms are subject to fine, but it takes a brave hotelier to collect. Nonsmoking rooms have migrated to nonsmoking hotels, but the retrofit is difficult. Smoke lingers in drapes and carpets and bedding.

Each issue, noise control, cleaner air, better light, and proper temperature, focuses on customer relations management. Ritz-Carlton's "Care Program" is a preventative approach, anticipative management. It inspects before the guest arrives to make certain there are adequate hangers, pillows, and towels. It also makes sure that everything is working: no drips in the bathroom fixtures and no issues with HVAC.

Total Quality Management Defined

Defining quality management is as difficult as delivering it. At its simplest, TQM is an attitude that drives actions. It is inadequate to define it by actions alone. Nevertheless, some attempt it with oft-told tales. There are three favorites: A bellperson delivers a lost attaché case to the airport just in time; a housekeeper launders clothes at home in order to meet a guest's deadline; a door attendant lends black shoes for a formal affair. Focusing only on delivery (the bellperson, the housekeeper, the door attendant) ignores attitude: the need for acceptance within management and the workforce. Only then can the tools, training for one, achieve improvement in process and service.

Quality service and the management of quality service have few objective measures. Definitions are broad and imprecise; delivery is inexact. Part Each of Buyers and sellers have different perspectives. QM must consider the buyer-receiver as well as the seller-giver. No wonder a single, satisfactory definition of quality is so difficult. How fortunate that everyone "knows it when they see it."

THE BUYER'S VIEW Guests measure quality by comparison. To what degree does the level of service actually delivered compare to expectations. If surprised by a better stay than anticipated, guests perceive quality to be high. If the visit fails to meet expectations, the property is downgraded. Nowhere is this more obvious than the website comments of previous guests.

Advertising, word-of-mouth comments, price, previous visits, and publicity create a level of expectation. Unfortunately, this defining barrage is received differently by every guest and changes over time within each guest. Furthermore, guest expectations have components that are outside the hotel's control: late flight, rude cabdriver, and bad storm.

Guests hold different expectations about different hotels, even different ones within the same chain. Quality is measured against the expectations of that particular property at that particular time more than against different hotels in different categories. Arriving at an economy hotel with a loaded family van and a pet but without reservations carries one expectation. Planning and saving over many years and flying around the world to an expensive resort creates different expectations. Coming to a busy convention with reservations made by the company's travel desk evokes still another level of expectation. Each hotel must deliver at the highest level of expectation for that circumstance. What a challenge!

Unlike manufacturing, the service industry lacks measurable specifications. Unlike manufacturing, the product is not created until it is delivered. So managing for quality in service must include standards derived from the consumer. Management's standards and measurements must be based on guest expectations. Then it is time enough to set the procedures for achieving them. Successfully implemented, the buyer's expectations are met by the seller's ability to deliver. When matched carefully, both parties know that quality service has been delivered.

THE SELLER'S VIEW   Like every policy created and every practice put into operation, TQM originates with management. Executives either make deliberate decisions to implement particular ideas or they passively accept ongoing practices. So it is with quality management. Management creates and implements a program of enhanced guest services, or there is none.

To deliver quality, management focuses on both employees and guests. The two are intertwined. Increasing guest service for the buyer requires attention to operational issues, the employee's side of QM. Staying close to the customer means ensuring consistency, remedying mistakes, and concentrating on the whole with a passion that hints of obsession. To do so, management must rely on the staff. Nothing can be accomplished without attending to those entrusted with the delivery.

Leadership   Adopting TQM as a company philosophy forces changes. Traditionally, management is said to be a series of functions. Planning, organizing, staffing, directing, and reviewing is the classic list. Quality management adds another—leadership. Leadership requires changes in both the style of management and the composition of the workforce. When both parties focus on delivering quality, the company has a *service culture*.

Developing that culture takes a fundamental shift in management style. Managers, supervisors, and staff must be bound into a closer relationship. Success depends in part to the degree of entrepreneurship extended to the staff. Employees must accept both the challenge and the power to make it happen. That requires management to balance its authority and discipline with delegation, flexibility, and leadership.

With a leadership mentality, management shifts from its traditional "review" function (see above) to a proactive style of management. The aim is error avoidance, rather than post-error review. Minimizing errors is what TQM is all about.

Quality management has come to mean almost any action that improves the operation. And that's what it is: a series of small steps taken within a service culture that has the customer as its central focus. Action follows the concept.

Sharing responsibility and credit requires sharing information. General meetings and departmental committees, called quality circles, keep staff members current and encourage participation and commitment to the new culture. A quality circle at the front desk might include members from the sales, housekeeping, and accounting departments. Then each of those members sits within his or her own department. Soon a hotelwide network exists. Quality goals and standards will then reflect the realities and limitations of the whole enterprise. Such broad input establishes fair standards to reward those who beat expectations. And, as we know, expectations are part of the buyer's view.

Empowerment   Having enlisted the help of the staff and opening once-restricted interests to employee-committees, the next step is anticlimactic. Some of management's powers are delegated down the organization. Operative employees are authorized to make on-the-spot decisions about problems that fall within the scope of their job assignments. Giving that authority to act is called *empowerment* (see Exhibit 5).

Empowerment comes at a good time. It creates leaner, flatter organizations just when leaner, flatter organizations are replacing the elongated organizational charts. This pancake structure allows each department to operate with a degree of independence that provides a quick response to unexpected issues.

Empowerment comes through understanding; knowledge is acquired through training and experience. Limits may apply, especially at first. Management helps by providing guidelines, a range of options (see Exhibit 11) that helps the guest-service agent gain confidence. Senior and more experienced associates have wider discretion and may serve as advisors to other staff members.

≡**V**

A Vallen Corporation Property

Dear Guests:

Welcome and thank you for your patronage.

During your visit, you'll come to realize that the Vallen Family of Hotels is unique among innkeepers. It is so because each associate offers exceptional levels of personalized service. In fact, our *Employee Empowerment Program* has gained national recognition as the very first winner of the Medal of Excellence. We're proud of the award, made possible because of our carefully selected and trained staff.

Along with the many complimentary amenities that you have come to expect (e.g., free wireless, a selection of newspapers, 24-hour self-serve coffee carts, and many more) you will also experience the finest in personalized guest service. That's the promise of each associate!

From the executive offices to the maintenance department, from our kitchen to housekeeping, all of us are pledged to act quickly on your behalf. Just ask the nearest associate... we'll accommodate your needs.

Enjoy your visit.

Gary K. Vallen

Dr. Gary K. Vallen, President
Vallen Hotels Corporation

EXHIBIT 5   This traditional welcoming letter says it all: Top management supports empowerment and wants the guest to know that every staff member can be relied upon to handle issues that may arise.

Initially, empowerment involves action by an individual. A misquoted rate is resolved by the receptionist/cashier. Apologies for an unmade room are reinforced with a free drink coupon in the bar. At its simplest, empowerment means courtesy and immediate response to issues and complaints. Once that's working well, management may elect to empower quality circles. Again, empowerment is done gradually. At first, quality circles are asked merely to identify problems. Step two, circles suggest possible solutions. Fully empowered, they begin to implement their own decisions. They tackle two kinds of problems. One deals with guest relations, how-to's. How to speed check-ins; how to reduce reservation errors; how to expedite group baggage within security guidelines.

The second class of problems also impacts guest services, but less directly. Attention is on in-house procedures (moving linens without tying up the elevators); cost reductions (reducing chargebacks by credit-card companies); or operational irritants (maintenance's slow response to guest-room repairs). None of which involves guest interaction, all of which improves TQM.

The Employee   TQM requires supervisors to adopt a leadership style of management. But that's just half the battle. Employees, the other half, must be won over as well: convinced to accept the empowerment offered. Just as some managers oppose empowering line employees, some line members reject the added responsibility. They decline to take on what they believe is management's job.

Similarly, the employer's willingness to share information may not be matched by the employees' interest in receiving it—or receiving it, having the capacity to understand it or the interest to use it. Even highly motivated associates may not comprehend what is offered or expected. Quality management is burdened with the development of both leaders and followers. Especially difficult with a workforce that has great diversity in language, education, and cultural expectations.

Diversity and Turnover   The lodging industry faces two labor challenges: workforce diversity and job turnover. They are often treated as one problem because finding and retaining competent staff requires management to look across the great diversity of America's workforce. Lodging relies heavily on a nonwhite, non-Anglo workforce. Within the hotel industry, diversity is a business necessity, not a hot social issue. Sensitive to different expectations among its employees, many hotels have adopted diversity programs to embrace the range of cultures. It seems contradictory, but the National Association for the Advancement of Colored People (NAACP) gives the hotel industry a low rank.[10]

Hotels are searching for staff continuously. Employees, and that term includes supervisors and managers, come and go at a costly pace. Many workers are in dead-end jobs. Boredom and monotonous repetition are blunted temporarily by moving to another hotel even though the new job has the same tasks. The loss is especially costly if the individuals who move do so because they are motivated; the very people one wants to keep.

Turnover at the lowest level of the organization, the spots where QM must shine, exceeds 200% annually in some jobs in some hotels. Said another way: Every employee is replaced twice each year! Less dramatic, but equally troublesome, rapid turnover also occurs among supervisors and managers. Turnover creates more turnover. Missing workers mean heavier loads for those remaining. Discontent grows so establishing, maintaining, and improving TQM is put aside as resources are assigned to searching, finding, and replacing a turnstile staff.

Retaining workers is smarter dollar-and-cent wise than replacing them. That is why retention tools, long used in other industries, are finding their way into the lodging industry. Identifying and training qualified associates for upgrades is one step. Financial incentives another, and one with broader applications. Retirement plans, year-end bonuses, and employee stock options are relatively new concepts for this old industry. Financial incentives enable low-paid workers to build savings and remain with the company. Marriott adopted employee-participation plans years ago. An occasional dip in the economic cycle keeps staff at work and brings candidates to the employment office. But that is a temporary blip, not a long-term trend.

QM demands a great deal from moderately paid personnel including those at the desk. Desk personnel are the first to see the arrival and the last to say goodbye. Although dollars and cents remain strong incentives, imaginative noncash rewards have a QM role. Others include cross-training, membership in quality circles, upgrade to a preferred shift, and language classes.

Employee-of-the-month is a sure standby. It is more effective if it carries a cash stipend and other perks such as reserved parking or a newspaper ad. Some departments can accommodate flexible work hours, which may be the best perk for working parents. So, too, might be job sharing. Local hotels could form a consortium to accommodate working parents by operating a nursery school. It is costly, but it may hold workers.

Cash incentives have a place for managers as well as associates. But since they are exempt from wage-and-hour laws, there is even a better reward, a day off. Long hours on the job cause hardships in personal life for many nonhourly (so-called exempt) workers. The best incentive might be an extra afternoon or a full-day off.

Good people at all levels is the measure of quality management. Finding and holding those persons is reflected in the salaries paid, the training offered, and the incentives rewarded. A hotel that concentrates on improving its human resources ensures the delivery of quality service. The effort begins with selecting and retaining the right persons.

Selecting and Retaining the Right Persons   Managing guest services requires enlisted and empowered employees. That means stretching backward to employment and forward to retention. Quality service begins at selection. How else can the right person be at the right place when customer service relations require? The personnel office is TQM's launch site! (See Exhibit 1.)

Selection—not hiring—is where good service begins. Just the expression, "You've been selected" changes the tone. Friendly, interactive associates who have the interest and ability to help will deliver better service than do more highly qualified technicians who lack those qualities. Just Wow! if the selection begins with an applicant who has both. The fact is, there are more guest complaints about employee attitude than about broken TV sets.

"If you don't have the right people, then you are the dummy that hired them."[11] Selecting the right person begins with finding the right pool of applicants. Personnel departments don't

[10]MGM Resorts International ranked 19 nationwide in an annual "Top 50 Companies for Diversity" list. (That is companies, not hotel companies.)

[11]Horst Schulze, one-time president and COO, the Ritz-Carlton Hotel Company.

always clear this hurdle because vacancies come frequently, are difficult to fill and funds are lacking for both the department and the wage. Often the first to come is the one hired.

Recruiting during good economic times takes special imagination. Nominees can be recruited through the current workforce especially with cash incentives. (Knowledgeable HR officials withhold bonuses until new recruits remain through a fixed period.) Websites are now widely used. They are great for college recruiting, but may not reach applicants on the lower end of the wage scale. That, too, is changing: The 2008–2011 downturn introduced many unskilled workers to Web applications. Success as well as greater diversity sometimes comes from advertising in the numerous ethnic newspapers that are available in large, urban areas. However accomplished, recruiting is costly. Turnover costs have been estimated at $2,000 for hourly workers and $6,500 for supervisors/managers. Retention is far less costly than recruitment.

Retention improves if new hires clearly understand what the work entails. Some companies ask the applicant to spend an hour observing the job before accepting it. Others go a step further. Applicants are interviewed by the very associates with whom they will work. The practice, called *peer-group hiring*, strengthens the TQM program and improves the hiring process.

Once hired, retaining that "right" worker should be the highest priority. Strangely, retention sometimes gets less attention than the original search. Induction, helping the new staffer ease into the company, is a common pitfall. After spending time and money, a new member may be alienated by the very next step: entering the work door. No "buddy" is assigned to walk along. Disenchanted, new hires sometimes leave within a day or two of employment. What a waste of time and money!

Labor Unions Labor unions are another recruiting resource. In fact, some labor contracts require hotels to first try the union hiring halls. Hotel and culinary unions are strongest in the big hotel cities. From east to west, they are New York, Chicago, Las Vegas, San Francisco, and Honolulu. Not all hotel-union relations revolve about employment. The union of Hotel Employees and Restaurant Employees (HERE) periodically faces off with the hotel industry over wages, rights to wear union bottoms, fringe benefits, and work rules. Recent challenges question the employer's right to require members to leave the premises after work. That's been in place for years!

Hotel chains have multiple properties in the same cities that unions have *locals* (regional divisions). At new contract time, HERE brings pressure in cities that are not up for renegotiation. Thus, hotels of the chain in, say, San Francisco may find pickets because the Chicago contract is under negotiation. So far, the lodging industry has averted a single national contract. Contracts expire on different dates in different cities. There are some 6,000 hotel workers in 31 Chicago hotels with a common contract date, August 31. Industry watchers believe the national unions are working toward a common contract date. This would increase the union's clout immeasurably.

Training TQM views training as an investment, not as a cost. Continuous training can be likened to the continuous upgrading of the physical plant. Both—employees and facilities—are critical to guest satisfaction. So training gives a bump up to the hotel, to the guest, and to the associate, who feels a real degree of personal satisfaction. Training also creates opportunities for long-run promotions and short-run gratuities.

Training has four different purposes. One improves work skills—better use of the reservation computer program, for example. A second, say security training, widens awareness beyond the immediate job and invites everyone to see the bigger picture. A third type of training enhances interpersonal skills—meeting and greeting guests in the corridor, for example. Still another focuses on personal needs: cleanliness, language skills, and retirement savings. The Ritz-Carlton chain has used a well-known motto: "We are ladies and gentlemen serving ladies and gentlemen." Training makes it so because we are not all born ladies and gentlemen.

Everyone is held responsible for his or her own actions. TQM doesn't ignore mistakes. It tries, rather, to substitute positive training for negative discipline. Coaching (positive suggestions) takes small steps to move the system toward error avoidance. Avoiding mistakes rather than reviewing them after the fact is the essence of good guest service. Pledging the costs to coach on a continuous basis is management's measure of commitment to the philosophy.

THE AUTHORS' VIEW   A brief phrase (an aphorism) has been used to summarize the culture of TQM. "The answer is 'Yes,' now ask me the question."[12] Such a can-do/will-do attitude represents the best that TQM can instill. Applications of the adage apply equally well to customer relations management, employee–management contacts, and employee–employee relations. Under so broad an umbrella of coverage, the motto offers a strong definition of TQM.

The adage also suggests a strong alignment between the culture of quality management and the culture of the concierge. Both cultures are expressed in Radisson Hotel's "Yes I can!" Hotels that promote QM understand that the concierge is neither an individual nor a department. It is an attitude that one hopes all employees will grasp. Hence, the first part of the authors' definition of TQM: *Quality Management is an attitude that has every associate acting like a concierge.*

The duality of quality assurance has been emphasized throughout the chapter. The guest's side, called the buyer's view, is balanced by the house side, called the seller's view. This second side, the operational side, is reflected in the second phrase of the authors' definition: ... *and thinking like a manager.*

Thus the authors' definition: Quality management is an attitude that has every associate acting like a concierge and thinking like a manager.

CUSTOMER RELATIONS MANAGEMENT

Unlike the individualized attention that was once the norm, modern hotels now serve mass markets. Responsive individuals, working in a democratic culture, have replaced the white-gloved authoritarianism of an era long past. It follows, then, that hotel companies have shifted from the formal to the informal, from pretense to expedited service, from rigid procedure to empowerment.

The shift has been easily accepted because the traveling public's attitude toward service has also changed. Aware of labor costs, functioning in a self-service environment, sensitive to employee's expectations of equality, today's guests no longer expect a servile attitude—and employees no longer deliver it. Guests do expect—and are entitled to receive—a friendly face, an attentive ear, and a twinkling eye. After all, quality service is an attitude that shines through.

Customer Relation Denied

Hotelkeeping is part of a vast industry whose trade is part service, part entertainment, part recreation, and part commerce. Hoteliers offer a product called hospitality. They consider their customers to be guests. And, above all, they deliver services. Because these positions have been verbalized so often, hotel patrons get confused by the antihospitality-antiguest-antiservice syndrome that is the wrong side of the industry.

All hotels are grouped under the lodging umbrella, but every property does not deliver the same product. Guests realize that but cannot understand why minimal service means antiservice and why a lack of personnel means a lack of courtesy. Management sometimes fails to distinguish minimal service justified by minimal rates from antiservice, which has no justification.

Customer relations management must be the industry's response to antiservice. CRM must ferret out the problems, train for the solutions, and reward those who demonstrate the right responses. Sometimes, however, the very structure of the operations thwarts the best intentions.

WHO KNOWS WHY?   Every organization develops standard operating procedures (SOPs). SOPs are to business routines as personal habits are to individual routines. Some are new and meaningful; some are bad, in need of change. Along with the new and the good, guests encounter the old and the useless. Like all bad habits, the old and the useless are hard to discard. Hotels that insist on keeping them irritate guests unnecessarily and undermine the concept of service. Some practices seem intentional, as if inconveniencing the guest is easier than fixing the problem.

Who knows why—Sleepers are aroused from their beds by:

Alarm clocks set by previous occupants?

Computerized calling systems asking for breakfast orders?

---

[12]Rick Van Warner, one-time editor of *Nation's Restaurant News*, attributes the aphorism to Keith Dunn, restaurateur, who cites Don Smith, restaurateur and one-time faculty, Michigan State University, as the source. *Nation's Restaurant News,* October 26, 1991.

Housekeepers knocking on the door, "Never mind, just checking?"

Running water in the neighbor's shower?

Who knows why—Guests are charged for:

Leaving a day earlier than their four-day reservation?

Incoming faxes, although incoming telephone calls are free?

Late check-outs even when occupancy is low?

Unannounced "service fees" that duplicate the very essence of the rate?

WHO KNOWS WHY?   Perhaps the decision makers are unaware because they have not built a communication staircase. *Who knows why?* Perhaps it is an old policy that has never been reexamined. Lots of old laws are on the books. *Who knows why?* Perhaps it was established by someone who doesn't know why.

Measuring Guest Services

Occupancy and ADR measure lodging's economic health. Their values rise and fall by such esoteric measures as the world's economy or the worth of the national currency. More immediately, these statistics also reflect management's commitments to maintenance, to expenditures for advertising, to employee attitudes. Surprising high occupancy and great rates come from satisfied guests served by positive employees. The contra-indication is that poor statistics come from unhappy guests served by grousing employee. Unfortunately, the economics of the business does not allow awaiting action until the statistics are in. The search for breakdowns in service must be ongoing.

MOMENTS OF TRUTH   A study measuring the cost of poor service was undertaken about the time that TQM was introduced to the industry. [13] The amount of dollars lost was calculated for each missed opportunity in each department. For example, overbooking, lost reservations, and discourtesy were charged against the front office. Although one incident does not cause bankruptcy, poor service is insidious. Single episodes mushroom from minor, miscellaneous costs to staggering totals, per week, per month, per year. Antiservice comes at a high cost.

Guest/staff interactions are more frequent in hotel settings than in other businesses. Each day, hotel associates are asked to deliver an exceptional level of service over and over and over again. Exhibit 6 emphasizes the cumulative impact of having one's customers in residence.

A 300-room hotel with 70% occupancy and 33% double occupancy generates 2,800 guest–employee contacts per day! The figure soars to over 1 million per year. Full-service hotels face a double whammy. Not only do more departments mean more contacts per day, but service expectations are higher. Plenty of opportunities to fail—or make good! These opportunities are called "moments of truth." It is during these encounters when the service provider and the service buyer meet eyeball to eyeball that the guest's perception of quality gets set. Some say the first 10 minutes are the most critical.

How does the staff respond? Does the final guest of the shift receive the same attention as the first arrival? For many, only a smile and an appropriate greeting are needed. More is expected by the next guest: the one with the problem, the one with the complaint, and the one with the special need. If the employee is empowered to act, to respond with alacrity, to evidence concern, it is a shining moment of truth.

Total quality management expects similar moments of truth between supervisors and staffers. No one shines outwardly unless there is an inward glow. Supervisors will not get positive results if they always second-guess subordinates who have been empowered. Supervisors will not get positive moments of truth if staffers are irritated, say, by late work-schedule postings that frustrate personal plans. Good service encounters begin with good work environments. Shining moments of truth come from a total quality program.

CONTROLLING QUALITY   Management uses several tools, including review and evaluation, in its oversight of operations. That is equally true whether it is customer relations management or, say,

---

[13]Stephen Hall, *Quest for Quality: Cost of Error Study.* American Hotel & Motel Association and CitiCorp Diners Club, n.d.

Counting the Moments of Truth		
Number of rooms in the hotel		**300**
Percentage of occupancy		**× 0.70**
Number of rooms occupied each night	210	
Percentage of double occupancy		× 0.33
Number of guest-nights	280	
Moments of Truth		
Arrival	1	
Inquiry at the desk	1	
Bellperson	1	
Chambermaid	1	
Telephone operator	1	
Coffee shop host(ess)	1	
Server/busperson	2	
Cashier	1	
Newstand	1	
Total encounters per guest-night		× 10
Daily number of moments of truth		**2,800**

EXHIBIT 6 Moments of truth are the points at which the service provider and the service buyer meet eyeball to eyeball. They may number in the thousands per day. Customer relations management (CRM) makes certain associates don't blink because each mistake impacts the bottom line.

cash management. Cash management requires standards and procedures to account for and control money. Service management employs similar standards and procedures. It is that very quality control, enforced by periodic inspections, that enables chains to maintain standards across broad holdings. Guests, too, rely on these standards, picking their destinations through company logos.

Controlling Quality Through Inspection Reinforcing standards through inspection is a critical element of TQM. Inspectors rate both the physical plant and the staff's response to moments of truth. Some companies use their own inspectors. Others, Preferred Hotels & Resorts, for example, employ third parties. So do Facebook and Twitter. Visits may be preannounced or not. Whichever, verbal reports are usually given to the unit manager before written documents are filed with headquarters.

Although they come for different purposes, inspectors from AAA, Forbes Travel Guide, and others are also on the road. Meeting planners are there as well. They are anonymously checking on staff and looking at the facilities before committing their groups.

Each chain sets its own standards, which cover both franchise and company-owned properties. So the number of inspections varies within the industry. Choice Hotels makes two annual visits; Hilton aims for three; Super 8, four. Depending on the contract, franchisees have 30–180 days to remedy serious defaults before the franchise is canceled. And they do get canceled. Radisson culls from the bottom up using, among other criteria, the guest comment cards that are discussed shortly. Holiday Inn had a 2010–2011 franchise shake-out.

Quality control has many parts, from the maintenance of the grounds, to general cleanliness, to the condition of FF&E (furniture, fixtures, and equipment). Are there holes in the carpet? burns on the bedcovering? paper in the stairwell? Checks sheets used by the inspectors deal with details: working blow-driers, cleanliness of air vents, number of hangers in the closet (see Exhibit 7).

Inspections like these must not be left to external agents only. Daily reports from housekeeping inspectors and periodic walk-throughs by managers of all levels must be part of the team's control of quality.

Mystery shoppers, a euphemism (nice word) for inspectors, eat in and report on all F&B outlets including room service. They check sales techniques as well: Does the foodserver push desserts? Does the room clerk sell up? Does the telephone operator know the hours of the cabaret? Good inspectors always visit the housekeeper's office. A neat and tidy office means a neat and tidy hotel; red flags go up if the office looks like a dormitory room.

INSPECTION REPORT

Auditor _____   Hotel _____

Identification no. _____   City _____

Date(s) _____

	Excellent	Good	Fair	Poor	Comments
Registration					
1. Waiting time		X			About 2 minutes
2. Greeting	X				Used my name in conversation
3. Friendliness		X			
4. Efficiency			X		PMS was slow
5. Staff on hand	X				Other clerks handled telephone
6. Grooming		X			Except for Grace's hair
7. Accuracy	X				
Rooming					
1. Bellperson offered				X	No, had to call housekeeping
2. Elevator wait	X				3:00 PM.
3. Floor signage	X				
4. First impression			X		Not too clean; stale odor
Guest Room					
1. Hangers	X				
2. Paper products			X		Facial tissue box nearly empty
3. Sanitation			X		Shower curtains need attention
4. Desk	X				
5. Telephone and book	X				Displayed card with fees listed
6. Bed and linens		X			
7. Lighting				X	Bulb burned out, standing lamp
Services					
1. Call housekeeping		X			Delay in acquiring extra pillow
2. Send fax to self	X				Prompt, no charge to receive
3. Get maid to let in				X	Took $3 tip and let me in
4. Ask for second key		X			Clerk remembered me, or said so
5. Ask for toilet repair			X		38-minute delay

EXHIBIT 7 Mystery shoppers make unannounced quality-control inspections to uncover and report (using forms similar to the illustration) weaknesses that need management's attention. Some shoppers are sent by the company; others represent rating agencies; still others are convention-service companies making unannounced inspections.

Security is another quality point. Both guest security (keys, locks, chains, and peepholes) and internal security (pilferage from the hotel and theft from guests) come under scrutiny during the visit. Still, mystery shoppers are neither police nor consultants. They are reporters of the scene. Quality control is maintained and improved when management acts on the reports. Good results are reinforced through rewards and recognition. Weak results bring increased training and review of procedures. Findings from the inspections should be widely circulated. How else would management's standards be known?

Controlling Quality Through Guarantees Quality guarantees (QGs) are simply assurances that the hotel will deliver on its promise of quality. If not, it will make amends; it will pay.

With a QG, the company puts its money where its advertising mouth is. Guaranteeing satisfaction takes gumption because it accepts responsibility. It flies in the face of the popular, "that's-not-my-fault." Quality guarantees announce unequivocally to customers and staff alike that management is confident standing behind its TQM program.

Quality guarantees must not be confused with discounted room rates, which are offered and withdrawn as occupancy changes. QGs become part of the company's operating philosophy. As such, they must be introduced slowly, evolving from a successful TQM effort. Guarantees are not the beginning of a TQM program. They should not be started because of an advertising idea. They must be the culmination of a proven, ongoing TQM program. Otherwise, they backfire badly.

Several years ago, a well-known chain announced a quality guarantee of "complete satisfaction." No modifiers or limiting exceptions—just "complete satisfaction." A guest, citing the guarantee, asked for a reduced rate one morning when there was no hot water. Request denied because a malfunctioning boiler was "beyond the hotel's control." What has that to do with "complete satisfaction"?

Obviously, quality guarantees need to be defined narrowly. The industry found that out after many incidents of the boiler type. A different guarantee can now be found on in-room tent cards. It reads, "We promise immediate action before you leave the hotel." If guests complain, there is a quality assurance guarantee that the hotel is listening. This is something quite different from the open-ended promise of "complete satisfaction." Nothing on the card says anything about payments.

Implementing guarantees in small steps as capabilities come on line announces to guests and staff that service quality is in place. Many hotels take the first step with room-service breakfast. It is free if not delivered within "x" minutes. Wrapped up in that simple promise is an advertisement, a departmental promotion, an employee empowerment, an assurance of quality, and a willingness to be measured. Time parameters are easier to measure than is "complete satisfaction." So guarantees might be: 10 minutes to deliver the car from the garage or breakfast coffee served within two minutes of being seated in the coffee shop.

Meeting planners have begun asking for and receiving guarantees. Groups have always guaranteed the number of guest rooms they will take and the number of covers for cocktail parties and banquets. Now they are asking hotels to do the same: Guarantee there will be no noise from adjoining meeting rooms; guarantee that coffee will be served within five minutes after the session breaks. Just as the group's missed guarantees carry monetary penalties, so must the hotel's.

Quality guarantees take on real meaning if staff members are empowered. Forcing a disgruntled guest to stew while searching for a manager intensifies the issue even if the resolution favors the customer. Similarly, failing to pay off after announcing a guarantee alienates the guest far more than the incident itself. Guarantees should be unambiguous, limited in scope, and focused on objectives that are easily understood. Then there is no quibbling about payment, which—when made promptly—leads to guest loyalty and positive word-of-mouth advertising.

Nothing highlights operational weaknesses more than paying off guarantees. Failure to deliver is evident to all. Guarantees, which were meant to forestall complaints, have fallen out of favor. So the search is on—a few pages ahead—for better methods of resolving complaints. Obviously, resolving complaints follows the incident whereas quality guarantees try to avert it.

Americans with Disabilities Act

The Americans with Disabilities Act (ADA) is a quality guarantee of a special nature. ADA requires changes in physical structures and hiring practices to accommodate the disabled, be they guest or employee. Title III of the law covers lodging, but the legislation applies to all industries.

This federal law (there are also state ADA laws) became operative in 1992. It was tweaked almost annually until 2010 when a major update was enacted. March 15, 2011, was the new effective date but construction enforcement was delayed one year until March 15, 2012. Specifics are available from the Department of Justice.

Unlike the quality guarantees of hotel companies, cash penalties are levied for failure to comply. Far worse than governmental oversight, civil suits, some filed for less-than-reputable reasons, plagued the hotel industry. Experienced now, hoteliers have fewer concerns than those that beset them in the years following 1992. For example, activists seeking cash settlements brought exotic animals representing them to be protected service animals. That was addressed in 2010, defined primarily as dogs.

Several years of court cases began because so much was left undefined in the law. It took time for everyone, those who wrote the regulations (not Congress), the disabled, and the hotel builders, to first understand and then to implement the provisions. What could not be resolved informally found its way to the desks of civil attorneys. Court rulings were far reaching, holding, for example, that a franchisor was responsible for the failure of a franchisee to build according to ADA specs. Savvy hoteliers worked with private groups (Society for the Advancement of Travel for the Handicapped, for example) to identify and correct barriers. Too soon to tell whether the revised law will reignite court cases; probably not.

Both the government's ADA and the lodging industry's TQM treat identical issues. One legislates; the other practices good business. The hotel industry was aware of the issue years before the government got around to legislating. Radisson was an early employer of the disabled. So was the Ritz-Carlton Company. Holiday Inn hired many handicapped persons, especially in its Worldwide Reservation Center.

Compliance with ADA standards is not the same as accommodating the handicapped within a quality assurance profile. Hotels can be accessible but not be hospitable. So chains refocused their training after ADA's passage. Embassy Suites called its ADA segment "Commandments of Disability Etiquette." Staff members across the industry were taught what to do and what not to do to help the handicapped.

Training differs in each department. Housekeepers learn to leave personal belongings in place (see Exhibit 8). Cashiers count aloud, announcing currency denominations. Enlarged folios and reg cards aid the visually handicapped. Enhanced lighting helps, particularly in corridors where lights have been dimmed to save energy. Those on staff are accommodated by moving, modifying, or replacing equipment and by adding new power sources for recharging wheelchair batteries. Human resources comply by revising hiring practices, including testing and job-description requirements.

SPECIFIC REQUIREMENTS   Because Congress didn't provide specifics, details were left to the regulation writers at both the federal and state levels.[14] Last time, California and the federal government needed seven years to reconcile conflicting legislation. As passed, the law had open-ended language. So the court battles were about the meaning of "disability" and the ambiguity of "undue hardship." After the rule-writers were done, the battle continued over specifications that were too rigid. Guest baths topped the failure-to-act list because bath renovations are expensive. Each wheelchair-accessible vanity was estimated at $750.

The approach area (floor space) to the tub must be at least 30 inches by 60 inches if the approach is parallel to the tub. If the approach is perpendicular to the tub, the area must be at least 48 inches by 60 inches. Tubs must have a seat or seating area with a width of at least 15 inches, extending the full width of the bath tub. Grab bars must be placed between 33 and 36 inches above floor level, must be 12 inches away from the shower head wall, and be at least 24 inches long

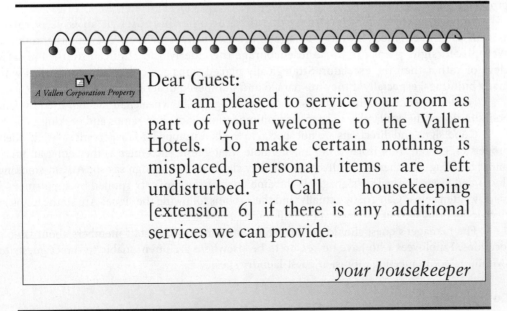

□V
A Vallen Corporation Property

Dear Guest:
I am pleased to service your room as part of your welcome to the Vallen Hotels. To make certain nothing is misplaced, personal items are left undisturbed. Call housekeeping [extension 6] if there is any additional services we can provide.

your housekeeper

EXHIBIT 8   Good ideas for providing extra service and attention are not limited to handicapped rooms. Many hotels personalize their room housekeepers with messages left in the room, often signing them with the individual housekeeper's name.

---

[14]Federal regulations [1992] limit shower heads to 2.5 gallons per minute. However, there is no restriction on the number of shower heads per shower. Forcing air to mix with the water in the shower head deceives the bather into thinking the pressure is pre-1992.

The original law stated that hotels standing before January 1993 need not comply with all the bath regulations. Hotels could delay changes until major renovations were planned. Missing was the definition of "major." Post-1993 hotels needed to make changes but only if they were—here are those words again—"readily achievable" and "without undue burden."

There are many specifications. The number of parking spaces for vans was legislated then revised. Door thresholds must be less than 0.5 inches high; roll-in showers no less than 36 by 60 inches; and drinking fountains no higher than 36 inches from the floor. A 300-room hotel is required to have eight handicapped guest rooms. Those rooms may be sold to the nonhandicapped and hotels do that as the house fills because rarely is there a call for eight handicapped rooms in one night.

Proposed new guidelines should not start the legal process anew because renovations made to meet previous standards would not need a redo until planned alterations are scheduled. Of course, there might be a court challenge to even that language.

Small offsets have been obtained because handicapped individuals represent both a new supply of workers and a new source of guests. Many executives viewed the Occupational Safety and Health Act (OSHA) of 1970 as a major intrusion of government into business. ADA's legislation appeared to be more of the same. Both laws have been around long enough so compromise and compliance has replaced confusion and anger. It is unlikely that the new regulations will reopen old wounds.

SIGNAGE   The ADA made innkeepers look more closely at their signage. Compliance requires both Braille and raised lettering. (Only 25% of the visually impaired read Braille.) The law brought attention to the whole issue of signage. Poor signs or the complete lack of them irritate every visitor, not only the handicapped. The American Automobile Association joined the push by adding sign requirements to its rating system.

Signage for the handicapped must be provided inside and outside of elevators, adjacent to handicapped rooms and on keys. Specifications are very exact: Wall mounted on the latch side of the room (to avoid being hit by an opening door while reading the number) and 60 inches above the floor. Audible elevator signals, once for up twice for down, supplement elevator panels. Some properties have tried audio signals that broadcast from small transmitters to the handicapped guests' receivers. The signals tell guests where they are and how to proceed to their destinations.

Signage, whether for elevators, exits, fires, or other purposes, is an issue of safety as well as convenience. Elevator locations are not always evident even to the sighted. Well-placed signs point the way and encourage the elderly and children to use the safer elevator rather than the escalator. Strategically placed signs are critical for properties with many buildings, especially if they are named and numbered differently.

Handicapped, but sighted guests, also rely on signs. The wheelchair symbol used by tour books indicates the availability of special accommodations including ramps and parking.

Good signs and directions are not special to the handicapped. Managers must "walk" their properties, get out from isolated offices, and note what guests encounter as they enter an unfamiliar building. Are there fire-exit signs? Are they alarmed? Does a sign say so? Are no-smoking floors and areas marked by signage? Is the ambiance of the property spoiled by supplemental hand-written signs? Can guests actually find their rooms following the signs? Are all the bulbs in electric signs lit? Go out and look at the building as a new arrival!

The manager's quest should go further, questioning various staff members about simple locations. Employees who have no reason to be elsewhere are often unable to direct guests to swimming pools, meeting rooms, or guest-laundry sites.

Complaints

Complaints, like quality guarantees, should direct management to troubled service areas. Unfortunately, too few guests complain and too few managers look below the surface of the rare complaint. Most guests and some (secretly thankful) managers mumble quietly and let the matter slip by. That is why those complaints that are registered must be resolved quickly and correctly.

HOW MUCH DO COMPLAINTS COST?   Measuring guest unhappiness is like measuring the value of the "moments of truth." Putting dollar amounts on them requires estimates and assumptions. Neither contains real mathematical accuracy, but one hears them over and over because they make believable points.

It is said that 10% of guests would not return to the property of their most recent visit. Using the same values as Exhibit 6, a hotel would lose 21 possible repeats each day (300 rooms at 70% occupancy times the 10% loss). With just 21 rooms lost nightly, the annual total is a whopping 7,665 guest nights. Make another assumption: The ADR is just $70. Then the total cost of 10% of nonreturning guests is over $500,000 annually! The cost stretches into the stratosphere of $5 million when hotels of 3,000 rooms are involved. Now add in the cost of replacing that number of guests in order to maintain the 70% occupancy.

Some maintain that labor-intensive industries such as lodging increase productivity only by improving the service encounter. The failure to do so, goes the argument, represents not merely additional labor costs but costs from lost business as well. Here, too, there is little empirical evidence to support the idea. Complaints do impact profits, but not every complaint takes dollars to resolve. One investigation reported just the opposite: Only one-third of written complaints were about money. Exhibit 9 suggests it is better to spend a bit to hold the guest than to invest five times that to solicit another.

Still Another Calculation   Exhibit 9, like others calculations, uses widely quoted but vaguely grounded assumptions. Still, the conclusions are startling.

Premise 1:   Some 68% of nonreturning guests stay away because of indifferent service. (Death, relocation, competition, and poor product account for the 32%.)

Premise 2:   About 2.5% or less of dissatisfied guests actually voice their unhappiness. There is an iceberg effect here. Below the surface floats vast complaints; never voiced, never resolved. Of this silent majority, it is estimated that over half will never patronize the hotel again. Worse yet, they will tell 10 or 11 others not to do so. Very angry ones may tell up to 20 others. This "fact" is so irrefutable in the view of many that a "rule" has been created, the 1-11-5 rule. One unhappy guest will tell 11 others and each of the 11 will tell 5 more.

Premise 3:   About two-thirds of the icebergs can be melted and won over by resolving the complaint. The other one-third can be converted from blasters to boosters if the complaints are handled quickly and properly. Implicit here is the guest's willingness to speak up. Guests will do so when they are very angry or when management has created an atmosphere that encourage guests to voice their complaints.

Cost of Lost Guests

Loss of Guests
68% of nonreturning guests quit because of indifferent service.
32% is lost to death, relocation, competition, and poor products.

Complaints
Less than 5% of dissatisfied guests speak out—so for every one that does there may be twenty who do not.
Over half of the silent majority refuse to return—an iceberg floating beneath the surface.
Noncomplaining guests do complain to friends and acquaintances.

   10 to 11 others will hear of the mishap.
   13% of the group will gripe to 20 others.

Two-thirds of the iceberg could be won over if they were identified—about half of these could become boosters.

Costs
It costs over $10 to answer a complaint by letter (including the cost of writing time, follow-up time, and postage).
It costs five times more to get a new customer than to keep an existing one.

EXHIBIT 9 Guest complaints are costly; few managers dispute that. Widely quoted but never documented values reinforce the concept and emphasize the importance of a proactive approach.

IDENTIFYING THE COMPLAINT   Identifying unhappy guests can be more challenging than resolving their problems. For certain, the rote question, "How was everything?" will elicit no meaningful reply. Desk personnel and managers from all operational and organizational levels must ask direct and specific questions. That means talking to guests, whether in the lobby, by the pool, or wherever. The dialogue may start with pleasantries such as a comment about the weather, an introduction, or the frequency of the guest's visits. Then, the conversation must elicit the negatives, if there are any. "Do you like our new bedding?" "Have you ever tried room service?" "Did you know we have a special lounge drink this month?"

Comments that flow from these solicitations are not complaints. They give management direction for improving service and, thus, preempting real complaints. Informal conversations highlight hidden issues that require no immediate action, no settlement costs, no allowances on the folios. Informal chats suggest grounds for operational changes and, secondarily, build guest relations, especially if followed with a letter of thanks.

Management must be knowledgeable if it hopes to prevent complaints. Executives who don aprons and work the floor create more than a pubic-relation photo-ops. They learn, for example, that the location of the dishwasher is, indeed, the cause for high chinaware breakage, that the housekeeper's vacuums really don't work, and that customer service does warrant the purchase of umbrellas for guest use. Managers who telephone their own hotels test departmental procedures and the temperament of their staff.

PREVENTING THE COMPLAINT: EARLY WARNING   Complaints can be forestalled if the staff is trained to tell it like it is. Alerting guests to bad situations allows them to participate or not. Of course, it may also cost business. So the reservations department must explain that the pool is closed for repairs during the dates of the reservation. A request for connecting rooms is impossible to promise. The request is noted but no guarantee can be made. A no-guarantee with apologies is stated by reservationists, not merely implied.

And so it should be across the hotel. Early warnings about other large parties in the house must be made by sales executives before finalizing the new booking. Likewise, room service would report elevator delays as it takes a breakfast order. Guest-service agents must offer reduced rates in the wing that is without air-conditioning.

Complaints may evolve around the prompt attention paid to the "squeaky wheel." Managers know that oiling the squeak out of turn may better serve everyone in the long run. Observant guests often side with the hotel when an obnoxious squeaker rolls up to the desk. They give away their priority in line to get the pest put away. Similarly, handling families with tired, irritable children outside the sequence may actually improve overall service. Just clear it with the next party in line.

Preventing the complaint by anticipating the problem and providing accurate information up front is preferable to quieting angry guests after the fact. Explaining the situation forestalls the complaint. "Yes, we can accept a 10:30 AM arrival, but please do not expect to be roomed before 1 o'clock because housekeeping will not get to your room before then. Perhaps you can plan to lunch first." Candor reduces complaints. Misleading statements either by omission or implication enrage guests who know "they've been had."

PREVENTING THE COMPLAINT: COMMENT CARDS   The effectiveness of comment cards is argued over and again. Distracters say the questions are tilted toward the hotel's strengths. Hotel managers grumble because guests use the questionnaires to gripe. Guests don't balance the good and the bad, managers say, but concentrate on operating weaknesses. Execs explain away negative comments by claiming the guest is simply wrong. Poor comments hurt managers doubly when results from the cards are part of bonuses or promotions.

Management's complaints aside, improving service requires every weapon to be mustered. Comment cards are one of those weapons, and like others, they have strengths and weaknesses. The better the questionnaire, the better the information obtained. Uncovering and remedying shortcomings is what managing for quality is all about. Anonymous guest cards help overcome the iceberg effect, the reluctance of guests to speak out.

Critics attack the statistical validity of comment cards. Responses are low, typically 1–2% of the guest population. Long questionnaires account for some of the low returns. Guests take the time only when they are really angry. Cards with a narrow focus get better responses. Short, one-topic questionnaires—cleanliness, for example—could be used throughout the property.

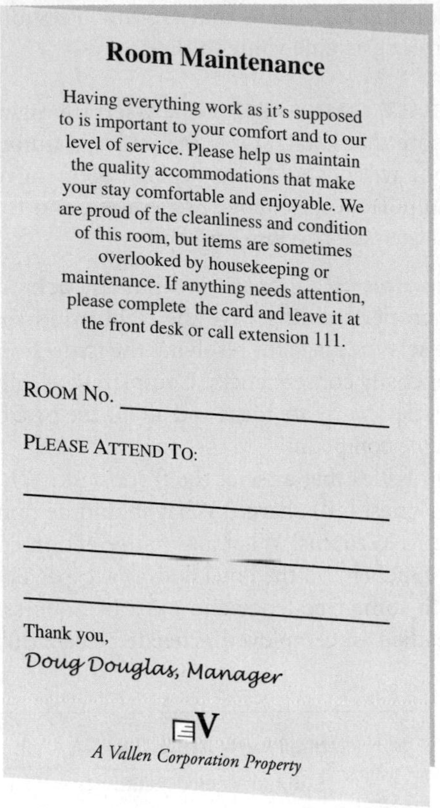

Room Maintenance

Having everything work as it's supposed to is important to your comfort and to our level of service. Please help us maintain the quality accommodations that make your stay comfortable and enjoyable. We are proud of the cleanliness and condition of this room, but items are sometimes overlooked by housekeeping or maintenance. If anything needs attention, please complete the card and leave it at the front desk or call extension 111.

ROOM No. _____

PLEASE ATTEND TO:

_____

_____

_____

Thank you,
Doug Douglas, Manager

▣V
A Vallen Corporation Property

EXHIBIT 10 Enlisting guest participation improves the quality of the room and of the guest's experience. It adds another source of information to guest comment cards, input from quality circles, inspections, and conversations. Management can forestall complaints with good recordkeeping provided it leads to corrective action.

The theme might change every quarter with specialized, equally brief forms used within each department. Although not a guest comment card, guests respond well when asked for help with in-room repairs (see Exhibit 10).

Comment cards are typically static: left in guest rooms or on coffee-shop tables. Returns increase greatly when guests are invited to participate. Guest-service agents do this by handing a pencil-and-paper questionnaires to guests at check-out. There is a better response if a private computer-screen questionnaire is close by. Requests can also be made on arrival accompanied by some incentive. How about lottery tickets; Carlson Hospitality tried that. Giving dessert coupons or wine with dinner doubles the benefits by drawing guests into the dining room. Lottery drawings are the best incentives. Guests complete the survey after the stay when they have had time to evaluate the property. Prize drawings, done monthly perhaps, identify each guest by name which facilitates follow-up, thank-you letters. (Careful: Some states outlaw lotteries.)

Before the Web, toll-free telephone numbers supplemented comment cards. 1-800-telephones are rarely staffed anymore. Besides, angry guests get angrier when the call is answered by a machine or a foreign outsourcer whose diction is, well, foreign. As guests have replaced their snail mail with email so have hotels replaced their telephones with software platforms that correlate the electronic responses and highlight the areas that need special attention.

Less formal, but equally helpful, are "comment cards" by bloggers. Unlike real comment cards, blogs are seen by everyone, not just by management. Blogs are helpful. Good ones reinforce the quality assurance effort. Bad ones require management to act faster than they might with confidential comment cards.

Different information is treated differently. Guest feedback supplements feedback from staff, which comes through quality circles or suggestion boxes. Management's response will not always be immediate and that must be explained. Some issues are operational and response is quick: placing an emergency telephone in the exercise room. Other issues are slower; they are strategic or involve large costs, building another elevator, for example.

Information from quality circles, from guest comment cards, from employee suggestion boxes, from computer programs, and from direct conversations needs to be analyzed. A simple spreadsheet highlights areas that get repeated comments. Management must analyze the input for trends in operating weakness and strengths. Good systems identify both functions that are working and those that are not. Previous, face-to-face encounters from agitated guests add immeasurable value to the analysis.

HANDLING THE FACE-TO-FACE COMPLAINT Guest-service management aims for error-free service, but that is a goal more than a fact. Only the number, timing, or place of the complaint is uncertain, not whether one will occur. As quality management reduces the number of complaints, each one gains in importance. Systems, procedures, and training notwithstanding, the unexpected happens: Door attendants do lose car keys!

Preparing for Complaints Preparing begins by acknowledging the likelihood of a slip-up. Employees with proper training have the right mind-set. They are aware and they recognize that their attitude sets the stage for resolving the issue. Preparation makes the best of a bad situation and minimizes costly consequences. Complaints usually follow themes within each operating unit. So quality circles can share ideas and adopt the best ones—best practices—as the starting point for the inevitable complaint.

Consider the common issues that arise at the front desk: What is the proper response to a guest who protests a folio (guest bill) charge? What should be done for a reservation-arriving guest when the house is full? No rooms! What alternative action can be taken for a guest who arrives with a travel agency voucher that the hotel doesn't accept? These are not rare, unexpected encounters. They occur with some frequency and must be addressed beforehand. Options for frequent glitches must be readied and employed as needed (see Exhibit 11).

Hotel Anywhere, U.S.A.
Internal Memorandum

To: Guest-Service Agents

From: Holly Wood, Rooms Manager

Subject: Empowerment Guidelines

Date: January 1, 20- -

A Vallen Corporation Property

Effective this date, all guest-service agents who have completed the four training hours have authority to make the following adjustments using their own discretion. Managers and supervisors are always available for consultation.

An Apology is the First Response! Apologies are free; we give away as many as necessary, but be sincere and listen carefully.

Where appropriate, verify information before acting.

Issue	Intermediate Response*	Maximum Response*
Noisy room	Relocate, if stay-over	Upgrade now or next visit; gift to the room
Incorrect rate	Correct the paperwork	Allowance for the difference; ticket to club or spa
Engineering problems: Heat and AC, TV, plumbing	Send engineer; change rooms	Upgrade; up to 25% off rate
Protested charges: Telephone	Allowance for local	Allowance for LD
In-room film	Allowance	One per day
Valet parking	Allowance	Full amount

*Awarding up to 500 frequent-guest points is always an alternative.

EXHIBIT 11 Empowering employees to take action requires them to understand what they can and cannot be done. Supplementing training with guidelines like these structure the procedure. Training must include which issues must be referred and what to do if that next management level is not available.

There are issues that fall outside the norm—issues that must be resolved by a higher level of authority. Preparing the staff must include directives about when and to whom the complaint must be referred. Rare is the session that trains for the next step: What is to be done when that next level of referral (authority) is not available. Leave the guest to wait ... to wait ... to wait? Complaints are not always of the hotel's doing. Tired, grumpy travelers, those who may have done battle with family members or business associates, who have fought canceled flights, and who have lost luggage, may find the hotel employee an ideal outlet for a week of frustrations. Preparing for the complaint means understanding that.

Preparing means putting up with drunks and being tolerant of the braggart performing for his group. Preparing means overlooking exaggerations, sarcasm, and irony. Preparing for the complaint recognizes that senior persons may berate younger ones replaying parent–child relationships. Preparing means understanding that some persons can never be satisfied no matter what the staff does.

Responding to Complaints   No complaint is ever trivial to the complainer. What appears to the hotelier as trivial often originates from a series of small unattended-to issues that smolder and then erupt.

By Listening   To bring remedy, the complaint must be heard and understood. That requires the one to communicate and the other to hear. Complaint-takers must listen actively, not passively. Careful listening is fundamental to resolution. Full attention moves the problem forward even before the explanation has been completed. Experienced complaint-handlers never allow other employees, guests, or telephone calls to distract them from paying attention to the complainant.

Complainers rarely begin with the real issue—which is true, of course, with many conversations. Questions are appropriate if they are not judgmental. Unnecessary questions interrupt the thought process, anger the speaker, and push up the level of frustration before all the facts are in.

Listening requires good eye contact and subtle supportive body movements. Appropriate nodding, tsh-tshing, facial attention, and hand movements encourage the speaker and convey attention, sympathy, and understanding. Contact with and empathy for the speaker's experience assures the right beginning.

Complainers don't want to be rushed; they want the whole story to be heard. Care in body language (a nodding head) and active listening (not preoccupied with other business) are minimum requirements as the story teller rumbles on. Observing the guest's nonverbal signals helps to interpret the guest's readings of one's own signals.

Attentiveness is particularly important in the resolution of accidents. Details can prove critical in court cases and court cases often result when the listener makes short shrift of the accident. Aggrieved guests want attention, whole-hearted attention. They want someone in authority to hear them out. Leave the investigation to security; management must handle the personal and public-relations issues. Together the team summons help. Then each handles what each is best able to do. Even as sympathy is evident no one admits mistakes. No one talks of financial aid or insurance coverage. Other parties (staff and guest) should be interviewed away from the scene but as promptly as possible.

In a Proper Venue   Complainers who grow hostile, overly upset, loud, or abusive must be removed from the lobby. Shifting to a new venue should be done quickly. Don't wait for the issue to intensify or the time commitment to outgrow the lobby discussion. Perhaps comfort can be the pretense: "Let's sit down in the office, we'll be more comfortable there."

Walking to another location offers a cooling-off time. There is a chance to change the topic and the tone of the conversation. Walking changes the physical stances of the parties and the defensive postures that may have been taken up. The office location reinforces the manager's authority and prestige.

The louder the complainer growls, the softer the response must come. There is an immediate reaction as the shouter quiets down to hear what may be an almost-whisper. Harsh answers to abuse and/or offensive language elevates a nonpersonal situation to a battle of personalities. The hotel's representative must retain dignity and if needed gently prod the other party toward the same. The facts are the issue, not the persons—certainly not the employee who may have been the original target of the guest's ire.

If need be, the manager may refuse further discussion until the guest moderates language and tone. The hotelier tells the complainer that he or she is being addressed politely and the listener expects the same courtesy. In worst-case scenarios, say with a drunk or drug-crazed individual, police may need to be called.

By Making a Record Asking permission to write-up the complaint indicates how seriously management views the matter. It allows the guest to restate the problem and modify it after second-thoughts. Recording upgrades the level of attention. It gives the hotel representative an additional opportunity to express sympathy and concern. Recording slows the conversation allowing emotions to cool. Watching the input makes the guest feel something is already being done. The stage is set for resolution.

Front offices maintain daily journals that include complaints. These logs improve communications between shifts since issues often carry over. Documentation helps the participants recall the incident, provide a basis for training, and support legal proceedings if the issue goes that far. Serious incidents are also documented by security and by medics and police if the situation so warranted.

The hotelier also examines registration cards and folios and reservation data if these help explain the problem. Inviting the employee into the office or interviewing him or her by telephone broadens the investigation. Pros and cons must be weighted: It is dangerous to do that with the guest present. Both the staffer and the guest must be addressed with civility using proper titles, not first names.

With a Settlement Once registered, the complaint must be settled, resolved somehow, and closed. The complainant expects some satisfaction or real restitution. The hotel wants to keep the customer, strengthen the relationship, and send the guest forth as a booster who tells the world about the fair treatment. Still, the hotel doesn't want to give away the house for real or imagined mistakes that caused no harm and little damage.

Apologies are free—give away as many as needed. And only an apology may be needed. Apologies are in order even if the complaint was baseless or unreasonable. The effectiveness of an apology depends on the guest's reading of the manager and the manager's delivery of the apology (see Exhibit 12). Does the unhappy guest see the hotelier as truly contrite or merely mouthing niceties? The apology must ring true and that sound can come only from sincerity. "I am sorry and I apologize on behalf of the hotel" goes a long way toward settling minor issues. "I am sorry" takes on different nuances with different levels of emphasis: "I *am* sorry" or additional words: "I am *so* sorry" or deleted words: "I'm sorry."

Voices can be shaped and honed to carry the right intonation and emphasis. Concern and belief can be communicated irrespective of the words used. Several standbys have a proper place in the list of apologetic inserts. "I know how you feel." "Yes, that is distressing." "I would have done the same." If the hotel was at major fault, citing "our mistake" may clear the air and end the crisis.

Regardless of fault, the traditional bowl of fruit or wine and cheese—even a box of bathroom amenities—is sent to the room to close the episode. Apologies are repeated on the enclosed

How Sorry—So Sorry		
Type	**Expression**	**Result**
The True Apology	Personally sincere, regretful, intense	Guest is very satisfied
The Next Best Thing	Institutionally sincere and apologetic	Guest is placated
The Premeditated Statement	Calls up a range of platitudes	Guest thinks it's OK
Mea Culpa	Yes, mistakes were made	Now, really!
A Defensive Offering	I'm sorry, but it isn't all our fault	Yes it is
OK, Here's an Apology	You want me to say something…	Complete dissatisfaction

EXHIBIT 12 Apologies are free—we give away as many as needed. Without careful attention to sincerity and delivery, the intended results may not be accomplished. Then the costs are very high.

card. Complaints that end with an apology are the least expensive and often the most satisfying. They should be reinforced with a followed-up letter or telephone call.

More substantial actions are needed if the issue balloons beyond an apology. Heading that list are moves that have just moderate costs. An upgraded room is an immediate response. Even here are degrees. Upgrade to the concierge floor or to a suite? Upgrade now or for a subsequent stay? If the latter, guests are given the manager's card with a "special" number. "Call me direct and I shall arrange it." By implication, these deviations from the standard recognize the desire to make things right.

A second-level incident might require a small gift. Tickets to an event within the house is one option. Athletic contests (tennis tourneys), art shows, distinguished speakers, and theater-style entertainment are upgrades almost without cost if seats are plentiful. Admission to the hotel's spa, tickets to local attractions (theme parks, boat rides), or limo transportation to the airport are still other options. Cash refunds are the very last choice but may be appropriate: Damage to guest property, for example. Compensation should be handled as an allowance against folio charges rather than handing over dollar bills.

More serious cases require more costly resolutions. Serious incidents are not settled easily. Smashed fenders, dentures broken on a bone, bites from bedbugs, and snared designer dresses are not remedied on the spot. Insurance companies or law firms (a fall in the tub) work their wares slowly.

Once resolved and whatever the level of complaint, experienced complaint-takers explain what will be done and how long it might take. The time should be overestimated because a more rapid response impresses the guest with the importance assigned to the issue.

By Asking the Guest   Guest demands soften if the episode is handled professionally and if the guest feels the ultimate resolution is apt to be fair. Having reached the guest and sensing empathy, a bold hotelier brings the complainant into the decision loop. Carefully, the guest's expectations are solicited. Often they are less than the hotel's. And to the guest's surprise, "Yes, let's do that; I think it's fair."

All of which is easier said than done. Listening to an experienced complaint-handler, what is said and how it is said, is the best learning experience a trainee can have. It is especially helpful if the claim is denied and the guest leaves disappointed but not angry.

Customers are always right! Except sometimes they aren't. Management can listen attentively, sympathize completely, and communicate caringly but still say "no" to outrageous requests based on nonevents. Refusing compensation—apologies are always offered—may cost the customer's patronage. It is a judgment call; the guest may already be lost. In denying restitution, inexperienced managers resort to "company policy," an ill-advised turnoff. Better to explain the decision—if one is really needed—in terms of fairness, safety, concern for other guests, or simple economics.

Disgruntled guests may ask see a higher authority. If that is appropriate, the next manager should be formally introduced and the issue recapped aloud. Thereafter, the first interviewer remains silent unless questioned, allowing the conversation to progress without interruption.

Quick and equitable resolutions make friends. Whatever the outcome, it is the attitude as expressed in words and actions that go far in minimizing (or aggravating) the damages, financial as well as reputation-wise.

Summary

Service is what the hospitality industry is all about. But service has a broader meaning than serving breakfast or opening a car door. Service means providing what is needed. Above all else, guests need the industry's basic product, sleep. Service also means providing guest needs within a cordial atmosphere generated by all employees, by associates committed to the service concept. Although hotel facilities differ across a broad range, the essence of the delivery remains the same: "Every staff member thinking like a manager and acting like a concierge." So broad a definition needs an equally broad conceptual base. That comes under the heading of *total* quality management. Every aspect of the operation is managed at the peak of quality. No

easy job, that, because management's scope of responsibility is broad and varied. For one, there is the physical hotel, which has been discussed briefly in topics such as room size, linens, and the ADA. It is the other, the attitude displayed by the staffers, that is the thrust of the chapter's discussion and the essence of service.

Each hotel delivers its product within its own type, class, and size. Those limitations notwithstanding, every organization can deliver a high standard of service if its members are imbued with customer relations. Instilling and installing customer relations management is part of the industry's drive toward TQM.

Guest satisfaction (and employee satisfaction, too) is at its highest when service is delivered by courteous, empowered staffers. Opportunities to do so occur often during the many "moments of truth" generated at busy hotels. Recognizing the associates' critical role, management is changing its methods of supervision. Winning the staff's commitment is an ongoing process that has redefined the role of everyone employed. Part of the change is management's empowerment of workers within their individual levels of authority. Part of the change is a flatter organization with fewer middle-management levels. Part of the change is a greater level of diversity within the industry and part of the change is the introduction of new language.

TQM, itself a term of recent origin, has introduced other language into human resources management. Fads in management come and go like other fashions. The language of CRM and of quality circles will soon fade away. Hotel management must retain the vision behind the language even as the actual terms disappear. Operating in a fast-changing society, innkeepers must hold on to the industry best practices. Total quality management ranks high among them.

Resources and Challenges

RESOURCES

Website Assignment

Submit a paper outlining what search-engine sources you, as Director of Human Resources, might pursue to fill an opening for (1) a national sales exec and (2) an assistant rooms manager.

Interesting Tidbits

- In 2010, Hilton settled a "spying" lawsuit brought by Starwood. Starwood alleged that two of its executives took company secrets about boutique hotels when they went to work for Hilton. Part of the court settlement stops Hilton from certain boutique hotel developments. A cash penalty was also paid.

- The U.S. Department of Justice provides free ADA materials, which may be ordered by calling 1-800-514-0301 (Voice) or 1-800-514-0383 (TDD). Publications are available in standard print, large print, audiotape, Braille, and computer disk. AAA also has a publication that lists properties which help the estimated 50 million disabled.

Challenges

True/False

Questions that are partially false should be marked false (F).

_____ 1. Hotels returned to smaller beds (twins and singles) as one profit-saving move during the economic turndown of 2008–2010.

_____ 2. Guests feel a sense of luxury when guest-room beds have a 180-linen count.

_____ 3. Guest-registers, where departing guests record their impressions and complaints, are basic to most hotels because they provide management an unbiased account of the visit, including any unresolved complaints.

_____ 4. Complaints are said to be like an iceberg, because, like an iceberg, most of the issues are hidden (below the water line).

_____ 5. A carefully drafted and enacted program of customer relations management does away with almost all complaints allowing management to focus elsewhere.

Problems

1. Using the computer, create a simple spreadsheet showing the form and functions that management can use to summarize and analyze complaints originating within departments of the rooms divisions.

2. Prepare and briefly discuss a list of three quality guarantees that are defined narrowly enough to be communicated easily and achieved successfully: for example, room service breakfast delivered within 30 minutes. Be certain to include the penalty to be paid by the hotel if the guarantee is not met.
   a. Explain why Marriott's guarantee of breakfast is, in the words of the authors, "an advertisement, a departmental promotion, an employee empowerment, an assurance of quality, and a willingness to be measured."

3. Compute how many moments of truth occur in a full-service convention hotel of 630 rooms during a typical month. Comment.

4. From readings and personal experience, discuss six of the most difficult elements of resolving a complaint.

5. You are the hotel's liaison with the architects designing guest rooms for a new tower. Present them a list of the 10 most important items that must be provided if the hotel is to meet its obligations under the Americans with Disabilities Act.

6. List five incentives that a hotel might offer to get guests to complete a guest comment card. Make a special effort to have the incentives encourage cross-advertising, by which one department awards incentives for use in another department.

AN INCIDENT IN HOTEL MANAGEMENT
Force Majeure

How to attract more customers from companies in the local business park was the topic of this month's meeting of departmental managers. The group was confident of its ability to deliver, so they adopted and widely advertised a quality guarantee for local businesses. "If anything goes wrong, the room rate is on us!"

An out-of-town representative of Allied Manufacturing, a nearby industry, has been in the hotel for two nights. There was no hot water last night or the morning of the third day. The guest mentions this to the guest-service agent as he goes through the check-out procedure. "I think I'll take advantage of your quality guarantee."

"Yes sir; please wait while I get the manager."

It was almost 15 minutes before the hotel manager appeared. "Good morning. The agent has told me about your request and I would like to comply. There's no hot water because the boiler is down. It's an act of God, a *force majeure*, so, as I have told other guests, the situation isn't covered by our guarantee."

Questions:

1. Was there a management failure here; if so, what?
2. What is the hotel's immediate response (or action) to the incident?
3. What further, long-run action should management take, if any?

Answers to True/False Quiz

1. False. Large beds are part of the basic service that hotels provide and guests expect. Moreover, just logically, the cost of disposing of perfectly good beds and acquiring whole new sets wouldn't make sense during a short-term dip.

2. False. Linen count of 180 is standard for most homes and hotels. Count needs to be higher, say 250, before the sleeper notices the difference.

3. False. There is no such record now! There were "Guest Registers" when registration books (rather than registration cards) were used, ca. 1930–1940. See the book's format (below).

Date 1937	Party	Address	Comments
8/4	M/M R. Jones	4322 Wyoming St New York, NY	
8/4	Mr. John Gilvert	21 Craig Drive Appleton, IL	Hope it's going to be a Great Hotel
8/4	Ms. M. Martin	Long Hill Rd Junction City, LA	

4. True. The bulk of an iceberg (almost 90%) is below the surface. Complaints are like that: unseen and portending an unexpected crash.

5. False Nothing does away with complaints; no program can do that no matter how well it is constructed.

From Arrival to Rooming

From Chapter 8 of *Check-In Check-Out*, Ninth Edition. Gary K. Vallen, Jerome J. Vallen. Copyright © 2013 by Pearson Education, Inc. All rights reserved.

From Arrival to Rooming

GREETED ON ARRIVAL

The arrival procedure appears routine and standardized. And so it is, although a wide choice of sizes, classes, and types of hotels means no two arrivals are exactly the same. Guests also contribute to the range of expectations. Some are seasoned travelers and some novices. Some know the brand well and some are first-timers. The arrival procedure mixes the personalities of each property, with its range of services and levels of training, with the personalities of each individual, both those arriving and those greeting the arrivals.

At one extreme are the road-warriors. Using self-check-in terminals, they arrive, register, and take occupancy without any staff interaction. First-time travelers fall at the other end. They need guidance, coddling, and reassurance. Both types arrive and register; both types must be greeted and roomed. Some come to mega resorts and some to roadside motor inns. So the arrival procedure is everywhere the same, even if it isn't. It is because the forms and format of the arrival are much alike. It isn't because some properties have all the steps outlined in Exhibit 1 and some properties skip the in-betweens, jumping from arrival to self-rooming. It is because all hotels strive for courteous and prompt attention. It isn't because the number of intervening staff encounters between arrival and occupancy range from one to four. All have a guest-service agent (that's one), but many have someone in parking or driving the airport shuttle (number two), someone at the door, number three, and a bellperson (four) before the desk's receptionist is even reached. (See Exhibit 1.)

Moments of Truth

Arrival is the guest's first physical encounter with the hotel. He or she comes with preconceived ideas of what it will be like. Arrival is, therefore, one of the "moments of truth." That is the point where the service providers and the arriving guests meet eyeball to eyeball. There can be but one opportunity to make a first, good impression. If all front-office functions are running smoothly and all systems are working in unison, the arrival is an auspicious one. The guest's presence is acknowledged. His or her vehicle, if there is one, is handled promptly and professionally—without skidding tires. Uniformed services make the initial greetings. Reception (guest-service agents) processes the registration quickly but courteously. Baggage is tended to; the guest is settled in, ready to use the services and incur the charges itemized at the bottom of Exhibit 1.

Arrival time signals the sharp distinctions among the industry's many levels of service. Full-service hotels make the arrival procedure part of the ambiance that creates the aura of something special. Exhibit 1 displays the ranks of associates who give emphasis to the occasion. Each contributes to the reception and creates the quality behind this initial moment of truth.

Limited-service properties are the other extreme. Only the guest-service agent stands between the guest's arrival and his or her occupancy of the room. In between lies the wide span of hotels. Some have a full arrival teams, some have none, and some fall in the middle. Whichever the grouping, the guest's first encounters often involve members of the uniformed services: valet parking attendant (or airport shuttle driver), doorperson, and bellhop.

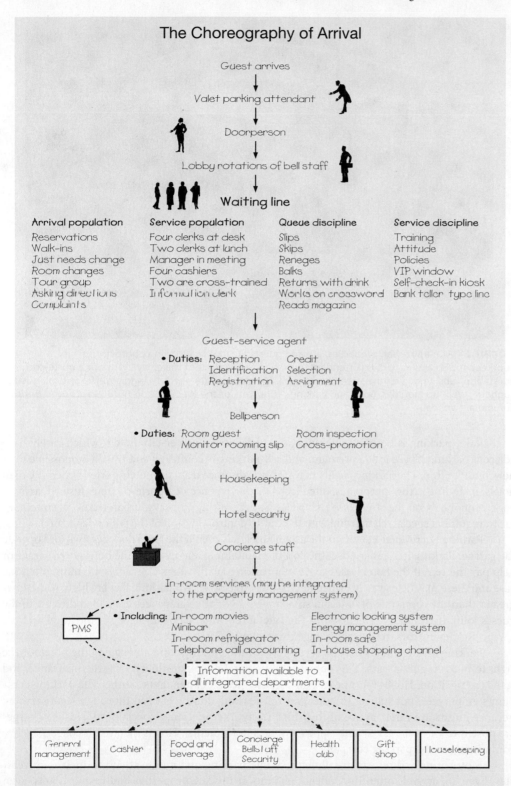

The Choreography of Arrival

Guest arrives

↓

Valet parking attendant

↓

Doorperson

↓

Lobby rotations of bell staff

↓

Waiting line

Arrival population	Service population	Queue discipline	Service discipline
Reservations	Four clerks at desk	Slips	Training
Walk-ins	Two clerks at lunch	Skips	Attitude
Just needs change	Manager in meeting	Reneges	Policies
Room changes	Four cashiers	Balks	VIP window
Tour group	Two are cross-trained	Returns with drink	Self-check-in kiosk
Asking directions	Information clerk	Works on crossword	Bank teller type line
Complaints		Reads magazine	

↓

Guest-service agent

• Duties: Reception   Credit
        Identification Selection
        Registration   Assignment

↓

Bellperson

• Duties: Room guest   Room inspection
        Monitor rooming slip Cross-promotion

↓

Housekeeping

↓

Hotel security

↓

Concierge staff

↓

In-room services (may be integrated
to the property management system)

• Including: In-room movies   Electronic locking system
          Minibar   Energy management system
          In-room refrigerator   In-room safe
          Telephone call accounting In-house shopping channel

PMS

Information available to
all integrated departments

| General management | Cashier | Food and beverage | Concierge Bellstaff Security | Health club | Gift shop | Housekeeping |

EXHIBIT 1   The arrival process is an exacting choreography of departments working together to make a seamless, positive experience for the guest. Luxury hotels add even more to this flow pattern; limited-service properties much less.

VALET ATTENDANT   The hotel's physical location dictates the need, if any, for parking attendants. There are no such positions in the many hotels with plenty of self-parking. In the absence of doormen, valet attendants take on some of that role. They greet guests arriving by auto, open car doors, and assist with luggage. Taking control of the vehicle, providing a receipt, and parking the car is the essence of the job.

EXHIBIT 2   At many urban properties, arriving guests are met by a smiling doorperson. This doorkeeper also acts as parking attendant (note sign to the right of the entry). Without a porte-cochère, guests and cabs unload on the street by the curb. The doorperson needs to juggle traffic control, guests, baggage, walk-up inquiries, taxis, and parking.   *Courtesy of the Wedgewood Hotel, Vancouver, British Columbia, Canada.*

Valet parking is both an amenity and a necessity in center-city hotels, which rarely have adjacent parking. Space is at a premium and self-parking is confusing and usually impossible for a newcomer to find. The parking facility may be some distance from the hotel's porte-cochère.[1] Urban hotels, including luxury properties, often lack the convenience of a porte-cochère. Instead, arrivals park temporarily on the street (see Exhibit 2). Street parking in heavy, urban traffic, even temporarily, requires a special relationship with the traffic-control division of the police department.

Parking is a revenue center for the urban hotel. It is even if the hotel does not own and operate the garage. Parking fees either offset the cost of maintaining and insuring the hotel's own garage or help pay the rent if the hotel leases space in a parking facility. Rental facilities are more often the case and these may be privately owned or city-owned. Downtown parking fees are high, sometimes greater than the room rate of hotels in small towns![2] Nightly garage fees are added directly to the guest's folio. In addition, the guest tips the valet attendants, who run between the hotel and the garage. Retrieving cars from urban garages may take 15–30 minutes.

Parking arrangements may be reversed with the parking company paying the hotel for the right to pick up guests' cars. This outside company takes responsibility, pays the insurance, and staffs the position. Hotels must be careful because the valet attendants are then the parking company's employees, not subject to hotel control. Parking contracts need thorough legal scrutiny because guests are rarely aware of this third-party intervention. Especially so because charges are posted to the folio. It certainly appears to be a hotel facility. Hotels then remit collections less commission to the parking company.

Motor inns and resorts usually have ample parking and guests attend to their own vehicles. Even so, arrivals often find valet attendants at upscale properties and casino/hotels, even those with convenient on-property parking. In their search for new revenue sources, some hotels charge a nightly parking fee even though space is plentiful and guests handle their own vehicles. And this is in addition to the resort fee.

---

[1]Port-ko-shar', French for coach gate. A covered drive-through on hotel property, not part of the public thoroughfare, that accommodates arrivals out of traffic and under shelter. May be heated or cooled. Porte cochere is a modern version of the horse-and-carriage courtyard where guests disembarked within the shelter of a U-shaped inn.

[2]Typically, urban parking fees for hotels are $50–$60 per night plus a charge of $5–$10 for each time in-and-out.

THE DOORPERSON   Door attendants produce no direct income for the hotel. Unlike parking attendants, this position falls early to the budget ax. (Many Asian hotels offer a contrasting view. Several employees staff the entryways including some who spin the revolving doors for arriving and departing guests.) Thus, the mere presence of a door attendant makes a strong statement about the hotel, its concern for guests, its level of service, but mostly about its location, urban.

The doorperson is part concierge, part bellperson, part tour guide, part host, and part friend. Like other uniformed personnel, gratuities are a mainstay of the doorperson's income. Guests and nonguests alike look to this person for suggestions, directions, and advice; and, not incidentally, for taxicabs.[3] They work closely with parking valets (see the sign of Exhibit 2). They keep the entry free of ice and snow and loiterers. They serve as an early-warning system for hotel security. Watching the comings and goings of regulars and strangers, doormen build an inner sense of who is who. Their antennae pick up the signals of something amiss from lurking strangers or suspicious packages. Without question, doorpersons in their splendid uniforms make an impressive impact and a comforting presence at the hotel's entry.

REGISTRATION

The sequence of arrivals discussed in Exhibit 1 is not applicable to every property. Guests may be greeted at the curb, or not. Guests may have help with baggage to the lobby, or not. Guests may find long lines at registration, or not. Large properties staff the desk, which may be hundreds of feet long, with numerous guest-service agents (see Exhibits 3 and 7). Smaller properties get along nicely with one clerk.

Segments of the larger front desks handle arrivals and departures separately. Arriving guests are guided by one of several signs: RECEPTION, or REGISTRATION, or ARRIVALS or CHECK IN.

Arriving guests may or may not hold reservations. Those with reservations are handled quickly because the information is already in the computer and an arrival list was printed as part of the night audit. The guest-service agent confirms the accommodations, has the guest sign the registration card, secures a credit-card imprint, selects a room, transfers a key, and exchanges pleasantries. The entire reception from A to Z is handled in a matter of minutes, (see Exhibit 3).

Provided rooms are available, registration is delayed but for a short time even if the desk has no record of the reservation. Basic information needs to be recaptured as unobtrusively as possible, but there is no reason to tell the guest that the reservation is missing. Registration is handled as if the guest were a walk-in. But guest-to-agent interaction changes dramatically when the house is full: 100% occupancy. "You mean there aren't any rooms?" Then speedy/cordial registration changes to angry/tension-filled reception. Little can be said to assuage an angry guest with a valid reservation. Guest-service agents must display great composure and immediately implement previously developed plans to accommodate the party elsewhere. A quick and caring response from the hotel staff might convert a traumatic experience into a positive moment of truth.

Walk-Ins

Registering walk-ins takes more time than registering reservation-holders. But, as with lost reservations, the process can be expedited. Guest-service agents collect the same information from walk-ins that is captured through reservations. To make the assignment and quote a rate, the agent needs to elicit the number in the party, the length of stay, and the accommodations desired.

Sales to walk-ins boost the hotel's bottom line. Walk-ins are the final tier of the yield management system. Motor hotels rely on walk-ins for a greater portion of their occupancy than do

---

[3]Clubs and restaurants may make "referral" payments to taxi drivers, who share with the doorpersons, when tourists are directed to participating properties. Many localities outlaw the practice.

Alphabetized Steps in the Guest's Arrival (Not a Chronological Sequence)	
...	Accommodations requested are obtained or re-confirmed
...	Bellperson summoned from the next front
...	Credit cards requested and processed
...	Due bill (if any) accepted
...	Greetings including small talk expected
...	Handicapped facilities noted and assigned
...	In-room facilities enumerated as part of an upsell
...	Just to be sure, sir, you're in a no-smoking room
...	Keys issued with rooming slips
...	Late check-out request noted
...	Mail and messages handed over
...	Names and numbers of party members verified
...	On-change rooms blocked
...	Pet accommodations and limitations explained
...	Quality assurance assured
...	Rates quoted in an attempt to upsell
...	Self-check-ins available
...	Travel agency vouchers processed
...	Upgrades assigned to loyalty-program members
...	VIPs flagged for future attention
...	Welcoming greetings is sincere and cordial
...	X-marks the spot for the guest's reg card signature and initials
...	Yield management in play
...	Zip-out check-out explained

EXHIBIT 3 An alphabetized (26 entries), but incomplete, listing of some of the activities that take place at hotels during arrival, registration, and assignment. *Courtesy of Rosen Hotels & Resorts, Orlando, Florida.*

urban, commercial hotels. Yet, the industry could do a better job of seizing the opportunity. The potential sale is standing in the lobby. It is not on the telephone, not on the Web, and not with some third party that takes a commission. An inviting lobby is the first means of capturing the sale (see Exhibit 4). A cordial, knowledgeable guest-service agent with the right message is the second. Prompt attention to the walk-in might be the real answer especially for motor inns (see Exhibit 5). Often these guests run into the lobby while the car idles, the kids fidget, and the spouse smolders. Given the right reception, these walk-ins will take the offer. Otherwise it is back to the tension in the car and another try elsewhere. Rate is a major factor in making such a decision. So while the motor inn's level of occupancy, its yield system, plays a role, so does the time of day and the likelihood of additional walk-ins. A decision that only a top-notch room clerk can make.

Registered, Not Assigned (RNA)

Early arrivals, especially those who appear before the check-out hour, may need to wait until a departure creates a room vacancy. (The industry has not seen 100% occupancy for a very long time.) Waiting guests are offered baggage-check service and sometimes a complimentary beverage. The registration card is completed but marked RNA, registered but not assigned. An actual room number is assigned only after someone checks out. Even then, the guest is kept waiting until housekeeping has finished its job and the on-change room is released. (Guests are never sent to unmade rooms.)

EXHIBIT 4 An inviting lobby, which includes bellhops posted in critical locations ready to serve in any capacity, helps capture walk-in guests and helps service arriving and departing guests. Bell service is essential to this hotel because it is adjacent to Orlando's Convention Center. Rosen Hotels was the first Orlando hotel company to offer baggage delivery to and from the airport.

Early arrivals who come after rooms have been vacated are assigned immediately, but not given the key while the room is on change. This is a slightly different procedure than the RNA. Occupancy takes place once housekeeping releases the room. Wait time is usually less for these early arrivals.

RNAs are very rare. They occur when hotels are full with simultaneous arrivals and departures such as large conventions or overlapping tour groups. Busy holidays cause RNAs at resorts because arrivals like to come early and departures try to stay late. Waiting for a room is a distressing experience; time ticks by so slowly. In extreme cases, guests may be roomed in accommodations that are not appropriate and moved later when the right room becomes available. This costly duplication is always avoided unless no other option is appropriate for the circumstances. Handicapped guests might warrant such an exception. Upgrading the room assignment may

EXHIBIT 5 A pleasant, open-looking desk is reinforced with a balanced design that separates functions but still allows staff to move between assignments. *Courtesy of Alamy.*

create an immediate solution. Checking guests in as RNAs allows them to incur charges and use the hotel's facilities until their rooms open. Having breakfast helps pass the time.

EARLY ARRIVALS   RNAs are rarely used because a full house, 100% occupancy, is rare even in very good times. Furthermore, no-shows create a mathematically full house that may still have empty rooms. No-shows with reservations are charged for rooms they never occupy. That room is ready for an early arrival the following day.

Two early-arrival issues face the guest and the hotel: an artificial check-in hour and the rate to be charged.

The Check-in Hour   Almost unknown a few years ago, most hotels now advertise both a check-out hour and a check-in hour. Check-in times are set somewhere between 1:00 PM and 4:00 PM. The check-out hour has been in place for a long time and has more validity because rooms need to be serviced before new arrivals. Moreover, individual cases are often accommodated by guest-service agents, who waive the check-out hour unless the space is really needed. Preferred-guest programs guarantee late check-outs for their members. Crown Plaza's Priority Club, for example, accommodates members for 7:00 AM arrivals and 3:00 PM departures. Starwood's is 4:00 PM. Club or concierge floors also extend hours, but the room charges are greater to begin with.

Refusing to room a guest before some arbitrary check-in hour seems to lack rationale. And that traveler, especially a business guest arriving for a meeting, is most indignant. Some are happy to check-in, leave their luggage with the bells, and go about their workday. They return later to a room that is ready with their baggage delivered. Other business travelers prefer to settle in, to change clothing, and arrive refreshed to their business appointments.

Obviously, room charges are the real issue with early arrivals! Why else would the hotel refuse to room a guest into a room that is vacant and ready? An argument could be made to just charge the regular nightly rate to, say, arrivals after the noon hour. Does that hold true then for an 11:00 AM arrival? or a 7:00 AM arrival if the published arrival time is, say, 3:00 PM? The answer has varied, in part, with the industry's cycle. When occupancy is low, almost anything goes. At the cycle's peak, guests can expect an additional charge.

Aside from the fee issue, an integrated PMS (property management system) holds one solution to very early arrivals. The PMS could match a list of early arrivals with another PMS report, that of expected early departures. Then, if need be, the linen room would call in enough floor house-keepers for very early shifts, say 6:30 or 7:00 AM, to ready the rooms between early departures and early arrivals.

Waiting Lines

Few check-ins occur early in the day so the early arrivals of the previous paragraphs get prompt attention. The busiest times vary with the type of hotel. Commercial arrivals peak between 4:00 PM and 7:00 PM. Their busiest check-out time is 7:00–9:00 AM. Arriving guests want in as quickly as possible. They have waited in innumerable lines and delays ranging from bad weather to lost baggage.[4] Security travel procedures have exacerbated the whole experience. Frustrated with travel, some arriving guests are quick to explode. Management must forestall arrival incidents through careful scheduling and sensitive hiring. It must balance budgets and sick calls, meal times and labor laws, and inexperienced agents and staff shortages. All this has to be done while checking in thousands of arrivals across the industry one guest at a time. Several innovations have helped offset these difficulties. One technique, queuing theory, has made the wait more acceptable. Other ideas, kiosks and pods and hand-held devices, are changing the procedure altogether.

BETTER LINES THROUGH QUEUING THEORY   A 20th-century mathematician, A. K. Erlang, introduced a theory known as queuing ("q-ing") theory. It was quickly dubbed *Waiting Line*

---

[4]There has been a steady growth of alternative baggage handling especially for travelers who expect to be away for some-time. A luggage-handling company picks up the traveler's baggage and ships it to the destination. Cost is higher than luggage charges levied by the airline, but traveler's move quickly through check-in, avoid delays at baggage carousels and save their backs from aches and pains.

Theory because of its application to customer lines at toll booths, 911 calls, traffic lights, and more. Queuing theory attempts to balance costs against waiting time. For lodging, the wait is on the telephone reservation call, or the Web window, or at the registration line. It is a balance between too much service, which increases operating cost, and too long a wait, which increases revenue losses.

Hotel executives must balance the four elements of waiting lines: arrival population, service population, queue discipline, and service disciplines (see Waiting Line of Exhibit 1).

Arrival Population   Arrival population like so much about the lodging industry varies with the type and class of hotel. Arrival configurations form around the hours of the day, the days of the week, and the months of the year. Tour and group hotels have different arrival dynamics than do motor inns or exclusive resorts. Preregistration options also impact the desk's workload, so does the hotel's size. Besides, there is no purity to "registration" lines. Some guests are waiting to ask questions; others need directions. Some are in line to complain; others need keys or mail. Many are in the check-in line in order to check out.

Service Population   Service population is best exemplified by the number and capability of guest-service agents. Cross-trained staffers, who support the regulars as needed, improve the service dynamics. Central to this component is the blueprint of the desk. Some designs limit the ability of guest-service agents by fixing the scope of their work, either as receptionists or cashiers. Better if everyone can respond to every guest request. Further improvements result from shuffling tasks. Simple modifications of longstanding procedures can produce quick upgrades to service. Two examples are shifting stamp sales from the desk to the gift shop and installing change-making machines to reduce desk traffic, as well as the size of front-office banks.

Queue Discipline   This behavior exhibited by waiting guests changes waiting-line theory from a mathematical process to a behavioral one. Queue discipline considers the guest's reaction to the line itself. Some guests balk and refuse to join the line. Some switch multiple lines as their respective lengths change. Others renege and drop out after waiting a while. If so, do others permit their return? and at what place? Skips and slips in the line push each member back a turn. Do guests cry "foul," rebuke the sinners, and force them out? What is the line's reaction when a late arrival is served first?

Little is known about queue discipline in hotel lines; the subject needs research.

Service Discipline   It examines employee attitudes and actions, including time lost to faffing.[5] Service discipline is the staff's side of the desk. Some of those issues: Is there a rationale for agents to service guests out of sequence? How are interruptions fielded from a "one-quick-question" interloper? Do VIPs, distinguished guests, and frequent-guest members receive special attention? Should they? Who answers the telephone? Does an agent stop servicing guests to help another agent who has problems? Many similar questions await management's attention.

CREATIVE SOLUTIONS   Check-in time might well be the guest's first encounter with the hotel and its staff. Management's failure to attend to the four parts of queuing theory creates negative moments of truth. Guests become agitated when wait times exceed expectations. Long waits, especially when there are just a few in line, translate to a poorly run hotel in the minds of the standees. Wait times angst can be mitigated! Empty minutes flow faster when the guest's time is filled with activity—so distract and entertain. Not knowing increases frustration—so communicate the estimated length of wait, even if the wait is long.

Line management is an issue for all service businesses. Banks respond with one line; that's *queue discipline*. Grocers advertise a *service discipline* by opening new lines whenever three customers are waiting. Airlines send an agent to the rear of the line: *service population,* and restaurants attend to *arrival populations* with their "early-bird specials." Hotels have used some of these ideas and made up some of their own (see Exhibit 6).

---

[5]*Faffing*—dithering and fussing—is a British word now entering the U.S. vocabulary. A faffer is a worker or a guest who works steadily and gets nothing done. So how quickly does agent A process the average guest versus, say, guest-agents B or C. The agent could fiddle with supplies while the guest faffers huge amount of time fumbling with purse or wallet, papers, and credit-cards before leaving the area to the next in line.

Hoteliers Manage the Distress of Long Queues with ...

… Animals: household pets and exotic creatures exhibited by qualified handlers

… Interactive participation: guests decipher codes; draw graffiti; converse with robots (actors in robot dress)

… Live entertainers: comedians; jugglers; magicians; ventriloquists

… Meet the people: hotel executives; entertainers playing the hotel; mimes

Preshows: informative videos describing the property (rooms, spas,) and events (entertainment venues and convention activities)

… Quiz shows: pose questions about the area or nonargumentive issues

… Rewards to guests: with complimentary drinks, reduced rates, or room upgrades

… Segmented queues: allow guests to see only small segments of the line in order to create an illusion of shorter lines

… Snaking the line: back on itself if lobby space allows

… Tasting: cookies, snacks, house favorites, and special wines or liquors

… Themed environment: something to see and wonder at (Exhibit 7)

… Time signs: estimated wait time is _____ minutes

… Video screens: entertaining video clips; national news; inhouse channel

EXHIBIT 6 Managing the line is not the critical issue that it once was. The stress of long queues has diminished as self-check-in terminals (see Exhibit 8), including mobile units, have gained favor with both guests and innkeepers.

The Mirage Hotel and Casino created one spectacular solution: placing a 20,000-gallon saltwater aquarium behind the desk (see Exhibit 7). Hundreds of flashing fish and lurking sharks distract those waiting, create conversations between strangers, and serve as one of the very best solutions to the irritating queue.

EXHIBIT 7 Wait-time issues are lessened by managing both those who wait and those who service the line. Directing the guests' attention to a 20,000-gallon saltwater spectacle with sharks circling a coral reef is memorable, whether it's for line management or word-of-mouth advertising. *Courtesy of MGM MIRAGE, Las Vegas, Nevada.*

BETTER LINES THROUGH INNOVATION Queuing theory treats the line. Other techniques approach the problem by eliminating it. Registration can be handled on the bus from the airport with radio-assisted techniques. Or it can be done right in the lobby by catching new arrivals at the door or working the back of the registration queue. After the information is captured by a hand-held computer, guests go to a special desk to sign in and collect a key.

Separating certain guests from the regular line speeds the line even as it acknowledges the special nature of those selected. Frequent-guest members, DGs (distinguished guests), VIPs, and premium corporate accounts are registered in a different area by the concierge or by a hotel executive.

Registration pods do not eliminate lines, but they make the experience more cordial. Pods may actually slow the process, but they generate a less institutional feeling and create a warmer environment. Guests are more relaxed.

Self-Check-in Kiosks The industry's adoption of self-check-in-check-out kiosks belies the call for more and more personal attention. Some guests are happy to bypass greetings from the desk in favor of what they see to be speed and efficiency (see Exhibit 8). Self-service-check-in like zip-out-check-out is viewed as a special accommodation rather than a reduction in service. Seasoned travelers see it as an extension of similar capabilities at the nation's airports. Most are pleased to find these ATM-cousins in the lobbies of even 4- and 5-star, upscale hotels.

Not only does self-registration save line-waiting time, it is actually faster than a manual check-in. Estimates put self-check-in times between 30 and 45 seconds—once the user is familiar with the procedure—in contrast to some 210 seconds required at the desk—that is, after one finally gets there. Much of the desk's longer time is attributable to the personal interaction with the guest-service agent. That's what's being given up.

Walk-ins require extra time to input the information, so the registration is slower. But that is also true of walk-ins with traditional desk registration.

The check-in kiosk is another extension of the property management system (see Exhibit 6). Guests select room types and rates from an online inventory of clean, ready rooms. It is the same inventory offered by the desk. Over time, some of the equipment has become portable and wireless. It can be located anywhere in the lobby to accommodate large group arrivals. It can even be moved to an airport baggage area to register a group while its members wait for their luggage. (For security, room keys would be issued later at the hotel.)

Initially, self-check-in terminals required the arriving guest to hold a reservation and a payment card, either credit or debit. Newer modifications accommodate walk-ins, accept cash, and "speak" foreign languages. Newer terminals are also more consumer-friendly, activated by touch screens rather than by slower keyboards. Terminal options, like ATMs, now

EXHIBIT 8 Self-check-in-check-out terminals are in widespread use. Updated versions serve up to eight languages, accept walk-ins, reduce waiting time, and enable departing guests to print airline boarding passes. Hyatt Hotels encourages their use with 1,000 bonus points for Gold Passport® holders, Hyatt's frequent-guest program. *Courtesy of NCR Corporation, Dayton, Ohio.*

go beyond their original concept. They accommodate speedy check-outs, provide community information, and advertise hotel services such as food and beverage.

The terminal displays an electronic map of the property showing the new arrival where to find the assigned room and where to park. Guests can opt for a different room or try for a different rate. The computer counters: It tries to upsell.[6] A room key and a printed receipt are dispensed once the assignment is finalized. With some systems, it is a blank key card that guests swipe through an electronic key writer adjacent to the terminal. Still newer systems instruct guests to use the credit card, which was just swiped to pay the bill, as the key.

Almost every hotel chain has joined the trend. Hyatt Hotels calls its system *Touch and Go*. Wyndham built *AutoCheck* into its Wingate Inns. Choice Hotel's MainStay Suites, whose rates are on the high end, encourage computer check-in by providing language options and downsizing the desk. Choice's system prompts by electronic voice. It asks for the same credit card that made the reservation. Guests also supply a personal identification number (PIN), which they use thereafter to access the system.

The industrywide hype over self-service kiosks may be overblown. Resort guests, for example, prefer the leisure and personal contact that desk personnel provide. And, unlike the measurable gains that PMSs have had for the night audit, the economic payback from the investment has been slow in coming. Location and type of hotel and the demographics of the clientele, as well as the time needed for travelers to adapt, are the real determinants of how quickly the equipment takes hold. Changes come quickly so the rise of remote check-in and cell-phone room keys may overtake the kiosk for electronic-savvy travelers.

Side issues, such as satisfactory identification required by some states and for some rate-purposes (government, military, and clergy), still need resolution. But then self-service elevators were once an oddity that many knew could not be sustained.

The Registration Card

Along with pleasantries, guest-service agents greet arriving guests with registration cards. Unlike the many variations in the arrival procedure of Exhibit 1, registration and registration cards vary little across the industry. Registration begins with a welcome. Pleasantries are part of all desk training, but the length of the greetings varies with the volume of business. A smile and a warm welcome are delivered when other guests are waiting; longer chats are appropriate when desk traffic is slow.

Timing applies to the registration cards as well. Guests with reservations are quickly accommodated when reg cards have been preprinted as part of the previous night's audit. Then, the property management system (the computer) has transferred the reservation information into a registration format (see Exhibit 9). Front-office clerks ask guests to verify the card's accuracy and then sign. Walk-in guests take longer because the agent must determine who the guest is and what accommodations are needed. The new arrival then completes and signs the newly printed card. Other countries have additional requirements, especially for foreign travelers (see Exhibit 10).

The guest's signature is not essential for the creation of a legal guest–host relationship in common law. It is required, however, by most state laws. In contrast, other countries view the card as a police document (see Exhibit 10) so guests must provide a great deal of personal information. Some countries require arrivals to surrender passports to the desk. Brazil asks registering guest to furnish the names of both parents. Information regarding age, birth date, nationality, and itinerary are required in many jurisdictions outside the United States.

RELEASE OF REGISTRATION INFORMATION U.S. hotels may not have as much information as their foreign counterparts, but they have quite a bit. Included are names, addresses, company affiliations, times of arrivals and departures, telephone and Internet records, credit-card data, and more. Guest history and frequent-guest memberships add information about previous visits and personal preferences.

---

[6]Some preliminary studies suggest a lower ADR results when guests self-register, hinting at the positive effects of guest-service agents selling up.

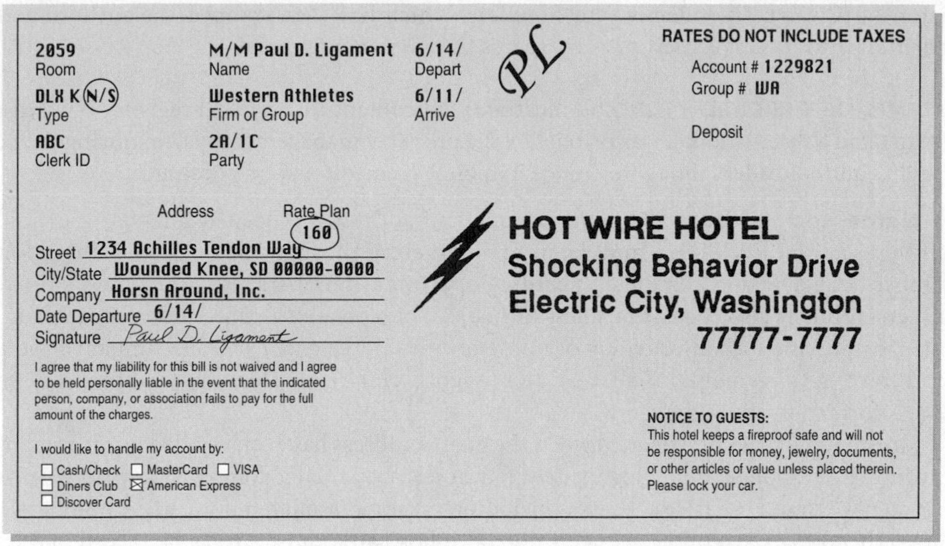
2059
Room
M/M Paul D. Ligament
Name
6/14/
Depart
PL
RATES DO NOT INCLUDE TAXES
Account # 1229821
Group # WA
DLX K (N/S)
Type
Western Athletes
Firm or Group
6/11/
Arrive
Deposit
ABC
Clerk ID
2A/1C
Party

Address   Rate Plan (160)

Street 1234 Achilles Tendon Way
City/State Wounded Knee, SD 00000-0000
Company Horsn Around, Inc.
Date Departure 6/14/
Signature Paul D. Ligament

HOT WIRE HOTEL
Shocking Behavior Drive
Electric City, Washington
77777-7777

I agree that my liability for this bill is not waived and I agree to be held personally liable in the event that the indicated person, company, or association fails to pay for the full amount of the charges.

I would like to handle my account by:
☐ Cash/Check ☐ MasterCard ☐ VISA
☐ Diners Club ☒ American Express
☐ Discover Card

NOTICE TO GUESTS:
This hotel keeps a fireproof safe and will not be responsible for money, jewelry, documents, or other articles of value unless placed therein. Please lock your car.

EXHIBIT 9 Computer-prepared registration cards speed the arrival process. Unless there are changes from the reservation, the guest merely signs in and arranges payment, usually by a credit card. The guest may be asked to initial the card (PL upper center) as acknowledgment of the rate, the date of departure, and recognition of the several stipulations. They include an agreement to be responsible for the debt and an acknowledgment of the availability of a safe.

Heretofore, innkeepers have released sensitive information to federal and local authorities only by subpoena or warrant. Time-sensitive emergencies—a heart attack, for example—were exceptions, of course. The conflict that hoteliers faced, help authorities or protect guest privacy, was resolved by the 2001 Anti-Terrorism Act. The law was passed immediately after the attack on New York City's World Trade Center. Law-enforcement authorities were given streamlined procedures to access information from private entities, hotels included. Hotelkeepers who respond to the written orders are protected from litigation arising from an

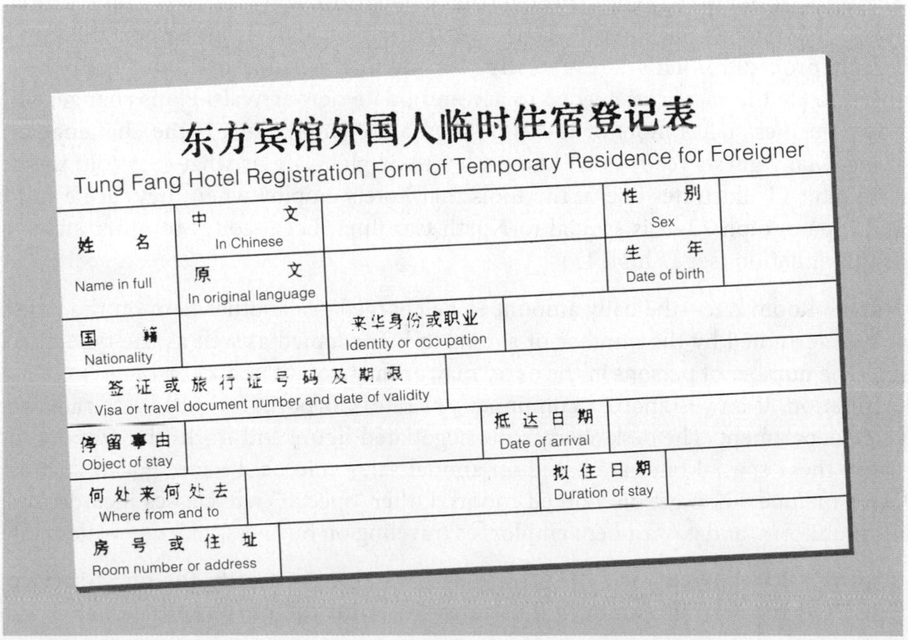
东方宾馆外国人临时住宿登记表
Tung Fang Hotel Registration Form of Temporary Residence for Foreigner

姓名 Name in full
中文 In Chinese
原文 In original language
性别 Sex
生年 Date of birth
国籍 Nationality
来华身份或职业 Identity or occupation
签证或旅行证号码及期限 Visa or travel document number and date of validity
停留事由 Object of stay
抵达日期 Date of arrival
何处来何处去 Where from and to
拟住日期 Duration of stay
房号或住址 Room number or address

EXHIBIT 10 International registrations require a surprising amount of personal information. Age, sex, travel plans, and parents' names are questions not posed at U.S. hotels. Arrivals overseas may also be required to surrender their passports to the desk. Changes may be coming to domestic hotels if the Anti-Terrorism Act is enlarged. Currently, registration is regulated by state laws as Exhibits 12 and 13 illustrate.

invasion of privacy. The dilemma for hoteliers, which has even trapped the authors, to help authorities or to preserve guest privacy, seems to have been resolved.

CONTENTS OF THE CARD   Exhibit 9 illustrates the contents of a typical registration card for a party that had a reservation. It was printed by the property management system during the previous night's audit. Readers should reference Exhibit 9 as the discussion continues.

Name and Address   Complete name and address are needed for identification, for credit verification, for billing, and, later, for marketing through mailing lists. The information must be legible and complete, including apartment numbers, city, state, and ZIP codes. Commercial hotels also request business affiliation, organizational title, and company address. Guests may provide such information or not. They must if the chain and the company have some special rate arrangements. Guest-service agents clarify nonlegible scribbles by printing the information above the scrawl.

Greater credit can be extended when the guest's address has been verified by an exchange of reservation correspondence. Unfortunately, few hotels are actually doing that anymore. Whereas those intent on fraud use false addresses including vacant lots and temporary box numbers, honest guests who inadvertently leave with unpaid folios can almost always be traced and billed. Moreover, most guests use credit cards, which simplifies the billing.

Number in the Party   Although not always, the number of persons in the room may determine the rate to be charged. Adults and children are identified separately especially at American-plan and all-inclusive resorts which charge less for children [see Exhibit 9: 2 (Adults)/1 (Child)]. The number of registered guests and the number of occupied rooms are important for statistical computations.

Room Number   Within the hotel community, guests are identified by room number. Once the registration is complete, hotels reference the room number rather than the guest's name. The room number is the major means of locating, identifying, tracking, and billing. Reservation numbers (or preassigned folio numbers) are *sometimes* used before the guest's arrival to locate reservations and record advance deposits. If the party is large or if a suite has been assigned, the reg card would have several room numbers whereas a separate card is used for each unrelated guest sharing the room.

Date of Departure   The expected date of departure is critical to the hotel's forecasting model and its yield management system. Verifying that date is an important step in the registration procedure. This is especially true during periods of high occupancy when departures create the vacancies needed to accommodate new arrivals. Plans change; emergencies arrive; business takes more or less time than anticipated. Such is the challenge of room forecasting. Many guests really don't know what their plans are or what they told the desk on arrival. Exhibit 11 illustrates one of the tools that hotels employ when they face a full house. Exhibit 12, paragraph 72-1, is special to North Carolina. Legal codes in other states do not address this situation (see Exhibit 13).[7]

Rate   Room rate—the daily amount to be charged—is another item on the registration card. It is determined by the number of rooms to be occupied as well as the type of room(s) assigned. The number of persons in the party may or may not influence the rate.

Affiliation, if any, is another component of rate. Corporations negotiate rates with the hotel's sale department. The desk charges the negotiated figure and tracks the number of arrivals because these special rates are based on annual sales volume. Leisure guests such as AAA and AARP members also get discounted rooms. Other "special" rate classes include the clergy, persons in uniform, and government employees traveling on business, called per-diem rates.

Agent's Identification   Registration cards always identify the guest-service agent who registered the arrival. Exhibit 9 illustrates this with the clerk's initials, ABC. Property

---

[7]Common law defines a hotel guest as one with an "indeterminable" stay. So ejecting a guest for overstaying a reservation runs the risk of losing an expensive lawsuit. Exhibit 12 is unusual because it is a statutory change to common law.

```
☐V
A Vallen Corporation Property
```

Just a Reminder

_____ Mr M.T.Wallet _____ Room _3308_

Thank you for staying with us. I hope you have had as pleasant a time with us as we have had serving you.

As you requested when you arrived, we are reminding you that tomorrow is your check-out date. Check-out time is 12 noon. The room is reserved for an arriving guest so it will not be possible to extend either the check-out hour or the day of departure.

If you need an additional time in the city, our assistant manager will be happy to help you search for accommodations nearby. All of our rooms have been reserved for tomorrow.

The assistant manager has a desk in the lobby, or call extension 123. The desk will also help with future reservations here or at another property in our group.

Ioona Carr
Reservations Manager

EXHIBIT 11 Check-out reminders may be placed on the bed or included with folios slipped under the door the night before the guest's anticipated departure. Reminders are used only when the hotel anticipates an overbooking the following night.

management systems identify the clerk from the password that he or she used to log into the computer. Management can then return to the source if issues about courtesy, rate, or clerical questions arise later. Better still, it is used if guests wish to compliment the agent.

Folio Number Whether computer-prepared or manually prepared, guests' accounts carry identification numbers. Folios can be accessed by this ID number, or by the guest's room number, or, of course, by the guest's name. Sequential numbering also serves as an internal accounting control when one staff member is clerk (and sells the room), cashier (and takes the money), and auditor/supervisor (and then prepares the control records, the night audit).

Folios and reg cards must be stored for seven years. Computerized records make that job easier because they are downloaded daily during the night audit onto disks or tapes. Everyone complies so old files are rarely disposed of and simply forgotten after seven years and numerous staff turnovers. However, if necessary (as discussed in *Release of Registration Information*), computerized and numbered documents make retrieval easier.

Disclaimer of Liability State statutes, not federal laws, control the innkeeper's liability for guest's luggage and personal belongings. If the innkeeper meets the provision of the state's law, liability for property loss is greatly reduced. Without statutory limitations, innkeepers would be liable under common law with an open-ended amount of damages. To gain this special protection, innkeepers must inform their guests of the hotel's limited liability and do so in the manner prescribed. The "manner" is not consistent state to state (see Exhibits 12 and 13).

Welcome to North Carolina

LAWS OF NORTH CAROLINA

LAW GOVERNING INNKEEPERS (From General Statutes of North Carolina)

72-1. MUST FURNISH ACCOMMODATIONS: CONTRACTS FOR TERMINATION VALID. (a) Every innkeeper shall at all times provide suitable lodging accommodations for persons accepted as guests in his inn or hotel. (b) A written statement setting forth the time period during which a guest may occupy an assigned room, signed or initialed by the guest, shall be deemed a valid contract, and at the expiration of such time period the lodger may be restrained from entering and any property of the guest may be removed by the innkeeper without liability, except for damages to or loss of such property attributable to its removal.

72-2. LIABILITY FOR LOSS OF BAGGAGE. Innkeepers shall not be liable for loss, damage or destruction of the baggage or property of their guests except in case such loss, damage or destruction results from the failure of the innkeeper to exercise ordinary, proper and reasonable care in the custody of such baggage and property and in case of such loss, damage or destruction resulting from the negligence and want of care of the said innkeeper, he shall be liable to the owner of said baggage and property to an amount not exceeding one hundred dollars. Any guest may, however, at any time before a loss, damage or destruction of his property notify the innkeeper in writing that his property exceeds value the said sum of one hundred dollars, and shall upon demand of the innkeeper furnish him a list or schedule of the same with the value thereof, in which case the innkeeper shall be liable for the loss, damage or destruction of said property because of any negligence on his part, for the full value of the same. Proof of the loss of any such baggage, except in case of damage or destruction by fire, shall be prima facie evidence.

72-3. SAFE KEEPING OF VALUABLES. It shall be the duty of innkeepers, upon the request of any guest, to receive from said guest, and safely keep money, jewelry, and valuables to an amount not exceeding five hundred dollars; and no innkeeper shall be required to receive and take care of any money, jewelry or other valuables to a greater amount than five hundred dollars. No innkeeper shall be liable for the loss, damage or destruction of any money or jewels not so deposited.

72-4. LOSS BY FIRE. No innkeeper shall be liable for loss, damage, or destruction of any baggage or property caused by fire not resulting from the negligence of the innkeeper or by any other force of which the innkeeper had no control. Nothing herein contained shall enlarge the limit of the amount to which the innkeeper shall be liable as provided in preceding sections.

72-5. NEGLIGENCE OF GUESTS. Any innkeeper against whom claim is made for loss sustained by a guest may show that such loss resulted from the negligence of such guest or of his failure to comply with the reasonable and proper regulations of the inn.

72-6. COPIES OF THIS ARTICLE POSTED. Every innkeeper shall keep posted in every room of his house occupied by guests, and in the office, a printed copy of this article and of all regulations to the conduct of guests. This chapter shall not apply to the innkeepers, or their guests, where the innkeeper fails to keep such notice posted.

72-8. ADMITTANCE OF PETS TO HOTEL ROOMS. (a) Innkeepers may permit pets in rooms used for sleeping purposes and in adjoining rooms. Persons bringing pets into a room in which they are not permitted are in violation of this section and punishable according to subsection (d) of this section.

(b) Innkeepers allowing pets must post a sign measuring not less than five inches by seven inches at the place where guests register informing them pets are permitted in sleeping rooms and in adjoining rooms. If certain pets are permitted or prohibited, the sign must so state. If any pets are permitted, the innkeeper must maintain a minimum of ten percent (10%) of the sleeping rooms in the inn or hotel as rooms where pets are not permitted and the sign required by this subsection must also state that such rooms are available.

(c) All sleeping rooms in which the innkeeper permits pets must contain a sign measuring not less than five inches by seven inches, posted in a prominent place in the room, which shall be separate from the sign required by G.S. 72-6, stating that pets are permitted in the room, or whether certain pets are prohibited or permitted in the room, and stating that bringing pets into a room in which they are not permitted is a misdemeanor under North Carolina law punishable by a fine not to exceed five hundred dollars ($500.00), imprisonment not to exceed 30 days, or both.

(d) Any person violating the provisions of this section shall be guilty of a misdemeanor and upon conviction shall pay fine not to exceed five hundred dollars ($500.00) or be imprisoned for not more than 30 days, or both.

(e) The provisions of this section are not applicable to assistance dogs admitted to sleeping rooms and adjoining rooms under the provisions of Chapter 168 of the General Statutes.

EXHIBIT 12 Every state has special innkeeping laws, but many of them have been standardized (see also Exhibit 13). North Carolina has two unique provisions: Paragraph 72-1 requires the guest to sign or initial the check-out date; 72-8 regulates pets in guest rooms.

Two legislative components are similar in every state: The hotel must maintain a safe for guest valuables and give notice of that safe (see Exhibit 9, lower right corner). Also, notices must be "posted," along with the excerpts of the code.[8] One invariably finds that posted notice on the inside of the guest-room door. Liability limitations have been extended by many states to include checkrooms, in-room safes, spa facilities, and goods too large to fit into the safe—salesman's samples, for example. In some states, hotels may simply refuse to accept guest valuables (see Exhibit 13, paragraph 509.111).

---

[8]"Posted" means just that. Notices laid on the bureau top—not hung, not posted—have been declared invalid and the protective dollar limits of the statutory law were lost.

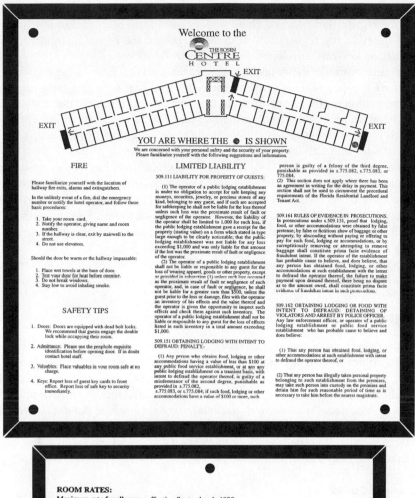

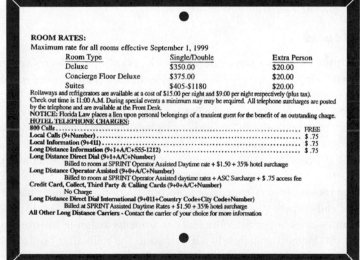

EXHIBIT 13 Posting notices about the availability of a safe and the maximum room rate are standard provisions of most state laws. Innkeepers who comply with all the provisions of the code have limited liability for the loss of the guest's belongings. Limitations do not apply to harm of the guest's person. Fire-conscious states and localities also require fire-safety directions. *Courtesy of Rosen Hotels & Resorts, Orlando, Florida.*

Posted notices that list the room rates (see Exhibit 13) contain a trap for the unwary. Hotels can put any value they want on that posting, but they exceed that amount at risk. Once a maximum rate is posted, as required by law, it is the maximum. Exceeding that figure invalidates the notice and makes the hotel liable under common law. Statutory limits are a safeguard no longer. Too frequently, old notices are left despite inflationary increases in room rates.

POINTS OF AGREEMENT   New legal language is being added to reg cards even as hotels work to speed up the registration process. These notices meet legal niceties, but few harried guests actually read them during registration. So hotels highlight the issues again: on rooming slips (see Exhibit 19), on key-card envelopes, and verbally by desk clerks.

To minimize misunderstandings, the agent repeats several facts as the registration closes. Among them are the date of departure and the room type that were just assigned. Room rates have always been high on the list of after-the-fact protests. To forestall later complaints, clerks close the registration process by circling the rate and asking the guest to initial the card (see Exhibit 9 with the guest's initials, *PL*). Now is the time for guests to raise issues about room charges, special rates, and ultimate liability for their bills.

Guests are expected to settle their folios at check-out time, but almost no one pays with cash. Credit cards and other third-party payers (companies, agencies, associations) are the norm. Guests assign their debts to these third parties, but sometimes the intermediaries won't pay. Credit-card companies, for example, occasionally charge back claims. So still another disclaimer appears on all reg cards. Arriving guests may not read the statement, but they agree to ultimate responsibility for their own folios (see Exhibit 9, lower left).

New social issues have added to the guest-service agents' responsibilities. Where appropriate, talking points have been expanded to include no-smoking rooms, pets, and "green" facilities.

ASSIGNMENT

Many things are going on during registration. Exhibit 3 presented them in an alphabetical listing, but events do not flow in any particular order even in the same hotel with the same guest-service agent. Besides, the alphabet's 26 letters are insufficient to cover every situation. Nor are all the items applicable to every arrival. Special handling is required for the rare due bill (advertising contract) that is presented. Travel-agency vouchers are more common, but not an everyday event. Even rates may need adjusting. Pre- and postconvention rates often differ from the convention rate. Special clarification is needed for those convention guests and special emphasis may be warranted for those assigned to no-smoking rooms.

No-Smoking Rooms

A decade ago, no-smoking rooms were rare. Gradually, as calls for no-smoking grew, hotels set aside entire floors or wings for nonsmokers. Today, some hotels are entirely smoke-free. Public contention between smokers and nonsmokers has spilled over to hotel rooms. Nonsmokers want a fresh room without the stale odor of smoke or the sweet scent used by housekeeping to mask the smell. Smokers want matches and ashtrays and less harassment. Hotels supply both, but are designating more and more rooms as nonsmoking. The issue comes to a head when space limitations require smokers be assigned to nonsmoking rooms. The politics of smoking aside, economics is the issue for innkeepers.

Nonsmoking rooms are very expensive to reconstruct once a smoker has lit up. Wall coverings, bed linens, and carpets absorb the smoke. Opening a window—and that is not possible in many hotel rooms—does not remedy the foul air. Smokers assign to no-smoking rooms must be alerted to the cost. Hotels typically add $200 or so to the folio after housekeeping alerts the desk. This contentious issue must be foreclosed by the desk clerk when a guest is assigned a nonsmoking room. Otherwise, every bit of a manager's skill will be required to answer an irate smoker who faces this hefty "fine." Guest-service agents circle the N/S letters to confirm their no-smoking discussion with the guest. Guests such as Mr. Ligament in Exhibit 9 initial the card for nonsmoking as well as for rate. His assignment is a deluxe, king, no-smoking room. That's what the initials DLX K N/S on the upper left of Exhibit 9 tell us.

Pets

Strangely, as the hoopla over smoking has accelerated, hotels have welcomed more pets into guest rooms. Forget the smoker/nonsmoker issue; many guests are allergic to pet dander! Pet-friendly rooms should be separated and designated with signs on corridor doors just as hotels do with no-smoking rooms. It is not done and although hotels charge special cleaning fees, housekeeping may not expend the extra effort needed to—or know how to—desensitize the room.

Denver's most famous hotel, the Brown Palace, has had a welcoming bed and bowl for nearly a century. During that time, pet-friendly hotels have developed into a sizable U.S. market. AAA reports that some 13,000 hotels allow pets.[9] And well they should because catering to pets can be a profitable decision. A pet-friendly policy attracts not only new, human business, but also adds to the revenue stream through special pet fees. A $100 nonrefundable charge is not unusual. Then there are the extras: The Soho Grand (New York City) charges $20 for pet toothpaste and $20 more for a pet pillow! Other properties increase the animal's registration fee and then deliver pet goodies (beds, bowls, pet-walking services) without special charge.

Almost every chain has some type of pet accommodation. Loews offers "puppy pagers" to call pet owners when barking disturbs other guests. Sheraton's Four Points chain has launched a pet-friendly program. Marriott's Residence Inns and some InterContinental properties have joined the march. All have recommended or established rules (see Exhibit 14).

Pets are not welcomed everywhere. Innkeepers who are sensitive to the noise, to the appearance of unclean accommodations, and to guest allergies arrange for local pet hotels—and these are everywhere—to accommodate the animals. Only seeing-eye dogs and other animals that support the disabled are welcomed. If the hotel has pet-designated rooms, they would be part of the assignment process, discussed next.

The Assignment Process

Each morning and throughout the day, the desk estimates the number of rooms available for sale. Reference is made to the Housekeeper's Report and to the departure dates that guests furnished during registration. Check-outs, which become available throughout the day, are added to last night's unoccupied rooms. The hotel's historical experience for this day and date is added to the mix. From the projected data come a forecast of how many walk-ins to accept. This decision is revised several times during the day.

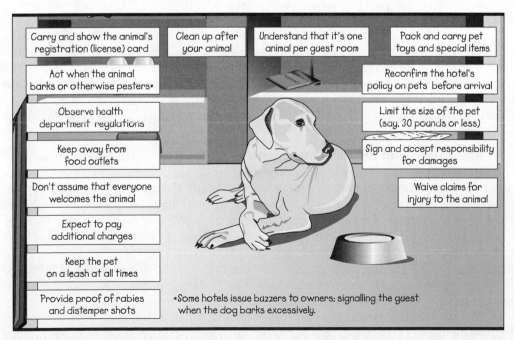

Carry and show the animal's registration (license) card

Clean up after your animal

Understand that it's one animal per guest room

Pack and carry pet toys and special items

Act when the animal barks or otherwise pesters*

Reconfirm the hotel's policy on pets before arrival

Observe health department regulations

Limit the size of the pet (say, 30 pounds or less)

Keep away from food outlets

Sign and accept responsibility for damages

Don't assume that everyone welcomes the animal

Waive claims for injury to the animal

Expect to pay additional charges

Keep the pet on a leash at all times

Provide proof of rabies and distemper shots

*Some hotels issue buzzers to owners; signalling the guest when the dog barks excessively.

EXHIBIT 14 The pet market is a significant one, estimated at $300 million for pet food advertising alone. Petswelcome.com lists 25,000 hotels soliciting pet-owner business. Notwithstanding figures like these, there are many non-pet lovers among the industry's clientele. Established rules that are strictly enforced accommodate both groups. North Carolina's provision (see Exhibit 12) for guests with animal allergies strikes a balance for hotels that cater to this growing market.

---

[9] *Traveling with your Pet: The AAA PetBook®*. Updated annually.

Matching arriving guests with the proper accommodations is what guest-service agents do best. The better the agent knows the room inventory, the better the assignment. Every room has its own features. Some have better views; some are larger. Certain rooms are noisier: They are closer to the elevator or overlook the alley. Renovations with new baths and new bedding is done floor by floor. So even rooms in the same category are not the same.

Desk clerks are not clairvoyant. They cannot know the order of arrivals relative to the order of departures. Guests are not kept waiting in the lobby for someone to vacate a particular room if other rooms are open. So shifts in the assignment take place throughout the day. But certain circumstances require the desk to preassign rooms for reservation-holders who have not yet arrived.

BLOCKING THE ROOM Rooms are *blocked*, *preassigned,* to make certain the hotel can honor special requirements. Hotels match specific rooms against arriving parties whenever the room count is tight, as it would be with an approaching full house. Then, specific rooms are assigned to anticipated arrivals. Doing so minimizes the chance of overselling to walk-ins.

Special cases are preassigned whether the hotel is full or not. Handicapped rooms are an obvious need. Careful room managers also block early arrivals and requests for connecting rooms. Blocks are used especially for management-made reservations and for other VIP arrivals. Blocks are in order if specific rooms have been set aside for pets and no-smoking.

Guest-service agents sometimes "play solitaire" with the room rack. They shift this or that room block as the arrival sequence, mixed with walk-ins and check-outs, becomes apparent. Changes are needed if an arrival comes early and the designated room has not been vacated. Or, perhaps, the arriving party is larger or smaller than the original reservation. Maybe there has been a change in length of stay—a major issue at a busy resort.

CHOOSING—SELLING—THE ROOM Front-office staffers know that the fewer the rooms available, the easier the assignment. The same is true about room knowledge: Knowing the room, the easier the assignment. Front-office managers must make certain that their agents know their products. Lessons begin with detailed floor plans that can be referenced on computer screens or printed charts. Frequent inspections of guest rooms during slow periods at the desk offer the best means of knowing the room that the agent is selling. And agents should sell rooms not merely choose them.

Agents should sell up: Convince guests to take higher-priced rooms. Agents will upsell if they have been trained how to, if they know their products, and if there is a cash incentive system in place. Showing the room is an aid to selling it. It is an especially good technique for selling walk-ins at small resorts. Prospective shoppers can be taken to the actual room or images can be displayed at desk monitors. Guests are familiar with this because typical rooms are already displayed on the Worldwide Web. Photo albums at the desk serve nicely for smaller properties that lack the technology.

Algorithms and Property Management Systems Algorithms give structure to computer programs specifically to the window displays of the property management systems. Algorithms are a step-by-step procedure, a series of "if–then" statements, used in computer programming to accomplish a given task. There are different kinds of algorithms for different types of jobs. A display of room availability is one example. Without the algorithmic function, available rooms would be displayed in sequence. In which case, the first room would most likely be sold over and over. With algorithms, the display is controlled to achieve stated goals. These might be: (1) Rotate assignments equally. (2) Concentrate assignments on newly furnished facilities at higher rates. (3) Restrict assignments to particular wings, floors, or exposures to save energy, reduce wear and tear, and concentrate the labor force.

So algorithms are behind the display in the search for an appropriate room assignment. Suppose the agent is looking for a double-double. The system could display a *single* choice, if that was management's original criteria. Or, at the agent's prompting, the screen displays a broader selection of ready rooms, on-change rooms, and out-of-order rooms (see Exhibit 15). Then the agent's knowledge and discretion determines the assignment.

UPGRADES Upgrades—rooming guests in better accommodations than their rates warrant— are part of the assignment process. Members of frequent-guest programs are upgraded automatically, space permitting. "Space permitting" is the operative term for all upgrades. The better room has to be available. Business guests from companies with negotiated rates or other formal

THE LODGE AT RIVER'S EDGE

Room Status Report

Date: 06/06/___ 10:37

Room Number	Discrepancy	Room Type	Clean Sectn	Hskpg Credits	No. of Guest	Room Status	Description
102		DDSN	R1	1	0	VACANT, CLEAN	RIVER N/S CONNECT 103
103		DDSN	R1	1	2	OCCUPIED, CLEAN	RIVER N/S CONNECT 102
105		KEX	R1	1.5	0	VACANT, CLEAN	RIVER S
106		KKEX	R1	1.5	2/2	OCCUPIED, CLEAN	RIVER S
107		KN	N1	1	2	OCCUPIED, CLEAN	POOL N/S
108		DDN	N1	1	0	VACANT, DIRTY	POOL N/S
109		KK	N1	1	2	VACANT, CLEAN, BLOCKED	POOL S
110		KEX	N1	1.5	0	VACANT, CLEAN	POOL S
111		PEXN[a]	S1	2	0	VACANT, DIRTY	MTN VIEW N/S CONNECT 112
112		DDN	S1	1	0	VACANT, CLEAN	MTN VIEW N/S CONNECT 111
115		QSN	S1	1	0	VACANT, CLEAN	MTN VIEW N/S
116		DDSN	S1	1	2/3	OCCUPIED, CLEAN	MTN VIEW N/S
117		K	S1	1	3	VACANT, CLEAN, BLOCKED	MTN VIEW S
118		QS	S1	1	0	VACANT, CLEAN	MTN VIEW S
119		K	S1	1	2	VACANT, CLEAN, BLOCKED	MTN VIEW S
120		DD	S1	1	1	VACANT, CLEAN, BLOCKED	MTN VIEW S
121		PEXN	P1	2	1	OCCUPIED, CLEAN	SPA N/S
123		PEXN	P1	2	2	OCCUPIED, DIRTY	SPA S CONNECT 125
125		PEX	P1	2	1	VACANT, DIRTY, BLOCKED	SPA S CONNECT 123

MORE

Due check out: 30	Dirty: 67	Occupied: 114	Occupied/dirty: 52	Occupied/clean: 62
Blocked: 24	Clean: 193	Vacant: 146	Vacant/dirty: 15	Vacant/clean: 131

[a] PEXN indicates a no-smoking, executive parlor with a Murphy bed.

EXHIBIT 15 Computerized room-status reports can be displayed in a variety of predetermined formats. Here, the display is in room-number sequence. Other options include a listing by status (clean, vacant, occupied, etc.); by room type (double-double, connecting rooms, suites, etc.); or by other parameters (view, no-smoking, concierge floor, etc.). Rooms can be displayed in reverse numerical order to assure equal wear on all rooms.

relationships with the hotel get upgrades. "Regulars," guests who return on a recurring cycle, are recognized with an upgrade. Upgrades are used to settle minor complaints or to thank guests who have waited patiently in the queue.

Promises of or hints at upgrades became a marketing tool during the most recent downturn. Advertisement promised a suite, concierge floor, or ocean-view upgrade under certain conditions. The terms of those conditions varied, but they all meant the same: "if available," or "on a space-only basis," or "on a standby condition." Sometimes the upgrade is given free, "if available," and sometimes the upgrades require a modest charge, say $25. The arriving guest has been promised an upgrade, *if available*, for $25.

A variation on the theme has been made possible by Internet messaging. Acknowledgment of and a request for further details of the guest's reservation are emailed back from the hotel's res department. This "Request Upon Arrival" asks what else the hotel can do to please the guest. Don't ask for connecting rooms—can't be promised. Don't ask for pet-free rooms—can't be promised. Good managers distinguish good ideas from hype.

True upgrades are usually at the discretion of the desk, but they become necessary if no rooms are available at the rate reserved. Unless the agent can up sell to a higher rate, guests get better rooms but pay the reserved rates. Guests are always told about their upgrades. Otherwise, they will expect the same assignment on the next visit. These guests may be moved to the original rate on the following day "space permitting," but only if the rate spread is huge or the better facilities are absolutely essential for new arrivals. Guests are not moved if their stay is brief. Moving is costly to both the guest and the hotel.

Moving a guest is problem enough. Moving rooms while the guest is away is a drastic decision. It is unacceptable if done without the guest's knowledge. At least two individuals (a bellperson and a supervisor from some other department) inventory the guest's belonging, pack them up, and move them to the new assignment. There are no happy road warriors then.

VIPs   Very important persons are usually upgraded and comped. Hotels identify both the reservation and, later, the room rack identification by flagging them as VIPs or DGs (Distinguished Guests) or SPATT (Special Attention). STAR GUEST is also used. VIPs represent good publicity or major business for the hotel. Meeting planners, company and associations presidents, and celebrities get VIP treatment. So do travel writers. Each represents some business gain for the hotel. DGs, on the other hand, are recognized because of their accomplishments rather than their economic impact. DGs include politicians, heroes, prize-winners, and distinguished persons of every discipline.

Management staffers may walk these special arrivals to their rooms, which have been upgraded and/or comped. Registration may take place there away from the glare of the front desk unless the publicity is what both parties want. Fruit baskets, cheese trays, and wine or champagne await the new arrivals.

Did Not Stay

In very, very rare instances, the arriving party may register and leave immediately. Dissatisfaction with the hotel or an incident with a staff member may precipitate the hasty departure. The guest may or may not seek remedy. More likely, the hotel is not the issue. Either an emergency message is waiting at the desk or comes soon after the guest is roomed. Typically, no charge is made if check out takes place within a reasonable time even if the room was briefly occupied.

The completed reg card is marked DNS and given over to a supervisor. Management must make certain the issue does not rest with the hotel's reservations system or its employees.

Establishing Credit and Identity

Guests with reservations have already established a preliminary level of credit and identification. Both the guest-service agent and the registration card (see Exhibit 9, bottom left) prompt the next step by asking how the bill will be settled. Hotels, for certain, and most guests, usually, prefer credit-card payments. Guests sometimes offer several cards. Desk clerks should take the card that charges the smallest discount (processing) fee, even if the reservation used a different card.

Credit cards help establish the guest's identity, but some jurisdictions require additional identification. Driver's licenses, passports, or state-issued ID-cards are used. Required by law or not, asking for extra ID dissuades prostitutes and other undesirables. Identification is critical in case of guest injury or death, in recovering stolen items, and in collecting unpaid accounts or losses from room damage. Knowing the guest's identity facilitates the return of lost items, but *only after* the guest inquires. Lost items are never returned unsolicited!

The credit card is entered into the hotel's PMS through a credit-card terminal, which reads the encoded strip. Back comes the approval (or denial) with an authorization number.

A small number of guests still prefer to settle with cash. In which case, the hotel offers two options. Pay in advance or provide a credit card and settle with cash at check-out. Either one works. Hotels have the legal right to collect in advance and guests may always settle with cash. Guests must understand upfront that a check, be it personal or business, is not cash.

The second option is the better one. Guests can charge services throughout the hotel when a credit card is on file. The PMS closes that option if payment is made in advance with cash. Guests cannot then charge in the dining rooms and lounges and cannot use the room telephone for outside calls.

This cash-or-credit option is needed with other methods of payment as well. New arrivals might have prepaid the room, or paid through a travel agent, or offer a trade account, a due bill, or assign the bill to a third-party, say, the traveler's company. These are all acceptable billing arrangements. Still, the desk needs a credit card on file if the guest wants to charge services in other departments.

Associates throughout the hotel must be vigilant if the paid-in-advance system is to work. Guest-service agents must disconnect outgoing telephone service for paid-in-advance rooms. And cashiers in spas, restaurants, lounges, and clubhouses must use the PMS to verify the guest's status before accepting payment by signature. Without a card on file, all services must be paid in cash.

ROOMING THE GUEST

Registration and assignment completed, the new arrival is ready to be roomed. And someone from the uniformed services is standing by (see Exhibit 16).

EXHIBIT 16 Bellhops rotate tip-generating assignments, called fronts, in a predetermined sequence. The next front stands by the desk, close to the bellstand, ready to service the guest who has just finished registering. In some hotels, baggage (shown on the cart) is taken to the guest room via the service, or rear, elevator, while the guest uses the guest, or front, elevator. *Courtesy of the Fairmont Hotel and Tower, San Francisco, California.*

The Uniformed Services

Many guests prefer to room themselves, and few hotels, anymore, insist otherwise. Upscale hotels may prefer, and a few might actually require, a bellperson to accompany each new arrival. The escort handles the luggage, serves as guide, acts as host, promotes other hotel services, and makes a quick inspection of the guest room before leaving. With a bellperson present, the occasional error of sending a new arrival to an already occupied room is tempered.

Members of the bell staff are in a unique position to improve communications between management and guests. After "visiting" on the elevator and down the corridors, guests often develop a rapport with the bellhop who roomed them. Experienced bell staffers sense otherwise and respect a guest's preference for silence. But there can be a quick intimacy during the 10 or 15 minutes of the rooming process when the guest and the staff member are isolated in a one-on-one setting. Later, the staff reinforces the previous familiarity by smiling, greeting, and conversing with the guests during their stay. This guest–staff connection can serve well the hotel's quality assurance program. Serious operational problems can be forestalled if management keeps open a communication channel with the bells.

Bellpersons are the hotel's most mobile employees. They can and should play a key role as the eyes and ears of hotel security. That's one advantages of outfitting the staff with inconspicuous earpieces, voice-activated mouthpieces, and attached belt packs. Wiring the crew also improves communication between the desk and the individual employee wherever he or she is in the building. Several well-known companies have installed talk-about equipment as a means of improving both service and security. The Breakers, a five-star Florida property, was one of the first. Hyatt Hotels and the Ritz-Carlton chain have been advocates as well, confident that outfitting all members of the unformed department has proven well worth the investment.

ROTATION OF FRONTS   Bellpersons, if they exist at all—and in many properties they don't—take on a variety of duties, especially in small properties. They drive the shuttle, watch for arrivals at the door, deliver room service, serve cocktails in the lobby, and relieve a one-clerk desk for meals. Taking guests to their rooms—*rooming* them—remains their principal duty.

Uniformed service personnel are minimum-wage workers, but are at the top of all hotel wage-earners because gratuities, tips, comprise their main income source. They zealously guard access to that income flow by monitoring their turns. The one who comes forward to take the key and rooming slip from the desk clerk is called the *front* (see Exhibit 16). Fronts rotate in turn. The one who has just completed a front is called a . Lasts are assigned errands that are unlikely to produce tips. They would move luggage for lockouts and deaths or for room changes when guests are not present. They keep the lobby clean and neat.

Between the front and the last, bellhops rotate assigned positions in the lobby (see Exhibit 5). Each position has a purpose. The station by the entrance catches the incoming luggage of new arrivals. The elevator position assists departures. The bell desk might have several posts depending on the size of the crew. Staffing requirements depend on the class of hotel. A general range of one bell position for every 40–65 estimated check-ins contrasts greatly to the 1 for 20 ratio of San Francisco's Fairmont Hotel, illustrated in Exhibit 16.

Bell service is much less formal today than it was 25 years ago. Fronts rarely need prompting with bells, hand signals, and verbal calls, "Front," that were standards a generation earlier. Remote printers at the bell (captain's) desk provide the front with the arriving guest's name. Guest identity is also made from the rooming slip (which will be discussed shortly) or even the tags on luggage. Also helping is an expected-arrivals list that was prepared during the previous night audit.

A record of fronts assures each bellperson his or her proper turn. The sequence is broken only if a guest requests a particular person, or if the next front has not returned from a previous errand. Missing turns are recovered because a record is maintained. The old pencil-and-paper journal has been replaced with a computerized record. It tracks the members of this very mobile department with times in and out, destinations, and purposes. Reference to the "journal" tells who was where and for how long. Each entry explains a bellperson's presence on a particular floor if some issue arises later. Obviously, there is a role here for the talk-about equipment that was suggested previously.

GROUP LUGGAGE AND OTHER INCOME   Tour group business is important to both the hotel's bottom line and to the income of the bell department. Almost universally, but especially when the hotel is unionized, each suitcase of a tour group is assessed an in-and-out fee. The charge is added to the group's master bill, collected by the hotel and paid to the bells.

Baggage is unloaded from the bus and processed in either a group lobby or the regular reception area. Colored tags, previously fixed to the bags, help with identification throughout the tour. Each tag has the guest's number, which corresponds to that person's identity on the master rooming list (see Exhibit 17). Copies of that list, provided by the tour company, are distributed to the bells in advance. Numbers are used because they are easier than names to read when matching baggage with the room assigned. Another technique uses PMS-preprinted adhesive-backed tags with the name and previously assigned room number. The tag is peeled from the list and slapped onto the bag to expedite delivery.

Baggage is moved en masse to the group's floor and delivered to each room. Hopefully, the desk has done its job by assigning rooms that are close together. Hotels that do large groups back to back use the same floors and the same rooms for successive arrivals.

Tour guests room themselves. The master rooming list has preassigned room partners using instructions from the tour operator. Envelopes, marked with room numbers, containing keys and instructions are distributed to the tour members. Meal tickets and freebees (gaming coupons, for example) would be included. Information that would otherwise be covered during the rooming process is communicated by these written instructions or done orally on the bus before the group disembarked, or both.

HMS32G	FINNERMAN			VAIL SKI MEADOW'S LODGE				2/05/
REFER #	GUEST NAME		ROOM	GROUP	ARRIVAL	DEPART	COMPANY LINE	# PERS
1	ADAMS	ADAM	609	NEWMEX	2/05	2/08	NEW MEXICO ST. SKI TEAM	1
2	BURTON	BOB	607	NEWMEX	2/05	2/08	NEW MEXICO ST. SKI TEAM	1
3	CURTIS	CHARLES	612	NEWMEX	2/05	2/08	NEW MEXICO ST. SKI TEAM	1
4	DILARDO	DALE	612	NEWMEX	2/05	2/08	NEW MEXICO ST. SKI TEAM	1
5	ELAN	EVAN	616	NEWMEX	2/05	2/08	NEW MEXICO ST. SKI TEAM	1
6	FEINSTEIN	FRED	613	NEWMEX	2/05	2/08	NEW MEXICO ST. SKI TEAM	1
7	GRAY	GARY	604	NEWMEX	2/05	2/08	NEW MEXICO ST. SKI TEAM	1
8	HARRIS	HARRY	606	NEWMEX	2/05	2/08	NEW MEXICO ST. SKI TEAM	1
9	INGOLS	IAN	616	NEWMEX	2/05	2/08	NEW MEXICO ST. SKI TEAM	1
10	JEFFREYS	JEFF	606	NEWMEX	2/05	2/08	NEW MEXICO ST. SKI TEAM	1
11	KASTLE	KRIS	604	NEWMEX	2/05	2/08	NEW MEXICO ST. SKI TEAM	1
12	LANGE	LOUIS	605	NEWMEX	2/05	2/08	NEW MEXICO ST. SKI TEAM	1
13	MORRISON	MORRIS	602	NEWMEX	2/05	2/08	NEW MEXICO ST. SKI TEAM	1
14	NORDICA	NEWT	605	NEWMEX	2/05	2/08	NEW MEXICO ST. SKI TEAM	1
15	OLIN	ORSON	609	NEWMEX	2/05	2/08	NEW MEXICO ST. SKI TEAM	1
16	POWELL	PAUL	607	NEWMEX	2/05	2/08	NEW MEXICO ST. SKI TEAM	1
17	QUAIL	QUINN	618	NEWMEX	2/05	2/08	NEW MEXICO ST. SKI TEAM	1
18	ROSSIGNOL	ROBERT	602	NEWMEX	2/05	2/08	NEW MEXICO ST. SKI TEAM	1
							TOTAL PEOPLE:	18

EXHIBIT 17 A group arrival list, another computer-generated report (see Exhibit 15), is prepared before the group arrives. The rooming arrangement is sent earlier to the hotel by the tour operator or meeting planner. The list serves the desk for individual identification because group members do not usually register individually. It serves the bell staff, which assigns the individual's reference number (extreme left column) to lobby baggage for prompt delivery to the room assigned (third column). Group arrivals are housed on the same floor close to one another to facilitate baggage handling. Back-to-back groups are assigned to the very rooms occupied by the previous group.

Group luggage is the bell department's bread and butter. Each bag is worth between $1 and $3 each way, in and out. Payroll records reflect these in-and-out earnings because the contracts flow through the hotel's sales and accounting offices. Tips earned from fronts are different; they are not handled by the hotel. They pass directly from the guest to the bellperson. Bells earn other incomes as well. How much depends on the services offered and the presence of a concierge or not. Auto rental companies, event venues, and local tour operators pay commissions of 10–15% for business booked through the bell desk. The same arrangement may apply if the hotel sends guest's laundry and dry cleaning to an outside company. Commissions are paid to the bellcaptain, but sometimes the whole department shares. Rarely does the hotel get a cut although it furnishes the space, the labor, and the utilities.

Rooming Slips

Through the rooming slip, the front desk communicates with the bells and the bells with the guest. Without bell service, the guest-service agent hands the rooming slip directly to the guest. With bell service, the slip passes to the guest after he or she has been roomed.

The guest is able to verify three bits of information that the hotel is using: Name including spelling, date of departure, and the rate. Legal disclaimers that appear on the registration card may be repeated on the rooming slip: The availability of a safe, for example.

The bellperson uses the slip to obtain the guest name and the room assigned. Off the party goes toward the elevator and the room. Other information may be used en route to make conversation and act as host. The guest's city or state and the weather are good starting points for welcoming the new arrival. Other nonthreatening topics are athletic events and the convention in town. Performers in the hotel or the gourmet restaurant chef on premises are other conversational openers that cross-sell facilities.

Some items that the bellperson promotes verbally may also be on the rooming slip. Whereas, foreign rooming slips contain some external advertising, U.S. slips focus inward. They provide a range of information and product promotions (see Exhibit 18). Although the guest is

---

Informative

Floor plan of the property
Aerial view of the property
Emergency and fire exits
Telephone directory of services
Kinds of lobby shops
Foreign language capabilities of the staff
Airline, taxi, and limousine telephone numbers
Local sites to see and things to do
Airport bus: times of operation and rates
Currency exchange capabilities
Map of the city with highway designations

Marketing

List of restaurants: prices, hours of operation, and menu specialties
A message of welcome or a note of appreciation
WATS number for other hotels in the chain
Recreational facilities: tennis, golf, pool, sauna
Discount coupons to area retailers and attractions

Regulatory

Check-out hour and check-in hour
Rate of gratuity applied to the room charge
Regulations for visitors
Limitations on pets

Dress code
Availability of the safe for valuables
Settlement of accounts
Expectations for guaranteed reservation holders
Deposit of room keys when leaving the property
Fees for local, long distance, and 1-800 calls
Other hotel fees and surcharges

Identification

Clerk's identifying initials
Identification of the party: name, number of persons, rate, arrival and departure dates
Room number
Key code—where room access is controlled by a dial system key

Instructional

Express check-out procedure
Electrical capacity for appliances
What to do in case of fire
How to secure the room
Notification to the desk if errors exist on the rooming slip
How to operate in-room movies, Internet, and games; their cost
How to operate the in-room refrigerator; cost
Rate of tax applied to the room charge

EXHIBIT 18 The size and content of rooming slips vary with the size and content of the hotel. Small properties provide a slip of paper and a key. Period. Large hotels, anxious to market in-house attractions, to supply safety information, and to defend against legal issues, may include all sorts of information, as this rooming slip illustrates.

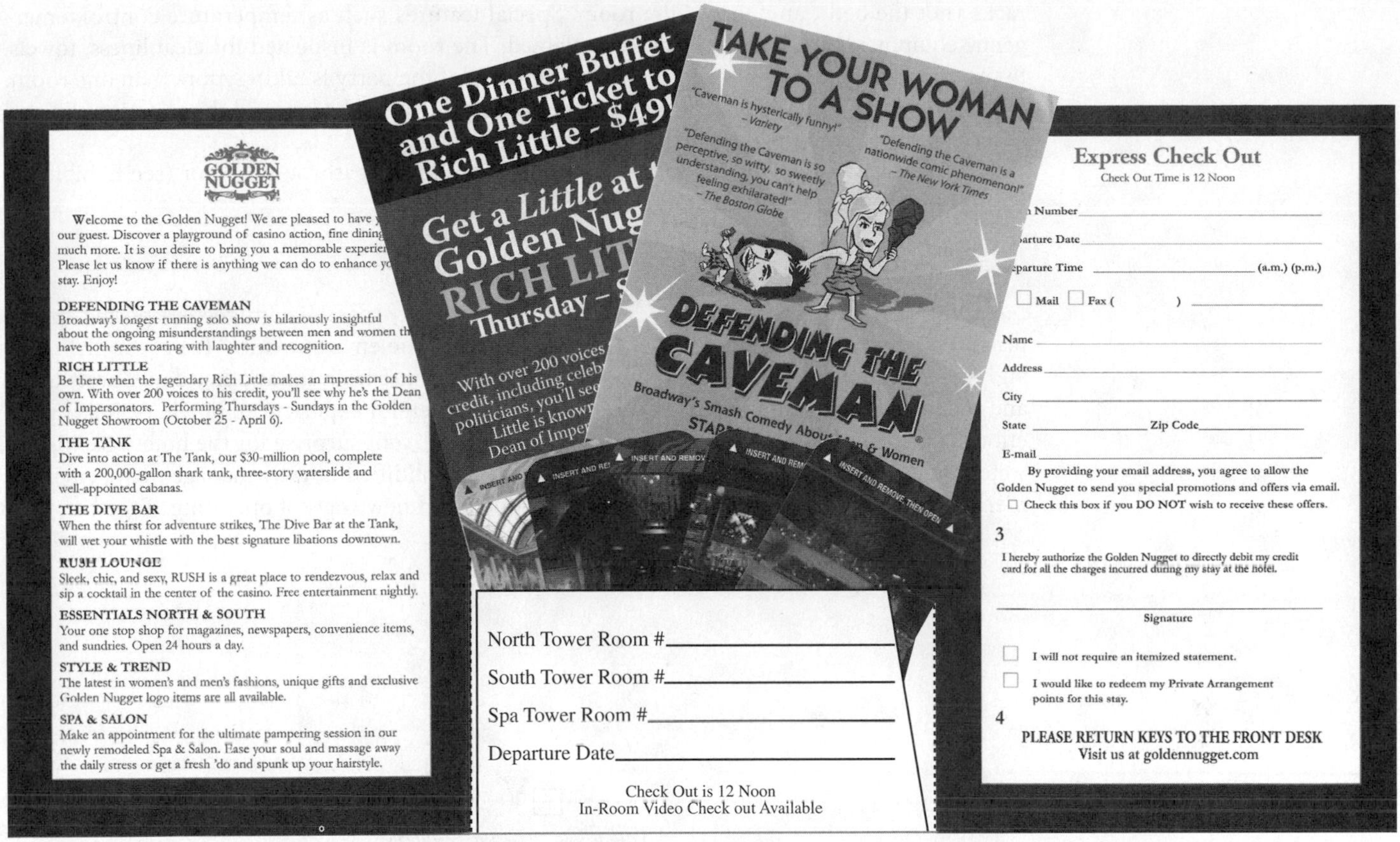

EXHIBIT 19 Example of a key envelope and welcome packet provided to arriving guests. Rooming slips are important vehicles for cross-promotions. Full-service hotels such as the Golden Nugget use the material to promote restaurants; shows; lounges and amenities, including spas, and salons, and, here, a $30 million pool. *Courtesy of the Golden Nugget Hotel and Casino, Las Vegas, Nevada.*

just arriving, rooming slips include check-out instructions. Safety alerts and recreational features are highlighted and sometimes special promotional items are included.

Sometimes rooming slips are used as identification cards. Both service and accounting improve when the staff knows who is who. Guests are asked to show them when signing for services throughout the hotel. Color-coding the slips adds extra value. VIPs have one color; all-inclusive guests another. Different colors distinguish American-plan guests, tour-group guests, paid-in-advance guests, and so on. Such use is limited to a small number of specialty properties. That is why, without being cautioned, the guest might toss away the slip.

The IRS, the Internal Revenue Service, has given the slips an unexpected use. Service employees must report gratuities as income. To verify the accuracy of the reported figure, the IRS estimates tip income from the bell department's call book or from copies of the individual rooming slips. Reported incomes are then compared to IRS estimates. It is the same approach that the IRS uses with bars and dining-rooms. Check values provide estimated tip incomes, which are then compared to tax payments made by food and beverage servers.

Rooming slips range from a simple piece of paper with the basic information scribbled by hand to a full spread of facts and advertisements (see Exhibit 19). Management's biggest hurdle: Get the guest to read them.

Arriving at the Room

Registration completed, the bellperson moves toward the elevators with the guest in tow. At some locations, baggage is carried on the service (or rear) elevators while guests take the guest (or front) elevators. The party reunites on the assigned floor and proceeds to the room. Bellpersons always knock on the guest-room door and announce themselves. The party enters only after a reasonable wait. Walking in on a half-clad guest is anywhere from awkward to extremely serious.

Guests proceed their guide into the room. The bellperson usually blocks the automatic door with a suitcase. Then he or she enters, hangs loose clothing, sets the suitcases on the baggage racks (not the bed), and checks the room. Special features such as temperature control, emergency equipment, and the minibar are explained. The room is inspected for cleanliness, towels, tissues, and hangers. Connecting rooms are unlocked if the party is taking more than one room. Unless there is a final request for service, the bellperson leaves the key and the rooming slip and accepts the proffered tip, if any, with thanks.

Hotels have gone "green" so explaining the sign on the bathroom mirror (see Exhibit 20) has become another commentary for the bellhop.

Green Hotels

Lodging's early efforts at "greening" the industry were chiefly cosmetic. Innkeepers posted appropriate statements a la Exhibit 20 about saving water and the environment. "Towels on the rack" and "cards on the bed linen" meant guests were willing to use both for another day. Guests did it and the savings in water and energy were eye-opening even for experienced hoteliers. Joining the efforts made guests feel better and produced a dollar-and-cent surprise for the hotels. Savings in water and energy were real.[10] Those savings have been solidified now by management's environmental awareness and its acceptance of new products and new ways of operating. Together, they

EXHIBIT 20 Typical notice hung on hotel doors, posted in the bath, or laid under the glass on the bureau top. Some 87% of guests support "green" travel, according to the U.S. Travel Data Service. The results are good for the hotel industry as well as the public. Savings in water, detergent, energy, and housekeeping time can be traced directly to the notice.

---

[10]By washing bed linens every other day, a 291-room hotel saved 6,000 gallons of water and 40 gallons of detergent each month. The program was voluntary so the results came without the participation of every guest.

What Does Green Really Mean?	
AAA identifies green hotels	– Beginning with AAA's 2010 TourBook®
Banquet menu program	– Hyatt's seasonal, local-grown foods
Bicycle stalls for commuters	– Orchard Garden Hotel, San Francisco
Biodegradable laundry bags	– Marriott Hotels
Building walls covered with perennial greens	– Athenaeum Hotel, London
Carbon calculator program	– Hilton International
Certification agencies	– LEED; Green Seal; MeetGreen
Content of Requests for Proposal (RFP)	– Meeting Professionals International
Dubai Green-Tourism Award	– Park Hyatt Dubai
Faucet aerators & toilet flappers	– Accor Hotels
Formal environmental department	– MGM Resorts International
Grading who is green	– Sustainable Travel International
Green roof using real grass	– Hyatt at Olive 8, Seattle, WA
In-room power-control key	– MTM Luxury Lodging, Yountville, CA
Landscaping with low-water using plants	– Harrah's
Meeting correspondence only electronically	– Kimpton Hotels
Fewer notepads, pens, menus at seminars	– Hyatt's "Meet and Be Green" programs
Recycled stationery paper	– Rodas Hotels, India
Roof panels heat 60% of hot water usage	– Proximity Hotel, Greensboro, NC
Separating hotel property from waste	– New Orleans InterContinental
Signage in baths	– With pledge to donate to environmental causes
Sustainable Travel Eco-Certification	– Grand Teton Lodge
Water-saving audit	– Marriott Marina Del Rey, CA
Wildlife Protection	– Amangani Hotel, Jackson Hole, WY

® AAA's TourBook and all other proper names cited here and throughout the text are registered trademarks.

EXHIBIT 21 Two dozen citations exemplify the spread and variety of "sustainable management" that hoteliers have undertaken. Today's efforts are profit-driven (light-emitting diodes replacing electric bulbs and recycled water on the golf greens), whereas much of the earliest efforts were political correctness.

have driven lodging toward the next environmental stage. Hotels big (such as Taj and Starwood) and small (such as Destination Hotels & Resorts and Grand Teton Lodge) have launched a range of new and real environmentally perceptive programs. Among them are "sustainable meetings," packages that focus on paperless meetings, alternatives for bottled water, recycled pens, and other green components. (See Exhibit 21.)

ECOTOURISM The greening of the American lodging industry is recent, but ecologically sensitive tourism, carrying an *ecotourism* label,[11] has been around for three decades. Most of it has taken place outside the United States. Ecotourism's major attractions have included animal life, rain forests, and natural phenomena such as The Red Rock of Australia or the Karsts of China's Pearl River. Closer to home is the Skywalk, a glass-floored platform 400-feet above the Grand Canyon, and Hawaii's Fairmont Orchid Hotel that features canoe trips to the coral reef.

Ecotourism often brings desperately needed foreign funds into economically poor locations, but it has detractors. Critics feel success may destroy the very attraction because the more visitors participating, the faster the environment degrades. The more tourists using showers and toilets and consuming local foodstuffs, the less pristine grows the environment and the greater the need for imports. A worrisome theme of ecotourism is: It is successful only so long as it does not succeed.

Very little of the total lodging industry is eco-sensitive. So rather than sell ecology, the industry has worked to reduce the impact of its operation on the environment. Some efforts are marginal and some are more sustainable (revisit Exhibit 21).

[11]The International Ecotourism Society defines ecotourism as "responsible travel to nature areas that conserve the environment and improve the well-being of local people."

SOME SPECIFICS Terminology is an important part of innovation and change. An early, but derogatory ecoterm, "tree-hugger," was replaced with "green." Green, which still carries some political baggage, has morphed to "sustainable development." Whatever the term, hotels that display sensitivity to the environment have come to the attention of LEED (Leadership in Energy and Environmental Design). LEED certifies environmentally desirable buildings. To win LEED endorsements, hotels have tested and installed a range of products, including bamboo sheets and towels (at twice the cost of cotton), recycled carpet, and chemical-free cleaning supplies. And that's just the beginning of a long list.

To achieve LEED accreditation, the building must also save energy. Two of many standards are rooftops covered with sod (see Exhibit 21; Hyatt at Olive 8) or white reflective toppings and windows that open. Neither of which are common in hotel construction. Real savings come from gadgets that turn off lights and energy when guests or employees leave an area. Equally important has been the switch to energy-efficient light bulbs. Big hotels have thousands of bulbs! An unexpected bonus comes from utilities, which rebate dollars when energy is reduced or water consumption drops or natural landscaping replaces water-hungry grass.

Storm water and some effluent water can be bio-cycled for landscaping and golf courses. Where location allows, ecosensitive hotels buy power from wind- and thermal-generated sources to provide a secondary level of support. Form turns into function when on-site thermal ponds are used for energy as well as for mud baths or landscaping.

Three components structure the greening of lodging: energy and resource management, maintenance and operations, design and construction. Moving sustainable development from a novelty to a workable commodity requires a large commitment of capital, especially

EXHIBIT 22 Mandarin Oriental has 400 rooms and 227 condo units as part of MGM MIRAGE's $7 billion project called City Center. City Center (Las Vegas) boasts the largest certified LEED project (Leadership in Energy and Environmental Design) in the history of the United States. All buildings associated with this project feature low-flow water systems, energy-efficient lighting, shaded design to reduce heat, underground parking to reduce "heat island" effect, and natural gas cogeneration plants to provide 10% of the electricity and 100% of the hot water needs. (Sales tax relief from both the state and the county helped in the completion of the project.) Mandarin Oriental, which has won awards for operating green hotels elsewhere, is a logical tenant. Shown here is a room in the Mandarin Oriental, New York. *Courtesy of Mandarin Oriental, The Hotel Group.*

for the design and construction elements. *CityCentre*, an 18-million-square-foot project, is a $7 billion venture of MGM Resorts International (previously MGM Mirage). The company received an unexpected surprise as it followed LEED recommendations. Projections now suggest that the construction costs of its green design will have an operational payback of fewer years than originally estimated.

Economies of scale have driven down costs as hotels and their suppliers invest in long-range planning. Innkeeping is not likely to be the leader of sustained development, but it has begun to do its share (see Exhibit 22).

Summary

Through its staff members, the hotel and the guest come face to face for the first time during the arrival sequence. There is plenty of opportunity for the hotel to make an impression, good or bad, during the several parts of the arrival process, including the greeting, the registration, the assignment, and the rooming. Each associates has a critical role to play. There are moments of truth for members of the uniformed services and for the desk agents who process the paperwork and the reception. Small hotels blend all these staffers into one individual, the guest-service agent.

Check-in time is a sensitive moment when the front-office staff communicates with the arriving guest in an unscripted interchange. Experienced guest-service agents balance business with reception. Some of the encounters are structured by long waiting lines, most of which are disappearing as guests turn to kiosks and electronic registrations. Whatever the mechanical techniques, a great deal of information must be taken from each new arrival. Identification, preferences and needs, length of stay, and method of payment are the most critical. Guests with reservations are processed quickly because the hotel's computer has already captured most of the information. Simultaneously, the hotel needs to communicate its own information, some of which is mandated by law. During very busy times, the check-in process can be an intense several minutes. During slower times, it can be a relaxed bit of hospitality.

Property management systems have enhanced the assignment part of the arrival as they have expedited much of the reservation and billing functions. Simultaneously, the role of the bell department has been diminished. Many guests now room themselves, but it is also true that the ax of economy has cut the size of the uniformed services. Fewer calls for the bells and its corresponding reduction in size have changed the security, inspection, and reception capability of individual hotels and, consequently, of the whole industry. These changes reflect, in part, shifting expectations and needs of the guest.

The dynamics of innkeeping are a work in this chapter. Simultaneously, but not consequentially, comes a new trend, sustainable development—the "greening" of the industry. *Change*—but within the context of hospitable reception—remains the industry's catchword.

Resources And Challenges

RESOURCES

Web Site Assignment

Reference the current websites of *green lodging news.com* or *whole-travel.com* or other Web or print sources and identify two specific efforts by hotel companies to save in energy and two in water. Cite the sources and comment in some detail about one of your four picks.

Interesting Tidbits

- The Bibles that arriving guests find in their room were probably left by the Gideons, a nondenominational evangelical group. Increasing diversity among the U.S. population and an increase in international travelers have many hotel chains (Marriott and Kimpton among them) adding other spiritual texts.
- Do Not Disturb signs hang in the inside of the guest-room corridor door until needed. Guests who want privacy move the sign to the outside knob to alert housekeeping.

Guest: (Telephoning the desk): "Help, I can't get out of my room, 1422!"

Desk: "I don't understand, sir. What's wrong; just open the door."

Guest: "Well, there are three doors. One opens into the bath; the second into the closet. And the third door has a 'Do Not Disturb' sign hanging on it."

Challenges

True/False

Questions that are partially false should be marked false (F).

_____ 1. The "It" in: "It is successful only so long as it doesn't succeed" refers to the algorithms that are used in building computer reports.

_____ 2. The hotel industry, but especially commercial hotels, has broadly adapted *queuing ("q-ing") theory* in order to streamline room service at breakfast.

_____ 3. "Road-warriors" are guest/travelers who require special attention in urban hotels because they arrive by car to nongarage properties that also have the animosity of the local police; when taken together on-street parking becomes nightmarish.

_____ 4. The abbreviation RNA (Registered, Not Assigned) is used at hotels to flag a reservation for a party that has not paid in advance or has not prepaid the reservation despite a request to do so.

_____ 5. Both the willingness of guests to self-serve and the need of hoteliers to watch budgets explain the decline of the once-large and important department of the uniformed service, the bells.

Problems

1. Reorganize the following jumbled list of events, persons, and job activities into a logical flow, from start to finish, of the guest arrival process:
   a. Room selection
   b. Establishing guest credit
   c. Registered, not assigned
   d. Bellperson
   e. Valet parking attendant
   f. Rotation of fronts
   g. Room assignment
   h. Obtaining guest identification
   i. Rooming slip
   j. Upgrading and/or up selling
   k. Rooming the guest
   l. Preblocking rooms
   m. Doorperson
   n. Ice bucket filled
   o. Guest queue
   p. Registration card signature
   q. Check-out reminder
   r. Room status report
   s. AAA discount
   t. Pet deposit

2. Foreign registration cards often require significantly more personal information than is required for domestic registration cards. Some management personnel feel that this extra data amounts to an invasion of the guest's privacy. Other managers, however, believe this extra information aids the hotel in providing better security and service levels to the guest. With whom do you side? Why might a hotel legitimately need to know your future and past destinations, your mother's maiden name, and your date of birth?

3. Intentional bias can be programmed (through computer algorithms) into the room-selection sequence of a property management system. Rooms will then appear in a prescribed order rather than in sequence or at random. Certain rooms can be offered first, or not, depending on management's criteria. Give examples explaining why management might wish to decide which rooms appear in which sequence in order to direct the clerk's selection.

4. A local merchant, whose attempts to service the hotel's guest laundry and dry-cleaning business have been frustrated, visits with the new rooms manager. (The laundry of this 600-room, commercial hotel does not clean personal guest items.) The conversation makes the rooms manager realize that she has never seen commission figures on any of the reports. She learns that the bellcaptain, who doesn't seem to do any work—that is, he doesn't take fronts—gets the commissions.

   The rooms manager initiates a new policy. All commissions from car rentals, bus tours, ski tickets, laundry, balloon rides, and so on will accrue to the hotel. An unresolved issue is whether or not the money will go into the employee's welfare fund.

   A very angry bellcaptain presents himself at the office of the vice-president of the rooms division. Explain with whom you agree (the rooms manager or the bellcaptain) and prepare an argument to support your opinion.

5. Some hotels upgrade corporate guests to nicer rooms when space is available. Usually, the guest need not even ask for this courtesy—it is offered as standard operating procedure. Managers of such properties believe that the corporate guest appreciates the courtesy and the nicer room. And since the room is not likely to sell anyway, why not make someone happy?

   The reverse side of this argument, however, suggests that the guest comes to expect this treatment and even feels slighted if only standard rooms are available. In addition, hotels that give upgrades away free are doing themselves a disservice in terms of upselling corporate guests to a higher rate. After all, why should corporate guests ever select higher-priced rooms (or concierge floor rooms) when they are given at no extra charge as a matter of standard practice? How would you respond to these arguments?

6. Ten weary, footsore travelers,
      All in a woeful plight,
   Sought shelter at a wayside inn
      One dark and stormy night.
   "Nine beds—no more," the landlord said,
      "Have I to offer you;
   To each of eight a single room,
      But number nine serves two."
   A din arose. The troubled host
      Could only scratch his head;
   For of those tired men, no two
      Could occupy one bed.
   The puzzled host was soon at ease—
      He was a clever man—
   And so to please his guests devised
      The most ingenious plan:

   |A|B|C|D|E|F|G|H|I|
   In a room marked A, two men were placed;
      The third he lodged in B.

The fourth to C was then assigned.
  The fifth went off to D.
In E the sixth he tucked away.
  In F the seventh man;
The eighth and ninth to G and H.
  And then to A he ran.
Wherein the host, as I have said,
  Had lain two travelers by.
Then taking one—the tenth and last,
  He lodged him safe in I.

Nine single rooms—a room for each—
  Were made to serve for ten.
And this it is that puzzles me
  And many wiser men.

—Excerpted from *Hotel News*,
Winnipeg, 1935.

Does it also puzzle you? How was the ingenious host able to lodge 10 men in only 9 rooms?

AN INCIDENT IN HOTEL MANAGEMENT
Barking Up the Wrong Lobby

A friend of a registered guest met with that guest in the lobby to get money to buy theme-park tickets for the two of them. The friend—and supposed visitor—had a large dog on a leash and was feeding it dog bones. Housekeeping had called the desk earlier to report evidence (dog bones and dog hair) of animal occupation in room 606.

When the guest came to the desk for change of a large denomination bill, she was told there would be a $50 cleaning fee for the dog and an additional $40 plus tax for a second occupant of the room. She denied that the dog had been anywhere but the lobby. This was contradicted by several complaints about loud barking that the desk had received from other guests. The staff had found those entries in the log left by the night shift.

Questions:

1. Was there a management failure here; if so, what?
2. What is the hotel's immediate response (or action) to the incident?
3. What further, long-run action should management take, if any?

Answers to True/False Quiz

1. False. "It" refers to ecotourism, not to computer technology. A concern of some tourism experts has been the degradation of an area's appeal by the very success of its appeal. The more visitors who come, the faster the unspoiled area declines.

2. False. The lodging industry never quite adopted queuing theory to line management. It would have been applied at the front desk, but two things happened. (1) The economy collapsed, so the need diminished and (2) self-service kiosks with the latest equipment fed self-registration into the industry's widening use of property management systems.

3. False. "Road Warriors" is a term given to individuals who travel a great deal; they "hit the road." The parking issues of urban hotels are real, but they have no reference to businesspersons who do a great deal of travel (i.e., "road warriors").

4. False. RNA (Registered, Not Assigned) means just that and no more. The guest has arrived and signed in, but has not yet had a room assigned because the house is full. If vacant but unmade rooms were available assignment could be made, but the guest held until housekeeping moves the room from "on change" to "ready."

5. True. The American public has grown accustomed to—and often prefers—self-service. After traveling for miles and handling personal luggage, most guests feel quite capable of finding their own room at their own pace. That coincides with the need of hoteliers to watch budgets by reducing labor costs in the bell department.

The Role of the Room Rate

The Role of the Room Rate

Room rates tell a great deal about the industry, the individual hotel, the traveler, and the economy. Small wonder then that everyone—the guest, the travel agent, the guest's travel desk, the guest-service agent, the management, the staff, the news media, the government, and the industry—focuses on room rates.

ROOM RATES AND THE ECONOMY

Supply and Demand

Room rates measure the economic health of the lodging business. When the economy is hearty and strong, so are room rates. When the economy is ailing and weak, so are room rates. The hotel industry experience dramatic downturn after the fall of New York City's Twin Towers on September 11, 2001. As fear gripped the nation, travel (demand) was curtailed and rates fell from the highs that had preceded that 2001 date. In the intervening periods between then and now, rates have followed the same cyclical pattern: Up and down between 2003 and 2008, but only down between 2008 and 2011, when a new recovery was sensed. STR Global[1] reported negative changes in RevPar in 2009 and 2010 before turning positive in 2011.

Few new hotels come on line during the dips and many tired properties close their doors when faced with bankruptcies. Obviously, the supply side—the hotels are already built—is not as sensitive and does not decline as quickly as the demand side. With plenty of rooms available, total occupancy declines during the dips.

Hotel construction lags and that is the positive side. When the recovery does start, demand exceeds supply and room rates move up rapidly. Five or so years into the recovery (it takes that long), new properties—indeed, whole new chains—bring equilibrium between supply and demand. Rate change stabilizes. Soon, too soon, it seems, the cycle reverses again. Excess supply and a general malaise in the reoccurring economic cycle restarts the sequence downward once again.

Competition

Supply and demand are not the only factors challenging hotel executives as they set rates. They must also weigh the competition across the street, down the road, and in far-away locales. Managers must comparison shop just as their customers do. The physical competition is easy to compare; it is there for the looking. Swimming pools, tennis courts, meeting rooms, restaurants, and lobby bars head a long list of differences that gives one property a competitive advantage over its neighbor. As external competition prescribes the general price range so do design differences determine increments within the rates. Room size, furnishings, modernization, location, and exposure differentiate the product still further. The variables are many and often difficult to monetize.

The property's physical presentation has a role in rate-setting. Hotels with burnt-out bulbs in exterior signage, wilted flowers in the planters, and litter on the airport bus lose out to hotels with lesser facilities that look fresher and newer. Much of that is housekeeping. "Clean and neat" sends an important subliminal message.

Differences in service are more difficult to discern, but they add to the room rate as substantially as the physical components. Twenty-four-hour room service, pool guard on duty, and an extensive training program for employees begin another, less visible list of competitive advantages. Like the capital outlays made to upgrade physical accommodations, these costs must be recaptured in the room rate.

---

[1]STR Global (Smith Travel Research, Hendersonville, TN) is the industry's best-known source of statistics. Its STAR program tracks occupancy, ADR, and RevPar across the industry and around the world. Researchers, hotel chains, and independently operated hotels rely on its output.

Elasticity

Elasticity is defined as the change in demand (number of rooms sold) resulting from a change in price (room rates). If demand increases with a drop in price or decreases when price is raised, demand is elastic. It bounces to price changes. If demand appears unaffected by changes in price, demand is inelastic. Elasticity has general economic applications; it is not limited to hotel rates. Applied to the hotel business, rate reductions in an elastic market generate new business through higher occupancy. Room-rate reductions in an inelastic market generate little or no new business.

There is a difference between increased occupancy and increased revenues!

Industry professionals have come to believe that reduction in rates produces less *total revenue* even if occupancy improves. They are saying: So what if room sales are elastic; so what if occupancy increases by lowering the price of rooms. Most hoteliers believe that the *total room sale dollars* generated from increasing occupancy, but decreasing rates, results in less take-home dollars than holding rates steady and taking a hit from falling occupancies.[2] So even if the market is elastic, most hoteleirs hold rates steady during the periodic dips in demand. In fact, there is some evidence that rates may creep upward even during bad times.

Within this broad industrywide view are two additional issues. If a property generates a large percentage of *total* income from nonroom sources (banquets, lounges, pools, clubs, etc.) increased occupancy from rate reductions may increase total sales even as room sales decline. This comes from more guests using these nonroom services.

The hotel's market is the second issue. It is quite clear that discretionary travelers, the tourists, are more elastic, and that business travelers are more inelastic. The former can travel or not; the businessperson has much less discretion. (See Exhibit 1.) So the hotel's primary market is a major factor in its degree of elasticity and therefore its posture about rate increases or reductions.

This split in markets was the catalyst for changing much of the travel industry. In the 1970s, customer profiles began to form into distinct buyer segments. After federal deregulation, the

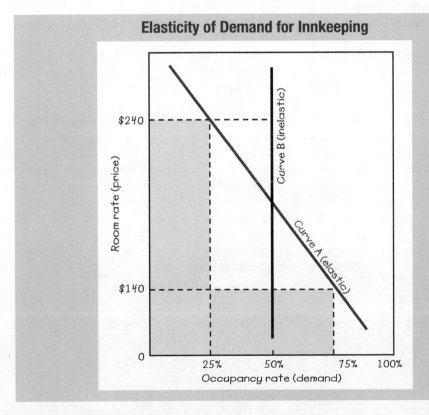

Elasticity of Demand for Innkeeping

EXHIBIT 1 The leisure market is chiefly an elastic market. Demand increases as rates fall and decreases as rates rise. The slope of Curve A illustrates the change in occupancy (demand) corresponding to the change in the rates being charged for the leisure market.

The business market is an inelastic market chiefly. There is no discernable change in demand (occupancy) up or down with fluctuations in rate, Curve B. This "truism" is tested whenever the economy goes through a serious shakeout.

---

[2]"This simple example [of a hotel decreasing its ADR by $5 in an attempt to maintain a 69% occupancy] shows that more money can be brought down to the profitability line by attempting to maintain rates than by trying to maintain historical occupancy levels." Lana Yoshii, vice-president, Product Development, STR, 23 February, 2009.

Two other researchers supported this position. They found that "rates [in Europe] are the key factor in maintaining revenue, rather than occupancy. While hotels that maintain an ADR below ... their competitor did gain somewhat on occupancy ..., these low-rate hotels recorded relatively low REVPAR." Cathy Enz and Linda Canina, *Strategic Pricing in European Hotels: 2006-2009. Cornell University. Ithaca, New York.*

airlines capitalized on the emerging distinctions between corporate and leisure travel. Each class was charged differently. The hotel industry followed suit. The shift was the beginning of a conscious attempt to segregate buyers by their price sensitivity, the concept behind yield management. Both industries discovered that demand in terms of time, price, and location was relatively elastic for the leisure market and relatively inelastic for the business segment.

Managing two distinct markets is both an art and a science. Success from discounting rates for elastic leisure markets may not carry over to the inelastic business market. Likewise, while leisure groups may respond positively to alternative, lower-rate dates, corporate groups travel on a need-to-go basis. Discretionary/leisure buyers may even change locations to save on the lodging budget, whereas corporate guests are often last-minute shoppers with little flexibility (see Exhibit 1).

The group market shares characteristics of the other two models. Group business from price-sensitive tours takes on characteristics of the leisure segment—elastic in terms of rate, flexible with regard to date. Conventions, trade shows, conferences, and corporate retreats have the characteristics of the corporate market—inelastic with regard to rate, inflexible in terms of dates. But even inelastic markets become elastic at some point. There may be little or no difference in corporate shopping when the rate fluctuates between $150 and $175. But even the corporate buyer takes a second look when the rate quote jumps, say, to $450. As corporate guests and/or their travel desk find last-minute bargains via Internet travel sites, the inelastic business guests shift ever so slightly toward an elastic buyer. It is something the industry has started to monitor.

RATE CUTTING Industry professionals are quick to distinguish rate discounting from rate cutting. Rate cutting functions in an inelastic market. That means lower rates do not generate new business in total. Unwarranted rate cuts generate new business for one property only by luring the customer away from a competing property. Too often, the competition meets the challenge in kind. Discounting, on the other hand, aims to attract new customers to the industry, benefiting all properties. Discounting seeks out the vacation-at-home customer, the bunk-in-with-friends-or-family customer, the let's-camp-out customer, and the do-you-think-we-can-afford-a-vacation-this-year customer. In contrast, rate cutting uses lower rates to entice the all-ready-committed guest who is considering a competitor's hotel at the market rate.

Rate cutting grows rapidly during economic dips. In soft markets, it tears down the region's entire price structure. And it does so much faster than it took to build. Where discounting is rampant, only the customer is the winner. When occupancy recovers, rate-cutters face customers who perceive full or even reasonable rates as very poor value.

Rate cutting is so destructive that some resort communities outlaw price wars. Posting rates on outdoor signs is made a misdemeanor. That is probably the explanation for the dollar name of several hotel chains: *Motel 6* and *Super 8*. Other communities require just the opposite. The lowest and highest rates must be posted externally. This establishes parameters for the shopper, and reduces the unsavory practice of "sizing up" the walk-in guest before quoting the rate.

Anyone who looks carefully at rate cutting comes to realize that recovering from even a small percentage price cut requires an even larger percentage increase in occupancy just to maintain dollar equilibrium, let alone gaining from the move (see Exhibit 2).

Rate Discounting Equivalency Table				
	Percent of Rate Discount			
Current Occupancy (%)	1. 10%	2. 15%	3. 20%	4. 25%
50	55.56	58.82	62.5	66.67
55	61.11	64.71	68.75	73.33
→ 60	66.67	70.59	75.00	80.00
65	72.22	76.47	81.25	86.67
70	77.78	82.35	87.5	93.33
75	83.33	88.24	93.75	100.00

EXHIBIT 2 The chart illustrates the additional occupancy needed to offset rate cuts and still maintain the same room revenue. Follow, for example, a hotel that enjoys a 60% occupancy before cutting rates (left column). If it cuts room rates by 10% (Column 1), occupancy must rise from 60% to 66.67% to *maintain the same dollar income*. A 20% cut in room rates (Column 3) necessitates a new occupancy of 75% just to stay even! A manager who contemplates rate cutting must ask whether the lower rates will increase occupancy by the new values.

ADDITIONAL FACTORS IN RATE

The quoted rate and the amount actually paid for a night's lodging are never the same. Several factors, some impacting the entire industry and some encountered less frequently, drive higher—frighteningly higher at times—the amount actually paid.

Surcharges

Excess charges for baggage and for the use of blankets and pillows are among the negative news facing the domestic airlines. As surcharges take hold elsewhere, innkeeping finds validity for doing the same. In both cases, these extra charge have a measurable impact on the consumer's cost. One of lodging's most irritating charges is the tax on room occupancy, but that one can't be blamed on the industry.

ROOM TAXES   Room taxes are also called bed taxes, hotel taxes, or TOTs (Transient Occupancy Taxes). Hotel managers have no control in setting these local lodging taxes. Even their trade associations are powerless against the revenue needs of local municipalities. Facing increasingly tight budgets, cities are lured into the easy money available from taxing out-of-towners. It is more palatable politically to increase that revenue base rather than taxing locals. So other political divisions also jump in. In New York City, guests pay a New York State sales tax, a New York City sales tax, and a New York City room occupancy tax. Spelled out: Total sales taxes are 8.875% of the room rate and the hotel tax is 5.875% more, plus a flat $3 per room. This adds $65.00 to the cost of a $400 room! That 16% boost to the bill is certain to awaken even a sleepy guest checking out.

Critics question the justification for taxing vistors to pay for new schools and local sports complexes (see Exhibit 3)! Even locals complain. By so doing, San Franciscans recently voted against a ballot measure that would have added an additional two percentage points to an already high 15.5% room tax. Increasing lodging taxes may actually hurt the local economy. More revenue may be lost in other taxes than is actually gained in room taxes. For example, at one time,

How Communities Use the Taxes Levied on Room Rates

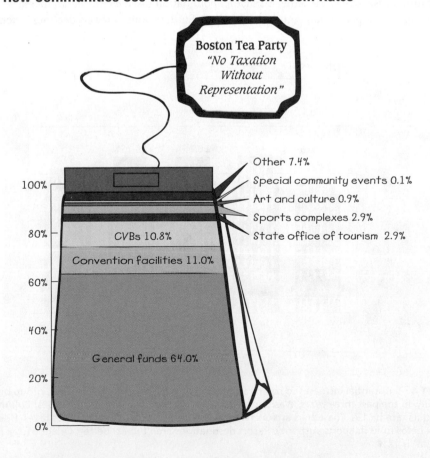

How Travel-Related Sales Taxes Are Used

EXHIBIT 3   Hotel guests have not yet staged a Boston Tea Party even though their room taxes (also called bed taxes) do little to promote tourism, innkeeping, or travel. Most of the funds are deposited in the community's general fund as the tea bag illustrates. A complimentary issue involves online travel companies. Are they paying the proper amount of bed taxes to the municipalities? And why are they subject to sales taxes when other Web retailers are not?

New York City had an effective rate of 21.25%! (See above; the tax is now approximately 15%.) In large part because of this tax, the city suffered a decrease in convention business estimated at 30%. With 30% fewer convention visitors, that were 30% fewer purchases of souvenirs, arts and crafts, taxis, meals and drinks, clothing, and related items. Each of those purchases had generated sales tax revenues. The increase in the lodging tax was purported to decrease total sales tax revenues across the city. It certainly impacted room demand.

Room Taxes Impact Demand   It is unlikely that the individual traveler changes plans because of high local taxes. However, negotiators for group business have become increasingly conscious of the impact of taxes on member attendance. Carefully negotiated group rates seem purposeless and inconsequential if the city then slaps an additional 15–20% levy on rates that have been shaved by just 5 or 10 dollars. No question that bed taxes are deterrents to the marketing efforts of numerous convention and visitor bureaus. Taxes between 10% and 12% seem acceptable to most group planners. Rates above 14% begin to meet resistance. Yet, cities such as Washington, Houston, and San Antonio—well-recognized destinations for groups—struggle with room taxes 16% and higher (see Exhibit 4).

To fight increasing taxation, industry associations have begun conducting research and educational campaigns aimed at local politicians. This research has uncovered some interesting findings. Twenty-five years ago, total room taxes (state and local sales and bed taxes) were just 3–4% of the room charge. Today, the national average is 11–12%—a threefold increase! More startling, as Exhibit 3 illustrates, less than 30% of the total raised goes to fund tourism. Bed taxes may represent the highest increase in taxation of any industry in the country, with casinos a possible exception. And it is not limited to the United States.

Looking at 50 destinations around the globe, the World Tourism Organization (WTO) concluded that taxes on tourism are proliferating. In some cases they stifle tourism resulting in a net loss in revenue for the localities. Some three-quarters of the destinations studied had raised tourism-related taxes over the past several years. Indeed, governments are finding creative ways to levy new taxes against tourists. More than 40 different kinds of taxes were identified, including an environmental tax.

Similar research by the American Hotel Foundation discovered that an increase in the bed tax has negative repercussions on room demand. Elastic room demand declines when the total

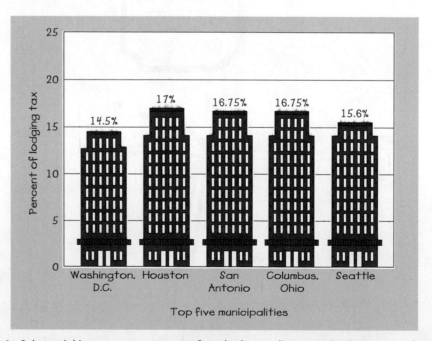

EXHIBIT 4   Substantial increases to room rates from bed taxes discourage business, group business especially. In the past three years, Washington, D.C., has lowered its rate from 20.25%; Columbus has boosted its rate by 1%. The others are unchanged. These rates do not include sales taxes. Houston's bed tax helps fund its sports authority. Resort destinations aren't much better: Orlando's tax is 14.5%; Las Vegas' is 12%.

room rate, including taxes, increases. A decrease in room demand doesn't just affect the hotel industry. Some suggest a multiplier, hypothesizing that a 2% increase in the lodging tax results in a 5.1% reduction in room sales and associated visitor spending. Certainly, New York City experienced that.

Room Taxes and Online Travel Companies Another room-tax issue, a big one, pits the online travel companies against the tax collectors with lodging only an interested bystander. Among the best known are Travelocity, Expedia, and Orbitz, but a lawsuit filed by the city of Atlanta actually listed 14 others. Similar suits have been filed by Philadelphia, Miami, Chicago, and many other cities. They all claim to have been shortchanged by the online companies. It is reminiscent of bed taxes in general: Municipalities need revenue. Some courts have ruled in favor of the companies; others in favor of the cities. Settlements have been huge. Anaheim, California, certainly not the largest plaintiff, was awarded nearly $18 million. Many suits are still pending. Las Vegas, with a 12% room tax, depends heavily on these partnerships and has not yet entered the courts.

It is a simple issue: Are the travel companies partners or customers? They obtain blocks of rooms at wholesale rates from hotels desperate to fill the house. For those rooms, the travel companies pay the municipal bed taxes, which are eventually paid to the cities. The travel companies (Travelocity, Expedia, etc.) resell the rooms on the Web at a higher price and collect tax on the higher price as well as a fee for their services. The cities lay claim to the difference between the taxes that the companies collect (on the higher room rate) and what they actually pay the municipalities (on the rate paid to the hotel). It makes for lawsuits.

RESORT FEES AND OTHER HIDDEN CHARGES Resort fee is probably a misnomer now because hotels of all stripes are adding fees, borrowing the concept that started at resorts. Although the fees per se are irritating, most complaints focus on notice. Often, guests first learned about them when checking out. There on the folio are additional charges that no one mentioned before. Such was the case with one of the most egregious add-ons. One dollar was automatically added to the guest's folio and that was done right across the whole chain. Management was surprised by the resulting hoopla. After all, the dollar was a donation to charity! Shouldn't everyone be willing to donate?

Typically, resort fees are explained away as a convenience. Supposedly, the fee incorporates many minor, irritating charges into one. Rather than add a daily fee for the newspaper, the health club, pool towels, and the in-room telephone, a daily charge is simply added to the folio, the resort fee. Left unresolved was whether the guest wanted to use those services or not. Moreover, many, many hotels provide those amenities as part of the rate—that is what hotels sell! (See Exhibit 5.)

The add-on-to-the-folio concept first took hold during the great energy shortage that began in 2001. California faced the highest energy costs in the country. Prices jumped to unprecedented highs. For example, the energy bill of the Hotel del Coronado rose to $200,000 per month

---

What Guests Might Be Told Their Resort Fee Includes

- Minibar restocking labor fee
- Local telephone calls
- Swimming pool & towels
- In-room coffee
- Cable television
- Gratuities
- Laundromat
- Business center usage
- Umbrellas on the beach
- Energy premium
- Use of the in-room safe
- Film disks
- Complimentary newspaper
- Administrative fees
- Internet usage
- Health club and gym
- Spa access
- Fax machine usage
- Library loans
- WIFI (or WI-FI; WiFi)

EXHIBIT 5 Resort fees are no longer special to resorts. All hotel types have levied charges over and above the room rate in an effort to leave quoted rates as low as possible. There may be costs even with the up-front fees, the Laundromat, for example. Unless guests are notified beforehand, they may opt out of the charge.

from the typical $50,000–$60,000! The San Diego Wyndham Hotel had a $46,000 energy bill for January of that year. That one month was half the cost of the entire previous year! Hoteliers just had to pass on these charges.

Wyndham added a $3.50 per room-night energy surcharge for its California-based hotels and $2.50 for Wyndham hotels located elsewhere. Starwood Hotels & Resorts Worldwide levied $2 per room-night in all of its west-coast properties. A month later, it levied energy fees across all its brands in most U.S. locations. Competing chains joined in. Like baggage charges for airlines, resort fees represent an important revenue source although they began as a cost offset.

Guests howled when the fees were not preannounced; many refused to pay. Then the attorneys general of several states considered the issue under Deceptive and Unfair Practices Acts. There were large fines against several chains. The Federal Trade Commission now requires mandatory fees to be disclosed at the time the room is reserved. Hotels that fail to disclose the fee in advance or provide information about the fee only at the time of check-in are required to make payment of such fees voluntary, or "opt-in" fees. If the guest first hears about the fee at check-in, the guest must "opt-in"—agree to the fee. Not "opt-out"—decline to pay.

Misrepresenting the resort fee as a type of occupancy tax was one of the charges levied against the hotels. From the trauma, the industry learned how to legally disclose extra charges and began training employees to fully disclose, in advance of the guest's arrival, the amounts and types of resort fees and surcharges.

Sometimes the fee has an actual payback: breakfast included with the rate and gratuities included with the rate— no tipping to the housekeeper or the bell staff. At a resort, it might cover one round of golf. More often the fee covers nothing specific. It is just another means of upping the rate. Upping the rate has a rare risk. If the rate charged exceeds the posted rate that state laws require, the hotel could lose the statutory protection of limited liability for property loses.

When negotiating rates, some meeting planners find resort fees more negotiable than room rates. Like any negotiation, it depends. It depends on the occupancy of the hotel, the time of the year, the group's size, and the agreed-upon rate on the rooms—the very conditions that determine all room charges.

Hoteliers have become inventive in their search for new revenues. For a fee above the room rate, say $20–$25, guests can "guarantee" having a king bed or a no-smoking room (or a smoking room). This concept of a la carte pricing (the airlines call it unbundling pricing) is spreading. So much so that a new revenue line may soon appear on profit-and-loss statements and guest folios.

One popular restaurant in Philadelphia has initiated the equivalent of a resort fee. Guests who gather to discuss business over lunch may hold the table for two hours by paying a "table fee." In their search for revenues, hoteliers adopt whatever pricing ideas seem viable. So room rates have been discounted for some time, and the next section examines these. Among them is a new type of discount, nonrefundable reservations. By whatever name, it is just another hidden charge; one that produces a bit of revenue, but, like several others, at the cost of customer goodwill.

Discounts were aimed originally at the elastic market, the leisure tourist, who responds to rate cuts more quickly than the business traveler. But nonrefundable discounts carry a penalty, one adopted from the airlines: No refunds. As the economy dipped, business travelers, who often change plans at the last minute, began buying into the discounts. Business travelers are accustomed to canceling room reservations at will, even up to 6:00 PM on the expected day of arrival. This is something that nonrefundable reservations do not allow. The terms are clear: risk the loss of the prepaid reservation versus the gain from a substantially reduced room rate (between 10% and 15%; say, $35–$50 on a $300 room). Less measurable is the long-term cost in customer goodwill.

Hotels have always had no-refund periods for special occasions: New Year's Eve, Homecoming Weekend, and the like. Widening the option is what is new and much of it has its origin with the online travel agencies. OTAs want to advertise the lowest possible rates. That's what a nonrefundable quote is, the lowest possible rate.

Discounts from the Rack

Folio add-on fees grab the public's attention, but everyone takes rate discounts for granted. And there are far more discounts than enhancements. Understanding discounts begins with an understanding of rack rates.

RACK RATES   All hotels have a rack rate against which other pricing structures are designed. A hotel's rack rate is the quoted, published rate that is theoretically charged to full-paying customers. The rack rate is the retail rate: The rate that appears in room racks. However, just as new cars rarely sell at sticker price, room rates rarely sell at rack rate. At one time, rack rates were distributed on rate cards (see Exhibit 6). Rates are so volatile now that what appears on the Web in the morning may be different by late afternoon.

Although reservationists try to sell at rack rate, travel-wise guests resist. Corporate discounts, affiliation discounts, frequent-travel discounts, nonrefundable purchases, and a host of other offerings erode the hotel's ability to charge rack rate. Indeed, sales executives often proclaim how much off the rack they are offering to close the group sale.

The average daily rate (ADR) computation is the best evidence of the breadth of discounting. Hotels never attain an ADR at the same value as their average rack rate. A lower ADR reflects

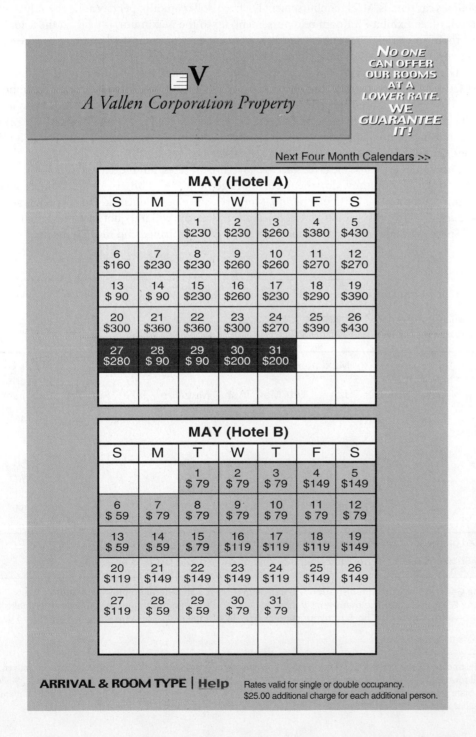

EXHIBIT 6 Rates are so volatile that hotels no longer print rate cards, a one-time staple of hotel marketing (see also Exhibit 10). Rates fluctuate widely based on occupancy forecasts, weather, citywide events, and other variables.

Two actual properties are illustrated here, taken from the Web. Rates are posted on the Web because changes can be made quickly or even taken down altogether. The price spread here tells us they're probably not competing properties. Go to any city and re-create this exhibit.

the vast discounting taking place at the property and throughout the industry. Corporate meetings, tour groups, and special transients head a long list of discounted customers. No way the ADR would ever equal the average of all the rates listed in the rack.

There are occasions when the room sells at a premium to the rack. Special, high-demand dates such as New Year's Eve or Mardi Gras justify selling rooms for rates higher than the rack price. (See Interesting Tidbits at the end of the chapter.) Multiperson occupancy, which is popular among skiers, also triggers a rack premium.

Group negotiations for room blocks far into the future call for rate quotes at higher-than-today's rack price. Inflation needs to be factored in when groups contract for two, three, or ten-years out.

Government per Diems   Federal, state, and local governments reimburse traveling employees up to a fixed dollar amount. This per-diem (per day) cap covers room and meals and sometimes car rentals. Meal reimbursement is a fixed dollar amount per day and generally requires no receipt (see Exhibit 7). Room reimbursement, up to the maximum, is paid on the actual cost of the room so a receipt is required. Since government guests are most reluctant to pay more than the amounts allowed, hotels have discounted rack rates, offering, instead, per-diem rates.

The General Services Administration (GSA) publishes the per-diem rates that apply to most federal employees, including civilian employees, military personnel, and cost-reimbursed federal contractors. Rates are reset annually on October 1.[3] That rate applies throughout continental United States with exceptions for 378 nonstandard cities. So the $94 rate (2012) that applies in Binghamton, up-state New York, is superseded by the $241.00 for New York City. That is if one can find a hotel offering per-diem rates there.

Difficulties arise if some chains accept government rates, but individual franchised properties do not. And if they do, the yield-management decision may reject these heavily discounted rates for that particular period. Moreover, since per-diems, like other special rates, are on a *space-available basis*, some central reservations systems will not quote the rate for confirmation. "Space available" means that rooms are not firmly confirmed and may not be until the date

2012 Per Diem Rates for the State of Utah

Cities not appearing below may be located within a county for which rates are listed.
To determine what county a city is located in, visit the National Association of Counties (NACO), (a non-federal website).

Primary Destination	County	Maximum Lodging, Excluding Taxes								Meals & Incidental Expenses**
		Oct	Nov/Dec	Jan	Feb/Mar	Apr	May/Jun	July	Aug/Sep	
Standard rate	Applies for all* locations without specified rate	77	77	77	77	77	77			46
Moab	Grand County	104	77	77	77	104	104			56
Park City	Summit County	94	94	94	163	94	94			71
Provo	Utah County	81	81	81	81	81	81			51
Salt Lake City	Tooele & County, Salt Lake Counties	96	96	96	96	96	96			61

*Note: Traveler reimbursement is based on the location of the work activities and not the accommodations.

**Meals and incidental Expenses, see Breakdown of M&IE for important information on first and last days of travel.

EXHIBIT 7   On October 1 of each year, the General Services Administration sets per-diem rates for all federal employees including the military. That information is available on the GSA's Web site. The many empty miles of Utah and the minimum number of large cities make that state a much easier illustration than might be with, say Texas. Check out your state at GSA, Washington, D.C.   *Source: GSA, Washington, D.C.*

[3]Adjustments are made as needed. They might be an across-the-board change or they might be a special waiver for a small town that is suddenly housing firefighters during fire season or agents staked out for long time periods. Since the U.S. State Department sets per diems around the world, savvy world travelers often use its site for personal planning: *aoprals.state.gov.*

of arrival when it will be known if space is available. Over all these hurdles, the guest must then prove per-diem entitlement. Without a standardized form or letter or government identification, the individual room clerk makes a discretionary call based on whatever evidence the guest can provide.

The Hotel and Motel Fire Safety Act of 1990 was passed after a federal employee perished in the Dupont Plaza Hotel fire (San Juan, 1986). The law required federal employees to stay only in hotels that complied with certain smoke detector and sprinkler regulations. Complying with this act was costly to the lodging industry. Eventually, nearly 40% of all hotel and motel rooms nationwide complied. Six years later, the federal government dropped the requirement and halted the physical inspection of properties.

Special Cases: Seniors, Military, and Others   Discounted or special rates come in a variety of shapes and sizes. None more pervasive than that granted to AAA (American Automobile Association) members. It is so well known a discount that guests who claim it are almost never asked for membership IDs. That tells us a great deal about room rates.

AARP (American Association of Retired Persons) members, and by extension, anyone classed as a "senior," find rate discounts throughout the industry. Estimates suggest that another person reaches age 50 every 7 seconds! The 2010 census reported that one in every eight Americans is over the age of 65. These are important statistics because seniors represent a significant travel market. If not a completely homogeneous market, they have several characteristics in common. Seniors have money—they are careful with that money—and they like to travel. They search out and find travel bargains because their travel schedules are flexible; they are elastic travelers. Elastic travelers look for value in discounted buffet breakfasts, complimentary newspapers, and free cable television. They opt for hotels where grandchildren can stay free, where menus highlight low-cholesterol and low-sodium items, where bathtubs have grab bars, and where large-digit alarm clocks and telephones are available. Among others, Ramada Inns and Howard Johnson's see seniors as an important market segment.

During and after World War II, uniformed personnel were give special rates as the hotel industry displayed support for the troops. The rationale continued so special discounted rates for anyone (police, fire personnel, nurses) in uniform are SOP across the industry. The definition of uniforms is broad; it includes clergy. The list of those entitled to special rates is limited only by the imagination of the marketing departments. One hotel chain has special rates for teachers, another for students. Almost all allow children in the room with their parents at no charge (see Exhibit 8). The *Worldwide Directory of Holiday Inns* advertises a sports rate for U.S. amateur and professional teams. Special introductory rates are a common tactic for launching a new hotel. Travel clubs from many sources enlist members with the promise of deep hotel discounts during off-peak periods. Discounts are also held out as an appeal to join credit unions and bank clubs.

Hawaii's *kamaʻaina* rate (literally, kama means "person"; aina means "land"; translation is "native-born") is an interesting case of special rates. A class-action suit was filed on the grounds that the 25% discount granted to Hawaiian residents was discriminatory. The argument was denied by the court. The judge found that "offering a discount to certain clients, patrons, or other customers based on an attempt to attract their business is [not] unlawful." The decision is important because it shows the other side of the issue. Rates that are raised to discourage business from certain persons might well be judged as discriminatory. Rates that are lowered to attract certain persons are viewed quite differently.

Discounts should be aimed at the development of new markets and should be phased out as that market stabilizes. It doesn't work that way in practice. Over time, special marketing rates have been introduced and tested only to become part of the established rate structure. So the list of room-rate discounts grows. Among them are discounted rates for employees.

Employee Courtesy Rates   Most hotel companies extend special, in-chain rates to staff members traveling on personal business. In fact, large chains identify employees as an actual market segment. Substantial discounts from the hotel's minimum rate plus upgrades whenever possible are very attractive fringe benefits. Special rates are always provided on a space-available basis. Employee-guests are accepted only if rooms are vacant when they present themselves. Some chains allow reservations a few weeks before arrival if projected occupancy is low. The Federal Deficit Reduction Law of 1984 reinforced this by taxing the employee for the value of a free room if paying guests were turned away. (Imagine policing that!)

A Historic View of an Early Form of Rate Cutting

Controversy is growing among American hotelmen about the family-rate plan method of basing hotel rates upon occupancy by adults only. Children of 14 years or less, accompanying their parents, are not charged for occupancy of rooms with their parents. For example, one adult and a child are charged a single rate for the double occupancy of the room. Two adults and children are charged a double rate for a room, or two single rates if two rooms are engaged. There are various other modifications of the plan, but fundamentally it represents complimentary accommodation of children below a certain age level.

At least three leading hotel chains have adopted the plan and report great success from the higher occupancy attributable to it. Why, then, the controversy? Certainly when hotel chains of the stature of the Statler, Eppley, and Pick chains favor the family-rate plan, it is well on its way to becoming a standard practice for most other hotels in the country.

The controversy rests on the issue of whether this plan is a form of rate cutting—the most disagreeable word in the hotelman's language. In this era of downward adjustment from high wartime levels of occupancy, naturally hotelmen are sensitive to any indirect methods of reducing rates. No hotelman wishes to see any kind of repetition of the rate-cutting practices of the 1930s.

In an attempt to evaluate the plan in its rate-cutting connotation, we believe that most hotelmen would be hard-pressed to define a rate cut in exact terms. For example, is the commercial rate to traveling men a type of rate reduction? Does a convention rate involve a hidden discount? We can remember the time when it was standard practice to compliment the wife of a traveling man, when a week's stay at a hotel resulted in having the seventh day free of charge, and when the armed forces, clergy, and diplomats got lower rates.

In our opinion, rate cutting is practiced only when hotels depart from their *regular* prices and tariff schedules in order to secure patronage from prospects who are openly shopping for the best deal in room rates. If, therefore, it is regular practice for hotels to have special rates for group business, this does not seem to represent rate cutting; and the same principle should apply to the family-rate plan. If this plan becomes widely adopted—as seems very likely—then it falls into the category of any other special type of rate for special business.

In some respects the plan is a form of *pricing accommodations by rooms instead of by persons*. In many resort hotels a room is rated regardless of its occupancy by one or two persons, and a similar concept is used in apartments and apartment hotels.

Although the arguments for or against the family-rate plan must be decided by hotelmen themselves, a strong point in favor of the plan is found in its adoption by other vendors of public service—the railroads and airlines. Family rates, weekday rates, seasonal rates, special-type carrier rates, and so on have been in vogue for several years. If the hotels adopt the family-rate plan, it seems that they will be falling into line with a national trend rather than venturing alone into a new and untried experiment in good public relations.

EXHIBIT 8 The family rate (ca. 1958) was based on the sale of the room, not on the number of its occupants. So it was viewed by many as an unacceptable form of "rate cutting, the most disagreeable word in the hotelman's language." Note the names of major hotel companies that no longer exist, Eppley, Pick, and Statler. *Source: The Horwath Hotel Accountant.*

Comps and discounted rooms are inexpensive ways for chains to supplement employee-benefits packages. Because these rooms are provided on a space-available basis, there is little cost associated, aside from housekeeping, with providing this perk. The benefits are increased morale and motivation among staffers. Some chains request visiting employees to fill out evaluation forms complete with comments and suggestions for improvement. This can be an important supplement to the company's regular secret-shopper program.

AUCTIONING Auctioning, a new form of discounting, has gained popularity with adventurous travelers. Auctioning begins when hotels, airlines, and rental-car agencies enter a product-available database marketed directly to the traveler through Web technology (see Exhibit 9). The guest decides where to travel and the dates and times to go, plus any other specs such as a four-star property, a midsized car, and so on. Next comes the gutsy part: Entering the amount that the potential traveler is willing to pay.

When the participating companies (hotel, airline, rental-car agency) accept the bid, the deal is on. Guests-to-be never know until the offer is accepted which airline, which hotel, or

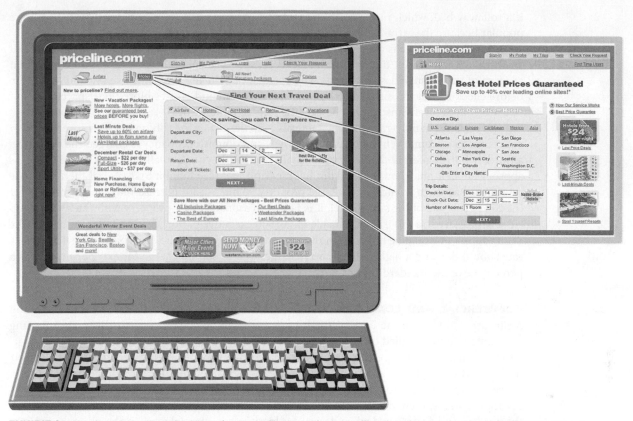

EXHIBIT 9 Third-party intermediaries such as priceline. com began selling hotel rooms on the Web in 1998. They have become major players in the sale of hotel rooms. Auctioning rooms is one of their services. Adventurous guests bid for accommodations and guarantee the bid with an up-front credit card. When and if some hotel accepts the bid, the room is booked and the deal is closed. Airlines and car-rental agencies also participate. *Courtesy of priceline.com, Stanford, Connecticut.*

which auto agency has agreed to the terms. If the bid is rejected, a time limit can be placed on the offer to await a more favorable response over the next few days.

In recent years, companies such as priceline.com (see Exhibit 9), Bid4Travel, LuxuryLink.com, and skyauction.com, among others, have taken inventory auctioning to new levels. By matching millions of potential buyers with millions of vacant rooms, travel-auction companies have created another market for the hotel industry. They search out deals for these most elastic consumers. These are travelers who, for very deep discounts, agree to non-prime-time flight schedules, less popular travel dates, and unknown destination hotels. To capture this new and growing market, hotels are discounting rates by still another means.

DOUBLE OCCUPANCY   Double occupancy refers to a second guest in the room. At one time, all hotels charged more, although not twice the single rate, for the second occupant. Today, many properties have only one rate for both single and double occupancy. The major costs (debt service, taxes, and depreciation) of a hotel room are fixed. Having a second occupant adds relatively few incremental costs in linen, soap, and tissue, but adds potential income from restaurants and bars. As such, one charge for both single and double occupancy has gained favor.

Convention rates are almost always negotiated with double occupancy at no extra charge. The more persons in the hotel, the more the hotel benefits from sales in other departments, but especially casinos, where the one-rate idea first caught on. There is a similar rational for suites. Rates are based on the number of rooms that comprise the suite, not the number of guests who occupy it. The room, not the guest, is the unit of pricing.

Price is a critical issue in package plans and tour bookings where double occupancy is the norm. Sales execs can shave rates closely because the second occupant represents so small an additional expense. The incremental cost is almost unnoticed if the extra person(s) share existing beds. That is what made family-plan rates attractive (see Exhibit 8). An extra charge is levied if a rollaway bed, which requires additional handling and linen, is required. All-suite hotels are popular because the extra bed is in the room, permanently available as a sofa.

Used rollaway beds are returned to the linen room. Linens are changed there and the bed is stored for future use. In contrast, housekeepers must inspect the permanent sofa beds that are part of the all-suite design. Guests who use that bed during their stay usually fold it back up before checking out. Closing it helps straighten the room and creates more floor space. Without housekeeping's careful inspection, new guests find an unmade bed.

Unless the family-rate plan is applicable, a charge is generally made for more than two occupants to a room. Even in hotels where single and double occupancy is charged the same rate, a third or fourth guest is charged extra, usually a small flat fee. A small flat fee of $20–$30 seems appropriate in a small house with a limited range of rates (see Exhibit 6). Not so if there is a wide rate spread as there would be in a large property. While a $20 increase may be appropriate for the $75–$100 rate of the small hotel, it is far less reasonable for a property with rates that go up from $100. An extra $20 isn't reasonable for a $500 executive parlor. Twenty dollars is 20% on the $100 room, but would be only 4% on the higher-priced room. That seems backward: The higher rate should demand a higher third-party charge. Best to set the charge for extra occupants as a percentage of the standard room charge.

COMMERCIAL AND CORPORATE RATES   Hotels have extended special rates to traveling businesspersons since the days of the itinerant "drummers." They do so still today, granting discounted rates, so-called commercial rates, to the traveling salesperson who returns on a regular cycle. Small hotels, especially, make such arrangements with small commercial clients. Their understanding might depend on five or ten room-nights per year for a manufacturer's rep or a no-room commitment to a salesperson traveling on a personal expense account. Unlike large, corporate clients, there usually is no official contract. The commercial rate is honored whether the house is full or not. And when demand is low, the commercial guest is always upgraded. It is a rare occasion, indeed, for a hotel to ever walk a commercial guest.

Commercial and *corporate rates* are discussed separately here, but the terms are often interchanged. Here, corporate rates refer to the synergy between large businesses and large hotel chains. Corporations have offices and plants worldwide; hotel chains have properties worldwide. Corporate employees at all levels (management, personnel, sales, engineering, accounting) travel in vast numbers. They visit the very countries and cities in which the hotel chains operate. It is but a short step to arrange special (discounted) rates between the two parties. By guaranteeing a certain number of room-nights per year, the corporation negotiates a better rate, a corporate rate, from the hotel chain.

Reducing room rates is only part of the discount. Reducing the number of rooms needed to close the deal is a more subtle form, a deeper discount. Not many years ago, corporate rates required a commitment of 1,000 room-nights per year. Recent figures place the level as low as 50 rooms. The number falls and rebounds with the economy, but a more ominous explanation is the appearance of aggressive third-party negotiators. Businesses that are too small to negotiate on their own get under a broader umbrella, which negotiates with hotels, airlines, and car-rental companies. Hotels have met this increased leverage by bypassing the consolidators and travel agencies and reaching out directly to small businesses. Big businesses have enough clot within themselves.

Technology has altered the corporate discount picture as well. In the past, major corporations negotiated favorable rates by promising a large annual room volume with a given chain. However, no one really counted, and room volume (actual or anticipated) was never verified. The improved capability of central reservations systems now allows hotel chains to accurately track a corporation's total room volume across the whole chain. Corporate room bookings at both franchised and parent properties are combined and counted. Renaissance Hotels, for example, produces quarterly reports for more than 1,800 of its major corporate accounts. These reports take the guesswork out of room-rate negotiations and give both the hotel chain and the corporation an accurate picture of utilized volume. The actual number of rooms occupied is less important with a different pricing agreement, dynamic pricing.

Negotiated Rates and Dynamic Pricing   The economic downturn of 2008 dropped rates considerably. Negotiated rates—the corporate rates discussed in the previous paragraphs—looked less appealing then. Some hotels began offering and some business began considering dynamic pricing. *Dynamic pricing* is a discount off the hotel's *best-available* rate whereas negotiated rates are a firm, known value. So dynamic pricing has not been widely accepted. The company/buyer is concerned that when rates move up again, a discount off the *best available* rate will be higher than the fixed corporate rate that was or could be negotiated.

Dynamic pricing is gaining favor in secondary cities and among smaller companies that may not be able to meet the minimum number of room-nights required by negotiated, corporate rates. The plus side is easier negotiations. Once a deal is struck—some percent off the best-available rate—annual meetings, negotiations, and request for proposals (RFP) are no longer needed. Such and such percent off the best available rate requires no new negotiations each year. Implicit, of course, is that the front desk will know and will book company rooms at the reduced rate. Companies are skeptical so they now reserve rooms at the hotel's lowest rate so long as it is below the negotiated rate and hold on to the negotiated rate for the eventual increase in room rates across the industry.

Most agreements contain penalty clauses if the hotel is not in rate compliance. If it is not, and it often isn't, the cause usually rests with the hotel's failure to load rates correctly. The major weakness lies in getting accurate rates into the several GDSs, global distribution systems. Getting that job done is the industry's responsibility; auditing the imput at least quarterly is the buyer's responsibility. (There are special companies that audit rates.) Although hotels get blamed for dropping rates, the real cause might lie with the initial negotiations. If the business client has access to only a small percentage of the hotel's standard-rate rooms, and if those rooms are often committed to group bookings, the likelihood of the client finding an available room is greatly reduced.

COMPS AND FAM TRIPS   One would think that hotel managers would be reluctant to give away (to comp) their product. But rooms are so perishable and the cost of housing a nonpaying occupant so low that comps are used readily as business promotions, as charitable giveaways, and as perks. It is not a free-for-all; comps are used judiciously for legitimate business purposes.

By custom, complimentary rates have always been extended to other hoteliers. The courtesy is reciprocated, resulting in an industrywide fringe benefit for owners and senior managers. Such comps rarely include food or beverage, which are high-cost items, even in American-plan hotels.

Travel agents and travel writers usually get free accommodations while they are on fam (familiarization) trips. At other times, a special 50% discount rate is extended except during high occupancy periods. Airline deregulation permitted the carriers to comp fam trips. They have now joined the hotel industry in developing site inspection tours for the travel industry.

Site inspections are also made by association executives, who are considering the property as a possible meeting place. Site visits are comped even though some association executives have been known to abuse the industry standard by using site inspection opportunities to vacation with their families.[4] Comp rooms are always included as part of a group's meeting package; its an acceptable and standard business practice.

Comps are given to famous persons whose presence have publicity value. Comps are used as promotional tools in connection with contests in which the winners receive so many days of free accommodations. In casinos, comps extend to rooms, food, beverage, and even airfare from the player's home. Parking is so difficult in Atlantic City that free parking is part of the high-roller's comp package. After all, in a brief period of table play, "a whale" can lose many times the cost of these promotions, which on close inspection proves to be relatively inexpensive.

Casino hotels have the most comps; it is part of the casino mystic. Where appropriate, the casino may charge the comp to other departments such as sales and marketing or entertainment. Departmental managers everywhere have accountability, and the dollar amount of comps is part of their departmental budgets.

---

[4]Now euphemistically called "buyer-education trips," in recognition of the need to upgrade the image and downgrade the frequency of free weekends with friends in tow that often passed as fam trips.

The Role of the Room Rate

SEASONAL AND WEATHER-RELATED RATES   In-season, off-season, and shoulder rates are quoted by most resort hotels. Incremental increases and decreases come and go as the season approaches and wanes (see Exhibit 10). The poor weekend occupancy of urban hotels has forced them to offer a seasonal rate of sorts—discounted weekend rates.

Resort communities are able to handle large number of tourists during peak demand. This means excess capacity during both the low and shoulder seasons. So rates are discounted then. It is the only alternative to what most resorts once did: Close completely during off-season. This practice changed many years ago. Today, very few resort properties actually close for the off-season. Reopening expenses, finding, training and hiring new staff, and paying a skeleton crew to maintain the closed facility changed the economics of closing the property. Instead, resorts remain open, steeply discounting rooms to value-conscious guests and competing fiercely for group business.

Weather-related discounts add another tier to the solicitation of both group business and social guests. Promising discounts for bad weather helps reduce the length of the low or shoulder season at some resorts. Rate discounts or other credits are offered to guests for each day it rains, stays unseasonably cool, fails to snow, or whatever else is appropriate. This is risky business, and resorts make the offer reluctantly. Several hotels are currently re testing it so others may follow.

▣V

A Vallen Corporation Property

The Lazy Λee

A Member of the
VALLEN FAMILY OF HOTELS

"Rate Sheet for This Year"

The ranch offers a variety of accommodations.
No two rooms are the same.
Rates are based on your selection and on the calendar.

Rooms in the Ranch House

Oct 1–Dec 8	$429	April 28–May 26	$495
Dec 9–25	$305	May 27–Sept 7	$205
Dec 26–31	$575	Sept 8–Dec 7	$495
Jan 1–Feb 14	$550	Dec 8–25	$290
Feb 15–April 27	$625	Dec 26–31	$575

Family and Group Accommodations in the Bunk Houses
(Each unit has a full-kitchen, laundry, and fireplace.)

	1-Bedroom	2-Bedroom	3-Bedroom	4-Bedroom
Oct 1–Dec 8	$515	$675	$775	$1195
Dec 9–25	$365	$480	$550	$749
Dec 26–31	$690	$902	$1040	$1450
Jan 1–Feb 14	$660	$865	$995	$1095
Feb 15–April 27	$750	$985	$1130	$1245
April 28–May 26	$595	$780	$895	$985
May 27–Sept 7	$245	$320	$370	$405
Sept 8–Dec 7	$595	$780	$900	$990
Dec 8–25	$350	$455	$525	$575
Dec 26–31	$690	$905	$1040	$1145

Rates subject to tax and daily service charges.

For reservations call	1-800-Vallen Hotels

EXHIBIT 10   Rate sheets like this one are rare in today's fast-changing rate environment. The exhibit illustrates the range of rates based on two criteria: the accommodations selected and the time of the year. High season in the desert is Christmas and the two months between mid-February and mid-April.

Discounts on Room Rates and Group Bookings

...   For every night paid at regular rate, the next night is _____
       (Free, 50% off, other)

...   Opting out of housekeeping services reduces the rate by $ _____ per night
       (Estimated savings to the hotel $20–$25)

...   _____ Percentage discount on all spa services

...   Limousine transfer to the airport or dock

...   Free: Internet fees/ breakfasts/ newspapers/ shoe shines

...   Priority access at the door for taxicabs

...   Group rates begin at _____ persons
       (less than the standard 20 rooms)

...   _____ Percentage discount on audiovisual rentals

...   Complimentary rooms for every _____ rooms booked by the group
       (50 rooms is the usual number)

...   Meeting planner earn personal points for group business*

...   First _____ guests booking from this website get a _____% discount
       (Each hotel would insert its own numbers)

...   Temperature falls below/ rises above _____ and the rate is reduced by _____
       (Each hotel needs to input its own values)

...   Guests receive a $ _____ voucher to be used for _____
       (Each hotel sets a value for shopping, tattoo, theater, etc.)

...   Increased attrition for groups

---

* Personal rewards to meeting planners raise questions of ethics.

EXHIBIT 11 These are actual advertised rate discounts taken from both the general and the trade press during the downturn between 2009 and 2010.

One resort already offers a "temperature guarantee" package that has been insured through Lloyd's of London.

OTHER DISCOUNTS OFF THE RACK Fighting for new business or retaining old customers taxes the imagination of hoteliers. Only after new ideas have been introduced and tested is it evident whether it was or wasn't a good move. Some that have been tested are outlined in Exhibit 11.

It is not easy to create special discounts with a positive net result. One idea is a reverse discount. Some upscale chains are holding rates steady but adding perks for guests who actually pay full rack rate. These include amenities such as free cellular telephone, free laundry and dry cleaning, and limousine service to the airport and nearby shopping centers. Even free meals, which have a smaller profit margin than rooms, have been included. Several high-end properties allow full rack-rate guests to extended check-out until 6 PM. One chain upgrades all rack-rate guests to deluxe accommodations. Like all discounts, these appear and disappear as occupancy and RevPar fluctuate.

TIME AS A FACTOR IN RATES

Arrival and departure dates are the main time measures of a guest's stay. But they are only part of the basis for the room charge. Weight must also be given to the number of hours of occupancy.

Arrival Time

The date and time of arrival appears on the registration card and the folio put there by the property management system. While the actual dates of arrival and departure are the primary drivers for establishing room charges, the number of hours of occupancy is receiving more attention from managers pressed for additional revenues.

CHECK-OUT TIME: 1 PM

We would like to ask your cooperation in checking out by 1 PM so that we may accommodate travelers who are beginning their stay. If you require additional time, you may request a two-hour grace period (until 3 PM) from the assistant manager or the front-office manager. If you wish to check out later, we regret that there must be a $12-per-hour charge, from 3 until 5 PM, for this added service. An additional half-day rate will be charged to guests who delay their departure until between 5 PM and 8 PM. After 8 PM, a full-day rate will be charged. Of course, you are then welcome to remain until the following afternoon at 1 PM.

As an incoming guest, your comfort and convenience depend on these stipulations. We hope you will visit again soon.

☐V
A Vallen Corporation Property

EXHIBIT 12   Reminders like this permanent one left in the guest room are supplemented during periods of tight occupancy with messages left on the pillow by the housekeeper and by telephone calls to the room from the assistant manager, the concierge, or the desk. A similar statement often appears on the rooming slip; see Exhibit 19.

The arrival time at an American-plan hotel, where meals taken are part of the rate, has always been critical. So much so that American-plan arrivals are flagged with special meal codes. The hour of arrival at a European-plan hotel is less critical, but cannot be ignored. How, for example, should a 1:00 AM arrival be billed; for a full night? Once that is decided, move that arrival up by three-hour increments and ask about 4:00 AM arrivals and 7:00 AM arrivals. Although very late arrivals are unusual exceptions, management must set policy. Somewhere in the early morning hours (5 to 7 AM) comes the break between charging for the night just passed and levying the first charge for the day just starting.

Most hotels have established check-in hours, but enforcing them seems petty. It means keeping a guest in the lobby even if there are plenty of vacant rooms. So advertising check-in hours and implementing them are two different decisions. The termination point of a night's lodging is more controllable, so every hotel posts an official check-out hour, the departure time (see Exhibit 12).

Departure Time

Check-in and check-out hours are eased or enforced as occupancies fall or rise. There are no governing laws. Each hotel sets its own check-out hour. The proper hour is a balance between the guest's need to complete his or her business and the hotel's need to clean and prepare the room for the next patron.

Seasoned travelers are well aware that check-out extensions are granted by the room clerk if occupancy is light. Under current billing practices, the effort should be made cheerfully whenever the request can be accommodated. When anticipated arrivals require enforcement of the check-out hour, luggage of the forced-out guests is stored in the checkroom of the bells.

Resorts are under more pressure than commercial hotels to expedite check-outs. Vacationing guests try to squeeze the most from their holiday time. American-plan houses usually allow the guest to remain through the luncheon hour and a reasonable time thereafter if the meal is part of the rate. Some 90% of the resorts surveyed in an AH&LA study identified their check-out hour to be between noon and 2 PM, in contrast to the 11 AM through 1 PM range used by transient hotels. These same properties assigned rooms to new arrivals on a "when-available" basis.

Special techniques in addition to that shown in Exhibit 12 have been tried to move the guest along. On the night before departure, the room clerk, the assistant manager, or the concierge calls the room to chat and remind the guest of tomorrow's departure. It is far less personal, but this task could be assigned to a computer. A more personal touch is a note of farewell left by the room attendant who turns down the bed the night before. If there is no turn-down service, the notice is left by the regular housekeeper.

The 24-Hour Stay

Some hotels are experimenting with true 24-hour stays. There is no official check-in time and no posted check-out hour. Rather, guests identify estimated arrival and departure times when the reservation is made. They are then welcome to stay at the hotel an entire 24-hour period for one set room rate.

Guests opting for the 24-hour stay pay rack rate; there are no discounted packages under this plan. Rate/time programs such as these are most often found at airport properties, where arrival and departure times coincide with flight schedules. A hotel that makes special accommodations like these develops a favorable reputation and eventually earns a higher market share.

It makes sense to view these 24-hour day programs as marketing tools. They drive higher rates and hopefully attract unique customer segments who appreciate the unusual policies. Initially, these programs are viewed as marketing "gimmicks," but so are any policies that differentiate a hotel from its competitor. Only time will tell if unique offerings usher in a new era of room pricing.

Day Rates

Special rates exist for stays of less than overnight. These are called *part-day rates, day rates*, or sometimes *use rates*. Day-rate guests arrive and depart on the same day. They boost the ADR and make possible an occupancy of greater than 100%.[5] Nevertheless, the industry has not fully exploited the possibilities. Sales of use rates could be marketed to suburban shoppers, day tourists, and to small, brief meetings. Airport properties have been the only hotel group to promote their locations as central, one-day-meeting places.

A new day-rate market is possible. Motels near campsites and along the roadways should attract campers as a wayside stop during the day. A hot shower, an afternoon by the pool, and a change of pace from the vehicle are great appeals when coupled with a low day rate.

Check-in time is often early morning. Corporate guests prefer to start their meetings early, and truck drivers like to get off the highway before the 7–8 AM rush hour. If clean rooms remain unsold from the previous night, there is little reason to refuse day-rate guests early access to the rooms. Breakfasts or room-service coffee add a revenue bonus.

Since rooms sold for day use only are serviced and made available again for the usual overnight occupancy, the schedule of the housekeeping staff has a great deal to do with the check-out hour. If there are no swing-shift room attendants, the day rate must end early enough to allow servicing by the day shift. On the other hand, low occupancy would allow a day-rate sale even late in the day. Nothing is lost if an additional empty room remains unmade overnight.

There are no guidelines for the day-rate charge. Some purists suggest that it must be half the standard rack rate. Others appreciate the extra revenue and are willing to charge whatever seems appropriate. Corporate hotels must remember that their day-rate rooms compete with their convention and meeting facilities that sell for two or three times the day-rate room. A small group of executives might prefer meeting in a day-rate suite with its attached bathroom and access to room service rather than the larger impersonal, more costly, convention meeting room.

Incentive Rates

Incentive rates have been tested as both a convenience to the guest and as a means of expediting check-outs. First, the check-out period for a normal day's charge would be established—say, between 11 AM and 1 PM. Guests who leave earlier than 11 are charged less than the standard

---

[5]One resort in the Mariana Islands has air service of both arrivals and departures in the early morning hours. Guests leave the hotel about 1:30 AM to meet the flight, and new arrivals check in about 3:30 AM. Both groups are charged for the night so occupancy can exceed 100% twice per week.

Guest	Rate Paid	March 15th Arrival	March 16th Departure	Total Hours Occupied
1	$225.00	1 AM (March 16)	Until 6 AM	5
2	225.00	2 PM	Until 11 AM	21
3	225.00	8 AM	Until 3 PM	31

EXHIBIT 13 Hoteliers are growing more sensitive to rates based on time as well as rate's traditional basis of overnight. Three guests pay the same room rate although their occupancy ranges from 5 to 31 hours! Guest #1 uses the room between connecting flights. Guest #2 adheres to the hotel's check-in and check-out hours. Guest #3 takes advantage of low occupancy to check in early and check out late.

rate; those who leave later are charged more. Like so many rate ideas, incentive rates have not caught on. Flexible charges require a whole new look at the unit of service, shifting from the more traditional measure to smaller time blocks. Hotels have yet to give weight to time as a factor in rate. Arrival and departure times establish broad parameters at best. It may be that increasing speeds of transportation will translate into new hotel rates with the hour being the basic unit of charge. Under current practices, a stay of several hours can cost as much as a full-day's stay (see Exhibit 13).

A popular journalist once observed facetiously that the length of time one spends in a hotel room is inversely proportional to the quality of the room. When one arrives at, say, 1 AM and needs to get some rest for a 7 AM flight the next morning, the room will be lavish—there will be vases of roses, trays of food and drink, soft music, a Jacuzzi tub, and candlelight. Conversely, when one has no time commitments and has all day to spend in the hotel, the assignment is invariably an establishment with no restaurant or lobby, fuzzy TV reception, and a drained swimming pool!

The American Plan Day

Meals are part of the American plan (AP) rate, as they are with the modified American plan (MAP). Accurate billing requires an accurate record of arrival and departure times as they impact on meals taken. Arrivals are registered with a meal code reflecting the check-in time. For example, a guest arriving at 3 PM would be coded with arriving after lunch but before dinner.

A complete AP stay technically involves enough meals on the final day to make up for the meals missed on the arriving day. A guest arriving before dinner would be expected to depart the next day, or many days later, after lunch. Two meals, breakfast and lunch, on the departing day complete the full AP charge, since one meal, dinner, was taken on the arriving day. MAP counts meals in the same manner, except that lunch is ignored.

Guests who take more than the three meals per day pay for the extra at menu prices, or sometimes below. Sometimes, guests who miss a meal are not charged. That is why it is very important to have the total AP rate fairly distributed between the room portion and the meal portion. Meal rates are set and are standardized for everyone. Higher AP rates must reflect better rooms, since all the guests are entitled to the same menu.

AP and MAP hotels have a special charge called *tray service*. It is levied on meals taken through room service. Room service in European-plan hotels typically contains inflated prices as a means of recovering the extra service. Menu charges are greater than the usual restaurant prices when the food is delivered to the room. This device is not available to the American plan hotel because meals being delivered to the room are not priced separately. Instead, a flat charge is levied as a tray service charge.

DETERMINING THE "PROPER" ROOM RATE

Because a sound room-rate structure is fundamental to a profitable hotel operation, every manager is sooner or later faced with the question of what is the proper room charge. Room rates reflect markets and costs, investments and rates of return, supply and demand, accommodations and competition, and, not least of all, the quality of management. Determining the proper room rate is a complicated undertaking. Heaped upon that difficulty is the strategy that the hotel must adopt vis-à-vis its competitors. Because even if the "right" rates were known for certain, room-rate strategy might involve charging a different figure altogether. Strategy starts with and involves competition, the economy, the age of the property, and its location.

Room-rate decisions have two major components. First, they must be large enough to cover costs and provide a fair return on invested capital. Second, they must be reasonable enough to attract and retain the clientele to whom the operation is being marketed. The former suggests a relatively objective, structured approach to cover costs and investments. The latter is more subjective. There is little sense in charging a rate less than what is needed to meet the first objective. There is little chance of getting a rate more than the competitive ceiling established by the second limitation.

Yield management, the balancing of occupancy and rate, has emerged as the number one component of rate making. Yield management has attracted attention because it introduces two new concepts to room pricing. (1) The industry is selling rooms by an inventory control system, and (2) the pricing strategy considers the customer's ability and willingness to pay. These ideas, especially that of price sensitivity, are of recent origin when viewed across the long history of lodging.

In years past, the rate structure was built around internal cost considerations. Yield management has not eliminated that focus. Important as customers are, they are not the only component of price. Cost recovery and investment returns, depreciation and interest, taxes, zoning restrictions, and land costs are outside the hotel–guest relationship but not external to the room charge.

The more traditional components of rate deal with recovering costs, both operating and capital. They deal with profits and break-even projections. Mixed into the equation are competition, price elasticity, and rate cutting. And the average daily rate earned by the hotel is also determined by the ability of a single reservationist or a room clerk determined to sell up.

So a hotel's room rates are derived from a mix of objective measures and subjective values. Expressing room rates numerically gives the appearance of validity, but when the origins of these numbers are best-guess estimates, the results must be viewed with some measure of skepticism.

Facts and suppositions are combined when hotel managers calculate the required room rate. As useful and respected as the following mathematical formulas may be, they are still merely an indication of the final rate. Fine-tuning the formula, establishing corporate and double occupancy prices, and adjusting the rate according to the whims of the community and the marketplace are still the role of management. That is the strategy of setting rates.

The Hubbart Room-Rate Formula

The Hubbart formula, which was created in the 1950s, offers a standardized approach to calculating room rates. The computation is based on the costs of operating the enterprise, not the price sensitivity of the guests. The computation focuses on the room rate, not the rate strategy. The average rate, says the formula, should pay all expenses and leave something for the investor. Valid enough—a business that cannot do this is short-lived.

Exhibit 14A illustrates the mechanics of the formula. Estimated expenses are itemized and totaled. These include operational expenses by departments ($1,102,800 in the illustration), realty costs ($273,000), and depreciation ($294,750). To these expenses is added a reasonable return on the present fair value of the property: land, building, and furnishings ($414,000). From the total expense package ($2,084,550) are subtracted incomes from all sources other than room sales ($139,200). This difference ($1,945,350) represents the annual amount to be realized from room sales.

Next (continuing with Exhibit 14B), an estimate of the number of rooms to be sold annually is computed. Dividing the number of estimated rooms (22,484) to be sold annually into the estimated dollars ($1,945,350) needed to cover costs and a fair return produces the average rate to be charged ($86.52).

SHORTCOMINGS OF THE FORMULA   Like many forecasts, the Hubbart room-rate formula is only as accurate as the assumptions on which it was projected. Several assumptions come immediately to mind. (1) What percentage is "reasonable" as a fair return on investment? (2) What

---

The Hubbart Room-Rate Formula

Operating Expenses

Rooms department	$467,400	
Telecommunications	60,900	
Administrative and general	91,200	
Payroll taxes and employee benefits	178,200	
Marketing, advertising, and promotion	109,800	
Utility costs	138,900	
Property operation, maintenance, and engineering	56,400	
Total operating expenses		$1,102,800

Taxes, Insurance, and Leases

Real estate and personal property taxes	67,200	
Franchise taxes and fees	112,200	
Insurance on building and contents	37,200	
Leased equipment	56,400	
Total taxes, insurance, and leases		$ 273,000

Depreciation (Standard Rates on Present Fair Value)

	Value	Rate	
Building	$_____ at	%	168,750
Furniture, fixtures, and equipment	$_____ at	%	126,000
Total depreciation			$ 294,750

Reasonable Return on Present Fair Value of Property

	Value	Rate	
Land	$_____ at	%	
Building	$_____ at	%	
Furniture, fixtures, and equipment	$_____ at	%	
Total fair return			$ 414,000
Total			$2,084,550

Deduct—Credits from Sources Other than Rooms

Income from store rentals	14,850	
Profits from food and beverage operations	131,400	
(if loss, subtract from this group)		
Net income from other operated departments	(7,050)	
and miscellaneous income (loss)		
Total credits from sources other than rooms		$ 139,200
Amount to be realized from guest-room sales to cover costs and		$1,945,350
a reasonable return on present fair value of property		

EXHIBIT 14A The Hubbart Room-Rate Formula, which was introduced in 1952, appears to be a series of simple mathematical steps. (That's true for the illustration, but it takes a great deal of work to get these values.) Incomes from nonroom sources (the lower quarter of the page) reduce total operating expenses as illustrated. The remaining expenses plus profits (called a "Reasonable Return on Present Fair Value of Property") are to be recovered by room income. Exhibit 14B explains the rate and occupancy needed to generate that room income.

occupancy rate appears most attainable? (3) What are the bases of the cost projections for payroll, utilities, and administration and general? And so begins a long list of questions.

The formula leaves the rooms department with the final burden after profits and losses from other departments. But inefficiencies in other departments should not be covered by a high, noncompetitive room rate. Neither should unusual profits in other departments be a basis for charging room rates below what the market will bring.

There is some justification in having rooms subsidize low banquet prices if these low prices result in large convention bookings of guest rooms. (Incidentally, this is one reason why the food and banquet department should not be leased as a concession.) Similar justifications could be found for using room rates to cover any expense, whether dining-room repairs, maintenance, or advertising costs. The trade-off is wise if these expenditures produce enough other business to offset lost room revenues resulting from poorly conceived room rates.

Additional shortcomings become apparent as the formula is studied. Among them is the projected number of rooms sold. This estimate of rooms sold is actually based on the very rate being computed. How can a hotel estimate the number of rooms it will sell before first knowing

1. Amount to be realized from guest-room sales to cover costs and a reasonable return on present fair value of property (from part A)		$1,945,350
2. Number of guest rooms available for rental		88
3. Number of available rooms on annual basis (item 2 multiplied by 365)	100%	32,120
4. Less: allowance for average vacancies	30%	9,636
5. Number of rooms to be occupied at estimated average occupancy	70%	22,484
6. Average daily rate per occupied room required to cover costs and a reasonable return on present fair value (Item 1 divided by Item 5)		$ 86.52

EXHIBIT 14B   As with Exhibit 14A, the mathematical steps are easy to make; the assumptions much less so. Here occupancy is projected based on a room rate that is determined, in part, by that very occupancy. The illustration is based on an 88-room, full-service resort.   *Courtesy of the American Hotel & Lodging Association, Washington, D.C. and used here with the Association's permission.*

the average rate for which it will sell each room? Yet that is exactly what the Hubbart formula requires! The ADR is also dependent on the percent of double occupancy. Yet the increased income from double occupancy, if any, is not a component of the formula.

The average rate that is computed ($86.52) is not the *one* actual rate used by the hotel. Hotels use a number of rate classes, with various proportions of the total number of rooms assigned to each classification (see Exhibit 10). The actual average rate will be a weighted average of the rooms occupied. Thus, the average rate reflects the range of accommodations offered and the guest's purchase of them, based, in part, on nearby competition.

SQUARE FOOT CALCULATIONS   A square footage calculation can supplement the Hubbart room-rate formula, although neither is in widespread use. Hubbart makes no distinction between rooms whereas the square foot calculation recognizes size. More expensive guest rooms are almost always larger than standard rooms at the same property. Therefore, rather than relying only on Hubbart, which equates one room to another, this variation calculates the rate on a per-square-foot basis.

To illustrate, assume that the small, full-service resort hotel presented in Exhibit 14 has a total of 27,250 square feet of space in its 88 guest rooms. With occupancy of 70%, there would be an average of 19,075 square feet sold per day. With an annual required return of $1,945,350, the daily required return is $5,329.73 (i.e., $1,945,350 divided by 365 days). Therefore, each square foot of rented room space must generate $0.27941 per day ($5,329.73 divided by 19,075 square feet sold per day) or almost 28 cents in daily revenue. As a result, a 300-square-foot room would sell for $83.82 (300 square feet times $0.28) and a 450-square-foot room would sell for $125.73. (Figures would be rounded, of course.) Assuming that the hotel sells all room types in equal ratios to the number of rooms available in each type, this square foot calculation offers another means for determining rates.

The Building Cost Rate Formula

Time and repetition have created an industry truism. It says that rates can be determined by a simple rule of thumb. The building cost rate formula bases room rates on construction costs. So the average room rate is easily computed at $1 per $1,000 of construction costs. Assume a 200-room hotel costs $20 million including land and land development, as well as the building and public space but excluding furniture, fixtures, and equipment. According to this formula, the average rate should be $100. That is $20,000,000 ÷ 200 rooms ÷ $1,000 (the rule) = $100. This formula, like Hubbart, makes no distinction between room types, sizes, or accouterments. It merely states that the ADR, the *average* daily rate, should be $1 per $1,000 in construction costs.

Despite some very radical changes throughout the years, the rule is still quoted on the theory that rising construction costs are matched by rising room rates. Higher construction costs are due, in part, to larger room sizes, as well as higher costs of building materials and labor. This generation of rooms is 100–200% larger than rooms of 50 years ago.

Cost of construction includes the cost of land and its improvements as well as the type of construction, the height of the building, and the cost of money (interest rates on debt). Luxury properties can cost five or six times as much per room as economy hotels. Land costs vary greatly across the nation. Comparing Los Angeles, California, and England, Arkansas is a lesson in futility. New York City may be stretching toward a $1,000 per-night room rate, but that is not the expectation of the manager in Dubuque, Iowa. That is why economy chains have stopped advertising a minimum national rate. Each locale has its own cost basis for building, borrowing, taxing, and paying labor. Budget hotels aim only for a percentage rate below that of local competitors. Advertising a single rate as part of the national company logo is no longer feasible.

Increases in room construction costs are startling. Even during economic downturns, a typical high-rise room costs between $200,000 and $250,000 today. Its figure was $8,000 in the 1960s. Consider what has happened in Hawaii over two decades. Twenty years after the Mauna Kea was built at $100,000 per room, it was sold at $1 million per room, and the hotel was 20 years older by then!

The situation is the same in New York. Regent Hotels, a super-luxury chain, built a 400-room hotel in New York with an average cost of $750,000 per room! With an actual average daily rack rate in the $550-range, the hotel was far from the $750 ADR dictated by the rule-of-thumb standard.

The Hotel Bel-Air in Los Angeles is another hotel that broke the mold. With only 92 rooms, the property sold in 1992 for a record $110 million (approximately $1.2 million per room!) to a Japanese hotel concern. Despite its incredibly high ADR *for that time* (about $400), the hotel earned far less than the $1,196 per average room-night that the building cost rate formula dictated. The hotel closed in 2009 (as did many other hotels nationwide) and reopened in 2011.

These examples are special cases of "trophy hotels." Viewing the trophy as an art asset, which gives satisfaction and pleasure to the owner, offers some perspective on the prices. Like an art piece, these eyebrow-raising prices are justified as long-term investments and by their uniqueness (location, reputation, etc.). In retrospect, the excessive prices of a generation ago have proven to be good deals—no one actually expected the hotel company that purchased the Hotel Bel-Air to make an operating profit. Profit, if any, would come from selling the resort several years down the road as it did with the seller. The buyer was one of four interested parties willing to bid in excess of $1 million per room for the Bel-Air. Rosewood hotels, which owned and sold the hotel, made an enormous profit, having purchased it just seven years earlier for $22.7 million, $247,000 per room.

Trophy hotels are extreme examples that do not set the rule for the remainder of the industry. With economy hotels costing about $70,000 per room, and standard properties nearing $250,000-plus per room, advocates of the rule take heart. The building-cost formula, a standard whose first known reference was in 1947, is still as roughly accurate today as it probably was back then.

THE RENOVATION COST RATE   The costs of additions, property rehabs, or new amenities such as swimming pools fall within the scope of the $1 per $1,000 rule. First, the cost of the upgrade is determined on a per-room basis. The installation of in-room air conditioners might be priced at $1,000 per room. A general-use item such as a sauna would need a per room equivalent. The cost (assume $150,000) would be divided by the number of rooms (100) to arrive at the per unit cost. Exhibit 15 shows the impact on room rates from management's decision to undertake a propertywide remodel.

The Ideal Average Room Rate

The firm of Laventhol & Horwath designed the ideal average room rate as a means of testing the room-rate structure. Although the L&H accounting firm is no longer in business, its ideal average room rate lives on. According to this approach, the hotel should sell an equal percentage of rooms in each rate class instead of filling from the bottom up (least expensive rooms selling first). A 70% occupancy should mean a 70% occupancy in each rate category. Such a spread produces an average rate identical to the average rate earned when the hotel is completely full—that is, an ideal room rate.

1. Renovation Project Parameters

	Guest Rooms: Cost per Room	Hallways: Cost per Door	Meeting Space: Cost per Square Foot	Lobby: Cost per Square Foot	F&B Outlets: Cost per Seat	Total Project
Soft costs[a]	$515	$194	$2	$3	$212	N/A
Hard costs[b]	3,305	755	5	18	1,342	N/A
Subtotals	$764,000	$189,800	$105,000	$73,500	$170,940	$1,303,240

2. Basic Hotel Information
- A 200-room full-service airport hotel
- 15,000 square feet of convention space
- 3,500 square feet of lobby space
- One 110-seat restaurant and bar
- 12% cost of funds interest rate
- Total renovation cost $1,303,240

3. Project Cost per Average Guest Room
- $1,303,240 project divided by 200 rooms equals $6,516.20 per room.
- Assume that the $6,516.20 project cost per average room is to be repaid over 15 years at a 12% cost of funds rate.
- The combined principal and interest charge is $956.74 per room per year.

4. Impact of the Building Cost Room-Rate Formula
- The $956.74 annualized cost per average room divided by $1,000 rule-of-thumb formula equals $0.96 increase per average room-night sold.

[a] Soft costs include professional and contractor fees, sales tax, and shipping fees.

[b] Hard costs include construction costs, labor, and materials.

EXHIBIT 15 Using the rule of thumb—the building cost room-rate formula— ($1 in room rate for every $1,000 in building costs), innkeepers can estimate the increases in room rates needed to recover propertywide renovations.

Exhibit 16 illustrates the computation used to derive the ideal rate. This formula assumes each room type (standard, executive, deluxe, and suite) fills to the same percentage of rooms sold as every other room type. At 70% occupancy, 70% of the standard rooms will be sold, 70% of the executive rooms will be sold, 70% of the deluxe rooms will be sold, and so on.

Once calculated, the manager is armed with a valuable figure, the ideal average room rate. If the actual average rate on any given day or week is higher than the ideal average rate, the front-office staff has been doing a great job of upselling guests. Either that, or the hotel has failed to provide a proper number of high-priced rooms. The market of this hotel may be interested in rooms selling above the average, so room types and rates may need to be adjusted upward.

An average room rate lower than the ideal, and this is usually the case, indicates several problems. There may not be enough contrast between the low- and the high-priced rooms. Guests will take the lower rate when they are buying nothing extra for the higher rate. If the better rooms do, in fact, have certain extras—better exposure and newer furnishings—the lack of contrast between the rate categories might simply be a matter of poor selling at the front desk. ("Upselling" is discussed shortly.)

Check-in at the front desk represents the last opportunity to upsell the guest to a more expensive room. Good salesmanship coupled with a differentiated product gives the hotel a strong chance to increase middle- and high-priced room sales. Such comments as "I see you have reserved our standard room; do you realize for just 20 more dollars I can place you in a newly refurbished deluxe room with a complimentary continental breakfast?" go a long way toward satisfying both the guest and the bottom line.

A faulty internal rate structure is another reason that the ideal room rate might not be achieved. The options, the range of rates being offered, might not appeal to the customer. Using the ideal room-rate computation, the spread between rates could be adjusted. According to the authors of the formula, increases should be concentrated in those rooms on those days for which the demand is highest. That begins with an analysis of rate categories.

The Ideal Room Rate

Room Type	Number of Rooms by Type	Percent of Double Occupancy	Single Rate	Double Rate
Standard	140	30	$ 80	$ 95
Executive	160	5	105	105
Deluxe	100	25	120	140
Suite	75	70	160	160
Total rooms	475			

Calculation Steps

1. Multiply all standard rooms (140) by their single rate ($80) to get a product of $11,200. Then take the double occupancy percentage for standard rooms (30%) times the total number of standard rooms (140) to get 42, the number of double-occupied standard rooms. Next, take the 42 double-occupied standard rooms times the differential between the single and double price ($95 double rate minus $80 single rate equals $15 differential) to get $630. Finally, add the room revenue for standard rooms calculated at the single rate ($11,200) to the additional room revenue received from standard rooms sold at the double rate ($630) to get the full-house room revenue for standard rooms, a total of $11,830.
2. Follow the same procedure for executive rooms: 160 rooms times $105 equals $16,800. The differential between single and double occupancy for executive rooms is zero, so there is no added revenue for double occupancy. The full-house room revenue for executive rooms is $16,800.
3. Follow the same procedure for deluxe rooms: 100 rooms times $120 single rate equals $12,000. In terms of double occupancy, there are 25 deluxe rooms (25% double occupancy times 100 rooms equals 25 rooms) sold at a $20 differential ($140 double rate minus $120 single rate equals $20 differential) for a total double occupancy impact of $500. The full-house room revenue for deluxe rooms is $12,500.
4. Follow the same procedure for suites: 75 rooms times $160 equals $12,000. The differential between single and double occupancy for suites is zero, so there is no added revenue for double occupancy. The full-house room revenue for suites is $12,000.
5. Add total revenues from standard rooms ($11,830), executive rooms ($16,800), deluxe rooms ($12,500), and suites ($12,000) for total revenues assuming 100% occupancy—ideal revenues. That total ($53,130) divided by rooms sold (475) is the ideal average room rate of $111.85.

No matter what the occupancy percentage, the ideal average room rate remains the same.

Try this problem again, assuming, say, 70% occupancy. The end result will still be an ideal average room rate of $111.85.

EXHIBIT 16   Regardless of the occupancy level, The ideal room rate generates an ADR equal to the ADR at 100% occupancy. That means rooms in each rate class are sold in the same proportion as they are at full occupancy. At 100% occupancy, each rate class has optimum occupancy. Accomplishing this at less than a full house is ideal.   *Courtesy of Laventhol & Horwath, which closed ca. 1990.*

RATE CATEGORIES   The discrepancy between the rates the hotel offers and those the guests prefer can be pinpointed with a simple chart. Guest demands and the hotel offerings are plotted side by side.

Guest demands are determined by examining registration-card rates over a period of time. The survey should not include days of 100% occupancy when guests had no rate choice. Special rate situations would also be excluded. Using elementary arithmetic, the percentage of total registrations is determined for each rate class. Exhibit 17 illustrates the contrast between what the guest buys and what the hotel offers. It also points to the rates that need adjustment.

Exhibit 17 assigns 40% of the hypothetical hotel to the median room rate. Two additional categories of 20% and 10%, respectively, appear on both the lower and upper ends. It is the sad history of our industry that hotels fill from the bottom up. Lower-priced rooms are in greatest demand. This means that low occupancy is accompanied by a low average daily rate. It is felt,

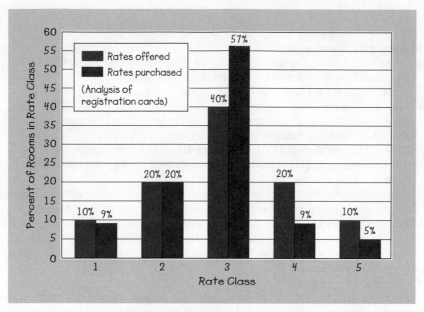

EXHIBIT 17 A simple analysis of registration cards highlights guest's preferences for certain room rates (the red columns) versus the rates being offered by the hotel (the gray columns). The obvious differences help management revisit its room-rate structure.

therefore, that hotels should offer more categories at the lower end of the price scale. These lower categories would be bunched together, while the higher rates would be spread over fewer categories. That might be the reason that Hilton advises its franchisees to concentrate on the minimum single rate as the key in competition.

Upselling

The hotel's policy on room rates faces a moment of truth when the front-office employee and the buying public come face to face. Fashioning a room-rate policy is a futile exercise unless management simultaneously trains its staff to carry out the plan. The selling skills of reservationists and clerks are critical to the average daily rate. Guest-sevice agents can relax only when the house nears capacity. Since 100% occupancy is very rare, earning a consistently higher ADR on the 60–70% occupancy days requires a program for selling up!

The final sell comes from the guest-service agent. A guest who approaches the desk with a reservation in hand has already decided to buy. Already committed, the new arrival will listen to a carefully designed and rehearsed sales effort (see Exhibit 18). The hardest job rests with the reservationists, who doesn't even see the buyer. Too hard a sell, too firm a price and the guest is lost early on. Teamed up, the reservationist and the guest-service agent deliver a one-two punch to the ADR, although they could be 1,000 miles and 30-plus days apart.

A firm sale begins with product knowledge. That is why good sales executives travel to the central reservations office to brief the operators there. On property, both the reservationists and the guest-service agents need continuous training about the facilities and accommodations of the hotel. This is rarely done. Few hotels ever assign 15 minutes per week for staff visits and room inspections. Hotels spend millions of dollars upgrading rooms and modernizing facilities, but the guest-service agents never see the changes. A simple and consistent training program assures management that employees know their product.

If the desk staff knows the product, a repertoire of reasons can be developed to upsell. An upsell of $10–$20 is not a large increment in terms of today's rate. Since every dollar of the increment goes to the bottom line, it represents a large annual figure, even if only a portion of the attempts are successful. The focus might be to sell the commercial guest from standard service to a concierge floor. The leisure market needs a different approach. These discretionary buyers must be convinced that the new rates being quoted at check-in are additional options and not a refusal to honor the price originally booked during the reservation. In every case, the guest-service agent needs price discretion to close the sale. With empty rooms, a $25 upsell is meaningful even if the better room normally carries a $100+ tab! It would be empty otherwise.

Mastering the Basics of Selling

1. **Impressing the Guests**
   - Maintain an appealing physical appearance, including good posture. Don't lean or hang over the front desk. Bring to the job your own sense of spirit and style.
   - Organize and keep the front-desk area uncluttered.
   - Get to know your property's every service and accommodation type thoroughly. Make frequent forays around the property to learn firsthand about each kind and category of room so that you can better describe the facilities to potential guests.
   - Memorize or keep close at hand an up-to-date list of the locations and hours of operation of all food and beverage facilities; entertainment lounges; recreational and sports rooms; and banquet, meeting, exhibit, and other public areas.
   - Learn the names and office locations of the general manager and all department heads, including directors of marketing, sales, catering, convention services, and food and beverages.
   - Be friendly to guests, greeting them warmly and, whenever possible, by name and title. For instance, when requesting a bellperson's service, ask him or her to take "Mr. Smith to room 340." (To ensure the guest's privacy, be discreet in mentioning the room number to the bellperson.) Call the bellperson by name as well.
   - Give guests your undivided attention.
   - Answer all questions completely, but concisely and accurately, based on your in-depth knowledge of hotel operations. Refrain from boasting about accommodations and services; instead, offer simple, to-the-point descriptions of features.
   - Assume a polite, patient manner in explaining the various options available—for example, the size of rooms, kinds of reservations (confirmed or guaranteed), and the terms *American, European,* or *modified American plan.*

2. **Winning the Guests**
   - Expand prospects' accommodations horizons with descriptions of the room and service possibilities awaiting them. Potential guests may think of a hotel as simply a building filled with bedrooms, but you know better. So inform them about rooms with views, rooms near the health spa, twinbed rooms, suites, rooms furnished according to a certain historical period, or ultramodern accommodations with Jacuzzis. Lay everything out for prospects, dwelling on the positive, distinctive appeals of each choice. Throw in the tempting intangibles associated with each type of room; for instance, the prestige of having a room on the same floor as the hotel's exclusive club for special guests, or the pleasure of staying in a room equipped with a VCR or a fireplace.
   - Attempt to sell a room to suit the client. Observe people and try to read their particular hankerings. If a guest is new to the hotel, a room with a nice view might be impressive. Business travelers might prefer a quiet room at the back. Guests with children, people staying for an extended visit, honeymooners, and celebrities are among those who might be interested in suites.

EXHIBIT 18 Increasing the ADR rests almost entirely with those at the desk. Guest-service agents must be taught to upsell, but to do so with finesse and professionalism. Mastering the basics of upselling is explained in this pamphlet, titled *The Front Office: Turning Service into Sales.* *Courtesy of the Hospitality Sales and Marketing Association International (HSMAI), McLean, Virginia.*

Each guest looks at the incremental dollars differently, and so does the employee. Management must be cognizant that the basic room rate and especially the incremental upsell may seem excessive to someone working for an hourly wage. Part of the training must, therefore, attend to the employee's frame of reference. Having some type of monetary incentive plan helps change attitudes and gets the staffers onboard.

INCENTIVES TO UPSELLING Every hotel manager works to better the property's ADR. The most astute among them looks to guest-service agents to do that job. That is because a person-to-person moment of truth across the desk is better at boosting the ADR than any advertisement or giveaway gimmick. Moreover, upselling is less expensive, even with an incentive-pay plan in place. A good incentive plan coupled with proper training will produce results, that is, higher ADRs.

Incentive systems stimulate interest among the staff and emphasize the goals of management. Rewards are especially important during heavy discounting periods when guests know that low rates are available and sales resistance is high. Unlike other cultures, clerks in the United

- Sell the room, not the rate. If a guest asks flat out for rates, avoid quoting a minimum or just one rate, instead, offer a range, portraying in detail the difference in accommodations that each rate affords.
- Should a prospect look unsure or reluctant to book a room, suggest that the guest accompany a hotel employee on a walkthrough. A tour of the premises gives guests a chance to settle any doubts they might have and demonstrates the hotel's policy of goodwill and flexibility.
- Keep abreast of special sales promotions, weekend packages, and other marketing strategies, and dangle these offerings to prospects. (To make sure you're informed, you might ask your sales department to hold regularly scheduled presentations to front-office staff on their latest schemes.)
- Look for opportunities to extend the sale—there are many. If a guest mentions that he or she is hungry or arrives around mealtime, promote the hotel's dining facilities; if a guest arrives late, talk up the entertainment lounge or room service. As the person most in contact with guests throughout their stays, you are in the enviable position of being able to please both your guest and hotel management. You can delight guests merely by drawing their attention to the multitude of services your hotel offers, whether it's quick dry cleaning or a leisurely massage. And you can thrill the boss by advancing a sale and hotel revenues through your promotion of in-house features.

3. **Wooing the Guests**
- When a guest arrives, upgrade the reservation to a more luxurious accommodation whenever availability allows, ask whether the guest would like to make a dinner reservation, and ask whether he or she would like a wake-up call.
- Record and follow through on all wake-up call requests.
- Deliver mail and messages promptly.
- Avoid situations that keep guests waiting. For instance, if you're unable to locate a guest's reservation and a line is beginning to form on the other side of the counter, assume that the hotel has plenty of the desired accommodations available and go ahead and book the guest. Finish registering anyone else who is waiting, and then search for the missing reservation.
- Should mishaps occur, whether a reservation mix-up or a housekeeping error, handle the matter with aplomb without laying the blame on any individual employee or department.
- Dispatch each departing guest with a favorable impression of the hotel. In other words, treat the guests with care and courtesy during check out. Regardless of whether guests enjoyed their stay, they will remember only the hassles experienced at check out if you allow them to occur. Therefore, don't. That is, be sure there are useful, comprehensive procedures for dealing with guests who dispute postings and payments, and follow those procedures with assurance and professionalism.

EXHIBIT 18 Continued

States do not share in mandatory service charges, which means management must establish a special cash pool.

Incentive systems require an accurate and easily understood formula. Flat goals can be established, or the focus can be on improvement from last year, last month, or last week. Most incentives are keyed to ADR. Since occupancy is a factor in total revenue, other bases are needed for reservation-takers. In most small hotels, the reservation-taker is the guest-service agent. Most systems create a pool that is shared by a team that includes guest-service and reservation staff. Some plans enlarge the pool to include telephone operators. Because of their proximity to the desk, even the bell staff is included sometimes.

The cash pool is generated from a percentage, perhaps 10%, of room sales that exceed projections. The basis must be clear. It could be total room sales that must be exceeded or average daily rate or the ideal room rate (see Exhibit 16) or the budget forecast. If actual sales exceed target sales, the bonus becomes payable. The bonus period is important. It must be long enough to reflect the true efforts of the team but short enough to bring the rewards within grasp.

To be effective, all reward systems must be timely!

Higher ADRs are a three-win situation. Staffers see an increased pay envelope; managers record higher P&L profits; guests enjoy better digs. None of which comes easily. A carefully planned and enunciated system must be installed, dollars must be allocated, and training must be intensive and ongoing.

Summary

A proper room rate is as much a marketing tool as it is a financial instrument. The room rate needs to be low enough to attract customers (marketing) and high enough to earn a reasonable profit (financial). Easier said than done. Even in this day of sophisticated computer technology, setting a room rate still involves guesswork and gut instincts. There is an unquantifiable psychology involved in the room rate. An attractive rate for one guest may appear unreasonable to another. For some, high rates suggest too pretentious operation; for others, a low rate suggests poor quality. So determining the room rate differs from setting a rate strategy.

Searching for and working toward the perfect rate is difficult. Even after the rate has been determined and established, it is changed immediately. Rates fluctuate by season, they change according to room type, they vary with special guest discounts, and they shift as a function of yield management (see Interesting Tidbits).

The well-established methods for calculating the proper rate should not exclude the wisdom of experience or the common sense of market demand. So the room-rate strategy that management adopts, including incentive payments, might well override the calculation of the room rate per se. Among the calculations are the Hubbart room-rate formula and the building cost rate. The ideal average room-rate formula adds a dimension of retrospection to understanding the appropriateness of a rate in terms of the local marketplace.

Get out there and upsell!

Resources and Challenges

RESOURCES

Web Site Assignment

Report and compare the total cost of lodging taxes (bed taxes plus sales taxes; state taxes plus local taxes) for your hometown to the total costs of all room taxes levied in Boston. Select a second city if your hometown is Boston or if your hometown is too small to be impacted by bed taxes.

Interesting Tidbits

- In June of 2011, Las Vegas hosted a three-day rave show, Electric Daisy, with an estimated attendance of 240,000 revelers. Occupancy was very high even for a city with 150,000 hotel rooms. The rate contrast between that weekend and the weekend preceding shows the yield management system in operation. (Listed by descending rate during the rave.)

Weekend Rates

Hotel	Preceding Rave	During Rave
Flamingo	$155	$775
Vdara	190	540
Venetian	189	529
New York, New York	125	525
Harrah's	125	450
Treasure Island	137	449

- A small boutique chain, Affinia Hotels (some seven properties), and a larger counterpart, Kimpton Hotels (about 50 properties), are among industry members using Twitter to give early notice of special rates and to award gifts to Twitter followers who book space.

Challenges

True/False

Questions that are partially false should be marked false (F).

_____ 1. An elastic market is one that bounces back from poor economic times, so the commercial (business) market, which remains the base of much of the hotel industry's room sales, is a good example of an elastic market.

_____ 2. Dynamic pricing refers to the activity (the dynamics at the desk) when a walk-in is subjected to a rate upsell or when a guest with a reservation has to be walked to a higher-priced competitor.

_____ 3. Many hotels, casino hotels especially, charge the same room rate whether the room is single or double occupied, but levy an additional charge for a third person.

_____ 4. The family plan was one of many discounted rates that the hotel industry introduced and tested to promote tourism and travel when the economy faltered between 2008 and 2012.

_____ 5. Per diem (meaning "watch each dime") is a well-known expression—a professional shorthand—used by hotel executives as they carefully monitor their operating budgets in times of economic crises.

Problems

1. The hotel that you manage always has an ADR $5–$10 higher than its ideal average room rate of $87.25. What does this tell you about the front-office staff? What do you know about the price sensitivity of your customers? And what do you conclude about rate tendencies in the surrounding marketplace? Armed with this knowledge, what type of action(s) might you now consider? Explain.

2. Although upselling is important to the hotel, it may cause guest discomfort if it is too aggressive. There is a fine distinction between professional upselling and intentional "hustling." Acting as the guest-service agent prepare a professional upsell dialogue for each of these situations. (Create details about room types, rates, and personalities as needed.)

   a. At the desk is an executive on your corporate-rate plan. He is stretching and yawning from a hard day of air travel and long, local meetings.

   b. About to check in is a mother with three young children. She is alone, but says her husband arrives tomorrow. The kids are obviously excited about the prospects of swimming and running around the courtyard/pool.

   c. Two gentlemen from a recently arrived bus tour approach the desk. They and the rest of the tour group have been housed in queen doubles, standard accommodations for tour groups. The men are unhappy because their room is too small.

   d. A female executive with an extended-stay reservation checks in. She wants assurance that the reservation is firm for at least 10 days. How can she possibly survive 10 days with the pressure from the upcoming assignment?

3. A commercial hotel offers deeply discounted rates on Friday, Saturday, and Sunday nights. Discuss what should be done or said in each of the following situations:

   a. A guest arrives on Saturday but, unaware of the discount possibilities, makes no mention of the special rate. The desk clerk charges full rack rate. On check-out Monday morning, the cashier notices the full rate charged for two nights, but the guest (after reviewing her folio) says nothing.

   b. The situation is the same as that in (a), but this time the guest questions the lack of a discount.

   c. A corporate guest stays Wednesday through Tuesday night on company business. He receives the usual discounted commercial rate for all seven nights, but that rate is still higher than the special weekend rate. He knows about the special rate, is surprised that no adjustment was made for the weekend nights, and asks for an adjustment.

   d. Create a fourth scenario of your own.

4. Prepare a list of similarities and differences between *discounting* and *rate cutting*. Are there substantial differences? If so, what are they? Or are these simply two different terms for describing exactly the same practice? Explain why hoteliers differentiate the two.

5. The Hubbart room-rate formula calls for an average room rate that will cover expenses and provide a fair return to the investors. Compute that rate from the abbreviated set of data that follows:

Land	$3,000,000
Building	$25,000,000
Furniture and equipment	$6,000,000
Nonappropriated expenses, such as advertising, repairs, etc.	$1,200,000
Income from all operating departments except rooms, net of losses	$3,200,000
Rooms available for sale	563
Nonoperating expenses, such as insurance, taxes, and depreciation	$510,000
Desired return on investment	16%
Interest on debt of $25,000,000	14%
Percentage of occupancy	71%

6. Using the data from Problem 5, compute the room charge according to the building cost rate formula.

AN INCIDENT IN HOTEL MANAGEMENT
So What Does FSG (Frequent-Stay Guest) Stand For?

Occupancy has been so high this year that the hotel has "regretted" a large number of reservation requests.

A registered couple was scheduled to leave at 6:00 AM on the morning of March 31. A family emergency with their young child called them home late on March 30. The airline accommodated the couple on a red-eye flight without charging for the ticket change. They ask the desk for a late check-out, 9:00 PM, and a half-day rate of $110.

The hotel was full that Sunday; most of the business crowd had already filled the house. The manager on duty denied the request because of the late hour and the unlikelihood of servicing and reselling the room. A full night's charge was made, $220.

In his letter of complaint, the husband asks to be reimbursed and questions the meaning of being a FSG. He notes that "I am not a big customer of yours." Adding, "You'll probably see me even less frequently now." The FSG profile shows three stays from the family since their membership was launched almost three years earlier.

Questions:

1. Was there a management failure here; if so, what?
2. What is the hotel's immediate response (or action) to the incident?
3. What further, long-run action should management take, if any?

Answers to True/False Quiz

1. False. The term does not refer to the economics of the time. An elastic market is one that responds significantly to changes in costs; for lodging that means changes in rate. Leisure travelers are viewed as an elastic market. They are more sensitive to rate changes: buying more when rates are low and buying less when rates rise.

2. False. Dynamic pricing refers to a negotiated method of charging room rates. The room rate for business travelers of a participating company is an agreed-upon discount (perhaps 10%) from the lowest available rate at the time of check-in. This contrasts with more traditional pricing negotiation that guarantees the buying company a fixed dollar rate for its traveler.

3. True. The statement is true as it stands. Many hotels, casino hotels especially, do charge the same room rate whether the room is single or double occupied, but levy an additional charge for a third person.

4. False. The family plan was launched in the 1950s, not between 2008 and 2012. It was somewhat revolutionary when first introduced as was the whole idea of changing rates to accommodate changing markets.

5. False. Per diem means "per day" not "each dime." The expression is used especially by governmental agencies—a professional shorthand—to identify the amount of reimbursement allowed for hotel rooms and meals by public employees traveling on government business.

Billing the Guest Folio

Billing the Guest Folio

There is a rhythm to the flow that marks the guest's passage through the hotel. Reservations sound the first drumbeat, followed by arrival and registration. The tempo of the visit ends with the guest's departure and payment. Between check-in and check-out, guests buy the services of the hotel. Selling those services is what hotelkeeping is all about. Recording those sales is what this chapter is all about.

WHAT THE CHAPTER IS ALL ABOUT

The Sale and Recordkeeping of Services

The services that hotels sell depend on their size, class, and type. Budget hotels offer room sales only. The offerings of full-service properties range broadly from room service, to wedding chapels, to spas. The more offerings, the more detailed the system of recordkeeping.

Hotels and their customers (guests) have a different relationship than do other retailers and their customers. Guests register as they arrive. Names, addresses, business associations, and—most important—credit-card numbers are known to the innkeeper. Having this information allows the sale of services without immediate payment. Unlike other retailers, the hotel merchant waits for payment. The wait may be a few hours or even an entire week. In the meantime, guest purchases are recorded on a bill, called a *folio*. The folio is presented as the guest checks out. But, as we shall see, it may not be paid even then.

Preparing the Folio

The folio is a current, accurate record of what the guest owes. It is available on demand to both the guest and the hotel's management. Whereas other retailers—department stores, for example—send monthly statements, the hotel's statement is ready at a moment's notice. The folio is ready even though the exact moment of departure is unknown, even unknown to the guest. Of course, the hotel is as anxious as the guest to have an accurate accounting available. Incorrect bills delay the check-out procedure and create ill will. *Charges* (amounts the guest owes) not on the folio are difficult to collect after the guest has departed. Collecting these *late charges* by mail is costly in both clerical expenses and guest relationships.

Recording (Accounting for) Each Transaction

> Understanding accounting is not essential to a clear understanding of this chapter. Hereafter, accounting rules are set in a box like this one. Students unfamiliar with the debits and credits of accounting may choose to read these accounting fundamentals or not. The text will make good sense even if the accounting information is skipped.

ACCOUNTS RECEIVABLE

Except at the retail level, most commerce is carried on without immediate payment. Businesses buy and sell to one another without a direct exchange of money. Both buyer and seller understand that payment will be delayed. Hotels also work that way. Guests are not disturbed during their sleep in order to collect the room rates! Instead, charges are made to the folio and collections are made later. Guests usually settle at check-out time. During the period between the sale (room, food, beverage, etc.) and the payment (at departure), the guest

Definition of Terms to Be Used	
Accounts Receivable (A/R)	Customers who owe for services already rendered
City Receivables	Accounts receivable who are not registered
Transient Receivables	Accounts receivable who are currently registered
Charge	The amount that the hotel asks for its service
Late Charge	Service charged to the folio after the guest has left
Folio	Guest bill; also called account card. Folios are A/R
Ledger	Group of folios
City Ledger	A ledger of city receivables
Transient Ledger	A ledger of transient receivables; also called a rooms ledger, a front-desk ledger, a guest ledger
Posting	The process of recording a charge or credit on the folio

owes the hotel. A customer who owes a business for services that have not been paid is known as an *account receivable*.[1]

Types of Accounts Receivable (A/R)

Hotels have two types of accounts receivable because there are two types of hotel guests. The most obvious guest (or account receivable) is one who is currently registered and occupying a room. Oddly enough, this most visible class of guest is not the largest dollar debt (accounts receivable) that the hotel is owed. More money is owed by the second type of accounts receivable: persons or companies that owe for services but are *not* registered, *not* occupying a guest room. Registered guests are called *transient guests*; nonregistered accounts receivable are called *city guests*. Both owe the hotel for services rendered and sold. One group, the city receivables, are not even in the hotel and may never have been.

Guests can and do change categories; transient accounts receivable usually become city accounts receivable. When guests check out, leaving their transient classification, they usually settle their folios (i.e., pay the bill) with a credit card. The amount owed is now a debt of the credit-card company. The hotel will be paid by a city-ledger receivable: Visa, MasterCard, or other credit-card companies. Credit-card companies obviously are not registered guests occupying a room. The credit-card debt is owed by an account receivable who is not registered: a city account receivable.

THE LEDGERS There are numerous individual accounts in both the registered and city-guest categories. Large hotels have several thousand registered guests and about the same number of folios. Accountants call a group of folios *a ledger*. (Any group of records can be called a ledger.) Since all the parties are registered, that is, transient guests, the folios at the front desk are viewed as one record, *a transient ledger*.

City accounts receivable are similarly combined. The total of individual city accounts, debtors who are not currently registered (Visa, for example), is viewed as one record, *a city ledger*.

In the preelectronic age, ledgers were actual piles of paper with each folio on a separate form, such as Exhibit 2. Today's folios are in computer memory. We still call them folios and their location is still identified either as transient folios (transient ledger) or city accounts (city ledger). The language has carried over although the format is no longer used.

Professional Lingo: The Transient Ledger Transient ledger is shorthand for the transient accounts receivable ledger. Hotel professionals use other jargon to identify this particular ledger. Because the ledger (i.e., the total record of debt to the hotel by registered guests) is available at the front office, it is frequently called the *front-office ledger*. Since it is made up of registered guests, it is also called the *guest ledger*. Room rates are the largest source of charges to guest folios, so *rooms ledger* is still another term used for the transient ledger.

The variety of terms used to identify the transient ledger spills over to the folios that make up this ledger. Thus, the single transient folio may be called the *folio*, or *guest folio*, or *front-office folio*. Since the folio is a record of the guest's account with the hotel, the folio is also called an *account card* or *guest bill*.

Professional Lingo: The City Ledger There are subcategories of the city ledger. But only one general term is used: *city ledger*. So a city-ledger reference

---

[1]Remember the spelling for receivable: Place *i* before *e* except after *c*, or when sounded like *a*, as in *neighbor* and *weigh*.

is easier to remember than the transient ledger with its variety of names: guest ledger, rooms ledger, and front-office ledger.

The guest ledger is located at the front desk, the city ledger in the accounting office. With computerization, ledgers have no real physical location. They can be accessed wherever a control terminal allows. Timing is the major difference between the two ledgers. Charges, which are the records of services rendered, are *posted* (recorded) immediately to the guest ledger since the guest might choose to leave at any time. City guests, who must establish credit in advance, are billed periodically. This permits some delay in posting city-ledger charges. Like many other businesses do, hotels bill city accounts monthly. Often, a three-day cycle is used for the first billing. These variations in timing are accommodated by different ledger forms as well as by different posting and billing procedures.

WHAT IS AND ISN'T ACCOUNTED FOR   Each folio is a record of the guest's debt to the hotel. Folios deal only with accounts receivable. Persons who pay cash for services, as they might in cocktail lounges and restaurants, are not billed at the front desk. It makes no difference whether the buyer is a registered guest or a stranger. There is no debt, hence no account receivable, when settlement is made immediately with cash!

Strangers, nonguests without front-office folios, can still purchase on credit. They do so with credit cards. Such a credit-card purchase creates an account receivable within the city ledger, not with the guest ledger (front-office ledger). Using the credit card means the credit-card company will pay the hotel. The credit-card company is a nonregistered account receivable. That's the definition of a city-ledger account. If services are purchased with a credit card by anyone, guest or nonguest, the purchaser owes the credit-card company and the credit-card company owes the hotel.

In summary, both registered guests and nonguest customers use the hotel's dining rooms and lounges. Nonguests pay by one of two methods. Either they pay with cash or credit card. This chapter concentrates on the third method of settlement, available only to registered guests. Such guests sign for services when delivered. That debt is recorded on the folio. During checkout, the guest settles all the charges on the folio. Settlement is almost always with a credit card, but need not be.

The Folio: The Individual Account Receivable

The terms *folio*, *bill*, *guest account*, *account card*, *guest account card*, and *guest bill* are used interchangeably. Some parts of the world use *visitor accounts*. All refer to the single folio that is opened for each guest. "For each guest" is not entirely accurate, because one folio may serve several persons, as it does with a family. Better to say "each party."

Definition of Terms to Be Used	
Account	A guest's transient folio, or a city-ledger record
Asset	Something owned by the hotel (building, A/R, furniture)
Balance of the Account (or Account Balance)	The net difference between charges and credits
Cashier's Bucket (or Well or Pit)	A front-office file, sometimes recessed in the desk
Charges	Amounts owed by guests for services received
Credits	Amounts by which guests settle the charges they owe
Direct Billing	Bill goes to the entity that created it, not to a credit card
Incomes	Earnings that the hotel enjoys from the sale of services
Master Account	Front-office folio for *group* charges and credits
PMS	Property management system, the hotel's computer
Sales	Same as income
Split (Billing or Folios)	Distribution of charges between a master account and a folio

LOCATION AND FILING OF FOLIOS Without exception, modern hotels use the computerized folios (see Exhibit 1) that property management systems (PMSs) create. There are no physical folios because the records are in computer memory. Folio information can be viewed on computer screens, by guests on their in-room television sets, or by a printed copy, a *hard copy.* Guest-service agents need skills on keyboards, scanners, display screens, and printers in order to record and access folio information.

Unlike computer-prepared folios, hand-prepared, pencil-and-paper folios (see Exhibit 2) were actually stored at the desk. They were kept in a *cashier's well,* also called a *bucket* or *pit* because many are recessed still in desk tops (see Exhibit 3). Folios were maintained there in room-number sequence separated by cardboard dividers. Room numbers were used—as they are now—because

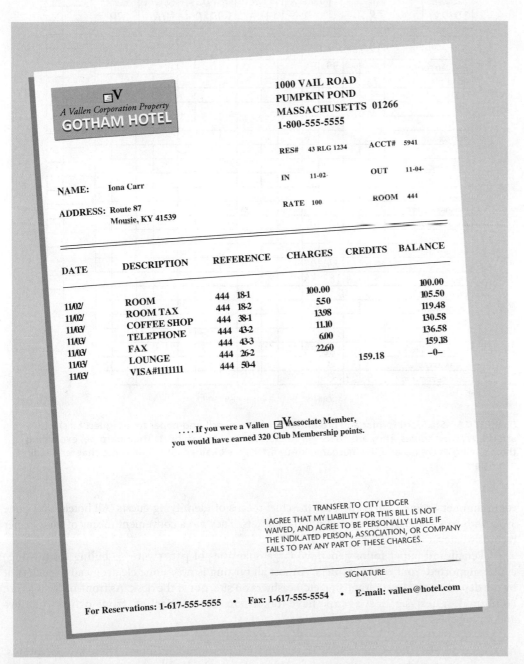

EXHIBIT 1 Standard format and presentation of a computer-prepared folio (guest bill) printed at the end of the guest's stay by a property management system (PMS). Information above the double line (reservation number, rate, arrival, and departure dates) is obtained from reservation and/or registration data. Services rendered to the guest are recorded below the double lines, and their meanings are the focus of this chapter.

ROOM NO.	409					E69080		CLERK

m M/M Art E. Fishal

86 Bates Boulevard

Hitchcock, Texas 01020

ROOM NO.	409					E69080		CLERK
								SB

m M/M Art E. Fishal

86 Bates Boulevard

Hitchcock, Texas 01020

ARRIVED	RATE	PERSONS	COT	REG. CARD #	PREV. INV. #	CLERK
12/23/	78	2	N/A	69080	N/A	SB

DATE	12/23/		12/24/												
BROUGHT FORWARD			99	24											
ROOM	78	–													
TAX	6	24													
RESTAURANT	15	–													
"															
TELEPHONE-LOCAL															
-LONG DISTANCE															
TELEGRAMS															
LAUNDRY & VALET															
CASH ADVANCES															
"															
NEWSPAPERS															
TRANSFERS from 407 *69081			84	24											
TOTAL DEBIT	99	24	183	48											
CASH															
ALLOWANCES															
CITY LEDGER:															
-ADVANCE DEPOSITS															
-CREDIT CARDS			183	48											
-TRANSFERS															
BALANCE FORWARD	99	24	0												

ALL ACCOUNTS ARE DUE WHEN RENDERED

EXHIBIT 2A Standard format and presentation of two pencil-and-paper folios (guest bills) with attached carbon copies. They are no longer in use, replaced by Exhibit 1. Their purpose, explaining the meaning of *credits* and the mechanics of *transfers,* is explained later, under the chapter heading "Transfers."

room numbers, more than names, are the chief means of identifying guests. All hotels have done away with hand-prepared folios, but not the buckets. They are a convenient means of filing paper records whatever the system being used.

Pencil-and-paper folios generated large quantities of paperwork so billing (or posting) clerks supported front-office cashiers. Almost all posting is now done electronically, much of it by the departmental (restaurant, bar, etc.) cashiers on site, not at the desk. As front-office jobs are combined, guest-service agents have taken on the duties of front-office cashiers and billing clerks.

NUMBER OF FOLIOS One folio is the norm for each occupied room. There are exceptions. A room with several unrelated persons would need several folios if each is to pay an equal share. Moreover, each would have signed in on a separate reg card. On the other hand, just one folio would be used for a single occupant in a two- or three-room suite. Likewise, one folio would do for a family of four assigned to a queen double.

ROOM NO. _____ 407 _____   **E69081**

m ___ *Benny Fishal* ___

12345 Education Avenue
Reading, Pennsylvania 98765

							CLERK
ROOM NO. _____ 407 _____   **E69081**

m ___ *Benny Fishal* ___

12345 Education Avenue
Reading, Pennsylvania 98765

ARRIVED	RATE	PERSONS	COT	REG. CARD #	PREV. INV. #	CLERK
12/23/	78	2	N/A	69081	N/A	SB

DATE	12/23/		12/24/							
BROUGHT FORWARD			84	24						
ROOM	78	–								
TAX	6	24								
RESTAURANT										
"										
TELEPHONE-LOCAL										
-LONG DISTANCE										
TELEGRAMS										
LAUNDRY & VALET										
CASH ADVANCES										
"										
NEWSPAPERS										
TRANSFERS										
TOTAL DEBIT	84	24	84	24						
CASH										
ALLOWANCES										
CITY LEDGER:										
-ADVANCE DEPOSITS										
-CREDIT CARDS										
-TRANSFERS TO 409	#69080		84	24						
BALANCE FORWARD	84	24	0							

ALL ACCOUNTS ARE DUE WHEN RENDERED

EXHIBIT 2B   Continued

EXHIBIT 3   A *cashier's well,* also called a *bucket* or *pit,* separated pencil-and-paper folios (see Exhibit 2) by heavy cardboard dividers. Folios were kept in room-number sequence. Buckets are still used at some front desks for filing vouchers and correspondence.

There is no relationship between the number of city-ledger accounts and the number of occupied rooms. City-ledger accounts are opened for nonregistered guests (individuals, companies, associations) who want credit privileges, not room occupancy. Before credit cards were adopted, large hotels had upward of a thousand city-ledger accounts. Individual accounts are not needed today because almost everyone carries a credit card. Now the bulk of the city ledger can be accounted for in a half-dozen credit-card accounts. Electronically tying city-ledger accounts to the computers of credit-card companies and banks speeds processing and reduces administrative costs.

The Folio: The Group Account Receivable

MASTER ACCOUNTS Master accounts accommodate tour companies, trade associations, convention organizations, and single-entity groups. The master account (master folio) is its own person, much like a corporation has a legal identity separate from its individual owners. Charges that are incurred by the group—not billable to any one person—are accumulated on the master account. Master accounts are transient accounts receivable, not city-ledger accounts. So long as the group is in the house, the master account is a front-office account. It uses a standard folio (see Exhibit 4).

As with all folios, master accounts are settled at check-out. Settlement involves a joint review of the many charges by representatives of the hotel and the organization. Then the folio is transferred to the city ledger for direct billing. Obviously, then, the city ledger has more than just credit cards. Individual accounts receivable with *direct billing*—to be made to the person, company, or organization (rather than through credit cards)—are also part of the city ledger.

Master accounts are complex. They may number 25 pages and more. It takes telephone calls and faxes and emails to resolve what the hotel believes it is owed and what the association believes it owes. Conflicts arise over the number of persons at each function, over who signed for services, over the number of comp rooms, over sales taxes due, and so much more.

HOW MASTER ACCOUNTS ARE STRUCTURED Decisions about master account billing are made well in advance of the group's arrival. Service details, credit terms, and authorized signatures are part of the negotiations between the hotel and the organization. How charges are to be distributed between individual folios and the master account is the group's decision, not the hotel's. The hotel is responsible for billing as instructed.

Single-Entity Groups Employees gathering for company business or groups traveling together, say, to perform, are examples of single-entity groups. Charging all the room rates to a single master account is one method of billing such closely related groups.

Convention Groups Unlike single entities, convention delegates hail from many locations and companies. Delegates pay their own room and personal charges. No master account would serve for room rates, since delegates have no relationship other than their mutual attendance. However, the association staging the event has a master account for banquet costs, cocktail parties, and meeting expenses. Other general costs, such as telecommunications and room charges for employees or speakers, also go onto the master account (see Exhibit 4). All charges must be authorized by a signature from the person or persons identified during prenegotiations. If not so signed, it becomes an issue at settlement.

Many master accounts are created during a large convention. Participating companies in attendance at the convention may have exhibits, employee rooms, hospitality suites, and other services that require charges to that subgroup. As affiliated or allied members, they may see public relations benefits from, say, sponsoring a meal. Each, then, has its own master account separate from the master account of the association. Hotels track and bill each separately.

Tour Groups Master accounts for tour groups differ from master accounts for convention groups. Unlike convention attendees, tour-group participants pay the tour company in advance,

GOTHAM HOTEL
A Vallen Corporation Property
☐V

1000 VAIL ROAD
PUMPKIN POND
MASSACHUSETTS 01266
1-800-555-5555

NAME:	Alumni Associates of America
ADDRESS:	#1 College Campus Road
	Any University Town

RES# LG 1235   ACCT# 1206
IN   5-14   OUT   5-16
RATE   MASTER   ROOM   2323

DATE	DESCRIPTION	REFERENCE		CHARGES	CREDITS
5/14	BD DIRECTORS LUNCHEON	2323	38-3	550.00	
5/14	AUDIO/VISUAL	2323	50-1	100.00	
5/14	COCKTAIL RECEPTION	2323	26-2	12,000.00	
5/14	ROOM 2323	2323	18-1	200.00	
5/14	ROOM 2325	2323	18-1	200.00	
5/14	ROOM 1618/1620	2323	18-1	600.00	
5/14	ROOM TAX	2323	18-2	80.00	
5/15	BREAKFAST BAR	2323	38-4	800.00	
5/15	ROOM RENTALS	2323	38-1	1,500.00	
5/15	BUFFET LUNCHEON	2323	38-3	10,500.00	
5/15	FLAG RENTALS	2323	50-4	250.00	
5/15	ROOM 2323	2323	18-1	200.00	
5/15	ROOM 2325	2323	18-1	200.00	
5/15	ROOM 1618/1620	2323	18-1	600.00	
5/15	ROOM TAX	2323	18-2	80.00	
5/16	FULL-SERVICE BREAKFAST	2323	38-3	3,500.00	
5/16	ROOM ALLOWANCES 1/50	2323	18-6		2,000.00
5/16	ADJUSTMENT FOR FLAGS	2323	50-8		250.00
5/16	DIRECT TRANSFER	2323	C/L		29,110.00
5/16	THANK YOU				-0-

. . . . If you were a Vallen ☐VAssociate Member,
you would have earned 58,220 Club Membership points.

TRANSFER TO CITY LEDGER

I AGREE THAT MY LIABILITY FOR THIS BILL IS NOT WAIVED, AND AGREE TO BE PERSONALLY LIABLE IF THE INDICATED PERSON, ASSOCIATION, OR COMPANY FAILS TO PAY ANY PART OF THESE CHARGES.

SIGNATURE _____

For Reservations: 1-617-555-5555 • Fax: 1-617-555-5554 • E-mail: vallen@hotel.com

EXHIBIT 4 Folios are used for both individual guests and master accounts. Master accounts, such as this one, accumulate charges for groups. Nightly charges for rooms 2323, 2325, and 1618/1620 (under "Description") are for the association's use, probably for staff members or guest speakers. The folio is settled with "credits." The $2,000, fourth line from the bottom, represents a typical group allowance: One free room-night for each 50 room-nights sold. There was also some issue with flags that warranted a second adjustment (allowance) of $250. The folio was brought to a zero balance at check-out (as must all folios) by transferring the balance to the city ledger for direct billing. (Figures are rounded for clarity.)

and the tour company negotiates with the hotel. So the tour company is responsible for payment of all charges included in the package. Most likely, the tour company's master account includes the room charges for everyone in the group, plus whatever else was sold with the package: meals, drinks, shows, golf and so on. Personal expenses – those not within the package could be meals, drinks, shows, golf, and so on – are charged to the guest's personal folio. Obviously, some of the very same items could be in the package or not.

SPLIT BILLING   The distribution of charges between the master account and the guest's personal folio is called *split billing* or *split folios*. Both the master folio (also called the *A folio*) and the guest or *B folio* are standardized forms of the types illustrated throughout the chapter. A and B are used merely to distinguish the group entity from the individual person. The A folio is the major folio where the large charges of the association, tour company, or business are posted. Sometimes, the hotel itself is the A folio. Such is the case with casino comps and frequent-stay customers.

Casino Comps   Casino hotels usually provide complimentary (free) accommodations to "high rollers" (big players). Split billing is used to account for the comps. To the A folio are posted all the charges that the hotel/casino will comp. Depending on the size of the guest's credit line, that could be everything: rooms, food, beverage, and telephone. Even the airfare is reimbursed for whales (very high rollers). A lesser player might have only the room comped. Items not covered are posted to the B folio, which the guest pays at departure.

Preferred-Guest Programs   Preferred-guest (or frequent-traveler) programs employ the flexibility of split billing. Two different folios are opened when a guest checks in with frequent-traveler points. The full rate of the room is charged on the A folio. On departure, the guest pays the nonroom charges, which have been posted to the B folio. The A folio is transferred to the city ledger, and either the parent company or the franchisor is billed. According to the frequent-traveler contract, one of them is now a city-ledger account receivable obligated to pay the room charge.

The actual amount the parent company or franchisor pays to the hotel under the preferred-guest program is always less than the rate quoted to the guest. Most programs pay the hotel full rack rate only if the occupancy of the hotel is above a given figure—90% perhaps. Below that figure—and the hotel is usually below that figure—the program reimburses the participating hotel for its operational expenses: linen, labor, and energy. So reimbursement may be 20–30% of the room rate. No provision is made for recovering fixed costs such as taxes, interest, or fair wear and tear. There is an offset. Guests pay on the B folio for services other than rooms.

The burden falls heaviest on resorts. Frequent travelers go to resorts to spend the points that were earned at commercial hotels. Resorts are reimbursed from the parent company based on their previous months' ADRs. Resorts discount room rates during both the off-season and the shoulder season. The result: Reimbursement for frequent-guest stays during the high season is often based on the months when ADR is at its lowest.

Understanding Charges and Credits

Familiarization with accounting and with its system of charges and credits is a great assist to guest-service agents handling folios. This knowledge is especially helpful in understanding the interface between front-office records (the transient ledger) and back-office records (the city ledger). Nevertheless, folios are designed for use by anyone, with or without an accounting background.

> Bracket materials are used hereafter to repeat the same discussion using accounting terminology. Explanations are complete even if the bracketed paragraphs are skipped. Students are urged to read the bracketed content for a broader understanding of the folio and its relationship to the hotel's accounting system.

Charges for services rendered *increase* the guest's debt to the hotel. The posting to the EL CAFE restaurant on the folio of Exhibit 5 is an example. *Credits reduce* the guest's debt. ADJUST PHONE of Exhibit 5 is an example. Credits *must* offset charges when the guest checks out. At departure, the guest's folio *must always be zero* (Exhibit 5).

Charges and credits are identified with separate columns in Exhibits 5 and 6. Another technique, illustrated in Exhibit 13, uses one column with plus (+) for charges and minus (−) for credits. Exhibits 10 and 15 illustrate still a third approach, which uses only one column. Credit values are marked CR. Since most folio postings are charges, there is no need to mark them. Charge is understood with the one-column folio.

THE MEANING OF DEBITS AND CREDITS

Accounting language speaks of debits and credits instead of charges and credits. Debits (or charges) increase the values of certain accounting records. In this chapter, the focus is on folios, which are accounts receivable. Other records, cash, for example, are also increased with debits. Cash and accounts receivable are among the many assets (things that hotels own) that follow the same accounting rules. Accounting records, assets among them, that are increased with debits are decreased by credits.

Increases in assets, including *accounts receivable* and *cash*, are made with debits.
Decreases in assets, including *accounts receivable* and *cash*, are made with credits.

Accounting students will recognize the folio as a T-account, where debits are on the left side and credits on the right. Exhibit 5 is highlighted with horizontal and vertical lines to reinforce the visual similarities between an account receivable folio and an account receivable T-account. But not all folios have two columns.

ASSETS An asset is something a business owns. Hotels own many assets, including land, buildings, furniture, and kitchen equipment. Only two of the numerous assets owned are important to the front office and its folio responsibilities. Accounts receivable, which are debts that customers owe the hotel (the hotel owns the debt), is one of those assets. Cash is the other. Cash is money: money in the bank, money at the desk, money in the bar till. Cash has become less important to the records of the front office because both guests and innkeepers prefer folios to be settled with credit cards, which are accounts receivable. Be they guests or strangers, customers who buy services *with cash* in the lounge, the coffee shop, the newsstand, or other hotel departments increase the hotel's cash asset. There is no record on the guest's folio, but there is an increase in the hotel's cash.

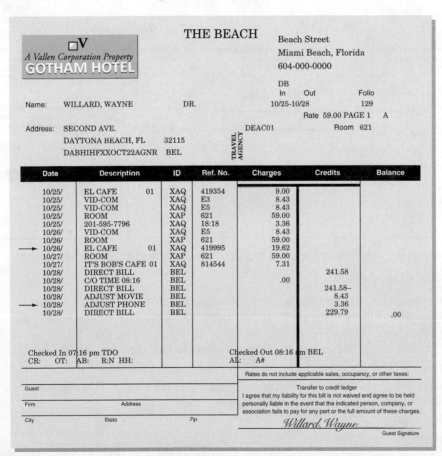

EXHIBIT 5 Another example of a modern folio. The final entry is similar to that of Exhibit 4. "Direct bill" or "direct transfer" indicates the folio balance is moved from the transient ledger to the city ledger for direct billing to the client's headquarters. The heavy vertical line between charges and credits is added here to show accountants the similarity between the folio and a simple T-account. Note the travel agency reference and number, DEAC01, above the charge line.

V

A Vallen Corporation Property
GOTHAM HOTEL

THE INN AT THE OTTAWA CENTER
OTTAWA, CANADA, K3P
613-555-5555

ROOM/CHAMBRE	NAME/NOM	RATE/TAUX	DEPARTURE/DEPART	TIME/HEURE	
1406	**STEIN, FRANK N.**	**75.00**	**14/10/**		**ACCT#**
ROOM/CHAMBRE	FIRM OR GROUP/COMPAGNIE OU GROUP	PLAN	ARRIVAL/ARRIVEE		**205**
1K1A	**AMERICAN**		**09/10/**	**12:29**	
					GROUP
4	**P.O. BOX 1211**	**DB**			**566**
	LANSING MI 90125-0012				
CLERK COMMIS	ADDRESS/ADRESSE		METHOD OF PAYMENT MODE DE PAIEMENT		

DATE	REFERENCE/RÉFÉRENCE		CHARGES	CREDITS/CRÉDITS	BALANCE DUE/SOLDE DÛ
09/10	ROOM	28, 1	75.00		
09/10	ROOM TAX	28, 1	3.75		
10/10	COFFEE SHOP	000000	17.12		
10/10	LNG DIST	315-386-	.57		
10/10	ROOM	28, 1	75.00		
10/10	ROOM TAX	28, 1	3.75		
11/10	ROOM	28, 1	75.00		
11/10	ROOM TAX	28, 1	3.75		
12/10	LNG DIST	315-386-	1.14		
12/10	LNG DIST	315-386-	1.14		
12/10	ROOM	28, 1	75.00		
12/10	ROOM TAX	28, 1	3.75		
13/10	COFFEE SHOP	000000	9.86		
13/10	COFFEE SHOP	000000	16.58		
13/10	ROOM	2228, 1	75.00		
13/10	ROOM TAX	2228, 1	3.75		
					440.16

FIRM / COMPAGNIE	ADDRESS / ADRESSE

I AGREE THAT MY LIABILITY FOR THIS BILL IS NOT WAIVED AND AGREE TO BE HELD PERSONALLY LIABLE IN THE EVENT THAT THE INDICATED PERSON, COMPANY, OR ASSOCIATION FAILS TO PAY FOR ANY PART OR THE FULL AMOUNT OF THESE CHARGES.

CITY _____ PROV. _____ POSTAL _____
VILLE   POSTALE
ATTENTION _____

IL EST CONVENU QUE MA RESPONSABILITÉ DE CETTE FACTURE N'EST PAS ABROGÉE ET JE CONSENTS A L'ASSUMER DANS L'ÉVENTUALITE OU LA PERSONNE INDIQUÉE, SOCIÉTÉ OU ASSOCIATION REFUSE DE PAYER LE MONTANT EN TOTALITÉ OU EN PARTIE.

GUEST SIGNATURE   X _____
SIGNATURE DU CLIENT

EXHIBIT 6 Another group folio. This one identifies the group by name, American; its identification number, #566; the identification of the guest-service agent who registered them, #4; the group's account (folio) number, #205, which could be the same as the room number; and the assumption of liability (bottom right). There's a folio balance so the account is not yet checked out.

An increase in the hotel's cash requires a debit to cash according to the accounting rule:

First Illustration:

> Increases in assets, including accounts receivable and *cash*, are made with debits.
> Increases in incomes (sale of rooms, *food*, beverage, spa, etc.) are made with credits.

Debit: Cash   33.00
  Credit: Proper Department (room, *food*, beverage, spa, etc.)   33.00
Explanation: Sold coffee-shop meal *for cash.*

Hotel guests may make the same purchases by signing for the charges. That requires an entry on the folio, a debit to the asset accounts receivable.

Second Illustration:

> Increases in assets, including *accounts receivable* and cash, are made with debits.
> Increases in incomes (sale of rooms, *food*, beverage, spa, etc.) are made with credits.

Debit: Accounts Receivable/Guest's Folio   33.00
  Credit: Proper Department (room, *food*, beverage, spa, etc.)   33.00
Explanation: Sold coffee-shop meal *on account (to registered guest).*

SALES OR INCOMES   Hotels are in the business of selling services. It is those sales that produce incomes and, eventually, profits for the business. The sale of rooms is the hotel's major product. Depending on the size, class, and type of property, income is also earned from the sale of other products and services. Guests pay for these services by charging them to the folio (establishing an asset called account receivable) or paying for them with credit cards or sometimes with cash. The delivered product or service is the same; they are just paid for differently. The record of service (the sale) is different from the record of payment (charge, or cash) although the two records take place simultaneously, as we shall see next in the discussion of equality.

Debit/credit rules are different for sales (incomes) than for assets. Just as all assets follow one asset rule, so all incomes follow one income rule. It is an opposite rule.

Increases in assets, including *accounts receivable* and cash, are made with debits.
Increases in incomes (sales of *rooms*, food, beverage, etc.) are made with credits.

Debit: Accounts Receivable/Guest's Folio   100
   Credit: Proper Department (*room*, food, beverage, spa, etc.)   100
Explanation. Guest occupied room.

Sometimes, but not too often, incomes are decreased. Assume that as a result of a serious mistake on the hotel's part, the guest's room charge is waived. The room income, which was recorded yesterday with a credit (see above), must now be reversed. Allowances, which are the opposite of sales, are used to do that.

Decreases in incomes (sales of *rooms*, food, beverage, etc.) are made with debits.
Decreases in assets, including *accounts receivable* and cash, are made with credits.

Debit: Proper Departmental (*room*, food, spa, etc.) Allowance   100
   Credit: Accounts Receivable/Guest's Folio   100
Explanation: Room allowance (reduction) because of housekeeping failure.

This room-sale debit offsets the original room-sale credit made when the room was occupied. The net result is no charge in the guest's folio. Both postings, the sale and the sale adjustment (an allowance), appear on the folio (see Exhibit 5, telephone $3.36).

Every accounting event has two parts. This dual accounting system always requires equal dollar amounts of charges and credits. For example, two things happen when a bar bill is paid with cash. One, the hotel has more cash in the till. Two, bar sales, or bar income, has also increased. Both increase by the same dollar amount. The first illustration, the $33 food example discussed earlier, illustrates that equality.

If the bar tab is charged to the room rather than paid with cash, the accounting entry changes somewhat, illustrated by the second $33 example, but the equality of debits and credits remains the same.

Reexamine the room sale and then the room adjustment discussed above, giving special attention to the equality of charges and credits—first, when the room sale was recorded, and then when the room was adjusted because of the complaint. Do you see that the adjustment (the room allowance) balances the original room charge? The complaining guest has been comped.

POSTING TO THE FOLIO (THE ACCOUNT RECEIVABLE)

Hotels readily extend credit to guests because their identities have been confirmed through reservations, registrations, and credit cards. Guests charge goods and services to their front-office accounts, their folios. Folios are accounts receivable, debts *owed by the guest* and *owned by the hotel.* "Posting" to the folio means recording the event, usually a sale (the charge), or a payment (the credit).

Guests may also buy goods and services by paying cash or using a credit card at the time the service is rendered. Paying for a bar drink or a breakfast buffet with cash or credit card does not impact the folio. The cash goes into the till. The credit-card charge appears eventually on the credit-card mailing sent to the guest's home or business. Most registered guests sign for such services. Then the debt appears on the folio to be settled at some later time, usually at check-out.

Room charges and telephone calls made from the room must appear on the folio. There is no practical way for the hotel to collect cash when those services are rendered. No one expects collection for the room occupancy in the middle of the night. Telephone calls are posted (recorded) on the folio automatically, electronically. So both room sales and telephone sales are made to the guest only on credit, charged to the folio. There are no cash sales for these.

Cash and credit cards do have a role at the front desk. They are used by guests to settle (pay for) the folio charges. That discussion appears at the end of this chapter.

Definition of Terms to Be Used	
Allowance	Reduction of the debt owed by an account receivable
Departmental Control Sheet	*Pencil-and-paper record* of departmental (food, beverage, etc.) charges made to various guest rooms. Control sheets have been placed by property management systems (computers)
Transfer	Movement of a folio balance between ledgers or folios
Zero Balance	After check-out, every folio has a balance of zero

Overview of the Billing Procedure

Electronic folios gained favor in the mid-1980s, gradually replacing the paper-and-pencil folios of Exhibit 2. Better carbon paper and then duplicating paper without messy carbons came during the transition. Stationery companies introduced packaged forms that reduced the need to rewrite the same information over and over. Then came property management systems (PMSs), which did away with all the paper. Records are retained in computer memory and printed only on demand.

PREPARING THE FOLIO The property management system formats the folios as guests arrive and register (see Exhibits 5 and 6 and others.) The data to open the folio come from the registration card. Some hotels use reservation information instead. Those hotels preprint the reg cards as part of the previous night's audit so they await the guests' arrivals. Preprinted cards speed up registration, but new ones may be needed if the information changes in the interim.

Many bits of information appear on the folio, including the times of arrival and departure (Exhibit 5, on the bottom). There are no rules, so information may appear anywhere or not at all. Exhibit 6 shows arrival time of 12:29 at the folio's top. Group affiliation is also shown there. Exhibit 6 indicates membership in the *American* group, whose GROUP billing code is 566, right side above the center.

There is common information on every folio. Exhibit 6 can serve as the standard. Illustrated are the room assigned (1406), the rate charged ($75), and the dates of arrival and anticipated departure (9/10 and 14/10).[2] Included, of course, is the guest's name, Frank N. Stein, and address. The number of persons is usually shown, but not in Exhibit 6; see instead Exhibit 9, top right.

---

[2]In many nations, the day of the month is written before the month of the year. So a date of 9/10 would be the 9th of October, not the 10th of September.

Folios may be numbered sequentially as a means of identification and accounting control. The folio account number of Exhibit 6 is 205. Folio numbers were especially important for internal control when the hotel used pencil-and-paper folios, and almost always appeared in the upper right corner, Exhibit 2.

Information of all kinds is being added to the folio to protect the hotel from unwarranted lawsuits. Notice of the availability of a safe for the protection of the guest's valuables is one such disclaimer. This fits better on the registration card, which the guest sees on arrival, rather than on the folio, which the guest normally sees at departure.

Nearly every folio now carries at the bottom of the page a statement about liability for the bill (see Exhibit 1 and others). With so many persons (employers, associations, credit-card companies) other than the guests accepting the charges, hotel lawyers want to make certain that eventually someone pays. The odd part about the statement is how rarely guests are asked to sign or initial it.

PRESENTING THE BILL   Common law protects the innkeeper from fraud. Guests who are unwilling or unable to pay may be refused accommodations. Extending credit, as most hotels do, is a privilege that may be revoked at any time. Nervous credit managers do just that whenever their suspicions are aroused. The folio is printed and presented to the guest with a request for immediate payment. Even the traditional delay of paying at check-out is revoked. The entire industry has gone one step further by collecting in advance with cash (rare) or by obtaining credit-card identification.

Since most guests are not credit risks, bills are normally presented and paid at check-out time. It works that way for the vast majority of guests who stay for several nights. A folio is printed on demand as the guest departs. If there are any adjustments, an amended copy is printed for the guest to take away. Many hotels deliver the customer's initial copy under the guest-room door sometime during the previous night. If a hard copy is not needed, the folio can be viewed on a front-office monitor or more leisurely on the television in the guest room.

Long-term guests are billed weekly, and they are expected to pay promptly. Regardless of the length of the stay, folios are also rendered whenever they reach a predetermined dollar amount. The class of hotel, which reflects room rates and menu prices, determines the dollar figure that management sets as the ceiling. No charges are allowed beyond that value once the guest has had ample notice.

COMMUNICATING THE CHARGES   Guests buy services—that is, incur charges—throughout the house. Perhaps there is a drink by the swimming pool, a dinner in the grill, or laundry for overnight service. Getting the information (name, room number, and dollar value) about the charge from the point of origin to the folio requires some type of communication.

Before the Age of Electronics   Paper-and-pencil systems required close cooperation and fast footwork between departments. The department making the sale had to communicate manually to the desk where the charge on the folio was entered. And it had to be done quickly. To illustrate, assume a guest takes breakfast in the coffee shop. By signing the $15 guest check, the guest orders the meal charged to the folio.

{*Reminder:* Folios are not used if payments are by cash or credit card!}

The signed check, now called a *voucher,* was used to communicate with the desk. As a precaution against its loss (it's just a piece of paper) the coffee-shop cashier recorded the information on a *departmental control sheet* (see Exhibit 7). Both the voucher and the control sheet showed the guest's name and room number, the amount of the charge, and the voucher (coffee-shop check) number. The cashier retained the control sheet.

Sending the voucher to the desk was easier said than done. Hand-carried vouchers moved slowly because the coffee-shop cashier had to wait for a runner: a busperson, a bellperson, or a foodserver. Several vouchers were accumulated before a runner was summoned. That minimized the inconvenience of frequent calls; after all, the cashier had no authority over these runners. Busy runners sometimes forgetfully pocketed the voucher as they ran off to perform their regular duties. (That is when the control sheet became a back-up.)

VOUCHER NO.	ROOM NO.	GUEST NAME	AMOUNT	MEMO
		Restaurant **DEPARTMENT CONTROL SHEET**		
	NAME	*Sally Newport*		
11870	409	*Fishel*	$ *16*	
11871	1012	*James*	*27*	

THIS REPORT MUST BE SENT TO NIGHT AUDITOR BY 12 O'CLOCK EACH NIGHT.

EXHIBIT 7 Segment of a departmental control sheet. The form is used no longer. Guest checks (called vouchers) were recorded as a precaution against loss. They were then dispatched to the front office for pencil-and-paper posting to the folio. This system has been replaced by electronic posting at the point of origin as illustrated in Exhibit 8.

Vouchers were often late in arriving at the desk. Charges that appear on a folio after the guest has checked out, called *late charges*, are difficult to collect. If the amount is small, the hotel doesn't even try.

With the voucher in hand, the guest-service agent began the posting (recording) sequence. A search was made for that particular guest's folio, filed in room-number sequence in the cashier's well (see Exhibit 3). The folio was removed and the $15 was posted (see Exhibit 2). Each posting had to be located in the correct vertical column (the date) opposite the proper department, "RESTAURANT," as Exhibit 2 illustrates.

With Electronic Systems   The hotel's PMS has done away with vouchers, control sheets, runners, and late charges. Communication is electronic and instantaneous. The distant department is tied to the folio electronically. Cashiers throughout the hotel enter the charge onto the folio by means of an electronic cash register, called a *point-of-sale terminal (POS)*. The system bypasses the front desk and the guest-service agent altogether (see Exhibit 8). Folios are always current; late charges are practically unknown. There is an extra: Information furnished through the POS terminal enables the departmental cashier to verify the guest's identity, if that is an issue (Exhibit 8).

EXHIBIT 8 Point-of-sale (POS) terminals are located in revenue centers (restaurants, bars, gift shops, etc.) throughout the hotel. The POS interfaces with the hotel's PMS, permitting cashiers at distant locations to post electronically to guest folios, eliminating control sheets (Exhibit 7) and vouchers.

POS installations involve cost. Management might make an economic decision to leave certain minor departments, which generate small revenue streams, without POS capability. Then the property operates with a mix of the pencil-and-paper system and the PMS.

Recording Charges to Accounts Receivable

Charges (increases to accounts receivable) and credits (decreases to accounts receivable) are posted (entered on the folios) to keep guest accounts current. The discussion now focuses on the meaning of each charge. Next, we'll examine the meaning of each credit.

UNDERSTANDING THE LINE OF POSTING Each *charge* line on the folio represents two things. One is the change in the value of the folio. The amount owed by the guest grows larger with each charge posting. The more services the guest buys, the more dollars are owed.

Each folio line has a second message. It tells the reader the source of the charge, the department providing the service. Hence, the second meaning reflects the income that the hotel earns from the delivery of the service. Exhibit 9 illustrates several of these departmental charges.

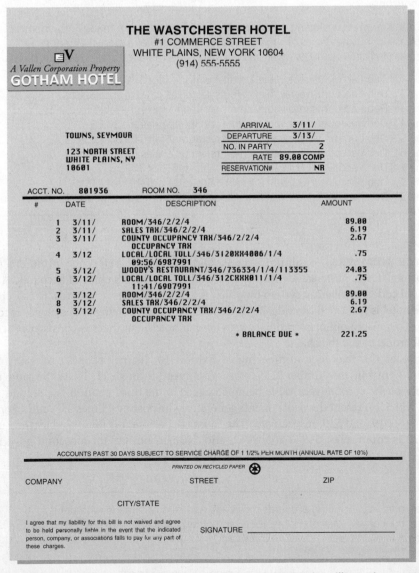

EXHIBIT 9 Electronic folios are all much the same. This one isn't. Previous illustrations contain two columns, charges and credits. This illustration has but one, leaving the user to distinguish charges from credits. Note the sales tax posting on lines 2, 3, 8, and 9. (The guest is a walk-in. There's a NR (no reservation) on the top right.) Still, someone knows him; his rate is comp.

Among them are room sales (Exhibit 9, lines 1 and 7); restaurant sales (Woody's Restaurant, line 5); and telephone sales (lines 4 and 6).

{*Reminder:* The folio would not be used if Woody's charge was paid with cash or credit card. Folios are accounts receivables, guests who *still* owe the hotel.}

Each folio illustrated in this chapter and each used in reality have the same format. There is a horizontal, single line entry for each activity. The printed information in the center of the folio line identifies a source of income for the hotel. The fact that there is a posting means that the guest (the account receivable) has purchased some service from the hotel and owes the same amount that is recorded as departmental income. That amount is added automatically to the previous folio balance, the right-hand column.

Examine Exhibit 9 or any of the other folio exhibits. Each line is read as a two-part accounting entry. One is a debit, the other the balancing credit. Since folios are accounts receivable, every folio line represents either an accounts receivable debit or an accounts receivable credit! With charges, each line is an accounts receivable debit, and the credit is to the department printed on the horizontal line.

Increase in assets, including *accounts receivable* and cash, are made with debits.
Increase in incomes (sales of *rooms, food, telephone*) are made with credits.
Increase in liabilities (debts owed to banks and *governments*) are made with credits.

Line 1 Debit accounts receivable, credit room sales for $89.
Line 2 Debit accounts receivable, credit sales taxes payable for $6.19.
Line 3 Debit accounts receivable, credit occupancy taxes payable for $2.67.
Line 4 Debit accounts receivable, credit telephone sales for $0.75.
Line 5 Debit accounts receivable, credit restaurant sales for $24.03.
Line 6 Debit accounts receivable, credit telephone sales for $0.75.
Line 7 Debit accounts receivable, credit room sales for $89.
Line 8 Debit accounts receivable, credit sales taxes payable for $6.19.
Line 9 Debit accounts receivable, credit occupancy taxes payable for $2.67.

REFERENCE NUMBERS Exhibits 5, 6, 9, and 10 display reference numbers on each line of posting. These numbers identify departments in the hotel's chart of accounts. A chart of accounts is a coded numbering system by which the hotel classifies its records. Each department within the hotel is identified by code, but it isn't a secret code. Having codes makes recordkeeping easier. There is no uniform coding system among hotels, but there is consistency within the individual property and the chain.

Consider the reference numbering of Exhibit 10. In the second column, under the "description" portion, the number 2315 appears on lines 2 through 11. That's the room number, the number of the account receivable being charged. In the third column is a second series of numbers, which represent the departments generating the postings. Lines 2, 3, and 4 contain the numbers 518, 519, and 520, respectively. The rooms department is identified by the number 5. Hence, 518 is room sales, 519 is room tax, and 520 is room tax for a second governmental agency.

Increases in assets, including *accounts receivable* and cash, are made with debits.
Increases in incomes (sales of *rooms*, food, and other) are made with credits.
Increases in liabilities (debts owed to banks and *governments*) are made with credits. Values for Exhibit 10:

Line 2: Debit accounts receivable, credit room sales for $125.
Line 3: Debit accounts receivable, credit excise taxes payable for $5.21.
Line 4: Debit accounts receivable, credit room taxes payable for $6.25.

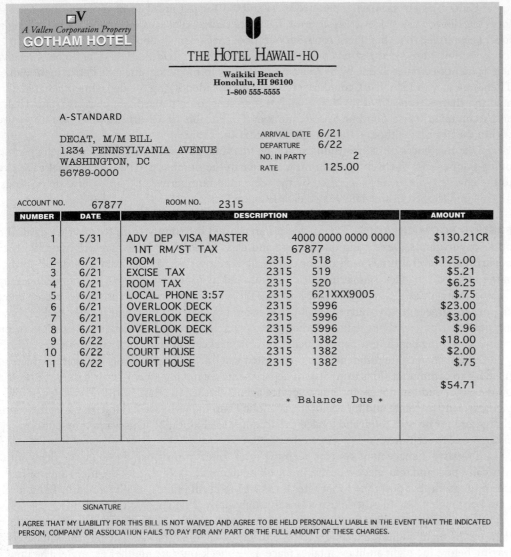

The folio image reads:

A Vallen Corporation Property
GOTHAM HOTEL

THE HOTEL HAWAII-HO

Waikiki Beach
Honolulu, HI 96100
1–800 555-5555

A-STANDARD

DECAT, M/M BILL
1234 PENNSYLVANIA AVENUE
WASHINGTON, DC
56789-0000

ARRIVAL DATE	6/21
DEPARTURE	6/22
NO. IN PARTY	2
RATE	125.00

ACCOUNT NO. 67877   ROOM NO. 2315

NUMBER	DATE	DESCRIPTION			AMOUNT
1	5/31	ADV DEP VISA MASTER 1NT RM/ST TAX	4000 0000 0000 0000 67877		$130.21CR
2	6/21	ROOM	2315	518	$125.00
3	6/21	EXCISE TAX	2315	519	$5.21
4	6/21	ROOM TAX	2315	520	$6.25
5	6/21	LOCAL PHONE 3:57	2315	621XXX9005	$.75
6	6/21	OVERLOOK DECK	2315	5996	$23.00
7	6/21	OVERLOOK DECK	2315	5996	$3.00
8	6/21	OVERLOOK DECK	2315	5996	$.96
9	6/22	COURT HOUSE	2315	1382	$18.00
10	6/22	COURT HOUSE	2315	1382	$2.00
11	6/22	COURT HOUSE	2315	1382	$.75
					$54.71
		* Balance Due *			

SIGNATURE

I AGREE THAT MY LIABILITY FOR THIS BILL IS NOT WAIVED AND AGREE TO BE HELD PERSONALLY LIABLE IN THE EVENT THAT THE INDICATED PERSON, COMPANY OR ASSOCIATION FAILS TO PAY FOR ANY PART OR THE FULL AMOUNT OF THESE CHARGES.

EXHIBIT 10 Line I of the folio indicates an advanced deposit made with a credit card; a very unusual entry. Under the "description" column, this folio references the chart of accounts that the hotel maintains. Each record (posting) has two parts! One is always understood as a charge to the account receivable, room 2315. Equal and opposite credits are recorded in their respective departments. The code tells us that the 500s (518, 519, and 520) are rooms; the 5900s are beverage, and the 1300s (1382) are food. The balance still due is net of the $130.21 deposit (one night's stay plus tax) and will be settled in all likelihood with the same credit card.

The number 5996 appears on lines 6, 7, and 8. In this case the number 59 indicates beverage sales and 96 indicates the Overlook Deck, so 5996 is beverage sales on the Overlook Deck. The number 5997 might be beverage sales in the Court House, 5998 might be beverage sales through room service, and 5999 might be beverage sales in banquets. Line 6 is the actual sale of beverages, line 7 is the tip that the guest added to the bill, and line 8 is the tax due.

Increases in assets, including *accounts receivable* and cash, are made with debits.
Increases in incomes (sales of *rooms*, *beverage*, and other) are made with credits.
Increase in liabilities (debts to *employees* and *governments*) are made with credits.

Line 6: Debit accounts receivable, credit beverage sales for $23.
Line 7: Debit accounts receivable, credit tips owed to employees for $3.00.
Line 8: Debit accounts receivable, credit sales taxes payable for $0.96.

Food sales are similarly referenced in Exhibit 10 using number 13. The number 1382 is food sales in the Court House Restaurant. Just as beverage sales had several divisions, so might food sales: coffee shop, banquets, room service, pool snack bar, and buffet, 1383…1387.

Exhibit 9 follows the same concept although the presentation differs. The account receivable is identified on each line by its room number, 346, immediately after the department name. Then, just as with Exhibit 10, comes a series of numbers identifying the departments that generated the charge. Code 2/2/4 (lines 1, 2, and 3) represent room department charges (rooms sales and room taxes) corresponding to code number 5 of Exhibit 10. Clearly, there is no uniformity within the industry, although there might be within the chain.

The references of Exhibit 5 do not follow the same pattern. The ID column is the person doing the posting. The Ref. No. column may refer to the number on the voucher that gave rise to the charge. That idea is supported by the sequential numbering of the two El Cafe postings, 419354 on October 25 and 419995 two days later, on October 27.

POSTING ROOM CHARGES   Room charges are posted differently from the charges of all the other departments. Depending on the type and class of hotel, charges may originate in other departments several times each day or not at all. Among them are laundry and dry cleaning, garage and parking fees, saunas and health clubs, and in-room bar charges. In-room films may also be charged (see Exhibit 5, lines 2 and 3). Full-service resorts have sports and recreational charges for greens fees, watercraft, ski tickets, skeet, horseback riding, and the like. All of these are posted as previously explained. Either posted directly through the departmental POS or by runners carrying pencil-and-paper vouchers (say from skeet) to be input by the desk.

Room charges are different. They are posted just once, at night. Room charges originate at the desk so communications from distant departments are not an issue. Room charges are posted by the night auditor, not by the guest-service agents during the day. With the old pencil-and-paper system, the night auditor removed each folio from the well (see Exhibit 3); wrote the room charge and tax on each folio; and totaled the account (see Exhibit 2). This was a time-consuming, error-prone procedure.

Property management systems keep the room rates in memory, compute the taxes automatically, post and total electronically and print on demand. With a PMS, the night auditor initiates a program that posts the room rates and taxes to all the folios, as illustrated in Exhibit 10, lines 2 through 4, and in other illustrations throughout the chapter.

Four exceptions, all infrequent ones, require room rates to be posted during the day rather than by the night auditor. Exception one is a day rate: Guests arrive and depart the same day—leaving before the night audit even takes place. Late check-outs are another example. The previous night's room charge is posted in the normal manner by the auditor, but the premium for staying beyond the check-out hour is added by the cashier/guest-service agent as the guest departs. Situation three is a recent innovation that has evoked industrywide angst and is not likely to be retained. Guests who leave earlier than their original reservation are penalized. Where inflicted, these outrageous charges are also posted by cashiers/guest-service agents. Obviously, the night auditor would be unaware of the early departure.[3]

Paid-in-advance guests, usually those without luggage, are the fourth and final exception to who posts the room rates. Here again, it is the cashiers/guest-service agents. Beside posting, they also collect for the night *before* the paid-in-advanced guest is roomed. Payment is night by night and no other charges are allowed against the folio. Without a cumulative folio balance, paid-in-advance guests must use cash or credit cards in the bars and restaurants. Guests are given receipts when they pay for the room, so they rarely come to the desk to check out. The general availability of debit and credit cards raises a caution flag for an arrival without either cards or baggage.

In each of the four cases (day rate, late check-out, reservation overstay, and paid in advance), the night auditor finds the room charge has already been posted just as other charges (food, telephone, etc.) have been.

---

[3]It has never been challenged in court, but the fee might run counter to the common-law description of a "guest;" one whose stay is indeterminable.

Although posted at a different time and in a different manner, room sales have the same impact as sales in other departments. All increase the amount owed by the guest, the account receivable. Most folio postings, including sales taxes, do just that: Increase the amount owed by the guest.

Sales Taxes Taxes levied on room sales by local, county, and state governments are universal to hotelkeeping. Government finds taxing visitors easier than taxing residents. Making the hotel collect the tax adds insult to injury. With rare exceptions, every jurisdiction requires each room charge to be followed by one or more tax charges. The amount owed by the guest (the account receivable) increases with the room sale, which belongs to the hotel, and with the room tax, which the hotel collects for the government.

Taxes collected and payable to the government make the hotel an account receivable to the government just as the guest is an account receivable to the hotel. An account receivable becomes an *account payable* when situated on the other side of the owe–owed relationship. The government considers the hotel's debt as an account receivable. The hotel, which owes the amount collected from guests, considers the government an account payable. So, the amount due is labeled *taxes,* meaning *taxes payable.* Exhibits 6, 9, and 10 reflect those taxes.

Periodically, perhaps quarterly, the hotel pays the governmental agencies the taxes due.

WHEN TAXES ARE LEVIED ON THE GUEST (SEE EXHIBIT 9)

Increases in assets, including *accounts receivable* and cash, are made with debits.
Increases in incomes (sale of *rooms*, food, beverage, spa, etc.) are made with credits.
Increases in liabilities (debts to employees and *governments*) are made with credits.

Debit: Accounts Receivable/Guest's Folio	97.86	
Credit: Room Sales		89
Credit: Taxes Payable		8.86

Explanation: Collected taxes on guest's room charges.

WHEN TAXES ARE PAID BY THE HOTEL TO THE GOVERNMENT

Decreases in liabilities (debts to employees and *governments*) are made with debits.
Decreases in assets, including accounts receivable and *cash*, are made with credits.

Debit: Debit Taxes Payable	8.86	
Credit: Cash		8.86

Explanation: Paid government sums collected from guests.

Recording Credits to Accounts Receivable

Having enjoyed the hotel's services (while the charge [debit] balance of the folio grew), the guest prepares to check out and settle the account. This is when the debt is paid and the active account receivable (the folio) is reduced to zero. At the end of the stay *the active account receivable (the folio) is always reduced to zero.*

As the guest folio (an account receivable) is increased by charges (room sales, food sales, and so on) so it is decreased by credits (payments). It is simple: Paying the bill reduces the debt.

Although charges occur and are posted numerous times throughout each day, settlement of the account usually waits until check-out time. Of course, guests can and do make payments during their stay. With reservations, payments are sometimes made in advance, prepaid. Irrespective of when and how the payment is made, the transient folio (the guest bill, the front-office account) *must* always have a zero balance at check-out! That is, total charges posted throughout the stay and total credits, whenever posted, must be equal at departure. Departed guests can have no transient folio balance if they are no longer registered. The first few pages of the chapter made clear that only registered guests can have accounts in the transient ledger.

THREE METHODS OF SETTLING ACCOUNTS Unlike the many charges itemized earlier (room charges, bar charges, green fees, saunas), there are only three ways to "pay" the bill. They can be applied separately or in combination.

1. Cash is one method, but it is used infrequently. Cash means any kind of money: bills and coin, foreign currency, domestic and international traveler's checks, personal checks, bank checks, cashier's checks, even casino chips.

2. Allowances, reductions to the amount owed, are a second method of settlement. One study suggested that billing errors that require allowance adjustments may occur as often as one in four postings!

3. Transfers—shifting the amount due to someone else—is the third method, and the most frequently used one. Credit-card transfers are the best examples. Departing guests shift their folio balances in the front-office ledger (the transient ledger) to the credit-card company's account in the city ledger. Earlier, the chapter pointed out that front-office ledgers (with their folios) are for registered guests only. Similarly, the city ledger is for nonregistered accounts receivable. When the guest leaves—is no longer registered—the charge must be moved to the city ledger, usually to a credit-card account. The credit-card company eventually settles with the hotel. However, other transfers are possible and frequent.

SETTLING WITH ALLOWANCES   Just as retailers permit the return of unsatisfactory goods, hoteliers give credit for poor service, misunderstandings, and mathematical errors. The retailer's exchange of goods is the hotel's allowance. Part or all of a folio settlement (by which the guest pays the bill) can be made with an allowance.

Legitimate adjustments to guest complaints are high on management's radar. So much so that lease contracts often contain provisions for hotels to grant allowances against privately owned concessionaires renting shop space in the hotel.

A record of every allowance highlights the issue for both the hotel and the guest. Using a pencil-and-paper allowance voucher (see Exhibit 11) provides guidance for the company anxious to avoid future errors in guest service. Improving operations starts with knowing what the failures have been. The dollar and cents of allowances emphasize the point.

Allowance reports summarizing the day's experience are prepared as part of the night audit. Reports to management take on extra significance when employees have been empowered. So granting allowances could become abusive. Employee empowerment aside, good fiscal management requires a supervisor's signature (see Exhibit 11, bottom line) when the allowance exceeds a certain value. This limit would vary with the class of the hotel.

Allowances or *rebates* are given to adjust the folio after the fact. Better to first correct the problem if possible. Allowances are warranted only if it is too late to rectify the situation.

Comp Allowances   Allowances are also used for room comps. "Professional courtesy" is a comp room that one hotelier gives to another when space is available. Rooms are often comped for convention executives making on-site visits and for VIPs.

The authority to compliment rooms or other services—professional lingo calls it "the power of the pen"—should be restricted and carefully monitored. Because comps, like

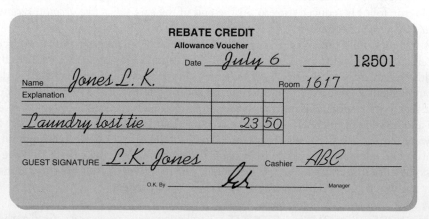

EXHIBIT 11   Allowance (or rebate) vouchers, which are credits to the guest folio, are issued to settle guest claims. They are numbered for internal control and serve to alert management to the quality of guest service.

allowances in general, are subject to abuse, management requires a comp report as an adjunct to the night audit's allowance report. Misuse of comps starts when comp policy allows comp guests to bypass registration. With no record, there is no room count, no house count, and no dollar income. Proper handling of room comps starts with a daily posting of the full room rate. To allay the guest's concern, the rate is flagged on the rooming slip, "$189 COMP," for example. An allowance, valued for the total of the daily room charges, is granted as the comp guest checks out.

This allowance illustration builds on the previous illustration dealing with room taxes and uses the same values. This comp guest (see Exhibit 9) stayed for two nights. The room and tax posting appeared twice. (See Exhibit 9 for the actual folio postings.) Here the folio entries appear in accounting form.

Increases in assets, including *accounts receivable* and cash, are made with debits.
Increases in incomes (sales of rooms, food, beverage, etc.) are made with credits.
Increases in liabilities (debts owed to banks and *governments*) are made with credits.

Debit: Accounts Receivable/Guest's Folio   97.86
    Credit: Proper Department (*room*, food, beverage, spa, etc.)   89.00
    Credit: Sales Taxes Payable   8.86
Explanation: Entry for *each night* of the guest's two-night stay.

Reversing the room sale (or any other sale) with an allowance results in no charges to the guest and no room (or other) income earned by the hotel. However, a clear record of what occurred is now on the books. Most jurisdictions require room taxes to be paid on comp rooms. Sometimes the hotel pays; sometimes the comped guest pays, as illustrated next.

Decreases in incomes (sales of *rooms*, food, beverage, etc.) are made with debits.
Decreases in assets, including *accounts receivable* and cash, are made with credits.

Debit: Proper Departmental (*rooms*, food, beverage) Allowance   178.00
    Credit: Accounts Receivable/Guest's Folio   178.00
Explanation: Comped two nights (leaving guest to pay the $17.72 tax bill).

Allowance for Poor Service Accidents happen: A shirt is scorched in the laundry; a skirt is torn on a rough cocktail table. And service delivery fails: A foodserver spills coffee on a guest; a child's crib is never delivered. Service mishaps are bound to occur when servicing hundreds of visitors each day.

If the problem is caught immediately, management remedies the mistake (delivers the crib). If not caught immediately, or if the problem has no remedy (the shirt is burned), there is little to do but reimburse with an allowance. Every allowance, whether for comps or adjustments, results in reductions of both the account receivable (the guest's folio) and the departmental income. If the original charge was made to a credit card (as it might be in the lounge where the skirt was torn), the adjustment would be made to the credit card, not to the folio.

All allowance entries follow the same format as the room comp allowance. The specific departmental allowance is substituted for the room allowance of the illustration above.

Allowance to Correct Errors Handling small late charges is one of several clerical errors requiring correcting allowances. A late charge is posted to the folio of a guest who has already checked out. If the charge is large enough to pursue by mail, a transfer—soon to be explained—is used. If the late charge is too small to warrant the costs of collection, including guest annoyance, it is wiped off. Accounts receivable is credited; the income of the department is reduced so the hotel absorbs the error.

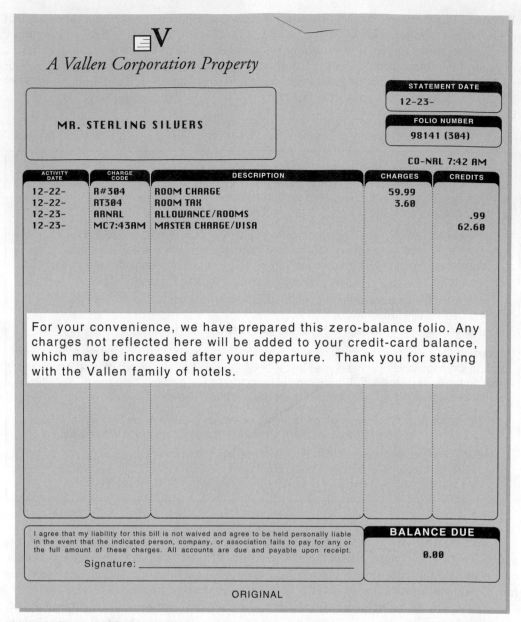

EXHIBIT 12 At check-out, all folios must have a zero balance (see lower right corner). This folio is balanced with two credits: an allowance and a transfer of the balance to a credit-card company. Exhibit 14 illustrates the third possible credit, payment with cash. Note the sequential folio number on the top right and the charge codes in the second column. Note also the "heads-up" alerting guests to possible late charges.

Some errors are just carelessness in posting. Exhibit 12 shows the allowance for $0.99 that was inadvertently posted as part of the room charge by the night auditor. Exhibit 5 (third line from the bottom) adjusts for a dual posting of an in-room film (lines 2 and 3).

Many errors originate in misunderstandings or lack of attention. For example, a couple arrives for several days but one spouse leaves early. Although the desk is aware of the situation, the double occupancy rate continues for the entire stay. An allowance is needed to reduce the charges by the difference between the single and double rates multiplied by the number of nights overcharged.

In theory, it should not happen, but sometimes a guest folio is carried one night beyond the actual departure day. An allowance corrects the error. This happens most frequently with one-night, paid-in-advance guests who do not bother to check out.

Every protested charge is not the hotel's error. This is why having old vouchers accessible to the cashier is helpful and PMS programs do that. When shown a signed voucher (the check), guests often recall charges that they had vehemently protested only moments earlier. Large bar charges fall into this category when viewed with a sober eye the following day. This also happens when two persons share a room and one makes charges but the other pays. Especially when the first guest has already checked out is it necessary to prove to the remaining guest that the charge was made.

Although computers reduce the number of errors, they do not compensate for guest forgetfulness, for honest misunderstandings, or mistakes by either party.

Extended-Stay Allowances Some resorts and extended-stay properties allow a rate reduction if the guest remains an extended length of time. To make certain of the guest's commitment to remain, the full daily charge is posted and not the pro-rata charge of the special rate. Either an allowance is given on the final day to adjust the weekly rate or the charge of the final day is reduced to meet the special weekly total.

Recording the Allowance Allowances as well as the other two means of settlement, cash and transfers, are usually resolved as the guest departs. Once the amount has been settled, a voucher is completed (see Exhibit 11). Empowered employees are authorized to sign off within a given dollar range. The allowance is used with either or both other methods of payment to settle the bill. Exhibit 12 illustrates settlement with an allowance and a credit-card transfer. Cash, not illustrated here, is the third method of settlement.

> Using the vouchers and computer records, the accounting department, not the front desk, will charge (debit) each allowance against the sales of the department from which it originates.

SETTLING WITH TRANSFERS Allowances, cash payments, and transfers are usually—but not always—recorded as the guest checks out. A transfer simply moves the balance of one record (say, a front-office folio) to another record (most often, a city-ledger credit-card account). The balance of the front-office folio gets smaller, falling to zero if part of the check-out. The balance of the other record gets larger by the same transfer amount.

All or part of a folio balance can be transferred. Transfers can be made between accounts in the same ledger (registered guest to registered guest in the transient ledger) or between accounts in two ledgers (registered guest in the transient ledger to city accounts in the city ledger). The first transfer type, registered guest to registered guest, is easier to track because both folios are available to the front-office staff. Transfers between transient folios and city accounts, usually credit-card companies, may appear incomplete to the front-office staff if the city ledger is not accessible to the front desk. City-ledger records are the accounting office's responsibility.

> Every accounting event (entry) must have equal dollar debits and credits.

Folio Transfer of Registered Guest to Registered Guest The two pages of Exhibit 2 illustrate how transfers were recorded on the old pencil-and-paper folios. Note that both parties have folios and both stay one night, December 23 (the first vertical column). Both folios reflect room and tax charges of $84.24 ($78 + $6.24). When the new day starts, December 24 (column 2), both have beginning balances, BROUGHT FORWARD. The BROUGHT FORWARD value is larger in Room 409 than in 407 because of the previous day's restaurant charge. As the second day unfolds, Room 407 *transfers* its balance to Room 409. Both check out before the second day ends. Room 409 pays the total of both folios.

At check-out, the balance on each folio is zero. Room 407 has paid by transferring the balance to another front-office folio, 409. Transferring is the topic of this chapter segment.

At check-out, Room 409 also has a zero balance. Room 409 has paid both folio charges. by transferring the balance to the city ledger. That's the topic of the next segment, transfers to the city ledger. In both exhibits of 10-2, the balances of the departing guests are zero. Closing balances must always be zero!

The same sequence and results can be seen in Exhibit 13, on modern PMS folios. Guest Berger, room 301, settles his account by transferring his folio to another folio, Meade's, room 723. Berger's folio falls to zero at check-out and Meade's increases by the same value, $230.80. Then

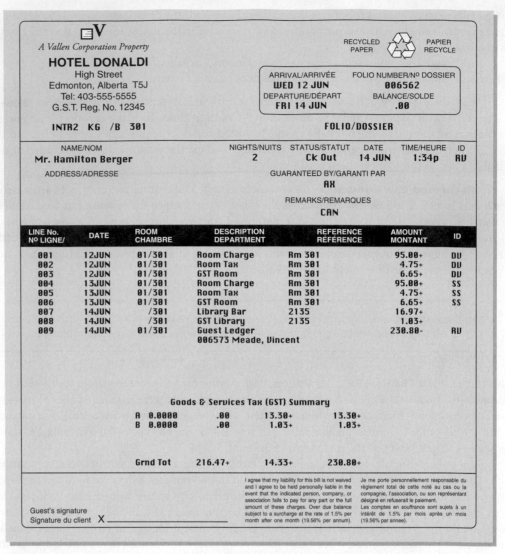

EXHIBIT 13A Line 9 (left column) of both folios illustrates a transfer from room 301 to room 723. That transfer zeros room 301 and the guest checks out. Room 723 also checks out after making a second type of transfer, one from the guest ledger to the city ledger using an American Express credit card. Two items to note: Sales taxes (GST in Canada) are summarized on each folio and charges and credits are indicated by + and − signs instead of two columns. (Another folio-to-folio transfer is illustrated in Exhibit 2.)

Meade departs, transferring his account including Berger's balance to the American Express card's city-ledger account. His front-office balance is now zero also.

Transfer of Folios to the City Ledger: Credit Card Most guests pay by transferring their folio balance to a credit-card account in the city ledger. That's what Meade did in the paragraph above. The cashier/guest-service agent sees Meade's front-office folio settled, brought to zero. Collection from the credit-card company is left to the accounting office.

Three exhibits in this chapter illustrate the folio-to-city-ledger transfer. Exhibit 2A, room 409 and Exhibit 13B, room 723 have been reviewed several times. Exhibit 12 offers another example, employing two of the three means of settlement. An allowance is granted in conjunction with the credit-card transfer. The two credits there balance the total charges, the guest departs, and the accounting office is left to collect from the credit-card company.

Transfer of Folios to the City Ledger: Direct By far the greatest number of transient ledger transfers are those just discussed, transfers to credit cards. But there are other transfers, too. The obsolete pencil-and-paper folio had one major advantage. It showed these other transfers, and that's significant enough for the text to reproduce the otherwise outdated example.

```
        ☐V
     A Vallen Corporation Property          RECYCLED    ♻    PAPIER
                                             PAPER            RECYCLÉ
     HOTEL DONALDI
        High Street              ┌─────────────────────────────────────┐
   Edmonton, Alberta  T5J        │ ARRIVAL/ARRIVÉE  FOLIO NUMBER/Nº DOSSIER │
     Tel: 403-555-5555           │  WED 12 JUN           006573          │
   G.S.T. Reg. No. 12345         │ DEPARTURE/DÉPART   BALANCE/SOLDE      │
                                 │  FRI 14 JUN            .00            │
   INTR2  KG  /B  723            └─────────────────────────────────────┘
                                        FOLIO/DOSSIER
```

NAME/NOM	NIGHTS/NUITS	STATUS/STATUT	DATE	TIME/HEURE	ID
Mr. Vincent Meade	2	Ck Out	14 JUN	1:34p	RU

ADDRESS/ADRESSE

GUARANTEED BY/GARANTI PAR
AX

REMARKS/REMARQUES
USA

LINE No. Nº LIGNE/	DATE	ROOM CHAMBRE	DESCRIPTION DEPARTMENT	REFERENCE RÉFÉRENCE	AMOUNT MONTANT	ID
001	12JUN	01/723	Room Charge	Rm 723	95.00+	DU
002	12JUN	01/723	Room Tax	Rm 723	4.75+	DU
003	12JUN	01/723	GST Room	Rm 723	6.65+	DU
004	13JUN	01/723	Long Distance	0 - 54-6 8	4.68+	
005	13JUN	01/723	Long Distance	0 - 51-1 6	5.57+	
006	13JUN	01/723	Room Charge	Rm 723	95.00+	SS
007	13JUN	01/723	Room Tax	Rm 723	4.75+	SS
008	13JUN	01/723	GST Room	Rm 723	6.65+	SS
009	14JUN	01/301	Guest Ledger		230.80+	RU
			006562 Berger, Hamilton			
010	14JUN	01/723	American Express Thank you		453.85-	RU

Goods & Services Tax (GST) Summary

A	0.0000	.00	13.30+	13.30+
B	7.0000	9.58+	.67+	10.25+
Grnd Tot		209.08+	13.97+	223.05+

I agree that my liability for this bill is not waived and I agree to be held personally liable in the event that the indicated person, company, or association fails to pay for any part or the full amount of these charges. Over due balance subject to a surcharge at the rate of 1.5% per month after one month (19.56% per annum).

Je me porte personnellement responsable du règlement total de cette noté au cas ou la compagnie, l'association, ou son représentant désigné en refuserait le paiement. Les comptes en souffrance sont sujets à un intérêt de 1.5% par mois après un mois (19.56% par année).

Guest's signature
Signature du client X _____

EXHIBIT 13B Continued

Exhibit 2 lists the several options that guests can use to settle their folios. Reader: look at 10-2! Six credit lines appear below the TOTAL DEBIT (total charge) line. One is CASH. One is ALLOWANCES (previously discussed), and one is CITY LEDGER (meaning transfers). There are three city-ledger choices. Exhibit 2 lists them in sequence: ADVANCE DEPOSIT (the final topic of this chapter); CREDIT CARDS, discussed immediately above; and TRANSFERS (meaning transfers other than credit cards).

Two transfer types have already been discussed at length: transferring one folio to another (Exhibits 2 and 13), and moving the folio to a city-ledger credit-card account (also Exhibits 2 and 13). Now a third is highlighted: transferring a folio to the city ledger but *not* to a credit card. The form and procedure are no different than the credit-card transfer. The difference is the destination in the city ledger. *Recall*: The city ledger is made of accounts receivable not now registered. Among those "persons" may be credit-card companies, business enterprises, associations, airlines, travel agents, individuals, and others. Creditworthiness is not an issue with credit-card companies in the city ledger. Since it may be with the other accounts receivables, hotels usually require city-ledger credit to be established beforehand.

Master Accounts   Master accounts are a good example of the direct city-ledger transfer. And they are quite common in hotels doing a large group business. Exhibit 4 illustrates a transfer in which the Alumni Association shifts its transient folio to a city account of the same name. Billing is direct—not to a credit-card company, but to the headquarters of the Alumni Association. Exhibit 5 is exactly the same, but the billing is to an individual. In both

≣V

A Vallen Corporation Property

VALLEN CORPORATE REQUEST FOR MASTER BILLING

Date(s) of the Function(s) _____

Hotels/Cities That Might Be Used _____
_____

Thank you for choosing the Vallen Hotel Company. To better serve you, we shall quickly process the credit information furnished. Extension of credit requires accounts to be settled within 30 days or be subject to a charge of 6% per annum. Your signature below grants us authority to verify the information provided.

NAME OF THE ORGANIZATION OR
PERSON REQUESTING MASTER BILLING _____

ADDRESS _____
      Street   City   State   Zip

CONTACT _____
      Telephone   Fax   Email

CREDIT REFERENCES: (PLEASE PROVIDE NAMES, ADDRESS, AND TELEPHONE NUMBERS)

COMPANIES _____

BANKS _____
_____

PREVIOUS _____
HOTELS _____

DOES YOUR ORGANIZATION REQUIRE A PURCHASE ORDER?   Yes/No _____
WHICH CHARGES WOULD BE AUTHORIZED FOR THE ACCOUNT?

_____ All room charges and incidentals   _____ Organization's functions only

_____ Room charges only for identified persons   _____ Other _____

_____
Authorized Signature   Title   Date

Sales Manager's Estimate of Charges: Rooms_____   F&B_____

Approved Yes_____ No_____   Credit Manager _____

EXHIBIT 14 Companies and associations that request direct billing of their city ledger accounts must first establish their creditworthiness. First, the hotel sales executive estimates the cost of the event(s). Then the credit manager reviews the application by checking references with other agencies, especially previous hotels, before giving the applicant an OK.

illustrations, payment comes from the source, not a third party—not a credit-card company. The extension of credit is not done lightly. Exhibit 14 illustrates a form that initiates the hotel's verification of the organization's credit credibility.

Coupons Direct city-ledger transfers may involve coupons. A guest whose reservation was made by a travel agent or airline may settle the front-office folio with a coupon. A coupon is a receipt by which a third party, the travel agent, acknowledges that it has already been paid by the guest. By accepting the coupon, the hotel agrees to bill the travel agent or other third party. This is accomplished by transferring the front-office folio of the guest to the city-ledger account of the agent. Then the agent is billed by mail. Obviously, the agent must have previously established credit with the hotel.

Skippers Despite increased credit vigilance, hotels sometimes get stuck by skippers, persons who leave (*skip*) the hotel without paying. Some skippers are accidental or the results of a misunderstanding. Since honest guests leave a trail of reservation and registration identification, collection after departure takes place without difficulty.

Real skippers make their living by skipping. Their moves are deliberate, even though states have legislated skipping to be a prima facie case of intent to defraud the innkeeper. Because it is a crime, a police report should be filed.

It often takes a day or two to verify the skip. Charges for additional nights are added to the folio. It makes little difference, actually, since collection is very rare. Once discovered, the room is checked out and the folio balance is transferred to a section of the city ledger called *Skippers*. After a while, the account is written off as a bad debt.

Transfer from the City Ledger to the Guest Ledger: Advance Deposits This interledger transfer differs from anything previously considered. The transfer flows in the opposite direction from earlier discussions. The balance is moved *from* the city ledger *to* the guest ledger. Earlier discussions were just the opposite; the balance flowed *from* the guest ledger (the folio) *to* the city ledger.

For this to happen, there must be some balance in the city ledger to be transferred. Perhaps there is an unpaid balance from a previous visit. Sometimes, guests are asked for a prearrival deposit. This is not very common because rooms are usually guaranteed with a credit-card number, but that charge is *not* processed. Some hotels, resorts especially, may want cash in advance of arrival (see Exhibit 15, line 1) or may wish to process the credit-card guarantee (see Exhibit 10, line 1).

What is to be done with the money when it arrives? It cannot be posted to a front-office folio. Front-office folios are for registered guests, and the guest has yet to arrive. Accounts receivable who are not registered are recorded in the city ledger. So a city-ledger account called *Advanced Deposits* is opened for the yet-to-arrive guest, who has already paid for one or more nights. Actually, of course, the guest is not a receivable; the guest owes nothing. The hotel owes the guest; so the guest is a negative account receivable; in other words, an account payable.

The account payable situation is similar to the tax issue raised earlier. The hotel collects taxes from the guest (taxes payable) and eventually pays the government. Here the hotel collects from the guest and eventually applies it to the account receivable.

When a deposit (check) is received,

> Increases in assets, including accounts receivable and *cash*, are made with debits.
> Increases in liabilities, including *debts to guests* or governments, are made with credits.
> Debit: Cash
> Credit: Accounts Payable/Advanced Deposits (City Ledger)
> *Explanation:* Cash deposit received for future arrival.

The record of the hotel's liability to the guest remains in the city ledger until the guest arrives days or weeks later. Then the balance is moved (transferred) from the city ledger to the arriving guest's newly opened front-office folio (see Exhibits 10 and 15). These two illustrations show the transfer *from* the city ledger *to* the guest ledger on the first line. Actually, they could appear on any line, depending on how many services the guest buys before the transfer is made.

The deposit is applied to the arriving guest in the following accounting entry, which appears in folio format on line 1 in Exhibit 15.

> Decreases in liabilities, including *city-ledger debts to guests*, are made with debits.
> Increases in liabilities, including *front-office folio debts to guests*, are made with credits.
> Debit: Accounts Payable/Advanced Deposits (in City Ledger) 680.00
> Credit: Accounts Receivable/Guest's Folio (in Guest Ledger) 680.00
> *Explanation:* Guest with advance deposit arrives; liability is transferred.

The hotel still owes the guest; the transfer has not changed that. Purchases during the guest's stay (rooms, food, and so on) are applied against the original deposit. Either the hotel still owes the guest at the end of the stay or the guest has charged more than the original deposit. With the former, a refund is necessary. More likely, the guest

□V

A Vallen Corporation Property

THE SYDNEY OUTBACK
1 PITT STREET
SYDNEY, AUSTRALIA
(02) 259 – 5555

GUEST		
M/M WILLIAMS	ROOM	2003
EASTER PACKAGE	RATE	170.00
2ND AVE BEACHSIDE APPTS	No. PERSONS	2
BURLEIGH HEADS QLD 4220	FOLIO No.	152490
	PAGE	01
	ARRIVAL	04/12/
	DEPARTURE	04/16/
CH-A	DEPOSIT	$680.00

DATE	REFERENCE No.		DESCRIPTION	CHARGES / CREDITS
		00754	DEPOSIT	680.00CR
APR12	401	01859 99	LOCAL CALL	.70
APR12	011	02003 00	ROOM CHG	170.00
APR13	131	04071 61	THE BISTRO	22.00
APR13	401	02145 99	LOCAL CALL	.70
APR13	011	02003 00	ROOM CHG	170.00
APR14	181	02003 43	MINI BAR	2.50
APR14	011	02003 00	ROOM CHG	170.00
APR15	401	01736 99	LOCAL CALL	.70
APR15	011	02003 00	ROOM CHG	170.00
APR16	001	00001 23	PAID CASH	26.60CR
			TOTAL-DUE	.00

TRAVEL AGENCY

*TRAVEL AGENCY #1,
SOUTHPORT, QUEENSLANDS 4215*

CHARGE TO

I AGREE THAT MY LIABILITY FOR THIS BILL IS NOT WAIVED AND AGREE TO BE HELD PERSONALLY LIABLE IN THE EVENT THAT THE INDICATED PERSON, COMPANY, OR ASSOCIATION FAILS TO PAY FOR ANY PART OR THE FULL AMOUNT OF THESE CHARGES.

SIGNATURE

EXHIBIT 15 A credit balance, a cash advanced deposit transferred from the city ledger, is the first line of this folio. This unusual entry is similar to Exhibit 10. Another cash payment closes the account as the guest checks out. Cash payments like these are one means of settling a folio balance, but are rarely used. Exhibit 12 illustrates the other two methods, allowances and credit cards.

checks out owing an additional amount because deposits are usually one night's room rate only. Then the cycle begins again with payment at check-out.

Payment at check-out brings us back to the beginning of the chapter. Guests settle their transient accounts (the folios) in the front-office ledger by one of three methods: cash, allowances, or transfers. Most settlements will be by transfer because departing guests usually shift their folio balances to credit cards in the city ledger.

Summary

Hotels sell services to strangers and to registered guests. Whereas strangers must pay immediately for services like food and beverage, guests may delay payment until check-out. In the interim, guests owe the hotel; they are accounts receivable (A/R). A record of that debt, called a folio, is maintained in the front office. All the folios together are called a ledger. Hence, the billing records of registered guests are in a front-office (or transient) ledger. Nonregistered parties—credit-card companies, for example—may also owe the hotel. Their records are maintained in a different ledger, the city ledger, by the accounting office.

Usually, guests settle their individual folios as they check out. This is when they pay for all of the services (room, room taxes, food, beverage, spas, golf, etc.) that have been charged to them. Payment is by cash (rare), by allowances (for service adjustments), and by credit cards (the usual method). Credit-card settlements transfer the balance of the front-office folios to the records of the credit-card companies in the city ledger. The accounting office bills and collects from credit-card companies.

Master accounts, which track the charges of groups, are also maintained on folios. These too are transferred to the city ledger when the association or company checks out. (Every folio must have a zero balance after check-out.) Master accounts are billed directly to the group's headquarters. That is different from billing credit-card companies for third-party folios. Both types of billing originate in the city ledger, having been transferred there from the front-office ledger.

Hotels have not only accounts receivable but also accounts payable. Receivables are something the hotel owns. Payables are something the hotel owes. Hotels owe governments for room taxes collected but not yet paid. Hotels owe employees for tips collected but not yet paid. Hotels owe guests with advance deposits (not common) for services not yet delivered.

Resources and Challenges

Web Assignment

Assume you are responsible for the city-ledger segment of your hotel's back-of-the-house records. Use the *dphs* website to identify four products that you would buy in order to update your system. Explain why you chose one of them.

Interesting Tidbits

- For guests who "record their profiles"—join frequent-guest programs, FGPs—Marriott, Hilton, and others have added a third method for checking out. Heretofore, guests went either to the front desk or to their in-room TV screen to process the checkouts. Now, FGP members can access folios online for up to 90 days after departure, and even track the number of FGP points they own.

- Organizers of a dental conference walked away without paying the master account. After the default—in an unprecedented shift in procedure—the hotel began billing the credit cards of conference attendees a pro-rata share of the unpaid bill. If a court case ensues, it might focus on the agreement at the bottom of most folios; see Exhibit 1.

Challenges

True/False

Questions that are partially false should be marked false (F).

_____ 1. Folio, bill, guest account card, and guest bill all refer to the same form; that used to register an arriving guest.

_____ 2. The city ledger is maintained by the city in which the hotel is located to track the sales taxes collected by the hotel and due to the city.

_____ 3. *Split billing* is the term used to explain the differences between purchases in the coffee shop made by (1) credit card or (2) room charge; that is, "split."

_____ 4. The term "allowances" is a take-off on a child's allowance; in innkeeping, it means time off for the desk due to vacations, sick leave, or scheduling.

_____ 5. Folios are not standardized. One hotel might include an arrival time; another may not. One might include the number in the party; another may not. And so on.

Problems

1. Differentiate the following:
   a. Charge from credit.
   b. Master account from split account.
   c. A folio from B folio.
   d. Transient guest from city guest.
   e. Charge from payment.

2. Use a word processor to replicate the folio that would be produced when the Arthur Jones family checks out. Mr. and Mrs. Jones and their infant son, George, reside at 21 Craig Drive in Hampshireville, Illinois, 65065. Their reservation for three nights at $125 per night plus 5% tax was guaranteed May 17 with a $200 cash (check) deposit for one night, indicating that they

will arrive late. They check in at 10 PM on June 3 and take one room (1233).

a. Breakfast charge on June 4 is $12.90.

b. Mrs. Jones hosts a small luncheon meeting for her company, and a $310 charge for the meeting room and meal is posted to the folio.

c. The family decides to leave earlier than planned and notifies the desk of a 7 PM check-out.

d. A long-distance call of $8 is made.

e. The family checks out. They raise the issue of no clean linen—the laundry had a wildcat strike—and argue for an allowance. One is given—$25. The rooms manager then charges 30% of the normal room charge for the late departure.

f. Payment is made with an American Express card, no. 33333333333.

3. Create a pencil-and-paper folio; use Exhibit 2 as a guide. Post the events of Problem 2 as they would appear on a hand-prepared folio.

4. Under which of the following circumstances would management grant an allowance? What would be the value of that allowance? What else might be done if an allowance were not granted?

a. Guest sets the room alarm clock, but it fails to go off, which causes the guest to miss a meeting that involves thousands of dollars of commission.

b. Same circumstance as part (a) but the guest called the telephone operator for a morning call, which wasn't made.

c. Guest checks out and discovers the nightly room charge to be $15 more than the rate quoted two weeks earlier by the reservations center.

d. Same circumstance as part (c), but the discrepancy is discovered soon after the guest is roomed.

5. How would the following transfers be handled? (Answer either by discussion, by offering the accounting entries, or both.)

a. A departing guest discovers that a $60 beverage charge that belongs to another guest, who is still registered, was incorrectly posted yesterday to the departing guest's account.

b. Same circumstance as part (a) but the $60 beverage posting was made today.

c. Same circumstance as part (a) but the other guest has departed.

d. Two days into a guest's four-day stay, the reservations department realizes the guest's advance deposit was never transferred to the front-office account.

e. Same circumstance as part (d) but the discovery is made by the guest, who writes to complain about the omission one week after check-out.

6. Check your understanding of accounting by proving the debits and credits for each of the following situations, which were not discussed in the text.

a. The hotel pays the quarterly sales taxes of $8,925.00 due the local government, the city of Popcorn, Indiana.

b. The hotel receives a check from Diners Club for payment of credit-card balances due of $1,000.

c. Same as part (b), but Diners Club withholds 4% for a fee.

d. The hotel receives a check from its parent company for $1,500, representing the total payment due for several frequent-stay guests who used their points at your hotel. The amount of room charges generated by those guests was $5,500.

AN INCIDENT IN HOTEL MANAGEMENT
Just a Hole in the Wall

Last month's security report contained three items dealing with noise and heavy traffic one night in the Kit Carson suite. The following day, housekeeping reported a huge hole in the wall between two of the bedrooms. It had not been there four days earlier, the last time the suite was used. Other damage included a broken chair, a smashed vase, and a cracked mirror. Engineering estimated $1,300 for repairs; that amount had been posted to the folio of the 18-year-old guest. She signed the folio as she checked out. It was posted to her father's city-ledger account and billed at month's end. He is president of a large local business.

The dad stops by the GM's office after a business luncheon in the gourmet room. "Good grief! $1,300? It's only a hole in the wall."

Questions

1. Was there a management failure here; if so, what?
2. What is the hotel's immediate response (or action) to the incident?
3. What further, long-run action should management take, if any?

Answers to True/False Quiz

1. False. These terms all have the same meaning; they refer to the guest's bill or folio. The answer is false because it references the registration card, not the folio.

2. False. The city ledger represents the hotel's nonregistered accounts receivable (debts owed to the hotel by individuals, companies, and organizations); has nothing to do with sales taxes.

3. False. Split billing refers to the split between A folios and B folios. Onto A folios go specific charges that the guest or association has arranged for, whereas the B folio accumulates personal charges, those not covered by the A folio.

4. False. Allowances are reductions to the guest's folio given to offset charges. They can be likened to returning goods to a retailer. The result is a reduction in the sale and, thus, in the debt owed. Allowances are given on the folio for poor service, errors, and adjustments.

5. True. Folios are not standardized. One hotel might include an arrival time; another may not. One might include the number in the party; another may not. At a minimum, the form contains the guest name, room number, address, and rate.

Cash or Credit: The City Ledger

The chapter deals on noncash settlements and the special class of accounts receivable these create, the city ledger.

CASH

Under common law, arriving guests "must be willing and able to pay." Most do so with plastic (credit or debit cards). Fewer than 5% opt to pay with cash (money) and those are chiefly in budget properties. However, payment at registration is just the start. Transactions involving cards and cash are not limited to the desk, especially not in large, full-service properties. This chapter examines the role of cash in operations and the role of cards in credit. With credit cards so pervasive, cash transactions take place much less frequently than, say, a generation ago. Fewer dollars have not diminished the importance of cash handling. Cash is a fragile asset that must be protected from intentional (criminal) and unintentional loss (poor cash management). Balances must be monitored: Enough on hand to meet business transactions; not so much as to idle this valuable asset. Carefully managed, cash produces cash.

Cash is very negotiable, easily pocketed, and a continuing target of the unscrupulous. Counterfeiters, bad check artists, photocopiers, and short-change manipulators work their wares at hotel desks. They prefer hotel desks over other retail outlets because guest-service agents handle less currency than do most retailers. That makes them less skilled at identifying bogus paper (see the end of the chapter).

Honest guests also turn to the desk, but for legitimate cash transactions. These may involve traveler's checks and personal checks, change, and foreign-currency transactions. Cashiers might make cash advances to guests and upfront money for some hotel uses. So cash is not disappearing in what many term "a cashless society."

Cash Paid-Outs

Cash at the front desk flows both ways: *cash receipts* and *cash paid-outs*. In other departments (food, beverage, newsstand) cash only flows in, cash receipts. Even that truism may not hold. Some properties allow dining room and lounge cashiers to reimburse servers for gratuities added to the tab by the guest. Just as often, gratuities are accumulated by accounting and payment is made along with the wage.

TIPS TO EMPLOYEES   Sometimes, especially in smaller properties, disbursement is made at the front desk. This was common in precomputer days when the hand-carried guest check arriving from the dining rooms and lounges contained an added gratuity. The cashier gave the runner carrying the charge slip the tip and received a signed receipt which became part of the front-office cashier's cash drawer. Charge slips—vouchers (tabs)—are no longer processed this way. They are entered into the property management system by the departmental cashiers of the food and beverage department. There is no traffic to the desk. Paid-outs to staff members still take place. An arriving guest might ask the desk to give a gratuity to the door, bell, or delivery person. That item appeared regularly on pencil-and-paper folios as a cash advance. The procedure is rarely used today.

From Chapter 11 of *Check-In Check Out*, Ninth Edition. Gary K. Vallen, Jerome J. Vallen. Copyright © 2013 by Pearson Education, Inc. All rights reserved.

Schedule of Hypothetical Costs Associated with Paying Employee Tips upon Receipt

1. **Assumptions**
   - A 525-room hotel staffs 7 bellpersons per day, who average $20 per day in charged tips.
   - 22 waitpersons and room servers per day, who average $45 per day in charged tips.
   - 4 bartenders per day, who average $40 per day in charged tips.
   - Some 75% of all charged tips are paid by credit card. The average merchant discount fee for all types of credit cards is 2.25%.
   - The average time for settlement of the bill (including those who pay by credit card, those who pay by direct bill, and those who pay by cash) is two weeks past the date the charge was made.
   - Approximately 0.5% of all folios are noncollectible.

2. **Float-Related Costs**
   - Total employee tips paid out per day are $140 for bellpersons, $990 for waitpersons, and $160 for bartenders. That's $1,290 per day for 365 days equals $470,850 per year.
   - Assuming a 9.0% internal rate of return and an average 2 weeks before collection, the hotel's cost of floating employees' tips equates to $1,629.87 per year.

3. **Merchant Discount Fees**
   - Assuming $470,850 per year in total employee tips and that 75% of all tips are paid to credit cards, the total amount of tips paid by credit cards is $353,137.50.
   - If the average merchant discount fee is 2.25%, the hotel's annual cost of paying employees tips in full (rather than discounting them) is $7,945.59.

4. **Noncollectible Accounts**
   - Assuming $470,850 per year in total employee tips and that 0.5% of all folios are noncollectible, the hotel pays employee tips of $2,354.25 but never receives payment from the guest.

5. **Grand Total Annual Costs**
   - The hotel's cost of floating employees' tips equates to $1,629.87 per year.
   - The hotel's cost of paying the employees' share of the merchant discount fees is $7,945.59.
   - The hotel's cost of paying employee tips on noncollectible accounts is $2,354.25.
   - For this hypothetical scenario, the total cost to the hotel for paying employee tips in full is $11,929.71.

EXHIBIT 1 The cost of gratuities and other cash advances made for guests is rarely computed. Strange, because they represent a significant, but hidden, cost to the hospitality enterprise and a significant benefit to the staff. It's an issue worth raising during wage negotiations.

Cost to the Hotel: Float   Reimbursing employees for tips has a direct hit on the hotel's operational profits. Three hidden costs become very apparent when the procedure is examined (see Exhibit 1). Float, the period between the hotel's cash outlay and its repayment, is one such cost.

Assume that on arrival, a guest asks the desk to pay a tip to a bellperson. Several days later the guest checks out charging a credit card. Ten days later, the credit-card company makes payment. For some two weeks, the hotel's cash has been "floating." It has earned no interest for the hotel and has always been in jeopardy of nonpayment.

Cost to the Hotel: Discount Fees   National credit-card companies charge merchants (hotels) fees for accepting their credit cards. Those fees range from 1–5%, depending on the sales volume of the hotel, the credit card in use, and a number of other variables. Assume that the hotel pays a 2% fee for the use of an American Express card. With a 2% fee, the hotel receives only $98 for every $100 charged. Therefore, the hotel will be reimbursed $9.80 for the bellperson's $10 tip, which the hotel has already paid in full. Twenty cents may sound trivial but it illustrates what is happening throughout the entire industry (see Exhibit 1).

Cost to the Hotel: Uncollectible Accounts   An uncollectible account is the most costly subsidy of paid-out tips. When the guest folio becomes uncollectible, the hotel loses more than departmental revenues. Whether the uncollectible folio was a direct bill gone bad, a personal check with insufficient funds, or a fraudulent credit card, the hotel has also lost the amount of the paid-out tips.

Recovering uncollectible tips from employees months after the service was rendered has a negative effect on morale for what employees perceive as trivial sums. It is hardly trivial as Exhibit 1 points out. Other options are equally fraught: Refuse to allow guests to charge tips against their folio (ludicrous); delay paying employees until the guests' bills are actually cleared (an accounting nightmare); reimburse employees at postdiscount rates (fosters discontent).

CASH LOANS   Historically, hotel desks were almost bank branches. Checks were cashed with alacrity and cash loans were not unusual. Not so today. Hotels are no longer in the banking business. Actual loans to hotel guests are very rare, occurring under unusual circumstances and only to those guests well known by the hotel's management. It is now more difficult to cash a check than it was to obtain a loan years ago. This is especially true on weekends when banks are closed. Some hoteliers believe that it is better to have a small loan skip than to have a large check bounce, so they grant the former if forced to choose. Companies that use the hotel on a regular basis may establish "loan" arrangements for their staff by guaranteeing the advances. Check-cashing is one privilege of PGP (preferred-guest program) membership. Other guests have other options and that explains the innkeepers' reluctance to play the banker.

Third-Party Sources   ATMs (Automatic Teller Machines) offer the easiest access to cash, but certainly not the only means. Guests can fall back on credit-card advances, person-to-person pay services such as iKobo, Internet money services (PayPal), payday loan companies, and expedited money order services (MoneyGram). Each of these options provides cash to the guest without jeopardizing the hotel or putting it into a business for which it lacks expertise.

Credit-card advances (Comcheck) and money order services (Western Union's Quick Collect or Send Money) transfer the related costs and risks (float, discount fees, and loss from uncollectible accounts) from the hotel to the guest. In essence, guests send themselves the cash and pay their own costs. And there are costs, 10% and up. Guests who would howl at the hotel for charging such usury fees pay third parties without protest.

Automatic Teller Machines (ATMs)   ATMs are the most common means of accessing cash (see Exhibit 2). They are everywhere: From *A*-loft hotels in New York City to *Z*-Palace Hotels in Xanthi Thraki, Greece, and all the lobbies in between. Two networks are particularly popular because of their accessibility overseas. Cirrus (linked to MasterCard) and Plus (linked to VISA) are accessible by over 90% of the bank cards circulating in the United States. An added appeal: ATMs' foreign exchange rates are usually lower than those of foreign banks.

EXHIBIT 2   The proliferation of ATMs has reduced the call for cash advances, those made by the desk to or for the guest. The more advanced ATMs offer additional services including check-cashing, biometric recognition, and payroll checks. *Courtesy of Mr. Payroll Corporation, Fort Worth, Texas.*

Their popularity is more than guest convenience. The machines are a new revenue source for hotels. Tied to the World Wide Web, ATMs offer more than cash. Users can pay utility bills, apply for car loans, even trade stocks. Tickets, postage stamps, and other commissionable services are the incentives for lobby ATMs. Contractors install and maintain the equipment, load it with cash, and pay the hotel a commission. Other vending contracts for news racks, cigarette, and soda dispensers work the same way. So did lobby phone-booths before cell phones put them out of business.

Many ATMs allow the hotel to custom-design promotional coupons on the back of the printed receipts. A coupon might entice the recipient to the bar with a free drink or to the coffee shop with a free appetizer. ATMs also flash messages and promotional screens to guests who are waiting for the transaction to process.

Paid-Outs to Concessionaires   Hotels often arrange for local merchants to provide services to supplement those offered by the hotel. Such merchants may have shops (beauty salon, florist, gifts) inside the hotel, or they may contract services off-premises (laundry/dry cleaning, print shop). These private vendors are referred to as *concessionaires;* their shops are known as *concessions*. Located within the hotel, they pay rent. Located outside the hotel, they pay commissions.

Concessionaires need the hotel to act as their middleman. Guests charge the concessionaire's services (laundry, hairstyling, gift purchases) to their folios as if these nonhotel departments were an integral part of the hotel. The hotel collects as the guest departs and reimburses the concessionaire. Accounts are usually settled monthly with the hotel keeping the negotiated percentage as its share for providing supplies, labor, storage, and accounting. Fees may be included in the rental and not captured separately.

Under some contracts, especially with small hotels and small concessionaires, the desk pays the merchant immediately. Cash is handed over and charged to the guest folio. It may appear on the folio as laundry, dry cleaning, florist, and so on, but it is a cash advance to the merchant for the guest. Posting it as departmental income—even though it isn't—makes it easier for the guest to understand. The merchant signs for the money if payment is made daily. That receipt becomes part of the cashier's daily turn-in. At the end of the shift, the cashier's report reflects the reduction of cash in the money drawer replaced by the concessionaire's signed voucher.

Whether the concessionaire is paid immediately or periodically, the hotel has loaned the guest and awaits repayment. All of the costs of Exhibit 1 (float, discount fees, and uncollectible accounts) are at issue for negotiation between the hotel and the concessionaire. So, too, are resolutions of problems or complaints. Guests are not interested in learning that the concessionaire is a different company. A quality guest experience requires the hotel to provide seamless service and solve problems on behalf of the guest. The contract with the concessionaire must account for this.

REFUNDS AT CHECK-OUT   On rare occasions—very, very rare occasions—the hotel owes the guest a cash refund at the conclusion of his or her stay. Either there was a substantial *cash* deposit with the reservation or a large cash payment was made on or after arrival. A refund is necessary if the total cash received exceeds the folio charges. In this unusual circumstance, the closing balance on the folio is a credit—the hotel owes the guest—not the traditional debit balance—the guest owes the hotel. Zeroing the credit balance requires a paid-out voucher for the guest's signature and the money tendered to the departing guest. At the end of the shift, the cashier subtracts the amount of that paid-out from the day's receipts.

Cash is refunded only if the original payment was made in cash! If the original payment was by credit card, any refund would be by credit card. Moreover, large cash deposits made by the guest may not be refundable on check-out. Before accepting a large cash deposit, the desk must explain hotel policy regarding paid-outs. Some hotels restrict the size of a paid-out: Perhaps to $100. Anything above that amount requires a check to be processed by the hotel accounting department and mailed to the guest's home or business. This prevents scammers from depositing fraudulent funds (traveler's checks, personal checks, counterfeit money) and then attempting to collect legitimate cash against that amount the following day.

HOUSE EXPENSES   Because of its central location and accessibility, the desk of small hotels may handle house-related disbursements as well as guest-related transactions. Small disbursements—petty cash expenditures—may be reimbursed by the desk. The amounts and reasons range far afield. Included might be payments to a farmer for produce delivered to the kitchen, COD shipping required by ICC regulations, postage for the marketing department, payroll for a

PETTY CASH

AMOUNT _29 90_   Date _Dec. 18_

FOR _Purchase 10 Bags Flour by Bellperson Joe for Chef Don_

CHARGE TO _Food and Beverage Purchases_

SIGNED _Joe Harris_

KAYCO FORM NO.1046

Tom's Market
135 Rio Plaza
San Diego, CA 13579

5# GOLD BRAND FLOUR	2.99 F
5# GOLD BRAND FLOUR	2.99 F
5# GOLD BRAND FLOUR	2.99 F
5# GOLD BRAND FLOUR	2.99 F
5# GOLD BRAND FLOUR	2.99 F
5# GOLD BRAND FLOUR	2.99 F
5# GOLD BRAND FLOUR	2.99 F
5# GOLD BRAND FLOUR	2.99 F
5# GOLD BRAND FLOUR	2.99 F
5# GOLD BRAND FLOUR	2.99 F
SUB TOTAL	29.90
TAX NON FOOD	0.00
CASH	30.00
CHANGE	0.10

EXHIBIT 3 Signed petty-cash vouchers (with or without supporting documentation) are used at the front desk when it acts as a cash-disbursing agent for house business. Later, the cashier/guest-service agent's bank will be reimbursed by the general cashier.

discharged employee, and so on. Each paid-out is evidenced by a signed voucher, which allows the cashier to reconcile the cash drawer at day's end (see Exhibit 3).

The general cashier reimburses the front-office cashier(s) periodically, daily in some hotels. Other properties bypass the desk entirely and have the general cashier handle these paid-outs directly from a central petty-cash fund.

Cash Receipts

Cash is very negotiable so guests can make deposits at any time. They rarely do. Cash is one method of settlement. Allowances and transfers (credit cards) are the other options. Settlement with allowances are rare and payment by cash, which includes currency, traveler's checks, and personal checks, equally so. Both guests and innkeepers prefer credit-card transactions or direct billing, both handled through the city ledger without the transfer of money.

Still, guests have the right to make interim payments with cash or settle their bill with cash. Doing so delays check-out. It requires the guest to come to the desk, stand in line, and process the payment. Express check-out, on the other hand, is a quick, self-service procedure that uses the credit card on file. Guests process express check-out through their in-room television set or by simply leaving the forms at the desk as they depart. Very few guests carry large sums of cash and very few make periodic payments or settle their folios that way.

Code[a]	Room	Last Name		First Name	Account	Rate	Time	Amount	Author
Cashier: Ardelle			Report Date: 03/09/--						15:28:41
		Cashier's Balance Report by Code							
0001	217	JOHNSON		LINDA	CASH	RACK	06:57:23	48.52	48.52
TOTAL	CASH		0001					48.52	
0011	319	WILSON		BILL	CHCK	DISC	07:17:17	82.50	82.50
0011	337	ADAMS		JOHN	CHCK	RACK	07:21:50	65.21	65.21
0011	711	GREGORY		GARY	CHCK	TOUR	09:10:10	111.77	111.77
0011	315	GONNE		CONNIE	CHCK	RACK	09:44:30	96.20	96.20
0011	211	JACKSON		ANDY	CHCK	DISC	11:04:41	46.31	46.51
0011	6371	WASHINGTON		TOURS	CHCK	TOUR	11:57:01	1,278.71[b]	452.51[c]
TOTAL	CHECKS		0011					1,682.70	
TOTAL	AMERICAN EXPRESS		0021					0.00	
TOTAL	CARTE BLANCHE		0022					0.00	
TOTAL	DINERS CLUB		0023					0.00	
0024	678	HARRISON		GEORGE	DSCV	TOUR	07:12:12	87.50	
0024	212	JONES		ROBERT	DSCV	DISC	08:34:20	242.59	
TOTAL	DISCOVER		0024					330.09	
0025	456	LENNON		JOHN	MC	TOUR	07:16:44	87.50	
0025	371	ORTIZ		RAUL	MC	RACK	10:40:29	68.57	
TOTAL	MASTERCARD		0025					156.07	
0026	1171	VANLAND		TOM	VISA	GRP	07:11:10	179.37	
0026	842	STUART		LYLE	VISA	GRP	08:10:15	161.40	
TOTAL	VISA		0026					340.77	
0031	902	GREEN		LOTTA	POUT	RACK	07:24:01	−17.50	
0031	107	MOORE		MANNY	POUT	TOUR	10:10:15	−20.00	
TOTAL	PAID-OUTS		0031					−37.50[d]	

[a] The reporting code is the hotel's chart of accounts.

[b] Washington Tours is a city ledger receivable that is settling its account at the desk, not directly through the accounting office as one would expect. Follow the $1,278.71 onto Exhibit 5, line #1.

[c] The Author's Column *would not appear* on an actual form. Follow the $452.51 onto Exhibit 5, line #1.

[d] The minus signs represent cash paid-outs. Follow the $37.50 onto Exhibit 5, line #1.

EXHIBIT 4 Each front-office cashier prepares a daily report, which accompanies the actual cash turn-in. The form reports receipts and paid-outs; cash and credit cards *as they pertain to accounts receivable*. Similar reports, which *pertain to cash sales*, are prepared by departmental cashiers in dining rooms, lounges, etc. (This exhibit does not coincide with any text material, but does precede Exhibit 5, line #1.)

HOUSE RECEIPTS Just as miscellaneous disbursements may pass through the desk, so might miscellaneous receipts. Cash from magazine, candy, and newspaper sales may be collected by the desk. Coins from vending machines might be similarly routed. Banquet deposits, meal-ticket sales in American-plan hotels, and concessionaire reimbursements might all be routed through the cash drawers of the front office. Small properties use their desks as the first cash records for everything from kitchen-fat sales to insurance settlements.

The Cashier's Daily Report

At the close of each shift, cashiers throughout the hotel turn in their net proceeds (cash received minus cash paid out) along with a daily cash report. The reports of the front-office cashiers (see Ardelle's Report, Exhibit 4) become part of both the night audit, which audits accounts receivable, and the day audit, which audits incomes of all operating departments.

Combined, funds from all cashiers plus any from the general cashier constitute the hotel's daily bank deposit (see Exhibit 5).

THE BANK Each guest-service agent/departmental cashier receives and signs for a permanent supply of cash called the *bank*. The amount depends on the position and shift that the cashier works. Busy commercial hotels need large front-office banks, but the night clerk at the same desk might get along with $250. It is a question of both safety and good cash management. Funds should not be tied up unnecessarily; temporary increases can be made for busy holidays

		Cash Sales	Collection Transient Receivables	Collection City Ledger Receivables	Total Cash Receipts	Paid-Outs Transient	Paid-Outs City Ledger	Net Cash Receipts	Add: Overages Less: Shortages	Turn in for Deposit
Department	Cashier									
FRONT OFFICE	ARDELLE		ᶜ452.51	ᵇ1,278.71	1,731.22	ᵈ−37.50	0.00	1,693.72	−.76	1,692.96
FRONT OFFICE	BABETTE		1,171.14	622.50	1,793.64	−49.00	−25.00	1,719.64	1.20	1,720.84
FRONT OFFICE	CHARLES		850.19	1,460.51	2,310.70	−11.50	−5.00	2,294.20	0.00	2,294.20
FRONT OFFICE	DIANE		67.10	0.00	67.10	0.00	0.00	67.10	0.00	67.10
FRONT OFFICE	EDWARD		572.46	604.27	1,176.73	−12.90	0.00	1,163.83	−2.41	1,161.42
FRONT OFFICE	FRANCES		934.72	210.58	1,145.30	−18.65	−14.00	1,112.65	.87	1,113.52
GIFT SHOP	GARY	687.14	0.00	0.00	687.14	0.00	0.00	687.14	0.00	687.14
GIFT SHOP	HARRY	901.73	0.00	0.00	901.73	0.00	0.00	901.73	−1.47	900.26
LOUNGE	ILONA	1,262.85	0.00	0.00	1,262.85	0.00	0.00	1,262.85	1.01	1,263.86
LOUNGE	JEROME	2,411.59	0.00	0.00	2,411.59	0.00	0.00	2,411.59	0.00	2,411.59
RESTAURANT	KATE	816.44	0.00	0.00	816.44	0.00	0.00	816.44	−.25	816.19
RESTAURANT	LOUISE	1,017.55	0.00	0.00	1,017.55	0.00	0.00	1,017.55	−.61	1,016.94
SNACK BAR	MARC	469.68	0.00	0.00	469.68	0.00	0.00	469.68	2.71	472.39
SNACK BAR	NANETTE	371.02	0.00	0.00	371.02	0.00	0.00	371.02	0.00	371.02
DAILY TOTALS		7,938.00	4,048.12	4,176.57	16,162.69	−129.55	−44.00	15,989.14	.29	15,989.43

Clerk: Thomas Report Date: 3/10/-- 09:39:17
Cash Receipts Summary Report

EXHIBIT 5 The general cashier summarizes the daily turn-ins from all of the hotel's cashiers to create the day's deposit—actually the morning after the day. So both the accounts receivable cash flows (in and out) from the desk (Ardelle: see *a*, *b*, *c*, *d* of Exhibit 4) and the cash intake from the operating departments are shown.

or conventions. A review of all house banks may release sizable sums for more profitable use. One measure suggests that the total of house banks be 2% of total sales. Careful monitoring and frequent reimbursement by the general cashier improves cash management.

The bank is not the employee's personal fund. So cashiers lock their banks in the hotel's safe after each shift. To ensure that all funds are properly held, the accounting office randomly schedules surprise counts. The cashier comes on duty to find tape has been placed across the box. Access requires two keys. One is the cashier's and the other is the accounting office's master key. The cashier must summons an auditor, who takes a few minutes with the cashier to count and verify the contents.

Unfortunately, common banks shared by several employees are not unusual. These are seen in every department from the bar to the front office. With shared banks, control is difficult to maintain and responsibility almost impossible to fix. Custom and convenience seem to be the major reasons for continuing this poor practice, although it obviously requires fewer hotel dollars to stock shared banks. Everyone handling money should be covered by a surety bond (insurance). Surety bonds offer blanket coverage or individual coverage, whichever best meets the hotel's needs.

NET RECEIPTS Net receipts is the difference between cash receipts and cash paid-outs. Since only front-office cashiers make paid-outs, net receipts in the bars and coffee shops is the same as total receipts. (The exception comes when tips are paid to employees by these specialty-room cashiers.) Front-office net receipts is computed by subtracting total paid-outs to accounts receivable from total receipts, accounts receivable receipts, plus miscellaneous inflows. House paid-outs (house expenses) would not be subtracted if they are reimbursed by the general cashier in a separate transaction. If not, house paid-outs would also be subtracted. Cashiers turn in their net receipts each day plus or minus cash over or short.

OVER OR SHORT The day's close occasionally finds the cash drawer over or short. Sometimes the error is simple addition or subtraction. Either the cashier finds it without help or it is uncovered later by the audit. Cash errors in giving change are usually beyond remedy unless they are in the house's favor. Guests may not acknowledge overpayments, but they will complain soon enough if they have been shortchanged.

Overages and shortages become an employee–management issue if cashiers are required to make up shortages but turn in overages. Better systems allow overages to offset shortages, asking only that the cumulative record be reasonable. Management should avoid systems that encourage the cashier to reconcile at the expense of ethical standards. Shortchanging, poor addition, and altered records accommodate such requirements. It is a better policy to have the house absorb the shortages and keep the overages. A record of individual performance is then maintained to determine if individuals balance over the long run. They should unless the cashier is inept or dishonest.

Over or short is the difference between what the cashier should have in the cash drawer and what is actually there. It is the comparison of a mathematically generated net total against a physical count of the money. The cashier *should* have the mathematical: The sum of the original starting bank plus the net receipts. What money is on hand in the drawer is what the cashier *does* have. Over or short is the difference between the *should have* and the *does have*. Assume net receipts of $2,664.09 plus a $500 starting bank. The drawer should have $3,164.09. It would be composed of cash (bills and coin) and other monetary units: traveler's checks, foreign monies, and personal checks. (Credit-card vouchers are not cash.) The cashier recaps the count; it might look so:

Cash on Hand—Physical Count:	
Travelers checks	$1,000.00
Personal checks	1,204.60
Currency	356.00
Coin	62.13
Casino chips	542.50
Total cash and cash equivalents on hand	$3,165.23

In the drawer is $3,165.23, which is more than the $3,164.09 (bank plus net receipts). Cash over is $1.14 and should be turned in. (Cashiers sometimes hold overage to offset another day's shortages, but get caught when addition/subtraction is the cause of the error.)

THE TURN-IN Front-office cashiers deposit net receipts plus or minus overage or shortage. But not all hotels handle turn-in that way! As a frequent alternative, cashiers do no calculations. They simply count and keep the bank. Everything else goes into a turn-in envelope. (see Exhibit 6). Cashiers who are permitted to total their receipts and count their drawers know exactly how much they are over or short. Not so with this alternative method. In such operations, front-office cashiers function no differently than departmental cashiers. They, too, retain their bank and turn in everything else. Sometimes, to get a due back, they even turn in part of their bank.

DUE BACK The turn-in of front-office cashiers and guest-service agents acting as cashiers has an issue not faced by departmental cashiers. The front-office bank makes change, it may make cash advances, and it accepts receipts that are not negotiable cash: traveler's checks/foreign currency, and so on. Assume that during one shift only traveler's checks were cashed. At the close of the day, the front-office bank would contain nothing but nonnegotiable paper. It would be impossible to do business from that drawer the next day. Banks must contain enough small bills and coins to carry out the cashiering function. There is no value in a $500 bank comprised of five $100 bills.

Examine the over-short computation above. Although there is $3,165.23 in the drawer, there is only $418.13 in negotiable money ($356 in currency and $62.13 in coin). This cashier operates with a $500 bank. The bank is short $81.87 ($500–$418.13). This cashier must turn in more than the net receipts ± overage or short. The excess turn-in requires a refund of $81.87, called a *due bank*. Others call it *due back*, or *U-owe-me*, or *difference returnable* or *exchange*.

The amount is calculated thus:

Due bank = Turn-in − (Net receipts ± Over or short)
Due bank = Turn-in ($1,000 + $1,204.60 + $542.50) − Net receipts ($2,664.09 + $1.14)
Due bank = ($2,747.10) − ($2,665.23)
$81.87 = $81.87

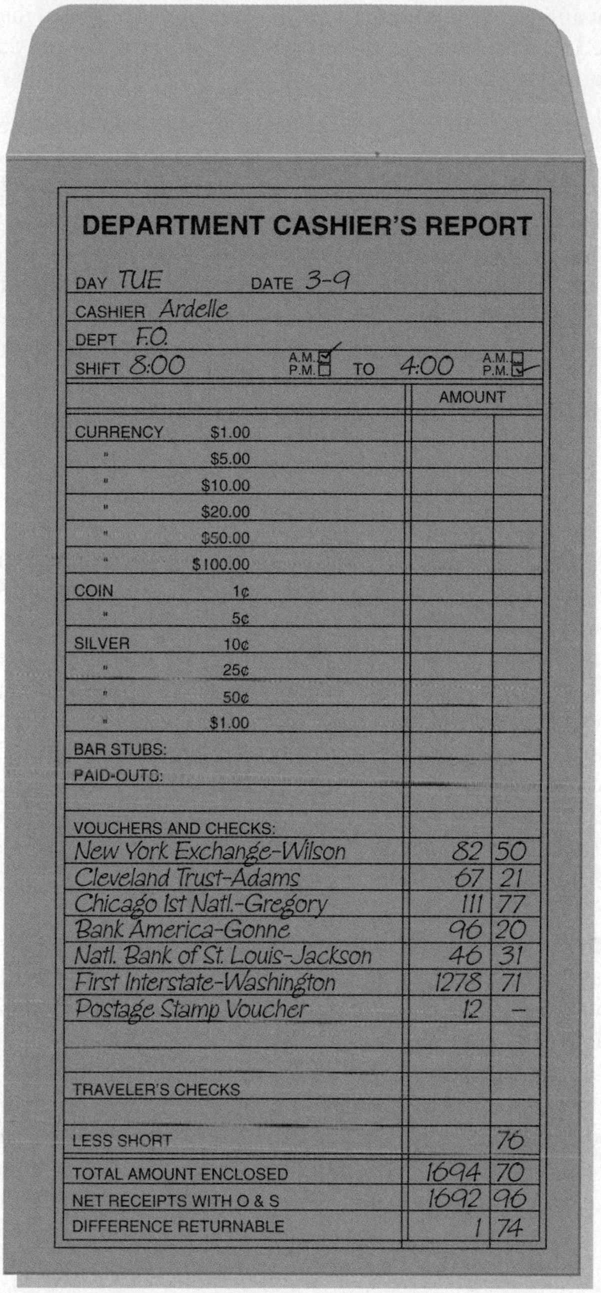

DEPARTMENT CASHIER'S REPORT

DAY _TUE_   DATE _3-9_

CASHIER _Ardelle_

DEPT _F.O._

SHIFT _8:00_   A.M. ☑ P.M. ☐   TO   _4:00_   A.M. ☐ P.M. ☑

	AMOUNT	
CURRENCY $1.00		
" $5.00		
" $10.00		
" $20.00		
" $50.00		
" $100.00		
COIN 1¢		
" 5¢		
SILVER 10¢		
" 25¢		
" 50¢		
" $1.00		
BAR STUBS:		
PAID-OUTS:		
VOUCHERS AND CHECKS:		
New York Exchange-Wilson	82	50
Cleveland Trust-Adams	67	21
Chicago 1st Natl.-Gregory	111	77
Bank America-Gonne	96	20
Natl. Bank of St. Louis-Jackson	46	31
First Interstate-Washington	1278	71
Postage Stamp Voucher	12	—
TRAVELER'S CHECKS		
LESS SHORT		76
TOTAL AMOUNT ENCLOSED	1694	70
NET RECEIPTS WITH O & S	1692	96
DIFFERENCE RETURNABLE	1	74

EXHIBIT 6 A typical envelope for a cashier's turn-in (or drop). This one would have accompanied Exhibit 4, at the close of Ardelle's shift. The list of checks here (Wilson, Adams, etc.) corresponds to her report. So does the total turn-in (Exhibit 5, line #1). The postage-stamp voucher was a paid-out for house business, so it's treated as if it were cash. See the text's discussion to understand overage and shortage and the due bank or difference returnable. There was no impact on currency and coin; apparently the bank is complete enough to avoid a larger due bank (due back).

Refunding the Due Back   To keep their banks balanced, cashiers specify denominations for the coins and currency that are to be returned. Due backs may be requested simply because the cashier has large bills even if the turn-in is not otherwise excessive, as it is in the illustration above.

Counting the turn-ins the next morning are the general cashier and at least one other member of the accounting department. The amounts enclosed are compared to the records including the faces of the cashier's envelopes (see Exhibit 6). There are two ways to proceed. Either the total dollar turn-in is deposited, in which case a withdrawal is needed to reimburse the due banks. Or the cash-rich envelopes of the operating departments "buy" the nonnegotiable monies from the envelopes of the front-office cashiers and the net is deposited (see Exhibit 5).

Most operations use a signature and witness system for returning the due banks. One person is given the due-back envelopes identified with the name of each recipient. Each recipient signs for the sealed envelope. The contents of the envelope are counted and added to the recipient's cash drawer, bringing it back to the initial bank. The envelopes were prepared during the cash audit and were witnessed as to the correct amount sealed inside. Some provision is needed to safeguard the envelopes of cashiers who are off the following day. Although simple, this signature and witness systems work well.

Refunding House Vouchers Some hotels utilize the front-office cash drawer as a petty cash fund. Cashiers pay out house expenses and hold the signed receipts (vouchers) until they reach a predetermined amount (say, $200). House vouchers might include soda-machine or video-game refunds, gasoline for the shuttle van, or emergency grocery purchases (see Exhibit 3). The receipts are kept in the cash drawer as part of the bank until they reach the predetermined amount. Then the vouchers are enclosed as part of the turn-in envelope (see Exhibit 6, postage stamp voucher) to become part of the due bank. An extremely large house voucher, say, a large COD shipment, may trigger an immediate due-bank turn-in or even a mid-day call to the general cashier.

Other Related Issues

TOUR PACKAGE COUPONS Hotels that market tour-and-travel packages must provide for the redemption of coupons. Coupons are processed primarily through the turn-ins of departmental cashiers, not front-office cashiers.

Package tours include more than hotel rooms. That is their appeal: A free round of golf, a drink at the bar, a dinner show, perhaps a gaming coupon. All are wrapped into the one-price package. Members of the tour are given booklets with specific coupons redeemable for each includable event. Guests use a coupon to pay for a particular service, say breakfast.

At this point the system sometimes breaks down. The breakfast cashier, who carefully monitors cash and credit payments, may overlook what appears to be a complimentary breakfast. What's the harm if tour guests forgot their coupon books? The harm, of course, is a loss of revenue. Each coupon that the cashier turns in is redeemed by the travel wholesaler for whatever payment was negotiated. Redeemed coupons are proof that services (breakfast, golf, drinks) were rendered and payment can be verified. Without the redeemed coupons, breakage accrues to the wholesaler. It accrues to the hotel when it is the hotel's package.

FOREIGN CURRENCY Unlike their counterparts worldwide, U.S. hotels do not deal in foreign currencies. They even refuse Canadian dollars despite their stability and similarity to greenbacks. Yet international tourism to the United States is rising, accelerating whenever the U.S. dollar weakens. Foreign currencies could be tendered across hotel desks if U.S. hoteliers would open currency-exchanges facilities. Some do have them, but only as lobby concessionaires.

Cities with large numbers of foreign visitors, such as New York, Los Angeles, and Miami, have developed good foreign-exchange facilities. These privately owned business are encouraged by local tourists bureaus and chambers of commerce. Foreign-exchange desks could do the same for hotels and enhance their incomes as well. International visitors prefer the safer environment of the hotel desk even though exchange costs are higher.

Foreign exchange at hotels flows in only one direction. Hotels do not repurchase U.S. currency as visitors prepare to go home. Foreign currency flows in, never out. This eliminates the need to inventory any foreign monies. The hotel's concern is the buy (bid) rate—only the bid rate. Money brokers quote both a buy (bid) rate and a sell (ask) rate.

The desk buys foreign currency from the guest at a rate that is lower than the bank/broker's bid rate, reselling later to the broker/bank at the bid rate. The hotel might buy euros at, say, 6 cents less than it sells, although the official spread might be only 3 cents. This extra spread between buy and sell may be further enriched by a supplemental exchange premium, which currency dealers call agio. Agio fees help offset bank charges or unexpected variations in foreign currency values. The latter makes it especially important to quickly process foreign currency. Foreign currency must be included in the turn-in every day and even more frequently in very volatile markets.

Obtaining daily quotes and avoiding banks that are not brokers themselves, but rather just middlemen, will maximize foreign exchange profits. The hotel could become an intermediary broker by converting funds for taxi drivers and servers throughout the community in addition to its own personnel. Of course, this opens a whole new business with the large risks that accompany foreign exchange. Not understanding "the business" is why many hoteliers have stayed away.

If the hotel is dealing in foreign currencies, the accounting office must furnish cashiers with a table of values for each currency traded (see Exhibit 7). (Several airlines quote rates on

Country	Currency	Country	Currency
THE AMERICAS		**CARIBBEAN**	
Argentina	Peso	Barbados	Dollar
Bahamas	Dollar	Curacao	Guilder
Bolivia	Boliviano	Jamaica	Dollar
Canada	Dollar	Martinique	Euro
Chile	Peso	Trinidad	Dollar
Columbia	Peso	Turks and Caicos	Dollar
Ecuador	Dollar	Virgin Islands	Dollar
El Salvador	Colon		
Guatemala	Quetzal	**AFRICA**	
Honduras	Lempira	Algeria	Dinar
Uruguay	Peso	Egypt	Pound
Venezuela	Bolivar	Ethiopia	Birr
		Ghana	Cedi
EURO-BASED		Libya	Dinar
Austria	Belgium	Morocco	Dirham
Cyprus	Estonia	South Africa	Rand
Finland	France	Sudan	Pound
Germany	Greece	Tanzania	Shilling
Ireland	Italy	Zambia	Kwacha
Luxembourg	Malta		
Monaco	Montenegro	**THE EAST AND OCEANIA**	
Netherlands	Portugal	Australia	Dollar
Romania	San Marino	Bahrain	Dinar
Spain	Vatican City	China	Yuan
		Hong Kong	Dollar
EUROPE		India	Rupee
Czech Republic	Koruna	Indonesia	Rupiah
Denmark	Krone	Israel	Shekel
Hungry	Forint	Japan	Yen
Latvia	Lat	Jordan	Dinar
Lithuania	Lita	Kuwait	Dinar
Norway	Krone	Lebanon	Pound
Poland	Zloty	Macau	Pataca
Russia	Ruble	Malaysia	Ringgit
Slovakia	Koruna	New Zealand	Dollar
Slovenia	Tolar	Pakistan	Rupee
Sweden	Krona	Singapore	Dollar
Switzerland	Franc	South Korea	Won
Turkey	Lira		
United Kingdom	Pound		

EXHIBIT 7 An abbreviated list of the world's currencies. Not every country using the euro is a member of the European Union! Similarly, not every country using a dollar-denominated currency (the Hong Kong dollar; the Canadian dollar) is using U.S. dollars!

foreign currencies and foreign traveler's checks as part of their reservations systems.) If currency values fluctuate over a wide range, a daily or even hourly quote is necessary to prevent substantial losses. More likely, the hotel will opt out of that particular currency.

Automated Currency Conversion Systems U.S. hotels have always quoted and sold rooms in U.S. dollars. Even foreign hotels often quote rates in dollars. International guests have had to do their own currency conversion calculations—at least that was the mind-set until recently. Hotels have begun implementing DCC (Dynamic Currency Conversion) software in their property management systems. The driver is twofold. (1) It is required by major credit-card companies as a software enhancement for international guests; and (2) hotels offering this service have experienced growth in international business—especially Web-based reservations.

DCC software quotes rates in both local and U.S. currencies. Guest access the information with the reservation or at registration. At check-out, folios are calculated in the currency selected and presented for approval. Once approved, the transaction is complete, and the cost of the hotel stay, including conversion fees and exchange rates, is shown. Payment is still in dollars unless the hotel has a currency-exchange option.

Example from the Land of Nod Let's see what needs to be done when a guest from the Land of Nod tenders a ₦5,000 bill in payment of a $234 account. Each ₦ (Nod dollar) is exchanged at 5 U.S. cents by the hotel, although the official rate may be somewhat higher—say, 5.3 cents. Therefore, the ₦5,000 is exchanged at $250, which is $15 less than the official rate of exchange. The cashier would return $16 in exchange for the ₦5,000 and the charge of $234. Change is given only in U.S. dollars even if the cashier has Nod dollars. If, on the other hand, the guest had offered only a ₦500 bill ($25) the cashier would have collected an additional U.S. $209 to settle the $234 account in full. The cashier would never offer change in ₦ currency even if Nod currency were in the cash drawer. Doing so would offset any profit earned on the exchange rates.

CREDIT AND THE CITY LEDGER

Cash, the discussion that just closed, is not the primary exchange for guests doing business in hotels. Most guests use credit, primarily credit cards, which ends up in the city ledger.

Review of the City Ledger

Registered guests enjoy the services offered by the hotel, but don't pay for them immediately. Many businesses work that way. Customers who have not yet paid for goods and services are called *accounts receivable, A/R*. Hotels have two types. Guests who are still in the hotel are called *front-office* (or *transient*) accounts receivable. Their debts are tracked by guest-service agents at the desk. A/R who are not registered are *city-ledger* receivables. Their debts are tracked by the accounting office.

In the age of computers, the records of both guest types are maintained electronically. The term "ledger" survives although the records are no longer ledgers, bound books. Thus, the city ledger references the accounts receivable of all nonregistered guests. Front-office ledgers are tracked through the room numbers of the registered guests. City-ledger records are assigned account numbers because these A/R are not registered in any room. Moreover, they may never have been—and may never, ever be—registered guests, although many start out as such.

As registered guests depart, they shift their account balances to credit cards. Credit-card companies, which then owe the debt, are nonregistered A/R, which means they are tracked through the city ledger. Other A/R types are also in the city ledger. The list is large: travel agents, associations, wholesalers, and client companies. Almost all of these non-credit-card receivables originate in the guest ledger as the hotel sells services, but delays collection. Credit-card accounts hold the largest amount of dollar debt, far more than these other city-ledger categories. So this discussion of hotel credit starts with credit cards.

Credit Cards

Credit, as a means of payment, traces back to the Biblical inns of Ancient Rome. Innkeepers issued negotiable tokens that were used as money. Similar coinage appeared 2,000 years later during America's colonial period. The concept reappeared about 1915 when Western Union, the telegraph company, issued special cards (no longer tokens) to preferred guests. As the credit action heated up, hotels chains joined the rush; but not for long. The financial and administrative burdens (precomputer age) were too heavy. By the 1970s, the lodging industry had come to understand that credit cards were financial instruments and not the marketing tools that the industry had hoped for. Preferred-guest programs, which came later, (and are discussed later) now serve that marketing need.

KINDS OF CREDIT CARDS All credit cards are much alike; but they did not start out that way. Although the number of cards seem endless, consumer cards fall into three categories. *Bank cards* are the most common, followed *by travel and entertainment cards* (T&E). All others (including Discover Card and *private-label cards,* which hotels might issue) have much smaller structures.

Card Types	
Airline	Earns frequent-flyer miles
Affinity	Issued to groups with an affinity (some relationship)
Bad credit	Helps re-establish poor credit record
Bank	MasterCard and Visa; used by many individuals
Business	Available to businesses, large and small
Cash back	Gives user cash rewards
Charge	Paid in full monthly; no balance allowed; annual fee
Co-branded	Contains a company name as well as that of the credit-card issuer
Debit	Removes cash from bank; hence there is no float
Efolio	Eases expense reporting by summarizing travel costs
Gift	Celebrates birthdays and other occasions
Gimmick	For funky market segment; aromatic or touchy/feely
Incentive	Supplements salaries and wages with bonus
Instant-approval	Issued by select banks
Limited use	Restricted, say for business travel
Low-interest	Zero introductory rates and/or low fixed rates
Memory	Component of many of the other cards
Payroll	Wages can be withdrawn from ATMs; see Exhibit 2
Perishable	Limited use; perfect for Web purchases
Prepaid	Cash is loaded before use; works like a debit card
Procurement	Or Purchasing pays for company procurements
Private label	See co-branded
Rewards	Reward with gifts, tee times, etc. rather than cash
Smart	Miniature computers a la smart phones
Stored	Has a prepaid but limited amount; see prepaid
Student	Targets high school and college students
T&E	Travel and entertainment

EXHIBIT 8 Financial institutions have followed a general marketing trend: Give consumers choice, whether with autos, bottled waters, or credit instruments. These are card types, not all are credit cards.

Each of the three types was designed initially for different consumer markets. T&E cards were for *T*ravel and business *E*ntertainment. That is the very name of the card class. Bank cards were visualized as retail cards for the general public. The distinctions hold true no longer. The original bank cards, Visa and MasterCard,[1] are now private corporations competing for T&E business. In turn, American Express and Discover Card reach out to nonbusiness cardholders. What started in 1950 as an experiment when Diner's Club launched the first retail (restaurant) card has become a mainstay of worldwide commerce (see Exhibit 8). There are more cards than people in the United States.

Competition between and among the cards is fierce. Lawsuits are frequent and rivalry intense. Most telling was the legal settlement that allowed nonbank cards (Discover, American Express, Diners) to clear through the banking system (see Exhibit 9). In 2009, Uncle Sam entered the fray with new rules, dealing primarily with interest rates. Credit cards are consumer loans so the legislation was designed to even the field between the card holder and the gigantic card issuers.

HOW THE SYSTEM WORKS The system works because there is something for each participant: Convenience for guests, security for merchants, and profits for the owners, the credit-card companies, some of which are traded on the stock market. Merchants/hotels foot the bill (see Exhibit 9), but make sales that might otherwise be missed and do so with far less risk of loss. Many hotels have been able to eliminate the position of credit manager, assigning those duties part-time to other accounting personnel.

---

[1] Trademark names are used throughout this chapter. Read registered trademark® adjacent to each registered name.

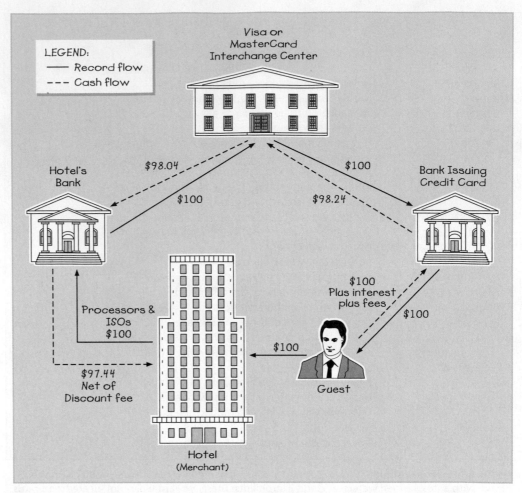

LEGEND:
— Record flow
--- Cash flow

EXHIBIT 9 The full burden of interchange fees, 2.56% ($100–$97.44) in this example, falls on the merchant/hotel. Other costs (see Exhibit 10) push the percentage upward by a point or more. Federal legislation in 2010 brought competition to the process by allowing merchants to promote less costly cards. That wasn't previously allowed under the credit-card contracts that merchants signed.

Fees Card companies charge merchant/hotels discount fees. Bank cards charge the smallest fees, 1–2% of the transaction; T&E's 3–5%. Card fees, like other business expenses can be negotiated. Large-volume merchants (hotel chains including their franchisees) are especially able to negotiate. Independent hotels in umbrella organizations have had much of their negotiating gains offset by administrative costs. Competition among rival banks is so keen that even small operators—especially those that have other relationships with their banks—can dicker successfully.

Competition is coming to credit-card fees. Part of the lawsuit brought by the Justice Department (2010) allows retailers/hotels to offer discounts if guests will use one card in preference to another. That's revolutionary! The choice might be between card companies or card types within one card brand (see Exhibit 8). As the hotel's first line of contact, guest-service agents must be conversant with the options to bring about savings in fees.

However, fees based on card types and dollar volume are but two of the many costs associated with credit cards. Handling, authorization, and settlement procedures add to costs. The credit business has grown so large that local banks have outsourced much of the business (see Exhibit 10). With these services come more fees. There are setup fees; per-transaction fees; programming fees; statement fees; authorization fees; minimum volume fees; telecommunication fees and lease fees. These costs push total outlays to 3–5% of sales even for bank cards!

Chargeback fees (when the credit-card charge fails to clear) are the most costly (see Exhibit 21). Chargebacks are voided transactions resulting from either processing errors or guests successfully disputing the charge. The hotel loses the original sale and still pays a hefty chargeback fee. Losses are even greater if the bill includes tips that the hotel has paid to service employees and/or cash advances for concessionaires (see Exhibit 1).

<table>
<tr><td colspan="2" align="center">**Credit Card Terminology and Definitions**</td></tr>
<tr><td>*Associations*</td><td>Affiliations of member banks to form the MasterCard and Visa systems.</td></tr>
<tr><td>*Card-processing company*</td><td>Handles electronic transactions at the *POS*, which includes verifying the card, transferring the funds, and issuing approval codes. May also be an *independent service organization*.</td></tr>
<tr><td>*Card-service provider*</td><td>See *Merchant-service provider*.</td></tr>
<tr><td>*Chargeback fee*</td><td>Credit-card company's charge added to the original value of a service when the charge is protested because of error or guest dispute. (See Exhibit 21.)</td></tr>
<tr><td>*Credit-card companies*</td><td>Technically, firms that appoint their own merchants and issue their own cards. Best known are American Express, Diners Club/Carte Blanche, and Discover. Generically used to include bank cards as well.</td></tr>
<tr><td>*Discount rate*</td><td>The percentage of each sale that the card companies charge the merchant; one of several fees, including a flat fee.</td></tr>
<tr><td>*Handling*</td><td>The method, manual or electronic, used to generate a sales slip.</td></tr>
<tr><td>*Independent service organization*</td><td>ISOs are contracted by banks to sell merchant status to businesses (hotels). May simultaneously be *card-processing companies* or may purchase wholesale services from one, reselling the services at retail.</td></tr>
<tr><td>*Interchange fee*</td><td>Charge paid by the merchant's bank that issued the card to compensate in part for the waiting time—float time—until payment is received.</td></tr>
<tr><td>*Merchant-service provider*</td><td>Also called a *card-service provider*. Any company, including banks, *card-processing companies*, and *independent service organizations*, that arrange for and service *merchant status*.</td></tr>
<tr><td>*MOTO*</td><td>Mail order/telephone order; nonelectronic communications.</td></tr>
<tr><td>*Merchant status*</td><td>A business (hotel) authorized to process credit-card charges. Authorized merchants may not process (factor) cards for nonmerchants.</td></tr>
<tr><td>*POS*</td><td>A widely used abbreviation for point-of-sale.</td></tr>
<tr><td>*Processor*</td><td>See *Card-processing* company.</td></tr>
</table>

EXHIBIT 10 The large size of the credit-card industry requires support from an army of indirect agents. Banks and nonbank (Discover; AmEx) issuers of credit cards can no longer do the job alone. With so many agencies involved, clients (hotels) of processing companies must now use the new PA-DSS (Payment Application Data Security Standards) to safeguard guests' credit-card information.

Fees are offset with certain credits: Installing point-of sale terminals (POSs, see Exhibit 8) and electronic scanners (see Exhibit 11) is among the offsets.

Other Cards

Debit cards and smart cards are neither credit instruments (see Exhibit 8) nor categories of the city ledger. They are discussed here because both card types are issued by the same credit-card companies/banks and both impact on hotel guests.

DEBIT CARDS Debit cards transfer funds (money) electronically. Thus comes the term *EFT*, electronic funds transfer. Money is switched instantaneously from the cardholder's bank account to the hotel's bank account. If payment is by EFT, there is no debt. No debt means no accounts receivable, no ledger postings, no transfer of front-office folios to city-ledger accounts, and no subsequent collections. Payment is up-front and immediate. Processing costs are much, much less.

Debit cards transfer cash to the hotel, but no cash changes hands at the front desk. Losses from change-making mistakes, dishonest employees, shortages and bounced checks are an issue no longer. Whereas credit-card fees may cost up to 5% of the bill, debit-card fees now cost less than

EXHIBIT 11 Swiping a card through an electronic reader brings instant validity. The cost of buying or leasing this equipment is partly offset by savings in discount fees, faster settlement, and reduced losses from chargebacks (see Exhibit 21). *Courtesy: Hypercom Corporation, Phoenix, Arizona.*

50¢! Cost was one of the issues that caused the Justice Department to bring its lawsuit. A lower dollar cost notwithstanding, debit cards carry a higher percentage fee. They are used, usually, to pay for small transactions; using credit cards (with their delayed float) for larger purchases. So although absolute cost is lower, the bite, as a percentage of the transaction, is usually higher.

Debit-card users enter a personal ID number; credit-card users sign a charge slip (see Exhibit 12). The former is an online transaction; the latter an off-line transaction. Both payments follow the same pattern and infrastructure. The holder's one card may do either depending on the user's mood at settlement time. The main differences: No float. No float is a negative for the consumer/guest, but a positive for the merchant/hotel, which doesn't wait for its money. Besides no float, there is no time lag and no question about the user's ability to pay. The consumers' switch to debit cards gained momentum after credit-card companies reduced grace periods for payment (reduced float time) and increased late fees for consumers. Theft is a major debit-card negative; imposters can clear out a victim's entire bank account. Debit-card issuers now cover that contingency loss as they do with credit cards.

Debit cards may be the first step in the march toward the cashless society that futurists predict. If so, smart cards are next.

SMART CARDS   Smart cards were introduced in France during the 1950s, but they are just now approaching the level of success that was envisioned. Part of the delay has been a search for universal application and part is the concern over privacy. Broader acceptance is coming because American Express, MasterCard, and Visa recently agreed on the technology.

Smart cards are miniature computers almost indistinguishable from standard cards. They have electronic chips instead of magnetic strips. Hence comes the terms *chip cards* or *digital cash*. Smart cards carry a quantity of information. Their 8K memory equates to about 15 typewritten pages. Smart cards are seen to be the future because they are everything in one[2] They are credit or debit cards; stored-value cards; and ATM cards. Identification, electronic door keys, medical and insurance records, and more can be stored for immediate recall. They hold promise for Internet commerce and Web access. They're apt to be wedded one day to the ubiquitous, smart cell phones.

Retailers, especially supermarkets, are already using low-level smart cards to track customer demographics and preferences. These cards provide marketers with names and addresses, purchasing patterns, and income levels. The hotel industry has had much of the same information for years. Guest's identity, address, company affiliation, room preferences, and more are available

---

[2]Smart cards (using both chip and PIN) are widely used in Europe and their rapid globalization represents a challenge for lagging U.S. card companies.

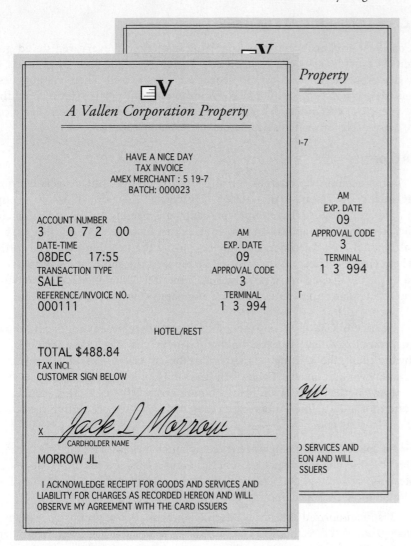

EXHIBIT 12 Although credit-card charges are processed almost 100% electronically, guests still need a printed receipt and merchants need a signed voucher. Exhibit 21 itemizes issues that even electronic systems have.

to every hotel and hotel chain with a property management system. Privacy concerns have arisen anew as recently issued *contact-less* cards containing embedded radio chips (called radio frequency identification, RFID) grow in popularity. The new cards can be swiped through the traditional terminal (see Exhibit 11) or waived before a special reader. Promoters praise the waived cards because they never leave their owner's hands. Critics fear electronic eavesdropping.

STILL OTHER CARDS Although less popular today, some organizations still opt for *affinity cards*. Affinity cards carry two designations. The name of the affiliated association or charity is identified along with the credit-card company. By doing so, the card company gains access to the organization's membership list. For this, it promises the organization a small commission. Cobranded cards are another marketing device. Affinity cards are associated with user groups, but cobranded cards attached the merchant's logo. For example, Chase Bank's Visa card might cobrand with Marriott. A second Chase card could carry Hilton's logo, and so on (see Exhibit 8).

Cobranded card users get special hotel privileges such as check-cashing, room upgrades, and free Continental breakfasts. Many are the same goodies that go with memberships in frequent-guest programs (FGP). A wider reward structure is the key to these cards. Points earned apply to the hotels FGP or to an airline's FFP, frequent-flier program. Hotels sometimes resolve complaints with points instead of with cash. Marketing is one more use of FGP points. Hotels double the award to lure guests; many do that to offset dips in the cycle. The industry needs to be cautious lest it piles up huge, unmanageable liabilities.

OTHER CITY-LEDGER CATEGORIES

Credit cards are found in every city ledger because almost every registered guest—and certainly almost every hotel—favors a credit-card settlement of the folio. Most hotels, excepting limited-service properties, have other city-ledger accounts as well. There are nonguest charges from banquet room rentals (charity dances, for example) and parties (retirement dinners, for example).[3] There are outstanding debts from travel agencies and wholesalers. Large convention hotels have master accounts, often several from just one convention.

Master Accounts

Master accounts accumulate charges for all types of groups, but especially conventions. Master accounts are front-office folios. However, the "guest" is a group or an association, not an individual. Entertainment, banquets, meeting space, and room charges are some of the items that may appear on master accounts. Outside vendors (florists, bands, and audiovisual rentals) are sometimes, but rarely, paid by the hotel and charged to the master account. These charges appear on the front-office folio. At the end of the stay, total charges are transferred to the city ledger from the master-account folio. Billing and collection are directed to the group's headquarters, not to a credit-card company. This creates a new category of the city ledger.

Functions that involve hundreds/thousands of persons represent huge sums of money. The hotel wants prompt payment! To expedite that payment, the master account folio is carefully reviewed by the client (the meeting planner and/or the association executive) and the hotel (the sales manager and/or accountant). Folios with thousands of dollar charges, may have errors, but they're not always in the hotel's favor. Four common errors irritate meeting planners and delay payment, often for a long time. Attending to these beforehand—preventing the complaint—is what good service is all about.

Error 1 is split billing. Meeting planners complain that charges are incorrectly split between master accounts and individual, personal accounts. Group events should be charged on the master folio and not on the personal folio of the executive who signs the tab. Front-office employees grow careless despite specific, written instructions from the client.

Error 2 is unauthorized signatures. Meeting and convention groups have many honchos: an elected board of directors, association officers, and paid professional staff. There are also informal leaders and past officers who forget they are no longer in authority. So they sign for charges to be posted to the master account. Meeting planners complain about these unauthorized charges by unauthorized members especially when the hotel was provided with an advanced list of authorized signatures.

Error 3 is the sequence of posting. The breakfast charge of day 2 of the meeting should not appear on the folio before the dinner of day 1. Picky clients require the entire bill to be reposted to show each event in sequence. Comparisons to the original contract and to the function sheets are facilitated thereby. That pleases the meeting planner, but the hotel could have done it beforehand.

Error 4 is comp rooms. Complimentary rooms are based on a widely used formula: 1 free room-night per 50 paid room-nights. Meeting planners complain that hotels deduct the lowest room rates against the free allocation instead of the highest rates. The comp should go against the suite housing the VIP speaker, they argue, not against the room housing the associations' clerical staff.

Although it is best to resolve billing differences while they are still fresh, it may not be possible to do so before the group departs. Agreed-upon items should be resolved and billed promptly without waiting to reach accord on the few differences. Otherwise, small sums keep thousands of master-account dollars unpaid. Associations sometimes take advantage of that intentionally.

---

[3]Some hotels open temporary front-office folios for such events and immediately transfer the balance to the city ledger.

Groups, Packages, and Company-Sponsored Functions

Master accounts are not limited to conventions. They are also used for single entity groups (traveling teams, glee clubs) and company-sponsored events (new product shows). Prepaid tour packages offered by wholesalers also use master accounts. One master account accumulates all the room charges on one folio. The entity (the team's manager, the company's treasurer, the wholesaler who has collected in advance from the tour members) pays the master account.

Attendee's personal purchases and services are rarely ever covered by the package. So they do not appear on the master account. Split folios are the answer. Major items, room and tax and included meals, are posted to the master account, the A folio. Personal charges are posted to the individual's room, the B folio. B folios are settled by the individual at check-out. Upon arrival, group members are reminded of the arrangement by computer-generated notices, which are distributed along with the room keys (see Exhibit 13), room assignments having been made before the group's arrival. The master folio is settled by the group's sponsor, almost always by a transfer to the city ledger.

The advertised package tells the buyer what is and, by inference, what is not included. Colored and dated coupons are issued to the package guests along with the keys. Guests use the proper coupon to pay for meals, drinks, golf, whatever was included with the package. As explained previously, cashiers in the various departments treat the coupons as part of their daily turn-in.

Individual City-Ledger Receivables

The city ledger contains individual accounts receivable, actual persons or companies, as well as credit cards and master accounts. Dollar volume is smaller, but that doesn't make them less an account receivable.

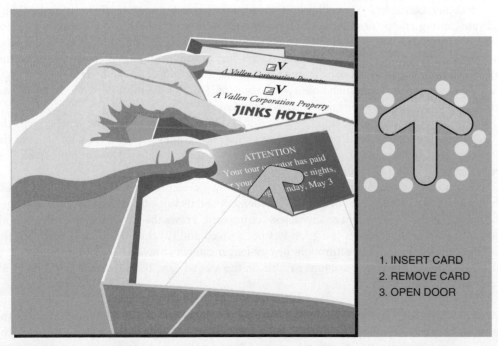

EXHIBIT 13 Room keys, meal coupons, and information about the division of expenses between the group (A folios) and its members (B folios) are distributed as those members arrive. The letter reads:

"Welcome! Here is your room key, *1217*. Your tour operator has paid for your room for three nights beginning *Sunday, May 3* and for all meals covered by the attached tickets. You are responsible for purchases in shops, dining rooms, and lounges. Laundry and telephone calls are also personal expenses. The desk will be happy to help with these arrangements. Thank you for choosing the Vallen family of hotels.

Cash or Credit: The City Ledger

THE ORIGINAL CITY-LEDGER ACCOUNTS Local individuals and companies were the original nonregistered accounts receivable. That is where the term *city* ledger originated. Individual accounts still exist, but they have been replaced in the main by the widespread use of credit cards. Hotels still favor individual city accounts with good credit because payment is made in full without fees.

These "city" accounts may not be local and charges may not originate at the front desk. They include individuals and companies that preestablish credit in order to use the hotel's facilities. A distant company may send employees to the hotel on a regular basis. A local business might use guest rooms for visitors and public rooms for business meetings and social affairs. Neighboring establishments use their credit for meals and drinks. Once credit has been established, the authorized user merely signs for the charges. Bills go out monthly, sometimes more frequently.

Airline crews are part of this city ledger. They provide a basic occupancy even though the average daily rate is very low. Layover crews charge rooms to the airline's city account and periodically the hotel bills. Airline contracts sometimes require the hotel to accommodate stranded travelers as well as crews. Typically, the airline pays for the rooms and meals by giving passengers miscellaneous charge orders (MCOs). Stranded passengers pay with the MCOs, which the hotel uses to balance the front-office folios. Those accounts receivable are transferred to the city ledger and the airline is billed. MCOs are also used when an airline acts as a travel agency and books rooms for travelers.

TRAVEL AGENTS (T/AS) The future of travel agencies is threatened by Web shopping, satellite ticket purchases (Japanese convenience stores sell airline tickets), and ticketless travel. Agencies are consolidating, diversifying, charging new fees, and disappearing from the hotel's city ledger.

Hotels have had a love-hate relationship with travel agencies. They contend that TAs earn commissions on the industry's own customers. (That animosity is also directed to Web-based reservations). In turn, TAs complain about not getting paid promptly. At least hotels still pay commissions; airlines stopped a decade ago. Some hotel chains outsource commission payments to companies such as Pegasus Solutions and Utell's Pay-Com. For a fee, these agencies consolidate T/A commissions.

Not all travel agents are small proprietorships. But even big agencies fight online bookings and rate-cutting competitors. Size aside, travel agents complain that they are heavily solicited when business is slow, but neglected when occupancy improves. Of course commissionable business is turned away during peak occupancies just as room rates are increased at that time. Notwithstanding the occasional carping, certain agencies and certain hotels develop strong profitable relationships. Hawaiian hotels rely heavily on TAs. For the most part, hotels are pleased to take agency business and pay the 10–15% commission.

Once the agency and the hotel have established a credit relationship, the hotel accepts the TA's coupon (see Exhibit 14) from the arriving guest. It becomes payment for all or part of the room charge. The TA could also forward a check (less commission) before the guest arrives. This prepaid deposit would be credited to the guest folio on arrival.

If not prepaid, the hotel honors the coupon only if credit relations have been established. The coupon is accepted as part of the folio's settlement and its value transferred to the city ledger. The hotel bills the TA. Payment received, less commission, erases the city-ledger account. In both cases [(1) cash is received but the guest has not arrived and (2) the guest has arrived, but the cash has not] the accounting is through the city-ledger category, travel agencies. In the first case, the hotel owes the agency, an account payable. In the second case, the agency owes the hotel, an account receivable.

BANQUET CHARGES Open-book credit, nothing more than a personal signature, was once the norm for banquet sales. Party givers and banquet chairpersons signed the tab and left—left the hotel waiting for payment. Catering managers still extend this courtesy in very special instances. More likely, they charge a credit card or obtain a deposit before the event begins. Open credit charges and unpaid balances still remaining from deposits become city-ledger accounts and are billed within three days. Three-day billing is standard procedure for banquet charges, master accounts, speedy check-outs, and late charges.

LATE CHARGES Late charges are departmental charges (food, spa, etc.) that show up after the guest has checked out. They're abbreviated LC or AD (after departure). There's been a time

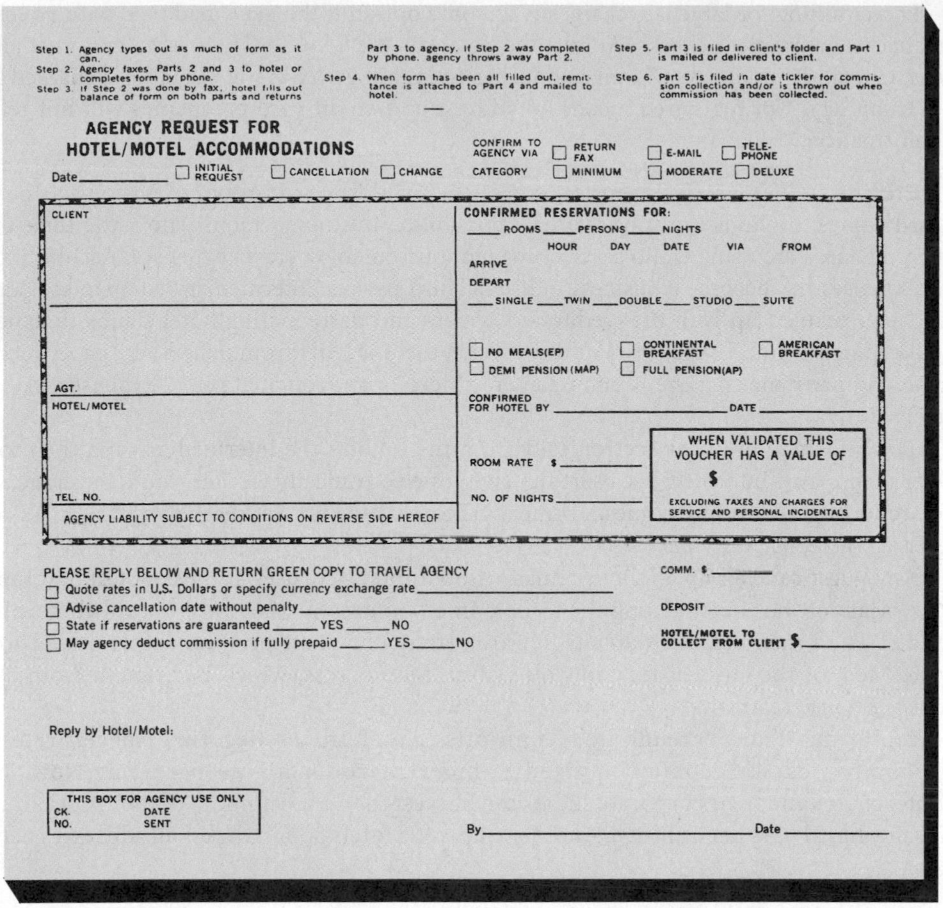
Step 1. Agency types out as much of form as it can.
Step 2. Agency faxes Parts 2 and 3 to hotel or completes form by phone.
Step 3. If Step 2 was done by fax, hotel fills out balance of form on both parts and returns Part 3 to agency. If Step 2 was completed by phone, agency throws away Part 2.
Step 4. When form has been all filled out, remittance is attached to Part 4 and mailed to hotel.
Step 5. Part 3 is filed in client's folder and Part 1 is mailed or delivered to client.
Step 6. Part 5 is filed in date tickler for commission collection and/or is thrown out when commission has been collected.

AGENCY REQUEST FOR HOTEL/MOTEL ACCOMMODATIONS

Date_____ ☐ INITIAL REQUEST ☐ CANCELLATION ☐ CHANGE

CONFIRM TO AGENCY VIA ☐ RETURN FAX ☐ E-MAIL ☐ TELE-PHONE

CATEGORY ☐ MINIMUM ☐ MODERATE ☐ DELUXE

CLIENT

AGT.

HOTEL/MOTEL

TEL. NO.

AGENCY LIABILITY SUBJECT TO CONDITIONS ON REVERSE SIDE HEREOF

CONFIRMED RESERVATIONS FOR:
____ ROOMS ____ PERSONS ____ NIGHTS

	HOUR	DAY	DATE	VIA	FROM
ARRIVE					
DEPART					

____ SINGLE ____ TWIN ____ DOUBLE ____ STUDIO ____ SUITE

☐ NO MEALS(EP) ☐ CONTINENTAL BREAKFAST ☐ AMERICAN BREAKFAST
☐ DEMI PENSION (MAP) ☐ FULL PENSION(AP)

CONFIRMED FOR HOTEL BY _____ DATE _____

ROOM RATE $_____

NO. OF NIGHTS _____

WHEN VALIDATED THIS VOUCHER HAS A VALUE OF
$
EXCLUDING TAXES AND CHARGES FOR SERVICE AND PERSONAL INCIDENTALS

PLEASE REPLY BELOW AND RETURN GREEN COPY TO TRAVEL AGENCY
☐ Quote rates in U.S. Dollars or specify currency exchange rate _____
☐ Advise cancellation date without penalty _____
☐ State if reservations are guaranteed ____ YES ____ NO
☐ May agency deduct commission if fully prepaid ____ YES ____ NO

COMM. $_____

DEPOSIT _____

HOTEL/MOTEL TO COLLECT FROM CLIENT $_____

Reply by Hotel/Motel:

THIS BOX FOR AGENCY USE ONLY
CK. NO. DATE SENT

By _____ Date _____

EXHIBIT 14 The format for travel agent/hotel communications was never standardized despite several attempts. That shortcoming is an issue no longer. Credit-card payments and electronic communications have replaced these written, hand-carried forms. This design served the two industries for many years.

lag getting the charge into the system. Most likely, the delay was inputting a pencil-and-paper voucher at the desk because it arrived late from a distant department.

POSs, point-of-sale terminals, have almost eliminated late charges. Those that slip through are irritants to both parties. Guests may need to modify their business expense-accounts. Hotels may need to absorb the late billings that guests won't pay. In fact, small amounts are not even billed. Processing costs and the loss of guest goodwill often exceed the amount sought. So small AD charges are posted to guest folios and balanced out with allowances. This provides a record of the charges. If a charge is too large to erase, the reopened folio is transferred to the city ledger and billed directly.

If late charges are numerous—certainly, management would look into that—they may be posted to a separate folio called "Late Charges." Then the whole day is erased with one allowance. Either way, management gets a Daily Allowance Report from the night audit.

There are no late-charge issues with express check-outs because guests use credit cards. Although the guest may have seen a copy of the folio, the hotel has not yet processed the card. The late charges are simply added to the folio and transferred, along with other charges, to the guest's credit card. The card company is billed from the city ledger. The guest receives the final folio several days later with its balance identical to the charge on the guest's credit-card statement. These folios are also being delivered now as efolios, discussed next.

Reconciling late charges is not so easy if the guest settled at the cashier's window and not by express check-out. Then the guest has a signed credit-card receipt and a folio marked "Paid." Card companies do not allow changes to be added after the signing. If the late charge is substantial, the hotel will bill the guest at the folio address. This second chance has an obvious public-relations cost.

Direct billing for large late charges is the only option if the guest had paid with vouchers, cash, checks, or traveler's checks. At least the hotel has the address. There is no option at all if a *nonregistered* individual pays a lounge or dining-room bill with a credit card that is charged back (see Exhibit 21). Not registered means no address and credit-card companies will not release that information.

Efolios   Guests review their folios using lobby kiosks or in-room television sets or they get hard copies. Efolio accounting is a new possibility. Businesspersons who settle their folios with credit cards are using efolio services for reimbursement of travel expenses. Accounting for travel expenses has become a business in itself. Third parties, intermediary companies, Concur is one, have teamed up with the credit-card issuers and participating hotel chains to expedite recordkeeping for travel expenses. For the traveler, there is relief from pencil-and-paper records. For the company making the reimbursement, there is a reconciliation of expenses with the traveler's itinerary.

The information flows electronically from the folio to the intermediary and then to the traveler's company. Intermediaries sort the charges electronically (rooms, food, beverage, etc.) before reporting details to the guest's company. Efolios have not yet reached critical mass so all hotels are not yet aboard.

Any guest can call up a folio by email without intermediaries at those hotels offering the service. Marriott has been among the leaders in efolio access. Marriott began with corporate accounts. Then members of Marriott Rewards (frequent-guest program) were added to the service. Most of the large chains now offer this efolio access, which is different from efolio business-expense reporting.

Efolio may have serendipitous spin-offs. Hotel chains negotiate special rates for large companies that commit a fixed number of room-nights per year. Now, both the hotel chains and their corporate clients can harvest the actual number of room-nights used. That value has always been elusive. Another spin-off: Hotels obtain the email addresses of their guests.

DELINQUENT ACCOUNTS   Receivables that may not be collectible are placed in the delinquent, or bad-debt division, of the city ledger. Such is the case with late charges that are too large for allowances and too small for legal action against the offending parties. Unrecoverable receivables, including chargebacks (see Exhibit 21), are eventually written off as bad debts.

Returned (bounced) checks are also tracked in delinquent accounts. Checks come back for many reasons: insufficient funds; no such account; account closed; illegible signature; incorrect date. Hotels accept very few checks any more so this is no longer a major issue. Passing bad checks is a criminal offense so hotels should support the prosecution of offenders even when restitution is made.

EXECUTIVE ACCOUNTS   Hotel executives can be city-ledger receivables in their own hotels. Managers at certain levels use the hotel for both personal and house business. Company policy dictates how charges are to be made. House entertainment might be distinguished from personal charges on the guest check by an "H" (house business) or an "E" (entertainment) added under the signature. Without that symbol, the accounting department bills the executive as a regular city account. Depending on the employment agreement, payment may be just a percentage of the actual menu prices.

DUE BILLS   Hotels have traded room-nights for products since the Great Depression of the 1930s. Swaps with media (radio and television stations, billboards, newspapers, and magazines) involve free rooms for free advertising. Trades with manufacturers for capital goods such as beds and televisions are a later development. Evidence of the hotel's obligation to meets its half of the bargain is a contract called a *due bill* (see Exhibit 15). *Trade advertising contacts, trade-outs,* and *reciprocal trade agreements* are other names for due bills. Temporary accounts receivable in the city ledger are needed when the due-bill user checks out. The negotiated items—preferably just the room portion—of the folio are paid with the due bill. That value is not the usual city ledger receivable! It is, rather, an offset against the liability (the hotel's promise to provide space) created by the due-bill contract. Due-bill users pay in the usual manner for items not covered by the agreement.

VALLEN CORPORATE TRADE ADVERTISING CONTRACT

The_____[MEDIA OR MANUFACTURING COMPANY'S NAME AND ADDRESS]_____

agrees to____[DELIVER A PARTICULAR PRODUCT; OR BILLBOARD SIGNAGE, OR INSERT ADVERTISING, ETC.]____

in the amount of $_____ to be paid for by room accommodations at any of the Vallen Corporation's member hotels. This trade contract expires on _____[Date]_____. Accommodations will not be available until the product has been delivered to the hotel or until the first advertisement appears. Claims for accommodations or for goods or services not used by the date above are hereby cancelled.

Charges for services in excess of this trade order or services other than those specifically identified above are the responsibility of the party using the contract and must be paid in full at departure (or more frequently if the stay is extended). The company or organization named above is responsible for full payment whether or not its owners, employees, or individuals in due course actually use this due bill.

No guarantee of room availability is made or implied; reasonable advanced noticed is recommended. Every effort will be made to accommodate the dates requested.

This contract must be presented to the guest-service agent upon arrival, but neither the hotel nor the Vallen Corporation will accept responsibility for identifying the validity of the user. The hotel and the Vallen Corporation retain the right to eject undesirable guests and to charge the full amount of the reservation against the contract. The hotel and the Vallen Corporation assume no liability for personal injuries or property damages to the person or persons using this contract whether or not the personal injuries or property damages were caused by the negligence of the corporation, the hotel, or its employees.

Date   _____

Merchant_____   Hotel_____
        Authorized Signature   Authorized Signature

            Title   Title

EXHIBIT 15 Trade advertising contracts, also called trade-outs or due bills, swap hotel space for goods (TVs, beds) or services (chiefly advertising). Both parties trade at sales value but deliver at cost. Hotels employ due bills aggressively during economic dips. Not all trade-outs can be negotiated with terms that so strongly favor the hotel, as these do.

Rationale for Due Bills   Airlines and theaters, arenas, and the media deal in highly perishable products. There is no means of recapturing an unsold seat or an unused television spot for resale another day. The same is true for lodging. Not one of these businesses can inventory its product to use sometime later. Once the newspaper is printed, that day's ad space is lost. Once the night has passed, that empty hotel room cannot be sold again. Trading a lost opportunity for something useful is the rationale behind due bills.

Hotels try to restrict due-bill usage to rooms, the hotel's most profitable item, and for use during the lowest occupancy periods and by specifically named persons. The due-bill user would then pay for all other services including food and beverage. F&B costs are much higher and, unlike unused rooms, can be inventoried. The media set restrictions too, making no promise as to the location of the print or the time it will be heard on the airwaves or the location of the billboard. With hard bargaining, each party gives up something.

Some due bills are so negotiable that they are traded on the open market. Brokers buy the bills at reduced prices from the original receiver or buy directly from the hotel. Due bills may be sold and resold with an additional markup each time. In due course, they are used at the hotel by the final buyer in lieu of cash. The hotel accepts the bills at face value, which is still greater than the user paid to acquire the contract and much less than it cost the hotel to deliver.

The concept and the markups work because two prices are involved. Both parties exchange due bills at retail prices but deliver goods or services at cost. The media might accept a $100 room for a $100 TV spot that costs only $40 to deliver. The TV station may resell the due bill at $65 and still make $25. The end user gets a $100 room for 65 bucks. It might cost the hotel $20 to deliver, for which it received $100 in advertising. That is the impetus behind the trading.

Due bills, which are often brokered by middlemen, are favored during low occupancy periods. Their usage declines as the economic cycle recovers.

Processing the Due Bill   The due bill must be presented as the holder registers. This enables the guest-service agent to assign the most expensive accommodation, which uses up the bill as quickly as possible. (The cost of delivering a suite is not much more than delivering a standard room.) The clerk also verifies the agreement's expiration date. Amounts unused after that date are lost to the due-bill holder. The bill is held at the desk until the guest leaves when the value of the used accommodations is recorded. An unexpired contract is returned to the holder for use by subsequent guests.

The transient folio, which was used to accumulate charges during the due-bill user's stay, is transferred to the city ledger in the usual manner. However, the city ledger account is treated differently. There is no billing. Instead, the account is charged off against the liability incurred by the contract. As hotel accommodations are furnished, that liability is decreased. Either it is balanced off against the city-ledger accounts that are created from the transfer of the users' folios as they check out or it expires.

FREQUENT- (PREFERRED-) GUEST PROGRAMS (LOYALTY PROGRAMS)   Frequent-guest programs (FGP) are to hotels as frequent-flier programs are to airlines. Each enables users to earn points toward free accommodations or catalog awards. Catalog gifts gained favor as travel declined (2008–2013). This shift was costly to hotel chains[4] which had to buy the gifts (cameras, necklaces), whereas inexpensive room occupancy is accounted for internally. Hotels countered by creating their own gifts. Using points, guests could join the performing group or cook with the celebrity chef. Some hotels partnered with local attractions using due bills.

Obviously, FGPs work best when frequent guests spend their points internally. Often they go to resorts within the chain, not to the commercial hotels where the points were likely earned.[5] The destination hotel accepts payment using the guest's FGP points and looks to the parent company's FGP division for reimbursement.

Split folios are used to process the awards that frequent guests tender. B folios accumulate all incidental charges, those not covered by the awards program. Guests are responsible for these and settle as they check out. Settlement is identical to any other check-out: by transfer, allowance, or cash.

Room charges plus any other services included in the FGP are posted to the A folio. That folio is also transferred to the city ledger for billing. Unlike other city accounts, the chain's itself is the account receivable. It is charged either for the full rack rate or for a lesser amount as the FGP contract provides. Reimbursement at full rack rate is almost unknown. Everyone knows that rooms have a high profit margin. Besides, sales of food and beverage, not usually covered by the program, are additional income to the host hotel. A room allowance reduces the amount between the rack rate that the guest was charged and the FGP rate that the parent company will reimburse. The allowance can be recorded either when the bill is sent or payment is received.

Payment from the parent company is not always by cash. Some FGP programs offset the amount *due to* the hotel with the amount *due from* the hotel. Franchise fees, reservation fees, and FGP fees are among those due. Other programs separate the accounting. Hotels collect the FGP debt from the parent and pay the parent whatever fees are due.

MANAGING CASH AND CREDIT

Cash and credit, like everything else that innkeepers oversee, must be managed. Doing so falls heavily, but not exclusively, on personnel at the front desk.

---

[4]That cost is estimated at $500,000 for one-year for one chain.

[5]There's an ethical poser here asking, "If points were earned at commercial hotels while traveling on company expense-accounts, should those be spent for private vacations or should they off-set costs of later commercial trips?" Similar questions arise when convention planners accept frequent-flier miles (or even cash) because they booked business on behalf of a client.

Managing Cash

Losses were dramatically lowered when hoteliers stopped treating personal checks as if they were actual cash. A similar scrutiny is now being applied to currency, which is actual cash.

COUNTERFEIT CURRENCY   Computer technology has improved the "business" of counterfeiting. And it is big business, estimated at $1 billion. The counterfeit $20 bill is the one most likely to pass across the front desk. Overseas it is the $100 bill. That suggests special scrutiny of $100 bills when they are tendered by foreign guests.[6] The Treasury Department has fought bogus bills ever since it first issued notes, 1861. Series 2004 (updated in 2010 with new $100 bills) contained the most aggressive new security features ever. By making counterfeit bills easier to recognize, the Treasury enlisted the aid of everyone handling money, including front-office cashiers.

Exhibit 16 details the newest embedded features. Held to the light, one sees a polymer security thread running top to bottom down the bill, just to the left of the portrait. A watermark, to the right of the portrait, is visible from both the obverse[7] and reverse sides of the bill. These two features are difficult to replicate on counterfeits. The most difficult of all, however, is the color-shifting ink found in the numerical denomination of the bill at the bottom right corner. Looking at it head on, the number appears green; brought closer it shifts colors.

Counterfeiters have countered with Supernotes, which use the same quality paper as genuine U.S. currency. They even simulate the color-shifting ink of genuine bills because they are produced on an intaglio press. Intaglio is an advanced form of printing technology that pressures paper and plate together. It is almost impossible for the desk to spot these fakes even when armed with counterfeit-detection equipment.

Detection Devices   Hotel cashiers rely on a number of inexpensive detection devices. First among them is the human eye searching for features highlighted in Exhibit 16. The marker-pen detector, made by Dri-Mark Products and others, is another popular device. All U.S. currency is made from 100% cotton rag—there is no paper content. Detector pens react with the starch found in paper to turn counterfeit bills brown.

Another device searches the bills for magnetic ink. Magnetic ink is found on the portrait and around the edges. Counterfeit currency that is created on copiers or printing presses lacks that magic ingredient. Other detectors use UV lamps to highlight the security threads on bills and on the hidden logos of credit cards and driver's licenses as well.

Awareness and detection are essential because the loss from counterfeit currency mounts quickly. Counterfeiters typically pass multiple bills in rapid succession. Counterfeits are like ants—there is never is just one! Adding injury to insult: Counterfeit bills are confiscated by the Treasury Department without restitution.

Managing Checks

Management cannot make every cash/credit decision every hour of the day. Instead, it creates the policies and procedures that minimize loss and still retain customer goodwill. Experienced guest-service agents find that procedures for handling checks, both personal and traveler's, are much alike hotel to hotel. Computer technology has aided the bad-check passer as it has the counterfeiter. Basic desktop publishing and scanning equipment is all one needs to copy or alter personal checks. Since there is no recourse in either case, the first rule in accepting checks is: Try not to.

---

[6]Seizures of counterfeit bills are highest in Colombia, Bulgaria, Germany, and the Dominican Republic in that order. The North Korean government is also highly suspect. Estimates of these $100 bills, called Benjamins, because Benjamin Franklin is pictured, reach as high as $500,000,000.

[7]The side with the principal design.

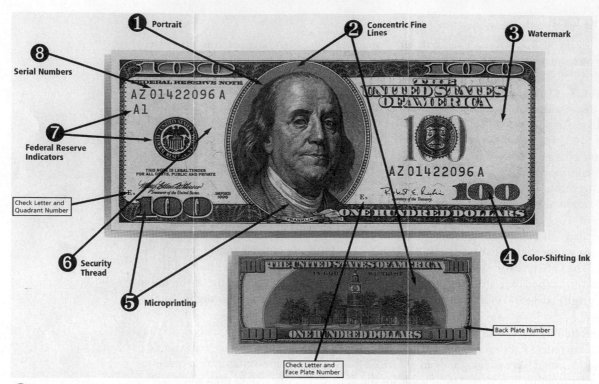

1 Portrait
2 Concentric Fine Lines
3 Watermark
8 Serial Numbers
7 Federal Reserve Indicators
Check Letter and Quadrant Number
6 Security Thread
5 Microprinting
4 Color-Shifting Ink
Back Plate Number
Check Letter and Face Plate Number

❶ **Portrait** The enlarged portrait of Benjamin Franklin is easier to recognize, while the added detail is harder to duplicate. The portrait is now off-center, providing room for a watermark and reducing wear and tear on the portrait.

❷ **Concentric Fine Lines** The fine lines printed behind both Benjamin Franklin's portrait and Independence Hall are difficult to replicate.

❸ **Watermark** A watermark depicting Benjamin Franklin is visible from both sides when held up to a light.

❹ **Color-Shifting Ink** The number in the lower right corner on the front of the note looks green when viewed straight on, but appears black when viewed at an angle.

❺ **Microprinting** Because they're so small, microprinted words are hard to replicate. On the front of the note, "USA 100" is within the num-

ber in the lower left corner and "United States of America" is on Benjamin Franklin's coat.

❻ **Security Thread** A polymer thread is embedded vertically in the paper and indicates, by its unique position, the note's denomination. The words "USA 100" on the thread can be seen from both sides of the note when held up to a bright light. Additionally, the thread glows red when held under an ultraviolet light.

❼ **Federal Reserve Indicators** A new universal seal represents the entire Federal Reserve System. A letter and number beneath the left serial number identifies the issuing Federal Reserve Bank.

❽ **Serial Numbers** An additional letter is added to the serial number. The unique combination of eleven numbers and letters appears twice on the front of the note.

EXHIBIT 16 Currency is upgraded continuously to thwart counterfeiters, who favor $20 bills in the United States and $100 bills overseas. Among the changes are relocated security threads, borderless portraits, and metallic pigmented ink.

THREE QUICKIES A large number of faulty checks can be detected because bad-check passers often fail to cover three frequent, but obvious, mistakes:

(1) Is the check perforated? Most are, on the left edge, except for government-issued and bank counter checks.
(2) Do the Federal Reserve district numbers (1–12) match the location of the issuing bank? (See Exhibit 17, item #9, which is flagged twice.)[8]
(3) Is the routing code printed in magnetic ink? (See Exhibit 17, items #2 and #8.)

Although these are three quick criteria, there are others; enumerated in Exhibit 18.

---

[8]The 12th district of the Federal Reserve stretches from Oregon to Arizona and includes Hawaii and Alaska.

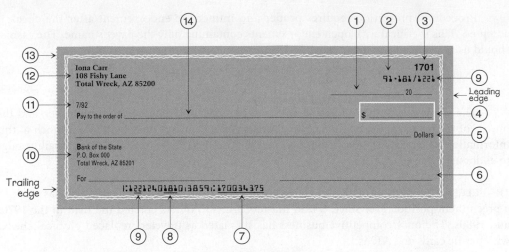

EXHIBIT 17 Fourteen locations flag a possible bad check: (1) Is the date current? (2) Do the routing numbers correspond to the magnetic numbers? (3) Has the account existed for some time? (4) Is the amount more or less than the statutory definition of grand larceny? (5) Are the values of the handwritten dollars and the numerical dollars identical? (6) Does the signature correspond to the registration card or the endorsement? (7) Are the account numbers in agreement with a bankcard that is being proffered? (8) Is the magnetic ink dull or reflective? (9) Is the number of the Federal Reserve region accurate? (10) Does the bank directory list this bank as shown? (11) When was the account established? (12) How does the maker's identity compare with the hotel's records? (13) Is the check perforated? (14) Is the payee a third party, a corporation, or cash?

SIMPLE DETERRENTS   Every available weapon including closed-circuit television and photography must be employed. Dual-lens cameras are available to simultaneously record the check-passer and the instrument. Other systems develop latent fingerprints without the use of ink or other messy substances. Signs help. One explains the surveillance equipment in use; another cites the penalty for passing bad checks. The cashing procedure may include a telephone call at the guest's expense to his or her office or bank.

When Cashing Checks, Watch For …

1. Values that separate petty larceny from grand larceny; the larger check, the safer.
2. The guest's age, hair and eye color compared to the ID (driver's license) offered.
3. Misspellings, incorrect dates and serial numbers of more than four digits.
4. Cash-back techniques, checks larger than the folio balance, which compound the loss.
5. Payroll checks of even-dollar denominations; tax withholdings make this very unlikely.
6. Identifications that lack photos, including library-, social security- or business-cards.
7. Cashier's checks (checks drawn on the bank by the bank) that lack an apostrophe "s."
8. Checks that are altered, illegible, stale (over 30 days old), postdated, or from a third party.
9. Pre-endorsed checks. Require a new endorsement be made in your presence.
10. Locations. Is the guest registered from the same city as the bank's location.
11. The date when the account was opened (Item #11 of Exhibit 17).
12. Restrictive or conditional endorsements that limit negotiability.
13. Similarity of signatures between the check and the reg card. Should they be? Are they?
14. Photo-copy paper that can be smeared with a wet finger; safety paper cannot.
15. Responses to questions: What does your middle C stand for? What's your address again?
16. The check's number. Most bad checks are numbered between 101 and 150.
17. Timing. No one should be above suspicion on weekends, holidays, or after hours.
18. Certified checks by asking why would the passer have one/need one.
19. The calendar. Most bad checks pass during the holiday season, the year's final quarter.
20. Policy adherence including dollar limits and membership in frequent-guest programs.

EXHIBIT 18 Twenty critical hurdles that check-cashing guests must clear and guest-service agents must evoke before the check-cash exchange is completed.

Procedural protection requires proper and immediate endorsement after the check is accepted. This is critical with open endorsements containing only the payee's name. The cashier should use a rubber stamp that reads:

> For Deposit Only
> The ABC Hotel

The stamp should provide for identification, credit-card number, room number, and the initials of the person approving the check. Because endorsements once blotted out much of this information, federal legislation (1988) assigned the first 1.5 inches from the check's trailing edge to endorsements.

TRAVELER'S CHECKS American Express (AmEx) pioneered traveler's checks and has retained a preeminent position ever since. VISA, MasterCard, and others entered the field in the 1970s and 1980s. The once competitive business has stagnated as travelers replaced physical checks with plastic cards and ATMs.

Traveler's checks are purchased prior to a trip. They are used as if they were cash, with the issuing company guaranteeing their replacement against loss or theft. The charge is usually 1% of the face value, but checks are often issued without charge. Even without charge, there was plenty of competition for the business. Large sums of interest-free money accrue from the time lag (the float) between the purchase and the use of the check. More than 15% of traveler's checks are never claimed! No wonder AmEx's advertising once encouraged buyers to hold their checks for some distant emergency.

Buyers sign the checks at the time of purchase and countersign when they cash it. Signature comparison is the main defense against fraud. Checks must be countersigned under the scrutiny of the cashier or re-signed if the first endorsement was elsewhere. Comparing signatures is all that is required; no need for supplemental identification. Examining identification takes the cashier's focus away from the signature line. This gives the passer time to switch the check to one professionally forged. Moreover, the owner's identification was mostly stolen along with the checks.

Guest-service agents/cashiers must watch the check's denomination. Many countries use dollar-based currency (see Exhibit 7). Cashing a $100 dollar Jamaican or Hong Kong traveler's check as if it were a U.S. bill sometimes traps a distracted cashier. Prompt refund of lost or stolen checks is more than a mere advertising. Hotel desks, with their 24-hour service, represent a logical extension of the issuing company's office system.

Managing Credit

This chapter has focused on the mechanics of credit, including the records of city-ledger receivables. It now examines the management of credit, including the decision to grant or withhold it. Policy and implementation often rest with a committee comprised of the rooms manager, the convention/catering manager, and a rep from accounting—the credit manager, if the hotel has one. The GM, who holds veto power, might sit in as well.

A COST/BENEFIT DECISION There is no perfect credit policy. Any business that extends credit becomes vulnerable to loss, but so do those that deny credit. Each credit decision weighs immediate, determinable gains against possible, uncertain losses. Recognizing this, the lodging industry has dramatically reduced its level of open credit, mere promise to pay. Open credit is still used for advances to concessionaires, outlays for employee gratuities and even occasionally for banquet or convention sales.

Successful credit policy cannot be measured by accounting figures alone. Hotels with small bad-debt losses are not necessarily the best managed ones. A conservative credit policy means few credit losses, but how much profitable business was turned away? Low credit losses are easily measured on the books; lost business has no entry. The conundrum is that the increase might not have been achieved; there is no way to know.

The issue is not always credit/never credit. With different conditions, credit could be severely curtailed, moderately administered, or liberally issued, even to the same customer with the same credit standing (see Exhibit 19).

Factors in Administrating Hotel Credit		
Credit Severely Curtailed	**Moderately Administered**	**Credit Liberally Issued**
High occupancy	...	Low occupancy
In-season	...	Off-season
No competition	...	Price cutting
Established property	...	New hotel
Interest rates are high	...	Interest rates are low
Reputable hotel	...	Disreputable hotel
Item of high variable cost	...	Item of low variable cost
Inexperienced lender	...	Low losses from debt recovery
Hotel's credit overextended	...	Hotel has good credit rating

EXHIBIT 19   Hotels extend credit based on their internal circumstances as well as the credit-worthiness of the group. Because each company has different priorities at different times, the same piece of business may be refused at one hotel and accepted at another or accepted at one time and denied at another.

Good occupancy, the first item of Exhibit 19, enables a hotel to adopt a conservative credit policy. There is no reason to replace already committed low-risk guests with those of uncertain credit standing. When occupancy is high, a bad debt loss is the sum of full rack rate plus administrative costs, not just the marginal cost of providing a room. Marginal cost is the measure at low occupancy.

Food and beverage sales, which have a high variable cost, are different. More caution is needed to justify banquet sales during low periods than room sales during low periods. A banquet bad debt may well cost the hotel two-thirds of the bill (food, call-in labor, flowers, special cake, etc.). Room losses are substantially less, a marginal cost of 20–25%.

Hotels reduce rates or adopt more liberal credit policies when occupancies are low. Too dismal a circumstance means the hotel will do both to book business. Fighting for market share and/or competing with better appointed properties means liberalizing credit still further (see Exhibit 9).

The obvious cost of poor credit decisions is the out-and-out loss from nonpayment. To that must be added bank charges, attorney fees, collection expenses, and administrative costs (forms, printing, credit checks, postage, telephone, and employee time). Equally costly is the permanent loss of a customer. Try pricing that. Expanded sales volume is the offsetting benefit to credit risk. Not all new customers are bad risks. Furthermore, hotels with good credit ratings may also gain from a spread in interest rates. If the hotel self-finances or borrows at low rates, it can extend credit at 18% (1.5% per month). The caveat: Provided it eventually collects.

COLLECTING, BILLING, AND CHASING   Hotels use a three-day billing cycle for city accounts. In reality, processing and mailing usually delay that first notice. Moreover, reviewing and agreeing on an entire master account may cause a more serious delay, but agreed-upon values can be and should be paid promptly.

Second and third notices follow in 15 and 30 days. The collection procedure, which has been routine during these first 30 days, now requires a telephone call to inquire about the delay and about the intended disposition of the bill. It is a careful balancing act of empathy with a valued client and gentle bullying with a recalcitrant debtor. Each statement should contain notice of the additional interest charges that are accumulating and the age of the account. Early efforts at collection are essential because the longer a bill is unpaid, the less likely it will ever be paid (see Exhibit 20).

Chasing unpaid debts should not be a random assignment. It must be in someone's job description. Without follow-up, debtors get the impression that the hotel has forgotten or decided it isn't important. Nor should the collector be apologetic—the late payer is the wrongdoer. Settlement arrangement should be specific in both amounts and dates. Partial payments plus interest are acceptable, provided when and how much are fixed and enforced. Small payments should be avoided. They are costly to administer and tend to be overlooked as insignificant when payments are missed.

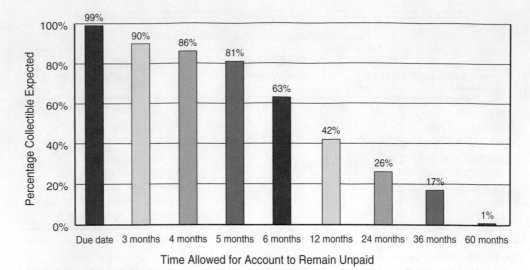

EXHIBIT 20 Managing credit cannot be an on-again, off-again affair. The likelihood of collecting debts (city-ledger receivables) decreases the longer they remain unpaid. Credit management requires prompt billing and an aggressive pursuit of late, unpaid accounts.

No matter how carefully credit requests are screened or how diligent the follow-up, some bad debts will materialize. The responsible manager must then decide to continue the internal collection efforts or employ a third party. The first step may be an in-house attorney, if the hotel has one. Or take action in a small-claims court, which does not require an attorney. Collection agencies and outside attorneys are other options. Either way, substantial collection costs now become part of the process.

Similarly, hotels that choose the internal option must be prepared to invest in recovery. Credit collection is not a sometimes affair. To be effective, collection must be systematic and thorough. It takes a flow of information and a stack of records, manual or computerized, to track debtors. Yet the job is one more task added to the office of controller when there is no full-time credit manager. Knowledge of federal and state legislation is another hurdle. If the in-house staff is insensitive to the rights of the debtor (and they have many legally protected rights), the process might best be left to a collection agency.

Oddly enough, a collection agency's basic technique is writing letters and telephoning, much like the hotel could do. Still, collections are light, especially for small accounts, which have the lowest priority with agencies. Less than 25% of accounts turned over are ever collected. If no collection is made, there is no fee, but the fee rakes 20–40% of what is collected.

The psychological effects on the debtor, who realizes that the matter has grown more serious, is the agency's most potent weapon. Debtors see the agency as more relentless and threatening than the hotel. Whatever softening existed through the customer–client relationship has dissolved with the appearance of this third party. The debtor is aware that the agency knows more about his entire credit record than the hotel knew. Credit ratings may suddenly be in jeopardy. Sometimes the debtor simply tires of the battle and willingly makes arrangements. "Arrangements" is a good word for any collector to use because it says that some kind of settlement can be negotiated and worked out. That is, after all, the intent of the collection effort.

AT THE DESK Identification of arriving guests was more reliable when reservations involved correspondence. Then the name and address, and perhaps even a company name, was verified by mail. This must now be done at registration with complete name, not just initials; complete address, not just post-office box, office building, or city. Scribbled, illegible signatures must be translated. Some hotels photocopy drivers' licenses. The line between information gathering and invasion is a thin one, as is the line between guest understanding and anger. Guest-service agents must be masters of diplomacy.

Early suspicions (missing or light baggage; nervous or poorly dressed guests) need to be confirmed quickly using ZIP-code and telephone directories, as well as websites, city directories, colleagues at other hotels, and telephone calls. Once it was Standard Operating Procedure (SOP) to have the bell staff record car license numbers on the hotel's copy of the rooming slip. Walk-ins pose additional credit risks so they are flagged with special identifications. All these are unnecessary exercises if the guest proffers a valid credit card. Then the responsibility shifts to the card company and its fraud division. Even then, the hotel is not entirely free.

MINIMIZING CHARGEBACKS   Hotels rely heavily on credit-card protection, but charges sometimes come bouncing back. The card-company seeks clarification: Either the guest has refused to pay or a procedural error has occurred (see Exhibit 21). Merchant/hotels have 30 days to respond, but too often accounting offices don't! Nearly half of these challenges, called *chargeback*s or debit memos,[9] is disallowed.

Reservation no-shows are common chargebacks. Guests guarantee the reservation using a credit card. One night is charged when the guest fails to show. With a credit-card number and no record of a cancellation, the hotel can counter the guest's challenge of the charge. A successful response requires just that, a response. Of course, not demanding payment may be more about guest relations than about credit. Whatever the decision, it should be dictated by policy, not rest with the disposition of accounting personnel.

Not all chargebacks originate from unclaimed reservations. Some stem from efforts to recover room damage and property theft. Smoking in nonsmoking rooms, theft of pictures and towels, damages during conventions, and prom nights account for special charges by the hotel and corresponding refusals by the guests.

Mistakes in procedures account for some chargebacks. Procedural snafus originate with departmental cashiers. Training programs concentrate on the do's and don'ts of taking and processing cards (see Exhibit 21).

Two special credit restrictions need extra attention. One is hotel derived; the other, a credit-card issue. Hotels retain the right to bill at any time. They do so whenever management becomes concerned, but especially when a folio nears a preset value. This amount varies with the class of hotel, its ADR. Upscale properties set a higher ceiling than do budgets. Collection

---

Avoiding Chargebacks

1. Check credit cards for both expiration and starting dates.
2. Scrutinize credit cards signed with felt pens; they may cover original signatures.
3. Decline requests to split charges on two vouchers to avoid floor limits.
4. Remember that MasterCard begins with number 5; Visa with 4; AmEx with 3.
5. Place no telephone numbers on credit-card slips.
6. Refuse to post fictitious items in order to give cash against the card.
7. Maximize recovery by retaining original, signed vouchers.

For Immediate Action
a. Replace the printer ribbons frequently.
b. Replace the printer's paper roll as soon as colored streaks appear.
c. Handle carbonless paper with care to prevent black marks.
d. Retain the white copy of the two colored draft print-out.
e. Store sales drafts carefully within a retrieval system

8. Issue credit-card refunds, not cash, against original credit-card charges.
9. Respond promptly to all chargebacks and furnish evidence for the charge.
10. Watch for altered cards: rearranged numbers; glue; misaligned numbers; color changes.
11. Compare suspicious card signature with driver's license signature.
12. Insure against false arrest caused by inaccurate information from the card company.
13. Exercise no force to retrieve cards or restrain users.
14. Anticipate some employee misuse such as increasing the gratuity.

EXHIBIT 21 Losses from chargebacks and other credit-card transactions offset the efforts of sales teams and service personnel. Losses can be minimized with training at the cashier's level and prompt attention to chargeback notices at the accounting level.

---

[9]"Debit" because hotel debt is a liability (i.e., a credit) to the credit-card company. Now the charge is being reversed; the reverse of a credit is a debit. "Memo" is another term for "notice."

efforts begin as soon as the folio total creeps toward that figure. Two reports prepared during the night audit alert management. One identifies unusually high daily charges; the other flags high cumulative values. Property management systems enable management to monitor these questionable folios throughout the day.

Credit-card companies also establish dollar ceilings, called "floors." Every hotel has a floor,[10] the maximum credit to be extended to any one guest and still retain protection from the card company. The hotel negotiates as high a floor as it can. Just as the hotel's own ceiling reflects its ADR, so does the card company's floor. If the guest's credit card is swiped at registration and accepted, the card company stands behind the charges up to the floors. Above that, the hotels must seek clearance.

Guests have their own floors. Credit-card holders have specific limits that also jeopardize the card's validity. Cards swiped for arriving guests may be refused if that card is close to the guest's personal limit. The hotel and the card company may be partners in credit, but each has its own interests to safeguard.

Summary

Having marketed, sold, and serviced the business, hoteliers expect to be paid. More and more often that payment takes form in plastic cards. Both guests and innkeepers prefer them over cash. Preference or not, the volatile cash asset need special attention and protection from bad check-passers and counterfeiters.

What cash there is flows inward at the operating departments (dining rooms, lounges, etc.). Even here, cash is tendered less and less frequently. These operating departments report only sales—cash sales and charge sales—whereas the desk reports payments from and advances to accounts receivable. So its cash flows two ways. Some guests settle their folios with cash (cash in) and some need cash advances (cash out). Paid-outs are also made for the house, although not every hotel runs house business through the desk.

Electronic communication and recordkeeping have relegated paper-and-pencil ledgers to the recycle bin. So cashiers in all department make their daily cash turn-ins accompanied by reports prepared by the property management system. The cash becomes part of the bank deposit; the reports part of the hotel's audit. All the while, cashiers/guest-service agents remain vigilant for bogus money and over-friendly short-change artists.

The desk focuses on registered accounts receivable; the city ledger focuses on the records of nonregistered accounts receivable. Credit-card companies are the city ledger's largest division, but there are other receivables. Among them are conventions, banquets, tour groups, travel agencies, and individuals. The credit standing of these city-ledger accounts must be vetted by the hotel itself. And when necessary, collection for nonpayment has to be pursued vigorously by the accounting staff or collection agencies. The sooner the better. Collection becomes less and less likely the older the debt becomes.

Recent federal legislation has wrought changes in the use of credit and debit cards. Most likely, other changes will materialize as cards' contents and forms evolve into an electronic purse of sorts. The ultimate form may even become an accessory to the hotel's electronic door key.

Resources and Challenges

RESOURCES

Website Assignment

Many websites broaden the topics covered in this chapter. Here is one:
http://retail.about.com/od/storeoperations/qt/drawer_balance.htm (A look at how, why, and when to balance a cash drawer and related articles.)

Required:
(1) Identify two more sources (websites by addresses; periodicals by name, date, and page).
(2) List two recommendations that have not been discussed in this chapter. List one for cash (including checks) and one for credit. Identify the sources.

---

[10]A carryover term from the preelectronic age when credit decisions were made on the retailer's floor.

Interesting Tidbits

- Hoteliers can encourage business from foreign groups by suggesting ways to minimize currency risks. Small groups coming to the United States with short lead times should be advised to simply pay with credit cards. Because of volume, card companies offer some of the best foreign-exchange rates.
- Large groups with long lead times should buy "forward contracts." Forward contracts lock in the price of the U.S. currency needed to pay the hotel bill sometime in the future. Commercial banks sell the contracts. There is a fee, of course. It is another cost of holding the meeting/convention, but it is an investment that a foreign meeting planner must make to avoid catastrophic changes in currency values.
- The administration of some loyalty programs (preferred-guest programs) is causing disloyalty among franchisees. Some franchisors are sweeping guests into the program without their knowledge or consent: Guests have to opt out. Under most franchisee agreements, the franchisor charges franchisees a "loyalty" fee of between 2.5% and 4.0% of room sales booked by these unknowing guests. Franchisees have filed lawsuits over what is seen to be a loyalty charge with a hint of disloyalty.
- International guests arriving from overseas may see an unusual paid-out posted to their folios. Intercontinental Hotels & Resorts prepares small cash packets for arriving guests who have not yet acquired local currency. (Intercontinental calls them "Little Touches," or "Currency Exchange Kits.") The $25 or $50 bundle is charged to the guest folio as a paid-out, but this small attention to detail is priceless.

Challenges

True/False

Questions that are partially false should be marked false (F).

_____ 1. Most persons distinguish credit cards from debit cards based on the time and method of payment; whereas the major distinction is smart card (debit card) versus one that isn't (credit card).

_____ 2. At day's end, the desk reports on accounts receivable and their room sales; each operating department reports on its own sales, both charge sales and cash sales.

_____ 3. *Due bank* is the value that a commercial bank credits to the hotel's account based on the checking-account arrangements between the two parties.

_____ 4. *Due bill* is the form prepared by sales and accounting and presented to a convention manager before the event closes, allowing a full review before payment.

_____ 5. By using cobranded cards, hotel chains have entered the profitable credit-card business as one means of offsetting the economic cycles that plague the hospitality business.

Problems

1. In terms of both the front office and the city ledger, explain how a reservation request from a travel agent is processed if:
   (a) The hotel and the agency have a good credit relationship and the guest pays the agency;
   (b) The hotel and the agency have no credit relationship and the guest pays the agency;
   (c) The guest makes no payment to the agency, and
      (1) The hotel and the agency have a good credit relationship
      (2) The hotel and the agency have no credit relationship

2. An international guest tenders $171 in U.S. funds and #2,000 from his native land to settle an outstanding account of $206.20. #s are being purchased by the hotel for 51.50 per U.S. dollar. What must the cashier do now to settle the account?
   (1) Assume that the guest has more U.S. dollars
   (2) Assume that the guest has no more U.S. dollars.

   (3) Explain the quick check-out system (speedy check-out) in terms of the front office and the city ledger.
   (4) A noticeable squeeze on profits had brought the management team to a brainstorming session. Noting the large amount of credit-card business that the hotel is doing, the controller suggests that each tip charged to a credit card be reduced by 3.77% when paid to the employee. (That is the average discount fee the hotel is paying to credit-card companies.) The controller further suggests that an additional 1.1% be subtracted, representing the percentage of card charges that prove uncollectible. Then round the total to 5%. A $10 tip would net the hotel $0.50. What comments would the food and beverage manager be apt to make? The rooms manager?

3. Explain the role of international tourism on the balance of trade (deficient or surplus) of any nation.

AN INCIDENT IN HOTEL MANAGEMENT
It's Not My Mistake; Must Be Yours

A late arrival is standing at the desk waiting to be roomed. The night manager stays silent allowing the guest-service agent to handle the situation. There are no rooms. "You don't seem to understand; I have a reservation. It was guaranteed with my credit card because I knew I was going to be late." "Sir, you made that reservation nine weeks ago on credit-card number 4300 0000 0000 0003. The card company dishonored that card; so we cancelled the reservation. We have no rooms and the citywide convention means the closest accommodations are in the next town, 18 miles away. Their rate is $165; my guess is the cab will be about $60. They're on the telephone, what should I tell them?" "I need a room. Have them hold space." The reservation confirmed, the guest turned toward the manager. "I feel you should pay the cab fare and the $75 difference between the rates. Since apparently we have both made mistakes; make it an even $100 and we'll each take a hit!"

Questions

1. Was there a management failure here; if so, what?
2. What is the hotel's immediate response (or action) to the incident?
3. What further, long-run action should management take, if any?

Answers to True/False Quiz

1. False. Neither card is a "smart card." The difference between credit and debit cards *is* the time of payment. Credit cards allow for a delay in payment, a float. Debit cards do not: The value entered is immediately removed from the bank account and transferred to the seller. Moreover, debit cards hold the possibility of loss from the bank account; credit cards do not. Smart cards contain electronic memory; neither credit cards nor debit cards do.

2. True. The front desk deals with accounts receivable, which includes room sales. The operating departments deal with sales, some of which are made on account and charged to the guest's front-office folio. Some on-account charges are also made directly to the buyer's credit card.

3. False. *Due bank* is an internal hotel term that has no connection to a commercial bank. Hotel cashiers sometimes turn in more money at the end of their shifts than the day's net receipts. They do this because some of the turn-in is made of nonnegotiable money (checks, vouchers, chips) that needs to be exchanged for smaller bills or coin. The excess is returned as a due bank.

4. False. A *due bill* is a contract between the hotel and another entity. It enumerates the conditions by which the two businesses agreed to swap hotel space for whatever product or service (often advertising) the other company can provide.

5. False. Cobranded cards contain the hotel chain's identification along with that of the issuer, VISA, for example. By no means does that put the hotels in the credit-card business.

The Night Audit

The Night Audit

THE AUDITOR AND THE AUDIT

The night audit closes the hotel's business day. It does so by reconciling the balances of the folios, the accounts receivable. Because of the audit, corrected, updated, and accurate guest bills can be rendered at any time. That is critical to the traffic flow of a hotel where guests come and go at all hours.

Audits have a secondary purpose. Sales (incomes) are the offsetting charges to folio postings. Folios are charged when guests buy something. So the audit also proves the charge sales of all the departments, beginning with rooms, food, and beverage. That is *charge* sales to the *folios*. Sales made by cash or by credit card are not covered by the night audit because these sales do not appear on folios. The night audit audits only account receivable sales charged to folios. Other sales types are audited by the income (or day) audit, a topic for an accounting text.

Uncovering clerical mistakes was the original focus of the night audit. This procedure, which dates to the 1920s, used a paper-and-pencil form, called a transcript (see Exhibit 12). This chapter retains the transcript as a means of explaining what takes place within the heart of the computerized audit, which is now carried out by a property management system (PMS). PMSs and hand-posted records have the same goals. With tedious hand-prepared audits, balancing the folio was the main thrust. With PMSs, the emphasis changes. Folio errors are still being repaired; they just are not visible. Readers can see the pencil-and-paper folio, voucher, and transcript that make the records. With a PMS report, they see only the output: a printout. Readers who follow the pencil-and-paper explanations of the chapter will better understand the not-very-visible electronic audit.

The Night Auditor

Despite the title, the night auditor is not a trained accountant and is an auditor only by the broadest definition. In general terms, an *auditor* is an appraiser/reporter of the accuracy and integrity of records and financial statements. One type of auditing, internal auditing, involves procedural control and an accounting review of operations and records. Internal auditing also reports on the activities of other employees. It is these final two definitions that best explain the role of the hotel night auditor.

No special knowledge of accounting or even of bookkeeping's debits and credits is required of the night auditor. That is why this chapter identifies accounting explanations in a different format and font. Having this knowledge is helpful and desirable, but it is sufficient for the auditor to have good arithmetic skills, self-discipline, and a penchant for detailed work. Auditors must be careful, accurate, and reliable. The latter trait is an especially redeeming one because the unattractive working hours make replacements difficult to recruit and almost impossible to find on short notice.

WORK SHIFT The audit crew works the graveyard shift, arriving between 11 PM and midnight. The shift ends 8 hours later, at 7 or in the morning. The night audit reconciles records that are needed to start the new day. Failing to reconcile keeps the auditor on the job until everything is in balance, regardless of the hour.

GENERAL DUTIES The audit staff of a large hotel consists of a senior auditor and one or two assistants. Other front-office staff (guest-service agents and cashiers) may also be on duty. Their presence frees the auditors to do their job without interruption. In smaller hotels, the audit team—often just one person—relieves the entire desk, filling the jobs of reservationist, guest-service agent, cashier, telephone operator, and auditor. Whether or not auditors assume these jobs, they must be conversant with them. These are the very duties covered by the night audit.

When the actual tasks are taken on, the night auditor is likely to be the only responsible employee on duty. The auditor assumes the position of night manager, whether the title is there or not. Problems are no different at night than they are during the day. Emergencies, credit, mechanical breakdowns, accidents, and deaths are some of the nonaudit duties of the night auditor/manager.

Security and incident reports must be filed by either the night auditor/manager alone or cooperatively with the security staff. Without a security contingent, the auditor may be the one who walks security rounds and fire watch. At one time—prior to self-service elevators—auditors had the company of a uniformed elevator operator.

Few hotels of less than 150 rooms employ a night engineer. So, often without adequate preparation, the night auditor/manager faces serious engineering problems. Fire, plumbing issues, power failures, elevator mishaps, and boiler troubles are matters that often take the auditor's time. Equally time-consuming are guest relations: A noisy party going into the early hours of the morning, the victorious football team converging in the lobby, a sick guest waiting for a physician, visiting conventioneers on the 11th-floor, paid reservations yet to arrive, and the hotel 100% occupied. Such are the nonaccounting matters for which a lone night auditor is often responsible.

Mature judgment and experience are needed to carry out these nonaudit functions. The combination of audit skills, working hours, and responsibility merit a higher salary for the night auditor than for the average guest-service agent, but the spread is not noticeably larger.

Overview of the Audit

The night audit is an audit of accounts receivable, an audit of guest folios. Most hotel sales are account-receivable sales. Guests obtain services such as room, food, and beverage with a signature, a promise to pay—an account receivable. Cash sales throughout the hotel are not the night auditor's responsibility. Income auditors (day auditors in contrast to night auditors) review cash sales in conjunction with the general cashier. Folio sales (the night auditors' work) passes the next morning to the same income (or revenue or day) auditors. Then both types of sales, cash and credit, are combined. From that step comes the daily report to the manager (see Exhibit 14) and, ultimately, entries into the hotel's sales journal, the permanent records of the business.

RECONCILING ACCOUNTS RECEIVABLE   Every business authenticates its accounts receivable periodically. Whereas most businesses do this monthly or even less frequently, hotels do the job nightly: the night audit. The night audit verifies the accuracy and completeness of each folio each night. In so doing, it also verifies all charge sales made throughout the hotel that day.

Hotel auditors lack the luxury of time because hotelkeeping is a very transient business. Arrivals and departures keep coming and going without notice at all hours of the day and night. Each new day brings more charges and more credits whether or not the previous day has been reconciled. There is no holding a departing guest until the folio is ready. The night audit makes certain that it is ready!

The pressure of immediacy is missing with city-ledger guests. City-ledger receivables are not registered, so their billing cycle is more like the accounts receivable of other businesses. Depending on the nature of the original charge, city receivables are billed for the first time three days—sometimes 10 days—after the charge is incurred.

THE CLOSEOUT HOUR   The night audit reconciles the records of a single day. Since hotels never close, management selects an arbitrary hour, the *closeout hour* or *close of the day*, to officially end one day and start the next. The time selected depends on the operating hours of the lounges, restaurants, and room service of that particular hotel. Each new charge changes the folio, so the audit is prepared when changes are infrequent—in the early morning hours when guests are abed. Departmental charges before the closeout hour are included in today's records. Departmental charges after the closeout hour are posted to the folio on the following date, after the night audit is done.

A late closeout hour captures the last of the day's charges, but pressures the auditing staff. Its job needs to be finished before early departures begin. Too early a closeout hour throws all the charges of the late evening into the following day. This delays their audit for 24 hours. Many guests are gone by then. Standardized, off-the-shelf stationery lists midnight as the closeout hour, but the actual time is set by management.

Posting Room Charges

Posting room charges during a pencil-and-paper audit is an onerous task in a large hotel. Posting room charges during an electronic audit allows the staff time for coffee.

POSTING ROOM CHARGES MANUALLY   Posting (recording) room charges is one of the night auditor's major tasks. Before the advent of the PMS, room charges were posted manually. That required each folio to be removed one by one from the cashier's well. The room charge and the room tax were recorded in pencil, the column totaled, and the folio returned to the well in room number sequence. Exhibit 1 illustrates postings on a manual folio: $60 recorded on the horizontal line labeled "rooms" and $3 for the tax.

Once the room charge and tax are posted, the night auditor adds the column, which includes the previous day's total. The second columns of Exhibit 1 illustrates that addition. The new balance is carried forward from the bottom of one column to the top of the column of the following day. In this manner a cumulative balance is maintained, and the manual folio is ready at any time for the departing guest.

THE CITY HOTEL
ANYWHERE, U.S.A.   #8001

NAME _B. M. Oncampus_
ADDRESS _1 Campus Rd., University City_
ROOM NUMBER _1406_   RATE _60_
NUMBER IN THE PARTY _1_   CLERK _ABC_
DATE OF ARRIVAL _10/5_   DATE OF DEPARTURE _10/7_
CHANGES: ROOM NO. _____   TO ROOM NO. _____   NEW RATE _____

DATE	10/5	10/6	10/7				
BAL. FWD		(19)	70				
ROOMS	60	60					
TAX	3	3					
FOOD	10	12					
BAR		6					
TELEPH							
LAUNDRY							
CASH DISBR GARAGE	8	8					
TRANSFERS							
TOT CHRG	81	70					
CASH							
ALLOWANCES							
TRANSFERS	100						
TOT CRDS	100						
BAL DUE	(19)	70					

EXHIBIT 1   Pencil-and-paper folios (see also Exhibit 2) accumulate daily charges in separate vertical columns. Figures from the column of a given day are copied onto a transcript sheet for balancing during that night audit. Column 10/6 appears on line 1 of Exhibit 12. The initial value of ($19) is a credit; the hotel owes the guest.

Pencil-and-paper folios are no longer used. They are included throughout the text to illustrate the relationship of the folio to the audit. That relationship is not visible with folios and audits prepared by electronic property management systems. *(For ease in reading, several illustrations use small dollar values, which may not seem realistic.)*

Included in the cumulative total are departmental charges other than room. These are posted throughout the day by the front-office staff as the charges arrive at the front desk from the operating departments. Exhibit 1 shows these as food, bar, and garage. At this hotel, garage is a concession. So the posting is a cash paid-out by the hotel to the garage company for the guest.

MANUAL SYSTEM ERRORS   With a manual (pencil-and-paper) system, the same values are written repeatedly. Names, room numbers, and dollar values are recorded many times by different individuals on reg cards and folios, vouchers, and control sheets. The night auditor rewrites the figures once again: room rates, departmental charges, credits, and others. Writing, rewriting, and adding columns manually create numerous human errors that property management systems avoid. Point-of-sale (POS) terminals (see Exhibit 2) communicate electronically with PMSs. They bypass the need for written vouchers between the department and the desk.

Additional errors are inherent in a manual system. Poor handwriting is the most obvious one. When handwritten, figures such as 1 and 7, 4 and 9, and 3 and 8 are often confused. Recopying also causes slides and transpositions. Slides are misplaced units, which may involve decimals. Saying 53 21 mentally or aloud may result in either 53.21 or 5,321 being recorded. Transpositions are similar errors, where the digits are reordered—53.21 may become 35.21.

Even simple addition causes problems. The auditor may create errors by incorrectly totaling the folios, the control sheets, or the packets of vouchers. Adding machines help, but there is no guarantee that the figures are entered accurately. Hand audits required

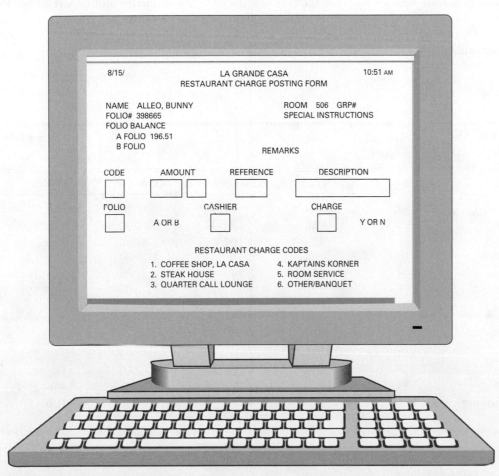

EXHIBIT 2   The display screen of this point-of-sale (POS) terminal guides departmental cashiers through the posting sequence. (See also Exhibit 8.) The posted charge appears instantaneously on the folio maintained in memory by the property management system. Before a POS, cashiers communicated by written vouchers, which had to be hand carried to the desk for posting, either with a POS located there or manually. Poor handwriting and frequent handling increase the number of errors when a POS is not used. That then becomes the focus of the hand-prepared audit.

adding-machine tapes. These tapes were used for comparing the actual figures and those entered into the adding machine.

Subtracting one total from another highlights errors. Errors of addition usually appear as differences of 1 in the unit columns. If the difference in the totals is 1 cent, 10 cents, $1, $10, and so on, the culprit is likely to be an error of addition. If not an error of addition, it might be a slide or transposition. Slides and transpositions are flagged when the difference in the total is evenly divisible by 9. For example, the difference between 53.21 and 35.21 is 18, evenly divisible by 9. Searching for mistakes begins by looking for errors of addition, transpositions, or slides.

POSTING ROOM CHARGES ELECTRONICALLY Electronic posting is easier and faster than manual posting. There are no physical folios. Labor is saved in simply not moving 100, 500, or 1,000 folios in and out of a cashier's well (cashier's bucket). Room charges and taxes are not posted individually. Folios are not totaled arithmetically. The property management system does the work. Memory stores the room rates and taxes, updates the individual folios, and prints them on demand. There are no errors of addition with a PMS. But they do crash! Not often, but an emergency backup is part of every night audit. Exhibit 3 illustrates the nightly report that is prepared at the close of each electronic audit. In form and content, it is much like the hand-prepared transcript illustrated in Exhibit 12. Guest-service agents can work from the closing balance of each folio (available by room number) even if the PMS crashes on the following day.

ROOM CHARGES NOT POSTED DURING THE NIGHT AUDIT In four special circumstances guest-service agents, rather than night auditors, post room charges. (1) *Day rates* (also called *use rates* or *part-day rates*) is one instance. Guests arrive and depart before the audit begins. (2) Extra room charges for late check-outs are another special case. (3) During the heady days of the late 1990s, when occupancy was high and hotels thought they could do no wrong, a penalty rate was posted by the day shift if guests failed to stay through

THE CITY HOTEL, ANYWHERE, U.S.A.						Page 1
03/16 Guest Ledger Summary Report						
Room #	Name	Folio #	Open Bal	Charges	Credits	Close Bal
3004	Huent	0457	–0–	81.30	.00	81.30
3005	Wanake	0398	65.72	91.44	.00	157.16
3008	Lee	0431	132.00	101.01	.00	233.01
3110	Langden	0420	–0–	99.87	100.00	0.13–
3111	Nelston	0408	233.65	145.61	.00	379.26
3117	O'Harra	0461	789.75	121.10	.00	910.85
6121	Chiu	0444	32.60–	99.87	.00	67.27
6133	Valex	0335	–0–	165.30	.00	165.30
7003	Roberts	0428	336.66	109.55	.00	446.21
7009	Haittenberg	0454	19.45	87.43	.00	106.88
Totals			44,651.07	18,632.98	950.00	62,334.05

EXHIBIT 3 A hard (printed) copy of closing folio balances is prepared nightly as part of the PMS audit and left at the desk. The new day's opening balances (last night's closing balances, Close Bal) are then available in case the computer fails the following day.

Each column of the report corresponds to a column of the pencil-and-paper audit. For example, the counterpart of the Charges column of this exhibit is Column 16, Total Debits, of Exhibit 12. "Charges" and "debits" are interchangeable terms.

their reservation commitment. (4) Guest-service agents sometimes post rates for paid-in-advance guests. The posting coincides with the payment.

Revenue Verification

Night audits have two objectives. Reconciling accounts receivable is one. Each folio (receivable) is updated nightly so an accurate bill can be presented on demand. By the time the night audit begins, dozens, hundreds, or even thousands of charges will have been posted to guest folios. Full-service hotels have charges from dining rooms and bars; local and long-distant telephone calls; laundry and valet; greens fees; saunas; ski tows and in-room safes, films, and bars. A small highway property may have room and tax postings only. But in both cases, the night audit proves two things. One, that the income (the sale) has been recorded accurately; and two, that the guest has been charged.

Every departmental charge has equal debits and credits. Each service that guests buy has an offsetting income to one department or another. What takes place individually—one folio being increased and one sale being recorded—has application to the audit. A rule of mathematics—the total is equal to the sum of the parts—plays a fundamental role in balancing the audit. Total income earned by any one department, say, room service, must equal the total of individual room-service charges posted to guest folios. If each individual room-service event increases a guest's folio and simultaneously increases income to the room-service department, then the totals of each should agree, that is, be in balance. Since there may be hundreds of posting and hundreds of folios, this simple fact is not evident immediately. The night audit reconciles the two by making evident this equality. In a nut shell, the audit asks:

Is the total income earned by each department from accounts receivable sales the same total charged to guest folios?

The accounting rules are given below:

Increases in assets, including *accounts receivable* and cash, are made with debits.
Increases in incomes (sales of rooms, food, beverage, etc.) are made with credits.

> Debit: Accounts Receivable/Guest's Folio   50
>   Credit: Proper Departmental (room, food, beverage, spa, etc.) Sale   50
> *Explanation:* Guest charged service in the whatever department. This single representation takes place with each service delivered. The audit proves, by departments, that the total charged to each department (the aggregate of this individual entry) agrees with the total charged to the many guests.

RECONCILING USING A PROPERTY MANAGEMENT SYSTEM

Property management systems have grown essential to hotel services as Exhibit 6 illustrates. To many, the night audit provides the most spectacular demonstration of all. Only those who have machine-posted using the NCR 2000 or 4200[1] system or hand-copied pages of transcript sheets (see Exhibit 12) can appreciate the savings in time and efficiency. Labor savings, the often touted but seldom delivered advantage of computer installations, is certainly evident in the PMS night audit. Since a minimum crew is always needed, the greatest labor savings are at the largest hotels.

The computer altered the mechanics of the audit, its purpose, and its scope. Traditionally, the night audit concentrated on finding and correcting errors—except the errors were caused by the system itself. Initial errors, transmittal errors, posting errors, and errors of addition are inherent in a pencil-and-paper audit. The entire thrust of the hand audit is discovery and repair. The computer audit has no such problems. The information that is input with the departmental POS appears everywhere, and everywhere it appears the same. Of course, there are errors of input, and these are discussed next.

---

[1]NCR is the abbreviation for the National Cash Register Company, which developed an electro-mechanical posting machine for hotel folios and bank passbooks. The initial product was the NCR 2000, ca 1921. It was an economic success because Ellsworth Statler bought the 2000 for his entire chain. Then came a second try, a much-improved, easier-to-operate product, the NCR 4200. It, in turn, was replaced by the rooms module of the earliest version of the property management system, ca mid-1980s.

Interfacing Different Systems

The property management system began life as a rooms-department device—a replacement for the NCR audit. (In turn, the NCR posting machine had been a replacement for the pencil-and-paper audit.) Additional tasks, called interfaces, were affixed to this new rooms-department device as it gained capacity. Linkages were added to support point-of-sale (POS) terminals in food and beverage outlets. Then came call accounting systems (CAS), a type of automated POS for telephone charges. These and other interfaces, including linkages between equipment made by different manufacturers, created equipment issues. One manufacturer made the PMS, another the POS, and still a third created the interface linkage. The system grew willy-nilly. Additional interfaces such as in-room minibars, housekeeping status, and reservation programs were added again and again. The more the merrier, but the more frequently the early systems crashed.

The American Hotel & Lodging Association along with large franchisors and hotel chains encouraged manufacturers to develop and adopt Hospitality Information Technology Integration Standards (HITIS). HITIS improved the compatibility of different products by different manufacturers and reduced the frequency of computer downtime. HITIS allowed for seamless connectivity, particularly communications between franchisor's res centers and the franchisees' properties. Common reservation equipment and programs have made last-room availability widely accessible.

TURNKEY SYSTEMS With a turnkey installation, the buyer/hotel merely "turns the key" to activate the PMS. The vendor has programmed the system including the reports. Nothing is ever quite that easy, but it is unlikely that the industry would be so far along if the burden of development had not shifted from individual hotel companies to industrywide vendors.

Prior to the turnkey concept, each hotel shopped among manufacturers for its own hardware. Then it developed its own software by employing computer specialists, who at that time knew nothing about the business of keeping a hotel. The large data processing departments that appeared as a result of in-house programming disappeared quickly with the introduction of the turnkey package.

Now systems are purchased off the shelf, shopping among suppliers for an existing system that is close to what the hotel needs. And systems are close to what is needed. Generic programs are much alike because hotels are much alike. What differences there are in off-the-shelf products diminish as the latest programs are developed. Each generation improves flow and screening. To remain competitive, new or missing functions are added. The movement has been toward a Windows/Intel environment with dragged icons, touch screens, and reduced training time.

Turnkey companies now dominate the field. Single suppliers furnish both the hardware and the software. If the supplier specializes in one segment, other vendors supply the missing parts. Responsibility remains with the primary vendor, who puts together the package, gets it up and running, trains the staff, and services the installation—not without some major grief for the hotel, of course.

Vendors who adopted Hospitality Information Technology Integration Standards succeeded because their systems interfaced with the other manufacturers who complied. Hotels that specified HITIS in their bid solicitations enjoy reduced risks, lower costs, and savings in installation time. Access to the World Wide Web changed the hotel's PMS from one with dedicated hardware to one using Web technology. As that happened, the front-office workstation became a general-purpose rather than a specific-purpose screen.

Verifying Basic Data

Both pencil-and-paper audits and electronic audits summarize the day's activities at the closeout hour. Although either could be done at any time, preference is for the quiet hours of the business day when there is little posting activity; hence the term "night audit." The late hour is especially important for the PMS audit because departmental POS terminals are shut down temporarily. Changes to guest folios must wait until the audit is finished. Manual audits were not quite as limiting. With much erasing and rewriting, pencil-and-paper audits accommodated folio changes during the audit process.

CLOSING ROUTINE   Every night audit has a fixed routine to follow. For the PMS, the major procedure is monitoring. Room charges and taxes are posted automatically. So is the cumulative balance on each folio. In contrast, the pencil-and-paper auditor had to write the values and add the columns.

The PMS audit sets the stage for tomorrow with a summary printout illustrated by Exhibit 3. It does so because the closing balance of one day (the summary printout) is the same value as the opening balance of the following day. That is also true of the pencil-and-paper transcript sheet, Exhibit 12. This is so because the audit is an inventory of accounts receivable. And with any inventory count, the value that closes one period's is clearly the value that opens the next period.

It is somewhat redundant to point out again that verifying departmental revenues is part of the audit. Each time an account receivable (folio) is charged, a counterbalancing record should appear as income for one of the operating departments. Unlike pencil-and-paper systems, PMS discrepancies are rare. POS terminals automatically record the same figure on the folio and the departmental revenue. Pencil-and-paper audits have numerous handwritten entries. First by the departmental cashier, then the guest-service agent who posts to the folio, then the auditor. Each contributes handwriting errors, misplaced values, and mathematical mistakes.

The night auditor finishes the PMS audit with an end-of-the-day routine much like that of the hand audit (see Exhibit 4). A trial balance of debits and credits is made. Debits are charges to the receivable folios; credits are earnings in the several departments. The day and date are closed and the next day opened. The POS terminals are put back online. Monthly and annual totals are accumulated as part of the reporting process that follows next. The sequence varies at

---

Closing Routine for Position of Combined Night Auditor/Guest-Service Agent

Attend to Relief of the Previous Shift
- Compare late arrivals (reservations) with room availability
- Examine the front-office log
- Retrieve keys to drawers; watchman's clock; etc.
- Review issues: messages to be delivered; equipment failures; noisy revelers
- Set wake-up-call clock if equipment is not yet automated
- Verify cash drawer if cashier's banks are carried over
- Walk the first safety patrol/fire watch while previous shift is still on duty
- Witness cash turn-in of previous shift's deposit

Before the Income Audit
- Check cashier's bucket; many desks use it for special messages
- Close POS interfaces
- Post any vouchers not yet posted
- Prepare non–dollar denominated reports such as:
  - In-house list (night clerk's report)
  - Tomorrow's arrival list
  - Tomorrow's departure list
- Sell nonguaranteed room reservations

During the Income Audit
- Identify special-case folios: high balances
- Match due-bill folios with due bills, if any
- Post room and tax charges
- Print folios for under-the-door delivery
- Reconcile audit: Source documents agree with folio totals and departmental incomes
- Total and reconcile coupons

EXHIBIT 4   In many hotels, the positions of night auditor and guest-service agent are combined. But even small properties support the auditor with security personnel. A chronological/alphabetical list such as this gives order to the night's work and assures everyone that the required tasks have been completed.

Following the Income Audit
> Back up data
> Charge no-shows who have guaranteed arrivals with credit cards
> Complete the night auditor's report to the manager
> Leave completed materials properly sequenced for the day auditor
> Prepare reverse housekeeper's report
> Prepare dollar-denominated reports
> Prepare statistical reports
> Reconcile credit cards and prepare reports
> Reconnect POS interfaces
> Reset all systems for the new day
> Verify credit-card revenues and prepare appropriate reports

Other Duties
> Coordinate with incoming shift
> Deposit cash collections with cashier's report after relief shift arrives
> Interact with guests as needed
> Maintain log
> Monitor lights and door locks
> Set up continental breakfast
> Walk a fire/security watch

EXHIBIT 4 Continued

each hotel. At some properties, the routine is preprogrammed; at others, the update proceeds by prompts from the system to which the auditor responds. Almost every hotel anticipates tomorrow's check-outs by printing copies of the folios. That is part of the zip-out check-out routine.

ZIP-OUT CHECK-OUT Express check-out is one of the exciting spin-offs of PMS installations. Standing in line to check out is the bane of hotel guests, who are always in a hurry to depart. Flexible terminals able to shift quickly between registration and departure were an early PMS innovation. This increased the number of front-office stations when demand was greatest. Lines were shortened, but not enough because early output printers were very, very slow.

Hoteliers responded. Folios of guests who were departing the following day were printed as part of the audit. Preprinting folios sped the check-outs when they came to the desk. Copies were filed by room number sequence in the cashier's well and produced without delay when the departing guest appeared at the desk. If subsequent charges—breakfast, for example—altered the previous night's balance, the old folio was merely discarded and a new one printed.

This routine fell into disuse as express check-out gained favor. From printing folios to delivering them under the guest-room door was not a large conceptual jump, but it created *express check-out* or *zip-out check-out*, also called *speedy check-out, no-wait check-out,* or *VIP check-out.* Zip-out check-out is only for guests using direct billing or credit cards—but that is almost everyone. At first, guests who wanted the service completed a request card. Later, every departure using a credit card had a folio under the door. If the folio is accurate, the guest leaves after completing one additional step. Notice is given by telephoning a special extension, using the TV, or dropping the room key and a form into the lobby box (see Exhibit 5). The final folio is mailed or emailed to the guest within a day or two, and the charges are processed through the credit-card company.

Express check-out leaped ahead with the interface of Spectradyne's TV pay-movie system into the hotel's PMS. Delivering folios to the rooms was supplemented by showing the folio on the TV set—showing it any time the guest wanted. From then on, the procedure was the same. With a click of the remote control, the guest signaled departure. As with zip-out check-out, the folio followed in the mail, and the credit-card charges were processed. The integrated PMS can transfer those charges, which have been accumulating in the front-office folio, to the city ledger module.

Interfacing the ever-expanding PMS with self-service check-in/check-out terminals was another progression. At freestanding lobby locations, self-check-out terminals present guests with their folios and accept their credit cards to speed them on their way. Having guests leave using

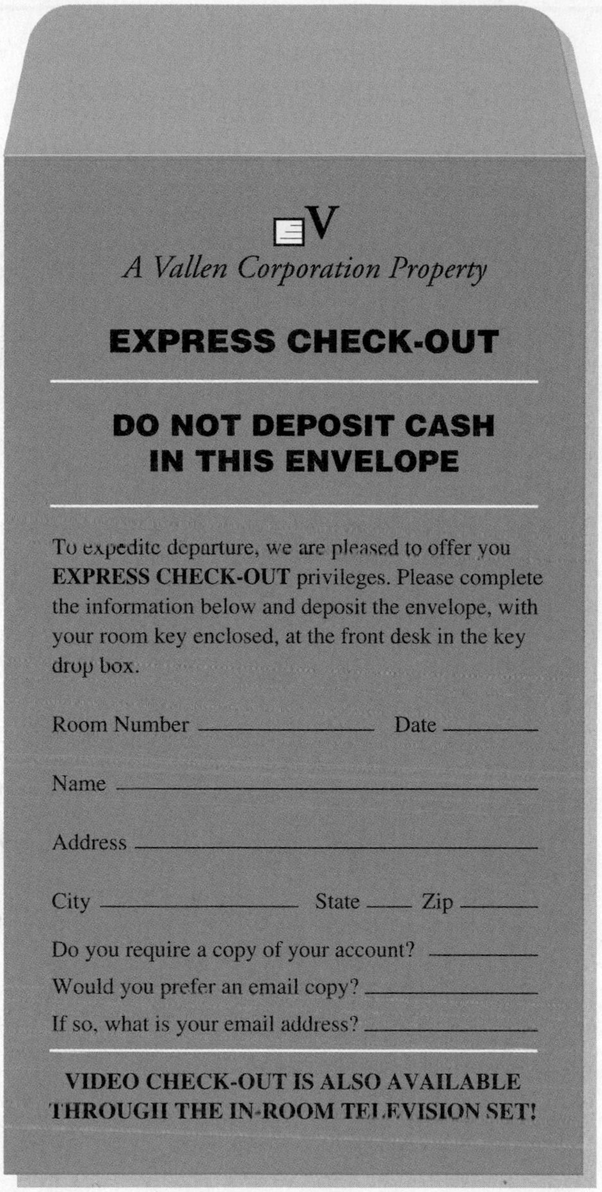

≡V

A Vallen Corporation Property

EXPRESS CHECK-OUT

DO NOT DEPOSIT CASH
IN THIS ENVELOPE

To expedite departure, we are pleased to offer you **EXPRESS CHECK-OUT** privileges. Please complete the information below and deposit the envelope, with your room key enclosed, at the front desk in the key drop box.

Room Number _____ Date _____

Name _____

Address _____

City _____ State _____ Zip _____

Do you require a copy of your account? _____

Would you prefer an email copy? _____

If so, what is your email address? _____

**VIDEO CHECK-OUT IS ALSO AVAILABLE
THROUGH THE IN-ROOM TELEVISION SET!**

EXHIBIT 5 Express check-out began with the procedure described on this envelope. As property management systems matured, zip-out check-out sequenced to the TV set, then to lobby consoles and most recently to efolios. The PMS allows guests to make a speedy departure but keeps the system updated on room status and accounts receivable.

the very terminal at which they registered was another giant step.

Each expansion of the PMS (see Exhibit 6) brings the industry a step closer to the fully electronic hotel.

PMS POSTING ERRORS   Property management systems are not error free. Staffers make mistakes whether the system is manual or electronic. Human errors are not offset by high-priced equipment. Computerized front offices minimize errors and facilitate corrections, but they do not create error-free environments.

Getting a detailed list of transactions is the first step in reconciling total departmental sales that differ from total departmental charges on guest folios. A hard copy (a printed copy) itemizes transactions by POS terminals and by reference codes. Cashiers must enter a code number and usually a voucher number before a charge can be recorded on a folio. The code number is automatic with many POSs that are permanently located in a particular service area, say, the coffee shop. The voucher number is the guest check.

A third code, the guest's room number, is also required. Some terminals require another element, the first three letters of the guest's surname. Postings will not clear without the required information. Exhibit 2 illustrates the screen that a dining room cashier uses to post charges.

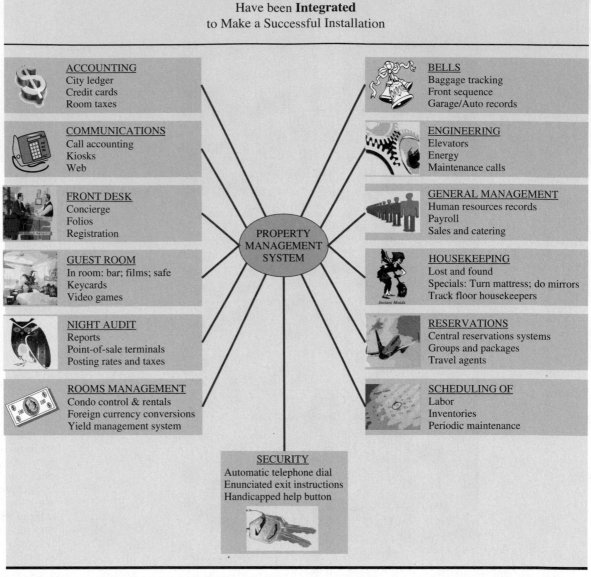

**The Many Interfaces of the PMS
Have been Integrated
to Make a Successful Installation**

ACCOUNTING
City ledger
Credit cards
Room taxes

COMMUNICATIONS
Call accounting
Kiosks
Web

FRONT DESK
Concierge
Folios
Registration

GUEST ROOM
In room: bar; films; safe
Keycards
Video games

NIGHT AUDIT
Reports
Point-of-sale terminals
Posting rates and taxes

ROOMS MANAGEMENT
Condo control & rentals
Foreign currency conversions
Yield management system

PROPERTY
MANAGEMENT
SYSTEM

BELLS
Baggage tracking
Front sequence
Garage/Auto records

ENGINEERING
Elevators
Energy
Maintenance calls

GENERAL MANAGEMENT
Human resources records
Payroll
Sales and catering

HOUSEKEEPING
Lost and found
Specials: Turn mattress; do mirrors
Track floor housekeepers

RESERVATIONS
Central reservations systems
Groups and packages
Travel agents

SCHEDULING OF
Labor
Inventories
Periodic maintenance

SECURITY
Automatic telephone dial
Enunciated exit instructions
Handicapped help button

EXHIBIT 6   Property management systems began life as front-office-records devices. They matured to interface and integrate many functions of a busy hotel. Touchscreen technology facilitated the consumer's role.

Matching the guest-room keycard (with its magnetic strip) to the PMS's registration data file is another means of verifying the user's identity. The guest inserts the keycard into a POS and the system verifies the identification. Implementation of this system has already begun, but it may be replaced even before it goes into general use. Credit card may become the keycard for the next generation of electronic locks. The POS reduces receivable losses by rejecting invalid postings. The guest may have checked out already, be a paid-in-advance customer with no charges permitted, or have exceeded the credit-card floor or other credit ceiling set by the hotel. Late charges are reduced dramatically when POS terminals are in place.

Departing guests sometimes challenge the accuracy of departmental postings. Denying that the charges were ever made, they ask the front desk for offsetting allowances. Obtaining a copy of the check (voucher) signed by the guest to show its accuracy was a slow process with a pencil-and-paper system. So time-consuming was it that front-office cashiers simply granted the allowance without further investigation. Until recently, the results were the same with a PMS.

Now disputed charges are being met with proof in a program first introduced at the Boca Raton Resort and Beach Club. The PMS is able to display the protested, signed voucher!

Reports from the Night Audit

It is difficult to say whether a uniform need created the turnkey system or whether mass production created standardization across the industry. Perhaps, it was a bit of each. The resulting uniformity is most evident in the reports that the night audit churns out—reports that provide management with critical information. Many are viewed on screens throughout the day as circumstances change and management decisions are needed. They are also formalized by nightly printouts covering a range of topics. Exception reports and the daily report to the manager, discussed later, are the most carefully examined.

An unlimited number of reports can be generated once the PMS captures the information. Data can be arranged and reordered in a variety of ways. The registration card is a good example. From it the PMS creates reports about the geographic origin of guests; the membership of group attendees; company affiliations; the frequency of double occupancy; average length of stay and more.

The ease of obtaining reports undoubtedly contributed to the vast numbers that were demanded when PMSs were first introduced. Much of that has shaken out. Management took control and pared the numbers by emphasizing exception reports. One no longer sees piles of trashed reports, which the night auditor prepared, unread by the recipient the next day.

Still, the night audit produces a wide range of reports. Many of these are day-end summaries, since unit managers use (through display terminals or hard-copy print) the same data several times throughout the day. Some reports are carry-overs from the traditional pencil-and-paper audit. The balance of each accounts receivable, credit alerts, and statistical reports to the manager are among them.

EXCEPTION REPORTS   Exception reports highlight digressions from the norm. Reporting everything that happens overwhelms the user. Reports by exception alert the reader to problem areas and do so without a time-consuming inspection of all data. A credit-limit report best illustrates the group. Listing the folio balance of every guest requires a tedious search to uncover possible problems. An exception report lists only those folios close to the hotel's ceiling. There is no need to scrutinize pages of data to find a problem. Such reports grab management's immediate attention and action whereas cumbersome reports are usually put aside for later examination, which never takes place.

Allowance Report: identifies who authorized each allowance, who received the allowance, the dollar amount, and the reason behind it.

Cashier's Overage and Shortage Report: pinpoints, by stations and persons, overages, and shortages that exceed predetermined norms.

Comps Report: is similar to the allowance report; identifying who authorized each comp, who received the comp, the amount and the reason.

No Luggage Report: lists occupied rooms in which there is no baggage (see Exhibits 15 and 16).

Room Rate Variance Report: compares actual rates to a standard rate schedule and identifies the authority for granting the variance. (Not meaningful if the hotel is discounting frequently and deeply.)

Skipper Report: provides room identification, dollar amount, and purported name and address.

Write-Off Report: lists daily write-offs, usually late charges whose account balances are too small to pursue or less than a specified amount. Includes the occasional bad debt that is deemed uncollectible.

DOWNTIME REPORTS   These reports, used when the computer crashes, provide insurance against disaster. Like a great deal of insurance, the reports usually go unused because emergencies rarely materialize. Downtime reports are dumped 24 hours later when the contingency has passed and the backup reports of the following day have been printed.

> **Folio Balance Report:** itemizes the previous day's record of each account receivable (the folio) in room number sequence. Exhibit 3, the Guest Ledger Summary Report, is a balance of folios comparable to Columns 1, 2, 4, and 5, 16, 20, 21, and 22 of a pencil-and-paper transcript (see Exhibit 12).
>
> **Guest-List Report:** alphabetizes registered guests with their room numbers. It is a computer version of a manual information rack. It would remain at the desk as a reference until tomorrow's new arrivals and departures made last night's record obsolete.
>
> **Room Status Report:** identifies vacant, out-of-order, on change, and occupied rooms for the beginning of the new day (the close of the old day); a computerized room count sheet (see Exhibit 13, a pencil-and-paper report).
>
> **Disk Backup:** is not a report, but part of the closing sequence of the auditor's shift. Data are replicated onto a disk to be retrieved if a malfunction erases the working disk.

CREDIT REPORTS The night auditor is the credit department's first line of defense. In that capacity, the night auditor reports both routine matters and special credit situations.

Mention has already been made of the auditor's responsibility to preprint the folios of expected check-outs. Although not nearly as numerous, folios must also be prepared for guests who remain longer than one week. On the guest's seventh night, the auditor prints the folio for delivery to the guest the next day.

The night auditor also makes an analysis of guest account balances. With a manual system, the auditor scans the last column of the transcript (see Exhibit 12, column 21) and itemizes those rooms with balances at or near the hotel's limit. The computer makes the same list, an exception report. If the audit team has time, additional credit duties may be assigned. All credit reports are time sensitive and may be viewed as exception reports:

> **Credit-Alert Report:** lists rooms whose folio charges exceed a given amount in a single day. That value varies with the class of hotel.
>
> **Cumulative Charges Report:** is similar to the credit-alert report except that it includes cumulative charges for the guest's entire stay.
>
> **Floor Report:** lists guests whose folio balances approach the maximum allowed the hotel by the credit-card company (the hotel's floor) or the maximum the credit card allows on the guest's own card.
>
> **Three-Day Report:** highlights folios unpaid three days after billing.

RESERVATION REPORTS Computerizing reservations added a new dimension to the process. The toll-free WATS number globalized the reservation network. Instant confirmation was given for dates that were months away to persons who were miles apart. In so doing, reams of information—fodder for reports—were generated.

Information is the power to decide. Reservation managers must know the number of rooms sold and the number available, by type, rate, and accommodations. They must know the number of arrivals, departures, stay-overs, cancellations, out of orders, and walk-ins. This information comes to the reservations department in a variety of reports.

Supplemental information flows from the same database. Which rooms are most popular and at which rates? Do no-show factors vary with the season and the day of the week? If so, by how much? How many rooms in which categories (i.e., kings) are turnaways? How many reservations were walked? How many in-WATS calls were there? How many were initiated by travel agents? Questions of this type illustrate again the dual management–operations capability of the property management system.

An alphabetical list of arrivals is an example of the computer in operations. It reduces the number of lost reservations and facilitates the recognition of VIPs. It helps the bellcaptain schedule a crew. It identifies group affiliations, which improves reservation and billing procedures.

As with all of these reports, reservation data can be displayed on a monitor or preserved on hard copy for further digestion and evaluation. A permanent copy turns the data into a report. Then it serves more as a management tool than an operational one.

Arrivals Report: alphabetizes a list of the day's expected arrivals, individually and by groups.

Cancellation and Change Report: lists reservation changes including reservations and cancellations for the day and for later dates.

Central Reservations Report: analyzes reservations made through the central reservations system, including numbers, kinds, rates, and fees paid.

Convention (Group) Delegates Report: is a compilation of group (and tour) room blocks, the number of rooms booked, and the number still available by rate category and name of group. Also called a Group Pickup Report when used for a specific day.

Daily Analysis Report: computes in one or more reports the number and percentage of reservations, arrivals, no-shows, walk-ins, and so on, by source (travel agent, housing bureau, etc.) and by type of guest (full rack, corporate rate, etc.).

Deposit Report: lists deposits requested and received, deposits requested and not received, deposits not requested. Could be treated as an exception report.

Forecast Report: also called (extended arrival report, future availability report) projects reservation data forward over short or long durations.

Occupancy Report: projects occupancy by category of room.

Overbooking (Walk) Report: identifies by names the reservations walked, the number of walk-ins denied, and the number farmed out to other properties.

Regrets Report: provides a count of the number of room requests denied.

ROOMS MANAGEMENT REPORTS   The PMS has brought major procedural changes to the front office but not to the functions that need doing. Comparisons of the old and the new are best illustrated through the room rack. Unlike manual room racks (see Exhibit 9), which one can see and physically manipulate, computerized racks are in memory, viewable only on the monitor screens (contrast Exhibits 7, 8, 9, and 10). Whether the clerk turns to the manual

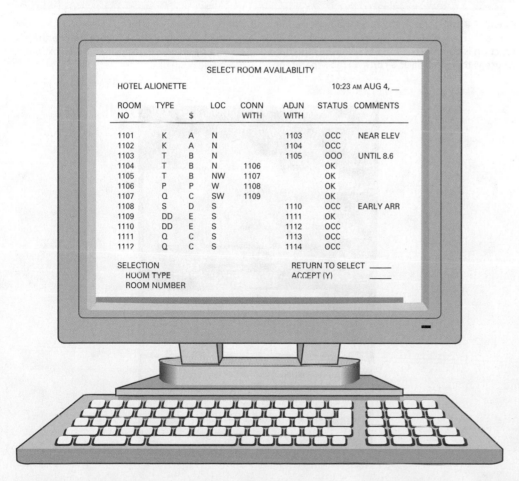

EXHIBIT 7 Computer screens, such as this one, have replaced the front-office room rack (Exhibit 9). Both pieces of equipment display the same information. Here, it's room availability by type, location, rate, and status. The guest-service agent completes the assignment, exiting with a "Y" (Yes)—lower right—once the selection that's made agrees with the previous input of room type requested. (See the master screen of Exhibit 8.)

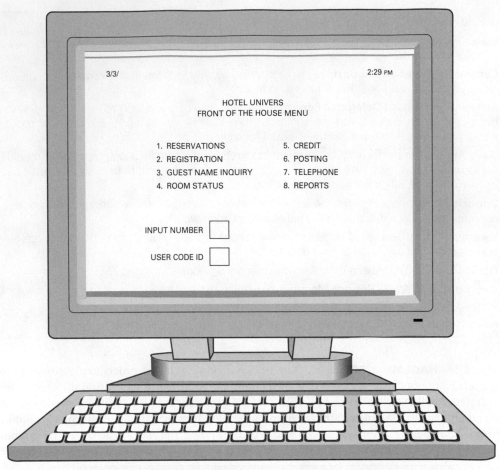

EXHIBIT 8 Pictured is the PMS' main rooms menu. It offers 8 screens, of which Exhibit 7 is one, as the equivalent of a room rack (Exhibit 9). Several screens are used in sequence before the function is completed. The PMS captures the data during other procedures, registration for example, whereas the room rack is constructed separately.

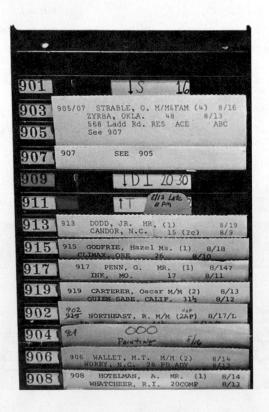

EXHIBIT 9 The manual room rack was in place well into the 1970s. One glance told the room clerk which rooms were vacant (no room-rack slip), which were occupied (names appeared on the rack slip), and which were reserved (Room 911). The slips showed the guests' arrival and expected departure dates (right corner of the slip); their rates and hometowns. Different-colored slips (not shown) identified group members, paid-in-advance, permanent guests, VIPs, and more. *(For ease in reading, several illustrations use small dollar values, which may not seem realistic.)*

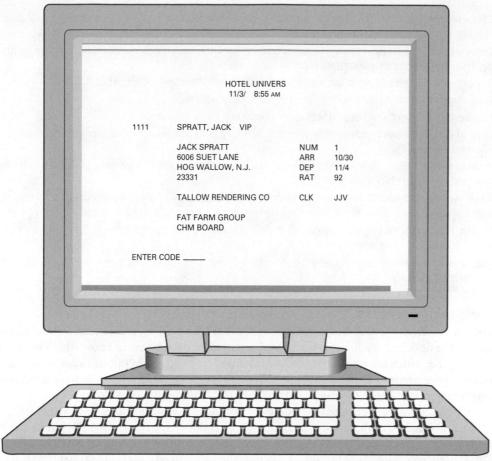

```
                    HOTEL UNIVERS
                    11/3/   8:55 AM


    1111          SPRATT, JACK   VIP

                  JACK SPRATT            NUM    1
                  6006 SUET LANE         ARR    10/30
                  HOG WALLOW, N.J.       DEP    11/4
                  23331                  RAT    92

                  TALLOW RENDERING CO    CLK    JJV

                  FAT FARM GROUP
                  CHM BOARD


       ENTER CODE _____
```

EXHIBIT 10   Code 3 of Exhibit 8 (Guest Name Inquiry) opens the screen that identifies individual guests. Compare this information with the room-rack slips of Exhibit 9. Both contain the same facts including the guest's name and address, number in the party, rate, arrival and departure dates, group membership, and the initials of the guest-service agent who registered the party.

rack (Exhibit 9) or the computerized one, the information is the same: room rates, connecting and adjoining rooms, bed types, and room status.

The computer restructures the data. It separates into different windows (see Exhibit 8) what is visible with one glance to the user of the manual rack (see Exhibit 9). The separate menus of Exhibit 8 are needed to view what the manual rack identifies as one class of information.

With a glance at the manual rack (Exhibit 9) one sees the rooms vacant and occupied, the rooms out of order and on change, the names of the guests and their city of residence, the number in the party and their company or group affiliation, the rate on the room and the anticipated check-out date. It doesn't work that way with an electronic system, where separate programs are needed for each function. Room identification (see Exhibit 7) is different from guest identification (see Exhibit 10). Not so with the manual room rack.

Far more information is available from the computer rack than from the manual rack of Exhibit 9, but the information has to be manipulated to provide the data. For example, the computerized rack can display all the vacant rooms on a given floor. All the king rooms in the tower or all the connecting rooms in the lanai building can be listed. Facts that would take many minutes to ascertain, if at all, from the manual rack, are flashed onto the screen in seconds.

Information is more complete and can be processed more rapidly with the computerized rack than with the manual one. This is true for the whole, although a greater amount of time may be required for the computer to process a single fact. In a contest to identify a guest whose name begins with either "Mac" or "Mc," for example, the manual user of an information rack (a manual alphabetical listing, not illustrated) should be able to beat out the computer user.

Change Report: identifies changes in rooms, rates, and numbers in the party of guests who are already in the house.

Convention-Use Report: summarizes room use by different convention groups in order to justify the number of complimentary rooms.

Expected to Depart Report: lists anticipated departures. The converse would be a Stay-over Report.

Flag Report: alerts desk to rooms flagged for special attention.

House-Use Report: counts and lists rooms occupied by hotel personnel.

Out-of-Order Report: advises the number, identity, and reason for of out-of-order or out-of-inventory rooms.

Pickup Report: identifies by name and room numbers the identity of group members to be charged against its block.

Rate Analysis Report: displays the distribution of rates by sources—reservations, walk-ins, travel-agency, res system, hotel sales department, packages, and company made.

Room Productivity Report: evaluates housekeeping's productivity in total time and by individual room attendant. (See Exhibit 11.)

VIP Report: identifies distinguished guests (DGs) and very important persons (VIPs) including casino high rollers.

ROOMS STATUS REPORTS The PMS's Rooms Status Reports offer one of the best examples of an old function with a new face. That function, room status, relies on frequent communication between the desk and the linen room, housekeeping. The desk needs to know which rooms are ready for sale; which are on-change; and which are vacant and ready, out-of-order, or occupied. Housekeeping needs to know which rooms require attention. Room status is referenced innumerable times throughout the day by both ends of this communication link.

Computers haven't changed the framework of room-status reporting. The cashier still puts the room on change as the guest checks out. (This is done electronically if the guest uses the speedy check-out option.) That is how the room clerk learns that a given room will be available soon. On-change status tells housekeeping that the room needs attention. When the room is clean, the housekeeper updates the system, switching the on-change room to ready. Immediately, the desk clerk has the information. The room is sold and the cycle begins anew. The faster the process goes around, the quicker the new guest is settled and the room sale consummated.

Prior to the computer, the cashier–desk–housekeeping link took different pathways. Either there were direct person-to-person conversations—the housekeeper would walk to the desk—or pencil-and-paper notations were sent back and forth or the telephone was used. Frequently, there was no contact at all. Regardless of the system used, floor housekeepers—the very persons who did the job—were not in the communication loop. That critical link, the floor housekeeper, couldn't be reached at all. Today's housekeepers communicate by telephone, but it is not a conversation. It is as an electronic input device to the computer. The message is input either through the room telephone or by a terminal located in the linen closet. PCs that have been introduced into guest rooms as an upgrade to guest service provide housekeeping with still another terminal. Hand-held devices are still another.

With access to the computer, the housekeeper's office tracks room attendants as they dial in and out of the system (see Exhibit 11). Daily job assignments can also be computer designed. At the start of the shift, employees get a hard-copy list of rooms that each is to do service. The print-out also includes special assignments such as mirrors in the corridors, attention to sick guests, or messages from management to the staff. Other room status reports include the following:

ADA Report: lists rooms occupied by handicapped guests. Copies go to the bell department and the desk, but especially to security in case evacuation of the building is required.

Out-of-Order Report: includes the dates and reasons that rooms were placed out of order (OOO) or out of inventory (OOI), expected ready dates, and the reasons behind the designations.

Permanent Guest Report: lists permanent residents by name and room number.

Room Status Report: identifies the status (occupied, vacant, ready, on-change, out-of-order) of every room. The room status report also serves as one of the downtime reports.

Sick Guest Report: includes guests' names and room numbers.

Room Attendant's Schedule							01:53 PM Nov 11						
Name							**Number**	**Duty H**		**Message Signal Off**			
		Number of Rooms Assigned								**Beginning Room Number**			
Room	U-R	In	Out	SL	HK	CO	Room	U-R	In	Out	SL	HK	CO
1200	A	9:35A	9:49A	SG	OK	SO	1209	A			SD	D	SO
1201	A	9:50A	10:14A	SS	OK	SO	1210	A	8:44A	9:02A	SD	OK	SO
1202	A	11:50A	12:12P	SS	OK	SO	1211	A	1:13P	1:48P	OK	I	OK
1203	A	9:20A	9:35A	SS	OK	SO	1212	A	9:03A	9:19A	SG	OK	SO
1204	A	10:54A	11:17A	SM	OK	SO	1213	A	1:48		OK	57	DO
1205	A	11:17A	11:50A	SD	OK	SO	1214	A			OK	D	DO
1206	A	10:31A	10:54A	SS	OK	SO	1215	A			OK	D	DO
1207	A	10:14A	10:31A	SS	OK	SO							
1208	A	12:12P	1:13P	OK	OK	OK							
										END DISPLAY			

EXHIBIT 11 Property management systems enable the linen room to communicate with and track each floor housekeeper (see Exhibit 6). This report monitors the room attendant's productivity, which is very high at 12 of 16 rooms completed. Stay-over rooms take less time than check-out rooms; note Room 1208. (Apparently, no lunch break?)

ACCOUNTS RECEIVABLE REPORTS Whether by PMS or pencil-and-paper, the night audit focuses on accounts receivable. Viewed at its simplest, the night audit is nothing more than a cumulative inventory of accounts receivable. Throughout the day, accounts receivables are increased through charges or decreased through payments. That count—the inventory of A/R— is treated like any other inventory, be it linens in the closet, liquor at the bar, or canned peas in the storeroom.

Each day's computation starts with the opening balance. This opening balance (yesterday's closing balance) is the amount already owed to the hotel (peas on hand in stores). New charges (new pea purchases) made by guests that day (account receivable debits) are added to the opening balance:

	Accounts Receivable in Dollars	Peas in Cans
Opening Balance (Yesterday's Close)	$186,000.00	186
Today's Charges (Purchases)	+ 24,000.00	+24
Total	$210,000.00	210

Subtracted from that sum are payments (credits) made by guests (cans opened and consumed) that day.

The new closing balance (*tomorrow's opening balance) is thus obtained for both accounts receivable and peas, or any other item being inventoried. This closing value becomes the opening balance of the following day when the sequence begins anew.

	Accounts Receivable in Dollars	Peas in Cans
Total (See Above)	$210,000.00	210
Today's Payments (Consumption)	−60,000.00	−60
A/R owed at day's close	$150,000.00*	
Peas on the shelf at day's end		150*

*Opening balance tomorrow—day three.

Several reports track these receivables:

Alpha List: inventories the entire guest (accounts receivable) population and the amount each owes. (This would be comparable to a list of each can of peas on the shelf if each had a name.)

City-ledger Transfers: itemizes all the accounts transferred from the front-office ledger to the city ledger that day; a journal of city-ledger transfers. (Identifies specific cans of peas shipped to the kitchen from the storeroom).

Credit-Card Report: includes amounts and identities of credit-card charges made this day.

Daily Revenue Report: analyzes revenue from all sources by outlet and by means of payment. (Sometimes called a D Report because it is comparable to the once-used NCR-machine D Report.)

Departmental Sales Journals: report the totals and individual transactions of each operating department. (Comparable to the vertical columns #5 through #15 of the transcript (see Exhibit 12).

Guest Ledger Summary: displays the daily opening balances, charges, credits, and closing balances of guests' A and B folios. Exhibits 3 and 12 contain the same information. One is a property management report (Exhibit 3); the other a paper-and-pencil form (Exhibit 12). Compare specifically Exhibit 3's Room # column and 12–12's column 2. Similarly, 12–3's Opening Bal(ance) column equates with 12–12's columns 4 minus 5. Continuing: 12–3's Charges, Credits, and Closing Bal(ance) columns are the same as Exhibit 12's columns numbered 16, 20, and 21 minus 22.

Late Charge Report: identifies the late charges transferred to the city ledger that day.

Posting Report: lists the postings made by each departmental POS terminal. (Comparable to pencil-and-paper departmental control sheets; see Exhibit 7).

Room-Revenue Report: displays the room rates and taxes posted to each room that day. Because room revenue can be obtained floor by floor, it is comparable to a once-used manual room count sheet (without taxes). It, too, was called an Occupancy and Room-Revenue Report (see Exhibit 13).

Reports to the Manager

The night auditor addresses and reconciles account-receivable sales. The income auditor (day auditor) casts a wider net, auditing cash sales and credit-card sales that have not passed through the folios. Both are combined during the income audit and presented in a *Daily Report to the Manager*. That report also becomes the basis of the daily entries into the permanent books of account.

There is obviously some delay between the time the day auditor reports to work and the completion of the Daily Report to the Manager. In the interim, the general manager relies on the *Night Auditor's Report to the Manager* (see Exhibit 14). Although the night auditor's report contains less information,[2] it does reflect total room sales, the hotel's largest revenue source. That room sales figure is accurate and complete because room sales are sold only to receivables, which comprise the core of the now-finished night audit.

Exhibit 14, an abbreviated night auditor's report, contains four segments. (1) Accounts-receivable sales—not total sales—in the several departments appear in the upper left. These values originate in the night audit. They would agree with columns 6 through 16 of Exhibit 12 were the hand transcript still being used. (2) The receivable charges, $18,632.98, of today, March 16th, are entered in the lower left corner of the report to obtain a cumulative balance of accounts receivable. The earlier pea-inventory discussion reinforced this concept of a cumulative accounts-receivable balance. The right side of the report, statistics and ratios, is the next topic.

---

[2]It contains less information because it deals only with accounts receivable sales. The night audit does not audit cash sales. Neither does it audit, and therefore does not include in its report, credit-card sales made throughout the hotel.

DAILY TRANSCRIPT OF
ACCOUNTS RECEIVABLE

DATE 10/6 _____ 20 ___

1 ACCOUNT NO.	2 ROOM NO.	3 NUMBER OF GUESTS	4 DEBIT	5 CREDIT	6 ROOMS	7 RESTAURANT	8 BEVERAGES	9 LOCAL CALLS	10 LONG DISTANCE	11 LAUNDRY	12 VALET	13 CASH DISBURSEMENTS	14 TRANSFERS	15 ROOM TAX	16 TOTAL DEBITS	17 CASH RECEIPTS	18 ALLOWANCES	19 TRANSFERS	20 TOTAL	21 DEBIT	22 CREDIT
8001	406	1		19 -	60 -	12 -	6 -					8 -		3 -	70 -					70 -	
8811	1817	2	63 60		30 -	5 -			4 -					60	39 60					103 20	
8123	824	1			18 50	6 40						1 -		37	26 27	37 -			37 -		10 73
7188	906	2	21 93		21 56									43	21 49					43 42	
7913	1907	2	39 96		30 -		6 -					47 96		60	84 56					124 52	
TOTAL	**40**	**51**	768 20	25 32	676 50	52 10	61 70	7 20	18 40		4 -	17 -	47 96	13 53	898 39	167 50	2 10		169 60	1488 70	17 03

DEPARTURES

8106	1616	3	46 20			4 40									4 40			50 60	50 60		
8007	1047	1	18 87													18 57	30		18 87		
7772	1234	2	39 96															39 96	39 96		
8282	1600	1	- 0 -				4 -	40	3 60						8 -	8 -					
TOTAL			105 03			4 40	4 -	- 40	3 60						12 40	26 57	30 90	56	117 43		
CITY LEDGER																					
Cum			500 -			40 -	30 -						90 56		160 56		47 96	47 96	612 60		
TOTALS	**40**	**51**	1373 23	25 32	676 50	96 50	95 70	160 22		4 -	17 -	138 52	13 53	1071 35	194 07	2 40	138 52	334 99	2101 30	17 03	

Courtesy: American Hotel Register Co., Northbrook, IL.

EXHIBIT 12 The transcript is a summary of accounts receivable. The vertical column of each folio is entered horizontally. (Exhibit 1 appears here as line #1.) Cross-footing (adding and subtracting) the totals verifies the mathematics of each folio since the total equals the sum of its parts. The transcript also verifies departmental incomes by comparing vertical column Totals 6 through 15 with departmental income reports. The property management system does the same audit electronically.

N:B There are two methods for completing a transcript. *Only one or the other would be used, but both are illustrated here!* Line 1 illustrates one method. Column 16, total debits (charges), includes the values of Columns 4 and 5, the day's opening balances. The remaining horizontal lines illustrate the second method where Column 16 does NOT include the opening balance. Both systems produce the same closing balances, Columns 21 and 22. *(For ease in reading, several illustrations use small dollar values, which may not seem realistic.)*

ROOM COUNT, HOUSE COUNT, AND ROOM INCOME Room count (the number of rooms sold [occupied]), house count (the number of guests [persons] registered), and room income (dollar sales) are computed during the night audit on the PMS's Occupancy and Rooms Revenue Report. (When this report was done in a pencil-and-paper format, it was called a room count sheet; see Exhibit 13.)

These three values are computed by the night audit and verified by the income audit, using a formula exactly like the earlier cans-of-peas illustration. The first step adds today's arrivals to the opening balance. Iterating: Today's opening balance is always yesterday's closing balance. We already know that this opening/closing relationship applies to every inventory count, be it cans of peas, accounts receivable, room count/house count/room income, or bottles of scotch. Consider the scotch.

When the bar closes at 2 AM, there are six bottles of scotch. Twelve hours later, when the bar reopens, the same six bottles are there. The closing balance of day one and the opening balance of day two are always the same.

The reasoning applies to room statistics. The number of rooms occupied, the number of persons, and the dollar income is increased by today's arrivals and decreased by today's departures. The values determined by the income auditor using the computation that follows should agree with the results of the night audit's report. So it is a mathematical check on the physical listing of the night audit's Occupancy and Room-Revenue Report. The counts of rooms, guests, and dollars shown on that report should agree to the mathematical inventory of rooms, guests, and dollars.

OCCUPANCY AND ROOM REVENUE REPORT			**Hotel Gary**				DAY _Monday_	DATE _9-18-_									

EAST WING

ROOM	No Guests	RATE	ROOM	No Guests	RATE	ROOM	No Guests	RATE	ROOM	No Guests	RATE	ROOM	No Guests	RATE	ROOM	No Guests	RATE
3101			3319			3615			3910			4206			4501		
3102			3320			3616			3912			4207			4502		
3103			S3322	4	80	3617			3914			4208			4503		
3104			3401			3618			3915			4210			4504		
3105			3402	2	66	3619			3916			4212			4505		
3106			3403	2	66	3620			3917			4214			4506		
3107			3404			S3622			3918			4215			4507		
3108			3405	2	68	3701			3919			4216			4508		
3110			3406			3702			3920			4217			4510		
3112			3407			3703			S3922			4218			4512		
3114			3408	1	58 –	3704			4001			4219			4514		
3115			3410			3705			4002			4220			4515		
3116			3412	3	72	3706			4003			S4222			4516		
3117			3414	1	59 50	3707			4004			4301			4517		
3118			3415	3	66 –	3708			4005			4302			4518		

ROOM	No Guests	RATE	ROOM	No Guests	RATE	ROOM	No Guests	RATE	ROOM	No Guests	RATE	ROOM	No Guests	RATE	ROOM	No Guests	RATE
3312			3606	2	66	3903			S4122			4418			4712		
3314			3607	2	66	3904			4201			4419			4714		
3315			3608	3	71	3905			4202			4420			4715		
3316			3610	1	66	3906			4203			S4422			4716		
3317			3612			3907			4204						4717		
3318			3614			3908			4205						4718		
TOTAL			TOTAL	57	3,731 00	TOTAL			TOTAL			TOTAL			TOTAL		

EXHIBIT 13 A Room Occupancy Report is prepared nightly by both the electronic and hand-prepared audits. This partially illustrated report would have been copied from a room rack like that of Exhibit 9. The totals: number of guests, number of rooms occupied, and total room revenue should agree with Columns 2, 3, and 6 of Exhibit 12 and with the totals obtained in the discussion called, *Room Count, House Count, and Room Income.* This report is also called A Night Clerk's Report (see Exhibit 4, "Before the Income Audit").

(For ease in reading, several illustrations use small dollar values, which may not seem realistic.)

The City Hotel, Anywhere, U.S.A.   **Page 1**
03/16 Night Auditor's Report

SALES			ROOM STATISTICS	
Rooms	$12,900.00		Total Rooms	320
Coffee Shop	1,524.80		House Use	–0–
Steak House	CLOSED		Out of Order	–0–
Cap'tn Bar	896.00		Complimentary	–0–
Telephone	990.76		Permanent	2
Laundry	100.51		Room Count	180
Total Sales	$16,412.07		Vacant	140
			House Count	210
Other Charges:				
Cash Advance	987.76			
Taxes Payable	540.00			
Transfers	693.15			
	$18,632.98			

ACCOUNTS RECEIVABLE			ROOM RATIOS	
Opening Balance	$44,651.07		% Occupancy	56.3
Charges	18,632.98		% Double Occupancy	16.7
Total	$63,284.05		Average Daily Rate	$71.67
Credits	950.00		RevPar	$40.35
Closing Balance	$62,334.05			

EXHIBIT 14 The Night Auditor's Report to the Manager is one of many reports prepared from the night audit. Since the audit deals only with accounts receivable, some values (Coffee Shop, Steak House, and Bar Sales) are under reported. Final figures will appear on the Daily Report to the Manager after the day audit is completed. All account receivable values (room income, closing balance, statistics, and ratio) are complete, but small changes may result from the day audit.

Typically, an inventory count is yesterday's close plus additions and minus reductions. There is an extra step with this computation. The extra step accommodates occasional changes that involve neither arrivals (additions) nor departures (subtractions). These internal changes must be accommodated simply because they are neither arrivals nor departures. Guests change rooms, hence a rate change might occur. Guests move to or from larger/smaller accommodations, hence a change in the number of rooms occupied might occur. Sometimes, additional members of a party join later and sometimes one or more of the original members leave. Both cases impact the three counts, which are captured on the night audit's Change Report—see the section above called "Rooms Management Reports." The simple mathematics is illustrated so:

	Room Count	House Count	Room Income
Opening Balance	840	1,062	$174,200
+ Arrivals	316	391	80,100
= Total	1,156	1,453	$254,300
− Departures	88	122	16,400
= Total	1,068	1,331	$237,900
± Changes	+ 6	− 2	+ 1,730
− Closing Balance	1,074	1,329	$239,630

ROOM STATISTICS Both the night auditor's report to the manager and the income auditor's report to the manager contain statistics. Statistics are merely special ways of grouping data in an orderly and usable manner. Statistics are the facts expressed in dollars, cents, or numbers. For example, instead of itemizing each identity:

Guest A	Room 597	$150
Guest B	Room 643	$130
Guest C	Room 842	$160

one might say there are 220 guests in 189 rooms paying a total of $27,198. A great deal of information has been grouped, classified, and presented to become a statistic.

Taking the next step, these room figures are expressed in ratios, which are more meaningful than statistics. So the 189 rooms sold is expressed in relation to the number of rooms available for sale, 270. The result is a percentage of occupancy, a mathematical expression of how many rooms were sold in relation to how many could have been sold. Using those values, the percentage of occupancy is:

$$\frac{\text{number of rooms sold (room count)}}{\text{number of rooms available for sale}} = \frac{189}{270} = 70\%$$

A frequent companion to the percentage of occupancy computation is the average daily rate (ADR). Both ratios appear in the night auditor's report to the manager. Sales per occupied room, as this figure is sometimes called, is the income from room sales divided by the number of rooms sold.

$$\frac{\text{room income}}{\text{number of rooms sold (room count)}} = \frac{\$27,198}{189} = \$143.90$$

A similar computation, RevPar, once called *sales per available room*, is derived by dividing room income by the number of rooms available for sale rather than by the actual number of rooms sold:

$$\frac{\text{room income}}{\text{number of rooms available for sale}} = \frac{\$27,198}{270} = \$100.73$$

The Night Audit

The fourth most frequently cited ratio in the manager's daily report is the percentage of double occupancy. Double occupancy is the relationship of rooms occupied by more than one guest to the total number of rooms occupied. That is what the following ratio expresses:

$$\frac{\text{number of guests} - \text{number of rooms sold}}{\text{number of rooms sold}} = \frac{220 - 189}{189} = 16.4\%$$

Having finished the audit with the preparation of the night auditor's report to the manager, the night auditor lays aside pencils and erasers—or did once, now it is more likely rubbing stiff shoulders from working at the keyboard—and goes home to bed.

THE HOUSEKEEPER'S REPORT   Earlier, the chapter highlighted the importance of communication between the linen room, the desk, and the floor housekeeper. How well this is done is highlighted by another report. This one comes from the linen room to the desk at day's end. In many properties, housekeeping forwards the report to the desk twice daily. Although the illustration that follows is presented in written form, the report is now filed electronically to be viewed on a monitor.

Room status is communicated by means of abbreviations that are widely understood across the industry (see Exhibit 15). Occupied rooms are reported with checkmarks (√), meaning OK. Sleep-outs, which are rooms with baggage but no overnight guests, are flagged with a B, for baggage. Occupied rooms with no baggage or just light baggage get an X mark (for nothing). Other codes mix handwritten and alphanumeric symbols.

The housekeeper's report is a composite report. It is a summary of reports coming from the floor housekeepers. Each sleeping floor is serviced by one or more floor housekeepers, who report room status to the linen room. The linen-room staff merges the floor reports (see Exhibit 16) to complete the final report.

Discrepancies between the housekeeper's report and the desk are usually resolved by emailing and telephoning between the two locations. When differences still remain, someone is dispatched to look at the room. A bellperson, or a security officer, might be sent. Or a more senior management type: The housekeeper, the assistant manager, or the chief of security might "take a look." Credit managers are especially interested in light luggage reports and skippers.

Several recent lawsuits have highlighted the need to investigate Do Not Disturb signs. Guests who leave DND signs on the door must be checked before the day is out. An alert is warranted if the floor housekeeper notes a DND on both the morning and afternoon reports. It is

Baggage: no occupant (sleep-out)	B
Check out: room on change	c/o
Cot	C
Do not disturb	DND
Double-locked room	DL
Early arrival	EA
No service wanted (Do not disturb)	NS
Occupied	√
Occupied, but dirty	OD
Occupied, with light baggage or no baggage	X
OK	ok
Out of order	O (also OOO)
Out of inventory	OOI
Permanent guest	P
Ready for sale	/
Refused service	RS
Stay-over	s/o
Stay-over, no service	SNS
Vacant	V (also no symbol at all)
Vacant and dirty (on change)	VD

EXHIBIT 15   To speed communication, a series of widely accepted alphanumeric symbols have taken hold throughout the hotel industry. They're used especially in housekeeping reports. They still hold sway despite the spread of electronic communication. (See also Exhibit 16.)

Floor Report

Floor # 16

01	V	28	RS
02	V	29	✓
03	✓	30	✓
04	✓	31	OOO
05	B	32	V
06	✓	33	X
07	✓	34	C
08	V	35	✓
09	V	36	✓
10	DND	37	✓
27	✓	54	✓

Code:
V = Vacant	RS = Refuse Service
B = Baggage	DND = Do Not Disturb
X = No Baggage	C = Cot
✓ = Occupied	EA = Early Arrival

EXHIBIT 16 It's critical that floor housekeepers keep the linen room and the front desk apprised of room status. That's done electronically throughout the day. At day's end, each housekeeper reports a floor summary such as this one to the linen room. Consolidated, these individual floor reports are combined into a daily Housekeeper's Report to the Desk. Electronic capability enables the report to be filed twice a day. In some hotels, the desk files its own report back to the housekeeper.

one fact if the guest forgot to remove the notice and something different if the guest is in distress, unable to remove the sign. Wise hoteliers telephone the room to verify the condition of the occupant. If no one answers, the room is entered, always by more than one person. Recording the circumstances in the front-desk log is an extra, prudent step.

The second report of the day is the chief means of uncovering sleepers, skippers, and whos. *Sleepers* are guests who have actually checked out but are still listed as occupants. *Skippers* are guests who have left without paying. *Whos* are unknown guests; someone is occupying a room but the desk doesn't know who it is.

Originally, the housekeeper's report was sent to the income auditor. Internal control is an issue when one person, the guest-service agent, sells the rooms, handles the payments, and keeps the records. Having another party check the status of the house versus the records of the desk established a degree of internal control. This is still important for small hotels. As front-office staffs grew larger, the housekeeper's report was no longer needed for internal control.

Property management systems have also altered the floor housekeepers approach to reporting occupied rooms. No longer do they bang on guest-room doors early in the morning. PMSs now prepare a *reverse housekeeper's report*, also called a *room occupancy status report*. It is one of the many night-audit reports listed previously. The linen room gets the report early the following morning. Now, the housekeeper knows the room count and the configuration of the floors before the day's work begins. Work schedules are refined before the crew arrives. Extra housekeepers are called in, or days off are scheduled for full-time staff. Assigning jobs earlier means the arriving staff gets right to work.

Summary

This chapter accomplished two tasks, two linkages. It looked rearward by auditing the accounting records (folios) and their dispositions—cash or credit. In so doing, this chapter closes the

hotel's day ending the sequence from reservations to arrival, from residency to departure, and from payment to audit.

PMS that was first conceived as equipment for the front office has grown to be an amazing tool for all of hotel management. That introduces the technological changes.

All businesses reconcile their accounts receivable, but only hotels do it nightly. They close the business day by means of the night audit. Guest folios (accounts receivable) are balanced and reconciled to accommodate the comings and goings of hotel guests at all hours. Their folios must be current and accurate on demand. That is the primary job of the night audit. Since most hotel sales are recorded on folios—guests charge purchases to their rooms—reconciling the folios enables the night auditor to report the bulk of the day's income. That is the second aim of the night audit. With so much data gathered, the third purpose evolves almost automatically: Present the information in reports that help management do its job.

Uncovering clerical mistakes made by the desk throughout the day, getting accurate folios, was the original focus of the night audit. Its paper-and-pencil procedure (the transcript) dates to the 1920s. A new system appeared in the 1980s, the property management system. As it matured, new capabilities such as point of sale (POS) terminals and call accounting (CA)

systems were added. These electronic upgrades reduced the human errors substantially, almost to none. So at one and the same time, the tedious work of the night audit, such as posting room rates and taxes or transcribing transcript sheets, was reduced and the number of errors minimized.

The chapter retains these outdated procedures as a means of explaining what takes place within the heart of the computerized audit. PMS and hand-posted records have the same goals. With tedious hand-prepared audits, balancing the folio was the main thrust. With PMSs, the emphasis changes, but the almost automatic repair of folio errors is not visible. Readers can see a pencil-and-paper folio, voucher, and transcript that make the records. They can see only the output, the results, of a PMS audit, a printout. Readers who follow the pencil-and-paper explanations of the chapter will better understand the modern PMS audit.

The PMS has jumped ahead. No longer is it a tool of the audit only. Rather than a piece of equipment for the front desk, the hotel's computer is now the heart of its operation, as Exhibit 6 illustrates. New capabilities have appeared, and many more are yet to come.

Resources and Challenges

RESOURCES

Web Assignment

List three accessories (supporting programs) that you might add to your property management system. Identify the programs and the suppliers by searching the Web under property management systems and note whether the items selected are innovations or old standbys.

Interesting Tidbits

- There are numerous job openings for night auditors. Poor working hours that are not offset by high enough wages impair the search. Websites and newspaper advertisement advertise salaries of between $10 and $20 per hour with $12–$15 a typical offer. A composite advertisement might read:

  "Audit and reconcile all revenue flows by checking figures, postings and documents. Prepare, maintain and distribute statistical, financial and accounting reports. Check figures, postings and documents for accuracy. Maintain confidentiality of proprietary information. Protect privacy and assets of the company its guests and staff members. Record, store, access and/or analyze computerized financial information. Control and secure cash and cash equivalents. Organize and maintain files and records. Audit and reconcile all revenue postings. Act as receptionist and night manager with particular attention to courtesy, security and safety of guests and of hotel property."

- Installing a PMS was a great uncertainty when the MGM Grand Hotel (now Bally's) opened in Las Vegas in 1973. So uncertain was management of the PMS's capability (ten years before their general availability) that a dozen NCR 4200 machines were purchased as backup. They were never used. Electronic locking systems were untested and, therefore, also rejected by the hotel. Soon after the opening, both systems were in place.

Challenges

True/False

Questions that are partially false should be marked false (F).

_____ 1. An acute shortage of night auditors has come about since the industry's trade association, the AH&LA, has required auditors to have the equivalent (but not the actual qualifications) of a CPA.

_____ 2. The night audit reconciles the cash sales made by each department with the actual cash turned in by departmental cashiers.

_____ 3. The closing balance of one day's inventory is the opening balance of the following day with only a few, rare exceptions.

_____ 4. A hotel's closeout hour depends upon its location; different municipalities mandate different closing times.

_____ 5. Across the lodging industry, the transcript has replaced the room count sheet as the major format for completing the night audit.

Problems

1. Explain how the three backup reports discussed in the section "Downtime Reports" would be used in the event of a computer malfunction.

2. A guest checks in at 4:30 AM on Tuesday, January 8. Under hotel policy, the guest is to be charged for the room-night of Monday, January 7. The closeout hour of Monday, January 7, was 12:30 AM, January 8, and the room charge postings were handled automatically by the PMS at approximately 3 AM on that morning. The room rate is $72 and the tax is 5%; no other charges were incurred. Sketch a computer-prepared folio as it would appear when the guest departs on Wednesday, January 9, at 10 AM. Identify each posting by day and hour and briefly explain who made which posting.

3. **Given**

Rooms occupied	440
Rooms vacant	160
Total rooms sales	$32,330
House count	500

Required

The percentage of occupancy	_____
The percentage of double occupancy	_____
ADR	_____
RevPar	_____

4. Use Exhibits 3 and 12, and identify your answers by room numbers.
   a. Which guests, if any, arrived today?
   b. Which guests, if any, had advanced deposits?
   c. Which guests, if any, checked out today?
   d. Which guests, if any, used credit cards at departure?
   e. Which guests, if any, had amounts due from the hotel?

5. The discussion on Reservation Reports cites a central reservation report that includes fees. Explain who pays what fees and to whom. About how much might those fees be?

6. Is this transcript in balance? If not, what error or errors might account for the discrepancy? What percentage of sales tax is being charged in this community?

Allowances	$ 100.00
Telephone	670.70
Transfers to	395.05
Rooms	9,072.00
Cash advance	444.25
Debit transfer	395.50
Beverage	1,920.00
Credit-card charges	14,482.07
Cash	10,071.22
Closing balance	3,670.41
Opening balance	48,341.50
Rooms tax	725.76
Food	3,000.10
Closing balance	43,007.33
Opening balance	185.00
Total charges	$64,384.81

AN INCIDENT IN HOTEL MANAGEMENT
When a Body Meets a Body

What a day! A traveling couple has stopped overnight at this airport hotel to break up 27 hours of travel from almost around the world. It is already late, almost 11:00 PM, when they finally get to their room.

What's that noise? A party in the room across the hall. After giving the partygoers an additional hour to finish up, the distraught guest calls the desk. No answer after some 10 rings. Every 10 minutes the caller rings the desk because the party has grown louder and louder. No answer. No answer. No answer.

Two hours after arriving, the man pulls on his trousers and goes down to the lobby. The lobby is pitch dark except for emergency lighting. "Wow, something has happened. Oh Gosh! There's a body on the sofa!"

The guest is startled even more than the guest-service agent/night auditor, who jumps up from the sofa and his deep sleep.

Questions

1. Was there a management failure here; if so, what?
2. What is the hotel's immediate response (or action) to the incident?
3. What further, long-run action should management take, if any?

Answers to True/False Quiz

1. False. There are no specific or required qualifications for night auditors.

2. False. The night audit reconciles transaction that involve accounts receivable, not cash.

3. False. There are no exceptions. Inventories counted as one day closes (say, bottles of rye at the bar) are the same count when the next day begins (say, bottles of rye at the bar).

4. False. Municipalities may control the bar's hours of operation, but the hotel's closing day is determined by management based on the closing hours and the amount of activity in the various food and beverage departments.

5. False. Both the transcript and the room count sheet are vestiges of an earlier era and are no longer in use. The property management system is the modern vehicle for the night audit.

Hotel Technology

Thirty years ago, it was easier for hotels to impress their guests, because the hotel room was usually more advanced than the guest's own home. The challenge today is to provide a hotel room which is more technologically sophisticated than guests' homes. And that has grown increasingly difficult in light of the Wii-, PS3-, Xbox-, Netflix-, Hulu-, iPad-, Kindle-, iPhone-, and Droid-generation of today!

State-of-the-art hotels have virtually eliminated the front desk, opting instead for handheld devices. These tablets perform all the functions of a traditional desk without the space constraints. The staff member host can check the guest into the hotel room, swipe the credit card, and even provide a keycard or RFID doorlock program while walking the guest toward the room, or enjoying a coffee in the lobby, or driving toward the property in the hotel's courtesy limo.

The hotel room greets the guest upon arrival by opening the curtains, turning on the lights, and setting the television to a welcome screen. Upon entry, the guest readily programs one-touch settings which manipulate the room to their personal preferences (see Exhibit 1). The guest might program a "good morning" setting, an "evening" setting, or a "bedtime" setting. The bedtime setting, for example, would close the drapes, turn-on the privacy function at both the door lock and telephone, power-off the 50+ inch high-definition television and all lighting (except the one nightlight in the bathroom which this guest prefers to remain on all night long), adjust the HVAC system, and turn-on the radio to a very low volume. Whether or not the privacy setting is in place, the guest doorbell features a housekeeping "silent doorbell" feature which allows housekeeping to scan the room with an infra-red sensor to determine whether or not it is occupied.

Newly built properties are wiring today's hotel rooms with fiber optics that carry at least one gigabit of bandwidth. This allows a fully integrated Internet Protocol property, whereby each room acts as an antenna providing wireless speed across the facility which is at least eight times faster than the best traditional hotel rooms. Enough to play games on-demand, download video, and work seamlessly online. But the property's IP network provides so much more than Wi-Fi; it also accesses better than 3,000 global television channels, thousands of world radio stations, assorted professional tools which integrate to the hotel's business center, electronic concierge assistance, and hotel and local area information. Additionally, the Internet Protocol infrastructure interfaces a number of hotel applications like VoIP telephony; point-of-sale tablets; in-house music; and locking, property management, back-of-house, energy, and fire-safety systems. In the lobby, the guest might find an electronic pad the size of a table-top surface on which to view and share weather, jogging maps, and citywide attractions. Heck, even the hotel's wall art is electronic: able to change themes, artists, and genres at a moment's notice.

TECHNOLOGY IN THE GUEST ROOM: HISTORICAL VIEW

Innkeepers have never been technology leaders. Lodging is so segmented that no one company has had the resources for research and technological innovation. The hotel industry was at the forefront of the credit-card revolution, but was unable to sustain its leadership; it lacked capital. The hotel industry was quick to adopt the computerized advantages of property management systems, but relied on outside industries to make them work; it lacked technical know-how.

Guests are pleasantly surprised to find cutting-edge technology in their hotel rooms, but they shouldn't be. Innkeepers have always marched ahead of their times. Hotels had bathtubs before the White

Room Control

Guest Services

Alarm Clock &
Digital Radio

2-Line
Speakerphone

EXHIBIT 1 Guest-controlled touch panels are the wave of the future. Newly built properties are hard-wiring the hotel room so that one-touch panels can control everything from the curtains to the lights; the television(s) to the locking system; the telephone to the sound system; and the coffee maker to the minibar. Imagine a guest who likes a certain "sleep" setting; he programs the touch panel accordingly (let's say one of his preferences is to dim the light above the bathroom sink) and enjoys a one-touch sleep mode each night of his visit. How much brand loyalty will there be when he visits a different property in the chain and finds that his one-touch sleep mode setting follows him property-to-property through the guest database! *Courtesy of INNCOM International Inc., Niantic, Connecticut.*

House; elevators were first tested in hotels; "tubular connectors" (mail chutes) sped letters down from the upper floors; telephones first appeared in New York City's Netherland Hotel in 1894. Hoteliers have always seized the moment, but they slipped behind over the past decade as the electronic technology revolution crossed the nation's threshold.

A Look Back

Neither the general public nor the lodging industry experienced much change in in-room technology before 1970. Small refrigerators with ice-cube makers were one early innovation. In part, this was a means of reducing labor, as the uniformed services division was responsible for delivering ice to guest rooms. Like other innovations (massage beds and television sets) either an extra charge was made for the room or a coin was needed to activate the equipment.

New telephone systems were introduced early in the decade of the 1970s (see Exhibit 2). Previously, hotels often had but one trunk line (outgoing connection to the telephone company's lines). Long waits for connections, especially for long-distance calls, were not unusual. Although nothing like today's cell phones, the in-room telephone soon became ubiquitous. HOBIC (Hotel Outward Bound Information Center) was a 1980 telephone innovation (see Exhibit 2), which enabled front desks to track calls originating in guest rooms and charge them to folios. That was sweetened in 1981 when it became legal for hotels to add service charges, especially for interstate calls. Telephone profits rose even further after AT&T's telephone monopoly was broken up in 1981. Those decades were the heyday for hotel telephone profits. Today, hotel telephone systems are a cost center, not a revenue center. And one which many experts predict will be all but gone from the hotel room landscape with a decade.

Hotel Guest-room Technology Between 1970 to 2007

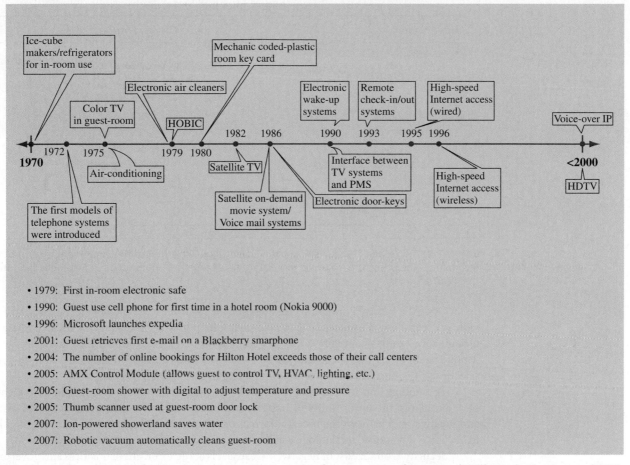

- 1979: First in-room electronic safe
- 1990: Guest use cell phone for first time in a hotel room (Nokia 9000)
- 1996: Microsoft launches expedia
- 2001: Guest retrieves first e-mail on a Blackberry smarphone
- 2004: The number of online bookings for Hilton Hotel exceeds those of their call centers
- 2005: AMX Control Module (allows guest to control TV, HVAC, lighting, etc.)
- 2005: Guest-room shower with digital to adjust temperature and pressure
- 2005: Thumb scanner used at guest-room door lock
- 2007: Ion-powered showerland saves water
- 2007: Robotic vacuum automatically cleans guest-room

EXHIBIT 2 Almost four decades of technological innovations ranging from in-room refrigerators (1970) to robotic vacuums (2007). Since 2007, the rate of innovation has been too rapid to include in this small chart. This chapter describes literally dozens of enhancements which have become standard fare over the past several years.

Color television sets were well established in private homes before the industry introduced them. In 1975, hoteliers intent on differentiating their property from the competition, began installing them in special guests rooms and eventually throughout the property.

Electronic key systems came on the scene in 1986 and with them increased security and convenience. The 1990s brought new ideas. Television sets were interfaced with the hotel's PMS, enabling guests to view their folios. Guests began using the television for speedy check-out and by the mid-decade this had replaced the pencil-and-paper zip-out check-out.

The technology revolution accelerated as the new century began. High-speed Internet access (1995) was widely available. Gaining ground were Voice-over Internet Protocol (VoIP) telephone systems, high-definition TV, wireless Internet access, interactive entertainment systems, and more (see Exhibit 2).

Costs and Benefits

Technology is part of today's culture; so is innkeeping. Technology increases the efficiency of the staff and enhances the experience of the guest. Technology can be overdone, however, and detract from the guest experience (just try holding on through minutes of automated telephone directions before reaching, a live voice, if ever).

At first, hotels were notorious buyers of products that failed to work as promised, or worked but provided no real benefit to the operation. Most of the companies that foisted products on the industry during the 1990s are no longer in business or no longer support the product that they once sold. Only three of the original 12 technology vendors that placed advertisements in the first issue of *Hospitality Upgrade* are still in business. That is a function of the rapid rate of innovation—technology vendors matured as their products matured. Early efforts seemed to focus on buying technology just to buy technology.

The Pluses and Minuses of Hotel Technology	
Advantages	**Disadvantages**
• Accurate information	• Amenity creep
• Better operational controls	• Crashed systems
• Closer fiscal scrutiny	• Ergonomic issues
• Ease of use; minimal training	• Higher-priced employees
• Enhanced guest satisfaction	• Initial investment
• Environmental sustainability	• Maintenance expenses
• Higher guest loyalty	• Periodic upgrades
• Improved labor productivity	• Rapid obsolescence
• Reduced operating costs	• Security losses
• Speedier decision making	
• Tighter fiscal controls	

EXHIBIT 3 Two alphabetized lists: one the advantages attributed to the implementation of hotel technology. The other, the potential disadvantages of hotel technology. The advantages far outweigh the disadvantages.

Once the industry sought technology for the right reasons, the benefits grew. Comfortable with the technology, innkeepers began applying its potential to a range of uses. The Mandarin Oriental, for example, actually tracks its guests' favorite fruits. Computerized guest profiles make it possible to stock the welcoming fruit basket with the guest's preference based on previous selections. It is the kind of "wow" factor that makes for repeat business.

Technology and the systems that it develops offer many tools. Among them, the ability to solve problems; the opportunity to improve profits through an effective utilization of resources; and positive returns from the use of information management. These advantages are highlighted in Exhibit 3. Of course, technology carries costs as well, and Exhibit 3 itemizes these also.

Security is on that list of negatives because it is at the forefront of business and governmental concerns. This places it high on the industry's watch list. One example is wireless Internet. It is a service that hotel guests expect. But private conversations are subject to security breaches. Guest credit-card information carries a similar risk. Hotel IT managers must assess these risks and implement steps to protect the hotel. Either a wireless security protocol such as Wi-Fi protected access (WPA) must be installed, or at a minimum, guests must be asked to sign a disclaimer at registration.

Ergonomics, the study of the relation between machines and humans, is another worry linked to increased technology. For the lodging industry, it focuses primarily on the employee who may be exposed to eight hours of poorly designed office facilities, or even worse, radiation from computer monitors. Management must attend to both issues, lest the potential for expensive litigation.

Cost plays a role in technology, as it does with every management decision. The relative price of technology has been in a downward spiral for many years, but new products come into the market at high initial cost. The operation may need to invest today even though the cost will be lower in the future. Waiting may be too late. Systems must be updated and maintained if they are to contribute to the bottom line. With technology, the outlay is evident; the gains much less clear. Technology investment is similar to marketing and advertising: Will my investment pay off? It is a management conundrum.

TECHNOLOGY IN THE ROOM: THE NEW GENERATION

This review of the latest technologies in hotel guest rooms will take you across a number of interdependent categories. From locking systems to minibars, energy management to fire alarm systems, each plays an important role in guest satisfaction, attraction, safety, and/or profitability. Some systems are a necessity in the modern hotel (locking systems) others an amenity (televisions which feature 3-d and/or interactive technologies). But whether a necessity or amenity, every system necessarily goes through a cost/benefit analysis. Does it improve the hotel's bottom-line? Does it positively impact guest satisfaction? Will it enhance our competitiveness? Is it legally necessary (as with locking systems, below)?

EXHIBIT 4 Old-fashioned iron keys and mortise locks were used by hotels into the 1960s. They were replaced with brass keys that could be cut on property for economy and convenience. Likewise, traditional locks were eventually designed with a quick replace feature allowing the hotel's maintenance department to pull one lock out and replace it with a different lock. Locks had to be replaced each time a guest failed to return the room key. That's why key inventory control (see Exhibit 4) was so important to guest safety. *Courtesy of Getty Images, Inc.*

Locking Systems

Just as the in-room telephone will eventually disappear in favor of the smartphone, so too have guest-room locking systems evolved from key and mortise locks to electronic, RFID, and biometric locks. A look at these futuristic locking systems is all the more valuable when first starting with a look back through history.

TRADITIONAL MORTISE LOCKS Colonial innkeepers roomed several parties together. Indeed, strangers often slept in the same bed. Keys were not part of an early inn's inventory. Room security and personal space improved when locks and keys were introduced (see Exhibit 4). But maintaining key inventories became a full-time job split between engineering, which made them, and the desk, which inventoried them (see Exhibit 5).

Iron keys had several issues. Made of metal with hanging metal tags, they were very heavy. The weight encouraged guests to return them each time they left the building. This approach is

EXHIBIT 5 Compared to a manual key system, which requires tracking thousands of keys, mechanical locking systems, electronic locking systems (ELSs), and today's audible key technology are easier to manage. Mechanical locking systems (keycards with numerous small holes which match a mechanical lock code) were the first invention, following several highly publicized security lawsuits. Electronic locking systems quickly became the standard in the 1970s and 1980s, and remain the minimum standard for guest safety in today's industry.

still seen in Europe today, where smaller inns request guests to hand over their bulky room keys each time they exit the property.

Brass keys became the standard for several decades from the 1950s through 1970s. Because they were less cumbersome, brass keys disappeared at an alarming rate. Way back in 1980, when a dollar had real value, Holiday Inn reported key replacement reached $1 million annually. And since the hotel had several keys already cut and waiting in inventory for a given room, when one key was not returned by the guest, hotels were reluctant to change the door locks. Thieves knew this, and readily burglarized rooms with found keys.

The American Hotel Association, forerunner of the American Hotel & Lodging Association, convinced postal authorities to accept keys in the mail and return them to the individual hotel, which would pay postage due. That information was printed on the key tag. When such keys fell into unauthorized hands, it wasn't difficult to figure out to which hotel room the key belonged.

Something needed to be done. Plastic tags was the first modification (see Exhibit 5). Though there were a number of variations, plastic tags all worked around one main premise. Keys followed the lock, not the room. When a room was rekeyed, the plastic tags would be quickly changed and the previous keys, retagged, now worked the lock in the new room. This provided substantial key savings to hotels.

MECHANICAL LOCKING SYSTEMS In the early 1980s, plastic keys (not plastic tags) encoded with punched holes forever changed guest lock security (see Exhibit 6). Locks were now available which allowed a series of keys to be produced in an established hierarchy. The first key in the hierarchy opened the lock for as long as it was used—possibly through a succession of guests. But when that key was eventually kept by a guest and not returned to the hotel, the next key in the hierarchy would be handed out. At this time, the lock accepted the new key in the hierarchy and was designed to reject the previous key(s) in the hierarchy. In other words, the design of the lock establishes which keys will open the door (this key and anything higher in the order); previous keys are rejected by the lock.

Not only did guests like these keys because plastic was lighter and easier to carry, especially to the beach or the pool, but hotels favored them since they carried no hotel identification. They were inexpensive enough that the hotel did not worry about the costs of unreturned keys. Room numbers were still required for the convenience of the guest and because keys returned to the desk were recycled for the next occupant of that room. They were also popular with hotel lawyers because they exceeded the standard of care previously provided through the traditional brass key and mortise locks.

The best thing about the key code hierarchy is that it allows a number of parallel levels to operate in conjunction with each other. So, even as the guest continues to use the assigned

EXHIBIT 6 An example of the first type of keycard available to hotels. Rather than an encoded magnetic stripe (as with electronic locking systems), these mechanical locking system keycards were encoded with punched holes. In terms of hierarchical locking systems—whereby the next card used invalidates all previous cards used—these keycards represent the first generation. Even so, many of the benefits associated with today's most sophisticated electronic locking systems were still available to hotels using these keycards in the early 1980s. Many hotels still utilize these systems. *Courtesy of VingCard Elsafe, an ASSA ABLOY company, Connecticut, U.S.A., and Stockholm, Sweden.*

key during a several-day stay, housekeeping can enter the room without disrupting the guest's key code. In fact, mechanical locking systems and electronic locking systems (discussed below) carry a number of parallel level hierarchies. From the lowest level, these usually include guest hierarchy, a guest failsafe hierarchy, housekeeping, hotel security, and hotel management. Even the deadbolt will open when keys are deployed from the highest two levels—allowing access to a room where a sick or injured guest may be unable to unlock the deadbolt from within.

ELECTRONIC LOCKING SYSTEMS (ELS)   The electronic lock became the third generation of locking systems. About 85% of all U.S. hotels now use one of the two versions of electronic locking systems: hard wired or microprocessor based.

Hard-Wired Systems   Hard-wired electronic locking systems are ideal for properties designed from the ground-up. They provide the highest levels of security and the most flexibility for adaptation to other in-room systems being developed in this age of technology. But hard-wired systems are extremely expensive to retrofit, because virtually every door lock across the property is physically wired to a central master console at the front desk. That is why they make the most sense for new construction.

The guest-service agent programs a new key (usually a set of two keys) for each arrival and transmits that code to the room door through the hard-wired installation. By the time the guest reaches the assigned room, the key lock has the new code and accepts the guest's key. Key codes issued to previous guests are invalidated simultaneously.

Microprocessor-Based Systems   Microprocessor-based systems are ideal for retrofit hotels because they function as stand-alone installations. The door lock is actually a miniature computer or "microprocessor." Microprocessor-based ELS's come in two forms: one-way or two-way communications.

One-way communication systems   These utilize an ELS console which functions as an electronic key encoder. This console is not very large—about the size of a shoe box—and sits at the hotel front desk. The console encodes a sophisticated lock combination on new guest keys at the time of guest registration. Minutes later, when the key is inserted into the guest-room door-lock (see Exhibit 7), the one-way communication is complete; the door lock accepts the new

EXHIBIT 7   There are dozens of electronic locking system vendors available to the hotel industry. Here are two examples. The one on the left is Onity's brass-plated micro-processor-based ELS. The one on the right is ILCO's Solitaire 710-11.   *Courtesy of Onity, A UTC Fire & Security Company, Duluth, Georgia. And courtesy of Kaba Lodging Systems, ILCO, Montreal, Canada.*

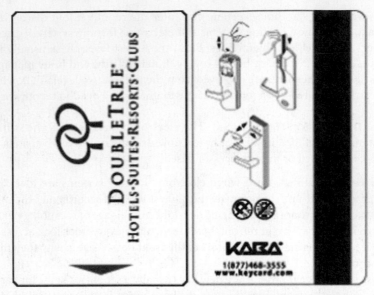

EXHIBIT 8 A keycard with operating instructions for the three types of locks available through this vendor. Notice the front of the key carries a DoubleTree logo. Hotel chains have experimented with all kinds of graphics; calendars, local area maps, etc. in an attempt to give the keycard a second life with the guest after check-out. It is the same logic hotels use with amenities (e.g., shampoo bottles) so guests hold on to them, re use them, and hopefully generate a bit of brand loyalty. *Courtesy of Kaba Lodging Systems, ILCO, Montreal, Canada.*

combination and automatically cancels any previous codes. This is very similar to the keycode hierarchy discussed above under mechanical locking systems.

ELS's featuring one-way communication systems offer several advantages over mechanical locking systems. Each is unique; every guest gets a new key (as many as they need). The keys are light weight; with a magnetic stripe that is generally not affected by water, sun, or sand; inexpensive (about 10 cents per key); and recyclable. Keys that are returned can be reprogrammed for another room and another guest (see Exhibit 8).

The door lock contains a battery-powered microprocessor (see Exhibit 9) and a card reader. And stored in the microprocessor is information related to previous users who accessed the room. Storing at least a few dozen of the last entries into the room, some ELS microprocessors store substantially more information than that. As guests and staff members enter the room (say the bellperson, housekeeping, or a security officer), they leave an auditable trail which can be downloaded from the lock using a special "interrogator" device available to hotel management (see Exhibit 10). In the case of burglarized rooms or any number of other reasons, the hotel

EXHIBIT 9 Electronic locking systems are either hard wired or microprocessor based. Hard-wired systems rely on electricity to operate (though they have a battery back-up for continuous operation during power outages). Microprocessor-based systems are retro-fitted and cannot use in-house electricity. They depend on a long-life battery to be a practical installation. *Courtesy of Kaba Lodging Systems, ILCO, Montreal, Canada.*

Guest Cards

Check-in:
Issue card to guest with relevant information.

Parking:
Access to parking facilities.

(Elevator) access:
Access to specified areas only.

Enter room:
Lock verifies that keycard has correct information (room #, unique hotel code, time frame etc.).

Payment:
Use keycard to pay for services at hotel (restaurant, souvenir shop etc.).

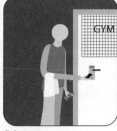

Other areas:
Guests have access to conference room, gym, etc., with keycard.

Lost keycard:
Hotel issues new keycard.

Enter room w/new keycard:
New keycard replaces previous guest keycard in lock.

Check-out:
Hotel system reports what to bill (restaurant, etc.). Guest leaves and keycard is cancelled for access upon departure.

Staff operations

Issue keycard to employee:
Employee gets individual keycard.

Access:
Only access to specified areas.

Locklink/program lock:
Upload software and data to lock (room #, unique hotel code, set clock).

Housekeeping:
Not able to access room if privacy function is turned on by guest.

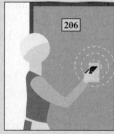

Low battery:
When low battery, employees will get 3 yellow flashes.

Lock link/read events:
Download lock events.

EXHIBIT 10 The advantages of two-way communication systems, whether hard wired or wireless, are highlighted here. Both guests and staff access various areas and services throughout the hotel. Security is increased, customer service enhanced, and an audit trail provided. *Courtesy of VingCard Elsafe, an ASSA ABLOY company, Connecticut, U.S.A., and Stockholm, Sweden.*

can know who entered, at what time the entry occurred, and even when the next time the door was opened from within (as when someone later exits the room).

One-way communication systems have disadvantages, as their name implies. There is no security alert if the wrong key is inserted in the lock. It also takes a trek to the desk for a new key if the party changes rooms. Their chief limitation is the "one-way" flow of information, as the following section on two-way communications explains.

Two-way communication systems   Two-way communication represents the next step in the evolution of electronic locking systems. Consequently, they are more expensive to install. With two-way systems, a central database communicates to each lock through either a hard-wired system or a wireless one. A major advantage of the two-way system is two-way programming—the guest key can open various locks throughout the hotel (this is not true with one-way communication). Guest-room keys can access the parking garage, the fitness room, the pool, the elevator, and the concierge floor (see Exhibit 10).

Similarly, floor housekeepers who are assigned to different stations can gain access remotely to both areas of the hotel. Once a two-way system is in place, interfaces can be installed with the property management system and the point-of-sale system,

KEY CARDS   Key cards are an essential element of every mechanical and electronic locking system. But even here, there are variations. Magnetic stripe cards (see Exhibit 6) are the most common of the four types.

Magnetic Stripe Cards   These cards contain three stripes or tracks embedded into the one ABA magnetic strip. Hotels use the first track to encode the ELS. In addition to the lock access codes, key cards also carry an expiration date. Most keys automatically stop accessing the room at 2 PM on the date of departure. Cards can also be created for one-time access, as when the bellperson escorts the guest to view a room before he or she decides to stay. Magnetic stripe cards can be encoded further to facilitate charges in dining rooms, lounges, and retail outlets. Personal information such as the guest's credit-card number is not on the key cards, although rumors abound that it is.

Memory Cards   As their name suggests, memory chips store data such as lock-access codes and other information. The smallest card stores about 2 kilobytes (Kbs) of data, enough to store 25 different key lock codes. Memory goes up from there: 8 Kbs can carry 125 different key lock codes; 64 Kbs as many as 1,350 key lock codes. Memory cards well serve staff members and managers who need access to multiple locks,.and hotels have locks everywhere. A memory card costs between $2 and $4 each, in contrast to 10¢ for a stripe card.

Smart Cards   Smart cards, chip cards, or integrated-circuit cards are any pocket-sized card with embedded, integrated circuits. They are capable of processing information. Smart cards store more information than memory cards. Because they also process data, smart cards can serve as an electronic purse or personal identification (ID). Their cost is upward of $10 each.

RFID Cards   Radio frequency ID (identification) is the fourth class of cards and the last of the group. We examine them next.

Radio Frequency Identification (RFID)

Identification using radio frequency is a recent innovation which appears perfectly suited to the hospitality industry. RFID technology stores and remotely retrieves data from devices called RFID tags or transponders. With RFID locking systems, the transponders or tags function as the room keys.

Because each transponder has a unique code, hotels have been experimenting with providing permanent tags to their frequent guests. Frequently they mail these RFID tags, but however they receive them, guests are encouraged to hold on to their RFID tag for each subsequent visit to the chain. This provides a major step in guest service, because it allows the frequent traveler direct access to the guest room while bypassing the front desk check-in process.

RFID-capable guests receive a text message upon arrival at the property. The message tells the guest which room number has been downloaded with the RFID code. The loyal customer walks right past the crowded front desk!

RFID LOCKS   RFID locks are known as "contactless" locking systems, because there is no need to slide a keycard into a slot (see Exhibit 11). Rather, the RFID lock only needs the transponder to be in close proximity to the lock. Many front desks instruct guests to tap the tag against the lock. But a nearby wave is really all it takes. Although the tag can look like a plastic keycard, it is more fun to make it into a key fob, wristband, necklace, or any number of creative ideas.

EXHIBIT 11 A radio frequency identification (RFID) lock contains no keycard slot. Access is made over radio waves with the encrypted code carried on a tag or transponder. Close proximity to the lock is all it takes for the door to open. Guest satisfaction has been extremely high in those properties which have converted from an ELS to an RFID system. No more demagnetized keys requiring the guest to trek all the way back to the desk! *Courtesy of Kaba Lodging Systems, SAFLOK, Troy, Michigan.*

A careful look at Exhibit 11 shows why RFID locks are quickly gaining popularity. There is no keycard slot and no keyhole. That provides the guest a number of advantages:

- No need to fumble for the lock opening in a dimly lit corridor
- Ease of access for the handicapped
- Less maintenance because dirt doesn't clog the aperture
- Less sensitivity to humidity, freezing temperatures (for motel rooms with outside access), and salty sea air.
- No more complaints about keycards failing to work at the guest-room door (such an inconvenience)
- No problems with keycard codes being erased when kept in the same pocket as the guests' cell phone
- "Open Sesame," even with hands full of suitcases or packages

OTHER RFID USES The RFID transponder has a number of other uses in the hospitality industry. It can identify where a guest has been (and when) across the hotel facility. This is especially handy with conventions, seminars, and conferences. For example, imagine a guest who is attending a medical training seminar. In order to receive continuous education points, the guest needs attend at least 7 hours of the 8-hour training. RFID would provide that information, tracking each time the guest left the seminar room and again when he returned to the training session. If a hotel wanted to promote a particular restaurant or lounge, it could market directly to those RFID guests who had entered the lounge over the previous 60 days. A trade show booth might want to send promotional materials to any RFID attendee who walked past the booth and lingered longer than 15 seconds. The potential for creative ideas using RFID technology is endless!

Biometric Locking Systems

The first generation of biometric ELSs was launched by Saflok in 2004. Saflok was one of the earliest companies to work in biometrics. Arriving guests register their fingerprints or iris scans during the registration process. The front desk forwards the information to the lock. And the guest enters without delay when he or she reaches the room. Similar to all two-way communication systems, access is easily made to other locks across the property: the pool, concierge floor, and so on.

In 2006, IBM introduced a biometric locking system that scanned the user's iris. *Guestroom 2010* featured IBM's system in an exhibition sponsored by the Association of Hospitality Financial and Technology Professionals. This organization was predicting success with biometric systems in just four short years.

The science might be in place, but its guest acceptance is not. Guests do not feel comfortable giving up sensitive information such as fingerprints and iris scans. Aversion grew greater after it was learned that even CIA and FBI files have been hacked. Replacing a key card is one thing; retrieving hacked iris IDs is something else entirely. Guests also do not feel comfortable staring into an iris scanner as other guests watch them enter their room or access the pool. Even as the extreme cost of such technology decreases with time, it may prove a hard sell for guests to accept biometric devices. Still, Boston-based Nine Zero Hotel uses an iris scanner to monitor access to its Cloud Nine suite.

Smartphone Applications

In 2011, the number of smartphone users in America finally equaled the number of mobile phone users, about 140 million for each category. Another way to look at this statistic is to understand that 91% of Americans carry some form of cell phone. And half of these are smartphones. No wonder the number of smartphone apps specific to the hospitality industry have been growing so rapidly.

GUEST-ROOM LOCK APPLICATIONS   Although RFID-capable locking systems have grown in popularity, it may be short-lived. Many lodging brands believe smartphones provide a better answer for tech-savvy travelers. You see, the service bottleneck for travelers—especially corporate guests—has always been the key hand-off, which is accomplished through the front-desk check-in. The RFID transponder (described above) has the potential to save the guest a major step in the check-in process by providing a key substitute through the mail, which becomes the guest's dedicated key. Yet critics suggest this only works in a perfect world. In a perfect world, the guest remembers to bring the transponder and has it readily available for access to the guest room. But those guests who leave the transponder at home, forget it in their car, or realize that it is buried in their luggage (and therefore can't place it in close proximity to the door lock)—those guests do not exist in the perfect world. The smartphone answers all of these issues. No longer does the industry need to burden its guests with additional items (keys, for example). The smartphone, which is practically attached to the ear of so many current travelers, provides access to the guest room. Once the guest downloads the free application (app) for the lodging brand, it is a simple matter to call up the confirmation for this particular reservation. With the confirmation displayed on the phone, a remote check-in completed, and a room number assigned, the guest needs to merely point the phone toward the door lock.

OTHER HOSPITALITY INDUSTRY SMARTPHONE APPLICATIONS   The airline industry has developed a seamless system: make an online reservation, print your boarding pass or arrive at the airport and print it at a self-serve kiosk, walk past airport security, and then turn over your printed boarding pass as you enter the plane. Seamless, with one small hitch—why make the customer print, retain, and hand over a boarding pass? The smartphone has proven to be even more seamless, because it hosts a unique barcode which was emailed to the phone after the reservation was booked. Pass the smartphone (barcode) in front of the scanner and enter the plane, easy as pie.

Other Airline Conveniences   The smartphone is as versatile as the Internet. Want to check the seat configuration on the airplane you are about to board? Use your smartphone. Want to reschedule your flight to a more convenient time? Use your smartphone. Want to receive delayed flight notices? Use your smartphone. Want access to special fares reserved *only* for smartphone users? Use your smartphone!

Hotel Check-In   Some chains are already boasting that 25% of their guests check in via smartphone. A simple email from the hotel to the user's phone the morning of arrival invites the soon-to-be guest to use a remote check-in app. The benefits are substantial. As more guests choose this smartphone remote check-in option, less guests wait in line, less employees are needed at the front desk, and better are the levels of service that can be provided to both types of guests.

Upselling and Suggestive Selling Even as reduced staffing has tremendous advantages to the bottomline, there are other benefits which accrue from smartphone check-in. Upselling is one such benefit. In a traditional face-to-face check-in, upselling is only as good as the employee training and willingness to attempt an upsell. Many employees are timid in this regard and either ignore the opportunity to upsell or, when they do try an upsell, quickly cease their attempt at the guest's first—"no thanks." The smartphone app is far less shy. With a top-down approach, the smartphone offers the guest the best room category (read: most expensive), requiring the guest to actively turn down the room choice option. Then, of course, the next category is offered. And so on, until the guest eventually makes the room choice. Research demonstrates great success with upselling via smartphone apps.

Additionally, chains are loading room service menus, spa services, and dining room reservations as follow-up apps to the guest check-in. These supplemental sales have been hitting record levels in recent months. There is something almost sci-fi like in being able to order— a steak cooked to your specifications, delivered according to your travel schedule, complete with a glass of wine and salad—before you even take off for your destination city!

Tap to Pay A number of vendors (Google, Visa, MasterCard, and Citibank, to name a few) have developed "single-tap" or "wave and pay" payment solutions. More secure than credit or debit cards, the smartphone becomes the vehicle for payment at the front desk, restaurants, or any number of various outlets across the property. While it is not uncommon to hear a guest exclaim, "I left my wallet (credit card, cash, debit card) in the room," guests are never far from their smartphones. That is what makes this system so attractive—the incredible convenience of having all systems work through one device. For a quick coffee at the snack bar, a single tap or wave might be all the operation requires. When closing a guest folio for potentially thousands of dollars, a signature on the screen is still recommended.

Single-tap systems don't really require the "tap" to process a transaction. Rather, they utilize "near field communication" hardware and software. An NFC chip comes standard in most smartphones, allowing the user to simply wave the phone (no tap actually required) within a few inches of the payment terminal.

The real question will be who is in the driver's seat with regard to smartphone transactions in the coming years. Although Visa and MasterCard have been experimenting with single-tap as well as wave and pay systems, the leaders may end up being the big four smartphone providers: AT&T, T-Mobile, Verizon, and Sprint. But other experts are betting on Google, Apple, and other Internet leaders to become the primary beneficiaries of smartphone transactions through clearing houses like Google Checkout and Apple iTunes.

While some paranoia still exists with users, smartphone transactions are actually safer than carrying a wallet. NFC-eavesdropping technology does exist. Yet it is not as advanced as some people fear, where the would-be thief can simply brush against your smartphone and steal the money in your accounts. NFC eavesdropping devices need to be physically inserted between the wave and the pay. That is unlikely except with a sophisticated inside job and a relatively naïve consumer. Anyway, consumers can simply encrypt their data transmissions for added security. Or they can voluntarily require the payment terminal to ask for a password for transactions above, say $50. The last point should certainly set users at ease; when your wallet is lost or stolen there is little you can do but contact each of your credit card companies and stop their usage. But with a smartphone, you can locate the phone by GPS and/or remotely deactivate the smartphone and/or require a password to access the phone.

Mobile Apps for the Meetings Industry Conventions, conferences, trade shows, and corporate meetings have benefited substantially from smartphone apps. A recent collaboration of key executives identified at least 500 different apps specific to the meetings industry. Many are designed to provide convenience to the user by replacing the conference program (often a bulky multi-paged program that is both a hassle to carry as well as expensive to print) with a smartphone app. Now the attendee can search the day's agenda, identify last-minute room changes, confirm events for which he or she is registered, read personal bios of key speakers, and chat with other attendees. Other features include a searchable list of all conference attendees, access to the conference's social media feeds like Twitter and Facebook, scheduling assistance programs by which to plan your conference day, brief synopses of each of the day's seminars, an interactive map of the exhibit hall, and an area map of local attractions. Maybe the coolest feature for networking during a conference is an app called "Bump," whereby two new friends can exchange contact details and personal information simply by bumping their individual smartphones together!

Proximity-Based Promotion Apps   Although it can be a bit unnerving the first time a smartphone user realizes how smart the phone really is, the advantages are mind-boggling. Proximity-based marketing is founded on the idea that the user—let's say John Smith, an executive in Las Vegas for two days of meetings—is interested in reading promotions specific to where he might be standing at the time. Walking through the lobby of Caesar's Palace, John's smartphone alerts him to a happy hour currently in progress at Payard's Patisserie & Bistro. How convenient, he is literally standing in front of the bistro right that moment. Later, as he walks past the Colosseum (Caesar's event center and showroom), his phone again alerts him; this time there are discounted show tickets available for this evening's show which starts in just 20 minutes. This is the concept behind proximity-based promotions.

While on the subject of casinos, there are a number of new casino gaming applications which are also proximity based. These apps allow the user to bet on sporting events, keno games, and a number of similar options provided he or she is ... you guessed it, within a certain proximity to the casino floor!

Energy Management and Climate Control Systems

After labor, energy is the industry's second largest operating expense, as it is for the nation's airline industry. According to the Environmental Protection Agency (EPA), the lodging industry spends nearly $5 billion annually on energy. And costs are rising. Energy usage in the guest room consumes 40–80% of the total utility expenditure, depending on the size, type, and class of hotel. The guest-room contribution to total energy usage is lower in those hotels which boast large public areas (spas, casinos, meeting space, etc.).

Utility usage spans a number of delivery formats, each with their own unique cost structures. Hotels use water, hot and cold, across the property in both the guest room as well as throughout the facility in such areas as laundry, kitchens, public restrooms, meeting rooms and banquets, landscaping, spa and pools, as well as décor (as in decorative fountains). Electricity, the largest single utility category for a hotel, is used in the guest room as well as all of the areas listed above. Additional sources of electricity usage would also include exterior and interior lighting; signage; all audiovisual uses across the property from the guest-room television to lobby background music; computers at the front desk, executive offices, and point-of-sale locations; fire and security systems; and the list goes on and on. Hotels are also large users of natural gas (less commonly, heating oil or steam systems) which is needed for hot water boilers; in-room and public space heating, ventilation, and air-conditioning systems; kitchen appliances; and other similar uses.

Energy costs vary by the time of day. Utility rates peak just about the time that guests leave their rooms. Signage that prompts guests to turn off the lights, television, and HVAC system when they leave the room has not been effective. Hotels began testing energy management systems (EMS) at the time of the first oil embargo in 1973. Now the industry has moved beyond the testing phase, using one of three approaches: centrally controlled systems, individually controlled systems, or network controlled systems.

Centrally controlled systems have not been well received and are, therefore, not in widespread use. Guests cannot adjust the room temperature. Control of the entire hotel rests with the engineering department. It sets a standard that old guests and young, northern guests and southern, national and international guests must all accept. They don't do so happily.

PTACS   Individually controlled units are commonly referred to as PTACs, or packaged terminal air conditioners. Individually controlled systems have been in place for a long time, because they have been the guests' preference. Guests have the comfort of setting their own in-room temperatures even as hotel management anguishes over controlling utility costs.

PTACs are an especially good fit for the lower- and mid-tiered lodging segments. This is because they have a low up-front cost in terms of initial investment, they require relatively little maintenance, and what maintenance is required is comparatively simple—ideal for the skill-set

EXHIBIT 12 PTACs are typically installed in hotel rooms. And while the manager of the property is concerned with energy efficiency, the typical guest usually is not. Here's the drill. It's a hot summer day and when the guest arrives in the hotel room, just before he throws himself onto the bed, he cranks up the air-conditioning. Then later, when he gets hungry, he heads out to the nearest restaurant. But did he remember to turn off the PTAC before he left?

The maker of this product, Amana, claims a 35% reduction in energy usage when their DigiSmart system is used. The bulk of these savings comes through the occupancy sensor, which shuts down or sets back the PTAC unit when no one is in the room. Additional savings come from setting certain heating and cooling limits on each unit. Establishing preset limits saves both utility costs as well as extends the life of the PTAC units. One unit for one room can cost up to $800.   *Courtesy of Goodman Manufacturing, Houston, Texas.*

found in many hotel engineering departments. When a unit does become inoperable, repairs are often straightforward because key parts are readily replaceable. When eventually a unit can no longer be repaired, the engineering staff merely slides out the old unit from its sheath underneath the guest-room window and replaces it with a new unit.

Newer PTAC installations have several advantages over the older units. They run quieter, control humidity better, and are more energy efficient (see Exhibit 12). They also allow for remote thermostatic control, a major step toward controlling energy usage in the guest room.

NETWORK-CONTROLLED ENERGY MANAGEMENT SYSTEMS   Connecting an in-room thermostat to a motion detector or infra-red sensor is an important first step to developing a network-controlled energy management system. Network-controlled systems strike a balance between centrally controlled and individually controlled systems. Guests control their own comfort even as hotel management is controlling propertywide energy costs. Guests have complete control over the HVAC/PTAC system while they are in the room. The hotel controls the temperature (and lighting, television, and power outlets) when guests leave the room. They do so with in-room sensors that operate across four levels of occupancy: sold, sold and occupied, sold but unoccupied, and unsold. Ceiling sensors electronically communicate the status of the room to the EMS. Three types are commonly in use.

Keycard Control Systems   As the guest enters the room, a wall-mounted unit at the entrance controls all electrical and HVAC systems. Aside from a single light shining inside the entrance to the room, nothing else operates until the guest inserts the keycard (see Exhibit 13).

EXHIBIT 13 A keycard-controlled system places the responsibility for energy conservation on the guest. It is the guest who needs to insert the keycard to turn on the electrical units across the room. It is the guest who, retrieving the keycard prior to exiting the room, actively shuts down guest-room utility usage. Though there are ample problems with keycard-controlled systems, they are inexpensive to install and work better than having no energy management system at all.

Conversely, when the guest exits the room and takes the keycard, everything turns off. A one- or two-minute delay allows the guest ample time to exit. Likewise, HVAC systems do not really shut down completely. Rather, they readjust to an energy savings setting. Shutting down completely would require too much recovery time (and energy) to return the room to a comfortable temperature each time the guest returns. The system recalls the last-entered temperature and operates until that is achieved.

Keycard control systems are the simplest energy control systems. They need no in-room sensors, installation costs are minimal, and energy savings are substantial. The downside with keycard control systems, however, is lack of guest satisfaction. Everything stops operating while guests are gone. They may return to find their cell phone has not charged while they were gone, their coffee pot did not brew, or any number of other electricity-based inconveniences.

Additionally, control is the system's weakness. The wall-mounted unit takes any card with a magnetic stripe. Savvy guests get two cards at check-in or carry one from another hotel and leave the extra in the slot. Then everything runs without disruption, defeating the very purpose of the system. For environmentally sensitive guests, it works well enough.

Motion Detection Systems A motion detection system requires the installation of in-room sensors. Hallway sensors are also commonly used, because the system is often extended beyond the guest rooms. When the ceiling sensor(s) detects no motion, lights, power, and the HVAC/PTAC system are shut down. These are sensitive instruments able to detect motion from adults, children, and pets. The chief disadvantage of motion detection systems is cost. The chief advantage is that the system does not require input (e.g., a keycard) from the guest. The system is on when it detects motion; it is off when no one is in the room.

Motion detection systems are not limited to guest rooms and corridors. They work well in public space such as banquet rooms, restrooms, and even offices. Here, too, nothing is absolute. Lights and temperatures are reduced, but a minimum of both assure safety for anyone passing through.

Like any equipment, the system doesn't work unless it is properly installed. Hidden angles and nooks in the room and bath may convey a nonoccupancy mode, which might shut down the system even when guests are present. Quiet sleepers may also fail to trigger the motion detector and wake surprised because the television they left on is now off. There are anecdotal cases, probably "urban myths," of such quiet sleepers waking hot and sweaty because the entire night passed without once triggering the HVAC.

Infra-Red Heat Detection Systems   Body heat detection systems are similar to motion detectors except they work from body heat generated by guests and pets rather than motion. Infra-red heat detection systems are thought to be more reliable. Although again, there are stories (myths) about guests who pull their bedcovers up so efficiently that they capture all the escaping heat. And, you guessed it, the infra-red heat detection system fails to register anyone occupying the room!

Both types of detection systems can and should be interfaced with the hotel's property management system. In this way, the EMS operates in conjunction with the PMS. The PMS provides the first important piece of information—that is, is the room occupied or not. If the room is unsold, the system will operate only at minimum levels. If the room is sold, energy utilization will be regulated according to the room's immediate status: sold and occupied or sold but unoccupied.

Housekeeping and engineering are the exception. When housekeeping enters a room, no matter what the status (sold or unsold), electrical outlets need to function, lighting needs to turn on, and HVAC systems need to power up. The television, however, will not operate when the room has been accessed by a housekeeping employee. Similarly, engineering maintenance visits, room tours by the sales department, and similar access to unsold rooms need to override the PMS's occupancy status.

"True" Detection Systems   A new dual-detection energy management system was recently developed by *Smart Systems International*. Increased accuracy and reliability are achieved by combining body-heat detection and motion detection systems (see Exhibit 14). The result is a truer, more accurate detection system. An added feature, an adaptive learning system, controls the amount of time needed to return the temperature to the guest's set point once the room is reoccupied. Recovery time is typically set at 12 minutes when the system is installed, but hotels have the option to change the program at any time. Unlike fixed setback thermostats, drifting recovery time around outside weather conditions enhances guest comfort.

EXHIBIT 14   The best of both worlds, a "true" detection system regulates guest-room energy consumption by providing both types of occupancy detection; motion detection as well as body heat detection. Wireless signals are then sent to the in-room energy controller regulating and conserving usage. Dual sensory systems such as this one increase reliability and guest satisfaction, but at a higher per room installation cost than single-sensor systems.   *Courtesy of Smart Systems International, Las Vegas, Nevada.*

EXHIBIT 15 Programmable digital thermostats designed for the lodging industry efficiently manage the guest-room temperature and operating cycles of HVAC and PTAC systems. Because these thermostats are programmable, they provide the hotel management team the ability to tailor usage to the unique operating requirements of their geographical setting.

For occupied rooms, hotel management can establish preset air-conditioning and heat levels designed to conserve utility usage while still providing a degree of guest comfort. Using the up/down buttons, the guest can fine-tune management's preset levels to match their particular comfort requirements. When the room registers unoccupied, the system defaults to a more conservative setting—a bit warmer in the summer or a bit cooler in the winter. Some hotels take an even more aggressive stance a day later; if the room remains unoccupied for the next day (and subsequent days), the system resets the temperature to levels outside of the comfort range to maximize energy savings. *Courtesy of Smart Systems International, Las Vegas, Nevada.*

Digital thermostats are integral to all types of EMSs (see Exhibit 15). Digital thermostats can be hard wired or wireless. They are standard equipment in many homes, so customers recognize them and easily use them to control their guest-room temperature. Because these thermostats are programmable, they provide the management team flexibility in tailoring HVAC usage to the unique operating requirements of the hotel.

For occupied rooms, managers establish preset air-conditioning and heat levels to conserve utility usage. Using the up/down buttons, the guest can fine-tune management's preset levels to match their particular comfort requirements. However, the guest's comfort range has limits—programmable digital thermostats allow management to establish parameters to prevent guests from overcooling or overheating the room.

By the way, all bets are off when the guest props open any of the doors or windows. Either through a hard-wired sensor or a remote sensor, both the front guest-room door as well as sliding glass door(s) and window(s) are linked with the HVAC system. An open door or window automatically turns off the system. No sense in heating or cooling the whole outside! (See Exhibit 16.)

Fire-Safety Systems

A 1946 fire in Atlanta was the nation's worst hotel conflagration until 1980, when an inferno at the MGM Grand in Las Vegas killed 85 and injured 700 persons. Unburned areas that were protected by a sprinkler system contrasted sharply with sections of the hotel which were not. Knowledge gained from the disaster spawned tighter fire regulations for hotels across the

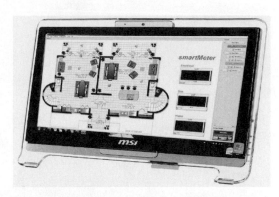

EXHIBIT 16 Here are some examples of products provided by one of the leading hotel energy management companies: Magnum Energy Solutions.

The motion sensor (left photo) is self-powered, using solar or ambient room light, and requires no hard-wiring. Because it requires no wiring, the hotel can place each sensor in its preferred location, providing maximum efficiency. And talk about efficiency, this product supports a "Fresnel" lens which allows the hotel to set various zones of detection. In that way, for example, traffic in the hallway or outside the guest-room windows won't accidentally trigger the parallel or perpendicular motion sensors.

The middle photo shows another wireless product for use at each window or guest-room door. These window contact sensors work in conjunction with the HVAC and/or other electrical units in the room. The sensor(s) sends a signal every 15 minutes updating the occupancy status of the room. When used on windows and sliding glass doors, the device automatically shuts down HVAC systems the moment a window or glass door is opened.

The hotel's energy management system all comes together with an energy management control module (right photo). This system allows the hotel numerous options. For example; management can visualize any single sensor anywhere on property; each sensor can be individually controlled and limits can be re programmed as warranted; timers can be set or any other event can be planned and programmed on an individual, zone, or property wide basis. The system also supports load-shedding, by reducing or shutting down in-room electrical usage during periods of peak demand and therefore peak utility costs. The control module alerts management to HVAC theft (an issue prevalent in the industry). And best of all, it is even controllable from the managers' cell phones or smartphones.   *Courtesy of Magnum Energy Solutions, Hudson, Ohio.*

nation. Several technologies were developed both to help control the spread of a blaze and to communicate the double danger of smoke and fire.

The Hotel and Motel Fire Safety Act was a delayed spinoff of the Las Vegas tragedy. Federal employees on official government business must stay in fire-safe accommodations. For the purpose of the act, every guest room must have no less than an AC-powered (hard-wired) smoke alarm. Installation must be in accordance with the National Fire Protection Association (NFPA) Standard 72. Battery-powered smoke alarms do not meet that criterion. Batteries wear out and guests "borrow" them. An AC-powered alarm with a battery backup is even more desirable, but is not mandated. Under the act, buildings of four stories or more must also have fire-suppression sprinkler systems. In-room sprinkler systems represent a significant safety upgrade. The fire code in Las Vegas was changed so all hotels in that city now have in-room sprinkler systems.

Stand-alone alarms, similar to those used by homeowners, are not adequate for hotels with public space and hundreds of guest rooms. Large areas of hotel buildings are unattended for long periods. Lodging facilities need a networked fire-alarm system. An integrated fire-safety system saves lives, reduces fire damages, lowers insurance premiums, and minimizes costly litigation. Components of such a system include a centralized computer or fire-command console that uses electronic and audiocontrol devices for fire alert, response, and protection.

A good fire system connects smoke detectors (see Exhibit 17) to a central management system by means of a wireless network. Sensing smoke, the detector notifies the closest receiving unit, which transmits the information to the central management system. Taken up a level, the fire system is also interfaced with a paging system. Security is paged and directed to the area or

EXHIBIT 17 Increased safety results when smoke detectors are interfaced to a central fire-control network. The federal Hotel and Motel Fire Safety Act requires these devices to be hard wired, not merely battery operated. *Courtesy of INNCOM International Inc., Niantic, Connecticut.*

specific room to check the status. (False alarms do occur; see the case incident at the end of this chapter.) Well-managed hotels respond with trained fire teams composed of individuals from several departments. The manager on duty also responds and decides whether or not to call the public fire department.

If there is a fire, management needs to determine if the property should be evacuated. When an evacuation is necessary (always erring on the side of safety—when in doubt, evacuate), the well-trained front-desk staff initiates the property's emergency evacuation procedures. The interfaced fire-safety system automatically communicates a calm, prerecorded message to every guest-room telephone.

The message asks the guest to remain calm, but leave the room immediately (grab your room key before leaving). The first stop for the guest is the fire evacuation route posted behind the guest-room door. A quick review of this map establishes the guest's evacuation route and proximity to the nearest exit. The map and the telephone recording both remind the guest not to use elevators. The recording also instructs the guest to feel the hotel room door before opening it. A hot door should never be opened—telephone the front desk immediately, seal the bottom of the door with a wet towel, close the window(s) or leave open a crack if fresh air is needed, turn off all ventilation (HVAC and/or ceiling fans), and fill the bathtub and/or sink with water (water pressure drops when the fire department arrives; a full bathtub becomes a valuable commodity should the guest need to actually battle the fire). Even if the hotel room door is cool, the guest should get low to the floor, brace his or her shoulder against the door and open it slowly—being ready to close it quickly if there are flames on the other side. During the exit, the guest should crawl low in the smoke to the nearest exit; the freshest air is near the floor.

FIRE-SUPPRESSION SPRINKLER SYSTEMS Hotels are equipped with fire-suppression sprinkler systems across the property. There are one or more such sprinklers in every guest room (depending on square footage and room configuration). There are sprinklers in all guest hallways, lobbies, executive offices, convention space, and public spaces. In the event of a fire, sprinklers are the first line of defense, working in conjunction with fire doors, fire walls, and ventilation systems to contain the fire and minimize its impact.

There are numerous types of fire-suppression sprinkler systems, including wet pipe, dry pipe, deluge, preaction, foam, and spray. However, most hotels use either wet or dry pipe systems (the other systems are designed for special applications like factories, hazardous storage facilities, warehouses, museums, etc).

Wet Pipe Systems   Wet pipe sprinklers are the most common systems installed in hotels. They are reliable, simple, and the only operating components are the automatic sprinkler heads and the alarm check valve. A continuous water supply provides water under pressure to the pipes. When an automatic sprinkler head is exposed for a sufficient time to a temperature at or above the temperature rating, the heat sensitive element (a glass bulb or fusible link) releases, allowing water to flow from that sprinkler.

Dry pipe systems are installed in hotels located in cold climates. Otherwise, in the winter, the cold external temperature could freeze the static water in a wet pipe system. There are numerous stories of this type of damage occurring. Flawed or cracked sprinkler systems have the potential to flood hotels in a matter of minutes, costing hundreds of thousands of dollars in water damage, drywall repair, and lost business. It even happens when the would-be bride—seeking something high above the floor on which to hang her wedding dress—finds the fire-suppression sprinkler head. She hangs her dress, inadvertently breaks the sprinkler head, and finds her room (not to mention her gown) soaked in minutes!

Dry Pipe Systems   Dry pipe systems are used in outdoor applications (in parking garages, above the porte cochere, or underneath canopies and awnings) as well as in ceiling installations above the insulation (above the heat source). There is no water present in the "dry" piping until the fire system calls for it. The piping is filled with air, designed to hold back the pressurized water. When one or more of the automatic sprinklers is exposed, for a sufficient time, to a temperature at or above the temperature rating, it opens, allowing the air in the piping to vent from that sprinkler and the water to flow in behind it (see Exhibit 18).

Industry Practices in Case of Fire

Before a Fire:

Management should have all front-office employees:

- Become familiar with the hotel's fire and life safety systems.
- Know where to locate and how to use:
  - Manual pull alarms.
  - Fire extinguishers.
  - Smoke detectors.
  - Fire alarm monitoring service.
  - Exit doors & stairwells.
  - Voice alarm system and/or intercom.
  - Sprinklers.
  - Fire doors.
  - The main water shut-off valve.

At the Time of a Fire:

The front-office employee should:

- Treat every alarm as though it is a real emergency (even if the initial source is unknown).
- Call the Fire Department immediately if the alarm sounds, or a fire is suspected. Never wait to investigate the situation before notifying the Fire Department. Any delay will allow a fire to grow and further endanger the building occupants and property.
- Send two employees with walkie-talkies and flashlights to the alarm's location to investigate whether it is a real fire or not.
- Call 911 and relay information to the Fire Department, if it is determined that there is no fire, but rather a malfunction of fire safety equipment or simply a false alarm.
- Not silence the alarm until given permission to do so by Fire Department personnel or by the emergency operator.
- Not reset the alarm until the Fire Department arrives and has investigated the source of the alarm.
- Remember to provide 911 calls the following information; hotel name, problem being reported, location of the problem, hotel address, nearest cross streets.

EXHIBIT 18   Some good industry practices to follow before and during a fire emergency.

- Retrieve the most up-to-date room status reports and be ready to provide such reports to the Fire Department.
- Contact each guest room (which may be an automatic feature of the interfaced fire-safety system) and keep track of any guest room which does not answer the telephone. Provide this list and master key(s) to the Fire Department.

In Case of Evacuation:

The front-office employee should:

- Be prepared to turn over operations to the hotel's fire director, an individual with sufficient knowledge of the hotel who has been preassigned and trained for this emergency.
- Be prepared to turn over floor responsibilities to floor wardens, preassigned employees who will locate themselves by exit doors on each floor to assist guests as they are exiting their hallways.
- Retrieve the most up-to-date room status reports and be ready to provide such reports to the Fire Department.
- Contact each guest room (which may be an automatic feature of the interfaced fire-safety system) and keep track of any guest room which does not answer the telephone. Provide this list to the Fire Department.
- Provide master key(s) and any assistance as requested by the Fire Department.

EXHIBIT 18   Continued

Minibars

Minibars have changed over time as technology improves and the cost and degree of automation makes new investment worthwhile. Some are still not automated; others are completely automated utilizing microprocessor-based technology. In between are semiautomated models.

The convenience of minibars plays an important role in guest satisfaction, especially in full-service hotels. They must be important because guests willingly pay a handsome premium for the soft drinks, candy, beer, wine, liquor, snacks, and personal items that minibars dispense. The minibar is a good profit center for the hotel. Mindful of guest expectations, some hotels provide (without charge) an empty refrigerator that occupants stock as they prefer. Complimentary bottled water is another step toward exceeding guest expectations.

TRADITIONAL (NONAUTOMATED) MINIBARS   Early versions of the minibar (see Exhibit 19)—and they are still popular—require a daily, manual count by a minibar employee. Minibar operations fall under the guest services department in most hotels, rarely under housekeeping. The minibar employee—armed with a master key and a rooming list—must enter every occupied room, open the refrigerator, and inventory the contents. Each room entry imposes on the guest and the guest's privacy. The minibar employee prepares a voucher for all the items consumed, restocks the minibar

EXHIBIT 19   Earlier versions of minibars—many are still in use—require daily, manual inventories to determine what charges need be posted to the guest's folio. Newer versions are interfaced directly to the property management system, so posting occurs automatically (see Exhibit 20). Even restocking is improved with automated minibars, because the minibar employee can prepare a dedicated bin for each room knowing in advance exactly which products were consumed and removed from inventory.   *Courtesy of Minibar North America, Inc., Bethesda, Maryland.*

back to par, and later delivers the voucher to the front desk so charges can be made to the folio.

To minimize labor costs some hotels tried eliminating the employee, relying on a honor system instead. It was penny wise and pound foolish. Labor was still needed to restock consumed items. Honor remains part of the procedure, nevertheless. The minibar inspector works during the day. Guests return to their rooms and use the minibars at night; they check out the following morning. Guest-service agents/cashiers routinely ask departing guests whether they used any minibar items in the past 24 hours. Some pay up; some do not.

Putting a "seal" on the minibar reduces labor costs. Guests must break the seal in order to retrieve an item. The staff member need only make a quick survey from the door. If the seal is intact, the associate moves on quickly to the next room. If broken, the count and restocking proceed as usual.

SEMIAUTOMATED SYSTEMS   Vendors came up with semiautomated minibars and completely automated ones in response to the several disadvantages of the initial equipment. One innovation built upon the "seal" idea used on the nonautomated equipment. Whenever the minibar door is opened, a door alert is posted to the property management system. Staff members get a report that shows which rooms have used the minibar (or, at least have opened the door to the minibar) and which rooms have not. If there is no activity, the room is skipped. This reduces both labor costs and imposition on guests.

Even this small amount of automation pays for itself quickly. This is because only one in four guests, on average, uses the in-room minibar. Knowing which rooms accessed their minibar and which did not saves dramatically on labor.

MICROPROCESSOR-BASED AUTOMATED SYSTEMS   Automated minibars monitor and process sales transactions electronically. Each tray in the minibar is programmed to inventory a certain item (see Exhibit 20). A weight-sensitive timer or electronic eye tracks whenever a product is removed from its designated space. The timer gives the shopper some 10–60 seconds (the amount of time is programmable to the hotel's wishes) for "inspection time." If the product is returned to its place in sufficient time, the system assumes the guest was curious but ultimately not interested in the purchase. For items which are not returned, a charge is automatically posted to the guest's folio.

Posting is accomplished through an interface between the automated minibar and the property management system. The PMS sends an unlocking signal to the in-room minibar as soon as the guest checks in. Some hotels actually ask guests if they would like to utilize their minibar during their stay. Such a query, though offered in the spirit of guest service, actually reduces spur-of-the moment purchases from hunger cravings, thirst, or forgotten toiletry items, thereby doing the guest a disservice. It is best to just unlock the minibar as a standard operating procedure with every new guest.

EXHIBIT 20   Each item in an automated minibar sits on a pressure-sensitive tray (some systems use an electronic eye). Guests have time to examine the product and return it if unused. Once the time is exhausted, a charge for the product is automatically documented to the guest's PMS folio. A record is maintained and quickly printed out should the guest protest the charges.   *Courtesy of Bartech System International, Millersville, Maryland.*

The automated minibar identifies each item removed for purchase, the time of purchase, the price of the removed item, and its tray location. A quick printout of minibar activity is possible if the guest disputes any charge at check-out. Here is usage for the guest in room 701:

Total Purchases
Minibar

Minibar Bill for Room: 701   **Time: 12:54 Date: Sunday 15 April**

Date	Time	Contents	Price (US $)	Tray Location
13 April	17:32:45	Imported Beer	5.50	Location 11
13 April	18:45:41	Tonic Water	2.50	Location 08
13 April	18:45:50	Beefeater Gin	6.50	Location 07
13 April	19:01:12	Mixed Nuts	7.00	Location 13
14 April	09:02:12	Spa Still Water	2.50	Location 15
14 April	09:03:01	Orange Juice	4.00	Location 17
14 April	16:32:34	Domestic Beer	4.50	Location 10
		Total Purchases	**32.50 (inc tax)**	

Guest checked in 11:25 13 April
**************THIS BILL FOR VERIFICATION PURPOSES ONLY*************

Relocking the minibar is an automatic function of the PMS's check-out procedure. Locking the minibar is performed as part of the same check-out procedure as putting the room on change. One side benefit is that housekeeping employees are no longer able to access the minibar prior to inspection and restocking by the minibar employee. This is another valuable benefit of automated minibars—no more theft loss from housekeeping employees!

Some systems even track expiration dates on products, alerting the department to items which have not sold in 30, 60, or 90 days. The interfaced microprocessor-based minibar system even helps with labor. A daily report of total minibar consumption is one of many reports generated by the PMS during the night audit. Minibar employees use the report to requisition and draw refills for the following day.

REFILL REQUIREMENTS REPORT
Automated Minibar System
Date: 15 April

Refill requirements report for the following rooms/groups/zones:
ALL

Item	Unit
Mixed Nuts	7
Spa Still Water	82
Beefeater Gin	12
Canada Dry Tonic Water	14
Orange Juice	48
Skyy Vodka	25
Coca-Cola (Can)	46
Evian Water (50ml)	76
Seven-Up (Can)	14
Domestic Beer	45
Imported Beer	23
Dorito's Cool Ranch Chips	17
Baked Lay's BBQ	11
Pretzels	3
Toothpaste	3

A refill requirements report, also produced during the previous night's audit, identifies which rooms get which inventory replacements from the total draw listed above. By way of our continuing the example, this refill requirements report shows the first few rooms from the seventh floor (including the guest from room 701, as discussed above). Note the usage of bottled water, still the most popular item sold in minibars. Bottled water sells four times more product than the next closest minibar purchase!

REFILL REQUIREMENTS REPORT
Automated Minibar System
Date: 15 April

Refill requirements report for the following rooms/groups/zones.

ALL

Seventh Floor/Room By Room			
	Quantity	Item	Tray #
Room: 701	1	Mixed Nuts	13
	1	Spa Still Water	15
	1	Beefeater Gin	7
	1	Canada Dry Tonic Water	8
	1	Orange Juice	17
	1	Domestic Beer	10
Room: 702	1	Spa Still Water	15
	4	Coca-Cola (Can)	1
	1	Dorito's Cool Ranch Chips	3
Room: 703	1	Spa Still Water	15
	1	Seven-Up (Can)	2
	1	Pretzels	5
Room: 704 +++	1	Mixed Nuts	13
	1	Evian Water (50ml)	16
	1	Toothpaste	27

Minibars began life as refrigerators. Guests still like to use them as such. They are perfect for storing half a sandwich, a baby's formula, or some medicine. Sometimes space is so tight that an item must be removed to make room for the guest's personal needs. Newer models need to accommodate this secondary use because getting charged for an unused item is irritating, and trying to obtain an offsetting allowance is frustrating and time-consuming.

In-room Safes

State laws require every hotel to maintain a safe or lose the protection of the limited-liability innkeeper statutes that each state has enacted. Large steel safes and safe-deposit boxes behind the desk were the standard until small, personal, in-room safes were introduced in 1979 (see Exhibit 2). Modern and secure, in-room safes need to be large enough to hold the personal electronics and jewelry, including the latest 17-inch monitors, carried by today's corporate (and leisure) travelers.

Initially, most hotels charged a fee for the use of their in-room safes. Purchase contracts were often based on a revenue split between the hotel and the safe provider. Hotels kept all the income after the purchase price (plus interest) was eventually recovered. Most dropped the charge thereafter, offering the in-room safe as another amenity. It was a messy arrangement otherwise; early safes did not interface with the PMS, so there was really no way to track their use or lack of use. So an "in-room safe fee" was charged to every folio during the night audit. Guests complained loudly about the charge, as they do still about "resort fees".

Use of in-room safes reduces theft. Electronic locking systems battle external theft; in-room safes reduce internal losses. Theft by employees (internal theft) is usually an impulsive act caused by temptation. Valuables in the safe remove the temptation. They also undercut the guest's effort at defrauding the hotel. Reduced insurance premiums are another savings. The safe is very heavy, almost impossible to carry, but bolted down nevertheless.

EXHIBIT 21 Located in closets, built into dresser doors, designed as end-tables, or free-standing, electronic safes are an important in-room guest amenity. This closet-located safe is opened by the guest's credit card or any other magnetic stripe card, including guest-room keycard or smart card. *Courtesy of VingCard Elsafe, an ASSA ABLOY company, Connecticut, U.S.A., and Stockholm, Sweden.*

Just as guest-room locks started with mechanical keys, so did in-room safes. Not nearly as heavy as the original door keys, guests signed for and obtained keys to fit the safe lock in their particular room. Lost keys required a locksmith to open the safe and rekey the lock at the guest's expense. Today's electronic safes carry an override feature. Management can override the guest's code or credit-card code if an emergency arises (like a forgotten PIN number). It takes two inputs: an instrument that looks like a cell phone and maintains an override audit trail, and an override security code.

Electronic in-room safes progressed through several steps since their introduction.

CREDIT-CARD ACCESS Many guests like the option of swiping their credit card for access to the safe. Credit cards are more user-friendly than the personal identification number (PIN) option (discussed below) and don't require the guest to memorize a particular code. Additionally, some guests are skeptical about using a PIN number because of exaggerated traveler stories suggesting there are hidden cameras, waxed keypads, or some other way for housekeeping to spy the guests' PIN. The credit card provides the most personal access. However, it means the guest must carry the credit card when leaving the room, even when going to the pool or spa (see Exhibit 21).

PIN-BASED ENTRY Exhibit 22 illustrates the PIN-based in-room safe. Digital safes are more common than lock and key or credit-card access safes. Some feel they are the best option, because

EXHIBIT 22 Digital code-based safes operate on a PIN number that each guest creates. This is the most popular type of in-room electronic safe. A well-designed safe, like this one, provides an easy-to-use override feature. In an emergency, hotel staff readily overrides the guest's PIN or credit-card code with an external processor (looks like a cell phone) and override security code. An audit trail is provided for each override performed, in case the guest should complain of unauthorized access. *Courtesy of VingCard Elsafe, an ASSA ABLOY company, Connecticut, U.S.A. and Stockholm, Sweden.*

EXHIBIT 23 Biometric safes use the same technology as biometric door keys. Neither is yet in widespread use. The reasons are two-fold. Biometrics is an expensive technology, one in which hotels are hesitant to invest. And guests appear to be reluctant to use biometrics because they are generally uncomfortable surrendering such highly personal data. Someday, biometric safes may be the ideal product for hotel in-room security; there is no key, PIN, or magnetic stripe card to lose or forget! *Courtesy of Minibar North America, Inc., Bethesda, Maryland.*

there is no secondary element (the metal key or credit card) to be lost. Each new guest enters a PIN. Although PIN encoding is a common exercise today, one would be surprised how many times hotel management (security or bell department) is called to open an in-room safe because the guest has forgotten the PIN. Safes lock out the guest after some few attempts at entry. So, a guest who is trying to guess his wife's PIN or has simply forgotten which of a series of various PINs he might have used today can easily be locked out of subsequent attempts.

Electronic safes must be easy to use. Directions need to be clearly present on the exterior of the safe. Large keypads are a must. Additionally, the LED display should be clearly legible and designed to display the guest's PIN code for a moment prior to the safe's lock being activated. This ensures the guest can verify the code and has not inadvertently entered a wrong digit. A lack of such simple features means hotel staff will be spending more time assisting guests with entry to their safes than appropriate.

BIOMETRIC SAFES Biometric safes use the same technology as biometric locking systems. Guests register either their fingerprint or their iris scan before using the safe. Biometrics are the most convenient of the systems because there is no key to lose or PIN code to forget. However, not all models accommodate multiple users at this time, so double occupancy poses an issue. The iris or fingerprint of one guest will not trigger the mechanism that was created with the biometrics of the room's companion. Exhibit 23 displays a biometric safe.

COMMUNICATION SYSTEMS

The in-room guest telephone may be one of the great hotel technology failures of the past decade. The dramatic increase in use of personal cell and smartphones, coupled with the ever-decreasing in-room telephone revenues, has led to a dim future for the guest-room telephone. Unlike most technologies, where the cost of purchasing equipment decreases with time, the cost of equipping a hotel room with telephone equipment has seen virtually no decrease over the past twenty years. That is why many industry experts predict the ultimate demise of the in-room guest telephone. This devise will be replaced by in-room one-touch programmable pads as well as by the guest's own mobile phone.

A Brief History of Telephone Service

Between the early 1980s and the late 1990s, the telephone department was a big contributor to the hotel industry's bottom line. Departmental income exceeded 2.5% of total hotel revenues. Telephones were profitable because they were deregulated and automated. But hotel telephone revenues fell victim to technological innovation. Departmental profits now contribute less than 1% of total industry revenue. In many hotels, the telephone department is a cost center more than it is a revenue center. Part of the decline was no fault of the hotel industry, but caused by the introduction of the now ubiquitous cellular phone. Part of the decline was due to the hotel industry's greed—that is, due to the excessive charges hotels levied on in-room telephone use.

To encourage the growth of hotel telephones, the Federal Communications Commission (FCC)—which regulates *inter*state calls, not *intra*state calls (calls within a state)—issued a 1944 ruling. Telephone companies were directed to pay a 15% commission for all calls originating in hotels. Before the installation of direct-dial telephones, hotel operators connected guest callers to the telephone company's operators. After the call was completed, the company's operator would call the hotel operator and quote "time and charges." To those charges, the hotel added its 15% commission and posted the total to the guests' folio.

The introduction of in-room direct-dial guest telephones bypassed the telephone company's operator. Now, guest telephone charges could be routed directly through the call accounting system (CAS). The CAS tracked the calls and the charges and reported them to the front-office cashier by means of a printer located at the front desk. Initially, such charges were posted manually to the guest folios. As progress continued, the CAS was interfaced with the PMS, and telephone calls were automatically charged to guest folios.

For almost 40 years, the hotel industry had to be satisfied with this paltry 15% telephone commission structure. But in 1981, the FCC changed the rules again. This time, the simple 15% commission structure was dropped, allowing each hotel to set its own surcharge. And charge they did! Revenue zoomed. Many hotels began charging 100–500% of their cost to the guest. In other words, a call which cost the hotel, say $5, would show up on the guest's folio at a rate of $10 to $30. Guests became irate.

At first, guests began utilizing payphone booths to avoid the excess surcharges. But even here, management was ahead of its guests because hotels were now legally allowed to own the lobby payphone (and charge whatever long-distance fee they wanted to). Some chains—understanding that telephone profits were not worth risking the reputation of the brand—began offering telephone services with no additional surcharges. That proved popular with corporate travelers, albeit short-lived. The cell phone was not far behind; the first cellular telephone usage by a hotel guest was in 1990 (see Exhibit 2). As the 20th century ended, in-room guest telephone revenue was becoming nonexistent.

Internet Access

Initial introduction of Internet access in hotel rooms followed much the same path as telephone systems. Some hotels charged excessive rates for Internet service in the guest room, hoping to quickly recover investment and make a profit. Other hotels saw guest-room Internet access as an amenity—and like all amenities, there is a cost to the property for providing such a service—a cost which is often not recovered through specific charges, but rather through increased brand loyalty.

Internet access is clearly an important element in the guest's overall satisfaction. Recent travel statistics suggest that more than 75% of corporate travelers carry their laptop when traveling. And 62% of corporate travelers spend at least 25 minutes per day online in the hotel room. These statistics are likely to change as the 45-year-old and under crowd quickly embraces smartphone technology as their preferred source of online access while away from home.

The interesting dichotomy of recent travel is that cheaper hotels (e.g., limited service) usually provide free Internet access, while higher-end (full-service) properties are more likely to charge for such service (see Exhibit 24). But the trend toward free Internet is growing, and has increasingly become one of the complimentary services offered to members of hotel loyalty programs. For those hotels which still do charge for Internet access, the charges for a 24-hour daily rate range from as little as $6.99 to as much as $49.99. One explanation for the rate spread is the type of access.

DIAL-UP ACCESS The first generation of Internet access was dial-up. An in-room connection to the Internet provider was made by means of a computer modem and data port built into the telephone. Speed was poor; transmission was limited to 56 kilobits per second (Kbps). Even today, a few users, especially business travelers, prefer dial-up access because of the heightened security, and willingly trade away speed to get security.

Parent Company	Chains Where Internet Access Is Free-of-Charge	Chains Where Internet Access Is Charged a Fee
Hilton Hotels & Resorts	Hampton Hotels & Suites Hilton Garden Inn Hotels Homewood Suites by Hilton	Conrad Hotels & Resorts Hilton Hotels & Resorts Waldorf Astoria Hotels & Resorts
Hyatt Hotels & Resorts	Andaz Hotels by Hyatt Hyatt Place Hyatt Summerfield Suites	Grand Hyatt Hotels Hyatt Regency Park Hyatt Hotels
Marriott International	Courtyard by Marriott Fairfield Inn & Suites by Marriott Residence Inn by Marriott Springhill Suites by Marriott	JW Marriott Hotels & Resorts Marriott Hotels & Resorts The Ritz-Carlton Hotel Company
Starwood Hotels & Resorts	None	Aloft Element by Westin Four Points by Sheraton Le Meridien Sheraton Hotels & Resorts St. Regis Hotels & Resorts The Luxury Collection W Hotels Westin Hotels & Resorts

EXHIBIT 24 A frustrating dichotomy in the lodging industry; limited service chains are more likely to offer free Internet access than are full-service brands. Here is a brief sampling, in alphabetical order.

HIGH-SPEED HARD-WIRED ACCESS Depending on the type of cable and bandwidth used by the hotel, the speed of the hard-wired Internet connection can vary between 1 Mbps and 1,000 Mbps (a gig per second). The cost outlay for the hotel varies as well, but hard-wired high-speed Internet is costly. Like all hard-wired systems (locking systems, energy management, minibars, etc.) the cost is associated with wiring every room to the main server. For existing construction, wireless is almost always the right choice. For new construction, there are current and future benefits associated with hard-wiring every room.

With wired access, guest rooms are furnished with an Ethernet cable. Guests attach their laptops by means of a network interface card. To minimize the hotel's liability, guests are asked to sign a liability waiver before using the equipment. Most hotels require the waiver, whether the wired access is free or not.

HIGH-SPEED WIRELESS ACCESS Lodging managers prefer wireless access to wired access for two reasons. Guests transact much of their business in public settings, such as lobbies and meeting rooms, where wired access is difficult to install and monitor. And, as discussed above, a wireless Internet installation is much less costly than a hard-wired one. That brings the issue back to security.

Wireless means just that: The data is transmitted through the air. The information can be captured by anyone and used for his or her personal gain. The user-guest as well as the innkeeper knows that, but security fears have not deterred the very rapid growth of wireless access.

The Institute of Electrical and Electronics Engineers (IEEE) has recommended standards for wireless and wired network communications. They are known as 802.11b, 802.11g, and 802.11a. Code 802.11b was one of the first standards for transmitting data up to 11 Mbps. The other two, newer standards, transmit at higher speeds.

TIERED BANDWIDTH The lodging industry has recently begun experimenting with tiered bandwidth options for guests. Like the menu of options high-end properties offer with regard to soaps, pillows, and room categories, Internet access appears to be taking a similar path. For those guests who just want to check their emails, Internet access at lower speeds is available free of charge. But those guests who need real surfing power to stream video, play interactive games, and access rich content would be charged for their access to premium bandwidth.

In early studies, tiered bandwidth seems a most satisfying arrangement for guests. They get what they pay for, or what they choose not to pay for. By the way, it is not uncommon for one guest room to consume more bandwidth today than an entire hotel did just three years ago!

CLOUD COMPUTING Another reason one guest room today can consume more bandwidth than an entire hotel of a few years ago is devices. Yes, that's plural—"devices," because today's guests travel with far more than one single laptop. Increasingly, guests arrive with multiple devices, each with its own particular need to access the network. The old logic suggested that Wi-Fi was the best technology for using a laptop and cellular service was best for voice. Today, both technologies are coupled together and embedded in such devices as laptops, smartphones, tablet PC's, gaming devices, Netbooks, and iPads.

The answer to this multitasking is just beginning to take shape: the cloud. Cloud computing is simple enough; it means that all your data is stored in a hazy cloud which hovers above all your devices. Really, it means that large computer companies (Apple, for one) provide—for fee or free—central servers on which all your data is stored. To the user, this means no device falls behind any other device. Download a movie on your PC but watch it on your Netbook, because each accesses the cloud and remains up to date with all your other devices. This provides a huge convenience for users, a large potential revenue source for computer providers, and an increasingly expensive trend for hoteliers, who will find their bandwidth demand growing faster than ever!

Future of Hotel Telephones

As telephone revenues are falling ever lower, the search is on for new revenue sources. Guests might be enticed back to paying for hotel services through one-price, telecommunications bundling. In their personal homes, guests are already accustomed to bundled rates. Wyndham was among the first to launch the format, testing it within their frequent-guest program. Currently, all *Wyndham By Request*® members get free Internet access and free local and long-distance calls. The Westin at Chicago's O'Hare Airport charges $9.99 for 24-hour Internet access, but also offers a "Telecom Bundle." Its $16 per-day package includes high-speed Internet access, long-distance calls within the United States, local calls, and operator assistance. Other properties are joining in the bundling, because they too are taking advantage of the rapid technical advances of VOIP.

VOICE-OVER-INTERNET PROTOCOL (VOIP) This upgrade is so new that the language has not yet solidified. One hears it called *VoIP, VOIP, IP telephony, Internet telephony, Broadband telephony, Broadband Phone*, and *Voice over Broadband*. Whatever the name, it routes voice conversation over the Internet or through any other IP-based network instead of the analog (twisted-pair-cable) phone lines. Improvements in VoIP have been rapid. Sound quality, which initially was poorer than analog transmission, has quickly reached analog levels.

Hotels need a broadband, high-speed Internet connection if they want to use VoIP in conjunction with their call accounting system (CAS). Hotels within a chain are usually connected by an IP network that supports the chain's data service. Telecommunication costs are drastically reduced if the individual hotel uses that same network for guests' long-distance calls. The property most likely pays a flat, monthly fee to the ISP (Internet service provider) for unlimited use of the network. Therefore, long-distance calls originating in the guest room add virtually no cost to the hotel. In return, the hotel can offer long-distance calls as a free amenity service, or can charge a reasonable price so guests are encouraged to consider this option.

Switching from traditional telephone lines to VoIP is not complicated. The traditional, handset telephone can be reconfigured to the new technology by an analog adaptor, which converts analog signals to digital signals. The cost is minimal, about $50 per handset. This is much less costly than the $500 needed to replace handsets with VoIP digital phones. Technology costs continue to fall, so both figures will likely be lower in short order.

EXHIBIT 25   Telephone equipment that accepts VoIP (Voice-over-Internet Protocol) looks no different from the traditional instrument. Lower fixed costs to the hotel (for equipment) and virtually no variable costs for long-distance calls are driving its spreading use. And ideally, will return the hotel's telephone department to a revenue center as opposed to a cost center.   *Courtesy of Cisco Systems, Inc., San Jose, California.*

VoIP telephones don't look much different than their analog cousins (see Exhibit 25), but they are a world apart. They are the future of hotel telephony. VoIP phones are a service and application delivery system all by themselves. The installation provides digital voice mail; alarm clocks; room service, spa, and golf interfaces; high-speed Internet access; an entry to interactive gaming; guest-room control of lighting, television, and temperature control; a digital hotel guide; and conference-call capability. A list which continues to grow as VoIP becomes more widely accepted.

Emergency 911 Calls   VoIP telephone systems are found to be lacking accurate data with regard to emergency 911 calls. This is because the 911 caller-identification system was developed for traditional landline telephones. Using a computer processor–based VoIP system leaves the 911 operator without knowing from where the call was placed. In some cases, the operator may see the address of the computer (say the hotel's address) but not understand that the call is originating from a hotel and, even if that information is available, not know from which of hundreds of the hotel rooms the call is being made.

The problem is exacerbated with cellular phones and smartphones. These phones draw their transmissions from cell towers. As the cell phone moves, the tower routing the call also shifts. Additionally, during periods of busy cell phone usage, less-busy towers handle cell calls from further distances. As such, in 911 emergencies, the 911 call center receiving the call is not always the closest call center to the guest's physical location.

As technology advances, certain basic infrastructures, like the emergency 911 system, fall behind. Maybe that is another reason to keep the traditional guest-room telephone in place.

Wake-Up Systems

Most telephone installations include both voice mail and wake-up service, of which there are four types.

MANUAL WAKE-UP SYSTEMS   There is an extended history of manual wake-up systems because they have been in use long before any technological advances. Guests used to call the telephone operator requesting a wake-up call. The operator then noted the room and time on a specially designed time sheet and set a special alarm clock (the brand name was Remind-O-Timer) that accommodated five-minute increments. At the appropriate time, the alarm would ring and the operator would call the room. Sometimes the call was early and sometimes it was late, depending upon the operator's call volume that morning.

SEMIAUTOMATIC SYSTEMS   These systems are one step up in automation. The guest still calls the operator, who manually enters the room number and time into the system. It is the system, not the operator, that makes the wake-up call. A prerecorded message might say, "This is your wake-up call. Today's weather is a brisk 37 degrees. Enjoy your day." Other options provide the date and day of the week and a marketing message (breakfast served until 10 AM). The message is repeated every five minutes until the guest answers. After four or five tries, the system either shuts down or—the preferred approach—alerts security to physically visit the room and make certain the guest is not in distress.

FULLY AUTOMATED AND INTERACTIVE TV-BASED WAKE-UP SYSTEMS   With fully automated wake-up systems, guests bypass the hotel's telephone operator and set their request by simply pushing a "wake-up" button on the guest-room telephone. A digital voice walks the user through the several simple steps. For example, for 7:00 AM, the instruction asks the guest to punch in 0700. Then it asks for a confirmation. The telephone rings at the desired time and an automated message similar to that of the semiautomated system plays its tune and/or delivers its message.

Interactive TV-based wake-up systems utilize an interface between the call accounting system and the guest-room television. Guests set the wake-up call with the TV remote. Technologically advanced or not, every hotel furnishes bedside alarm clocks. Paranoid guests, or those who have critical early-morning meetings, are known to set all three: their smartphone, the hotel's CAS wake-up system, and their bedside alarm clock!

Voice Mail

Voice mail enables a caller to leave a message for an absent guest. Historically, a telephone operator took such a message, wrote it down, and left it in the guest's mailbox (by room number) at the front desk; hence the term—*voice mailbox*. Technology has removed the operator from the message procedure, as it has with wake-up calls. By so doing, the system improved the accuracy of the message, reduced labor costs for the hotel, and made delivery more timely. A blinking light on the telephone alerts the guest to the waiting message. No longer is there any need to trek to the front desk.

The advantages of automated voice mail are numerous. Guests can leave messages as well as retrieve them. Messages can be forwarded to another room, in case one message were intended for several travelers. Messages can be personal and in the guest's native language. Access can be restricted, requiring callers to use a special PIN number that the guest has created.

Pressing the call-message button activates the system when the guest returns to the room. The guest is told there are a given number of messages, some old, some new. Messages can be saved or deleted.

The system is activated when each new guest checks in. Some systems hold messages up to 24 hours after check-out, unless the room is assigned to a new guest in the interim. In all cases, messages are deleted and a fresh, empty voice mailbox is initiated with each new check-in.

Where's My Phone?

The guest-room telephone may or may not be around in the future. On one side of the coin, experts predict the demise of the guest-room telephone because it is a costly piece of equipment which provides minimal revenue, it is readily replaced with an interactive television center and/or guest-room touch-screen tablet, and any emergency situations can be communicated through an in-room enunciator.

On the other side of the argument are experts who predict the guest-room telephone is here to stay. They argue that there are legal reasons for guest-room telephones (see 911 discussion above), they are critical in an emergency, and they remain convenient as a means of communication between guest and desk. Additionally, foreign guests are returning to the guest-room telephone for their international calls, which, when the hotel offers VoIP pricing, are cheaper than international calls on their cell phone/smartphone.

OTHER TECHNOLOGIES

In-room Entertainment Systems

Color television came to the hospitality industry in 1975 (see Exhibit 2). Within five years, almost every property offered it as an amenity. Today's generation of travelers expect rooms to have the same multimedia and entertainment choices that they use at home. In-room entertainment is a fast-growing revenue center. Visitors are willing to pay for movies, video-on-demand, in-room games, and high-speed Internet access. Hoteliers have shifted their offerings from conventional cable to high-tech options such as 3D televisions, high-definition, flat panel monitors, and video-on-demand equipment. Guests want to watch what they want and when they want. So when interfaced with other systems, "entertainment" systems offer:

- Personalized welcoming messages on the TV screens for new arrivals.
- Video-on-demand by means of pay-per-view (films and programs) that guests special order with options such as pause, rewind, and fast forward.
- High-speed Internet, which usually includes free news and weather.
- Wake-up calls interfaced to the television as explained previously.
- Room service with pictures of the menu items displayed on the television screen.
- Live feedback to management from surveys. Survey items that guests mark very low alert the manager on duty by means of a paging interface. Here's a unique opportunity for the hotel to "make it right".
- Different language options, especially useful as international tourism booms.
- Internet Protocol based radio that captures broadcasts over the Internet from around the world. Thus, say, a Turkish guest can tune in Power FM, a popular radio channel from Turkey.
- Folio viewing, billing, and settling as part of the departure process. Folios can follow guests to their homes or offices by land mail or Internet.
- Parental control of programming, blocking adult material from their children's sets.
- Compatibility with a multitude of portable devices that many guests now carry.
- Other two-way communication services like book spa appointments and golf tee times.
- Flash- and Java-capable systems which can deliver a full-range of graphics, content, and services.

And this is just the start of what is still to come. Some hotels are now experimenting with in-mirror televisions. Literally, as the guest combs her hair in the mirror she can see both her own face as well as the built-in television screen. The level of opaqueness can be adjusted—from maximum television viewability to more mirror and less TV. And, of course, the in-mirror television can be turned off completely if it proves too invasive. Who knows what else is on the horizon?

PROPERTY-BY-PROPERTY CUSTOM PROGRAMMING One of the most efficient improvements found in the newest in-room entertainment systems comes in the form of labor-savings. Today's most sophisticated television systems are now controllable through one central server. A hotel which chooses to reprogram channel numbers, remove certain channels from viewership, or arrange the television so that all like-channels are grouped can do so across all televisions from one central controller. Whether the room is occupied or not; the television is on, off, or switched to standby; or the television is located in the lounge, spa, or workout center, all televisions can be centrally reprogrammed.

This degree of controllability came in handy for Marriott International recently, when they began to deliver on a controversial decision to remove the availability of adult content from their new properties. The chain also plans to phase out adult content from existing Marriott properties as it switches them from traditional video systems to video-on-demand (VOD) systems. While Marriott International's official position states the move is due to declining revenues from in-room movies, many industry insiders believe it reflects a personal commitment by leaders of the chain. Bill Marriott has shared, for many years, his disdain for pornography. Although the largest, Marriott is by no means the first—Omni Hotels decided adult content was "not the way it wanted to make money" as far back as 1999!

STREAMING ON DEMAND More and more guests are opting away from video on-demand services provided by the hotel in favor of streaming their own video. Providers like Hulu, Netflix, and YouTube allow guests to view TV programs, movies, and videos through their laptops, iPads, and smartphones. The hotel's role in the experience: to provide bandwidth and televisions compatible with everything and anything the guest is carrying!

At the Desk

Maybe technology's greatest impact has been at the desk. The property management system has quickened the speed of service, reduced labor costs, improved accuracy, and modernized the look and flow of the lobby. The PMS has its relevance right from reservations and arrivals to billing and auditing.Because—contradictory as it seems—the nonpersonal, self-service aspects of an electronically supported hotel strengthen the guest's perception of a caring management. Guests know that staff is available—that desk personnel will respond when needed. Knowing help can be summoned, guests appreciate the speed and anonymity of self-service. Travelers (especially business travelers) dislike waiting in line, whether they are arriving or departing. So the self-service kiosk that speeds the guest along simultaneously saves the hotel labor. One study estimated the labor savings to be between 15% and 20%! Another anomaly: Self-service kiosks may actually increase revenue. Unlike self-conscious guest-service agents, kiosks easily prompt guests to buy up to higher rate rooms. Without awkwardness, kiosks promote the ancillary services of restaurants, lounges, spas, and nightclubs. Advertising revenue from lobby concessionaires and external merchants has proven to be another unexpected plus.

Self-check-in equipment accommodates arrivals with a swipe of their credit cards (see Exhibit 26). It accepts registrations, distributes keycards, and prints instructions for finding the room. Property management systems continue handling guests' records during their stay, tracking everything through point-of-sale(POS) terminals, telephone call-accounting systems (CASs), in-room minibars and safes, electronic locks (ELSs), and fire systems. And then the guest can return to the kiosk and its PMS interface for an electronic check-out.

Internet-based systems push the process forward. Check-ins via the hotel's website are accepted as early as seven days before arrival. Radisson Hotels led with this idea: "Express Yourself" features a three-step process. (1) Guests make reservations through any of the means, for example, telephone, Internet, agents, and so on. (2) Seven days before arrival the system sends emails inviting guests "to express" themselves by checking in. Personal preferences are accommodated: room location, no-smoking, king bed, and so on. (3) The key is waiting when the guest arrives and offers identification. And as discussed

EXHIBIT 26 Guests dislike front-desk queues. Strategically located self-serve kiosks get the guests into their rooms (and out of their rooms) more quickly with self-check-in and self-check-out services. The exhibit shows the benefits; a guest in the foreground is handling his account while guests in the background monopolize the front-desk agent. *Courtesy of Micros Systems, Inc., Columbia, Maryland.*

throughout the chapter, many hotels are now offering Internet-based check-in by smartphone or personal digital-assistant (PDA).

Similar handheld devices are used by guest-service agents. Cross-trained staffers exit the desk. Then from the middle of the lobby, the rear of the line, by the curb, or in the parking lot or garage, guests are registered by wireless equipment that communicates with the PMS. It is service with a technological smile.

STANDARDIZATION: FROM HITIS AND BEYOND Lodging now employs many technologies, but getting to this stage has been a bumpy road. Early systems were unable to talk to one another. That incompatibility was an industrywide issue that slowed progress. Initially, the industry lacked knowledge of the subject. Eventually, a decision was made to adopt an industrywide approach. The American Hotel & Lodging Association launched an initiative called Hospitality Industry Technology Integration Standards (HITIS).

The HITIS committee created a unified programming and hardware architectural structure for the PMS and all property-related interfaces. Previously, compatibility between, say, the PMS vendor and the POS vendor (or any other combination; PMS and CAS or PMS and ELS, etc.) did not exist. HITIS created standards and hoteliers were urged to specify them as part of their requests for proposal (RFPs) as early equipment was upgraded. And they did with good success.

OTA, Open Travel Alliance, the next generation of cooperative effort, expanded the horizon from "hospitality" to "travel." Its goal states: "...our primary focus is the creation of electronic message structures to facilitate communication between the disparate systems in the global travel industry." The organization's website goes on to identify membership, including "travel suppliers, defined as any company with primary control of inventory, including air carriers, car rental companies, hotel companies, railways, cruise lines, insurance companies, golf course owners, motorcycle, water or bicycle tour companies, etc."

Clearly, OTA's interest doesn't focus on lodging exclusively, but rather as one of its cross-industry sectors. Within the definition of a travel supplier, the hotel industry isn't as large as hoteliers imagine. As industry-buyers learned with HITIS, it takes cooperation among the immediate user-buyers to force uniformity from the manufacturer-sellers. A new association, Hotel Technology Next Generation (HTNG), returned the momentum to the lodging industry.

HTNG, a nonprofit organization, is more like HITIS than is OTA. All three organizations bring manufacturers, suppliers, consultants, and end-users together. HTNG's narrower universe concentrates on lodging, whereas lodging is but one segment within OTA. Within itself, lodging's focus is all inclusive, embracing the full scope of lodging technology: operations, telecommunications, in-room entertainment, customer information systems, and electronic installations.

Employing the initiatives of both of its predecessor organizations as well as its own, HTNG has begun certifying products, identifying them with an HTNG label and special logo. In so doing, it rejuvenates the work of HITIS. By using standardized interfaces rather than reinventing, as was done in the early effort, vendors save time and money. Knowing that larger companies will interface with them, smaller vendors are encouraged to participate. This broadens the scope of progress.

Whatever the organization one subscribes to, it works only when hoteliers buy from vendors that comply with universal standards. They have; so progress continues unabated.

Summary

No longer is hotel technology viewed as necessary cost. Today, it is a strategy which finds itself at the core of the entire operation. Technology impacts guests from the moment of reservation, through their arrival and departure, and into their next stay. It tracks, implements, and facilitates so many parts of the guest's stay and the hotel's operation that no summary list is practical.

For an industry as old as innkeeping, technology is the new kid. Still, it has shaken traditions and reformulated the delivery of "guest service." Few would say that service has diminished with the use of PMSs, or in-room technologies, or improved fire and security systems. Technology is a great differentiator, separating the "Mine Host" profile from the modern hotel executive. We find it in more than a dozen applications in the guest room alone. Just as the single bed with a connecting bath has been replaced with supreme bedding and multiple shower heads, so has the operator-assisted telephone and the open window been replaced by VoIP phones and sophisticated PTAC systems.

Resources and Challenges

Web Assignment

Visit http://www.hitec.org and report on either the next or the previous HITEC meeting. Explain what HITEC means, where the meeting was held (or will be held), the number of vendors, and two interesting aspects of the meeting's content.

Interesting Tidbits

- In 2011, Starbucks became the first major retailer to allow single-tap smartphone payment applications across all 6,800 of its stores.
- In a step toward regulating energy conservation, the U.S. government will no longer allow the manufacture of incandescent, halogen, and linear fluorescent bulbs. Beginning in 2012, the U.S. legislation begins phasing out certain bulbs—starting with the incandescent 100-watt bulb—the most common bedside light bulb in the lodging industry.
- The Lock Museum of Orange Country is located in Garden Grove, California. Among the exhibits are classic prison hardware such as leg irons and handcuffs, including those of the famous escape artist Houdini. Closer to the hotel industry are old keys and locks, including the lock from Elvis Presley's dressing room at the MGM Grand in Las Vegas.
- Robotics were not discussed in this chapter, but Hotelier Grace Leo-Andrieu, whose hotel company is based in Paris, and is a consultant for *Travel + LeisureMagazine*, foresees their use as part of an in-room vacuuming and disinfecting system, as a back-and-foot massage amenity, or even as a food and beverage delivery system!
- Marriott has launched an employee recruiting tool—a game found on Facebook called "My Marriott Hotel."

Challenges

True/False

Questions that are partially false should be marked false.

_____ 1. By changing the name of their "Telephone Departments" to "The Department of Communications (DOC)," hotels have been able to stop the decrease in revenue that began about 1990, caused partly by hotels overcharging for in-room calls.

_____ 2. Biometrics, the price of which has dropped substantially with time, has been widely adopted by the lodging industry, and is the best means yet of increasing security of both guests' assets and persons.

_____ 3. "True" detection systems are energy detection systems that sense both body heat and body motion, and therefore achieve a truer reading of room occupancy than utilizing just one or the other alone.

_____ 4. Four nonprofit organizations (in alphabetic order: HITIS, HTNG, OTA, PIN) have been launched during the past several years to establish standards for the manufacture and sale of hotel technology.

_____ 5. The hotel PMS has been interfaced with the POS, the CAS, the ELS, and the HVAC to provide better service to guests and improved costs for the business.

Problems

1. The relationship of the telephone and hotel industries has changed significantly since the 1960s. List three major pieces of legislation, court rulings, findings by the FCC, or decisions by members of either industry that caused or contributed to the changes. How did each alter the way in which the hotel's telephone department operates?
2. Undoubtedly, some PMS vendors will comply with HITIS standards and others will not. What are the benefits to a hotel manager who purchases software from a vendor in compliance? Are there any disadvantages to using a vendor in compliance with HITIS standards?
3. Most hotel operations charge a premium for the convenience of placing long-distance phone calls directly from the room. International guests prefer to use the guest-room telephone rather than their own cell phone because international calls are so expensive by cell phone. If such calls are placed through the hotel's VoIP, what is the cost per call to the hotel? If you were running the chain, would you charge a fee for in-room long-distance calls or give the calls away as just another amenity? Explain your logic.
4. Using professional terminology correctly is important to understanding and being understood. Identify the following acronyms or abbreviations and briefly discuss what they represent:
   a. HOBIC   b. WATS
   c. PMS   d. FCC
   e. ELS   f. OCC
   g. AT&T   h. PBX
   i. RFID   j. POS
   k. CAS   l. AH&LA
   m. PPC   n. VoIP
   o. HVAC   p. PTAC
   q. Tap to Pay r. Bandwidth
   s. Smart cards
5. Be creative and imagine the hotel room of the future. Describe several guest-operated interfaces or devices that might be available in your fictitious hotel room of tomorrow.

AN INCIDENT IN HOTEL MANAGEMENT
The Bare Facts

Stay Today, a small West-coast limited-service chain, decided to market themselves toward the Asian traveler. It used a well-respected Asian marketing firm to create the "buzz." Among the hype: a fully electronic hotel. The effort had already showed positive results when a Japanese couple arrived one afternoon. Luckily—because they spoke no English—all their reservation papers were in order, including a four-day deposit. After much nodding and smiling, they were provided a keycard to room 1714, a nonsmoking room as prescribed by the reservation.

As they let themselves into the room, they realized there were no lights operating, except one single light above the front door. They walked back downstairs and were escorted to the room by an employee who showed them that inserting the keycard would turn on all in-room systems. They thanked the employee.

After a while, they sensed the room was growing very warm. Yet they could not determine how to adjust the temperature. Again, they walked downstairs and were escorted to the room by a different employee. This time they were shown how to access the temperature control setting on the one-touch guest-controlled tablet. They thanked the employee.

Late that evening, as they prepared for bed, they realized there were no light switches anywhere on the walls. The husband removed the keycard from the control slot, the lights turned off (except the annoying single bulb above the front door), and they went to sleep. An hour later, they were awake because the room was growing too warm. The husband reinserted the keycard, but then all the lights came back on. They decided to sleep with all the lights on. The next morning they tried to make themselves understood at the front desk.

Questions

1. Was there a management failure here; if so, what?
2. What should be the hotel's immediate response to this morning's complaint?
3. What further, long-run action should management consider?

Answers to True/False Quiz

1. False. Changing the name is meaningless. Hotels need to change the structure in order to woo guests back, if that is even possible. Two strategies are being tested: (1) Bundle all telecommunications together to increase sales; and (2) Use ISPs (Internet service providers) to carry VoIP calls at a lower cost.

2. False. Guests are reluctant to surrender very personal attributes such as fingerprints and eye scans, and until that changes, biometric security systems will not gain position in hotels. Additionally, biometrics still remain relatively expensive even as other forms of technology decrease in price.

3. True. However, the more accurate sensing comes at a higher initial cost, because the hotel is supporting two systems (infra-red and motion detectors) rather than just one.

4. False. This is a "catch question." HITIS, HTNG, and OTA are organizations working to standardize equipment interfaces. PIN is a well-known abbreviation for one's personal identification number. So it doesn't belong in the grouping.

5. True. And these four interfaces are just the start of a long list of current and potential systems (minibars and fire-safety, for example) and many more to come.

Index